EQUITY AND THE LAW OF

AUSTRALIA

LBC Information Services
Sydney

CANADA AND THE USA

Carswell

NEW ZEALAND

Brooker's
Auckland

SINGAPORE AND MALAYSIA

Thomson Information (S.E. Asia)
Singapore

Equity and the Law of Trusts in Ireland

2nd edition

Hilary Delany

B.A. (Mod.), M.Litt., Ph.D, Barrister-at-Law
Fellow of Trinity College, Dublin
Lecturer in Law, Trinity College, Dublin

ROUND HALL SWEET & MAXWELL

This book was typeset by
Gough Typesetting Services for
ROUND HALL SWEET & MAXWELL
Brehon House, 4 Upper Ormond Quay,
Dublin 7.

A catalogue record for this title
is available from the British Library.

ISBN 1-85800-138-2 pbk
1-85800-137-4 hbk

Printed in England by
MPG Books

To my Mother,
and in memory of Douglas

Preface to the First Edition

The aim of this book is to provide a comprehensive modern text dealing with Equity and the Law of Trusts in Ireland. Although it is designed primarily to fulfil the needs of students in this area of the law, it is hoped that it will also prove to be of value to practitioners and others who for one reason or another need to acquaint themselves with the principles of equity.

While I have sought to set out and analyse the law as it presently exists in Ireland, this analysis extends to consideration of case law in other jurisdictions, particularly England, in areas where this is necessary to supplement our own developing jurisprudence. Indeed some aspects of equitable jurisdiction have yet to be considered adequately or at all here and in such instances I have endeavoured to provide an insight into approaches adopted elsewhere in the common law world. While a number of excellent English texts cover this area, particularly Hanbury and Martin's *Modern Equity*, since the book written by Mr Justice Ronan Keane on the subject, *Equity and the Law of Trusts in the Republic of Ireland* went out of print, there has been no text available dealing specifically with equity and the law of trusts in this jurisdiction. Although developments here have tended to a great extent to mirror those in England, this trend is far from universal and equitable principles as they exist in Ireland today differ in some important respects from those applied in other common law jurisdictions, e.g. in relation to secret trusts and trusts of family property.

A number of significant decisions have been handed down in areas covered by the text over the past year or so. In particular, the judgment of Keane J in *Re Worth Library* [1994] 1 ILRM 161 has provided a detailed and most useful overview of the general principles relating to charitable trusts and the exercise of cy-près jurisdiction. The scope of a trustee's powers of investment (*Stacey v. Branch* [1995] 2 ILRM 136) and the jurisdiction of our courts to grant Mareva injunctions, both on a domestic and extra-territorial basis (*Deutsche Bank Atkiengesellschaft v. Murtagh* [1995] 1 ILRM 381 and *Countyglen plc v. Carway* [1995] 1 ILRM 481), have also been addressed by the High Court in decisions delivered over the past year.

I have made every effort to include developments in this area up to 20

October 1995 although in some cases (e.g. the decision of Kinlen J in *Premier Dairies Ltd v. Doyle* (High Court 1995 No. 7008P, 29 September 1995) it was only possible to include a brief reference to this new material in a footnote. In addition, it should be noted that at the time of writing, judgment has been reserved by the Supreme Court in two important cases, *Lynch v. Burke* and *Bank of Ireland v. Smyth*.

I would like to record my thanks to a number of individuals who have greatly assisted me at various stages in the preparation of this book. First, I would like to thank Michael Adams of Four Courts Press and Terri McDonnell and Eilis Maguire of Round Hall Sweet & Maxwell for their guidance and practical advice and expertise. I am also most grateful to Gilbert Gough for his trojan work in typesetting the book so quickly and efficiently and to Julitta Clancy for preparing the tables and index in such a professional and user friendly manner. In addition, I would like to thank my colleagues in the Law School, Trinity College, Dublin for their advice and support and the staff of the Berkeley Library at Trinity College for their assistance while I was researching the book.

I wish particularly to thank my colleague and friend Paul Coughlan who read a draft of the text and made many useful suggestions and Ruth Heard, who also read the manuscript and greatly assisted me in the unenviable and rather laborious task of proofreading. I am greatly indebted to them both and to my friends, particularly Niall, for their support and encouragement in what proved to be a rather more time-consuming project than I had perhaps envisaged!

Hilary Delany
20 October 1995

Preface to the Second Edition

Less than four years have passed since the publication of the first edition of this book which was intended primarily as a student text. However, the number of significant judicial decisions, both in this jurisdiction and elsewhere, and the increasing amount of academic commentary on developments in this area of the law now justify a new edition.

Some decisions handed down recently in this jurisdiction have been particularly significant, such as *Lynch v. Burke* [1995] 2 IR 159 which changed the law in relation to the beneficial ownership of monies in a joint deposit account after the death of one of the depositors. This decision brought our jurisprudence into line with other common law countries and it now more accurately reflects the true purpose of a resulting trust which is to give effect to presumed intention. Other decisions such as *McQuillan v. Maguire* [1996] 1 ILRM 395 (voidable trusts), *Spencer v. Kinsella* [1996] 2 ILRM 401 (removal of trustees), *Mackie v. Wilde* [1998] 1 ILRM 449 (part performance), *Bentham v. Potterton* High Court (Barr J) 28 May 1998 (*donatio mortis causa*) and *Smyth v. Halpin* [1997] 2 ILRM 38 (proprietary estoppel) while they do not effect radical change are nevertheless noteworthy as they confirm or clarify existing principles. There has also been a significant number of cases dealing with injunctions of various types including *Szabo v. ESAT Digiphone* [1998] 2 ILRM 102 (*quia timet* injunctions), *Bennett Enterprises Inc v. Lipton* [1999] 1 ILRM 81 (Mareva injunctions) and continuing consideration has been given to the circumstances in which the *American Cyanamid/Campus Oil* principles, which are relevant to the granting of interlocutory injunctions, should not be applied, e.g in *Reynolds v. Malocco* [1999] 1 ILRM 289.

As mentioned in the preface to the first edition, developments in England in the area of equity and the law of trusts generally tend to be of considerable relevance in this jurisdiction and there have been a number of landmark decisions handed down by the House of Lords over the last few years, particularly *Co-Operative Insurance Society Ltd v. Argyll Stores (Holdings) Ltd* [1998] AC 1 (specific performance) and *Westdeutsche Landesbank Girozentrale v. Islington London Borough Council* [1996] AC 669 (tracing) which are considered in this new edition. Reference is also made to useful authorities in other common law jurisdictions e.g. to the decisions of the Canadian Supreme Court in *Soulos v. Korkontzilas* (1997) 146 DLR (4th) 214 and *Citadel General Assurance Co v. Lloyds Bank Canada* (1997) 152 DLR (4th) 411 on constructive trusts.

I would like to thank a number of people who have helped me in various ways in the preparation of this new edition. First, I would like to thank the staff at Round Hall Sweet and Maxwell and in particular Terri McDonnell for her practical advice and assistance in preparing the text for publication. I would also like to express my appreciation to Gilbert Gough who as ever did a superb job of typesetting and to Julitta Clancy who prepared the tables and a most comprehensive index with her usual skill. Finally, I would particularly like to thank Ruth Heard, Grainne Mullan and Finbarr McElligott who read the text in proof form; I am greatly indebted to them.

I have endeavoured to state the law as of 1 June 1999.

Hilary Delany
1 June 1999

Contents

Table of Contents

CHAPTER 1 INTRODUCTION

CHAPTER 2 MAXIMS OF EQUITY

CHAPTER 3 TRUSTS — AN INTRODUCTION

CHAPTER 4 TRUSTS — FORMALITIES AND ESSENTIAL ELEMENTS

CHAPTER 5 SECRET TRUSTS

CHAPTER 6 CONSTITUTION OF TRUSTS

CHAPTER 7 RESULTING TRUSTS

CHAPTER 8 CONSTRUCTIVE TRUSTS

CHAPTER 9 PURPOSE TRUSTS

CHAPTER 10 CHARITABLE TRUSTS

CHAPTER 11 VOID AND VOIDABLE TRUSTS

CHAPTER 12 ADMINISTRATION OF TRUSTS

CHAPTER 13 INJUNCTIONS

CHAPTER 14 SPECIFIC PERFORMANCE

CHAPTER 15 RECTIFICATION

CHAPTER 16 RESCISSION

CHAPTER 17 EQUITABLE ESTOPPEL

CHAPTER 18 TRACING

CHAPTER 19 EQUITABLE DOCTRINES

Table of Cases

Other Tables

CONSTITUTION

TABLE OF STATUTES

TABLE OF STATUTORY INSTRUMENTS

EUROPEAN LEGISLATION

TABLE OF EUROPEAN CONVENTIONS

CHAPTER 1

Introduction

GENERAL PRINCIPLES

Equity can be described as the branch of the law administered by the Court of Chancery prior to the enactment of the Judicature (Ireland) Act 1877 and is the body of principles which evolved with the aim of mitigating the severity of the rules of the common law. The original objective of the Court of Chancery which operated as a 'court of conscience' was to achieve a fair and equitable result in all cases which came before it and the principles which it developed became known as 'equity'. The court sought to avoid the injustice which might result from a strict application of the common law,[1] and to provide a remedy where an existing one might be inappropriate or even lacking altogether.

While equitable jurisdiction developed as a means of mitigating the harshness of the common law, it is important to stress that it is still dependent on the existence of the framework which the common law provides. Equity is essentially a supplementary and fragmentary jurisdiction, and as Maitland[2] has suggested it should be regarded as a gloss added to the common law and statute law, rather than as an independent system.[3] More recently Kenny J spoke in similar terms in the course of his judgment in *Hynes Ltd v. Independent Newspapers*[4] and referred to equity as being 'a gloss on or an improvement and reform of the common law'. For this reason it is difficult to define its scope and a more useful exercise is to point out the main areas in which equity operates today. However, it should be stressed that equity plays a role in a wide range of different situations and it would not be possible to delimit these in a fully comprehensive

---

1. As Lord Denning MR commented in *Crabb v. Arun District Council* [1976] Ch 179, 187: 'Equity comes in true to form, to mitigate the rigours of strict law.'
2. *Lectures on Equity* Lecture II. See also the comment of Lord Evershed MR to the effect that 'equity never denied the existence of the legal right. It said that the legal position was not the whole position, and added something to it.' (1954) 70 LQR 326, 329.
3. As Kiely states in *Principles of Equity as Applied in Ireland* (1936) p.7 'If a conglomeration of miscellaneous rules can be called a system then it is such'.
4. [1980] IR 204, 218.

manner. Lord Upjohn's statement in the course of his speech in *Phipps v. Boardman*[5] should also be borne in mind, namely that: 'Rules of equity have to be applied to such a great diversity of circumstances that they can be stated only in the most general terms.'

One of the most enduring and still one of its most important creations is the trust, which is the relationship which arises whenever a person, called a trustee, is compelled in equity to hold property for the benefit of some persons or persons, termed beneficiaries, or for some object permitted by law, in such a way that the real benefit accrues, not to the trustee, but to the beneficiaries or other objects of the trust.[6] This device is still of enormous practical significance today, particularly in view of the wide-ranging nature of taxation statutes and the desire to avoid or postpone their application whenever this is legally possible. The other area in which the influence of equity can be seen most clearly is in relation to the grant of equitable remedies such as injunctions and specific performance. Such remedies which are discretionary in nature continue to play an important role in increasingly diverse areas of the law.

One of the hallmarks of equitable jurisdiction is that it is discretionary in nature, as Black LJ made clear in *Conlon v. Murray*[7] in relation to the remedy of specific performance, although his comments could be interpreted as being of more general application: 'This discretion is not, of course, the arbitrary discretion of the individual judge but is a discretion to be exercised on the principles which have been worked out in a multitude of decided cases'. Similar sentiments were expressed by Greene MR in *Re Diplock*[8] where he said that 'if [a] claim in equity exists, it must be shown to have an ancestry, founded in history and in the practice and precedents of courts administering equity jurisdiction.' To ensure that equitable jurisdiction is not exercised in an arbitrary and unfair manner the courts must strive to reconcile the conflicting aims of achieving justice in an individual case and ensuring an element of consistency in decision making. It could be argued that the very nature of equitable jurisdiction lends credence to the belief that there is some concept of fairness of equity which renders precedent superfluous. The temptation to seek to do justice in an individual case may be great, but as Lord Evershed has pointed out, 'there is, I venture to think, great danger in practice in what is, in truth, palm tree

---

5. [1967] 2 AC 46, 123.
6. See Keeton and Sheridan, *The Law of Trusts* (12th ed., 1993) p.3 and *infra*, Chapter 3.
7. [1958] NI 17, 25. See also the *dicta* of O'Higgins CJ in *Smelter Corporation v. O'Driscoll* [1977] IR 305, 310-311.
8. [1948] Ch 465, 481-482.

justice'.[9] He is correct to the extent that the principles of certainty and consistency form an integral part of the fair administration of justice, and the sacrificing of settled principles and precedents in specific cases to meet the demands of justice in the name of equity would result ultimately in the development of an arbitrary and therefore unfair legal system.

Another important aspect in the overall development of equity, although it may have been lacking at certain stages of this development, is that equitable principles have been 'altered, improved, and refined from time to time'.[10] Certain areas, such as constructive trusts and the equitable remedy of tracing have developed considerably in significance over recent decades and are both now of primary importance as devices to combat increasingly sophisticated transnational fraud. The extent to which equity itself is still developing is a less straightforward question to answer. Although there have been signs of judicial willingness to extend the reach of existing doctrines in some areas,[11] in others there has been a marked reluctance to do so.[12]

Article 73 of the Irish Free State Constitution and Article 50 of the Constitution of Ireland 1937 made provision for the carrying forward of existing laws to the extent to which they were not inconsistent with these Constitutions and the practice has been to treat the established principles of equity as being applicable in our courts. It is fair to say that since the foundation of the State the attitude of the judiciary in this jurisdiction has been generally to follow the approach adopted by their counterparts in England — although there have been notable exceptions to this principle[13] — and equity as it exists in Ireland today plays an ever-increasing role across a broad range of activities, including commercial ones.

As Sir Peter Millett[14] has commented in an important recent article on the way forward for equity in England: 'It can no longer be doubted that equity has moved out of the family home[15] and the settled estate and into

---

9. (1954) 70 LQR 326, 329. See Halliwell (1994) 14 LS 15, 17.
10. *Re Hallett's Estate* (1880) 13 Ch D 696, 710 *per* Jessel MR.
11. *H.K.N. Invest Oy v. Incotrade Pvt Ltd* [1993] 3 IR 152.
12. See e.g. the attitude of the Supreme Court in *L. v. L.* [1992] 2 IR 77 in relation to extending the reach of the purchase money resulting trust.
13. E.g. in relation to half secret trusts (Chapter 5) and the division of family property (Chapter 7).
14. A Lord Justice of Appeal in England, writing extra-judicially. See (1995) 9 Trust Law Int 35.
15. However, it should be noted that equity still plays an important role in resolving property disputes between co-habitees, between spouses and third parties e.g. financial institutions and between spouses outside the context of separation and divorce proceedings. See further Chapter 7.

the marketplace' and in his view 'the intervention of equity in commercial transactions, long resisted by common lawyers, can no longer be withstood'. However, it is also fair to say that while the circumstances in which equity intervenes are changing and developing, the underlying rationale for its intervention remains essentially the same. Millett usefully summarizes the basis for equity's role as follows:

> The traditional objects of equity have not changed: to relieve against mistake, fraud, accident and surprise; to protect the weak from exploitation and trust and confidence from betrayal; to prevent the unconscionable assertion of legal rights; and to give relief against every kind of unconscionable conduct. It demands not merely honesty and a willingness to meet one's commitments, but integrity, good conscience and fidelity.[16]

HISTORICAL BACKGROUND

The 13th century saw considerable progress being made in the development of the common law in England. However, by the end of that century it had grown into a rigid set of principles which were slow to adapt to meet the needs of a developing system of justice, and hardship frequently arose as a result. A number of major defects had become apparent, principally that under the common law, many wrongs could not be remedied. An injured party could only bring an action at common law if his claim came within a recognised form of writ. To compound this difficulty, the *in consimili causa* clause in the Statute of Westminster II 1285 was interpreted very restrictively and was confined to varying the form of existing writs.

In addition, even where a remedy was available, it was frequently inappropriate or inadequate. The only remedy available at common law was damages, and orders which are of such importance in our modern system of justice, such as specific performance and injunctions, were unknown. A defendant might also suffer because a plaintiff might be entitled to a judgment at common law regardless of mitigating factors which would be relevant to the exercise of equitable jurisdiction as we know it today. A further shortcoming of the common law system as it existed at the end of the thirteenth century was its numerous procedural defects and inadequa-

---

16. *Ibid.* at 36-37.

cies. Often a defendant might not be allowed to give evidence or a jury might be subject to outside influences.

As a result of these defects in the system a practice developed of petitioning the king in situations where a litigant complained that he could not obtain an adequate remedy within the framework of the common law. The Lord Chancellor was the officer responsible for overseeing such matters and as the number of petitions increased, the king delegated his functions to the chancellor with the direction that a petitioner should be given a legal remedy if a litigant was entitled to one and where none existed, to give such a remedy as would be just. As the number of petitions increased, the chancellor and his office took on the role of a court which became known as the Court of Chancery.

The office of Lord Chancellor of Ireland was created in the early thirteenth century,[17] although it should be pointed out that until the seventeenth century Brehon law tended to prevail outside the settled areas in the country. The early chancellors in both jurisdictions were predominantly ecclesiastics and many of the principles which date from this time have their origins in canon law or, to a lesser extent, Roman law. During the Middle Ages, the Irish parliament seems to have played a significant role in exercising equity jurisdiction and it was not until the sixteenth century that the Lord Chancellor of Ireland started to play a meaningful role in dispensing justice on the basis of equitable principles.

The Court of Chancery never sought to deny a litigant's legal rights but rather aimed to ensure that such rights were not exercised in a manner which would cause undue prejudice to the other party or bring about an unjust or inequitable result to a dispute. The court began to issue injunctions to restrain a party from exercising his legal rights, a practice which effectively curtailed the authority of the common law courts. This caused increasing ill-feeling and matters came to a head during the reign of James I in the *Earl of Oxford's Case*[18] when a bitter dispute about the validity of these 'common injunctions' between the Chief Justice of England, Edward Coke and the Lord Chancellor, Lord Ellesmere, was resolved in favour of the Court of Chancery.

While the early chancellors in theory acted on a number of settled prin-

---

17. There is some dispute about the identity and the date of appointment of the first Lord Chancellor. Kiely suggests in *Principles of Equity as Applied In Ireland* (1936) p. 6 that it was John de Worchley appointed in 1219, but other commentators suggest that it was Ralph Neville, appointed in 1232. See Hand (1970) Ir Jur (ns) 291; Ball, *The Judges in Ireland* (1926) pp. 6-7; Wylie, *Irish Land Law* (3rd ed., 1997) p. 84 and Keane, *Equity and the Law of Trusts in the Republic of Ireland* (1988) p.13.
18. (1615) 1 Rep Ch 1. See Baker (1969) 4 Ir Jur (ns) 368.

ciples in granting or refusing relief, there was little uniformity in the judgments handed down and the types of remedies varied from one chancellor to the next. By the beginning of the 17th century the chancellors were generally speaking common lawyers, rather than ecclesiastics and while the court of chancery remained a 'court of conscience', a system of precedent did begin to develop. Much of this systemisation took place from the time of the chancellorship of Lord Nottingham (1673-1682), sometimes referred to as the 'Father of Equity',[19] until the time of Lord Eldon (1801-1806 and 1807-1827). However, the price of systemisation was that by the beginning of the nineteenth century, the principles of equity were nearly as rigid as the common law rules. As Lord Eldon commented in *Gee v. Pritchard*:[20] 'Nothing would inflict on me greater pain, in quitting this place [the office of chancellor] than the recollection that I had done any thing to justify the reproach that the equity of this Court varies like the Chancellor's foot.' A further difficulty which had come to the fore by this time was the inconvenience of the fact that two distinct court systems had developed, each applying their own often inconsistent principles. Reforms aimed at tackling this problem were begun in the mid-nineteenth century. In 1856 the Common Law Procedure Amendment Act, Ireland,[21] was passed which gave the common law courts power to grant equitable remedies in limited situations. Subsequently the Chancery Amendment Act 1858 (Lord Cairns' Act) gave the Court of Chancery power to award the common law remedy of damages either in substitution for or in addition to an injunction or a decree for specific performance.

A major reform of the system of the administration of justice was effected in England by the Supreme Court of Judicature Acts 1873 and 1875 (followed in Ireland by the Supreme Court of Judicature (Ireland) Act 1877) which established one Supreme Court of Judicature and replaced the system of separate courts exercising common law and equitable jurisdiction.[22] This court was to have two divisions, the High Court of Justice, which possessed both original and appellate jurisdiction and the Court of Appeal which exercised a purely appellate function. The High Court itself was initially divided into five divisions — Chancery, Queen's Bench, Common Pleas, Exchequer and Probate and Matrimonial. In 1887 the Common Pleas Division was merged with the Queen's Bench and in 1897 so were

---

19. *Kemp v. Kemp* (1801) 5 Ves 849, 858 *per* Arden MR.
20. (1818) 2 Swans 402, 414.
21. The equivalent legislation in England was the Common Law Procedure Act 1854.
22. See the comments of Palles CB in *Antrim County Land, Building and Investment Co Ltd v. Stewart* [1904] 2 IR 357, 364.

the Exchequer and Probate and Matrimonial Divisions so that by the end of the century, only the Chancery and Queen's Bench Divisions remained.

Palles CB summarised the effect of the Judicature Act as follows in *Barber v. Houston,*[23] a decision of the Exchequer Division:

> The same system of Jurisprudence now prevails in all Divisions of the High Court; and if, upon the facts pleaded, the Plaintiff could, before the Judicature Act, have had in Equity the relief which he seeks in this action, he is now entitled to it in this Court. That Act changed forms of procedure, but did not alter rights or remedies.

The fusion of the administration of legal and equitable jurisdiction was continued with the enactment of the Courts of Justice Act 1924 which established a High Court and Supreme Court to take the place of the Supreme Court of Judicature and this structure was continued by the Courts (Establishment and Constitution) Act 1961. However, as Kiely[24] has stated: 'The intrinsic difference between legal and equitable rights and remedies remains unaffected'.

One issue which was bound to lead to difficulties in practice was how this new court system was to deal with any potential conflict between legal and equitable principles. Section 28(11) of the Supreme Court of Judicature (Ireland) Act 1877 addressed this problem by providing that where any conflict arose between the rules of equity and common law that the equitable rule was to prevail. An illustration of how this provision operated in practice is provided by the decision of the English Court of Appeal in *Walsh v. Lonsdale.*[25] The defendant landlord agreed in writing to grant the plaintiff a lease of a mill for seven years although no deed was executed as required by law. The agreement provided for the payment of rent quarterly in arrears but that a year's rent would be payable in advance if demanded. The plaintiff tenant fell into arrears; the defendant demanded a year's rent in advance and when the plaintiff refused to pay, purported to exercise a right of distress. The plaintiff claimed an injunction and damages for illegal distress but the action failed. At law, the distress would have been illegal, as there was no deed in relation to the seven year lease[26]

---

23. (1884) 14 LR Ir 273, 276.
24. *Principles of Equity as Applied in Ireland* (1936) p.9.
25. (1882) 21 Ch D 9. In this case the equivalent provision, s.25(11) of the Supreme Court of Judicature Act 1873, was at issue. See Sparkes (1988) 8 OJLS 350.
26. S. 1 of the Statute of Frauds 1677 as amended by s. 3 of the Real Property Act 1845 provided that a lease for a period of time greater than three years would be void unless it was executed by deed.

and the yearly legal tenancy which had arisen because of the entering into possession and the payment of rent by the plaintiff would not have permitted the landlord to demand the payment of a year's rent in advance. However, in equity the agreement for the lease was treated as being as good as a lease and the Court of Appeal, in reliance on section 25(11), which required that in the event of conflict, the equitable rule must prevail, held that the distress was lawful. As Jessel MR stated: 'There are not two estates as there were formerly, one estate at common law by reason of the payment of rent from year to year and an estate in equity under the agreement. There is only one court and equity rules prevail in it.'[27]

FUSION OF LAW AND EQUITY — A PROCEDURAL FUSION ONLY?

The generally accepted opinion at the time of the enactment of the Judicature Acts was that the result of the legislation was to effect a fusion of administration rather than a fusion of the principles of the common law and equity. Jessel MR remarked in *Salt v. Cooper*[28] in relation to this issue: 'but it was not any fusion, or anything of the kind, it was the vesting in one tribunal the administration of law and equity in every cause, action or dispute which should come before that tribunal.' Similarly, Ashburner[29] has commented: '[t]he two streams of jurisdiction, though they run in the same channel, run side by side and do not mingle their waters.' This view is also well summarised by Delany[30] in the following terms:

> The Judicature Acts fused the courts of law and equity; they created a substantially uniform system of procedure and pleading; and they provided that in case of 'conflict or variance' the rules of equity should prevail. But there was nothing more than a fusion of jurisdiction, procedure and pleading; the substantive rules themselves remained.

---

27. *Ibid.* at 14.
28. (1880) 16 Ch D 544, 549. See also *Joseph v. Lyons* (1884) 15 QBD 280.
29. *Principles of Equity* (2nd ed., 1933), p.18.
30. (1961) 24 MLR 116, 117. Delany referred to Maitland's point that equity is not a self sufficient system in itself and presupposes the existence of the common law. He stresses that the so called 'fusion' effected by the Judicature Acts has not reduced the dependence of equity on the common law. See also the comments of Baker in (1977) 93 LQR 529, 531 that 'we may . . . conclude that it was the intention of the Judicature Acts to preserve the distinction between the rules of law and equity'.

While the development of common law rules since the enactment of the Judicature Acts have in some instances been influenced by equitable principles, there is no doubt that the distinctions between legal and equitable rights and remedies remain today. For example, to obtain an equitable remedy a litigant must rely on the court's discretion whereas if he seeks a common law remedy, once he has established that a right existing at common law has been breached, a remedy will be granted. In recent decades there has undoubtedly been greater interaction in this area and it has been accepted that a legal remedy may be given for breach of an equitable right, as in *Seager v. Copydex Ltd*[31] in which damages were assessed in respect of a breach of confidence, which is a right protected by equity. However, as a general rule the courts in England have been reluctant to apply this principle, as in *Metall und Rohstoff AG v. Donaldson Lufkin & Jeanrette Inc*[32] in which the Court of Appeal held that damages could not be awarded for a breach of trust. This reluctance has not been evident in some other common law jurisdictions, particularly New Zealand, where damages have been awarded in respect of breach of confidence[33] and breach of fiduciary duty.[34] This more radical view is well summarised by the comments of Cooke P in *Attorney General for the United Kingdom v. Wellington Newspapers Ltd*:[35]

> As law and equity are now mingled ... it does not seem to me to matter whether the duty be classified as equitable or not. The full range of remedies deriving historically from either common law or equity should be available.

Such an expansive approach would tend to suggest that the fusion effected by the Judicature Acts was more than merely procedural in nature and that the systems of law and equity themselves have merged as a result. This view was put forward by the House of Lords, and particularly forcefully by Lord Diplock, in *United Scientific Holdings Ltd v. Burnley Borough Council*[36] in which the essential issue was whether a landlord who had

---

31. [1967] 1 WLR 923.
32. [1990] 1 QB 391, 473.
33. *Attorney General for the United Kingdom v. Wellington Newspapers Ltd* [1988] 1 NZLR 129; *Aquaculture Corporation v. New Zealand Green Mussel Co. Ltd* [1990] 3 NZLR 299. See also the Canadian decision of *Lac Minerals Ltd v. International Corona Resources Ltd* (1989) 61 DLR (4th) 14.
34. *Day v. Mead* [1987] 2 NZLR 443; *Mouat v. Clarke Boyce* [1992] 2 NZLR 559.
35. [1988] 1 NZLR 129, 172. See also his comments in *Day v. Mead* [1987] 2 NZLR 443, 451.
36. [1978] AC 904.

failed to adhere strictly to the time requirements laid down by a rent re-view clause should be deprived of the right to increase the rent. The Su-preme Court of Judicature Act provided that stipulations in contracts which would have been deemed to be of the essence in a court of equity prior to the enactment of the legislation should henceforth receive that construc-tion in all courts. The lessee argued that as this question had not arisen prior to this, the relevant section[37] could not apply and that time was of the essence. The House of Lords held that the position prior to the enactment of the legislation was not of relevance and that since then a fusion of the rules of law and equity had occurred. It therefore held that the council was entitled to invoke the rent review provisions notwithstanding the fact that the time limits prescribed had expired as time was not normally of the essence under the rules of equity.

In reaching this conclusion Lord Diplock stated that Ashburner's meta-phor has become 'both mischievous and deceptive' and said that if that 'fluvial metaphor is to be retained at all, the waters of the confluent streams of law and equity have surely mingled now'.[38] In his view as a result of the Judicature Acts 'the two systems of substantive and adjectival law for-merly administered by courts of law and courts of chancery ... were fused.'[39]

The finding in this case appears to have been applied by a number of the members of the Supreme Court in *Hynes Ltd v. Independent Newspa-pers Ltd.*[40] The question at issue was a similar one, namely whether time was of the essence with regard to a rent review provision in a contract. The Supreme Court held that if the time stipulation would not have been deemed to be of the essence of the contract in a court of equity prior to the enact-ment of the Judicature Act then it would still receive the same construc-tion. As there were no grounds for implying a term that time was of the essence, the plaintiff tenant's appeal against the validity of the late service of a rent review notice was disallowed. O'Higgins CJ stated that in Ireland 'the fusion of common law and equitable rules ... initiated by the Supreme Court of Judicature Act (Ireland) 1877 ... was completed by the Courts of Justice Act 1924 and the Courts (Establishment and Constitution) Act 1961.'[41] Kenny J also spoke in terms of the decision of the House of Lords

---

37. S.25(7) of the Supreme Court of Judicature Act 1873. The equivalent provision un-der the Supreme Court of Judicature (Ireland) Act 1877 was s. 28(7).
38. *Ibid.* at 925. See also the comments of Lord Denning MR in *Federal Commerce & Navigation Co Ltd v. Molena Alpha Inc* [1978] QB 927, 974.
39. *Ibid.* See also the speeches of Lord Simon at pp. 944-945 and of Lord Fraser at pp. 957-958.
40. [1980] IR 204.
41. *Ibid.* at 216.

in *United Scientific* as being the 'restoration of a fundamental equitable principle which, unfortunately, has tended to be ignored in many recent decisions.'[42]

However, it would be a mistake to read too much into these comments. Coughlan[43] points out that the statement of O'Higgins CJ quoted above, in which he refers to the legal basis for the existing court structure, may suggest that he was referring instead 'to the uncontroversial principle of procedural fusion'. Keane comments that the opinions expressed by the Law Lords in *United Scientific* must be regarded as *obiter*,[44] and argues that it would be unwise to assume that *Hynes* indicates that these views have necessarily been accepted in this jurisdiction.

The better view would certainly seem to be that the substantive distinctions between the two systems of law and equity are still valid and there have been signs of this approach being reasserted recently in England.[45] So, in *Downsview Nominees Ltd v. First City Corporation Ltd*[46] the Privy Council refused to replace or supplement the equitable duties of mortgagees by liability in negligence, holding that such a result would lead to 'confusion and injustice'.[47] Similar reluctance to apply the principle of substantive fusion can be discerned from the approach of the House of Lords in *Lord Napier and Ettrick v. Hunter,*[48] in which Lord Goff stated that he could see no 'justification for sweeping the line of equity cases under the carpet as though it did not exist'.[49] Finally, in *Tinsley v. Milligan,*[50] Lord Browne-Wilkinson although he spoke of the fusion of law and equity[51] seemed to rely on common law and equitable principles which had

---

42. *Ibid.* at 221.
43. *Property Law* (2nd ed., 1998) p. 49.
44. *Equity and the Law of Trusts in the Republic of Ireland* (1988) p.25. Keane suggests that until the question is unequivocally resolved, the views expressed 'are most safely regarded as in the nature of premature funeral orations'.
45. *Bank of Boston Connecticut v. European Grain and Shipping Ltd* [1989] 1 All ER 545, 557 *per* Lord Brandon.
46. [1993] 2 WLR 86.
47. *Ibid.* at 99. This approach can be contrasted with that of the New Zealand Court of Appeal reported at [1989] 3 NZLR 710.
48. [1993] 2 WLR 42.
49. *Ibid.* at 59. Although the language employed by Lord Browne-Wilkinson who spoke in terms of 'the fusion of law and equity' (at pp.65, 66) might have suggested support for the alternative approach, the conclusion which he reached did not.
50. [1993] 3 WLR 126.
51. *Ibid.* at 147, 151. Although note that this first reference appears in the All England Reports as 'the fusion of the administration of law and equity', see [1993] 3 All ER 65, 86.

developed side by side rather than on the 'mingled' doctrine favoured by some judges in New Zealand.[52]

Millett[53] in a recent article has quite rightly suggested that the opinion that the Judicature Acts had the effect of fusing law and equity to the extent that they have become a single body of law rather than two separate systems of law administered together has been widely discredited, both in England and Australia.[54] In reviewing the recent English decisions, Martin[55] argues that the view that flexibility and capacity for development is best achieved by disregarding the legal or equitable origins of causes of action, remedies or defences is misconceived. She asserts that it does not seem that the fusion fallacy evidenced in cases such as *United Scientific* has become established in England; on the contrary she claims that there has been a return to orthodoxy. In her view, this is apparent from recent decisions of the House of Lords in *Napier* and *Tinsley* which, she says, contain 'meticulous analyses of the separate common law and equitable origins and principles' in the areas concerned. Hanbury and Martin's[56] concluding comments on this subject probably come closest to summing up the existing position:

> What can be said is that a century of fused jurisdiction has seen the two systems working more closely together; each changing and developing and improving from contact with the other; and each willing to accept new ideas and developments, regardless of their origin. They are coming closer together. But they are not yet fused.

---

52. See the *dicta* of Thomas J in *Powell v. Thompson* [1991] 1 NZLR 597, 615 who spoke of the 'happy mingling of law and equity'. However, this approach has been far from universal in that jurisdiction, see the *dicta* of Wylie J in *Equiticorp Industries Group Ltd v. Hawkins* [1991] 3 NZLR 700, 727. A more balanced view is that following put forward by Somers J in *Elders Pastoral Ltd v. Bank of New Zealand* [1989] 2 NZLR 180, 193: 'Neither law nor equity is now stifled by its origin and the fact that both are administered by one court has inevitably meant that each has borrowed from the other in furthering the harmonious development of the law as a whole'.
53. (1995) 9 Trust Law Int 35, 37.
54. See Mason (1994) 110 LQR 238. Mason also warns that over-concentration on the effect of the Judicature Acts is likely to result in undue emphasis being placed on the state of equitable doctrine as it existed at the time of their enactment. Similarly Millett asserts that not only did the Judicature Acts not fuse law and equity, 'they did not freeze them in their then state of development either'. See (1995) 9 Trust Law Int 35, 37.
55. [1994] Conv 13.
56. *Modern Equity* (15th ed., 1997) p.25.

CHAPTER 2

Maxims of Equity

INTRODUCTION

The maxims of equity constitute the general principles developed by the Court of Chancery over the years; as Mason CJ stated in *Corin v. Patton*[1] an equitable maxim is 'a summary statement of a broad theme which underlies equitable concepts and principles'. While they are not to be interpreted as positive rules of law which should always be applied in their literal sense, they do reflect general trends which can be discerned from the manner in which the equitable jurisdiction of the courts has been exercised. It is important to realize that some of these maxims overlap or may even appear to contradict one another and they should be treated with a certain degree of caution. Nevertheless a brief examination of the maxims and what they mean in practice provides a useful introduction to the manner in which equity operates.

EQUITY WILL NOT SUFFER A WRONG TO BE WITHOUT A REMEDY

The principle which lies behind this maxim is that equity will intervene to protect a recognised right which for some reason is not enforceable at common law and it reflects the basis for the origins of the equitable jurisdiction of the chancellor. However, as equitable jurisdiction became more established, it also grew increasingly formalised and based on precedent. As Greene MR commented in *Re Diplock*:[2] 'if a claim in equity exists it must be shown to have an ancestry founded in history and in the practice and precedents of the courts administering equity jurisdiction'.

Textbook writers have pointed out that this maxim should be treated with considerable caution today; Wylie[3] has commented that 'it is a grossly inaccurate statement of equity's approach in modern times' and Meagher,

---

1. (1990) 169 CLR 540, 557.
2. [1948] Ch 465, 481-482.
3. *Irish Land Law* (3rd ed., 1997) p. 121.

Gummow and Lehane[4] stress that it is misleading unless one realises that the maxim is now of 'purely historical importance'. It should also be made clear at the outset that in this context the word 'wrong' refers to conduct contrary to the law rather than simply immoral.

Despite its potentially misleading nature, there are nevertheless some important practical illustrations of the operation of the maxim which can still be seen today. Perhaps the most far-reaching of these is the recognition given by equity to the concept of the trust by virtue of which a beneficiary can enforce equitable rights which the common law would not recognise, as it simply regarded the trustee as the legal owner. Other notable illustrations of the maxim can be found in relation to the grant of equitable remedies. The injunction developed as a means of achieving justice where the common law remedy of damages could not provide an adequate remedy and will now issue e.g. to restrain an ongoing nuisance[5] or in *quia timet* form to prevent a threatened wrong from occurring.[6] Similarly, where specific performance of a contract for the sale of land is sought, it can be granted provided sufficient acts of part performance can be established despite non-compliance with the necessary statutory formalities.[7] Another illustration is the appointment of a receiver by way of equitable execution which can operate where a creditor is unable to levy execution at law owing to the equitable nature of the property concerned.

Despite the frequency with which the above illustrations of the maxim occur in practice, it would be fair to say that more recent attempts to develop the principle which it lays down have proved less successful. As Lindley LJ commented in *Holmes v. Millage*:[8] 'It is an old mistake to suppose that, because there is no effectual remedy at law, there must be one in equity'. A classic example of how an attempt to develop a new form of equitable relief has failed to become established is provided by the new model constructive trust,[9] a creature first devised by Lord Denning to be imposed 'whenever justice and good conscience require it'.[10] Maudsley[11] criticised this development saying that it was possible to read into the decisions the principle that 'in cases in which the plaintiff ought to win, but has no legal doctrine or authority to support him, a constructive trust

---

4.   *Equity Doctrines and Remedies* (3rd ed., 1992) p. 71.
5.   *Patterson v. Murphy* [1978] ILRM 85; *Kennaway v. Thompson* [1981] QB 88.
6.   *Whelan v. Madigan* [1978] ILRM 136.
7.   *Lowry v. Reid* [1927] NI 142.
8.   [1893] 1 QB 551, 555.
9.   See *infra* Chapter 8.
10. *Hussey v. Palmer* [1972] 1 WLR 1286, 1290. See also *N.A.D. v. T.D.* [1985] ILRM 153, 160.
11. (1977) 28 NILQ 123. See also Oakley (1973) 26 CLP 17, 39.

in his favour will do the trick.' More recent judgments show a considerable retrenchment from the position laid down in the early decisions[12] and it has been rejected outright in some common law jurisdictions.[13] While there is still some evidence of its existence in this jurisdiction,[14] there is certainly no sign of any wholesale adoption of Lord Denning's constructive trust of a 'new model'.

There is also evidence of a reluctance to further extend existing equitable devices for achieving justice between parties which is well illustrated by examining the concept of the purchase money resulting trust and the manner in which it has been used to confer interests in the family home. This type of trust has traditionally been employed to give relief to a party who has no legal interest in the property but has nevertheless contributed financially either directly or indirectly to its purchase. When the Supreme Court was faced with the argument in *L. v. L.*[15] that contributions of a non-financial kind, such as work in the home, should also give rise to a resulting trust, it declined to accept this proposition on the basis that such a step would involve the creation of an entirely new right and instead decided that the issue was one for the legislature.

EQUITY FOLLOWS THE LAW

This maxim might be more accurately stated as: 'Equity follows the law, but not slavishly nor always'[16] and it would be inaccurate to interpret it too strictly. It would be fair to say that although equity does not seek to question the existence of legal rights it will attempt to mitigate the often harsh results caused by their strict enforcement. Equity restricted or modified the application of common law principles where it was in the interests of fairness to do so. A classic illustration of this modification is the principle that equity will not allow a statute to be used as an instrument of fraud.[17] So, for example, equity would not permit a beneficiary to be deprived of an interest in land under the terms of a trust where this would amount to fraud even if there was insufficient compliance with the requisite statutory

---

12. E.g. *Ashburn Anstalt v. Arnold* [1988] 2 WLR 706.
13. E.g. in Australia, *Muschinski v. Dodds* (1985) 160 CLR 583, 615.
14. *H.K.N. Invest Oy v. Incotrade Pvt Ltd* [1993] 3 IR 152.
15. [1992] 2 IR 77.
16. *Graf v. Hope Building Corporation* (1930) 254 NY 1, 9 *per* Cardozo CJ.
17. *McCormick v. Grogan* (1869) LR 4 HL 82, 97 *per* Lord Westbury. See further Chapter 4.

formalities,[18] provided that there was some other evidence to establish the nature of his interest.[19] Equally, equity would recognise the existence of secret or half secret trusts[20] by waiving the requirement of strict compliance with the necessary testamentary formalities in the interests of preventing fraud.[21]

Having referred briefly to some of the equitable modifications to common law principles, it should be pointed out that in numerous situations, equity does indeed follow the law and as a general principle, equitable interests in land correspond with legal estates and interests.[22] This point is well illustrated by the manner in which equity tends to follow the law in relation to executed as opposed to executory trusts. These expressions refer to the creation of a trust and not to its performance. A trust is said to be executed where the settlor has specified precisely the limits under which the trust property is to be held and where no further instrument is required as the trust has been finally declared in the first instance. A trust is said to be executory where, although a valid trust is created, the settlor has only indicated his general intentions as to how the trust property is to be disposed of and the execution of a further instrument is required to define the beneficial interests with precision.[23]

In the case of executed trusts, equity follows the law and generally requires the same precise words of limitation in relation to an equitable interest as would be required for a legal estate. This proposition can be seen from the decision of the English Court of Appeal in *Re Bostock's Settlement*[24] in which it was held that where an executed trust is created, the requisite legal words of limitation must be used and a general intent to confer an interest in fee simple will not suffice. A similar finding was made by the Supreme Court in *Jameson v. McGovern*[25] where Murnaghan J cited with approval the following *dicta* of Lord Eldon in *Jervoise v. Duke of Northumberland*[26] in relation to executed trusts: 'These are cases where

---

18. S.4 of the Statute of Frauds (Ireland) 1695 requires that express trusts of land be evidenced in writing and signed by a person able to declare the trust, or by his will.
19. *Rochefoucauld v. Boustead* [1897] 1 Ch 196; *McGillicuddy v. Joy* [1959] IR 189; *Gilmurray v. Corr* [1978] NI 99.
20. See *infra* Chapter 5.
21. E.g. *Riordan v. Banon* (1876) IR 10 Eq 469.
22. There are exceptions to this general principle, see Megarry and Wade, *The Law of Real Property* (5th ed., 1984) p.120.
23. See *Davis v. Richards and Wallington Ltd* [1990] 1 WLR 1511, 1537-1538.
24. [1921] 2 Ch 469.
25. [1934] IR 758.
26. (1821) 1 Jac & W 559.

the testator has clearly decided what the trust is to be; and as equity follows the law, where the testator has left nothing to be done, but has himself expressed it, there the effect must be the same, whether the estate is legal or equitable.' In *Jameson* by virtue of a marriage settlement freehold premises had been conveyed to a husband for life, to his wife for life, then to any children, or if there were none, to those appointed by the husband and in default of appointment, for the survivor of the husband and wife absolutely. The parties had no children and no appointment was made by the husband. After his death, the question of the extent of the wife's interest under the settlement arose. The Supreme Court held, following *Re Bostock's Settlement*, that the wife only derived a life interest from it, although the court went on to hold that she had an equity independent of the settlement sufficient to give her an equitable fee simple in the property. A similar approach of requiring the necessary words of limitation was followed by Costello J in *Savage v. Nolan*,[27] although as in *Jameson* the court was able to find that the parties in question, in this instance children under a marriage settlement, were entitled to an absolute interest independent of the settlement. As Keane[28] points out it would be interesting to see whether the courts in this jurisdiction would adopt such a strict approach if a case arose in which there was no such 'escape route'.

HE WHO SEEKS EQUITY MUST DO EQUITY

Equity will only grant relief on terms which ensure that a defendant is treated fairly and to obtain equitable relief, a plaintiff must be prepared to act in an honourable manner. This maxim has many different applications and reflects the fact that equitable remedies are discretionary in nature. It is one of the few maxims that can be interpreted fairly literally; as Meagher, Gummow and Lehane[29] point out 'there are many illustrations of, and almost no exceptions to, the maxim'. It in a sense complements the maxim that 'he who comes to equity must come with clean hands' and while the latter principle focuses on the past conduct of the party seeking the intervention of the court, the maxim that 'he who seeks equity must do equity' is concerned with his likely future conduct.

The effect of the maxim is noticeable in the approach of equity towards the granting of remedies and is a feature of equitable jurisdiction

---

27. High Court 1976 No. 2395 P (Costello J) 20 July 1978.
28. *Equity and the Law of Trusts in the Republic of Ireland* (1988) p.29.
29. *Equity Doctrines and Remedies* (3rd ed., 1992) p. 77.

which distinguishes it from the common law. An illustration of this is the manner in which equity approaches a claim for rescission of a contract. Rescission will be granted to a plaintiff on such terms which the court considers just[30] and relief of an unconditional nature may not achieve this aim. So, in *Cheese v. Thomas*[31] an elderly plaintiff who had given the defendant, his great-nephew, approximately half of the purchase price of a house on the understanding that he could live there until he died, sought to have the transaction set aside on grounds of undue influence. Nicholls VC ordered that the property should be sold and that both parties should bear the loss on the sale in the same proportions as they had contributed to the purchase price. He pointed out that the court was concerned to achieve practical justice for both parties and not for the plaintiff alone and stated that 'the plaintiff is seeking the assistance of a court of equity and he who seeks equity must do equity'.[32]

Another example of the application of the maxim is that an interlocutory injunction will not be granted unless a plaintiff is prepared to give an undertaking as to damages in order to ensure that a defendant may be compensated in the event of the former being successful at the interlocutory stage but ultimately failing at the trial of the action. In addition, in specific cases a court may choose to withhold interlocutory relief where a claimant is unwilling to carry out his side of a contract or arrangement which may exist between the parties. So, in *Chappell v. Times Newspapers Ltd,*[33] the plaintiffs sought an interim injunction to restrain their employers from terminating their contracts of employment, although they refused to give the undertakings sought by the employers not to engage in disruptive behaviour. Although the plaintiffs themselves had not previously been directly involved in these activities, the Court of Appeal refused to grant the relief sought on the grounds that the plaintiffs had failed to establish that they intended to act equitably by abiding by the terms of their contracts of employment. As Lord Denning MR said: 'if one party seeks relief, he must be ready and willing to do his part in it.'[34]

Equally, a claimant will not be granted specific performance of a contract unless he can establish to the satisfaction of the court that he is willing and able to carry out his own contractual obligations. Specific performance may also be refused on the grounds of a lack of mutuality

---

30. *Cooper v. Phibbs* (1867) LR 2 HL 149; *Solle v. Butcher* [1950] 1 KB 671.
31. [1994] 1 WLR 129.
32. *Ibid.* at 136.
33. [1975] 1 WLR 482.
34. *Ibid.* at 502.

between the parties, a principle set out as follows by O'Connor LJ in *O'Regan v. White:*[35] 'Generally speaking, at any rate, it would not be even-handed justice to compel specific performance against the one party, where the same remedy would not be available against the other party in respect of matters to be by him performed under the contract.'

In deciding whether to grant or withhold equitable relief, a court will have regard to the conduct of both parties if it 'is truly to act as a court of conscience'.[36] This principle can be seen in the context of claims which may be defeated by a plea of estoppel and, where it would be unconscionable for a plaintiff to renege on an assumption which he has permitted a defendant to make, he will be estopped from asserting his claim.[37]

The operation of this maxim can also be seen in relation to the mortgagor's equity of redemption. If the mortgagor wishes to use the extension of time permitted by equity to exercise the right of redemption, it can only be exercised on equitable terms; he must be willing to pay all arrears of interest due to the mortgagee and to give him reasonable notice of his intention to redeem.

Finally, the maxim is the basis for the doctrine of election, i.e. that a person cannot take a benefit and reject an associated burden, which will be considered in detail in a later chapter.[38]

HE WHO COMES TO EQUITY MUST COME WITH CLEAN HANDS

This maxim also reflects the discretionary nature of equity and requires that a person seeking equitable relief must refrain from fraud, misrepresentation or any other form of dishonest or disreputable conduct if he wishes to be granted a remedy.[39] However unlike the maxim just considered, it refers principally to the past conduct of the plaintiff. The general principle

---

35. [1919] 2 IR 339, 393.
36. *McMahon v. Kerry County Council* [1981] ILRM 419, 421.
37. E.g. *Lim Teng Huan v. Ang Swee Chuan* [1992] 1 WLR 113. See further Chapter 17.
38. See *infra* Chapter 19.
39. See generally, Chafee (1949) 47 Mich L Rev 1065 and Pettit [1990] Conv 416. Pettit suggests (at p.424) that unclean hands seems to be a 'last resort defence' to be invoked where none of the so called nominate defences are applicable but where it would be unconscionable for the plaintiff to be granted relief by the court. For a recent restatement of the fact that this maxim applies to a plaintiff seeking equitable relief, see the judgment of Keane J in *National Irish Bank Ltd v. RTE* [1998] 2 ILRM 196, 207.

which the maxim lays down was stated by Eyre LCB in *Dering v. Earl of Winchelsea*[40] as follows:

> A man must come into a court of equity with clean hands; but when this is said, it does not mean a general depravity; it must have an immediate and necessary relation to the equity sued for; it must be a depravity in a legal as well as in the moral sense.

One classic illustration of the maxim in operation is the decision of Wigram VC in *Overton v. Banister.*[41] An infant beneficiary fraudulently misrepresented herself as being of age, although she was only 19, and thereby induced the trustees to give her possession of assets to which she should only have been entitled when she reached the age of 21. When she reached this age, she instituted a suit against the trustees to compel them to reimburse the trust fund of assets which they had improperly paid to her. Although at common law, her deceit was ineffectual to discharge the trustees of their duty, her claim was disallowed in equity because she had misrepresented her age. It is clear that where a beneficiary has instigated, participated in or even consented to a breach of trust, as the decision in *Overton* shows, the beneficiary will not succeed in any action brought against a trustee in respect of this breach.[42] Even where a beneficiary is not involved prior to the breach being committed, he may still be unable to bring a successful action against the trustees if he subsequently acquiesces in the breach,[43] provided that he does so with full knowledge of the surrounding facts and circumstances.

It is well established that a plaintiff will be refused a decree of specific performance if his conduct towards the defendant has been less than honest. This point was made in a general way by Black LJ in *Conlon v. Murray*[44] where he stressed that the remedy may be withheld in a situation where the conduct of the parties and the circumstances of the case demand it. In *Smelter Corporation v. O'Driscoll*[45] the plaintiff claimed an order of specific performance of a contract to sell lands. The plaintiff's agent had told

---

40. (1787) 1 Cox 318, 319-320. Cited with approval by Issacs J in *Meyers v. Casey* (1913) 17 CLR 90, 123. See also *Tinker v. Tinker* [1970] P 136, 143 *per* Salmon LJ and *NZ Netherlands Society 'Oranje' Inc v. Kuys* [1973] 2 All ER 1222, 1227 *per* Lord Wilberforce.
41. (1844) 3 Hare 503. See also *Cory v. Gertcken* (1816) 2 Madd 49.
42. *French v. Graham* (1860) 10 Ir Ch R 522; *Re Pauling's Settlement Trusts* [1964] Ch 303, 335 *per* Wilmer LJ.
43. *Walker v. Symonds* (1818) 3 Swans 1, 64 *per* Lord Eldon.
44. [1958] NI 17, 25.
45. [1977] IR 305.

the defendant that if she did not sell the land in question, the property would be compulsorily acquired, although, unknown to the agent, this was not in fact the case. The Supreme Court refused a decree of specific performance. O'Higgins CJ stressed that the remedy was a discretionary one and concluded that by reason of the plaintiff's misrepresentation, the defendant was under a fundamental misapprehension as to the true facts and that it would be unjust to grant specific performance in the circumstances. While the type of conduct which will disentitle a plaintiff to equitable relief will usually amount to impropriety of a fairly serious nature, because of the discretionary nature of the court's jurisdiction, a claimant would be well advised to follow the advice given by Barr J in the course of his judgment in *O'Connor v. Harrington Ltd*[46] where he concluded that the 'clean hands' principle applies with equal force to applications for injunctions made under section 27 of the Local Government (Planning and Development) Act 1976. Barr J stated that '[i]n seeking such relief an applicant should put before the court fairly and with candour all facts known to him which are relevant to the exercise of the court's discretion and he should satisfy it about his *bona fides* and the true purpose of his application.'[47]

It has been established that equitable relief may be refused to a plaintiff where his conduct in relation to the transaction at issue has been less than honest even where this conduct has not directly prejudiced the defendant. This proposition is well illustrated by the decision of Costello J in *Parkes v. Parkes.*[48] A husband bought land and the conveyance was taken in his wife's name to obviate the need for Land Commission consent.[49] After the parties divorced, the husband registered an inhibition on the land and the wife instituted proceedings claiming that it had been wrongly registered. The husband counter-claimed that he was entitled to the beneficial ownership in the property. It was claimed on behalf of the wife that the husband should not be able to obtain relief in equity 'by setting up his own illegality or fraud'. Costello J referred to other cases where a husband had bought a house and put it in his wife's name to protect it from creditors[50] and where a father had deposited money in his son's name to avoid death duties,[51] and concluded as follows:

---

46. High Court 1984 No. 69 MCA (Barr J) 28 May 1987.
47. At p. 14.
48. [1980] ILRM 137.
49. Under s.45 of the Land Act 1965 this consent would have been required had the conveyance been taken in the husband's name, but as the wife was an Irish citizen, it was not necessary.
50. *Gascoigne v. Gascoigne* [1918] 1 KB 223.
51. *McEvoy v. Belfast Banking Co.* [1934] NI 67.

> Just as the courts will not grant relief to a person who has allowed
> property to be placed in a wife's or son's name for the fraudulent
> purpose of defeating creditors . . . or for the illegal purpose of evad-
> ing liability to tax . . . so it seems to me that the court should not
> grant relief to a purchaser who has placed property in his wife's
> name dishonestly and by means of an illegal act performed for the
> purpose of evading the law relating to the transfer of land.[52]

Therefore, although the husband's dishonest conduct had in no way prejudiced the wife in this instance, it sufficed to disentitle him to the equitable
relief which he sought.

One important aspect of the application of this maxim which must be
stressed is that a court will decline to intervene on the basis of the 'unclean
hands' principle unless there is a sufficient connection between the inequitable conduct and the subject-matter of the dispute. This point was made
by Eyre LCB in *Dering v. Earl of Winchelsea*[53] and re-iterated in the following terms by Scrutton LJ in *Moody v. Cox:*[54] 'Equity will not apply the
principle about clean hands unless the depravity, the dirt in question on the
hand has an "immediate and necessary relation" to the equity sued for.'
The effect of this proposition is well illustrated by the decision of Ungoed-
Thomas J in *Argyll v. Argyll*[55] where he held that the alleged immorality of
the plaintiff's conduct which had led to divorce did not deprive her of her
entitlement to an injunction to restrain a breach of confidence by her husband. Ungoed-Thomas J stated that 'the plaintiff's adultery, repugnant
though it be, should not in my view license the husband to broadcast un-
checked the most intimate confidences of earlier and happier days' and he
continued 'a person coming to equity must come with clean hands but the
cleanliness required is to be judged in relation to the relief that is sought.'

The so-called 'clean hands' principle has been applied in a wide variety of situations where equitable remedies have been sought e.g. where
the plaintiff has acted unfairly and unreasonably,[56] or where he has attempted to mislead the court.[57] The Supreme Court has recently given some
consideration to the type of conduct which is necessary to bring the 'clean

---

52. [1980] ILRM 137, 144.
53. (1787) 1 Cox 318, 319-320.
54. [1917] 2 Ch 71, 87-88. The plaintiff's claim for rescission of a contract succeeded
    despite the fact that he had given a bribe to the vendor's solicitor, although admit-
    tedly in an unconnected matter.
55. [1967] Ch 302.
56. *Shell U.K.Ltd v. Lostock Garages Ltd* [1976] 1 WLR 1187, 1199 *per* Lord Denning
    MR.
57. *Armstrong v. Shepherd & Short Ltd* [1959] 2 QB 384, 397.

hands' maxim into operation in *Curust Financial Services Ltd v. Loewe-Lack-Werk Otto Loewe GmbH & Co. KG*.[58] There, it had to decide whether the alleged breach by the plaintiff of an exclusive licensing agreement, consisting of its sub-contracting the manufacture of a product without the prior written consent of the first named defendant, should disentitle it to relief. As a general principle, Finlay CJ accepted that the court has a discretion, where it is satisfied that a person has come to court otherwise than with 'clean hands,' to refuse equitable relief in the form of an injunction on that ground alone. However, he stated: 'It seems to me that this phrase must of necessity involve an element of turpitude and cannot necessarily be equated with a mere breach of contract.'[59] Finlay CJ made reference to the fact that what might be established as a breach by the plaintiff of the agreement not to sub-contract, namely the entering into an arrangement with a third party for this purpose, might also be established as having been provoked by a wrongful repudiation on the part of the first named defendant of its own contractual obligations under the licensing agreement. He therefore concluded that it would be unreasonable that such conduct should disentitle the plaintiff to an injunction to which it would otherwise be entitled and he held that this should not constitute a ground for rejecting the claim for relief.

This more flexible approach to the application of the maxim has also been adopted by the majority of the Court of Appeal and the House of Lords in *Tinsley v. Milligan*.[60] This case concerned a dispute in relation to the beneficial ownership of property registered in the sole name of the plaintiff but bought by the parties as part of a business venture on the tacit understanding that both should be joint beneficial owners of the house. The purpose of this arrangement was to assist in the perpetration of frauds on the Department of Social Security, although the defendant subsequently decided to disclose these irregularities to the department. The plaintiff sought possession of the property and the defendant counter-claimed seeking a declaration that the house was held by the plaintiff on trust for both parties in equal shares. The majority of the Court of Appeal held that since both the plaintiff and the defendant had been party to the fraud and since the illegality was not of a continuing nature, it would not be an affront to

---

58. [1994] 1 IR 450.
59. *Ibid.* at 467.
60. [1992] Ch 310 (CA) and [1994] 1 AC 340 (HL). See further, Lunney (1992) 6 Trust Law Int 110; Martin [1992] Conv 153, 161-166; Halliwell [1994] Conv 62; Buckley (1994) 110 LQR 3. For further analysis of the decision in *Tinsley*, see Thornton [1993] CLJ 394; Stowe (1994) 57 MLR 441; Enonchong (1995) 111 LQR 135; Rose (1996) 112 LQR 386.

the public conscience to grant the relief sought by the defendant and that her counterclaim did not arise *ex turpi causa* so as to deny her relief.[61] Lloyd LJ in considering the possible relevance of the maxim 'he who comes to equity must come with clean hands' seemed to countenance a flexible application of the principle and said that he saw no reason why the court should not in the exercise of its equitable jurisdiction, follow and adopt the more adaptable attitude shown by the common law in cases where issues of public policy have arisen. He continued:

> If the common law can discriminate, so can equity. So far as the joint fraud on the D.S.S. is concerned, the parties were admittedly *in pari delicto*. But when one looks at the overall equities, the balance comes down strongly in favour of the defendant. I do not think that the clean hands maxim should prevent us from giving effect to that balance. We are not obliged to draw up our skirts and refuse all relief.[62]

The majority of the House of Lords agreed with this more flexible ap-proach to the issues of 'clean hands'[63] and illegality.[64] In the opinion of Lord Browne-Wilkinson, illegality may render a proprietary interest un-enforceable in certain circumstances but only where the claimant had to rely on the illegality to prove the equitable right and this was not the case in this instance. Lord Goff in his dissenting judgment took a stricter ap-proach towards the equitable maxim and said that '[i]t is founded on the principle that he who has committed iniquity shall not have equity'. In his view, it was not desirable to distinguish between varying degrees of iniq-uity and he felt that to adopt a more flexible approach would 'open the door to far more unmeritorious cases'.[65]

---

61. Lunney comments in (1992) 6 Trust Law Int 110 that the basis of both the maxims *ex turpi causa* and 'he who comes to equity must come with clean hands' is public policy and that it is desirable that public policy achieves the same result whether the interest sought to be protected is legal or equitable.
62. [1992] Ch 310, 341.
63. Council suggests that the decision of the House of Lords in *Tinsley* leads one to ask whether the maxim 'He who comes to equity must come with clean hands' has now been modified to read 'He who comes to equity should keep unclean hands in his pockets', see (1993) 143 NLJ 1577.
64. Some commentators have sought to distinguish the 'clean hands' principle from the notion of illegality on the basis that the former merely operates to deprive the plain-tiff of his entitlement to equitable relief whereas the latter may destroy all his rights, whether legal or equitable. See Meagher, Gummow and Lehane *Equity Doctrines and Remedies* (3rd ed., 1992) p.82 footnote 15.
65. [1994] 1 AC 340, 362. Buckley (1994) 110 LQR 3, 5-6 has asserted that many of the

It is fair to say that while the earlier authorities suggested a rather rigid approach to the application of the 'clean hands' principle, there is now increasing evidence both in England, in this jurisdiction and elsewhere in the common law world[66] of a more flexible attitude being adopted.[67] However, one point which should be made about *Curust* and *Tinsley* is that both parties in these cases had been involved in some form of impropriety. It would be interesting to consider whether if one party alone had been guilty of this impropriety, the court would have taken such a benevolent attitude towards the wrongdoing.

DELAY DEFEATS EQUITY

This maxim is enshrined in the phrase *vigilantibus, non dormientibus jura subveniunt*; the law assists the vigilant not those who sleep, so delay is well established as a discretionary factor which may influence a court's decision to grant or withhold equitable relief.[68] A well known summary of its effect is provided by Lord Camden LC in *Smith v. Clay*[69] where he stated: 'A court of equity ... has always refused its aid to stale demands, where a party has slept upon his right and acquiesced for a great length of time. Nothing can call forth this court into activity but conscience, good faith and reasonable diligence.'

Two concepts are of relevance in examining the application of this maxim in practice, namely, laches and acquiescence. The effect of the doctrine of laches is that where there has been unreasonable delay in the bringing of proceedings which would render it unjust to grant relief, a plaintiff may find his claim barred in equity. Acquiescence on the other hand means that where one party infringes another's rights and that other party does nothing, equity infers that the latter has acquiesced in the former's

---

cases relied on by Lord Goff in support of the view that the 'clean hands' principle applied in this case were distinguishable as they involved unsuccessful attempts by participants in unlawful schemes to refer to these schemes so as to rebut the presumption of advancement to which their contribution has given rise.

66. See *Equiticorp Industries Group v. The Crown* [1996] 3 NZLR 586, 601 and *Unilever plc v. Cussons* [1997] 1 NZLR 433, 442.

67. However, Halliwell suggests [1994] Conv 62, 67 that neither the dissenting judgment of Lord Goff, nor the majority satisfactorily determined the scope of the underlying principle of unclean hands. She asserts that 'justice..was achieved in the case but the achievement was purely pragmatic and not purposeful'.

68. See e.g. *Lennon v. Ganly* [1981] ILRM 84; *Howard v. Commissioners of Public Works in Ireland* High Court 1992 No. 331JR (O'Hanlon J) 3 December 1992.

69. (1767) 3 Bro CC 639, 640n. See also the *dicta* of Lord Blackburn in *Erlanger v. New Sombrero Phosphate Co.* (1878) 3 App Cas 1218, 1279.

actions and he may not be permitted to pursue his claim. However, before examining these doctrines in more detail, it is first necessary to explain the effect of statutory limitation periods. As a general principle equitable doctrines will have no application to cases to which the Statute of Limitations 1957 applies,[70] and the statute lays down such express periods in relation to a number of equitable rights. A six year limitation period is laid down with respect to actions by beneficiaries to recover trust property or in respect of any breach of trust or to recover the estates of deceased persons.[71] A 12 year limitation period is laid down for actions for the recovery of land[72] and actions by a mortgagor to redeem a mortgage.[73] It was held recently by the Supreme Court in *Gleeson v. Feehan*[74] that a limitation period of 12 years as provided for under section 13 of the statute applies to an action by a personal representative of a deceased owner of land seeking recovery of such land in succession to the owner, rather than a period of six years laid down by section 45 as amended, which would apply to an action against a personal representative by a person claiming to be entitled to a share in a deceased's estate. As McMahon J had pointed out in *Drohan v. Drohan,*[75] section 45 applied to claims against, and not claims by, personal representatives and it had no application to a claim by a personal representative to recover a deceased's assets against a person holding adversely to the estate.

Section 43 of the Statute of Limitations 1957 provides that an action taken against a trustee in respect of a breach of trust must be brought within a six year limitation period provided that it is not an action to which any other statutory limitation period applies. However, section 44 excludes from the application of limitation periods a claim founded on fraud or fraudulent breach of trust in which the trustee was involved or to which he was party.

The only exception to the principle that equitable considerations will have no application to cases to which the Statute of Limitations 1957 ap-

---

70. S.5 of the statute provides that 'Nothing in this Act shall afford any equitable jurisdiction to refuse relief on the ground of acquiescence or otherwise' and it would seem in England that where a limitation period is prescribed by statute and a claim is brought within this period that a person cannot rely on the doctrine of laches to defeat the claim, see *Re Pauling's Settlement Trusts* [1964] Ch 303.
71. Ss.43 and 45 of the Statute of Limitations 1957, Note that a new s.45 was inserted by s.126 of the Succession Act 1965.
72. S.13 of the Statute of Limitations 1957.
73. S.34 of the Statute of Limitations 1957.
74. [1993] 2 IR 113.
75. [1981] ILRM 473.

plies, is the reasoning employed by Henchy J in *O Domhnaill v. Merrick*[76] based on the constitutional right to fair procedures to the effect that in certain circumstances 'inordinate and inexcusable delay' will bar a claim brought within the relevant limitation period where this will place an unfair burden on the person sued. The principle in *O Domhnaill* was applied by the Supreme Court in *Toal v. Duignan (No.2)*[77] where Finlay CJ said that the courts have an inherent jurisdiction to dismiss a claim in the interests of justice where the length of time which has elapsed between the events out of which it arises and the time when it comes for hearing is in all the circumstances so great that it would be unjust to call upon a particular defendant to defend himself.[78] However, as Keane[79] has pointed out, these principles are likely to only apply in a small number of cases, namely those relating to personal injuries claims by minors, in which the limitation period may be particularly long, and the recollection of witnesses of considerable importance.

While we have considered some of the most common situations to which express statutory limitation periods apply, it is important to stress that the principles of laches and acquiescence may also not be relevant to cases in which limitation periods are applied by analogy. While section 9(a) of the Statute of Limitations 1957 provides that the limitation periods laid down in section 11 for claims in contract and tort shall not apply to any claims for equitable relief, section 9(b) goes on to provide that the provision shall not be construed as preventing a court 'from applying by analogy' any provision of the section. One question which remains to be satisfactorily resolved is what the position will be where the cause of action in contract or tort is not statute barred. In *Cahill v. Irish Motor Traders Association*[80] Budd J stated: 'Mere delay will not of itself disentitle a plaintiff to an injunction in aid of his legal rights unless the claim to enforce the right is barred by a statute of limitations.' The effect of this approach would seem to be that where a cause of action is not statute barred and equitable relief is sought in relation to a common law right, the doctrine of laches cannot

---

76. [1984] IR 151.
77. [1991] ILRM 140.
78. Finlay CJ stated that while the existence of culpable negligence on the part of a plaintiff whose claim has been delayed is of considerable relevance, it is not an essential ingredient for the exercise of the court's inherent jurisdiction to dismiss a claim (p.143). McCarthy J dissented in part by saying that without culpable delay on the part of a plaintiff, the court's inherent jurisdiction to dismiss a claim may not be exercised. (p.159).
79. *Equity and the Law of Trusts in the Republic of Ireland* (1988) at pp.35-36.
80. [1966] IR 430, 449.

be applied. This approach seems to have been also followed in Australia and in *Orr v. Ford*[81] Deane J said that 'laches . . . is not available in answer to a legal claim'. However, in England it was held by the Court of Appeal in *Habib Bank Ltd v. Habib Bank AG Zurich*[82] that laches is always relevant where equitable relief is sought and that no distinction should be made between cases where such relief is sought to give effect to legal as opposed to equitable rights.

Laches and Acquiescence

The doctrine of laches which may operate to bar a claim in equity where no statutory period of limitation applies, either expressly or by analogy, was described as follows by Lord Selborne LC in *Lindsay Petroleum v. Hurd*:[83]

> [T]he doctrine of laches in Courts of Equity is not an arbitrary or a technical doctrine. Where it would be practically unjust to give a remedy, either because the party has, by his conduct, done that which might fairly be regarded as equivalent to a waiver of it, or where by his conduct or neglect he has, though perhaps not waiving that remedy, yet put the other party in a situation in which it would not be reasonable to place him if the remedy were afterwards to be asserted, in either of these cases, lapse of time and delay are most material.

In deciding whether the defence of laches has been established, a court must consider first, whether the plaintiff has delayed unreasonably in bringing his claim and secondly, assess whether prejudice or detriment has been suffered by the defendant as a result. Delay of itself is insufficient and clearly, the period of time necessary to invalidate a claim will vary according to the circumstances of each case. Often delay may be interpreted as evidence of an agreement by the plaintiff not to pursue his claim and where a plaintiff had acted in a manner which has induced the defendant to alter his position, it would be inequitable to allow the claim to proceed. A good example of how the doctrine of laches operates in practice is provided by the decision of Keane J in *J.H. v. W.J.H.*[84] The plaintiff signed a document in which she agreed to compromise her rights under the Succession Act 1965 to her late husband's farm in favour of her son. While Keane J ac-

---

81. (1989) 167 CLR 316, 340.
82. [1981] 1 WLR 1265.
83. (1874) LR 5 PC 221, 239-240.
84. High Court 1977 No. 5831P (Keane J) 20 December 1979.

cepted that the transaction was an improvident one which the courts would in the normal course of events have set aside, he refused to grant her relief in the circumstances. Keane J referred to the delay by the plaintiff for a period of four years in seeking to assert her claim and the time and money invested in the running of the farm by the defendant on the basis that she had abandoned her rights, and concluded that the lapse of time coupled with circumstances which made it inequitable to enforce the claim was sufficient to bar the plaintiff's action. Another illustration of the doctrine of laches is provided by the decision of the English Court of Appeal in *Allcard v. Skinner.*[85] The plaintiff, who joined a sisterhood of nuns, made her will in favour of the superior of the order and also transferred large amounts of money and stock to her. When she left the order, she revoked her will but made no attempt to reclaim her property until five or six years later when she instituted proceedings claiming that it had been transferred as a result of undue influence. The majority of the Court of Appeal held that the claim was barred by laches and acquiescence. As Lindley LJ stated it was a case which by no means rested on mere lapse of time and the plaintiff's conduct amounted in effect to confirmation of the gift.

Acquiescence arises where a plaintiff either expressly or impliedly represents that he does not intend to enforce a claim and as a result of this representation, it becomes unjust in all the circumstances to grant the relief which he subsequently seeks. The principle was summarised as follows by Lord Wensleydale in *Archbold v. Scully:*[86]

> If a party, who could object, lies by and knowingly permits another to incur an expense in doing an act under the belief that it would not be objected to, and so a kind of permission may be said to be given to another to alter his condition, he may be said to acquiesce.

It is well established that acquiescence may bar a claim for equitable relief[87] and it usually arises in circumstances where a party fails to seek a remedy when a violation of his rights is brought to his attention.[88]

Consideration has recently been given by Laddie J in his judgment in *Nelson v. Rye*[89] to the circumstances in which the equitable defences of laches and acquiescence operate, although he stressed that it can be mis-

---

85. (1887) 36 Ch D 145.
86. (1861) 9 HLC 360, 383.
87. See e.g. *Irwin v. O'Connell* [1936] IR 44; *Sayers v. Collyer* (1884) 28 Ch D 103; *Shaw v. Applegate* [1977] 1 WLR 970.
88. *McCausland v. Young* [1949] NI 49, 88-89 *per* Andrews LCJ.
89. [1996] 2 All ER 186.

leading to approach them as if they consisted of 'a series of precisely defined hurdles over each of which a litigant must struggle before the defence is made out'. The plaintiff musician sought an account of the moneys
received by the defendant, his manager, during the ten year period from
1980-1990 in which the latter had managed his business affairs. Laddie J
accepted that the plaintiff's delay in instituting proceedings was such that
it would be unreasonable and unjust to allow the plaintiff to assert his
right to an account against the defendant for the period prior to December
1985 and that the defences of laches and acquiescence were made out in
relation to that part of the claim. Laddie J made the following comment
about the circumstances in which the defences will operate:

> [T]hese defences are not technical or arbitrary. The courts have in-
> dicated over the years some of the factors which must be taken into
> consideration in deciding whether the defence runs. Those factors
> include the period of the delay, the extent to which the defendant's
> position has been prejudiced by the delay, and the extent to which
> that prejudice was caused by the actions of the plaintiff. I accept that
> mere delay alone will almost never suffice, but the court has to look
> at all the circumstances, including in particular those factors set out
> above, and then decide whether the balance of justice or injustice is
> in favour of granting the remedy or withholding it.[90]

This tendency to treat laches and acquiescence as a single defence has
been continued in the decision of the Court of Appeal in *Gafford v.
Graham*[91] and Milne has recently commented that there is 'no reason for
continuing to treat laches and acquiescence as two separate equitable
defences'.[92] In *Gafford*, the plaintiff, who was the successor in title to the
original covenantee, sought to enforce restrictive covenants to the effect
that lands should only be used for a stated purpose and that there should be
no building on them without the vendor's approval, against the defendant
who was the successor in title to the original covenantor. While the Court
of Appeal was satisfied that the works carried out by the defendant clearly
breached the restrictive covenants, it was satisfied that the plaintiff's claim
should be barred by acquiescence as he had failed to take any action to
enforce the covenants for a period of three years despite being aware of
his rights. Acquiescence was described by the court in terms of it being

90. *Ibid.* at 201.
91. The Times, 1 May 1998.
92. (1998) 114 LQR 555, 557.

unconscionable in all the circumstances for the plaintiff to assert his rights but as Milne has commented 'although the court consistently spoke of "acquiescence" it could equally well have said "laches"'.

EQUALITY IS EQUITY

In circumstances where more than one person is entitled to property, equity favours a principle of equal division. The most common illustration of the maxim in practice is the attitude adopted by equity towards the joint tenancy as a method of holding property. In this case the right of survivorship operates and on the death of a joint tenant, the estate belongs to the surviving joint tenant(s) to the exclusion of the deceased's successors. This can be distinguished from the position in relation to a tenancy in common where the interest of each party devolves upon his personal representatives on his death. Equity tends to lean in favour of a tenancy in common and in certain circumstances, even where persons are joint tenants at law, they may be regarded by equity as tenants in common of the beneficial interest. In such cases while the survivor(s) may be entitled to the entire estate, he will hold part of it as trustee for the deceased's personal representatives.

This presumption of a tenancy in common in equity arises in three recognised situations. First, where the purchase money for property is provided in unequal shares, equity presumes a tenancy in common proportionate to the contributions made. On the other hand, where the purchase money is advanced equally, the survivor becomes entitled to the entire estate in equity as well as in law. Secondly, where parties lend money on a mortgage, whether equally or unequally, the mortgagees are presumed to be entitled as tenants in common and the survivor is regarded as a trustee for the representatives of the deceased mortgagee to the extent of the amount of the loan advanced by the deceased.[93] Thirdly, where partners acquire property, they are presumed by equity to hold it as tenants in common on the basis that the principle of survivorship is inconsistent with the nature of the partnership relationship.[94] However, these three situations are not the only ones in which equity will presume a tenancy in common, a point made by the Privy Council in *Malayan Credit Ltd v. Jack Chia-MPH Ltd*[95]

---

93. *Morley v. Bird* (1798) 3 Ves 628, 631.
94. *Lake v. Craddock* (1732) 3 P Wms 158. Although see *Barton v. Morris* [1985] 1 WLR 1257.
95. [1986] AC 549.

where it was held that this result will follow where grantees hold premises for their several individual business purposes.

Even where an equitable interest in property is held jointly, for example where the purchase money is advanced equally, equity leans in favour of severance and an act of alienation by one tenant or even an agreement to alienate will be sufficient to sever the joint tenancy and create a tenancy in common.[96]

The maxim that equality is equity can also be seen in operation in a number of other circumstances. It has generally been applied where surplus funds remain on the dissolution of an unincorporated association as in *Re Bucks. Constabulary Widows' and Orphans' Fund Friendly Society (No.2)*,[97] where Walton J held that the surplus funds remaining should be distributed equally amongst the members of the association alive at the date of dissolution. There is still a lack of consensus in this jurisdiction on the issue of whether the distribution of surplus funds should be carried out on the basis of equal division or in accordance with the proportion of contributions made and in *Tierney v. Tough*[98] O'Connor MR favoured the latter approach. However, subsequently in *Feeney v. MacManus*,[99] Johnston J supported the principle of distribution on an equal basis and this is the approach which is more likely to be followed.

In addition, there was for some time a tendency to apply the maxim in England in relation to the division of matrimonial property in the absence of any other clear basis for carrying out this exercise. However, this approach never found favour with the judiciary in this jurisdiction and instead division is carried out on the basis of the respective contributions of the spouses or partners, and the non-owning partner has been held to be entitled to a beneficial interest to the extent of his or her contributions.[100] While the principle of equal division is still applied in England where there is evidence that it was the common intention of the parties that this should be the case,[101] Waite J has recently stressed in *Hammond v. Mitchell*[102] that 'this is not an area where the maxim that equality is equity falls to be applied unthinkingly'.

---

96. *Burgess v. Rawnsley* [1975] Ch 429.
97. [1979] 1 WLR 936. See also *Re GKN Bolts & Nuts Ltd (Automotive Division) Birmingham Works, Sports and Social Club* [1982] 1 WLR 774.
98. [1914] 1 IR 142.
99. [1937] IR 23.
100. *C. v. C.* [1976] IR 254; *W. v. W.* [1981] ILRM 202; *McC. v. McC.* [1986] ILRM 1.
101. *Grant v. Edwards* [1986] Ch 638.
102. [1991] 1 WLR 1127, 1137.

More recently Waite LJ delivering his judgment in the Court of Appeal in *Midland Bank plc v. Cooke*[103] stated that when the court is proceeding to determine what proportions the parties must be assumed to have intended for their beneficial ownership, the duty of the judge is to undertake a survey of the whole course of dealing between the parties relevant to their ownership and occupation of the property. Waite LJ said that the court will take into account all conduct which throws light on the question of what shares were intended and that it is 'only if that search proves inconclusive does the court fall back on the maxim that "equality is equity"'.[104] It should be noted that an attempt to pass legislation providing for automatic joint ownership of the matrimonial home in this jurisdiction proved unsuccessful,[105] and it is fair to say that the maxim no longer plays a role in this area and has been superseded by more precise methods of distribution in both jurisdictions.

The Supreme Court has recently commented in *E.B. v. S.S.*[106] that the maxim that 'equality is equity' should not necessarily apply where an application is brought under section 117 of the Succession Act 1965 by a child claiming that a parent has failed in his moral duty to make proper provision for the child in accordance with his means. Although the plaintiff's application was dismissed in this case, Keane J stated that it was not necessarily an answer to an application under section 117 that the testator had simply treated all his or her children equally. As he stated 'the maxim "equality is equity" can have no application where the testator has, by dividing his estate in that manner, disregarded the special needs . . . of one of the children to such an extent that he could be said to have failed in his moral duty to that child.'[107] However, Keane J acknowledged that the understandable desire of parents to avoid any friction amongst their children by effecting, so far as possible, an equal distribution of their property must also be recognised. In the circumstances the Supreme Court held that the defendant, who had divided her property equally between all her children, had not failed in her moral duty towards the plaintiff.

One other area in which the principle that equality is equity may be of relevance is where a 'trust power' is implied in default of any appointment being made by the donee of a power of appointment. So where a general intention in favour of a class of persons is expressed and no selection is

---

103. [1995] 4 All ER 562.
104. *Ibid.* at 574.
105. *Re Article 26 of the Constitution and the Matrimonial Home Bill 1993* [1994] 1 IR 305.
106. [1998] 2 ILRM 141.
107. *Ibid.* at 150.

made, a trust in favour of the members of the class in equal shares may be implied.[108]

EQUITY LOOKS TO THE INTENT RATHER THAN THE FORM

While this maxim does not mean that legal formalities will not be required by equity, it looks to the substance rather than the form of a transaction and does not require 'unnecessary formalities'[109] to be observed. Lord Romilly MR laid down this principle in *Parkin v. Thororld*[110] in the following terms:

> Courts of Equity make a distinction in all cases between that which is matter of substance and that which is matter of form; and if it find that by insisting on the form, the substance will be defeated, it holds it to be inequitable to allow a person to insist on such form, and thereby defeat the substance.

This maxim was applied in a number of situations. First, where land was used as security for a loan, equity regarded the transaction as a mortgage even though it might not be described as such.[111] In addition, equity provided relief against the payment of penalties on this basis. Where the parties to a contract agreed that in the event of its breach, a named sum of money would be paid by the defaulting party, equity would ask whether it was a genuine estimate of the damages which would result from the breach or whether it was a penalty to be held over the head of the other party. In deciding this, equity would look at the parties' intention rather than the form of the instrument. Another example of the operation of this maxim can be seen where there has been a failure to complete a contract for the sale of land within the time stipulated. While at law the party who failed to complete was in breach of contract, in equity he would be permitted to complete the contract within a reasonable time thereafter, provided time was not expressed to be of the essence in relation to completion of the contract.[112]

---

108. See e.g. *Re Kieran* [1916] 1 IR 289. Although note the comments of Lord Wilberforce in *McPhail v. Doulton* [1971] AC 424, 452 to the effect that 'a discretionary trust can, in a suitable case be executed according to its merits and otherwise than by equal division'.
109. *Sprange v. Lee* [1908] 1 Ch 424, 430 *per* Neville J.
110. (1852) 16 Beav 59, 66-67.
111. *Grangeside Properties Ltd v. Collingswood Securities Ltd* [1964] 1 WLR 140.
112. *Tilley v. Thomas* (1867) 3 Ch App 61, 67.

Another illustration of this maxim is the fact that a valid trust may be created without actually using the word 'trust'.[113] In limited circumstances a trust may be created by the use of 'precatory words' where a gift is made and the donee expresses the wish or hope that the property be dealt with in a particular manner. However, the use of such words will only be held to be sufficient to create a trust if this intention is clear from the language used in the instrument as a whole,[114] and they are more usually interpreted as being insufficient to achieve this result.[115]

This maxim is also the basis for the equitable remedy of rectification which allows an instrument to be rectified or corrected where it fails to record the actual intention of the parties to a contract.[116] Equity looks at the substance of the transaction and allows rectification in circumstances where it would be inequitable to allow a party to retain a benefit obtained e.g. as a result of mistake.[117]

EQUITY LOOKS ON THAT AS DONE WHICH OUGHT TO HAVE BEEN DONE

Where a specifically enforceable obligation exists, equity regards the parties as being in the position in which they would have been had the obligation been performed, and their legal rights and duties are assessed by reference to this position. So, in equity, a specifically enforceable contract for a lease is treated as being equivalent to a lease and the rights and duties of the parties are regarded as being the same as if the lease had actually been executed.[118] Similarly, a specifically enforceable contract for the sale of land transfers the equitable interest to the purchaser to the extent to which the purchase price is paid, and the vendor holds the legal title on a constructive trust until completion.[119]

It would seem that the maxim cannot be relied on in this context by a volunteer and equity will regard the obligation as carried out only in favour of persons who are entitled to specifically enforce the contract. Lindley LJ made this point as follows in *Re Anstis*:[120]

---

113. *Page v. Cox* (1852) 10 Hare 163, 169 *per* Turner VC.
114. *Comiskey v. Bowring-Hanbury* [1905] AC 84.
115. *Re Humphrey's Estate* [1916] 1 IR 21; *Re Sweeney* [1976-77] ILRM 88.
116. See *infra* Chapter 15.
117. *Irish Life Assurance Co. Ltd v. Dublin Land Securities Ltd* [1989] IR 253.
118. *Walsh v. Lonsdale* (1882) 21 Ch D 9.
119. *Tempany v. Hynes* [1976] IR 101, 114 *per* Kenny J, O'Higgins CJ concurring.
120. (1886) 31 Ch D 596, 605.

> Equity no doubt, looks on that as done which ought to be done; but this rule, although usually expressed in general terms, is by no means universally true. Where the obligation to do what ought to be done is not an absolute duty, but only an obligation arising from contract, that which ought to be done is only treated as done in favour of some person entitled to enforce the contract as against the person liable to perform it.

A similar approach seems to have been adopted by Scott J in *Davis v. Richards and Wallington Ltd*[121] in which he applied the maxim that 'equity looks on that as done which ought to be done' in considering the validity of a definitive trust deed establishing a pension scheme. Scott J said that the effect of the maxim was explained in the following terms in *Snell's Equity,*[122] namely: 'Equity treats a contract to do a thing as if the thing were already done, though only in favour of persons entitled to enforce the contract specifically and not in favour of volunteers.'

However, this requirement does not appear to have been enforced by Carroll J in *Shanahan v. Redmond.*[123] The deceased named his cousin as sole beneficiary of a trust, the assets of which comprised a life insurance policy. The parties fell out and the deceased attempted unsuccessfully to exercise a power of appointment over the trust funds in his own favour. Subsequently he instructed the insurance company to cancel the policy and to replace it with a similar one under which he would be the sole beneficiary. Although this direction had not been carried out when the testator died, Carroll J applied the maxim that equity looks on that as done which ought to be done and held that the existing policy should be treated as if it were a substitute policy in which the deceased was named as sole beneficiary.

Another controversial application of the maxim is contained in the decision of the Privy Council in *Attorney General for Hong Kong v. Reid*[124] where it held that when a fiduciary receives a bribe he holds it on a constructive trust for his principal. Lord Templeman explained this conclusion on the basis of the fiduciary's obligation to account to his principal for the bribe. As he stated: 'Equity considers as done that which ought to have been done. As soon as the bribe was received, whether in cash or in

---

121. [1990] 1 WLR 1511.
122. (28th ed., 1982) p.41. Now see 29th ed., 1990, Baker and Langan, p.40.
123. High Court 1994 No. 129 Sp (Carroll J) 21 June 1994.
124. [1994] 1 AC 324.

kind, the false fiduciary held the bribe on a constructive trust for the person injured.'[125]

The maxim that equity looks on that as done which ought to be done also underlies the doctrine of conversion which operates by regarding one form of property as being another where there is an obligation to convert it.[126] The effect of the doctrine is that in certain circumstances the nature of property is notionally changed so that realty may be treated as personalty with the legal incidents of personalty and *vice versa*. The reasoning behind it is that where a person is under a duty to convert one form of property into another, it will not be regarded as still being in its original form because the person concerned has failed to perform his obligations.

EQUITY IMPUTES AN INTENTION TO FULFIL AN OBLIGATION

Where a person is under an obligation to perform an act and does some other act which could be regarded as fulfilment of that original obligation, it will be regarded as such. This maxim forms the basis for the equitable doctrines of satisfaction and performance.[127] The effect of the first doctrine is that if a person is under an obligation and subsequently gives that person a benefit, it is presumed that the benefit is intended to satisfy the obligation or debt. Similarly, where a party is under an obligation to carry out a particular act and subsequently does an act which can be considered as performance of his obligation, equity will presume that this subsequent act was carried out in order to fulfil the earlier obligation.

EQUITY ACTS IN PERSONAM

This maxim has been described by Meagher, Gummow and Lehane[128] as 'historically of the greatest importance, theoretically the most elusive and practically of the most dubious significance'. It was originally one of the most fundamental principles of equity that equitable jurisdiction was ex-

---

125. *Ibid.* at 331. This reasoning has been criticised by a number of commentators. Gardner [1995] CLJ 60, 61 has suggested that 'the maxim's cryptic form has apparently led it to be applied in a fashion which cannot be squared with a proper articulation of the law in question.' See also Oakley [1994] CLJ 31 and Watts (1994) 110 LQR 178.

126. See further Chapter 19.

127. See *infra* Chapter 19.

128. *Equity Doctrines and Remedies* (3rd ed., 1992) p.96.

ercised against the person of the defendant rather than against his property. This is illustrated by the fact that failure to comply with an order granted where equitable relief is sought constitutes contempt of court. Where such a remedy was insufficient, the Court of Chancery had recourse to the writ of sequestration and since the enactment of the Judicature Act, orders can be enforced by any of the legal writs of execution e.g. *fieri facias*.

As Lord Selborne LC stated in *Ewing v. Orr Ewing (No.1)*:[129] 'The Courts of Equity in England are, and always have been, courts of conscience, operating *in personam* and not *in rem*; and in the exercise of this personal jurisdiction they have always been accustomed to compel the performance of contracts and trusts as to subjects which were not either locally or *ratione domicilli* within their jurisdiction.'

The maxim still has relevance to disputes relating to property outside the jurisdiction and it is immaterial that the property in question is not within a court's jurisdiction provided that the defendant himself is within its jurisdiction or can be served outside the jurisdiction. So, in *Penn v. Lord Baltimore*[130] specific performance was ordered in an English court of an agreement relating to land boundaries of property in the US although the defendant was in England. When the defendant objected to the jurisdiction of the court, Lord Hardwicke replied that the conscience of the defendant was bound by the agreement and that the dispute was a matter within the jurisdiction of the court which acted *in personam*.

A similar point was made by the Irish Court of Appeal in *Lett v. Lett*[131] in which an injunction was granted to restrain proceedings taken in an Argentine court which amounted to a repudiation of a settlement of divorce proceedings by virtue of which a wife had undertaken not to pursue any further claim against her husband. As Sir Samuel Walker stated: 'The jurisdiction asserted is not against the foreign tribunal, but against the person within the jurisdiction, who has made a contract not to resort to proceedings; and whether such proceedings are in a foreign court or not, is immaterial for the purpose of the equity on which the jurisdiction rests — an equity *in personam*.'[132]

A recent illustration of the maxim is provided by the decision of the European Court of Justice in *Webb v. Webb*[133] which classified the claim

---

129. (1883) 9 App Cas 34, 40.
130. (1750) 1 Ves Sen 444.
131. [1906] 1 IR 618.
132. *Ibid.* at 635.
133. [1994] QB 696.

of a beneficiary under a trust as a right *in personam* rather than *in rem*. A father had bought a flat in France in his son's name and subsequently sought a declaration that the son held the property as a trustee for him. Article 16 of the Convention on Jurisdiction and the Enforcement of Judgments in Civil and Commercial Matters 1968 provides, *inter alia,* that in proceedings which have as their object rights *in rem* in immovable property the courts of the state in which the property is situated shall have exclusive jurisdiction. Therefore if the action had been designated as one *in rem,* the French courts would have had exclusive jurisdiction in the matter. However, the European Court of Justice concluded that an action for a declaration that a person holds immovable property as a trustee did not constitute an action *in rem* within the meaning of Article 16 of the Convention which meant that the father was entitled to sue in the English courts.[134]

While it has been acknowledged that the 'rights and interests evolved in equity were originally conceived as purely personal'[135] it has also been recognised that the view that equitable interests convey no right *in rem* cannot be reconciled with the the right of a beneficiary to follow trust property.[136] However, it is still fair to say that to a large extent equitable relief is of a personal rather than a proprietary nature.

WHERE THE EQUITIES ARE EQUAL, THE FIRST IN TIME PREVAILS

WHERE THE EQUITIES ARE EQUAL, THE LAW PREVAILS

These two related maxims are relevant to the question of priorities as between competing interests in land. However, they cannot be looked at in isolation; it is necessary to examine the distinction between equitable interests as opposed to mere equities and the effect of the doctrine of notice on the operation of the maxims. Finally, it is also necessary to consider the impact which registration has had on the question of priorities between competing interests in land.

---

134. The decision in *Webb* was criticised by Briggs (1994) 110 LQR 526. However, MacMillan [1996] Conv 125, 129 is more supportive of the conclusion reached, asking 'is it not preferable that the determination of a trust created in England be made by an English court'.
135. *Re Cuff Knox* [1963] IR 263, 289 *per* Kingsmill Moore J.
136. *Ibid.*

Equitable Interests and Mere Equities

It is difficult to define the concept of a 'mere equity' with any degree of clarity or to explain the characteristics which distinguish mere equities from equitable interests properly so called. Equitable interests can be categorised as actual rights in property and include interests arising under a trust, equitable mortgages, equities of redemption, restrictive covenants and contracts to convey or create a legal estate in land. On the other hand, mere equities are better described as rights of a procedural nature which are ancillary to a property right and include e.g. the right to have a transaction set aside for fraud or undue influence or a right to have a document rectified for mistake.[137] Delany[138] has suggested that the term extends 'to all personal claims which *may* be converted into equitable estates and interests' and Everton has said that a mere equity might be defined as 'a right of an exclusively personal nature to pursue an equitable remedy'.[139] She suggests that many of the difficulties which have been encountered in endeavouring to distinguish between equities and equitable interests could be overcome if it were accepted that equitable interests can be variable in character and of different quality. Not all mere equities can bind third parties and a category sometimes referred to as a 'naked equity' was identified by the House of Lords in *National Provincial Bank Ltd v. Ainsworth.*[140] In the Court of Appeal, Lord Denning MR had held that a deserted wife had a 'licence coupled with an equity' entitling her to remain in possession of the family home which took precedence over the rights of the plaintiff bank which had taken a mortgage on the house. However, the House of Lords reversed this decision; as Lord Upjohn stated, the wife was seeking to assert rights over the land of another in relation to which she had no beneficial ownership. He said that he could not see how it was possible for a mere equity to bind a purchaser unless it was ancillary to or dependent on an equitable estate or interest in land. In the case before him the right of the wife was not ancillary to or dependent on an equitable interest and could not bind purchasers; it was a right of a purely personal nature.[141]

---

137. See Everton (1976) 40 Conv 209, 210.
138. (1957) 21 Conv 195, 201.
139. *Ibid.* at 220. Wade [1955] CLJ 158 at 160 has suggested that another distinction between equitable interests and mere equities lies in the fact that mere equities are discretionary in character but he concedes that a purchaser's right under a contract for the sale of land which must surely amount to more than a mere equity depends on the willingness of a court to award specific performance (at p.161).
140. [1965] AC 1175.
141. As Keane points out in *Equity and the Law of Trusts in the Republic of Ireland* (1988) p. 44 the point decided in *Ainsworth* is now academic in this jurisdiction as

The most practical significance of the distinction between mere equities and equitable estates can be seen where a question of priorities arises. As the maxim makes clear, where the equities are equal, the first in time prevails, but where one equity is superior to another, the time of their creation cannot govern priority. It would appear that the maxim should only be applied where the equities are in all respects equal. On this point Kindersley VC stated as follows in *Rice v. Rice*:[142]

> [I]n a contest between persons having only equitable interests, priority of time is the ground of preference last resorted to; i.e. . . . . a Court of Equity will not prefer the one to the other, on the mere ground of priority of time, until it finds upon an examination of the relative merits that there is no other sufficient ground of preference between them, or in other words that their equities are in all other respects equal; and that, if the one has on other grounds a better equity than the other, priority of time is immaterial.

While a *bona fide* purchaser of a legal estate for value and without notice of an earlier equitable interest may take the property free of that interest, a *bona fide* purchaser of an equitable interest without notice of an earlier equitable interest will take subject to it on the basis of the maxim that where the equities are equal the first in time prevails. However, while such a purchaser does not take free of prior equitable interests, he will take free of any prior mere equities on the basis that the 'equities' are not equal. An example of how this distinction may be of practical importance is provided by the decision of Lord Sugden LC in *Bowen v. Evans*.[143] There a dispute arose between the plaintiff, who sought to have a deed set aside for fraud and one of the defendants, who claimed under a settlement for value of the lands which constituted an equitable interest. Sugden LC held that this defendant could raise a plea of purchaser for value against the plaintiff on the basis that the plaintiff's right to have the transaction impeached for fraud was a mere equity and so could not take priority over the defendant's equitable estate acquired for value and without notice of the plaintiff's claim.

This decision is not entirely reconcilable with his subsequent judg-

---

a result of the enactment of the Family Home Protection Act 1976, s.3 of which renders invalid any disposition of the family home by one spouse without the written consent of the other.

142. (1853) 2 Drew 73, 77. Quoted with approval by Porter MR in *Bank of Ireland v. Cogry Flax Spinning Co* [1900] 1 IR 219, 230.
143. (1844) 6 Ir Eq R 569.

ment as Lord St Leonards in *Stump v. Gaby*[144] in which he found that where a person makes a conveyance in circumstances where it may be set aside for fraud, his equitable right to rescind amounts to a beneficial interest in the land conveyed capable of being devised by will. The better view would seem to be that expressed in *Stump v. Gaby* and this was re-asserted by Lord Westbury in *Phillips v. Phillips*[145] where he confirmed that the right to set aside a deed for fraud or correct it for mistake was a mere equity as distinct from an equitable interest. A similar conclusion was reached more recently in this jurisdiction by Kenny J in *Allied Irish Banks v. Glynn*.[146] The first named defendant conveyed land to his son, the second named defendant, subject to the former's right to remain in residence in a house on the lands. The son deposited the land certificate with the plaintiff bank as security for monies advanced to him by the bank. As a result of proceedings brought by the father, the conveyance was set aside on the grounds of undue influence. The plaintiff bank which was not aware of these proceedings, then brought a claim to enforce the equitable mortgage. Kenny J held in giving priority to the bank that the equitable mortgage took precedence over the prior right of the father to have the deed set aside which was described as a chose in action rather than an equitable interest.

Similarly, there has been some dispute about the status of a beneficiary's equitable right to trace trust property into the hands of third parties and specifically as to whether it can be categorised as an equitable interest or as a mere equity. The position in England would appear to be that it is recognised as an equitable interest. In *Cave v. Cave*[147] trustees improperly invested trust moneys in the purchase of land, the legal estate in which was conveyed to another party who made both legal and equitable mortgages. Fry J held that the mortgagees took without notice and that as between the beneficiaries and the equitable mortgagee, the beneficiaries took priority because they had a prior equitable estate as opposed to a mere equity. Therefore, although the equitable mortgagee was acting in good faith and took without notice of the beneficiaries' interest, he could not take priority over the prior equitable interest of the beneficiaries. The result in this case is a good illustration of the maxim that where the equities are equal, the first in time prevails, although as the decision of the Irish

144. (1852) 2 De GM & G 623.
145. (1862) 4 De G F & J 208.
146. [1973] IR 188. See also *Latec Investments Ltd v. Hotel Terrigal Pty Ltd* (1965) 113 CLR 265 *per* Kitto and Menzies JJ.
147. (1880) 15 Ch D 639.

Court of Appeal in *Re Ffrench's Estate*[148] shows, the result will be different where the equities are not considered to be equal. This decision also concerned a contest as between the right of beneficiaries to trace and that of an equitable mortgagee, although Porter MR reached the opposite conclusion on this issue to that arrived' at by Fry J in *Cave v. Cave.* Trust funds were mixed by an equitable tenant for life with his own funds and used to buy property. A question of priorities arose between the right of the beneficiaries to trace the trust funds and a bank in whose favour an equitable mortgage had been created, which had no knowledge of the fact that the trust funds had been converted. It was held that the rights of the equitable mortgagee must prevail over the rights of the beneficiaries who possessed a mere equity only i.e. the right of tracing. Porter MR said that the equity of the mortgagees was a 'superior equity' to that of the beneficiaries. In his view, the primary right of a beneficiary was against his own trustees and the right to trace the trust fund into its improper investment is ancillary to this. He concluded that such an ancillary right should not prevail against innocent purchasers and said that in this instance he was unable to regard the equities as equal. Porter MR regarded the beneficiaries' right as 'rather in the nature of a chose in action than an estate — an equity as distinguished from an equitable interest and inferior to the equitable interest of the mortgagees.' While Porter MR was the only member of the court who decided the case on the basis that a right to trace was a mere equity, this view has been applied in several decisions in this jurisdiction.[149] In *Scott v. Scott,*[150] the administratrix of an estate and her son had invested certain assets of the estate in a house and deposited the title deeds with a bank by way of mortgage. When a dispute over priorities arose between the next of kin and the bank, it was held that the former's right was a mere equity which could not prevail over an equitable estate such as was possessed by the bank which amounted to an equitable mortgage on specific items of property.

While this approach to the status of a beneficiary's right to trace appears to be established in Ireland,[151] Wylie has questioned its soundness on the basis that it seems to involve an 'unjustifiable limitation' of the beneficiaries' interests.

---

148. (1887) 21 LR Ir 283.
149. See *Re Sloane's Estate* [1895] 1 IR 146 in which Monroe J confirmed (at p.165) that the right to trace was a 'lower one' than the right created by an equitable mortgage by deposit. See also *Bourke v. Lee* [1904] 1 IR 280 and *Re Bobbett's Estate* [1904] 1 IR 461.
150. [1924] 1 IR 141.
151. See Wylie, *Irish Land Law* (3rd ed., 1997) pp. 129-130.

Priorities and the Doctrine of Notice[152]

The basic rule at law as in equity is that estates and interests rank in priority according to the order of their creation where they are otherwise equal and so it is important to distinguish legal estates, equitable estates and mere equities for this purpose. The other important factor which affects the question of priorities is the doctrine of notice. This in turn has been affected and to some extent displaced by the modern systems of registration. As regards notice, the rule developed by equity was that a *bona fide* purchaser for value without notice of a legal estate or interest in land would take free of an equitable interest of which he had no notice. Similarly, a *bona fide* purchaser for value of an equitable interest without notice will take free of a mere equity. As Keane[153] points out, there are two exceptions to this principle, first that a naked equity, such as the right of a spouse to possession considered in *National Provincial Bank v. Ainsworth*[154] will not be binding on a subsequent purchaser irrespective of the question of notice as the right is purely personal in nature and cannot be binding on third parties. In addition, a purchaser for value of registered land will not be affected by an unregistered equitable claim even if he has notice of it.

For the doctrine of the *bona fide* purchaser without notice to come into effect, the purchaser must be *bona fide* i.e. there must have been no fraud on his part in relation to the purchase. In addition, he must have been a purchaser for value although there is authority for the proposition that it need not be shown that the consideration given was adequate. Finally, the purchaser must establish that he took the estate without notice of any prior interest.

It is generally accepted that there are three forms of notice — actual, constructive and imputed and these can be identified in section 3(1) of the Conveyancing Act 1882 which provides as follows:

> A purchaser shall not be prejudicially affected by notice of any instrument, fact or thing unless:
>
> (i) It is within his own knowledge, or would have come to his knowledge if such inquiries and inspections had been made as ought reasonably to have been made by him; or
>
> (ii) In the same transaction with respect to which a question of notice to the purchaser arises, it has come to the knowledge of his

---

152. Sheridan (1950) 9 NILQ 33.
153. *Equity and the Law of Trusts in the Republic of Ireland* (1988) p.55.
154. [1965] AC 1175.

counsel, as such, or of his solicitor, or other agent, as such, or would have come to the knowledge of his solicitor, or other agent as such, if such inquiries and inspections had been made as ought reasonably to have been made by the solicitor or other agent.

Actual Notice

A person will be considered to have actual notice where he discovers information himself, so a subjective standard is imposed. The wording of section 3(1)(i) shows that unlike in the case of imputed knowledge referred to in paragraph (ii), it is not necessary that the actual knowledge was obtained in the course of the transaction in question. However, it is clear that merely hearing a rumour will not amount to actual notice.[155]

The question of actual notice was considered by the Supreme Court in *Bank of Ireland Finance Ltd v. Rockfield*[156] although in a different context. The question at issue concerned whether the plaintiff bank had notice of the fact that monies advanced to a company had been used to purchase its own shares in breach of section 60 of the Companies Act 1963, subsection 14 of which provides that any transaction in breach of section 60 is voidable at the instance of the company against any person who had notice of the facts that constituted the breach of the statute. The Supreme Court held that the company could not invoke section 60(14) as they had failed to establish that prior to the transaction in question the plaintiff had had actual notice of the facts alleged to constitute a breach of the section. Kenny J stated that the notice referred to in the subsection was actual notice and not constructive notice and said that there was strong authority to support the view that the doctrine of constructive notice should not be extended to commercial transactions. He said that he was using the term 'actual notice' 'as meaning in this case that the plaintiff bank, or any of its officials, had been informed, either verbally or in writing, that part of the advance was to be applied in the purchase of shares in the defendant company, or that they knew facts from which they *must* have inferred that part of the advance was to be applied for this purpose.'[157]

Constructive Notice

A person will be deemed to have constructive notice where he fails to make the inquiries and inspections which he ought reasonably to have

---

155. *O'Connor v. McCarthy* [1982] IR 161, 174. See also *Lloyd v. Banks* (1868) 3 Ch App 488, 491 *per* Lord Cairns.
156. [1979] IR 21.
157. *Ibid.* at 37.

made, judged by reference to standard conveyancing procedures. Snell[158] states that a purchaser will be treated as having constructive notice 'of all that a reasonably prudent purchaser, acting on skilled advice, would have discovered'. The question of constructive notice was considered by Henchy J in the Supreme Court in the context of the application of the Family Home Protection Act 1976 in *Somers v. W.*[159]

The plaintiff had purchased a house from the defendant's husband without the defendant's consent and sought to sell it to a purchaser who insisted on her written consent. The plaintiff then sought an order dispensing with the defendant's consent under section 4 of the Family Home Protection Act 1976. In finding for the defendant, the Supreme Court held that at the date of the purported assignment, the plaintiff was affected by constructive notice of the defendant's statutory rights as these would have come to the knowledge of the plaintiff's solicitor if such inquiries had been made as ought reasonably to have been made. The Supreme Court therefore concluded that the purported assignment by the defendant's husband to the plaintiff was void. Henchy J stated as follows:

> In earlier times the tendency was to judge a purchaser solely by the facts that actually came to his knowledge. In the course of time it came to be held in the Court of Chancery that it would be unconscionable for the purchaser to take his stand on the facts that had come to his notice to the exclusion of those which ordinary prudence or circumspection or skill should have called to his attention. When the facts at his command beckoned him to look and inquire further, and he refrained from doing so, equity fixed him with constructive notice of what he would have ascertained if he had pursued the further investigation which a person with reasonable care and skill would have felt proper to make in the circumstances.[160]

Further consideration was given to the question of what will constitute making reasonable inquiries by the Supreme Court in *Northern Bank Ltd v. Henry.*[161] The second named defendant purchased the leasehold interest in a house with the money which belonged to the first named defendant, his wife, but the assignment of the interest was made to him alone. The wife sought a declaration that she was entitled in equity to the leasehold interest. On the same day the husband mortgaged the house to the plaintiff

---

158. *Snell's Equity* (29th ed., 1990, Baker and Langan) p. 51.
159. [1979] IR 94.
160. *Ibid.* at 108.
161. [1981] IR 1.

bank which apart from making a search in the Registry of Deeds, made no investigation of the husband's title. The wife succeeded in obtaining a declaration that her husband held the leasehold interest in trust for her and claimed that her interest prevailed over that of the plaintiff bank because, she contended, it had constructive notice of her interest. Henchy J emphasized that section 3(1) of the Conveyancing Act 1882 gave statutory force to the 'existing judicial insistence that constructive notice could be found only when lack of knowledge was due to such careless inactivity as would not be expected in the circumstances from a reasonable man'. He stated:

> In my judgment, the test of what inquiries and inspections ought reasonably to have been made by the plaintiffs is an objective test which depends not on what the particular purchaser thought proper to do in the particular circumstances but on what a purchaser of the particular property ought reasonably to have done to acquire title to it.... . [Section 3(1)] because it is laying down the circumstances in which a purchaser is not to be prejudicially affected by notice of any instrument, fact or thing, is setting as a standard of conduct that which is expected from a reasonable purchaser. Reasonableness in this context must be judged by reference to what should be done to acquire the estate or interest being purchased, rather than by the motive for or the purpose of the particular purchase.[162]

Imputed Notice

This type of notice is referred to in section 3(1)(ii) of the Act of 1882. The effect of the subsection is that all knowledge, of which an agent of a purchaser is actually aware or of which he would have been aware if he had made the inquiries and inspections which he ought reasonably to have made, will be attributed to the purchaser. However, the subsection also stipulates that this notice must have been acquired 'in the same transaction' if it is to bind the purchaser and so any knowledge which an agent may have obtained from previous dealings will not be relevant in this context.

Onus of Proof

Finally, it should be noted that the onus of proving that a person had no notice of a prior interest lies on the party claiming that he took without notice. This was confirmed by O'Byrne J in *Heneghan v. Davitt*.[163] The

---

162. *Ibid.* at 9.
163. [1933] IR 375.

plaintiff entered into an agreement for the purchase of lands and while the agreement was awaiting completion the vendors entered into a further agreement for sale with another person which was carried into effect by a conveyance. The plaintiff brought a claim for specific performance. In the Circuit Court, the third party's plea of purchaser for value without notice was upheld but in the High Court it was held that it had been incorrect to impose the onus of proving that the other person had been a *bona fide* purchaser without notice on the plaintiff. The onus rested instead on the defendant and since he had not discharged this onus, the plaintiff was granted specific performance of the agreement. O'Byrne J stated as follows:

> In order to defeat a plea of purchaser for value without notice, it is not, in my opinion, necessary that the purchaser should have actual notice. If he has sufficient notice or knowledge to put him upon enquiry, and if he deliberately refrains from making such enquiry, he is thereupon deemed to have constructive notice of such facts as would have come to his knowledge if he had made proper enquiry; and such constructive notice is, in my opinion, sufficient to defeat the plea.[164]

Registration of Deeds, Priorities and Notice

There are two main systems of registration affecting land in Ireland; the registration of deeds system introduced by the Registration of Deeds Act (Ireland) 1707 which provided for the registration of memorials of deeds and conveyances affecting lands, tenements and hereditaments and the registration of title system which provides for the registration of ownership of land.

The registration of deeds system did not have any kind of comprehensive application; it was not compulsory and where there was no memorial or written document in existence relating to a disposition, there was nothing to register. However two provisions of the Act of 1707 are still of considerable importance to the question of priorities where a deed has been registered and must be examined. Section 4 provides that registered dispositions rank in priority according to their date of registration not according to their date of execution, so the maxim that where the equities are equal the first in time prevails has no application in this instance. Section 5 provides that a deed or conveyance of which a memorial is not registered

---

164. *Ibid.* at 379.

will be deemed 'fraudulent and void' against a deed or conveyance, a memorial of which has been registered and effectively provides that a registered disposition will take priority over a registrable but unregistered disposition.

However, the Act did not govern priorities where an unregistrable disposition was involved e.g. the deposit of the title deeds of land to create an equitable mortgage. In this case such a disposition will take priority over a subsequent equitable interest even though the latter is registered. So in *Re Burke's Estate*[165] it was held that an equitable mortgage by deposit of title deeds, unaccompanied by any memorandum in writing, took priority over a purchaser for value claiming under a subsequent registered deed, without knowledge of the mortgage.

Where two registered dispositions are involved in a conflict as to priorities, the provisions of section 4 of the 1707 Act will apply and they will rank according to the date of registration of the memorials of the transactions. The question of notice will not be relevant and a purchaser for value without notice cannot claim priority over a prior registered deed irrespective of whether the estates or interests created are legal or equitable.[166] However, where there is a conflict between a prior unregistered deed and a subsequent registered deed, the issue of notice does become relevant. It was held in *Forbes v. Deniston*[167] that the 1707 Act which was intended to prevent fraud should not be used to provide a means of achieving fraud. So, where a purchaser who registers a deed has notice of a prior unregistered deed he will not be permitted to obtain priority. In *Forbes* a subsequent lessee, whose lease was registered and who knew of a prior unregistered lease, was not permitted by the House of Lords to take priority over the holder of the earlier lease.

It has been established that for this qualification to the statutory scheme to operate, the purchaser/lessee must have actual notice of the existence of the prior unregistered deed at the time of the subsequent deed's execution or at least at the time of its registration or else have notice imputed to him by reason of the actual notice of his agent. Therefore, in this context constructive notice will be insufficient, a point re-affirmed by Costello J in *O'Connor v. McCarthy*.[168] A company contracted in writing to sell premises to a purchaser although the memorial of the contract was not registered in accordance with the provisions of the Registration of Deeds Act 1707. It

---

165. (1882) 9 LR Ir 24.
166. *Eyre v. Dolphin* (1813) 2 Ba & B 290.
167. (1722) 4 Bro PC 189.
168. [1982] IR 161.

subsequently contracted in writing to sell the premises to a second purchaser and this contract was registered in the Registry of Deeds. The second purchaser's solicitor had no knowledge of the existence of the first contract when he registered the second. However, the second purchaser had heard rumours of a previous contract, but being satisfied that he had in fact bought the premises, did not inform his solicitor of this. Costello J held that the registration of the memorial of the second contract in accordance with the provisions of the 1707 Act conferred priority on it subject to the equitable doctrine of notice. He held that neither the second purchaser nor his solicitor had had actual notice of the existence or nature of the first contract and that therefore the second contract must be given its statutory priority. Costello J effectively held that constructive notice was insufficient to defeat the statutory scheme. However, he proceeded to refer to the *dicta* of Lord Cairns in *Agra Bank Ltd v. Barry*[169] and suggested that where a purchaser has not acted in good faith e.g. where he has deliberately refrained from making inquiries, the court might not give effect to the statutory priority even though the purchaser only has constructive notice. In this instance, Costello J was satisfied that neither the second purchaser nor his solicitor had acted in any way *mala fide* and there was no reason to consider whether constructive notice might have sufficed to displace the statutory priority accorded to the second contract.

Registration of Title and Priorities[170]

Under the registration of title system, title to any land may be registered. In general the system operates on a voluntary basis although registration of title to certain types of land and of land situated in specified counties is compulsory,[171] and once land is registered, all dealings relating to it must be effected through the Land Registry. Where title has been registered, the register will to a large extent govern the question of priorities as between competing interests in land. However, certain types of rights and burdens listed in section 72 of the Registration of Title Act 1964 can affect registered land without being registered. In addition, other unregistered rights apart from those referred to in section 72 may be created in or over registered land, although these will not affect the registered owner of a charge created on land for valuable consideration and will only be effective where

---

169. (1874) LR 7 HL 135, 149.
170. For more detailed consideration of the registration of title system, see Wylie, *Irish Land Law* (3rd ed., 1997) Chapter 21 and Coughlan, *Property Law* (2nd ed., 1998) Chapter 7.
171. Counties Carlow, Laois and Meath.

the transferee is a volunteer.[172] So, where an equitable mortgage is created by the deposit of the land certificate, this equitable charge is subject to any prior equitable interests in accordance with the maxim that where the equities are equal the first in time prevails. In *Tench v. Molyneux*[173] the equitable interest of a purchaser of registered land who had failed to take the necessary steps to effect his registration as owner was held to take priority over a party with whom the vendor had subsequently deposited the land certificate to secure a loan. As the equities were equal in this case, the interest of the purchaser being prior in time prevailed.

---

172. *Devoy v. Hanlon* [1929] IR 246.
173. (1914) 48 ILTR 48.

CHAPTER 3

Trusts — An Introduction

GENERAL PRINCIPLES

The Origins of the Trust Concept

The modern trust developed out of the medieval concept of the use whereby the owner of land would give it to another to hold on his behalf.[1] Initially where the owner of property put his land in the possession of another person a mere moral obligation was imposed and the original owner had no remedy if his wishes were not carried out. However, the Court of Chancery intervened to provide for the enforcement of the use of land on the grounds that it would be unconscionable not to recognise the device.

The system of the use was adopted for a number of reasons. Perhaps the most significant of these, and the one which ultimately led to legislative intervention to curb its predominance, was that it facilitated the avoidance of certain feudal dues and incidents e.g. payments to a lord where an heir succeeded to land or the right of escheat where there was no heir. In addition, until the enactment of the Mortmain Act 1391, the concept also enabled property to be effectively transferred to bodies corporate, usually religious institutions, a practice which the earlier mortmain legislation had been designed to prevent. A further advantage was that despite the fact that it was not possible to make a devise of land in Ireland until after the passing of the Statute of Wills (Ireland) Act 1634, a landowner could effectively achieve this result by employing the device of the use. Another often fraudulent practice which grew up was to grant lands to the use of another to defeat the claims of a creditor or to delay actions for the recovery of land.

While the intervention of the Court of Chancery to give effect to the use proved a most useful and beneficial practice from the point of view of tenants of land, it grew increasingly unpopular with feudal lords and especially with the ultimate overlord, the King of England. As a result the

---

1. It became the practice to convey land 'to A to the use of B'. While B had no legal estate in the lands which remained at common law the property of A, the Court of Chancery would recognise B's beneficial or 'equitable' ownership of the land.

Statute of Uses was passed in England in 1535 and the equivalent legislation, the Statute of Uses (Ireland) 1634, was passed by the Irish parliament.[2] The statute provided that where any person or persons were seised of any lands or other hereditaments to the use, confidence or trust of any person(s) or of any corporation, the person or corporation having such use, confidence or trust in fee simple, fee tail, for term of life or for years, or otherwise, should be deemed in lawful seisin and possession of the lands or hereditaments for the same estate as he or they had in the use, confidence or trust.

Prior to the enactment of the statute, it was usual to grant land 'unto A and his heirs to the use of B and his heirs'. Its effect was to provide that the use should be immediately executed with the result that B would become the legal owner and A would have no further interest. As the Statute of Uses (Ireland) 1634 was not passed until nearly a century after the equivalent legislation had taken effect in England, it was recognised by the time of its enactment here that the legislation was far from comprehensive in nature. First, it applied only where a person was seised of land to the use of another, which effectively confined its application to freehold land. Secondly, it did not apply where the person to whom the freehold was conveyed had an active duty to perform e.g. to collect rent and pay it over.[3] Thirdly, the statute had no application where a body corporate, rather than a person or persons, was seised of lands to the 'use, trust or confidence' of any other person or corporation. However the most important exclusion, and the one which ultimately led to the creation of the modern concept of the trust as we know it was that a use upon a use did not come within the ambit of the statute. At common law there could not be a second use in a conveyance of freehold land so if the land was conveyed 'unto A and his heirs to the use of B and his heirs to the use of C and his heirs', the common law would not give effect to the use to C. This was established in

---

2. 10 Chas. I, sess. 2, c.1. It should be noted that this statute has never been repealed. Pearce suggested in an article written in 1990 (see (1990) 41 NILQ 43) that the Statute of Uses could still have effect and that interests in freehold land arising from a contribution to its purchase price should in many cases be treated as executed by the statute. However, in a reply to this article published in 1996 (see (1996) 47 NILQ 367) Mee argued convincingly against such a proposition and submitted (at p.376) 'that there is no possibility of the courts in Ireland deciding that the Statute of Uses should execute modern resulting or constructive trusts'.
3. If the statute executed the use in such a case, this person would be left with no interest in the property and would therefore be unable to carry out the duties imposed on him. However, the statute did apply if the use or trust was purely passive e.g. where land was conveyed to A on trust to permit B to receive the rents, A took no estate since there was no active duty to perform.

Tyrrel's case[4] where it was held that where there was a use upon a use, the second use would not be executed by the statute.

However, the Court of Chancery in England gradually came around to the idea of enforcing this second use in a manner similar to that in which the first use had been enforced prior to the enactment of the Statute of Uses. While some controversy remains about when this practice became established,[5] in time the second use became known as a trust and it became common to simply convey property 'unto and to the use of B (the trustee) in trust for C' (the beneficiary).

Definition of a Trust

Since the concept of a trust came to be recognised, numerous attempts have been made both by members of the judiciary and various academic commentators to define in precise terms the nature of the rights and obligations which it gives rise to, often with only a limited degree of success.[6] Underhill[7] provides the following definition:

> [A]n equitable obligation, binding a person (who is called a trustee) to deal with the property over which he has control (which is called the trust property) for the benefit of persons (who are called the beneficiaries or *cestuis que trust*) of whom he may himself be one, and any one of whom may enforce the obligation.[8]

This definition is insufficient to cover trusts for various purposes other than for the benefit of persons, so Pettit[9] makes the following addition 'or for a charitable purpose, which may be enforced at the instance of the Attorney General, or for some other purpose permitted by law though unenforceable'.

Perhaps the most comprehensive definition and one approved of in *Snell's Equity*[10] is that suggested by Keeton and Sheridan:

---

4. (1557) 2 Dy 1555a.
5. One view is that the courts had adopted this approach by the time of the enactment of the Statute of Uses (Ireland) 1634, (see Wylie, *Irish Land Law* (3rd ed., 1997) p. 171 and Baker (1977) 93 LQR 33, who relies on the authority of *Sambach v. Dalston* (1634) Toth 188), while another view is that the position was not clarified until later that century (see Strathdene (1958) 74 LQR 550 and Yale (1957) 15 CLJ 72).
6. See Hart (1899) 15 LQR 294 where a number of attempts at definitions dating back to 1734 are set out and analysed.
7. Underhill and Hayton, *Law Relating to Trusts and Trustees* (15th ed., 1995) p. 3.
8. This was quoted with approval by Cohen J in *Re Marshall's Will Trusts* [1945] 1 Ch 217, 219 and by Romer LJ in *Green v. Russell* [1959] 2 QB 226, 241.
9. *Equity and the Law of Trusts* (8th ed., 1997) at p.24.
10. (29th ed.,1990, Baker and Langan) p.89.

> A trust is the relationship which arises wherever a person (called the trustee) is compelled in equity to hold property, whether real or personal, and whether by legal or equitable title, for the benefit of some persons (of whom he may be one and who are termed beneficiaries) or for some object permitted by law, in such a way that the real benefit accrues, not to the trustee, but to the beneficiaries or other objects of the trust.[11]

It is not always correct to refer to the trustee as the legal owner and the beneficiary as the equitable owner as the trustee's interest may be equitable only as where for instance a beneficiary under a settlement makes a settlement of his interest where the legal interest remains in the trustees of the original settlement. So it is more correct to refer to the trustee as the nominal owner of the property and the beneficiary as the beneficial owner.

TRUSTS DISTINGUISHED FROM OTHER FORMS OF LEGAL INSTITUTION

Before examining the trust concept in any detail it is useful to distinguish it from other legal institutions. Some of these may in certain circumstances resemble a trust and the duties and obligations which it gives rise to, although none of them contain all the essential elements necessary to constitute a trust and it is therefore important to be able to distinguish them. It is proposed to examine these in turn.

1. Trusts and Bailment

Pettit[12] suggests the following definition of bailment:

> delivery of personal chattels upon a condition, express or implied, that they shall be redelivered to the bailor, or according to his directions, when the purpose of the bailment has been carried out.

There are certain similarities between the position of a trustee and bailee in that both are subject to fiduciary obligations, albeit of varying degrees, in relation to the property which is within their control.[13] However, there

---

11. *The Law of Trusts* (12th ed., 1993) p.3.
12. *Equity and the Law of Trusts* (8th ed., 1997) at p.25.
13. See the judgment of Mason J in *Hospital Products Ltd v. United States Surgical Corporation* (1984) 156 CLR 41 for a discussion of the nature of the fiduciary obligation owed by a bailee to a bailor.

are a number of basic distinctions between the concepts of a trust and a bailment. The first is that bailment is a creature of common law while trusts are equitable in nature and their enforcement is based on equitable rather than common law principles. Secondly, bailment applies only to personal property whereas a trust can apply to any type of property. Thirdly, while a bailor can enforce or vary the bailment, a settlor cannot carry out the same function in relation to a trust unless he has specifically reserved such a power to himself when setting it up. However, the most important practical significance of the distinction between the concepts of trust and bailment is where the person to whom possession of the property is given disposes of it to a third party. A bailee merely has special property in the goods which constitute the subject-matter of the bailment and cannot generally pass good title to the property which will be valid against the bailor.[14] On the other hand, a trustee can give good title in these circumstances to a person who acquires the legal ownership *bona fide* for value without notice of the trust.

2. Trusts and Agency

There are some similarities between the relationship of principal and agent and that of trustee and beneficiary to the extent that both the agent and the trustee have fiduciary obligations and must act in the interests of their principal or beneficiaries and not for their own benefit. While the agency relationship is governed mainly by common law principles, equity will intervene in certain circumstances. First, it will impose fiduciary obligations on an agent to make him liable to account where he has made a personal profit out of his position without the consent of his principal. In addition, he will be regarded as a constructive trustee where property has been entrusted to him by his principal for investment or safekeeping.

However, there are also a number of significant ways in which the relationships can be distinguished. First, the agency relationship is personal in nature, whereas the trust is proprietary. Secondly, there must be some form of agreement between an agent and his principal which forms the basis of their relationship, whereas this will hardly ever be either necessary or desirable between a trustee and the beneficiaries of a trust. Thirdly, the agency arrangement is normally terminated by the death of either the principal or the agent; this is not the case in relation to a trust where either a trustee or beneficiary dies. Fourthly, a trustee cannot commit the beneficiaries of a trust to liabilities towards third parties whereas an agent can commit his principal to such liabilities. Fifthly, an agent is bound to carry

---

14.   There are exceptions to this general principle, e.g. sale in market overt.

out his principal's instructions yet a trustee is not subject to such control either by the settlor or the beneficiaries and is simply bound to carry out the terms of the trust and discharge his functions as trustee according to law. A final essential element present in a trust relationship which is lacking in an agency agreement is that while an agent may have his principal's property in his possession, he will not usually have title to it.[15]

3. Trusts and Contract

From one perspective, contracts and trusts would appear to be completely distinct concepts with few characteristics in common; the former is a creation of the common law, an arrangement which requires valuable consideration for its validity and one which only the parties to it can enforce. A trust, on the other hand, is a species of equitable obligation which can be perfectly valid without the element of consideration being present,[16] and which can be enforced by a beneficiary who is not party to the original arrangement between the testator/settlor and the trustees.

However, in practice it is often difficult to draw a distinction between these concepts and the same transaction may even give rise to both a contract and a trust. Yet important practical consequences may flow from characterizing a relationship between parties as either a contract or a trust. For example, where property is vested in A, who then becomes insolvent, the likelihood of B recovering whatever is owed to him is substantially higher if A held the property in trust for him than if he is A's debtor and can only claim in A's bankruptcy. The most far-reaching consequence of the distinction is that beneficiaries can enforce a trust even though not party to its creation whereas only the actual parties to a contract can enforce it.[17] Although the wisdom of not recognising the right of a third party to a contract to enforce it has often been questioned,[18] it has been reasserted on a

---

15. *Cave v. Mackenzie* (1877) 46 LJ Ch 564, 567 *per* Jessel MR.
16. E.g. where a testator creates a trust in his will or a settlor declares himself trustee of named trusts for the benefit of a volunteer.
17. This latter principle has long been an accepted feature of the law in this jurisdiction and in England, see e.g. *Tweddle v. Atkinson* (1861) 1 B & S 393; *Dunlop Pneumatic Tyre Co. Ltd v. Selridge & Co. Ltd* [1915] AC 847 and has been the subject-matter of much academic debate. See Dowrick (1956) 19 MLR 374; Wylie (1966) 17 NILQ 351; Yates (1977) 41 Conv 49 and Andrews (1988) LS 14.
18. See Corbin (1930) 46 LQR 12 and the recommendations of the Law Revision Committee in 1937 Cmd 5449, section D paragraph 48. In addition, Lord Denning has often advocated a more liberal view, see *Smith & Snipes Hall Farm Ltd v. River Douglas Catchment Board* [1949] 2 KB 500; *Drive Yourself Hire Co. (London) Ltd v. Strutt* [1954] 1 QB 250; *Adler v. Dickson* [1955] 1 QB 158; Denning (1960) 3 Syd Law Rev 209, 214.

number of occasions by the House of Lords[19] and there has been no sign of any move away from that position in this jurisdiction. Instead there have been sporadic instances of the courts employing the concept of a constructive trust to provide a third party with a remedy by finding that one of the parties to a contract entered into it as a trustee with the intention of benefiting the third party. In *Drimmie v. Davies*[20] by virtue of a deed a dentist and his son agreed to become partners for five years; in the event of a dissolution the son was to have the right to purchase the property and, in the event of his father's death, was to pay certain annuities to his brothers and sisters. The father died and his executors and the brothers and sisters succeeded in an action to enforce payment of the annuities on the grounds that the son was bound by the obligation to his father which was now being enforced by his executors. It is clear from the judgment of Chatterton VC, which was upheld by the Irish Court of Appeal, that he felt it was not necessary to decide whether a fiduciary relationship existed between the executors and the beneficiaries for the purpose of maintaining the action. However, Chatterton VC referred to the *dicta* of Cotton LJ in *Gandy v. Gandy*[21] to the effect that the rule that a contract cannot be enforced except by a party to it is subject to an exception:

> [I]f the contract, although in form it is with A, is intended to secure a benefit to B, so that B is entitled to say that he has a beneficial right as *cestui que trust* under that contract; then B would, in a Court of Equity, be allowed to insist upon and enforce the contract.[22]

This statement was also quoted with approval in *Kelly v. Larkin*[23] by Andrews J who stated that, while he did not seek to question the common law doctrine that a contract cannot be enforced except by a party to it, he considered that the facts of the case before him came within the 'equitable exception' to this doctrine expounded in *Gandy*.

It can be argued that such an approach may often be called for to ensure that justice is achieved yet the courts both in this jurisdiction and elsewhere have shown a marked reluctance to infer the existence of a trust

---

19. *Scruttons Ltd v. Midland Silicones Ltd* [1962] AC 446 and *Beswick v. Beswick* [1968] AC 58.
20. [1899] 1 IR 176.
21. (1885) 30 Ch D 57.
22. (1885) 30 Ch D 57, 67. Also approved by Walker LJ in *Kenney v. Employers' Liability Assurance Corporation* [1901] 1 IR 301.
23. [1910] 2 IR 550, 557. Andrews J held that a person who is not named as a party to a covenant was nevertheless entitled to maintain an action upon it on the basis that he was in a position akin to that of a beneficiary under the covenant.

in these circumstances, unless it is clear both from the language used in creating the arrangement and from the surrounding circumstances that this was the clear intention of the parties.[24] In *Cadbury Ireland Ltd v. Kerry Co-operative Creamery Ltd*[25] the plaintiffs claimed an entitlement to a quantity of milk at a price to be determined in accordance with a clause in a contract which had been concluded between the defendants because, it claimed, the second named defendants were trustees of the benefit of the clause in question on behalf of the plaintiffs. The defendants pleaded that the plaintiffs were not party to the agreement and denied that they had any rights thereunder. Barrington J held that while the principle that parties to a contract can create a trust of contractual rights for the benefit of a third party which can be enforced by that third party is well established, in the circumstances, the plaintiffs had failed to establish that the second named defendants were trustees of any contractual rights on their behalf. A similarly unsuccessful attempt to rely on this principle was made by the plaintiffs in *Inspector of Taxes Association v. Minister for the Public Service.*[26] Murphy J referred to the judgment of Barrington J in the *Cadbury* case and to the 'well established proposition that parties to a contract can create a trust of contractual rights for the benefit of a third party'.[27] However, he said that he would find it very difficult to infer that the various staff associations, which were parties to the original conciliation and arbitration agreement on which the plaintiffs sought to rely, had purported to contract by implication as trustees for the plaintiff association which had been formed subsequently.

Finally, it is worth noting that in some jurisdictions, third parties are given statutory rights against the promisor in a contract, which as Jacobs[28] has noted, may even put them in a more favourable position than if they had been recognised as beneficiaries under a trust implied by the courts.

---

24. See *Re Webb* [1941] 1 Ch 225, 234 *per* Farwell J; *Re Schebsman* [1944] 1 Ch 83, 104 *per* du Parcq LJ and *Green v. Russell* [1959] 2 QB 226, 231 *per* Romer LJ: 'an intention to provide benefits for someone else and to pay for them does not in itself give rise to a trusteeship.'
25. [1982] ILRM 77. See also *Bula Ltd v. Tara Mines Ltd (No. 2)* [1987] IR 95, 101.
26. High Court 1981 No. 2846P (Murphy J) 24 March 1983.
27. *Ibid.* at 35.
28. Jacobs, *Law of Trusts in Australia* (5th ed., 1986, Meagher and Gummow) pp. 27-29. See e.g. the position in Western Australia and Queensland. In Ireland, ss.7 and 8 of the Married Women's Status Act 1957 confer rights on spouses and children to enforce certain types of contracts entered into for their benefit.

4. Trusts and Powers

There is a fundamental distinction between trusts and powers; while trusts are of an imperative nature, powers are discretionary. A trustee must carry out his functions according to the terms of a trust whereas the donee of a power has considerable discretion as to the manner in which he exercises the power, if indeed he exercises it at all. The beneficiaries under a trust are the owners in equity of the trust property while the objects of a power have only the expectation that the power may be exercised in their favour. The most usual type of power and the one which is relevant in this context is a power of appointment, which authorizes the creation or grant of beneficial interests in property and which gives authority to the donee to nominate objects of the power who will generally be chosen from a defined class. It is also relevant at this juncture to draw a distinction between general and special powers of appointment. A power will be characterized as general if the donee may designate any person even himself as the object(s) of the power, otherwise it will be termed a special power of appointment.

While these basic distinctions seem clear in theory, they are confused by the fact that a trust may confer a measure of discretion on a trustee e.g. he may be given a discretion to select beneficiaries from a specified class or to decide the proportions in accordance with which the trust property is to be divided, and this is known as a discretionary trust. While the beneficiaries under a discretionary trust cannot demand that trustees exercise their discretion in their favour, they can seek to ensure that the trustees make a selection as to who will benefit under the terms of the trust. This compares with the situation in relation to a power of appointment where the donee of the power cannot be compelled to make a selection.

To confuse matters further, there is also a concept known as a power in the nature of a trust or a 'trust power'[29]. This essentially denotes the situation which arises where a court implies the existence of a trust in default of any appointment being made by the donee of a power.[30] A gift over in

---

29. For a detailed consideration of these various distinctions, see Unwin (1962) 26 Conv 92; Hopkins [1971] CLJ 68; Cullity (1976) 54 Can Bar Rev 229 and Bartlett & Stebbings [1984] Conv 227.

30. Explained in the following terms by Lord Eldon in *Brown v. Higgs* (1803) 8 Ves 561, 570: 'there are (sic) not only a mere trust and a mere power, but there is also known to this court a power, which the party, to whom it is given, is entrusted and required to execute; and with regard to that species of power the court consider it as partaking so much of the nature and qualities of a trust, that if the person, who has that duty imposed upon him, does not discharge it, the Court will, to a certain extent, discharge the duty in his room and place.' Quoted with approval by Budd J in *Re Parker's Will* [1966] IR 309, 319.

default of appointment negatives the existence of a trust of this nature for the objects of a power.[31] Where there is no gift over in the event of non-exercise of a power, it may be construed as a trust for all the members of the specified class equally.[32] However, the absence of a gift over is not conclusive[33] and there must be a clear indication that the testator or settlor intended the power to be in the nature of a trust. Where the court is not satisfied that such a trust power exists and the person to whom the power is given has died without exercising it, there will be a resulting trust in favour of the testator's estate.[34]

The manner in which a court should determine whether a mere power or a trust power exists in circumstances where there has been a failure to exercise a power of appointment is in the words of Evershed MR a question of deducing the 'intention or presumed intention to be derived from the language of the instrument'.[35] Perhaps the most frequently cited example of such an intention being found by the courts is *Burrough v. Philcox*[36] where Lord Cottenham laid down the following principle:

> When there appears a general intention in favour of a class, and a particular intention in favour of individuals of a class to be selected by another person, and the particular intention fails, from that selection not being made, the court will carry into effect the general intention in favour of the class.[37]

A testator gave life estates in certain stock and property to his two children with remainder to their issue and provided that if they should both die without leaving lawful issue, the survivor of the children should have power to dispose by will of the estate amongst his nephews and nieces, or their children, either all to one of them or to as many of them as his surviving child should think proper. There was no gift over in default and it was held by Lord Cottenham that a trust was thereby created in favour of

---

31. *Re Mills* [1930] 1 Ch 654. Note that an ordinary residuary gift is not considered to be a gift over for this purpose, see *Re Hall* [1899] 1 IR 308, 320.
32. See *Re Llewellyn's Settlement* [1921] 2 Ch 281; *Re Arnold's Trusts* [1947] Ch 131.
33. *Re Weekes' Settlement* [1897] 1 Ch 289 applied in *Re Combe* [1925] Ch 210 and *Re Perowne* [1951] Ch 785.
34. See e.g. *Bank of Ireland v. O'Toole*, High Court 1979 No. 671Sp (Barrington J) 26 June 1980; *Tuite v. Tuite* [1978] ILRM 197.
35. *Re Scarisbrick* [1951] Ch 622, 635. See also the *dicta* of Buckley J in *Re Leek* [1967] Ch 1061, 1073.
36. (1840) 5 My & Cr 72.
37. (1840) 5 My & Cr 72,92. Note also the *dicta* of Lord Eldon in *Brown v. Higgs* (1803) 8 Ves 561, 574.

the testator's nephews and nieces and their children, subject to a power of selection and distribution in the surviving child.

A similar result was achieved in *Re Kieran,*[38] where a testator devised and bequeathed his farm and the rest of his property to his brother on trust for the latter's eldest son and, if this son should die before attaining the age of 21, to such of his other sons as his brother should appoint. The testator's brother's eldest son died before he reached the age of 21 and his brother died without making any appointment amongst his three surviving sons. Pim J held that in the circumstances these three surviving sons were entitled to the farm in equal shares as tenants in common. He commented that 'it is the recognized duty of every court to carry out a trust if it is possible to do so, and if it is possible, a court will avoid a construction which must result in an intestacy and in the carrying of the property, possibly wholly, probably largely, to persons whom the testator never meant to get it.'[39]

The intention of the testator appears to have emerged as the paramount consideration which will influence a court in deciding whether a gift should arise by implication in the absence of any appointment being made in these cases. In *Robinson v. Moore*[40] Dixon J was satisfied that the testator intended to deal exhaustively and completely with the property which formed the subject-matter of the power and did not intend that it should devolve as on an intestacy or lapse into residue. In these circumstances, he was satisfied that there was an implied gift to the objects of the power in default of appointment.

The rationale behind this approach is that the failure on the part of the donee to exercise the apparent power should not prejudice the donor's intended objects. Instead, the court will substitute its own discretion for that of the donee and in doing so seek to give effect as far as possible to the donor's original intentions.[41] Where the donor of the power has subsequently died, arguably this approach will come much closer to carrying his wishes into effect than if the property were to become the subject-matter of a resulting trust. Despite the existence of the fundamental principle that the courts will seek as far as possible to ascertain and give effect to a testator's intentions, the courts have on a number of occasions decided in

---

38. [1916] 1 IR 289. This was also the approach adopted by Budd J in *Re Parker's Will* [1966] IR 309.
39. [1916] 1 IR 289, 297. See also *Rorke v. Abraham* [1895] 1 IR 334.
40. [1962-3] Ir Jur Rep 29.
41. Where the court intervenes the objects of the power will take in equal shares as tenants in common whereas the actual donee might well have exercised his discretion to divide the property in unequal shares.

such circumstances that no 'trust power' arises and that a resulting trust in favour of a testator's estate should take effect.

In *Healy v. Donnery*[42] a testator devised freehold property to his daughter for life and gave her power to dispose of it amongst her children in such shares as she might consider proper. Pennefather B rejected the argument that the power to appoint amongst the children was tantamount to creating a trust in their favour and stated that the power was not coupled with a trust. This approach was confirmed by the English decision of *Re Weekes' Settlement*[43] in which the following statement of principle was made by Romer J:

> The authorities do not shew . . . that there is a hard and fast rule that a gift to A for life, with a power to A to appoint among a class and nothing more, must, if there is no gift over in the will, be held a gift by implication to the class in default of the power being exercised. In my opinion, the cases shew ... that you must find in the will an indication that the testatrix did intend the class or some of the class to take — intended in fact that this power should be regarded in the nature of a trust — only a power of selection being given, as, for example, a gift to A for life, with a gift over to such a class as A shall appoint.[44]

Here a testatrix bequeathed property to her husband for life and granted him a power of appointment over this property to be exercised amongst their children. The husband died intestate without having exercised the power and Romer J found that there was no implied gift to the children in default of appointment. A similar result was arrived at in *Clibborn v. Horan*,[45] where O'Connor MR stated that 'there must be something in the instrument creating the power from which the intention that the objects shall take in default of appointment can be gathered'.[46] He concluded that no intention that there should be a trust in favour of the objects of the power was expressed or could be gleaned from the will and in the circumstances there could be no gift by implication to these objects. This principle of giving effect as far as possible to the testator's intentions where

---

42. (1853) 3 ICLR 213. See also *Re Hall* [1899] 1 IR 308.
43. [1897] 1 Ch 289.
44. [1897] 1 Ch 289, 292.
45. [1921] 1 IR 93.
46. [1921] 1 IR 93, 97. This statement was quoted with approval by Dixon J in *Robinson v. Moore* [1962-3] Ir Jur Rep 29, 38 a case in which the opposite conclusion was reached.

these can be extracted from the will resulted in a similar conclusion being reached by McWilliam J in *Tuite v. Tuite*.[47] In this instance the testator's intention appeared to the court to be to seek to benefit those persons to whom he had bequeathed his residuary estate and McWilliam J concluded that the proceeds of the property in question should pass under the residuary clause in the will.

A further example of a situation in which a court was satisfied that a testator did not intend a power to operate by implication as a gift to all the potential objects equally in default of appointment is *Bank of Ireland v. O'Toole*.[48] A testator had conferred a power of appointment over his property on his widow intending her to exercise it in favour of one of his sons subject to the payment of a number of legacies to the other children. His widow died without exercising the power and Barrington J rejected the argument that it should be construed as a power in the nature of a trust and that the property, which was principally comprised of a farm, should go to the sons equally. He reiterated that the fundamental duty of the court was to attempt to ascertain and give effect to the testator's intentions and that it was clear that the testator intended that the farm should pass to one of his sons alone; it was quite inconsistent with any intention which could be gathered from the will that the sons should take equally.

Despite the conflicting results arrived at by the courts in this jurisdiction even in comparatively recent cases it is possible to deduce some general principles from these decisions. First, it seems clear that the court will seek to give effect as far as possible to the testator's intentions, which will usually[49] be achieved by construing a power as being in the nature of a trust in default of appointment. However, there must be some intention either expressed or implied in the will that the objects of the power should take a gift by implication in these circumstances. The question which is difficult to answer with certainty is what will constitute sufficient evidence of such intention and this problem of interpretation is to an extent responsible for the divergence in recent authorities in this area.

A final matter of considerable practical significance is that whether one is dealing with powers or trusts it is necessary for the objects or beneficiaries to be defined with a sufficient degree of certainty to enable the donees or trustees to carry out their functions in relation to distribution. The position in both England and in this jurisdiction in relation to the test

---

47. [1978] ILRM 197.
48. High Court 1979 No. 671Sp (Barrington J) 26 June 1980.
49. As in decisions such as *Re Kieran* [1916] 1 IR 289 although, as shown above, not in *Tuite v. Tuite* [1978] ILRM 197.

of certainty used to differ as between mere powers on the one hand and trusts, whether fixed, discretionary or trust powers on the other hand. In the former case the test was whether it could be said with certainty that any given individual was or was not a member of the class.[50] In the latter case the trust was void for uncertainty unless a comprehensive list of the beneficiaries could be drawn up.[51] However, the majority of the House of Lords decided in *McPhail v. Doulton*[52] that the test to be applied in ascertaining the validity of a discretionary trust should be the same as that outlined above in relation to mere powers. Clearly the assimilation of the test of certainty in relation to discretionary trusts and powers has from a practical perspective removed to a great extent the need to distinguish between them. It had been presumed in some quarters[53] that the approach of the House of Lords in *McPhail* would be followed in this jurisdiction but it now appears that this will not necessarily be the case. In *O'Byrne v. Davoren*[54] Murphy J stated, albeit *obiter*, that a trust for the division of income between members of a class to be selected by trustees will be invalid unless the entire class of potential beneficiaries is ascertainable. This issue will be considered in more detail below in the context of the requirement of certainty of objects in relation to express trusts, but for present purposes it suffices to make the point that in this jurisdiction at any rate the distinction between mere powers and discretionary trusts or trust powers may yet be of considerable significance in determining the validity of the trust or power in question.

5. Trusts and the Administration of a Deceased's Estate

While the roles of a personal representative and trustee are often confused in practice, their origins are quite distinct; the position of the former was regulated by the Ecclesiastical Courts whereas the latter as we have seen was a product of the developments brought about by the Court of Chancery. While the task of the personal representative could be said to be the limited one of realizing and distributing assets whereas the trustee's function is ordinarily of considerably more lasting duration in terms of admin-

---

50. *Re Gestetner Settlement* [1953] Ch 672; *Re Gulbenkian's Settlement* [1970] AC 508.
51. *IRC v. Broadway Cottages' Trust* [1955] Ch 20, 35-36. Approved by Budd J in *Re Parker* [1966] IR 309.
52. [1971] AC 424. It is interesting to note that a differently constituted House of Lords has confirmed the earlier approach only three years earlier in *Re Gulbenkian's Settlement* [1970] AC 508.
53. See Keane, *Equity and the Law of Trusts in the Republic of Ireland* (1988) at p.81.
54. [1994] 3 IR 373.

istering the trust on an ongoing basis, there are nevertheless considerable similarities between the offices.[55]

Both trustees and personal representatives are subject to fiduciary obligations in the performance of their functions and often the same individuals will fulfil both roles at different stages. In the first instance, an individual may act as an executor and once the deceased's estate is administered may take over the role of trustee of the trusts established under the testator's will. It is often difficult to determine precisely when one role ceases and the other commences but having said this, the individual concerned will rarely act in both capacities at the same time. Legislative provisions may cause confusion as for example section 10(3) of the Succession Act 1965 which provides that a personal representative holds a deceased's estate as a 'trustee' for those entitled to it. Despite the use of such terminology, until the estate is fully administered, the residuary legatee or next of kin will not be regarded as the beneficial owner of the testator's assets and a personal representative does not become a trustee in the strict sense of the word.[56] So when acting as a personal representative, he must be regarded as such for the purposes of deciding on the application of relevant limitation periods to any actions which these parties may take or which may be taken against them.[57]

A distinction between the offices which may have considerable practical significance is that while trustees only have joint authority to deal with or dispose of personal property, personal representatives have joint and several authority to do so and the lawful actions of one will be binding on all.[58] This is illustrated by *Attenborough & Son v. Solomon,*[59] where an executor, over thirteen years after the testator's death but before the distribution of the residuary estate had been completed, pledged property to a pawnbroker which formed part of this residuary estate without the knowledge of his co-executor/co-trustee. The pledgor died and when the transaction was discovered an action was brought to recover the property. The

---

55. *Re Speight* (1883) 22 Ch D 727,742 *per* Jessel MR.
56. See the *dicta* of Sargant J in *Re Ponder* [1921] 2 Ch 59, 61: 'when the estate has been wound up and the residue ascertained, the executor has ceased to be an executor and has become a trustee for the persons entitled to the residue.' See also *Eaton v. Daines* [1894] WN 32 and Ker (1955) 19 Conv 199.
57. See e.g. *Vaughan v. Cottingham* [1961] IR 184.
58. *Jacomb v. Harwood* (1751) 2 Ves Sen 265, 267. Although note that where one administrator purports to sign a contract on behalf of himself and his co-administrator and warrants that he has the authority to do so when this is in fact lacking, no specifically enforceable contract will exist, see *Fountain Forestry Ltd v. Edwards* [1975] Ch 1.
59. [1913] AC 76. See also *Astbury v. Astbury* [1898] 2 Ch 111.

result of the case turned on whether the pledgor had been acting as an executor or trustee; if he was adjudged to have been still acting as executor, the pawnbrokers would have obtained good title. However, the House of Lords held that at the relevant date the executors had assented to the trust dispositions under the testator's will taking effect and that the property was held by the pledgor as a trustee. Accordingly he had had no authority to act without the assent of his co-trustee and the property could be recovered.

A further distinction which can be made is that a personal representative holds his office for life except where the grant of probate or letters of administration is for a limited period or the court releases him from such duties.[60] However, by virtue of section 11 of the Trustee Act 1893, provided that there will be at least two trustees remaining to administer the trust, a trustee may by deed declare that he wishes to retire and if the consent of his co-trustees is forthcoming, he will be permitted to do so.

CLASSIFICATION OF TRUSTS

Trusts can be classified in a number of different ways; e.g. according to the manner of their creation, by virtue of the objects which they seek to benefit or from the perspective of the nature of the duties which they impose on the trustee. It is proposed at this point to set out briefly the main classifications which are recognised but it is important to note that these categories are not always mutually exclusive.

Public and Private Trusts

This classification is based on the reason for the creation of a trust. Private trusts are created for the benefit of an individual or a class of individuals irrespective of the benefit which they may confer on the public at large. Public trusts, otherwise known as charitable trusts, are set up for purposes beneficial to the community in general although in most cases they will incidentally confer a benefit on a specific person or class of persons. In the case of the former type of trust the so called 'beneficiary principle' applies i.e. there 'must be somebody in whose favour the court can decree specific performance'.[61] However, there is no such requirement in the case of public trusts which may be enforced by the Attorney General.

---

60. *Re Timmis* [1902] 1 Ch 176, 183 *per* Kekewich J.
61. *Morice v. Bishop of Durham* (1804) 9 Ves 399, 405 *per* Grant MR. Note that there is also an anomalous category of 'purpose trusts' which have been upheld as valid despite their failure to adhere to the beneficiary principle. See further, Chapter 9.

Express, Resulting and Constructive Trusts

Express Trusts

An express trust is one created by express declaration of the settlor or
testator either by instrument *inter vivos* or by will. Certain formalities must
be observed in the creation of *inter vivos* trusts of land and all trusts which
are set up by means of a will. In addition, all express trusts must contain a
number of essential elements known as 'the three certainties', and these
issues will be considered in detail in the following chapter. Further subdivisions in the classification of express trusts can be made; first, according
to the form in which the declaration of trust is effected, which can give
rise to either executed or executory trusts. A trust is said to be executed
where the settlor or testator has delimited precisely the circumstances under which the trust property is to be held and no further instrument is
required to effect this. However in the case of an executory trust, although
a valid trust has been created the settlor or testator has only indicated his
general intentions as to how the trust property is to be disposed of and a
further instrument is required to define the beneficial interests with precision.[62]

A further subdivision can be made between completely and incompletely constituted trusts. A trust is said to be completely constituted when
the trust property has actually been vested in the trustees for the benefit of
the beneficiaries; until this has been done the trust remains incompletely
constituted. The distinction between these last two subdivisions and their
practical implications will be considered in more detail below.

Resulting Trusts

A resulting trust[63] is one which arises from the unexpressed but presumed
intention of the settlor or testator. They are known as resulting trusts because the beneficial interest in the property reverts or 'results' to the settlor
(or if he is dead, to his estate) who transferred the property to the trustee in
the first instance. Resulting trusts are often divided into two categories:[64]
automatically resulting trusts arise where a trust has been declared but the
beneficial interest fails for some reason or is not disposed of in its entirety
and presumed resulting trusts which occur as a result of the inference drawn
by the law with regard to the donor's intentions. Due to the informal man-

---

62. *Egerton v. Earl Brownlow* (1853) HLC 1, 210 and see further *infra*.
63. The term 'implied trust' is sometimes used interchangeably with the term 'resulting
    trust'; alternatively resulting trusts may be considered to be merely examples of a
    wider category of implied trusts, see Wylie, *Irish Land Law* (3rd ed., 1997) p. 543.
64. *Re Vandervell's Trusts (No. 2)* [1974] Ch 269, 294 *per* Megarry J.

ner in which they come into being, resulting trusts are exempt from the formalities required in relation to the creation of express trusts.

Constructive Trusts

A constructive trust is a form of trust which arises by operation of law and which comes into being irrespective of the intentions of the parties concerned. The main distinction between resulting and constructive trusts is that in the case of the former, the courts assume that the creation of the trust was intended by the parties whereas in the latter instance a trust is imposed to satisfy the demands of justice and good conscience and may often be imposed in a manner contrary to the intentions of the individuals concerned. To the extent that there is no requirement to observe the formalities necessary in relation to express trusts in either case, there is often little practical significance in drawing a distinction between the two categories. Constructive trusts are generally regarded as constituting a residual category of trust but as we shall see they are adaptable and often dynamic in nature.

Simple and Special Trusts

This classification distinguishes between different types of trust according to the nature of the duties which are imposed on the trustees in each case. A simple trust[65] is one in which property is vested in a trustee but the trustee is given no active duties[66] to perform and merely holds the legal title to the trust property. A special trust is one in which a trustee is required to carry out duties imposed on him by the settlor or testator which necessitates him taking an active as opposed to a passive role in administering the affairs of the trust.

Fixed and Discretionary Trusts

In a fixed trust each beneficiary has a fixed current entitlement to a specific share or interest in the trust property. However, in the case of a discretionary trust, a beneficiary has no actual entitlement to any part of the trust property; instead the trustees are given the discretion to apply the property for the benefit of specified persons or classes of persons. Therefore in the latter case a potential beneficiary cannot compel a trustee to

---

65. Also known as a bare trust, see *Tomlinson v. Glyn's Executor & Trustee Co.* [1970] Ch 112, 125-126.
66. This has been construed as meaning that a simple or bare trustee is given no specific duties by the settlor and must merely carry out whatever duties are imposed on him by law. See *Snell's Equity* (29th ed., 1990) p.103.

exercise his discretion in his favour.[67] Within this category a distinction is sometimes drawn between 'exhaustive discretionary trusts' which impose an obligation on the trustees to dispose of the entire trust income and 'non-exhaustive discretionary trusts' which leave the issue of the extent of any distribution to the trustee.

Protective Trusts

A further category of trust which should be mentioned at this juncture is a protective trust.[68] The essence of such a trust is that the interest of a beneficiary is made determinable on the happening of certain events, most usually bankruptcy or an attempt to alienate the trust property. This determinable interest is then followed by the establishment of a discretionary trust, usually in favour of the beneficiary and members of his family or some other class of persons.

While a settlor cannot set up a protective trust to guard against his own bankruptcy,[69] he may do so to protect himself against alienation which will usually be of an involuntary nature. However, the most common type of protective trust will be one in which the interest of a beneficiary, other than the settlor, becomes determinable.[70] It is important to distinguish between such a determinable interest and an interest subject to a condition subsequent. A condition subsequent designed to terminate an interest in the event of bankruptcy or alienation will be void whereas an interest determinable in such cases will be valid.

Although there has been no legislative intervention in this area in Ireland, in a number of other jurisdictions legislation now provides a means whereby a settlor may direct that property be held on protective trusts without the necessity of setting out in detail the circumstances in which the interest will become determinable and the manner in which the discretionary trusts should operate.[71]

---

67. Although such a trustee can be compelled to at least make a selection amongst the beneficiaries.
68. Sheridan (1957) 21 Conv 110.
69. *Re Burroughs-Fowler* [1916] 2 Ch 251.
70. *Billson v. Crofts* (1873) LR 15 Eq 314 and *Re Ashby* [1892] 1 QB 872.
71. E.g. s.33 of the Trustee Act 1925 in England; s.42 of the Trustee Act 1956 in New Zealand and s. 45 of the Trustee Act 1925 in New South Wales.

CHAPTER 4

Trusts — Formalities and Essential Elements

FORMALITIES

Creation of Trusts Inter Vivos

Primarily with a view to preventing fraud, legislation has intervened to provide that in specific cases certain formalities must be observed in the creation of express trusts. However, no formalities are required for the creation of an *inter vivos* express trust of personalty and provided that the settlor manifests the intention of creating such a trust[1] it may be established orally.[2] In relation to the creation of express trusts of land, whether freehold or leasehold,[3] section 4 of the Statute of Frauds (Ireland) 1695 requires that the trust be evidenced in writing and signed by a person able to declare the trust, or by his will.[4] It is important to note that the declaration of trust itself does not need to be in writing but written evidence must exist to prove the declaration and its essential terms.[5] This written evidence need not be in any precise form,[6] and can even be extracted from two or more separate documents.[7] It has also been established that this

---

1. *Paul v. Constance* [1977] 1 WLR 521, 531 *per* Scarman LJ.
2. While the courts have accepted that such a trust may be validly created in this manner (*M'Fadden v. Jenkins* (1842) 1 Ph 153; *Re Kayford* [1975] 1 WLR 279, 281-282 and *Paul v. Constance* [1977] 1 WLR 521) in most cases fairly strong evidence will be required to establish this, see *Paterson v. Murphy* (1853) 11 Hare 88, 91-2 and *Maguire v. Dodd* (1859) 9 Ir Ch R 452, 458.
3. *Forster v. Hale* (1798) 3 Ves 696; *Donohue v. Conrahy* (1845) 8 Ir Eq R 679.
4. See Bridge (1986) 64 Can Bar Rev 58 for a comprehensive review of the authorities relevant to the similar evidential requirements imposed by the Statute of Frauds in relation to contracts for the sale of land.
5. *Morton v. Tewart* (1842) 2 Y & C Cas Ch 67, 80; *Smith v. Matthews* (1861) 3 De G F & J 139, 151.
6. E.g. it can be contained in correspondence *Forster v. Hale* (1798) 3 Ves 696; *Childers v. Childers* (1857) 1 De G & J 482 or in a telegram *McBlain v. Cross* (1871) 25 LT 804.
7. *Forster v. Hale* (1798) 3 Ves 696. See also *Timmins v. Moreland Street Property Co.* [1958] Ch 110 (Fridman (1958) 22 Conv 275) and *Elias v. George Sahely & Co. (Barbados) Ltd* [1983] 1 AC 646 which relate to the requirements imposed by s.40 of the Law of Property Act 1925 in England in relation to contracts for the sale of land.

written evidence need not come into existence at the time the trust is declared provided that it exists before the commencement of any action in which the validity of the trust is questioned.[8]

The generally accepted view is that section 4 of the Statute of Frauds (Ireland) 1695, or its equivalent,[9] only provides an evidential requirement which will affect the enforceability and not the validity of trusts, so in the absence of any written evidence to prove its existence, such a trust will be valid although unenforceable.[10]

Statute Not to be Used as an Instrument of Fraud
Notwithstanding these statutory requirements, the courts will not always insist on strict compliance with the provisions of the Statute of Frauds.[11] Possibly for the reason that these formality provisions which can be considered as merely a means towards an end should be used purposively,[12] the principle has been established that equity will not permit the statute to be used as an instrument of fraud. As Lord Westbury stated in *McCormick v. Grogan*:[13]

> The Court of Equity has, from a very early period, decided that even an Act of Parliament shall not be used as an instrument of fraud; and if in the machinery of perpetrating a fraud an Act of Parliament intervenes, the Court of Equity, it is true, does not set aside the Act of Parliament, but it fastens on the individual who gets a title under that Act, and imposes upon him a personal obligation, because he applies the Act as an instrument for accomplishing a fraud.

So, the court will not permit a beneficiary to be deprived of an interest in land under a trust in the absence of written evidence of the trust if such a result would amount to a fraud providing that there is some other evidence to establish the existence and nature of the trust. Where there has been a failure to comply with the statutory requirements the court must weigh up the desirability of ensuring adherence to these requirements against the likelihood of injustice being caused by insisting on their observance. This

---

8. *Rochefoucauld v. Boustead* [1897] 1 Ch 196, 206 and *Re Holland* [1902] 2 Ch 360, 382.
9. S.7 of the Statute of Frauds 1677, replaced by s.53(1)(b) of the Law of Property Act 1925.
10. See Youdan [1984] CLJ 306, 320-1.
11. See generally, Thompson (1985) 36 NILQ 358.
12. Langbein (1975) 88 Harv L Rev 489, 491-498 and Youdan [1984] CLJ 306, 315.
13. (1869) LR 4 HL 82, 97.

balancing exercise is illustrated by the decision in *Re Duke of Marlborough*.[14] The Duchess of Marlborough assigned a leasehold interest in property to the duke and after his death asserted that the transfer was made solely to enable her husband to raise money by mortgaging the lease and that they had agreed that the property would ultimately be re-assigned to her. It was held that the provisions of the Statute of Frauds could not be successfully pleaded in opposition to the duchess's claim to the interest on the basis that the duke's estate would benefit unjustly had the obligation to re-assign the lease not been enforced owing to non-compliance with the statute. Stirling J stated that 'the general principle that the statute is not to be used as a protection to fraud has long been recognised by the courts of equity'[15] but commented that this principle has not always been applied in a uniform manner.

Perhaps the most frequently cited example of the operation of this doctrine is the decision of the English Court of Appeal in *Rochefoucauld v. Boustead*.[16] The plaintiff was the owner of mortgaged property which was sold by the mortgagee to the defendant. The defendant had orally agreed to hold the property on trust for the plaintiff subject to repayment to the defendant of the purchase price and other expenses incurred in the transaction. The defendant subsequently sold the land and the plaintiff, who claimed that the land had been conveyed to the defendant as trustee for her, was held to be entitled to obtain an order for an account. Lindley LJ stated:

> [I]t is a fraud on the part of a person to whom land is conveyed as a trustee, and who knows it was so conveyed, to deny the trust and claim the land himself. Consequently, notwithstanding the statute, it is competent for a person claiming land conveyed to another to prove by parol evidence that it was so conveyed upon trust for the claimant, and that the grantee, knowing the facts, is denying the trust and relying upon the form of conveyance and the statute, in order to keep the land himself.[17]

This principle was applied in Ireland in *McGillicuddy v. Joy*.[18] The plaintiff and the defendants agreed to purchase a farm jointly and the contract was signed by one of the defendants. The plaintiff paid one-third of the

---

14. [1894] 2 Ch 133.
15. [1894] 2 Ch 133, 141.
16. [1897] 1 Ch 196.
17. [1897] 1 Ch 196, 206.
18. [1959] IR 189.

purchase price and the defendants then reneged on the agreement. The plaintiff sought a declaration that the defendant, who had signed the agreement, held the benefit of the contract in trust for him. Budd J held that the principle in *Rochefoucauld* applied even though here there was only a contract of sale, as opposed to a conveyance. He concluded that the defendant had purchased that part of the lands previously agreed between them in trust for the plaintiff and that the former's repudiation of that trust constituted a fraud. Similarly, in *Gilmurray v. Corr*,[19] the plaintiff had a leasehold interest in lands part of which were used as a golf driving range. After an unsuccessful attempt to buy the freehold, he came to an oral agreement with the defendant whereby the latter would purchase the lands with the plaintiff providing part of the purchase money, on the understanding that the defendant would then transfer the range to the plaintiff. The defendant subsequently told the plaintiff that he wished to incorporate in the transfer of the driving range a restrictive covenant that would prevent the use of the site for a licensed restaurant which might compete with the defendant's own premises. The plaintiff would not agree to this and the defendant proceeded with the purchase of the lands and refused to transfer the range to the plaintiff. The Northern Ireland Court of Appeal held that when the defendant offered to purchase the lands he was acting as a trustee for himself and the plaintiff and that the plaintiff was entitled to prove by parol evidence that the land was conveyed to the defendant as a trustee. Lowry LCJ referred to *Rochefoucauld* and said that the decision had established that it is a fraud in equity for a person to whom land is conveyed as a trustee and who knows that it was so conveyed to deny the trust and claim the land as his own. This principle clearly applied to the facts of the case before him and the defendant could not rely on non-compliance with the statutory requirements to defeat the plaintiff's claim.

A question which has provoked considerable debate in recent years is whether a third party beneficiary can rely on the principle enunciated in *Rochefoucauld* to enforce such an informal trust. Feltham[20] has argued that there is a strong line of authority against allowing a third party to rely on the doctrine and has stated that 'neither precedent nor policy' support the extension of the principle in this way. However, Youdan[21] has asserted that the relevant authorities[22] favour the view that such trusts can be en-

---

19. [1978] NI 99.
20. [1987] Conv 246.
21. [1984] CLJ 306; [1988] Conv 267.
22. *Neale v. Willis* [1968] 19 P & CR 839; *Binions v. Evans* [1972] Ch 359; *Lyus v. Prowsa Developments Ltd* [1982] 1 WLR 1044.

forced at the instance of a third party beneficiary and on balance this would seem to be the fairer approach.

Finally, it should be noted that section 2 of the Statute of Frauds (Ireland) 1695 requires that contracts to create a trust in consideration of marriage must also be evidenced in writing.

Dispositions of Equitable Interests Held Under a Trust

Section 6 of the Statute of Frauds (Ireland) 1695 provides that all subsequent dispositions of the beneficial interests held under a trust must be in writing and signed by the person making the disposition, or be included in a will. Two important points should be noted in relation to this requirement. First, it must be remembered that the requirement relating to the creation of trusts of land laid down in section 4 of the statute is that they must be evidenced in writing whereas this provision, which relates to the subsequent disposition of such interests, requires that the disposition actually be in writing. Secondly, section 6 applies to both personal and real property held under a trust and so while a trust of pure personalty can be created orally and subsequently be enforced, any disposition of this interest must be in writing.

Considerable uncertainty has surrounded the ambit of section 53(1)(c)of the English Law of Property Act 1925[23] and the circumstances in which a 'disposition'[24] takes place within the meaning of the subsection are far from clear.[25] It has been accepted that where a trustee is directed by a beneficiary to hold his interest on other trusts that this is sufficient to constitute a disposition of the beneficiary's interest.[26] However, the statutory requirement will not apply where the trustee conveys the legal interest to a third party on the instructions or with the consent of the beneficiary.[27]

Creation of Trusts by Will

Where a trust is created by will, the testator must comply with the statutory requirements laid down by section 78 of the Succession Act 1965 in relation to the making of statutory dispositions i.e. that the will be in writing, signed at the foot thereof by the testator or by some other person in his presence and at his direction and the testator's signature must be made or

---

23. This replaced the original equivalent to s.6 of the 1695 statute, s.9 of the Statute of Frauds 1677.
24. This phrase replaced the formula used in s.6 of 'grants and assignments of any trust or confidence'.
25. See e.g. *Oughtred v. IRC* [1960] AC 206.
26. *Grey v. IRC* [1960] AC 1; Green (1984) 47 MLR 385.
27. *Vandervell v. IRC* [1967] 2 AC 291.

acknowledged in the presence of two or more witnesses present at the same time, each of whom must attest that signature by his own signature.

However, as with trusts created *inter vivos*, equity will not always strictly enforce the statutory formalities required where the statute is being used as an instrument of fraud and it was in obedience to this principle that so called 'secret trusts', which will be considered in Chapter 5, came to be recognised.

ESSENTIAL ELEMENTS

Essential Elements of a Trust

Apart from ensuring compliance with the formalities outlined above, no technical or precise language is necessary to create a valid express trust. However, certain essential elements which have come to be known as 'the three certainties' must be present if such a trust is to be created. These three conditions of substance are as follows: certainty of intention or words, certainty of subject-matter and certainty of objects. These requirements were laid down by O'Byrne J in the Supreme Court in the decision of *Chambers v. Fahy*:[28]

> [I]t has been established that, in order that a trust may be created, the subject matter must be certain, the objects of the trust must be certain and the words relied on as creating the trust must have been used in an imperative sense so as to show that the testator intends to create an obligation.

Certainty of Intention or Words

The requirement that the words used to create a trust be imperative does not mean that any precise form of wording must be used,[29] so a trust may be validly created without actually using the word 'trust' and conversely the use of that word does not conclusively indicate the existence of a trust.[30] In determining whether this requirement of certainty has been met, the court will examine the substance and effect of the words used and a finding that a trust has been created will not be made unless it is satisfied that this was the settlor or testator's actual intention. So even where there is

---

28. [1931] IR 17, 21. This essentially re-iterated the statement of Lord Langdale MR in *Knight v. Knight* (1840) 3 Beav 148, 173.
29. *La Have Equipment Ltd v. Nova Scotia* (1994) 121 DLR (4th) 67, 77 *per* Chipman JA.
30. *Hunter v. Public Trustee* [1924] NZLR 882.

certainty of subject-matter and of objects, no trust can be created unless there is also certainty of intention.[31]

The words used must be examined with a view to ascertaining whether the intention was to make an absolute gift to the donee which he might, in the exercise of his discretion, dispose of in accordance with the settlor or testator's wishes, or whether the latter intended the donee to hold the property on trust.

This question of construction arises most frequently in relation to wills and historically the courts readily inferred the existence of a trust where the words used were hardly of an imperative nature,[32] as for example, where a gift was made by a testator who expressed the hope, wish, expectation or desire that the donee would deal with the property in a particular manner.[33] However, more recently these so called 'precatory words'[34] have usually been interpreted as being insufficient to create a trust. Before examining some of the authorities in this area in more detail, it is important to bear in mind that the type of language used is of itself not conclusive and the question of certainty of intention must be resolved by construing the whole of the instrument in question and thereby endeavouring to ascertain the intention of the settlor or testator.[35]

An examination of the decisions of the courts in this jurisdiction since the last quarter of the nineteenth century shows that the majority favour the conclusion that precatory words will not suffice to create an express trust.[36] Instead they may often be interpreted as merely expressing the

---

31. *Crownx Inc v. Edwards* (1994) 120 DLR (4th) 270, 280.
32. The reason for this approach, as suggested in Hanbury & Martin, *Modern Equity* (15th ed., 1997) pp.90-91 is that prior to the enactment of the Executors Act 1830 in England, the undisposed of residue which remained after an estate was administered might be retained by an executor. Thereafter, the residue was held on trust for the next of kin.
33. *Palmer v. Simmonds* (1854) 2 Drew 221; *Moriarty v. Martin* (1852) 3 Ir Ch R 26; *Gray v. Gray* (1860) 11 Ir Ch R 218.
34. Trusts created by the use of precatory words have sometimes been referred to as 'precatory trusts', although they are in fact ordinary express trusts and the use of this terminology has been criticised as 'misleading' by Rigby LJ in *Re Williams* [1897] 2 Ch 12, 27.
35. *Re Adams and the Kensington Vestry* (1884) 27 Ch D 394, 410 *per* Cotton LJ; *Re Hamilton* [1895] 2 Ch 370, 373 *per* Lindley LJ; *Re Williams* [1897] 2 Ch 12, 14 *per* Romer J.
36. *McAlinden v. McAlinden* (1877) IR 11 Eq 219; *Morrin v. Morrin* (1886) 19 LR Ir 37; *Murtagh v. Murtagh* (1902) 36 ILTR 129; *Berryman v. Berryman* [1913] 1 IR 390; *Re Humphrey's Estate* [1916] 1 IR 21; *Re Walker and Elgie's Contract* (1919) 53 ILTR 22; *Re McIntosh* [1933] IR 69; *Re Coulson* (1953) 87 ILTR 93; *Re Fitzgibbon* (1959) 93 ILTR 56; *Re Sweeney* [1976-77] ILRM 88. However, the opposite conclusion was reached in *Re Finnerty* [1970] IR 221.

motive for the gift[37] or as imposing some form of moral obligation on the donee to carry out the testator's wishes. Certainly there have been numerous statements to the effect that the 'tide has turned'[38] and which support the view that the trend is now against permitting the creation of a trust by the use of precatory words.[39] The position now appears to be that such words will not *prima facie* create a trust,[40] so any intention to the contrary must be clearly and unequivocally expressed by the testator. The statement of Monroe J in *Re Byrne's Estate*[41] provides a useful summary of the position:

> [I]t is impossible to lay down any general rule by which all the cases on this subject can be reconciled; but I think it will be found that, in the great majority of cases where the Court of Chancery has refused to establish a precatory trust, there is, in the first place, an absolute gift to a particular individual, the terms of which are sought to be qualified by subsequent words in a subsequent clause. No trust will be established unless the words of qualification are clear and definite, and so expressed as to be regarded as imperative.

In *Re Humphrey's Estate*[42] a testator devised and bequeathed all his property, real and personal, to his wife and added that he wished that she should leave by will or transfer during her life a house and demense to his son and that the remainder of his property should be left or transferred to his daughters. Ross J held that in the circumstances, the wife took an absolute interest. Similarly, in *Re Coulson*,[43] a testatrix left a farm and the furnishings of the farmhouse to her cousin in her will and went on to state that it was her wish that it should not be sold or divided but should be retained by the cousin for whichever of her children she thought fit. In these circumstances, Dixon J said that while the words used in the will were capable of being imperative they were not necessarily so and that the determining factor

---

37. *Re Fitzgibbon* (1959) 93 ILTR 56, 59 *per* Budd J.
38. *Re Humphrey's Estate* [1916] 1 IR 21, 24 *per* Ross J.
39. *Re Hamilton* [1895] 2 Ch 370, 374 *per* Lopes LJ; *Mussorie Bank Ltd v. Raynor* (1882) 7 App Cas 321, 330 *per* Sir Arthur Hobhouse; *Murtagh v. Murtagh* (1902) 36 ILTR 129, 130 *per* Porter MR; *Re Coulson* (1953) 87 ILTR 93, 94 *per* Dixon J.
40. *Re Walker & Elgee's Contract* (1919) 53 ILTR 22, 23.
41. (1892) 29 LR Ir 250. Note also the *dicta* of Chatterton VC in *Morrin v. Morrin* (1886) 19 LR Ir 37 where he stated that where these 'superadded words' do not cut down the interest given, it will not be held without more evidence that a trust has been created.
42. [1916] 1 IR 21.
43. (1953) 87 ILTR 93.

was 'what could be gathered from the will as a whole'. He was satisfied that the wording used amounted to no more than the expression of the hope that the cousin would act in the manner intended by the testatrix and held that in the circumstances, she took an absolute interest in the farm and furnishings. The most recent case to be decided in this area would appear to confirm the approach established in decisions such as *Re Humphrey's Estate* and *Re Coulson*. In *Re Sweeney*[44] the testator devised and bequeathed all his assets to his wife for her own absolute use and benefit 'subject to the express wish' that she make provision for the payment of certain legacies after her death. The question arose whether the words of the gift to the wife of all the testator's assets could be cut down by these subsequent words. Hamilton J commented that while they were capable of being imperative, if he were to so hold, he would be cutting down considerably the clear words of the gift and quoted with approval the statement of Ross J in *Re Humphrey's Estate*[45] to the effect that 'after a devise and bequest in clear and express terms, if a trust is intended to be created one would expect that this would be done in terms equally clear and explicit'. He concluded that it was the testator's intention that his wife should enjoy the assets for her own absolute use and benefit and that the words were not intended to create any trust in favour of the other defendants but were merely the expression of his wish for the guidance of his wife as to the manner in which she should dispose of her assets after her death.

Despite the general trend illustrated by these decisions, precatory words may be sufficient to create a trust if it is clear from the language used in the will as a whole that this was the testator's intention.[46] In *Comiskey v. Bowring-Hanbury*[47] a testator devised and bequeathed all his real and personal property to his wife absolutely 'in full confidence' that she would make such use of it as he would have made himself and that at her death she would devise it to one or more of the testator's nieces as she might think fit. The majority of the House of Lords held that on the true construction of the will there was an absolute gift of the testator's real and personal estate subject to an executory gift of the same at her death to such of his nieces as survived her, either in accordance with the shares provided for in the wife's will or otherwise equally.

So, it would be incorrect to assume that the use of any particular form

---

44. [1976-77] ILRM 88.
45. [1916] 1 IR 21, 24.
46. *Comiskey v. Bowring-Hanbury* [1905] AC 84, 89 *per* Lord Davey.
47. [1905] AC 84. See also *Re Burley* [1910] 1 Ch 215.

of words may or may not be sufficient to create a trust[48] and in any event the courts may find expressions used in other parts of the will which may be used as a guide in construing the precatory words.[49] Romer J summarized the position aptly in *Re Williams*:[50]

> [T]he rule you have to observe is simply this: 'In considering whether a precatory trust is attached to any legacy, the Court will be guided by the intention of the testator apparent in the will, and not by any particular words in which the wishes of the testator are expressed.'

The only situation where the use of identical language to that employed in a previous case may be decisive is where a testator can be shown to have used this particular language as a precedent with the intention of creating a trust. Where this is shown to be the case, it has been held that a trust may be created even though the words themselves, given a modern interpretation, might not otherwise have been held to be sufficient to create a trust.[51]

Where the test of certainty of intention is not complied with, as where precatory words are interpreted as being insufficient to create a trust, the donee will take an absolute gift of the property.[52] This should be contrasted with the situation which arises where the test relating to certainty of objects is not met, in which case a resulting trust arises in favour of the settlor or testator's estate.

Finally it should be noted that even where a settlor executes a declaration of trust, the courts may look behind such a declaration at the settlor's intention to ensure that he genuinely meant to create a trust. In *Midland Bank plc v. Wyatt*[53] the defendant and his wife purchased a property in their joint names and the defendant subsequently executed a trust deed giving the equity in the house to his wife and daughters. After the defendant's business ran into difficulties he sought to resist the making absolute

---

48.   *Re Hamilton* [1895] 2 Ch 370, 373 *per* Lindley LJ and *Re McIntosh* [1933] IR 69, 71 *per* Kennedy CJ. Contrast the decisions of *Re Williams* [1897] 2 Ch 12 where the words 'in the fullest trust and confidence' were insufficient to create a trust in this case, and *Comiskey v. Bowring-Hanbury* [1905] AC 84 where the opposite conclusion was reached where the words 'in full confidence' were employed.
49.   *Re Blackwood* [1953] NI 32, 46 *per* Black LJ.
50.   [1897] 2 Ch 12, 14.
51.   *Re Steele's Will Trusts* [1948] Ch 603. This decision should not be interpreted as authority for the proposition that if a particular form of wording has been held to create a trust, the use of this wording will necessarily without further evidence also create a trust. See the statement in *Snell's Equity* (29th ed. 1990) p.115 and (1968) 32 Conv 361.
52.   *Lassence v. Tierney* (1849) 1 Mac & G 551.
53.   [1995] 1 FLR 696.

of a charging order on the property obtained by the bank relying on the declaration of trust. However, the court held that the declaration upon which the plaintiff sought to rely was void and unenforceable on the basis that it was a sham and that the deed had been executed by the plaintiff 'not to be acted upon but to be put in the safe for a rainy day'.[54] The court was satisfied that the plaintiff had never intended to give his children any interest in the property but had merely sought to protect his family from commercial risk. If this approach is followed in this jurisdiction, it opens up the possibility of the courts looking behind a whole range of trust declarations with a view to examining the settlor's motives in such cases. It should be noted that in *Wyatt* it was stated that even if the deed was executed without any dishonest or fraudulent motive but was merely entered into on the basis of mistaken advice, it would still be an unenforceable transaction if it was entered into for some ulterior motive.

Certainty of Subject-Matter

To ensure the creation of a valid express trust, the subject-matter of the trust must be defined with sufficient certainty. This principle applies not just in a general way to the property which should form the subject-matter of the trust, but also requires that the beneficial interests to be taken by the beneficiaries are defined with sufficient clarity except in a situation where the trustees are given a discretion to decide what the extent of these beneficial interests should be.

One of the most common examples of a trust failing due to lack of certainty of subject-matter is where a testator gives property to an individual and directs that whatever is not required during that individual's lifetime and remains at the time of his death should go to another person or persons.[55] So, where phrases such as 'the remaining part of what is left'[56] or 'such parts of my ... estate as she shall not have sold or disposed of'[57] are employed, these gifts will usually fail to take effect. However, it would be incorrect to assume that gifts described in this way will invariably be considered too uncertain. As Karminski J commented in *Re Last's Estate*:[58]

In a matter of construction of this kind, it is clearly essential to pay

---

54. *Ibid.* at 707.
55. *Mussoorie Bank Ltd v. Raynor* (1882) 7 App Cas 321.
56. *Sprange v. Barnard* (1789) 2 Bro CC 585.
57. *Re Jones* [1898] 1 Ch 438.
58. [1958] P 137.

particular attention to the terms of the instrument which is being construed and to avoid too close comparisons with words used in wills in other cases.

There a testatrix left all her property to her brother and directed that 'anything that is left' should go to her late husband's grandchildren. Karminski J quoted with approval the statement of Joyce J in *Re Sanford*[59] to the effect that 'it is better to effectuate than to frustrate the testator's intentions' and held that when the testatrix's brother died intestate, her husband's grandchildren were entitled to the estate in equal shares.

It must be possible to determine with certainty what will constitute the trust property, so vague expressions such as 'the bulk of my ... residuary estate'[60] and 'remembering always ... the Church of God and the poor'[61] will be insufficient. The most usual result where a purported trust attached to an absolute gift fails due to the uncertainty of its subject-matter is that the donee takes beneficially,[62] but if it is clear that a trust was intended and the only uncertainty relates to the precise shares which the beneficiaries are to take, the trustees will hold the property on a resulting trust. In *Boyce v. Boyce,*[63] a testator devised all his houses in a particular location in trust to his wife for life and after her death in trust to convey whichever of these houses was chosen by her to one of his daughters, the other houses to go to another daughter. The daughter who was to have made the selection predeceased the testator and it was held that the trust failed for uncertainty. Had the trustees been given the authority to make the selection this problem could have been averted but in the circumstances the court felt that it had no choice but to find that all the properties should be held on a resulting trust for the testator's estate.

Where an objective criterion which can be applied by the court is provided by a settlor or testator, a failure to quantify precisely the extent of the subject-matter of a trust will not prove fatal to its validity. In *Re Golay's Will Trusts*[64] Ungoed-Thomas J upheld the validity of a gift directing the testator's executors to allow a beneficiary to use a flat during her lifetime and to receive 'a reasonable rent' from his other properties. The question which the court had to consider in such a case was 'whether the testator by

---

59. [1901] 1 Ch 939, 944.
60. *Palmer v. Simmonds* (1854) 2 Drew 221.
61. *Curtis v. Rippon* (1820) 5 Madd 434.
62. E.g. *Re Jones* [1898] 1 Ch 438; *Mussoorie Bank Ltd v. Raynor* (1882) 7 App Cas 321; *Curtis v. Rippon* (1820) 5 Madd 434.
63. (1849) 16 Sim 476.
64. [1965] 1 WLR 969.

the words "reasonable income" has given a sufficient indication of his intention to provide an effective determinant of what he intends so that the court in applying that determinant can give effect to the testator's intention.' Ungoed-Thomas J concluded that the yardstick indicated by the testator is what has been objectively identified as a 'reasonable income' and as the court was constantly involved in making such objective assessments, the direction in the will, in his view, could not be defeated on the grounds of uncertainty.

Difficulties have always arisen where a settlor seeks to create a trust of a definite but yet unidentified portion of an asset or assets. It was held by Oliver J in *Re London Wine Co Ltd*[65] that where wine beneficially owned by certain purchasers and stored in a warehouse had not been segregated no trust could arise over it and the purchasers could therefore not assert proprietary rights over the stock against the holders of a floating charge. However, where the asset in question is of an intangible nature, the courts in England have recently accepted that a trust may arise in these circumstances. In *Hunter v. Moss*[66] it was confirmed that the requirement of certainty of subject-matter in relation to a trust of intangible assets is not based on any immutable principle which demands segregation or appropriation of the specific property which is to form this subject-matter. The trust in that case was comprised of a number of shares in a company which were of their nature indistinguishable from other shares in the same company. They were all equally capable of satisfying the trust and it was unnecessary to identify any particular shares before determining that the subject-matter requirement was satisfied. In these circumstances, Colin Rimmer QC, giving the judgment of the Divisional Court in *Hunter* was of the view that 'any suggested uncertainty as to subject matter appears to me to be theoretical and conceptual rather than real and practical'[67] and his finding that the trust was not void on the grounds of uncertainty of subject-matter was upheld by the Court of Appeal.[68] However, Dillon LJ made no reference to the distinction drawn between tangible and intangible assets at first instance and simply reasoned that 'just as a person can give by will a specified number of his shares in a certain company, so equally, in my judgment, he can declare himself a trustee of 50 of his ordinary shares'.[69]

---

65. [1986] PCC 121.
66. [1993] 1 WLR 934 (DC) ; [1994] 1 WLR 452 (CA).
67. [1993] 1 WLR 934, 946.
68. [1994] 1 WLR 452.
69. *Ibid.* at 459.

Prior to the decision in *Hunter* it had been assumed in England that trusts of intangible property would only be valid if the settlor declared a trust of his entire interest in the *chose in action* or of a fixed proportion thereof. The decision has provoked controversy and it should not be suggested that it will be followed without question in this jurisdiction. Hayton is particularly critical of the reasoning employed by Dillon LJ and suggests that the latter's judgment 'should not be regarded as the last word on the subject'.[70] He points out that this reasoning 'overlooks a crucial difference between *inter vivos* and testamentary dispositions'.[71]

Martin[72] states that critics of the *Hunter* decision do not claim that there is any difference between one ordinary share in a company and another but difficulties could arise in relation to subsequent dealings with the shareholding of which an unsegregated part is subject to a trust. However, she submits that the solution achieved in *Hunter* is 'fair, sensible and workable'[73] and welcomes the decision as an example of the court's policy of preventing a clearly intended trust from failing for uncertainty. However, as Oakley[74] rightly suggests *Hunter v. Moss* has left the law in a somewhat uncertain state in England and it is quite possible that the courts in this jurisdiction will not follow it.

In any event, it seems clear that where the purported subject-matter of a trust is comprised of goods or chattels these must be properly segregated before there can be a valid trust. This point is made clear by the decision of the Privy Council in *Re Goldcorp Exchange Ltd.*[75] In this case the purchasers of bullion which had not been specifically allocated to them failed to establish proprietary rights over it after the company which had possession of it was put into receivership on the basis that there was no ascertained property to which a trust could attach. As Lord Mustill commented: 'It makes no difference what the parties intended, if what they intend is impossible: as is the case with an immediate transfer of title to goods whose identity is not yet known'.[76]

A final point which should be made about this certainty requirement is

---

70. (1994) 110 LQR 335, 340. Although as he points out, the House of Lords refused leave to appeal in *Hunter*, see [1994] 1 WLR 614. See also Hayton and Marshall *Commentary and Cases on the Law of Trusts and Equitable Remedies* (10th ed., 1996) p.146.
71. Hayton and Marshall *Commentary and Cases on the Law of Trusts and Equitable Remedies* (10th ed., 1996) p.146.
72. [1996] Conv 223.
73. *Ibid.* at 227. See also Hanbury and Martin *Modern Equity* (15th ed., 1997) p.97.
74. Parker and Mellows, *The Modern Law of Trusts* (7th ed., 1998) pp.89-90.
75. [1995] 1 AC 74.
76. *Ibid.* at 90.

that it should not be regarded as existing in isolation and is often closely connected with the requirement of certainty of words. Sir Arthur Hobhouse made this point in *Mussoorie Bank Ltd v. Raynor*[77] in the following terms:

> [T]he uncertainty of the subject of the gift has a reflex action upon the previous words, and throws doubt upon the intention of the testator, and seems to shew that he could not possibly have intended his words of confidence, hope, or whatever they may be ... to be imperative.

Certainty of Objects

The general principle that 'in order to be valid, a trust must be one which the court can control and execute'[78] has led to the development of a considerable body of case law and academic criticism[79] in relation to the objects of a trust. The fundamental rule which must be observed in this context is that the objects or beneficiaries of a trust must be defined with a sufficient degree of certainty to enable the trustees, or if necessary the court, to administer the trust according to the settlor or testator's intentions. The reason that this area of the law remains clouded by such a degree of uncertainty is that the requirements which must be satisfied will depend on whether the instrument being construed is characterised as a trust or a power and in addition may vary according to the nature of the trust involved.

Test for Fixed Trusts

Under the terms of a fixed trust, the interest which each beneficiary is to take is specified in the trust instrument and the trustees have no discretion to determine either who will benefit or the extent of that individual's share. The requirement in this case is that the persons who are to benefit under a trust must be clearly identified or identifiable by the time it comes into operation; 'the trust must have ascertained or ascertainable beneficiaries'.[80] Clearly where property is to be held on trust to be divided amongst the members of a class either in equal or other specified shares, this task cannot be carried out unless it is possible to draw up a complete list of the

---

77. (1882) 7 App Cas 321, 330.
78. *IRC v. Broadway Cottages Trust* [1955] Ch 20, 30.
79. See in particular, Hopkins (1971) 29 CLJ 68; Emery (1982) 98 LQR 551. See also Harris (1971) 87 LQR 31 and Grbich (1974) 37 MLR 643.
80. *Re Endacott* [1960] Ch 232, 246 *per* Evershed MR.

members of that class.[81] In addition, the class must be defined with sufficient conceptual certainty to enable the trustees or if they fail to act, the
court, to be able to decide in principle whether or not a given individual is
or is not a member of the class.[82] Where this requirement is met it will not
be fatal to the validity of a fixed trust that the whereabouts and even the
continued existence of a beneficiary cannot be ascertained; provided that
their identity as a member of the class is established, their share can be
paid into court.[83]

Test for Mere Powers

The donee of a power of appointment is under no duty to exercise it in a
particular manner, if indeed he exercises it at all and to this extent his
position differs from that of a trustee.[84] However, such a donee can only
make a distribution amongst the classes of individuals specified by the
settlor and to this extent the construction of special powers of appointment is a matter which requires the application of certain principles. While
Harman J sought to lay down a test of certainty in *Re Gestetner Settlement,*[85] it gave rise to some confusion as to the precise meaning intended
and in subsequent cases the requirement was variously stated as being that
a power would be valid if it could be said with certainty whether any given
individual fell within the class of objects,[86] or that it was sufficient that
any person should be found who clearly came within the class.[87] Much

---

81. *IRC v. Broadway Cottages Trust* [1955] Ch 20, 29 *per* Jenkins LJ. While Matthews
    argued in [1984] Conv 22 that there should be no requirement that all the objects be
    known in the case of a fixed trust and that the proper test should instead be that the
    description of the beneficiaries be conceptually certain, there is no sign of any judi-
    cial or even academic acceptance of this idea. Hayton argues ([1984] Conv 307) that
    this suggestion is based on a misunderstanding of Lord Upjohn's judgment in *Re
    Gulbenkian's Settlements* [1970] AC 508 and Martin ([1984] Conv 304) also dis-
    putes Matthews' suggestion and instead insists that the test for the validity of a fixed
    trust should continue to be that it should be possible to draw up a list of potential
    beneficiaries which is on the balance of probabilities complete.
82. See *infra* pp. 91-92.
83. *Re Gulbenkian's Settlements* [1970] AC 508, 524 *per* Lord Upjohn.
84. Although note the *dicta* of Lord Reid in *Re Gulbenkian's Settlements* [1970] AC
    508, 518 in relation to the situation which arises where a power is given to trustees as
    such and where a settlor or testator must be taken to be relying on them in their
    fiduciary capacity, sometimes referred to as a 'power fiduciary'. See Emery (1982)
    98 LQR 551, 580
85. [1953] Ch 672, 688.
86. *Re Gresham's Settlement* [1956] 1 WLR 573.
87. *Re Gibbard's Settlement Trusts* [1967] 1 WLR 42 and see the judgments of Lord
    Denning MR and Winn LJ in *Re Gulbenkian's Settlements* [1968] Ch 126, where the
    former stated at p.134: 'if the trustees can say of any particular person that he is
    clearly within the category the gift is good.'

needed clarification of the position came in the form of Lord Upjohn's judgment in the House of Lords in *Re Gulbenkian's Settlements* where his lordship formulated the test as follows:[88]

> A mere or bare power of appointment among a class is valid if you can with certainty say whether any given individual is or is not a member of the class; you do not have to be able to ascertain every member of the class.

In *Gulbenkian* a settlement contained a power of appointment in favour of an individual 'any wife and his children or remoter issue ... and any person or persons in whose house or apartments or in whose company or under whose care and control or by or with whom [he] may from time to time be employed or residing.' The validity of this power was unanimously upheld by the House of Lords, although four of the law lords[89] rejected the broader view which had been put forward by Lord Denning MR and Winn LJ in the Court of Appeal to the effect that a power is valid if any one individual clearly falls within its scope. As Lord Upjohn stated: 'the trustees or the court must be able to say with certainty who is within and who is without the power'.[90]

A similar viewpoint was put forward by Murnaghan J in the Supreme Court in *Re Bayley*,[91] where a power of appointment amongst such of the testator's 'Irish relatives' as his sister should appoint was upheld as valid. Murnaghan J stated:

> It is not, I think, necessary for the valid exercise of a power of appointment that the donee should be able to range in his mind every person capable of taking under the power. It is sufficient if the person chosen as an object comes properly within the description of the class amongst which an appointment may be made.[92]

While the Supreme Court did not go as far as following the broader approach adopted by the members of the Court of Appeal and rejected by the House of Lords in *Re Gulbenkian's Settlements*, Murnaghan J did show his willingness to adopt a flexible attitude by stating that the words of

---

88. [1970] AC 508, 521.
89. Lord Donovan reserved his opinion on the issue although he stated that he was inclined to share this view. (at p. 526)
90. [1970] AC 508, 525.
91. [1945] IR 224.
92. *Ibid.* at 229. See also the *dicta* of Budd J in *Re Parker* [1966] IR 308, 318.

Lord Brougham in *Winter v. Perratt*[93] laid down in that case with reference to a devise, were equally applicable to the construction of a power; namely: 'we ought not, without absolute necessity, to let ourselves embrace the alternative of holding a devise void for uncertainty. Where it is possible to give a meaning, we should give it, that the will of the testator may be operative.'[94]

Test for Discretionary Trusts

In the case of a discretionary trust, trustees are under an obligation to distribute the trust property to the beneficiaries, although they have a discretion to select which members of the class should benefit and to what extent. Trusts in this category are usually created by a settlor with a view to deriving the tax advantages which result from divesting himself absolutely of the property and often confer a discretion on trustees to benefit a wide class of potential beneficiaries. Another, similar concept, although much less common today, is that of a trust power,[95] which involves the court implying the existence of a trust in default of any appointment being made by a donee of a power.

Considerable uncertainty still surrounds the question of the correct test of certainty in relation to objects to apply to such discretionary trusts in this jurisdiction. Should the test laid down in *Re Gulbenkian's Settlements* in relation to mere powers apply or must the entire class of potential beneficiaries be ascertained or ascertainable in order for the trust to be valid? The test originally applied in England was as formulated by Jenkins LJ in *IRC v. Broadway Cottages Trust*,[96] namely that 'a trust for such members of a given class of objects as the trustees shall select is void for uncertainty unless the whole range of objects eligible for selection is ascertained or capable of ascertainment.' Where this test is applied the validity of a disposition may therefore depend on whether it is classified as a trust or a power.[97] The rationale behind such an approach was twofold: first, that a trustee's duty to distribute could only properly be carried out if he had before him a comprehensive list of the potential beneficiaries,[98] and sec-

---

93. (1843) 9 Cl & F 606, 687.
94. *Ibid.* at 230.
95. Considered *supra* pp. 60-64.
96. [1955] Ch 20, 35-36.
97. Criticised by Harman LJ in *Re Baden's Deed Trusts* [1969] 2 Ch 388, 397 as 'an absurd and embarrassing result'.
98. This rationale was rejected by Stamp LJ in *Re Baden's Deed Trusts (No. 2)* [1973] Ch 9, 27. Although he accepted as Lord Wilberforce had indicated in *McPhail v. Doulton* that a 'wider and more comprehensive range of inquiry' was necessary in the case of

ondly, that if the court was required to make a distribution where the trustees failed to act, it could only do so on the basis of equal division and this would not be possible without a complete list of the potential beneficiaries.[99]

Although the traditional *Broadway Cottages Trust* test for discretionary trusts was approved *obiter* by the majority of the House of Lords in *Re Gulbenkian's Settlements,*[100] a differently constituted House took the opportunity to reformulate the test of certainty the following year in *McPhail v. Doulton.*[101] A deed executed by the settlor provided that a fund was to be held on certain trusts for the benefit of the staff of a company and their 'relatives and dependants'. The House of Lords held that the deed created a trust rather than a power and Lord Wilberforce concluded that the test for discretionary trusts 'ought to be similar to that accepted by this House in *Re Gulbenkian's Settlements* for powers, namely, that the trust is valid if it can be said with certainty that any given individual is or is not a member of the class.'[102] When the matter was remitted to the Court of Appeal,[103] the court concluded that the test of certainty had been satisfied in the circumstances of the case and the trust was valid.

Despite these far-reaching developments in England, there is good reason for supposing that in this jurisdiction, certainly in relation to specific types of discretionary trusts, the law remains as formulated in *IRC v. Broadway Cottages Trust*. In *Re Parker*[104] the testator's will provided that certain income from a trust was to be divided amongst his 'necessitous nieces and nephews' and their children in such manner as his executors might think fit. Budd J, in holding that the trust was not void for uncertainty, stated that where trustees have a duty to distribute income under a trust it is essential that they know before performing this duty who the beneficiaries are. He formulated the test as follows:

---

a discretionary trust than in the case of a mere power, he said that provided an appropriate survey was made it did not matter that it was not absolutely complete.

99. This reasoning was adverted to by Lord Hodson in *McPhail v. Doulton* [1971] AC 424, 442, although as he pointed out, such a basis for division may lead to absurdity, particularly in the context of a typical modern discretionary trust. Note also the comments of Lord Wilberforce in *McPhail* at p.451 where his lordship pointed out that in the case before him equal division was 'surely the last thing the settlor ever intended.'

100. [1970] AC 508, although not by Lord Reid.

101. [1971] AC 424. Lord Wilberforce, Lord Reid and Viscount Dilhorne formed the majority. Lord Guest and Lord Hodson, who had supported the view of the House in *Re Gulbenkian's Settlements*, dissented.

102. *Ibid.* at 456.

103. *Re Baden's Deed Trusts (No. 2)* [1973] Ch 9.

104. [1966] IR 308.

> [A]n imperative trust for the division of income between such members of the class as the trustees may select is invalid unless the whole class of potential beneficiaries can be ascertained.[105]

This view has recently been approved, albeit in an *obiter* context, by Murphy J in *O'Byrne v. Davoren*.[106] The testatrix's will provided that the residue of her estate should be held on trust for the post-primary education of such members of a class consisting of the children, grandchildren and direct descendants of named persons whom the trustees in their discretion should decide would be most likely to benefit therefrom. Murphy J was satisfied that the gift was sufficiently certain but held that it was void because it infringed the rule against perpetuities and the rule against perpetual trusts. Nevertheless, it is interesting to compare the view which he expressed on the question of certainty with those put forward by the House of Lords in *McPhail v. Doulton*. Murphy J commented that not only was the judgment of Budd J a precedent of greater authority than that of the House of Lords but he also preferred the reasoning in the former case, namely that an imperative trust for the division of income between such members of a class as the trustees may select is invalid unless the whole class of potential beneficiaries can be ascertained. Murphy J also said that he approved Budd J's view to the effect that difficulties in interpretation should not be sufficient to render a gift void for uncertainty; as Budd J had said 'to be void for this reason it must be utterly impossible to put a meaning on it'.[107] So Murphy J concluded that the court should endeavour to resolve ambiguities and uncertainties where this was compatible with the expressed or implied wishes of the testator and concluded that this view would have been of decisive importance in upholding the validity of the residuary bequest if the class of relatives had been confined to those living at the date of the testatrix's death.

It can be argued that from a global perspective the *McPhail* approach is much more likely to lead to at least partial fulfilment of a testator's intentions in these circumstances, for the alternative is that the trust will fail for uncertainty. As against this it can also be said that the approach adopted in this jurisdiction, provided an effort is made to give effect to a testator's intentions in as liberal a manner as possible, is more likely to lead to a division of the trust property or income in equal shares amongst *all* potential beneficiaries. However, it is submitted that for a court in this jurisdic-

---

105. *Ibid.* at 318.
106. [1994] 3 IR 373.
107. [1966] IR 308, 320.

tion to consider itself faced with a stark choice between the *McPhail* and *Parker* approaches, irrespective of the nature of the discretionary trust involved, is unduly simplistic. As noted above, the rationale of the need for equal division which seems to lie behind *Parker* is far from suitable in the case of many modern discretionary trusts and is based rather on the type of 'trust powers' so common in the last century.[108] Perhaps before deciding which test is to be preferred in a given case, the question of how the court would exercise its discretion where the trustees fail to do so should be addressed.[109] Where the testator's intentions are likely to be fulfilled by equal division amongst all the potential beneficiaries, clearly the certainty requirement laid down in *Parker* is to be preferred. However, as the judgment of Lord Wilberforce in *McPhail* made clear, this is no longer the case in relation to many modern discretionary trusts which are designed to benefit a much wider class of beneficiary and it is difficult to fault the conclusion reached in the latter case on the basis of the nature of the trust involved.

Clearly such a flexible approach will itself lead to uncertainty and may be as undesirable as a rigid application of principle which fails to take into account the nature and circumstances of a discretionary trust. While it would be impossible to predict how the courts in this jurisdiction will resolve the dilemma, it is to be hoped that they will at least have regard to some of the pragmatic arguments advanced above.

Conceptual and Evidential Certainty

Irrespective of the nature of the trust or power involved,[110] the description used to define the class of potential beneficiaries must be conceptually certain. In some instances, the concepts employed to describe this class may be so precise that it is most unlikely that any uncertainty could arise, e.g. 'son' or 'daughter'. On the other hand there will be many cases where the terminology used is far from being free from some element of uncertainty e.g. 'relative' or 'friend'. So, as a general rule, whether one is dealing with a fixed or discretionary trust, the class must be defined with sufficient conceptual certainty to enable the trustees, or if necessary the court, to determine theoretically whether any given individual is or is not a member of that class. Where the words used are sufficiently precise to satisfy this test of conceptual certainty in principle, the question of who falls within this description is a matter of fact. As Sachs LJ commented in

---

108. E.g. *Burrough v. Philcox* (1840) 5 My & Cr 72.
109. See Emery (1982) 98 LQR 551, 569.
110. *Re Sayer* [1957] Ch 423,432 *per* Upjohn J.

Re Baden's Deed Trusts (No.2),[111] 'it is essential to bear in mind the differences between conceptual uncertainty and evidential difficulties'. This latter concept of evidential certainty relates to the practical question of whether it is possible to establish as a matter of fact that a given individual does or does not fall within the defined class; in the words of Sachs LJ: 'once the class of persons to be benefited is conceptually certain it then becomes a question of fact to be determined on the evidence whether any postulant has on inquiry been proved to be within it; if he is not so proved then he is not in it.'[112]

The point has been made in *Hanbury & Martin*[113] that 'to insist on complete certainty would be to defeat most gifts' and the courts have displayed a relatively flexible attitude towards this issue, as for instance in *Re Baden's Deed Trusts (No.2),*[114] where the Court of Appeal accepted that there was no conceptual uncertainty in the words 'relatives' and 'dependants'.

It would appear that the conceptual certainty required in the case of trusts for members of a class subject to the fulfilment of a condition precedent is not as strict, although arguably this is difficult to justify. In *Re Barlow's Will Trusts*[115] a testatrix directed her executors 'to allow any members of my family and any friends of mine who may wish to do so' to purchase any of her paintings at a reduced price. Browne-Wilkinson J upheld the validity of the gift as it was 'possible to say of one or more persons that he or they undoubtedly qualify even though it may be difficult to say of others whether or not they qualify.'[116]

Administrative Unworkability and Capriciousness

Even where a class is defined with sufficient conceptual certainty a trust may still fail for uncertainty 'where the definition of the beneficiaries is so hopelessly wide as not to form "anything like a class" so that the trust is administratively unworkable.'[117] This ground of uncertainty was put forward by Lord Wilberforce in *McPhail v. Doulton,*[118] where he suggested that perhaps a discretionary trust for 'all the residents of Greater London'

---

111. [1973] Ch 9, 19.
112. *Re Baden's Deed Trusts (No. 2)* [1973] Ch 9, 20.
113. *Modern Equity* (15th ed, 1997) p.102.
114. [1973] Ch 9.
115. [1979] 1 WLR 278.
116. *Ibid.* at 281.
117. *McPhail v. Doulton* [1971] AC 424, 457 *per* Lord Wilberforce.
118. [1971] AC 424. See also the *dicta* of Lord Eldon in *Morice v. Bishop of Durham* (1805) 10 Ves 522, 527.

might prove invalid for this reason. While there is no conceptual uncertainty in such a description and it would be theoretically possible to make a complete list of such persons, it would arguably not be possible for trustees to exercise their discretion in such a manner so as to give effect to a settlor's intentions when dealing with such a huge number of potential beneficiaries. A discretionary trust in favour of 'any or all or some of the inhabitants of the County of West Yorkshire' was found to be invalid for this reason in *R. v District Auditor, ex p. West Yorkshire Metropolitan County Council,* [119] on the grounds that the definition of the beneficiaries was, in the phraseology used by Lord Wilberforce, so hopelessly wide as to be incapable of forming anything like a class.

It should be noted that while administrative unworkability can invalidate a discretionary trust, the weight of authority [120] supports the view that it will not affect the validity of a mere power. The statement of Templeman J in *Re Manisty's Settlement Trusts* [121] that 'a power cannot be uncertain merely because it is wide in ambit' found favour with Megarry VC in *Re Hay's Settlement Trusts,* [122] where the latter concluded that he did not see how mere numbers could inhibit the donees of a power from considering whether or not to exercise it.

While it has been argued that this notion of basing a finding of uncertainty on the concept of administrative unworkability is 'incapable of solid justification on the basis of either administrative feasibility or judicial execution', [123] the better view would seem to be that it is a logical and necessary extension of the requirement of evidential certainty. Hardcastle has put forward the suggestion that while the court will not normally permit difficulties in ascertainment to defeat execution of a trust, a point may be reached where its performance 'becomes an exercise in futility ... when a potentially innumerable class of beneficiaries is coupled with a total lack of provable definitional criteria'. [124]

Another related concept which may form the basis for a finding of uncertainty is that of capriciousness. While the same set of circumstances, such as Lord Wiberforce's example of all the residents of Greater London may at the same time give rise to a finding of administrative unworkability and capriciousness, the latter concept has no necessary connection with

---

119. (1986) 26 RVR 24.
120. Although note the contrary view expressed by Buckley LJ in *Blausten v. IRC* [1972] Ch 256.
121. [1974] Ch 17.
122. [1982] 1 WLR 202.
123. See McKay (1974) 38 Conv 269, 284.
124. [1990] Conv 24, 33.

width of numbers which is an essential characteristic of the former. A further important distinction which should be drawn is that the notion of capriciousness has been held to apply to mere powers. In *Re Manisty's Settlement Trusts*[125] Templeman J commented that 'a capricious power negatives a sensible consideration by the trustees of the exercise of the power' and contrasted this with a 'wide power' which 'does not negative or prohibit a sensible approach by the trustees to the consideration and exercise of their powers.' So where a settlor seeks to benefit 'an accidental conglomeration of persons'[126] who have no discernible link with him, it may be unrealistic to seek to give effect to his intentions and the instrument, whether construed as a trust or a power, may be found to be invalid on the grounds of capriciousness.

---

125. [1974] Ch 17, 27.
126. *Re Manisty's Settlement Trusts* [1974] Ch 24, 27 *per* Templeman J.

CHAPTER 5

Secret Trusts

INTRODUCTION

As we have already seen in relation to trusts created *inter vivos*, equity will not always insist on strict compliance with the statutory formalities required when this would result in a statute being used as an instrument of fraud.[1] Similarly, the statutory formalities which must normally be complied with to create a valid testamentary trust may in some circumstances be waived to give effect to what has become known as a 'secret trust'. A fully secret trust usually arises where a testator makes a gift of property to a named person in his will without expressly stating that the latter is to hold it on trust. If either before or after making his will, but during his lifetime, he informs the legatee that he wishes him to hold the property on trust for a third party or a particular purpose and the legatee either expressly or by his silence impliedly agrees to do so, he will be bound by the trust.[2] A half secret trust on the other hand is said to exist where it is clear from the will that the legatee is to hold the property on trust but neither the terms of the trust nor the identity of the beneficiaries are disclosed in the will.

Historically, the reason for the creation of such trusts was to allow a testator to make provision for a mistress or an illegitimate child or another person whom he wished to benefit for some reason without his family or the world at large being aware of the gift. While this is rarely necessary today, a testator may still employ this device, often to prevent having to specify with precision at the time of making a will how he intends his property to be distributed. The practice of giving effect to secret trusts created for such a purpose has been criticised[3] as it effectively allows a testator to bypass the statutory requirements laid down in relation to the

---

1. See *supra Rochefoucauld v. Boustead* [1897] 1 Ch 196; *McGillicuddy v. Joy* [1959] IR 189 and *Gilmurray v. Corr* [1978] NI 99.
2. Such a trust can also arise where an individual refrains from making a will on the basis of a promise made by his intestate successor that he will carry out the former's wishes, see *Sellack v. Harris* (1708) 5 Vin Abr 521 and note the comments of Lord Westbury in *McCormick v. Grogan* (1869) LR 4 HL 82, 97.
3. Watkin [1981] Conv 335, 338.

execution of wills where the need for secrecy is not present. However, certainly in the case of a fully secret trust, fraud may still result if effect is not given to these trusts and the principles governing their enforcement are likely to be considered as being too firmly established now to be disregarded for policy reasons.

FULLY SECRET TRUSTS

Historically, the dilemma faced by the courts in deciding whether to enforce a fully secret trust was this; should it be permissible for a testator to disregard or bypass the statutory formalities laid down in relation to testamentary dispositions or should a legatee be permitted to take a gift beneficially when it was clearly intended by a testator to be held on trust? The conclusion reached was that equity should intervene to prevent the perpetration of a fraud[4] and the practice of giving effect to secret trusts developed. The next question was, should the legatee merely hold the property on a resulting trust for the testator's estate, which would be sufficient to prevent fraud, or should the courts go a step further and actually enforce the trust in favour of the beneficiary? It was decided to adopt the latter course and while the avoidance of fraud probably formed the basis for such a development, it is now often justified on the grounds that the testator had declared a valid trust *inter vivos* which merely became constituted on his death by virtue of the testamentary gift to the legatee.

From a practical perspective, it may be of relevance to note that where a testator leaves property to A in his will on the understanding that he will hold it for the benefit of B on a secret trust, B's interest is not considered to have arisen by virtue of the will. This is illustrated in *Cullen v. Attorney General for Ireland*,[5] where a residuary legacy was left to an individual to hold it on a secret trust for the benefit of a charity. Although a testamentary gift in favour of a charity would have qualified for an exemption from certain taxes, the House of Lords held that this tax was payable because the testamentary gift was construed as having been made to the individual; 'the charity has no place, and is not to be found either in anything that is expressed in the will, or in anything that is so referred to in the will.'[6] The most important practical result of this principle that such a trust is not

---

4.   See *McCormick v. Grogan* (1869) LR 4 HL 82, 97; *French v. French* [1902] 1 IR 172, 230.
5.   (1866) LR 1 HL 190. See also *Revenue Commissioners v. Stapleton* [1937] IR 225.
6.   *Ibid.* at 199 *per* Lord Westbury.

regarded as being a testamentary disposition is that a beneficiary will not forfeit his interest merely because he has witnessed the testator's will.[7] Therefore in *O'Brien v. Condon*[8] it was held that a witness to a will was not precluded from benefiting from a secret trust on the grounds that 'what she takes under the trust is something not under the will, but solely by virtue of the secret trust, not disclosed on the will.'[9]

Despite this theoretical independence from the will, the beneficiaries' interests are still dependent on the validity of the initial testamentary disposition.[10] If a testator makes a gift to a legatee in his will intending him to hold it on trust for another and the legatee predeceases the testator, the legacy and therefore the secret trust will fail.[11] However, there is some authority to support the proposition that even if the beneficiary predeceases the testator, his heirs will take the interest created by the secret trust on the testator's death provided that he was alive at the time when the undertaking to enforce the trust was given by the legatee.[12]

To create a valid fully secret trust, the terms of the trust must be communicated to the legatee and accepted by him during the testator's lifetime. In the words of Viscount Sumner in *Blackwell v. Blackwell*,[13] there must be 'intention, communication and acquiescence'. As Hammond J commented in the recent New Zealand decision of *Brown v. Pourau*,[14] communication of the deceased's intention to create a secret trust is an essential factor because otherwise the devisee can quite reasonably argue that he took the will to mean precisely what it said on its face. Hammond J was of the view that once communication was established, acceptance, though also crucial, could in an appropriate case be inferred from the silence of the devisee. This principle had been laid down in the following

---

7. S. 82 of the Succession Act 1965 provides that a witness to a will may not take a benefit under it.
8. [1905] 1 IR 51. See also *Re Young* [1951] Ch 344, 350 *per* Danckwerts J: 'the whole theory of the formation of a secret trust is that the Wills Act 1837 has nothing to do with the matter.'
9. *Ibid.* at 58 *per* Porter MR.
10. As Viscount Sumner commented in *Blackwell v. Blackwell* [1929] AC 318, 334: 'the doctrine must in principle rest on the assumption that the will has first operated according to its terms.'
11. *Re Maddock* [1902] 2 Ch 220, 231 *per* Cozens-Hardy LJ.
12. *Re Gardner* [1923] 2 Ch 230. As Wylie has pointed out (see *Irish Land Law* (3rd ed., 1997) p. 532) the reasoning in *Gardner* seems to ignore the fact that the trust is unlikely to be completely constituted at this point and some doubt must be cast on the validity of such a proposition for this reason.
13. [1929] AC 318, 334. This decision concerned a half secret trust and is dealt with in detail *infra*.
14. [1995] 1 NZLR 352. See further Rickett [1996] Conv 302.

terms by Lord Davey in *French v. French,*[15] from whose judgment
Hammond J quoted with approval:

> It is now well established, and has been settled since the time of
> Lord Hardwicke, that if a testator communicates in his lifetime to a
> proposed devisee or legatee that he has left him his property, and
> expresses a wish that the property should be disposed of in a par-
> ticular manner, and the legatee or devisee by acquiescence, or even
> by silence accepts that communication, and the testator dies without
> any repudiation, a trust is fastened upon his conscience.

Any attempt to communicate the testator's intention after his death, for
example by written instructions, will be ineffective as the legatee's conscience will not be affected by the trust at the time when the will becomes
effective. As Fleming has stated:[16] 'it is not the unilaterally expressed intention of the testator, but the conduct of the legatee in inducing the former,
on the faith of his promise, to make or revoke his will, which calls the
equitable doctrine into operation.' However, where a testator gives the
legatee a sealed envelope during his lifetime containing precise instructions about the terms of the trust and it is not opened until after the testator's death, this will be sufficient to give rise to a trust provided the legatee
agrees in principle to carry out its terms during the testator's lifetime.[17] On
the other hand, where a testator merely informs the legatee that he intends
him to hold the property on trust but does not disclose its terms prior to his
death, no secret trust will be created. This will also be the case where it is
established that the testator intended to create a trust and the trustee accepted the obligation but the trust fails for some other reason, e.g. because
the beneficiaries are unascertainable.[18] Similarly where a legatee agrees
to comply with a testator's directions with regard to a trust during the
latter's lifetime, but these instructions only come to light following the
testator's death.[19] In these situations where the evidence establishes that
the testator intended a trust and that the legatee undertook to give effect to
it, the legatee will hold the gift on a resulting trust for the testator's es-

---

15. [1902] 1 IR 172, 230.
16. (1947) 12 Conv 28, 29.
17. *Re Boyes* (1884) 26 Ch D 531, 536 and *Re Keen* [1937] Ch 236, 242. See also where
    the legatee had signed the document containing the testator's instructions although
    she had not seen its contents; *Morrison v. McFerran* [1901] 1 IR 360.
18. See *Brown v. Pourau* [1995] 1 NZLR 352.
19. *Re Boyes* (1884) 26 Ch D 531.

tate.[20] However, where the testator never communicated any intention to the legatee during his lifetime that the latter was to hold the legacy on trust, the legatee will take beneficially.[21]

The onus lies on the person seeking to show the existence of a secret trust[22] to establish this on the balance of probabilities. While earlier authorities suggested that a higher standard of proof would be required,[23] it was established in *Re Snowden*[24] that the ordinary civil standard of proof applies. In this case Megarry VC suggested *obiter* that this standard might be higher if any question of fraud arose,[25] although as Keane[26] points out the Supreme Court has rejected the suggestion that any higher burden of proof should be placed on a plaintiff where an allegation of fraud is made in a civil case.[27]

Secret Trusts Involving Joint Tenants and Tenants in Common

A question which must also be addressed is whether a secret trust will arise and who will be bound by it where a testamentary gift is made to more than one person but the testator's intentions with regard to the creation of a trust are not communicated to all of these persons during his lifetime. The traditional approach as set out by Farwell J in *Re Stead*[28] involves drawing a distinction between the position of legatees who hold as joint tenants and as tenants in common.

> If A. induces B. either to make, or to leave unrevoked, a will leaving property to A. and C. as tenants in common, by expressly promising or tacitly consenting, that he and C. will carry out the testator's wishes, and C. knows nothing of the matter until after B.'s death, A.

---

20. For the residuary devisees or legatees or if there is no residuary gift assuming that the residue is the subject-matter of a secret trust, for those entitled on an intestacy.
21. *Wallgrave v. Tebbs* (1855) 2 K & J 313.
22. *Jones v. Badley* (1868) 3 Ch App 362.
23. *McCormick v. Grogan* (1869) LR 4 HL 82, 97 *per* Lord Westbury.
24. [1979] Ch 528. This standard seems to have been accepted elsewhere in the common law world, e.g. see *Quinn v. Dean* High Court, Wellington, A 123/84 30 July 1986. The formula adopted by Dixon CJ in his dissenting judgment in *Voges v. Monaghan* (1954) 94 CLR 231, 233 was of establishing the elements of the trust 'to the reasonable satisfaction of the court'. Both these formulae were recently considered by Hammond J in the New Zealand High Court decision of *Brown v. Pourau* [1995] 1 NZLR 352.
25. For a criticism of this suggestion, see Rickett [1979] CLJ 260. See also Rickett [1996] Conv 302, 307.
26. *Equity and the Law of Trusts in the Republic of Ireland* (1988) p.92.
27. *Banco Ambrosiano SPA v. Ansbacher & Co.Ltd* [1987] ILRM 669.
28. [1900] 1 Ch 237, 241. See also the *dicta* of Monroe J in *Re King's Estate* (1888) 21 LR Ir 273, 278.

is bound, but C. is not bound. ... If however the gift were to A. and C. as joint tenants, the authorities have established a distinction between those cases in which the will is made on the faith of an antecedent promise by A. and those in which the will is left unrevoked on the faith of a subsequent promise. In the former case the trust binds both A. and C., ... the reason stated being that no person can claim an interest under a fraud committed by another; in the latter case, A. and not C. is bound, ... the reason stated being that the gift is not tainted with any fraud in procuring the execution of the will.

On the basis of this statement it seemed that in the case of tenants in common, only those to whom the testator's intentions were communicated during his lifetime were bound and that any other person took free of the trust and was entitled to his share beneficially. However, in the case of joint tenants, a distinction was drawn between a situation where one or more of these joint tenants had accepted the trust prior to the execution of the will and where the acceptance did not take place until after this. In the former case, all the joint tenants were bound and in the latter case only those who had accepted the secret trust were affected by it. Farwell J himself appeared unconvinced by the drawing of such a seemingly arbitrary distinction and admitted that he was unable to see the difference between 'a gift left unrevoked on the faith of antecedent promise and a gift left unrevoked on the faith of a subsequent promise'.[29]

Similar sentiments were expressed by Walker LJ in the Irish Court of Appeal in *Geddis v. Semple,*[30] although as the case before him concerned tenants in common, it was not necessary for him to reach any conclusion on the issue. At the time when the testator in *Geddis* executed his will, the effect of section 16 of the Charitable Donations and Bequests (Ireland) Act 1844 was to render void gifts of land for charitable purposes unless the testator's will had been executed at least three months prior to his death.[31] With the intention of avoiding this statutory restriction, the testator devised certain houses and a pecuniary legacy charged on land to three individuals as tenants in common, although at the time the will was executed only one of these individuals was aware of the testator's intention to create a secret trust for a charitable purpose. The Irish Court of Appeal held that while the gift to the individual who knew of the testator's wishes must fail, the other tenants in common, who knew nothing of the intended

29. *Ibid.* at 241.
30. [1903] 1 IR 73.
31. This provision was repealed by s.4 of the Charities Act 1961.

trust until after the testator's death, became beneficially entitled to their shares. However there is a suggestion in the judgment of Walker LJ that an 'innocent' tenant in common might be bound in such circumstances if it could be established that the testator was induced to make the gift by the promise of a co-tenant on the basis of the principle laid down in *Huguenin v. Baseley* [32] that 'no man may profit by the fraud of another'.

This inducement theory was developed by Perrins[33] who has suggested that Farwell J in *Re Stead* misinterpreted the authorities relied on to support the general principles set out above. In Perrins' view, the only question to which the court must address itself in such circumstances is whether the gift to the legatee who was unaware of the testator's intention to create a secret trust was induced by the promise of the legatee who knew of his intentions in this regard to carry out his wishes. If this approach is accepted, issues such as whether the legatees take as joint tenants or tenants in common and whether the promise was made prior to or after the execution of the will are merely matters of evidence which may be of assistance to the court in deciding on the question of inducement but will not of themselves determine the issue.[34]

There is certainly considerable merit in Perrins' views,[35] and on the basis of the comments of Walker LJ in *Geddis v. Semple* they will probably be followed in relation to a situation of tenants in common. Although there is no authority to support this approach in the case of joint tenants, Wylie[36] puts forward the suggestion that a court might regard the creation of a secret trust as severing a joint tenancy, thus allowing the principle of inducement to operate in any event. Until this question is resolved by the courts the result must remain a matter of speculation, but it is submitted that the most equitable result would certainly be to follow the approach laid down by Perrins.

---

32. (1807) 14 Ves 273.
33. (1972) 82 LQR 225.
34. As Perrins points out as a matter of evidence it may be easier to show inducement in the case of a gift to joint tenants and clearly where a secret trust is not communicated to any of the co-tenants until after the testator's death it will be difficult, if not impossible, to show that the gift to the other was induced by any promise made.
35. This is the approach taken in both *Snell's Equity* (29th ed., 1990) p.110 and Underhill and Hayton, *The Law Relating to Trusts and Trustees* (15th ed., 1995) pp. 223-224 although the view is expressed in Hanbury & Martin, *Modern Equity* (15th ed., 1997) p. 152 that while the argument is persuasive the case law suggests otherwise.
36. *Irish Land Law* (3rd ed., 1997) p. 529.

HALF SECRET TRUSTS

A half secret trust arises where a testator leaves property to an individual in a will and expressly directs that this individual is to hold the property on trust without specifying the terms of the trust. The principal advantage to be gained from employing this form of secret trust is that the possibility of the legatee taking the property beneficially and successfully perpetrating a fraud is avoided as it is clear from the face of the will that a trust was intended. However, by manifesting his intention to create some form of trust in this way, the testator is also removing the historical justification for non-compliance with the statutory formalities required in the case of secret trusts, namely the prevention of fraud. Perhaps for this reason, the courts have adopted a more stringent attitude towards the enforcement of half secret trusts and an examination of the case law in this area in the last century, particularly in England, shows a marked reluctance on the part of the judiciary to overlook non-compliance with the provisions of the Wills Act in the absence of any likelihood of fraud.

This trend was reversed in Ireland by the decision of *Riordan v. Banon*[37] and although Chatterton VC acknowledged that 'the same kind of fraud cannot operate'[38] in the case of trusts which appear on the face of the will, he was prepared to extend this principle to half secret trusts as the result of a refusal to enforce such trusts would be to defeat the expressed intention of the testator. In *Riordan*, the testator's will directed that a legacy be disposed by the legatee 'in a manner of which he alone should be cognizant, and as contained in a memorandum which I shall leave with him'. Prior to executing his will the testator had verbally informed the legatee that he intended to leave the legacy for a named person whom he did not wish to identify in his will and it was accepted that the legatee had accepted this obligation.[39] Chatterton VC held that a valid secret trust had been created.[40] He stated:

---

37. (1876) IR 10 Eq 469.
38. *Ibid.* at 473. Although Chatterton VC also commented (at p.478) that the principle which led the courts to hold that the Statute of Frauds and the Wills Act were not to be used as instruments of fraud appeared to apply to cases such as that before him where the will showed that some form of trust was intended.
39. One difficulty with this interpretation to which Chatterton VC did not refer was the possibility of inconsistency between the terms of the statement in the will which pointed to some form of subsequent communication and what the court accepted had actually transpired i.e. communication and acceptance prior to the execution of the will. This ground of inconsistency is considered in more detail *infra*.
40. See also *Re Ellis* (1919) 53 ILTR 6.

The result of the cases appears to me to be that a testator cannot by his will reserve to himself the right of disposing subsequently of property by an instrument not executed as required by the statute, or by parol; but that when, at the time of making his will, he has formed the intention that a legacy thereby given shall be disposed of by the legatee in a particular manner, not thereby disclosed, but communicated to the legatee and assented to by him, at or before the making of the will, or probably, according to *Moss v. Cooper*, subsequently to the making of it, the Court will allow such trust to be proved by admission of the legatee, or other parol evidence and will, if it be legal, give effect to it.[41]

To be valid a half secret trust, like a fully secret trust, must be communicated to and accepted by the legatee prior to the testator's death.[42] This requirement has been strictly enforced as in *Re Watters' Will Trusts*,[43] where a testator directed that his property should be applied for 'charitable purposes and objects known to my executors'. After executing his will but during his lifetime, the testator had a number of general conversations with one of his executors about the manner in which he wished his assets to be applied but failed to specify precisely the particular purposes or objects which he intended to benefit. A memorandum found after his death which contained such specific directions was held not to be admissible as there had not been sufficient communication and acceptance of the trust prior to the testator's death.[44]

One question which has led to considerable controversy and to an apparent divergence in the law as it applies in England and Ireland is whether there can be effective communication and acceptance of a half secret trust after the execution of the testator's will. As can be observed from the portion of Chatterton VC's judgment in *Riordan* set out above, he commented in that decision that such subsequent communication was 'probably' acceptable and this principle was re-iterated by Monroe J in the course of his judgment in *Re King's Estate*.[45] While on the facts of that case no secret trust of any nature arose, Monroe J laid down a number of proposi-

---

41. *Ibid.* at 477-478.
42. *Scott v. Brownrigg* (1881) 9 LR Ir 246.
43. (1928) 62 ILTR 61.There was no evidence to suggest that the trust failed on the grounds of inconsistency. See further *infra* p. 108.
44. Although in the circumstances as a general charitable intention had been manifested by the verbal communication an order was made that a scheme for the application of the assets should be directed by the court.
45. (1888) 21 LR Ir 273.

tions, drawn from the relevant authorities,[46] which it is useful to set out in full:

> 1. A testator cannot reserve to himself the right of declaring trusts by an instrument informally executed subsequent to the execution of his will. This would be to repeal the statute of wills.

> 2. If a testator at or before the execution of his will communicate to a person to whom he proposes to give a legacy that the legacy is given upon trust to be applied in a particular way, and if the legatee expressly or tacitly consents to take the legacy on these terms, the Court of Chancery will not permit him to be guilty of a fraud, but will compel the execution of the trust so communicated.

> 3. This rule applies whether the existence of the trust be indicated on the face of the will, or the legacy by the terms of the instrument be given absolutely.

> 4. The rule applies when the communication is made subsequently to the execution of the will: *Moss v. Taylor*.[47]

> 5. It is essential to the creation of a valid trust that the communication should be made to the legatee in the testator's lifetime, and that the legatee should not object to execute the trust.

> 6. If the bequest be to two or more legatees, a valid trust is created if the communication be made to any one of them, before or at the time of the execution of the will. If the communication be made after the execution of the will, it must be made to all the legatees on whom the trust is sought to be imposed.

> 7. The terms in which the trust is expressed must not be vague or uncertain.[48]

Further confirmation that communication and acceptance of a half secret trust may validly occur after execution of a testator's will provided this is done during his lifetime can be found in the judgment of Overend J in *Re Browne*.[49] Although Overend J found that the reference in the will before

---

46. *Riordan v. Banon* (1867) IR 10 Eq 469; *Re Fleetwood* (1880) 15 Ch D 594; *Scott v. Brownrigg* (1881) 9 LR Ir 246; *Re Boyes* (1884) 26 Ch D 531.
47. More commonly known as *Moss v. Cooper* (1861) 1 J & H 367.
48. *Ibid.* at pp.277-278. Quoted with approval by Barron J in *Prendiville v. Prendiville* [1995] 2 ILRM 578, 583.
49. [1944] IR 90. Although note the conclusion reached in *Balfe v. Halpenny* [1904] 1 IR 486.

the court to the testator's wishes was too ambiguous to disclose a trust on the face of the will and instead decided to enforce a fully secret trust on the basis of the latter's wishes expressed to the legatee during his lifetime, he suggested *obiter* that that even if he had found the existence of a half secret trust, it would have been immaterial that the trusts in question were communicated to the legatee after the execution of the will so long as they were communicated to him and accepted by him during the testator's lifetime.

The courts in England have not accepted the principle of subsequent communication and indeed it was not until the decision of the House of Lords in *Blackwell v. Blackwell*[50] that the validity of half secret trusts was finally recognised in that jurisdiction. A testator gave a sum of money on trust to legatees to apply the income thereof 'for the purposes indicated by me to them' in a codicil to his will. Detailed instructions were given to one of the trustees and the others accepted these terms in outline before execution of the codicil. Viscount Sumner recognised that a half secret trust existed which arose independently of the will: 'it is communication of the purpose to the legatee, coupled with acquiescence or promise on his part, that removes the matter from the provision of the Wills Act and brings it within the law of trusts'.[51] In the course of his speech Viscount Sumner also laid down the following fundamental principle:

> A testator cannot reserve to himself a power of making future unwitnessed dispositions by merely naming a trustee and leaving the purposes of the trust to be supplied afterwards, nor can a legatee give testamentary validity to an unexecuted codicil by accepting an indefinite trust, never communicated to him in the testator's lifetime. ... To hold otherwise would indeed enable the testator to 'give the go-by' to the requirements of the Wills Act, because he did not choose to comply with them.[52]

This statement although it is in some respects in line with a number of the propositions set out by Monroe J in *Re King's Estate*, has been subsequently interpreted in England as authority for the proposition that the communication and acceptance of a half secret trust cannot be effective if

---

50. [1929] AC 318.
51. *Ibid.* at 339. Quoted with approval by Barron J in *Prendiville v. Prendiville* [1995] 2 ILRM 578, 583.
52. *Ibid.* at 339. See also the *dicta* of Parker VC in *Johnson v. Ball* (1851) 5 De G & Sm 85, 91.

made after the execution of a will. In *Re Keen*[53] a testator gave a legacy to trustees 'to be held upon trust and disposed of among such person persons or charities as may be notified by me to them or either of them during my lifetime'. Before executing this will the testator had given a sealed envelope to one of the trustees containing the name of the intended beneficiary. The provision in the will was interpreted as the reservation of a power by the testator to make future testamentary dispositions in a manner which would be contrary to section 9 of the Wills Act 1837. However, in the view of Lord Wright MR, even if such subsequent communication had been permitted the trust would have failed independently on the grounds of inconsistency. On the facts of the case, communication and acceptance of the trust had taken place prior to the execution of the will, when the sealed envelope was handed over, and this was plainly inconsistent with its terms which provided for a future definition of the terms of the trust. While there has been a certain amount of confusion and academic debate about the true *ratio* of *Re Keen*,[54] it was re-affirmed in England in *Re Bateman's Will Trusts*[55] that communication and acceptance of a half secret trust must take place prior to the execution of the will.[56]

It is interesting to note that a refusal to accept the principle of subsequent communication in the context of a half secret trust has recently manifested itself elsewhere in the common law world. In *Jankowski v. Pelek Estate*[57] the majority of the Manitoba Court of Appeal found that the evidence disclosed the existence of a fully secret trust which in their view was valid as communication and acceptance of it had taken place during the testator's lifetime. However, Huband JA was satisfied that any trust intended was a half secret one as there was no possibility that the intended legatee might fraudulently retain the legacy as his own and in his view the rules relating to the enforcement of such trusts are 'much more stringent'. He continued as follows:

---

53. [1937] Ch 236.
54. See the judgment of Barron J in *Prendiville v. Prendiville* [1995] 2 ILRM 578; Coughlan (1991) 5 Trust Law Int 69 and Mee [1992] Conv 202. Huband JA suggests in the course of his dissenting judgment in *Jankowski v. Pelek Estate* (1995) 131 DLR (4th) 717 that *Re Keen* is authority for the proposition that the nature of trust instructions must be consistent with the wording of the will.
55. [1970] 1 WLR 1463.
56. This has been justified by Perrins [1985] Conv 248 on the basis that extrinsic evidence of prior communication is admissible as it does not contradict the terms of the will whereas to allow evidence of subsequent communication would be 'to give the go-by' to the Wills Act even where there is no danger of fraud. The suggestion has even been made that this stricter requirement should also apply to fully secret trusts, see Watkin [1981] Conv 335, 340. See also Wilde [1995] Conv 366.
57. (1995) 131 DLR (4th) 717.

> Specifically there must be communication of the terms of the trust
> to the proposed trustee before or contemporaneously with the mak-
> ing of the will. The word 'contemporaneously' in this context means
> 'at the same time'. It cannot include 'shortly after'. To have it other-
> wise would allow the testator to add to the terms of the will after its
> execution, in a form which does not comply with statutory require-
> ments.[58]

He concluded that in the case before him the fact that the instructions
regarding the trust were given after the will was executed was fatal to its
enforcement and said that this could not be redeemed by the fact that these
instructions were communicated only minutes after the execution of the
will. In his view 'the effect is the same whether the time differential is a
few minutes, a few hours, a few weeks or a few years'. This seemed a
particularly harsh conclusion to reach and resulted, as Huband JA himself
acknowledged, in the intentions of the testatrix being frustrated by purely
technical reasons.

The opportunity to resolve once and for all in an Irish context the question of whether communication and acceptance of a half secret trust must
take place before the execution of the will in order for it to be valid was
presented to the High Court in the case of *Prendiville v. Prendiville.*[59] There,
the testator left his estate to his wife for life 'to be used by her according to
my wishes — as she has been advised'. Before he died the testator had told
one of his sons that he had written out his wishes as to the passing of his
estate after his wife's death and had shown him a document containing
these instructions which included the provision that a named residence
and lands were to be offered for sale to another son at a reasonable valuation. Following the testator's death, his wife made a statutory declaration
acknowledging that her husband's instructions had been communicated to
and accepted by her. After her death a dispute arose between the next of
kin of the testator and the son in whose favour the option to purchase had
been made as to whether an enforceable secret or half secret trust existed.
Barron J said that *Re Keen* had been relied on as an authority for the proposition that a half secret trust could not be established unless its terms were
communicated and accepted prior to the execution of the will. He felt that
this proposition could not be taken from that case, which, in his opinion,
turned on the construction of the particular clause in the will and the issue
of inconsistency. Barron J concluded that the principles of law to be ap-

---

58. *Ibid.* at 730.
59. [1995] 2 ILRM 578.

plied to secret and half secret trusts are the same and were those as set out by Monroe J in *Re King's Estate*.[60] He held that in the case before him, a trust existed on the face of the will and found there was sufficient evidence that the terms of the trust in relation to the option to purchase the house had been communicated by the testator to his wife and accepted by her during his lifetime.

Although this judgment would appear to confirm the correctness of the *obiter* views on the timing of communication and acceptance of a half secret trust referred to above, *Prendiville* is not an entirely satisfactory authority for a number of reasons. Barron J failed to identify precisely the time at which communication and acceptance of the trust occurred although he did find that this had taken place at some stage during the testator's lifetime. The use of the words 'as she has been advised' would suggest that such communication was intended to take place either before or at the time of execution of the will and yet one must ask why Barron J took the trouble to refute the suggestion that *Re Keen* was authority for the proposition that communication must occur prior to the will, unless on the facts of the case before him, communication did not take place until after its execution. Because of his failure to be more specific about the timing of these events, it is therefore still not clear whether Barron J's rejection of the need for prior communication forms part of the *ratio* of the case. A further possible flaw in his judgment is the failure to address the potential problem of inconsistency. As Andrews[61] has pointed out, the most important requirement with regard to half secret trusts is the need for careful construction and communication in some other form or at a time other than that contemplated in the will cannot be permissible as it will lead to an attempt to contradict its express terms. Barron J appeared to endorse this ground of inconsistency as being the basis for the decision in *Re Keen* and yet, if as his rejection of the wider ground for that decision suggests, communication in the case before him took place after the execution of the will, this would itself lead to inconsistency with the terms of the instrument.[62] While it is unfortunate that the Supreme Court was not given the

60. (1881) 21 LR Ir 273. Note that Wilde has asserted in [1995] Conv 366 that there is a justification for the distinctions drawn by the courts between secret and half secret trusts.
61. (1963) 27 Conv 92,99.
62. See Coughlan (1991) 5 Trust Law Int 69, 73 and Mee [1992] Conv 202, 205. It would appear that the possibility of inconsistency was also effectively ignored by Chatterton VC in *Riordan v. Bannon* (1876) IR 10 Eq 469 and by Meredith J in *Re Watters' Will Trusts* (1928) 62 ILTR 61. However, it appeared to be accepted by Huband JA in his dissenting judgment in *Jankowski v. Pelek Estate* (1995) 131 DLR (4th) 717 that inconsistency between the instructions given and the scheme of the

opportunity of further clarifying these issues, the High Court decision in *Prendiville* does appear to confirm that in Ireland it is permissible for communication and acceptance of a half secret trust to take place after the execution of a will but during a testator's lifetime provided it does not contradict the terms of the will. Certainly, the view of Barron J that the principles to be applied to fully and half secret trusts should be the same has much to commend it and is based on sound practical arguments.[63] The passing of the beneficial interest in respect of either type of trust is not a testamentary disposition and so it should not be relevant whether communication and acceptance of the trust occurs prior to the execution of the will.[64] This argument is re-enforced if one accepts the modern justification for the enforcement of secret trusts and on this basis the approach of the Irish courts cannot be faulted either on policy grounds.

THE JURIDICIAL NATURE OF SECRET TRUSTS

As we have already seen,[65] a secret trust is not considered to have arisen by virtue of a testator's will. While to an extent its existence is dependent on the validity of this instrument and in particular on the disposition which is to form the subject-matter of the trust, it is considered to arise 'dehors' the will. A related question which has provoked considerable debate, and which can have practical significance is whether secret trusts are express or constructive in nature. Clearly, if they are characterised as express, where land forms the subject-matter of the trust there must be compliance with the statutory formalities.[66] Fully secret trusts have been variously characterised as implied[67] or sometimes express[68] in nature but the most acceptable view would seem to be that they are constructive and are imposed on a legatee to prevent him from abusing the fiduciary obligations which he

---

will would be fatal.There is probably merit in Mee's argument that inconsistency should be overlooked where it is merely inadvertent (see *infra* n. 64)

63. It would seem arbitrary to draw a distinction when the overriding reason for enforcing such half secret trusts is to give effect as far as possible to the testator's intention to create a trust. For a view of the academic arguments favouring such an approach, see Holdsworth (1937) 53 LQR 501 and Sheridan (1951) 67 LQR 413.
64. Mee [1992] Conv 202, 206 suggests that where inconsistency occurs as a result of mere inadvertence it would be 'unnecessary and unjust' to base a finding of invalidity on this ground.
65. See *supra* p. 96.
66. See *supra* Chapter 4.
67. Burgess (1972) 23 NILQ 263, 268-273.
68. Perrins [1985] Conv 248, 254. See also Wilde [1995] Conv 366, 371 and Rickett [1996] Conv 302, 305 and 308.

assumed on giving an undertaking to the testator that he would enforce the trust.[69] This conclusion would appear to be supported by the decision in *Ottaway v. Norman,*[70] where a fully secret trust of land was upheld as valid on the basis of oral evidence. However, it would be incorrect to place too much emphasis on this decision as the issue of the nature of the trust and the need for compliance with the statutory formalities was not discussed.

Half secret trusts on the other hand are usually accepted as being a species of express trust. Support for this proposition is derived from *Re Baillie*[71] where a half secret trust was held not to be enforceable in the absence of adequate written evidence. Burgess[72] has argued that this decision actually turned on the lack of evidence to establish the terms of the trust and that the very essence of a secret trust is that it operates in spite of the requirements as to form. While there is some merit in the arguments put forward by Burgess, the most widely held view is that half secret trusts are express in nature.

The issue of the classification of secret trusts as express or constructive was raised again recently in the New Zealand decision of *Brown v. Pourau*[73] where Hammond J had to consider whether an oral secret trust of land could be valid. He stated that whatever the correct theoretical explanation, the reported English decisions appeared to recognise that a fully secret trust of land could be valid independent of any requirement of written evidence. In his view contemporary New Zealand jurisprudence required the court to inquire into the obligation which it was being asked to uphold and then make an evaluation of the remedy which would best support or advance that obligation. Applying this reasoning he concluded that the court should support the intended trust by using a constructive trust as a remedy. While Hammond J's judgment therefore fails to resolve the express/constructive issue in the context in which it has arisen in England and in this jurisdiction, it confirms the practical point that for the purposes of compliance with the Statute of Frauds, fully secret trusts can be treated as constructive in nature.[74]

---

69. Andrews (1963) 27 Conv 92, 98. See also Sheridan (1951) 67 LQR 314, 327.
70. [1972] Ch 698.
71. (1886) 2 TLR 660.
72. (1972) 23 NILQ 263.
73. [1995] 1 NZLR 352.
74. It should be noted that Rickett [1996] Conv 302 is critical of Hammond J's reasoning and asserts that a secret trust is express in nature and therefore where necessary must satisfy the formal requirements in relation to trusts of land. She points out quite correctly (at p.306) that if judges persist – as Hammond J did in *Brown v. Pourau* – in applying the test of certainty laid down for express private trusts, it is a strong argument in favour of using the express rather than the constructive trust label.

So although this issue of the juridicial basis of secret trusts remains to an extent uncertain, it should be remembered that even if a secret trust is characterised as express, compliance with the formality requirements will not be enforced where this would lead to the perpetration of a fraud.

CHAPTER 6

Constitution of Trusts

INTRODUCTION

A trust is said to be completely constituted when the trust property has been vested in the trustees for the benefit of the beneficiaries; a trust remains incompletely constituted until this is done. The practical importance of identifying when a trust has been completely constituted by either of these methods lies in the fact that equity will not enforce or perfect an incompletely constituted trust in favour of a volunteer.[1] However a completely constituted trust will be enforceable at the suit of the beneficiaries irrespective of whether or not they are mere volunteers. This different attitude adopted by equity towards the enforcement of completely and incompletely constituted trusts was summed up by Lord Eldon in *Ellison v. Ellison*[2] as follows:

> I take the distinction to be, that if you want the assistance of the Court to constitute you *cestui que trust*, and the instrument is voluntary, you shall not have that assistance for the purpose of constituting you *cestui que trust*; as upon a covenant to transfer stock etc., if it rests in covenant, and is purely voluntary, this Court will not execute that voluntary covenant; but if the party has completely transferred stock etc., although it is voluntary, yet the legal conveyance being effectually made, the equitable interest will be enforced by this Court.

To fully understand the practical implications of this distinction a number of issues must be examined. First, the circumstances in which a trust may be regarded as completely constituted must be clarified and secondly, the question of who will be regarded as a volunteer has to be addressed. Fi-

---

1. As Johnston J commented in *Re Wilson* [1933] IR 729, 739: 'A gift is a gift, and of course, if a donor, while expressing an intention to give something and taking certain steps in the direction of giving it, has not gone the whole way, the expectant donee has no equity to compel the completion of the gift.'
2. (1802) 6 Ves 656, 662.

nally, it is necessary to examine the alternative remedies open to beneficiaries of an incompletely constituted trust who are regarded as mere volunteers.

COMPLETE CONSTITUTION OF A TRUST

An express trust may be completely constituted either by a transfer of property to trustees to be held on certain trusts, by will or *inter vivos*, or by a settlor declaring himself to be trustee of his own property for the benefit of specified beneficiaries. Since it is necessary to recognise whether a voluntary trust has been completely constituted if it is to be enforced, it is necessary to set out in some detail the manner in which this may be achieved. These principles were summarized by Turner LJ in the decision of *Milroy v. Lord*[3] as follows:

> I take the law of this Court to be well settled, that, in order to render a voluntary settlement valid and effectual, the settlor must have done everything which, according to the nature of the property comprised in the settlement, was necessary to be done in order to transfer the property and render the settlement binding upon him. He may of course, do this by actually transferring the property to the persons for whom he intends to provide, and the provision will then be effectual, and it will be equally effectual if he transfers the property to a trustee for the purposes of the settlement, or declares that he himself holds it in trust for those purposes; and if the property be personal, the trust may, as I apprehend, be declared either in writing or by parol, but in order to render the settlement binding, one or other of these modes must, as I understand the law of this Court, be resorted to, for there is no equity in this Court to perfect an imperfect gift.

Transfer of Trust Property

If a trust is to be validly constituted in this way, it is necessary to comply with whatever formalities apply to the method of transfer employed. A trust created by will can only be regarded as completely constituted provided that the relevant statutory formalities have been complied with. Similarly, where the transfer is effected *inter vivos*, the formalities applicable

---

3. (1862) 4 De GF & J 264, 274.

to the type of interest being transferred must be observed. So where for example the subject-matter of the trust is a legal estate in unregistered land the transfer must be effective to vest this interest in the trustee and will therefore usually require the execution of a deed. Where the trust property comprises an equitable interest, it will be completely constituted provided that a valid assignment of that interest to the trustees takes place.[4]

In *Milroy v. Lord*[5] a settlor executed a voluntary deed purporting to transfer shares in a bank to be held on trust for the plaintiff. Such a transfer could only be properly effected by registration of the name of the transferee in the bank's records. While the trustee held a power of attorney to act on the settlor's behalf, he failed to register the transfer. The Court of Appeal held that no enforceable trust in favour of the plaintiffs had been created. It should be noted that the statement of Turner LJ in *Milroy* set out above to the effect, *inter alia*, that in order to ensure that a trust is completely constituted, the settlor must have done everything which it is necessary to do to effect the transfer[6] is subject to some qualification in the following circumstances. Where the settlor has done everything in his power to transfer the title to the property but cannot ensure compliance with some formality which is outside his control, the trust will nevertheless be regarded as completely constituted. In *Re Rose*,[7] a settlor executed a voluntary deed which purported to transfer shares in a private company to trustees but died before the transfer was registered by the company's directors. The question arose whether the settlor was still the owner of the shares at the time of his death for the purpose of determining whether estate duty was payable. The Court of Appeal held that as the settlor had done all in his power to divest himself of the shares, although he remained in law the owner until the transfer was registered, in equity the transfer was regarded as being effective from the date of the deed. The reasoning in *Re Rose* has been criticised[8] and it has been argued that it is difficult to distinguish the circumstances of the case from those in *Re Fry,*[9] in which a donor was not regarded as having done everything in his power to effect a transfer of shares as it could not be registered without treasury consent. Nevertheless, the principle laid down in *Re Rose* has been applied subsequently in Eng-

---

4.   *Kekewich v. Manning* (1851) 1 De GM & G 176 and *Re McArdle* [1951] Ch 669.
5.   (1862) 4 De GF & J 264.
6.   It was suggested by Griffiths CJ in *Anning v. Anning* (1907) 4 CLR 1049, 1057 that the words 'necessary to be done' as used by Turner LJ in *Milroy v. Lord* mean necessary to be done by the donor.
7.   [1952] Ch 499.
8.   Sheridan (1955) 33 Can Bar Rev 284 and McKay (1976) 40 Conv 139.
9.   [1946] Ch 312.

land in *Mascall v. Mascall*[10] in the context of a transfer of registered land and more recently in *Brown & Root Technology Ltd v. Sun Alliance and London Assurance Co.Ltd*[11] which concerned the assignment of a lease-hold interest which had not yet been registered. In *Mascall* the plaintiff had executed a transfer of a property with registered title to his son but before the necessary documents had been sent to the Land Registry for registration, the plaintiff changed his mind about the transfer. The Court of Appeal held that there had been an effective gift to the son; as Lawton LJ commented 'the plaintiff had done everything in his power to transfer the house to the defendant'.[12] In *Brown & Root* the first named plaintiff, the original lessee, served a notice purporting to terminate the lease after an assignment to the second named plaintiff, its parent company, had taken place but before it had been registered at the Land Registry. The court refused the first named plaintiff a declaration that the notice served was valid to terminate the lease on the basis that the date on which the assign-ment took place was the date upon which it was completed and so the lease could not have been determined by a notice served by this plaintiff. Judge Paul Barker QC reiterated that the leading case in this area is *Milroy v. Lord* but pointed out that there are exceptions to the rule that 'an at-tempted but ineffectual or uncompleted conveyance or transfer of prop-erty to trustees to hold on certain trusts would not be enforced at the suit of a volunteer'. He accepted the defendant's submission that if it was neces-sary to fix a date on which the assignment took place, this was the date upon which it was completed. As he pointed out 'the tenant/assignor gives up the property on that date; he has no control over the stamping of the transfer, or its submission to the Land Registry'.

This approach appears to confirm the *obiter* view expressed in this jurisdiction in *Devoy v. Hanlon.*[13] There the owner of registered land ex-ecuted a voluntary deed transferring land to his son, but the transfer was not registered and was therefore ineffective. He subsequently devised the land to his daughter in his will and she was then registered as the owner. The son's claim to the land failed but only because he could not prove that the deed of transfer was ever delivered. The implication was that the court would have been willing to hold that the son, who was a volunteer and to whom the legal interest had not been transferred, would have been entitled to the land if he could have proved that the deed had been delivered. Once

---

10. (1984) 50 P & CR 119.
11. [1996] Ch 51.
12. (1984) 50 P & Cr 119, 125.
13. [1929] IR 246.

registered, the gift would have been completely constituted and could have been enforced even by a volunteer.

It follows from the proposition that a completely constituted trust is enforceable by a volunteer that such a trust is binding on a settlor and his personal representatives and will be irrevocable unless an express power of revocation is reserved at the time of its constitution. In *Re Bowden*,[14] a settlor by means of a voluntary settlement agreed to convey to trustees all the property which she might become entitled to under her father's will. She knowingly allowed this transfer to take place and it was held by Bennett J that she could not subsequently reclaim the property held on trust. As the trust was completely constituted, the fact that the settlement was voluntary did not affect its validity or enforceability. It should also be noted that in England there appears to be authority to support the proposition that a trust may be considered as completely constituted when property is vested in trustees although it did not come into their possession in their capacity as trustees of that particular trust.[15]

Declaration of Trust by Settlor

The alternative method of completely constituting a trust is for a settlor to declare himself a trustee of property for the benefit of third parties. Neville J summarised the requirements which must be satisfied to achieve this in *Re Cozens*[16] as follows: 'where a declaration of trust is relied on the Court must be satisfied that a present irrevocable declaration of trust has been made.' There must therefore be a clear manifestation of the intention to create a trust in this way and where it appears that a settlor's intention was to bring a trust into operation by transfer in the manner outlined above but he fails to achieve this objective, this ineffective attempt to transfer the property will not be construed as a declaration of trust. The general principle was set out by Turner LJ in *Milroy v. Lord* as follows: 'if the settlement is intended to be effectuated by one of the modes to which I have referred,[17] the Court will not give effect to it by applying another of those modes. If it is intended to take effect by transfer, the Court will not hold the intended transfer to operate as a declaration of trust, for then every imperfect instrument would be made effectual by being converted into a perfect trust.'[18]

---

14. [1936] Ch 71. See also *Paul v. Paul* (1882) 20 Ch D 742.
15. *Re Ralli's Will Trusts* [1964] Ch 288. However, note the conclusion reached by Farwell J in *Re Brooks' Settlement Trusts* [1939] Ch 993 which was not referred to in *Ralli*.
16. [1913] 2 Ch 478, 486.
17. See *supra* n. 3.
18. (1862) 4 De GF & J 264, 274-275. Quoted with approval by Lawson J in *Hayes v. Alliance British & Foreign Life & Fire Assurance Co.* (1881) 8 LR Ir 149, 153.

Similar sentiments were expressed by Fitzgibbon LJ in the Irish Court of Appeal in *O'Flaherty v. Browne*:[19]

> A voluntary trust may be created by a declaration of trust, or by a complete assignment of the legal ownership to a trustee; but it is impossible to turn an incomplete, conditional, or postponed gift into a trust, where there is no intention to create the relationship of trustee and *cestui que trust*.

This proposition is aptly illustrated by the decision of *Richards v. Delbridge*,[20] where the deceased who was the owner of leasehold premises endorsed and signed on the lease a memorandum in the following terms: 'this deed and all thereto belonging I give to Edwards Benetto Richards from this time forth, with all the stock-in-trade'. He delivered this document to the mother of the intended transferee and after his death the question arose whether the purported transfer was effective. The Court of Appeal concluded that there had been no proper assignment of the lease and in addition, that this ineffective attempt to transfer the interest could not be interpreted as a declaration of trust.[21]

Where the trust property is comprised of realty, the declaration of trust must be evidenced in writing and while strictly speaking this is not necessary in relation to personalty, it is clearly desirable from an evidential point of view. While the settlor 'need not use the words "I declare myself a trustee"',[22] he must unequivocally convey that this was his intention. As Lord O'Hagan LC commented in *Miller v. Harrison*[23] the effect of the declaration of trust must be to leave no reasonable doubt about the reason for its execution. In this case a dispute arose about the distribution of the property of an intestate who had died in America a naturalized US citizen. One of the next of kin executed a deed in which he agreed to share the property equally with the other next of kin and in reliance on this deed, these other individuals allowed a decree in the former's favour to be given by an American court in proceedings to determine ownership of the property. The Court of Appeal held that a subsequent attempt by this person to

---

19. [1907] 2 IR 416, 434.
20. (1874) LR 18 Eq 11.
21. Jessel MR stated at p.15: 'The true distinction appears to me to be plain, and beyond dispute: for a man to make himself a trustee there must be an expression of intention to become a trustee, whereas words of present gift shew an intention to give over property to another, and not retain it in the donor's own hands for any purpose, fiduciary or otherwise.'
22. *Richards v. Delbridge* (1874) LR 18 Eq 11, 14 *per* Jessel MR.
23. (1871) IR 5 Eq 324.

revoke the deed was invalid as its execution in the first instance had constituted a declaration of trust. As Lord O'Hagan LC stated:

> No future act is contemplated; no promise remains to be fulfilled; there is a gift, and not an engagement to give. The words of the donor denude him equitably of the shares which he bestows, save as a trustee for those so obtaining the beneficial interest, while the legal interest remains in himself ... and therefore it binds him, though it states no consideration, and uses no language expressly creating trusts.[24]

In some cases the courts have adopted a fairly rigorous interpretation of this requirement that the intention to declare a trust must be clearly shown. In *Jones v. Lock*[25] a father who had been reproved by his family for failing to bring home a present for his baby son on his return from a trip, placed a cheque in the child's hand having expressed the intention that the latter should have the money. The cheque was placed in a safe and six days later the father died. Lord Cranworth LC found that no valid transfer had been effected and stated that there was no evidence of an intention on the father's part to declare himself trustee on his child's behalf. However, more recently there has been evidence of some relaxation of this rather restrictive attitude and a more liberal view of the evidence necessary to establish a declaration of trust was taken by the English Court of Appeal in *Paul v. Constance*.[26] Scarman LJ acknowledged that on the facts it might be thought to be a 'borderline case' as it was not easy to identify a specific moment when the trust was declared. However, the court concluded that the repetition of the words 'the money is as much yours as mine' in relation to funds in a bank account was sufficient to constitute the deceased as trustee of these monies for the plaintiff.

EXCEPTIONS TO THE PRINCIPLE THAT EQUITY WILL NOT PERFECT AN INCOMPLETELY CONSTITUTED TRUST IN FAVOUR OF A VOLUNTEER

1. The Rule in Strong v. Bird

The effect of the rule in *Strong v. Bird*[27] is that where an incomplete gift is

---

24. *Ibid.* at 344.
25. (1865) 1 Ch App 25.
26. [1977] 1 WLR 527.
27. (1874) LR 18 Eq 315.

made during a donor's lifetime and the legal title to this property subsequently becomes vested in the donee, the donor's prior intention to make the gift is regarded as having been perfected provided that the intention has continued until the date of the donor's death. The result of the decision in *Strong* itself was that an executor did not have to account for a debt where a testator had manifested an intention to forgive the debt during her lifetime and this intention had continued until her death. This was extended to a positive application of the principle in *Re Stewart*[28] by a finding that an imperfect gift made by a testator *inter vivos* to his wife was subsequently perfected by her appointment as one of his executors. Neville J stated:

> [W]here a testator has expressed the intention of making a gift of personal estate belonging to him to one who upon his death becomes his executor, the intention continuing unchanged, the executor is entitled to hold the property for his own benefit. The reasoning by which the conclusion is reached is of a double character – first, that the vesting of the property in the executor at the testator's death completes the imperfect gift made in the lifetime and secondly, that the intention of the testator to give the beneficial interest to the executor is sufficient to counterveil the equity of beneficiaries under the will, the testator having vested the legal estate in the executor. The whole of the property in the eye of the law vesting in each executor, it seems to me immaterial whether the donee is the only executor or one of several; nor do I think the rule is confined to cases of the release of a debt owing by the donee.[29]

A number of aspects of the principle must be considered in more detail. The legal vesting of the property in the donee commonly occurs when this individual is appointed a personal representative of the donor. So the rule applies where a donee acquires legal title to the property by becoming an executor[30] of the deceased's estate and has been also held to extend to a situation where the donee is appointed administrator. While the latter principle was laid down in *Re James*[31] and now seems to be accepted, it has been criticised[32] on the basis that the identity of an administrator is often a

---

28. [1908] 2 Ch 251.
29. *Ibid.* at 254.
30. It suffices if a donee is appointed as one of a number of executors. See *supra Re Stewart* [1908] 2 Ch 251, 254.
31. [1935] Ch 449.
32. See the judgment of Walton J in *Re Gonin* [1979] Ch 16, although he did apply the principle as both counsel had accepted it.

matter of chance and it would seem unfair that such a person should obtain an advantage over the other beneficiaries by reason of this position.

An intention to make a gift in the future[33] or to make a future testamentary gift[34] will not come within the rule in *Strong v. Bird*. The distinction between a present intention to make an immediate gift of property and the intention to make a testamentary gift is well illustrated by the decision in *Re Wilson*.[35] The testator had manifested an intention to make an immediate gift of certain securities to his son, who was the executor of his will, although he did not complete or perfect this gift during his lifetime. Johnston J was satisfied that this intention had been proved and that the principle in *Strong v. Bird* applied to perfect the gift. However, the rule did not apply to other properties which the testator had promised to transfer to his son during his lifetime or by his will. In relation to the intended testamentary disposition, Johnston J quoted with approval[36] the words of Neville J in *Re Stewart*[37] as follows:

> [T]he intention to give, however, must not be an intention of testamentary benefaction, although the intended donee is the executor, for, in that case the rule cannot apply, the prescribed formalities for testamentary disposition not having been observed.

It is also important that the intention relates to specific property[38] and the gift must be perfected in all respects save for the formalities necessary to effect the proper transfer of the property. In addition, for the rule to apply the intention to make the gift must have continued until the time of the donor's death,[39] and it cannot have any application in cases such as *Re Wale*,[40] where the evidence showed that the settlor appeared to have forgotten the very existence of the settlement and had continued to treat the property as if it were her own.

The practical significance of the rule in *Strong v. Bird* is that the claim of beneficiaries under a will will be displaced by the donee's prior equity, although it is not clear in this jurisdiction or in England whether this priority will be effective over creditors.

---

33. *Re Freeland* [1952] Ch 110.
34. *Re Innes* [1910] 1 Ch 188.
35. [1933] IR 729.
36. *Ibid.* at 748.
37. [1908] 2 Ch 251, 25.
38. *Re Innes* [1910] 1 Ch 188, 193 *per* Parker J.
39. See *Re Gonin* [1979] Ch 16 where the lack of a continuing intention to make the gift resulted in the court's refusal to apply the rule in *Strong v. Bird*.
40. [1956] 1 WLR 1346.

2. Donatio Mortis Causa

A *donatio mortis causa* is the delivery of property to a donee in contemplation of the donor's death which is conditional on this event occurring and the gift is not regarded as complete until the donor dies. It should be regarded as a conditional present gift and must be distinguished from a straightforward gift *inter vivos* which is an absolute present gift, and from a testamentary gift which is a future gift. Buckley J described a *donatio mortis causa* in the following terms in *Re Beaumont*:[41]

> It is an act *inter vivos* by which the donee is to have absolute title to the subject of the gift not at once but if the donor dies. If the donor dies the title becomes absolute not under but as against his executor. In order to make the gift valid it must be made so as to take complete effect on the donor's death.

The general principle that equity will not perfect an imperfect or incomplete gift in favour of a volunteer does not apply to a *donatio mortis causa*, although in practice the assistance of equity will only be required in limited circumstances. Where the subject-matter of the *donatio mortis causa* is a chattel which has been delivered to the donee, title to this object is regarded as being complete on the donor's death. However, where the subject-matter is a chose in action or land, the legal title to this property will vest in the donor's personal representatives on his death. It is in these circumstances that the exception to the general principle becomes important as equity will compel the donee's personal representatives to take whatever steps are necessary to complete the donor's title.

The essential elements of a *donatio mortis causa* have been laid down in a number of decisions and are now clearly established.[42] There must have been a gift made in contemplation of the donor's death, the subject-matter of the gift must have been delivered to the donee and the gift must have been made on the basis that it becomes absolute only on the donor's death and therefore remains revocable during his lifetime. It is also necessary to consider whether the property is capable of forming the subject matter of a *donatio mortis causa*.

The attitude of the court in relation to these requirements has tended to be quite strict and they must all be satisfied to establish a valid *donatio*

---

41. [1902] 1 Ch 889, 892.
42. See *Cain v. Moon* [1896] 2 QB 283, 286 *per* Russell LJ quoted with approval by Molony CJ in *Re Mulroy* [1924] 1 IR 98, 103 and *Re Craven's Estate (No. 1)* [1937] Ch 423, 426 *per* Farwell J.

mortis causa. As Gallen J has recently commented in the New Zealand High Court decision of *Wilson v. Paniani*:[43]

> It is important . . . that there ought to be stringent requirements in respect of such claims since they are frequently made without any independent evidence to support them and in circumstances where they would be difficult to refute. Accordingly the law ensures that for such a claim to succeed the strict requirements of the law must be adhered to and satisfied.

Another reason why a strict approach has been taken in such cases is that the upholding of a *donatio mortis causa* may mean that the court is giving effect to a distribution of the deceased's property in a manner which may differ considerably from that set out by the deceased in his will. This point is well illustrated by the judgment of Barr J in *Bentham v. Potterton,*[44] the most recent decision in this jurisdiction on *donatio mortis causa.* The deceased in her will bequeathed cash legacies varying in amount from £1,000 to £3,000 to nine beneficiaries, including the first and second named plaintiffs, her grandnieces, and a residuary clause provided for the division of the remainder of the estate equally between all but one of the named beneficiaries. The deceased was hospitalised two months before her death and it was discovered that she was suffering from inoperable cancer. The trial judge was satisfied that there was no evidence that she had ever been told that her condition was terminal and it was not until a week before she died that she told her niece that she knew she was in fact dying. Three and a half weeks before her death the deceased asked the first named plaintiff to retrieve bank books from her home and put them in a safe in the latter's house, which she did. The following day, the first named plaintiff informed her great-aunt that she had carried out her wishes and the former deposed that the deceased had then told her that if anything was to happen to her, she was 'to keep the contents of the books and give [her sister] a few bob out of it'. After the deceased's death, an issue arose about whether this transaction amounted to a valid *donatio mortis causa* made in favour of the plaintiffs. Barr J made it clear that the onus lay on the party claiming the gift to establish to the court that the requirements for *donatio mortis causa* had been satisfied. In the first instance, he said that the facts fell

---

43. [1996] 3 NZLR 378, 384. The court held that on the facts the conditions necessary to establish the existence of a *donatio mortis causa* had not been made out by the plaintiff despite the fact that Gallen J was satisfied that the deceased had wished to benefit her.

44. High Court (Barr J) 28 May 1998.

short of establishing on the balance of probabilities that the gift had been made by the donor in contemplation of her death. He suggested that if it had been the deceased's intention to make a gift of the funds on deposit to the plaintiffs it seemed probable that she would either have made this clear on the first occasion on which she had referred to the deposit books or alternatively would have made a new will or codicil to give effect to her revised intentions. Barr J concluded that he was not satisfied that the deceased 'positively intended to make a radical change in the disposition of her property in contemplation of her death'. Although this might have been her intention, he said that the surrounding facts raised considerable doubt in this regard and in the circumstances he held that the plaintiffs had not established the validity of the alleged gift on the balance of probabilities.

(i) *In Contemplation of Death*

The gift must have been made in contemplation, although not necessarily in the expectation of death, but not simply in circumstances where the donor is acknowledging the general inevitability of death. So it is usually made where 'death for some reason [is] believed to be impending'[45] as a result of some form of serious illness or because the donor intends to embark on a particularly hazardous journey.[46] However, it is essential that the court is satisfied that the donor knew that he was dying at the time the transaction took place and this point is illustrated by the High Court decision in *Bentham v. Potterton,*[47] the facts of which are set out above. Barr J said that he had substantial doubts about whether the donor appreciated the gravity of her medical condition when the transaction in question took place. Although she was elderly and had been gravely ill two years previously, he adverted to the fact that there was no evidence that the deceased had been told that her condition was terminal and pointed out that it was only some two and a half weeks after the transaction had taken place that she had admitted to her niece that she thought she was dying. In these circumstances he said that the facts fell short of establishing on the balance of probabilities that the gift had been made by the donor in contemplation of her death.

Provided that death actually occurs it appears to be immaterial that it does so as a result of a cause different to that contemplated at the time of

---

45. *Re Craven's Estate (No. 1)* [1937] Ch 423, 426 *per* Farwell J.
46. The ordinary risks of travel by air will not suffice, see *Thompson v. Mechan* [1958] 13 DLR (2d) 103.
47. High Court (Barr J) 28 May 1998.

the gift. This is illustrated by *Wilkes v. Allington*,[48] in which a donor made a gift knowing that he was suffering from an incurable disease and then died two months later from pneumonia. It was held that the gift remained valid in such circumstances. A similar result ensued in *Mills v. Shields (No. 1)*,[49] where a donor made a gift while suffering from an oppressive form of neurosis and subsequently took his own life while travelling to Dublin for treatment for this condition. It is important to distinguish *Mills* from the decision in *Agnew v. Belfast Banking Co.*,[50] where it was held that a gift actually made in contemplation of suicide could not form the subject-matter of a valid *donatio mortis causa*. Porter MR commented that as suicide was recognised as a crime, it was 'fundamentally opposed to the first principles of our law ... that legal rights should be created by the intention to commit suicide followed by the actual commission of it'.[51] Fitzgibbon LJ agreed that it would be contrary to public policy to uphold a gift which was intended to take effect as a result of suicide and the policy arguments which lay behind the *Agnew* decision may still be recognised as valid.

(ii) *Delivery of the Subject-Matter of the Gift*
There must be delivery of the subject-matter of the *donatio mortis causa* made by the donor with the intention of parting with dominion over the property[52] and not just mere physical possession.[53] It is insufficient if the property is simply handed over for safe keeping and the result of such delivery must be that the donor can no longer exercise any control over the subject-matter of the gift.[54] As Evershed MR commented in *Birch v. Treasury Solicitor*[55] delivery must be made 'of the essential indicia or evidence of title, possession or production of which entitles the possessor to the money or property, purported to be given'.

Delivery may be made before[56] or after[57] the appropriate words of

---

48. [1931] 2 Ch 104.
49. [1948] IR 367.
50. [1896] 2 IR 204.
51. *Ibid.* at 216. Note that suicide is no longer regarded as a crime; see s.2 of the Criminal Law (Suicide) Act 1993.
52. There must be 'a complete parting with the dominion over the subject matter by the donor' *per* Molony CJ in *Re Mulroy* [1924] 1 IR 98, 100. See also *Hawkins v. Blewitt* (1798) 2 Esp 663.
53. *Birch v. Treasury Solicitor* [1951] 1 Ch 298.
54. *Re Craven's Estate (No. 1)* [1937] Ch 423, 427.
55. [1951] Ch 298, 311.
56. *Cain v. Moon* [1896] 2 QB 283.
57. *Re Weston* [1902] 1 Ch 680.

gift[58] are used and provided that it is achieved in an effective manner there is no requirement of any written evidence to substantiate it. It was held in *Mills v. Shields (No.1)*[59] that where delivery is made to an agent of the donor as trustee for the donee this will suffice. However this can be contrasted with the finding made in the earlier case of *Re Thompson's Estate*[60] that where the deceased simply handed her servant the property to keep for the donee this was not sufficient delivery. Meredith J quoted with approval the *dicta* of Knight Bruce VC in *Farquharson v. Cave*[61] to the effect that 'a mere delivery to an agent, in the character of agent for the giver, would amount to nothing' and concluded that in the circumstances where insufficient instructions had been given to the agent, no delivery, either actual or constructive, had taken place.

Where the subject-matter of the *donatio mortis causa* is a chattel, there must be either delivery of the chattel itself or of something which will enable the donee to obtain effective control over it. So the handing over of a key to a locked container or safe deposit box will constitute delivery,[62] although the reverse is not the case and delivery of a locked box without the key does not meet the requirements of a valid *donatio mortis causa*.[63] A good example of a case where no delivery was found to have taken place was *Re Mulroy*.[64] Shortly before his death, the deceased opened a cash box in the presence of the defendant and took out a deposit receipt and two 'stale' cheques and said to him: 'Here is all belonging to me; I am sorry I have no more to give you. You were very good to me.' He then replaced the documents and locked the box, putting the key in his pocket. The deceased subsequently died intestate and the Irish Court of Appeal held that there was no valid *donatio mortis causa* on the grounds that the deceased, by replacing the documents, had led the court to believe that he had never intended to part with them in such a manner as to lose dominion over them during his lifetime.

(iii) *The Gift Must be Conditional upon Death and Revocable*
The gift must have been made on the basis that although it is in form a

---

58. Note that words of gift are clearly not in themselves sufficient without actual delivery taking place, see *Re Mulroy* [1924] 1 IR 98, 104 *per* Molony CJ.
59. [1948] IR 367.
60. [1928] IR 606.
61. (1846) 2 Coll 356, 367.
62. *Re Wasserberg* [1915] 1 Ch 195; *Re Lillingston* [1952] 2 All ER 184. Although if the donor retains another key, it will probably not suffice, see *Re Craven's Estate (No. 1)* [1937] Ch 423, 428 *per* Farwell J.
63. *Re Johnson* (1905) 92 LT 357.
64. [1924] 1 IR 98.

present gift it is nevertheless conditional on the donor's death and it will remain revocable during his lifetime. As Lord Porter MR stated in *Agnew v. Belfast Banking Co.*:[65] 'A *donatio mortis causa* is incomplete till death, and depends upon it. If the sick man recovers it is of no avail. No property passes until death.' Such revocation may occur automatically where for example the donor recovers from the illness which led him to make the gift.[66] Equally, the donor may expressly inform the donee that the gift is being revoked, or may recover dominion over it, although recovery of possession for the purposes of safe keeping will not amount to revocation.[67] Clearly a purported revocation by will cannot be achieved as the instrument will not come into effect until the donor's death at which stage the donee's gift will be regarded as complete.

(iv) *The Property Must be Capable of Forming the Subject-Matter of a Donatio Mortis Causa*

Clearly, any property transferable by mere delivery can form the subject matter of a valid gift by way of *donatio mortis causa* and delivery of the documentation appropriate to effect a transfer of property will also suffice.[68] Until recently it had been thought that realty could not form the subject matter of a valid *donatio mortis causa*[69] but the Court of Appeal in *Sen v. Headley* [70] made it clear that a gift of land by the delivery of deeds should not be excluded. The deceased and the plaintiff lived together for ten years and remained on close terms thereafter. When the deceased was very ill he told the plaintiff that his house was hers and that the deeds to it were in a steel box to which she had the keys. He died intestate and the plaintiff claimed that he had made a valid gift to her in contemplation of death. The defendant, who was the deceased's nephew and the administrator of his estate, counterclaimed for the return of the deeds to the house. The Court of Appeal upheld the plaintiff's claim.

There is some authority to the effect that stocks and shares cannot form the subject matter of a *donatio mortis causa*[71] on the basis that a share

---

65. [1896] 2 IR 204, 216.
66. *Keys v. Hore* (1879) 13 ILTR 58.
67. *Re Hawkins* [1924] 2 Ch 47.
68. *Birch v. Treasury Solicitor* [1951] Ch 298, 311.
69. See the *dicta* of Lord Eldon in *Duffield v. Elwes* (1827) 1 Bli 497 and the Australian decisions of *Watts v. Public Trustee* (1949) 50 SR 130 and *Bayliss v. Public Trustee* (1988) 12 NSWLR 540.
70. [1991] Ch 425. See Halliwell [1991] Conv 307; Thornley [1991] CLJ 404; Baker (1993) 109 LQR 19.
71. *Moore v. Moore* (1874) LR 18 Eq 474; *Re Weston* [1902] 1 Ch 680, although note *Staniland v. Willot* (1852) 3 Mac & G 664.

certificate although it will constitute *prima facie* evidence of good title is not the vital document which forms 'the fundamental contract between a company and its members'.[72] Similar uncertainty surrounds the position of a savings bank book. In *M'Gonnell v. Murray*[73] Walsh MR rejected the argument that it could validly form the subject-matter of a *donatio mortis causa* on the grounds that the book did not embody the terms of the contract between the depositer and the bank. However, in the more recent Circuit Court decision of *Hearty v. Coleman,*[74] it was held by Judge Sheehy that the handing of a post office savings bank book by the testator to the defendant constituted a valid *donatio mortis causa* of the money standing to her credit in the account and other authorities seem to support this conclusion.[75] It would seem that neither an IOU[76] nor a donor's own cheque or promissory note can come within the ambit of the doctrine on the basis that these are respectively merely a revocable instrument and a gratuitous promise.[77]

In the last analysis perhaps the most useful test is that proposed by Evershed MR in *Birch v. Treasury Solicitor,*[78] which was set out above; namely whether delivery of the documents concerned amounts to a transfer 'of the essential indicia or evidence of title, possession or production of which entitles the possessor to the money or property, purported to be given'.

3. Proprietary Estoppel

Where an imperfect gift has been made and the donor knowingly allows the donee to improve the property or act to his detriment in some manner, equity may compel the donor to perfect the gift even where the donee is a volunteer. This will be considered *infra.*[79]

---

72. *Mills v. Shields (No. 2)* [1950] IR 21, 31 *per* Gavan Duffy J.
73. (1869) IR 3 Eq 460.
74. [1953-54] Ir Jur Rep 73.
75. *Re Weston* [1902] 1 Ch 680; *Birch v. Treasury Solicitor* [1951] Ch 298. In addition, in *Re Thompson's Estate* [1928] IR 606 Meredith J while he held on the facts that there was no valid *donatio mortis causa* on the grounds that there had been no delivery, did not raise any issue as to whether a Post Office savings bank book could have formed the subject-matter of such a gift.
76. *Duckworth v. Lee* [1899] 1 IR 405.
77. *Re Beaumont* [1902] 1 Ch 889; *Re Leaper* [1916] 1 Ch 579. However there might be a valid gift if the cheque was paid during the donor's lifetime or even after his death if the bank was not aware of the fact that he had died.
78. [1951] Ch 298, 311.
79. See Chapter 17.

THE POSITION OF A VOLUNTEER

As we have seen, once a trust is completely constituted it can be enforced by any beneficiary, even if he is a mere volunteer. However, where a trust is still incompletely constituted, it may be of crucial importance to determine whether the beneficiaries are volunteers or have given consideration; in these circumstances 'equity will not assist a volunteer' although it will enforce such an incompletely constituted trust if valuable consideration has been given by the beneficiaries.

A beneficiary will be regarded as a volunteer unless he had provided valuable consideration in the sense recognised at common law or comes within the scope of a marriage consideration. It is important to note that what is referred to as 'good consideration' comprised of natural love and affection is not considered to be valuable consideration and will not suffice to make an incompletely constituted trust enforceable in equity. A settlement made before and in consideration of marriage is regarded as being one for valuable consideration. However, a settlement made after marriage will only suffice provided it is made in fulfilment of a pre-nuptial agreement.[80] In any other circumstances a settlement made in consideration of a past marriage will not be regarded as being one for valuable consideration. This is illustrated by the decision of *Re Greer*,[81] where a settlement executed for the benefit of children of a former marriage on the occasion of a second marriage was not found to be a settlement for valuable consideration. The spouses[82] and issue[83] of the marriage are regarded as coming within the marriage consideration. The latter phrase has been variously interpreted as being confined to children[84] and as extending to grandchildren[85] but the better view would seem to be that it is usually confined to the children of the marriage.[86]

It has been clearly established that persons coming within the marriage consideration can enforce the settlement even though they might other-

---

80. *Re Holland* [1902] 2 Ch 360.
81. (1877) IR 11 Eq 502.
82. *Dennehy v. Delany* (1876) IR 10 Eq 377.
83. *Greenwood v. Lutman* [1915] 1 IR 266.
84. *Re Dixon's Trusts* (1869) IR 4 Eq 1.
85. *McDonald v. Scott* [1893] AC 642.
86. *Re Bromhead's Trusts* [1922] 1 IR 75. While some early authorities suggested a wider definition of those falling within the marriage consideration, these decisions are now explained on the basis that in the special circumstances of these cases the interests of these parties, often illegitimate children or children of a former marriage were so closely interwoven with the interests of the children of the marriage that they could not be separated.

wise be regarded as volunteers. In *Pullan v. Koe*[87] as part of a marriage settlement in which property was settled on a husband and wife and their prospective children, the wife covenanted to settle after acquired property to the value of £100 or upwards. She subsequently received a gift of £285 which was ultimately used to buy bonds which remained in her husband's name until his death. The question arose whether these bonds could be recovered from his estate and held on the trusts of the settlement. It was held by Swifen Eady J that the trustees, acting on behalf of the wife and children, could succeed in reclaiming the bonds on the grounds that the money had been subject to a trust in favour of those coming within the marriage consideration. Swifen Eady J distinguished the circumstances of the case before him from those where it had been held that a court would not intervene to assist a volunteer who did not come within the marriage consideration. In *Re Plumptre's Marriage Settlement*[88] a settlement in consideration of marriage contained a covenant providing for the settlement of property subsequently acquired by the wife on trust for herself and her husband for life, their issue and in default, for their next of kin. The husband gave some stock to his wife and it was held that after her death the covenant could not be enforced by their next of kin against her personal representative, her husband, on the grounds that the next of kin were volunteers and did not come within the marriage consideration.[89]

POSSIBLE ALTERNATIVE REMEDIES FOR A BENEFICIARY WHERE A TRUST IS INCOMPLETELY CONSTITUTED

Where a beneficiary is a volunteer and does not come within any of the exceptions outlined above, it is necessary to examine whether there are any other means of enforcing an incompletely constituted trust in his favour. A settlor may commonly enter into a covenant to create a trust by transferring existing or so called after acquired property to trustees. This is particularly common in the case of a marriage settlement where the parties may covenant to settle any property which they may subsequently acquire on the trusts of the settlement.[90] Where such a covenant is entered

---

87. [1913] 1 Ch 9.
88. [1910] 1 Ch 609. See also *Re D'Angibau* (1880) 15 Ch D 228.
89. It should be noted that a volunteer beneficiary who is party to a covenant may bring an action on the covenant at common law for damages, see *Cannon v. Hartley* [1949] Ch 213.
90. See *supra Re Plumptre's Marriage Settlement* [1910] 1 Ch 609; *Pullan v. Koe* [1913] 1 Ch 9.

into other than for valuable consideration, there are two main alternatives relating to its possible enforcement which must be examined. First, to establish that there is a completely constituted trust of the benefit of the covenant in their favour and secondly to consider indirect enforcement by means of an action by the trustees on the covenant at common law against the settlor.

The principal difficulty with the first option is in determining the circumstances when such a trust will arise and in particular in assessing whether sufficient intention to create a trust has been established. In the early decision of *Fletcher v. Fletcher*[91] a settlor entered into a voluntary covenant with trustees to the effect that if either or both of his natural sons should survive him, his executors should, within twelve months of his death pay a sum of £60,000 to the trustees to hold on trust for both or such one of them as might attain the age of 21. One of these sons survived the settlor and reached the age of 21 when he sought to enforce the covenant against the executors who had refused to take any action. The effect of the decision of Wright VC was that there was a completely constituted trust of the benefit of the covenant which could be enforced by the son. On the facts the court in *Fletcher* was satisfied that the testator had manifested a sufficient intention to create a trust, although it has been argued that these same facts would hardly satisfy a more modern approach to the question of certainty of intention.[92] A further difficulty is that *Fletcher* has been distinguished in the case of after acquired property and it has been held in a number of decisions that there can be no enforceable trust of the benefit of the covenant in such cases.[93] In *Re Cook's Settlement Trusts*,[94] by virtue of an agreement and subsequent settlement entered into by Sir Herbert Cook and his son, certain pictures became the absolute property of the son, who covenanted that if any of these pictures were to be sold during his lifetime the proceeds of sale should be held on the trusts of the settlement. The son gave one of the pictures to his wife who wished to sell it and the question arose whether the trustees were obliged to take any steps to ensure performance of the covenant. Buckley J distinguished *Fletcher v. Fletcher* as follows:

---

91. (1844) 4 Hare 67.
92. See *supra* Chapter 4. While at the time *Fletcher* was decided the use of precatory words was considered to be sufficient to show intention to create a trust, a more stringent approach is now applied.
93. *Re Pryce* [1917] 1 Ch 234; *Re Kay's Settlement* [1939] Ch 329; *Re Cook's Settlement Trusts* [1965] Ch 902.
94. [1965] Ch 902.

> The covenant with which I am concerned did not, in my opinion, create a debt enforceable at law, that is to say a property right, which, although to bear fruit only in the future and upon a contingency, was capable of being made the subject of an immediate trust, as was held to be the case in *Fletcher v. Fletcher.* ... In contrast ... this covenant on its true construction is, in my opinion, an executory contract to settle a particular fund or particular funds of money which at the date of the covenant did not exist and which might never come into existence. It is analogous to a covenant to settle an expectation or to settle after-acquired property. The case in my judgment, involves the law of contract, not the law of trusts.[95]

It has been argued that there is no good reason for drawing such a distinction[96] and perhaps the decision in *Cook* is better explained on the grounds that there was clearly no intention to create a trust of the benefit of the covenant in that case.

So, in theory a completely constituted trust of the benefit of a covenant to settle either existing or after acquired property may be found provided the settlor has manifested the appropriate intention and it is likely that in the absence of such a clearly expressed intention no trust will exist. This would allow voluntary covenants to settle property to be enforced where there is sufficient evidence of the settlor's intention to create a trust of the benefit of the covenant; any more radical approach would seem inconsistent with a considerable number of authorities.

A second option, which derives little or no support from the relevant case law, is that where a beneficiary is unable to enforce a covenant to settle in the manner outlined above it might be possible to secure enforcement of the covenant by means of an action on it at common law by the trustees against the settlor. However, the authorities in this area have clearly established that there is no obligation on the trustees to take action in such circumstances; *a fortiori* it has been suggested that they should be restrained from taking any such proceedings.[97] In *Re Kay's Settlement*[98] a spinster executed a voluntary settlement in favour of herself for life and after her death for her issue which contained a covenant to settle after acquired property. She subsequently married, had children and acquired further prop-

---

95. *Ibid.* at 913-914.
96. Barton (1975) 91 LQR 236; Meagher & Lehane (1976) 92 LQR 427; Goddard [1988] Conv 19.
97. *Re Pryce* [1917] 1 Ch 234.
98. [1939] Ch 329.

erty and then refused to comply with the trustees' request to bring this additional property into the settlement. The trustees sought the direction of the court on the issue of whether they should take proceedings against the settlor to compel performance of the covenant or to recover damages for her failure to implement it. Simonds J followed the decision of Eve J in *Re Pryce*[99] and directed the trustees not to take any steps either to compel performance of the covenant or to seek damages in respect of the settlor's failure to implement its terms.

However, even if the courts were to re-appraise their approach, there would be difficulties from the point of view of the beneficiaries in having recourse to this option. First, the extent of the damages to which the trustees would be entitled in these circumstances is far from clear and in any event, any damages which might be recovered would in all likelihood be held by the trustees on a resulting trust for the settlor rather than for the beneficiaries. Therefore, unless a beneficiary is recognised as being an actual party to the covenant, in which case he can maintain an action at common law for its breach,[100] he will not be able to secure a remedy at law for failure to give effect to the terms of the covenant.

---

99. [1917] 1 Ch 234. Criticised in Jacobs, *Law of Trusts in Australia* (5th ed., 1986, Meagher and Gummow) pp. 91-93.
100. *Cannon v. Hartley* [1949] Ch 213.

CHAPTER 7

Resulting Trusts

INTRODUCTION

Resulting trusts can be said to arise by implication and are founded on the unexpressed but presumed intention of the settlor.[1] This label is used to describe such trusts because the beneficial interest in the property in question comes back or results to the settlor, or, if he is dead, to those entitled to his estate, where the law presumes that this was the settlor's intention. They are also sometimes referred to as implied trusts because they are presumed to arise as a result of the settlor's implied intention. Due to the informal manner in which they come into being, such trusts are exempt from the formalities required in relation to the creation of express trusts. A division of resulting trusts was suggested by Megarry J in *Re Vandervell's Trusts (No. 2)*[2] in the following terms:

> (a) The first class of case is where the transfer to B is not made on any trust. If, of course, it appears from the transfer that B is intended to hold on certain trusts, that will be decisive, and the case is not within this category; and similarly if it appears that B is intended to take beneficially. But in other cases there is a rebuttable presumption that B holds on a resulting trust for A. . . . The presumption thus establishes both that B is to take on trust and also what that trust is. Such resulting trusts may be called 'presumed resulting trusts'.

> (b) The second class of case is where the transfer to B is made on trusts which leave some or all of the beneficial interest undisposed of. Here B automatically holds on a resulting trust for A to the extent that the beneficial interest has not been carried to him or others. The resulting trust here does not depend on any intentions or presumptions, but is the automatic consequence of A's failure to dispose of what is vested in him. . . . Such resulting trusts may be called 'automatic resulting trusts'.

---

1. See generally Chambers, *Resulting Trusts* (1997).
2. [1974] Ch 269, 294. See Clarke (1974) 38 Conv 405; Harris (1975) 38 MLR 557.

The extent to which the trusts which may arise by implication in either of these two categories will actually reflect the settlor's real intentions in a given case is open to question and particularly in the context of automatically resulting trusts, the result, which the law presumes, is often quite contrary to that which a settlor could be said to have intended.[3]

AUTOMATICALLY RESULTING TRUSTS

Failure of the Trust

Where an express trust fails completely for any reason, a resulting trust of the trust property will arise in favour of the settlor or his estate. This may occur for a variety of reasons; there may have been a total failure of the beneficiaries; the settlement deed defining the scope of the trust may have been lost,[4] the trust may be void for uncertainty,[5] or may fail to qualify for charitable status in circumstances where it cannot operate as a valid purpose trust.[6] In *Re Ames' Settlement*[7] property was settled on the trusts of a marriage settlement by the husband's father. The marriage was subsequently declared void and it was held that this property should be held on a resulting trust for the settlor's estate after the husband's death, rather than passing to those entitled under the settlement in default of issue.

Another situation in which a resulting trust will arise is where property is given to trustees and yet no trusts are defined. This can arise in the context of a half secret trust,[8] where a testator makes it clear on the face of a will that property is to be held on trust without specifying the nature and extent of the trust and the identity of the beneficiaries. In those circumstances where such a trust fails because there has been no adequate communication and acceptance of the terms of the trust during the testator's lifetime,[9] or if it were to fail on the grounds of inconsistency between the terms of the will and the events which transpired,[10] a resulting trust in

---

3. *Vandervell v. IRC* [1967] 2 AC 291. See *infra* p. 135.
4. *Cummins v. Hall* [1933] IR 419.
5. *Re Pugh's Will Trusts* [1967] 1 WLR 1262; *Re Atkinson's Will Trusts* [1978] 1 WLR 586.
6. *Re Diplock* [1948] Ch 465.
7. [1946] Ch 217.
8. See *supra* Chapter 5.
9. See *Scott v. Brownrigg* (1881) 9 LR Ir 246; *Re Watters' Will Trusts* (1928) 62 ILTR 61. This seems to be now accepted as being the requirement in Ireland rather than communication and acceptance prior to the testator's will which still appears to be the position in England, see *supra* Chapter 5.
10. *Re Keen* [1937] Ch 236.

favour of the testator's estate would arise. A similar result will ensue where a testator makes an unsuccessful attempt to create a fully secret trust and the intended trustee admits that it was not the testator's intention that he should take as a beneficiary.[11]

One of the most important cases in this area is that of *Vandervell v. IRC*,[12] in which the appellant transferred shares in a private company to a college which he wished to endow with the intention of declaring dividends on the shares. The effect of the arrangement was that the college would grant an option to a company which acted as trustee for various family trusts enabling the shares to be acquired by the company, although it was not stated on what trusts these shares were to be held. The House of Lords held that the option was held on a resulting trust for the appellant with the result that not having divested himself completely of his interest in the shares, he was liable for surtax on the dividends paid to the college. As Lord Wilberforce stated: 'the conclusion on the facts found, is simply that the option was vested in the trustee company as a trustee on trusts, not defined at the time, possibly to be defined later. But the equitable, or beneficial interest, cannot remain in the air: the consequence in law must be that it remains in the settlor'.[13]

Failure to Exhaust the Beneficial Interest

In practice a trust does not often fail completely but a situation may quite frequently arise where there has been an incomplete disposal of the beneficial interest under a trust. Even though it may appear at the time a trust instrument or will is executed that this interest has been fully disposed of, subsequent events may occur, or fail to occur, which may change this position. In *Re Lane's Trusts*[14] by virtue of a marriage settlement a husband and wife each contributed the sum of £1,000 to a fund to be held on certain trusts with the intention that it would ultimately benefit their children. No issue of the marriage survived the husband and he died before his wife. On her death, it was held that a resulting trust in favour of the husband's administrator and the wife's executor arose. The resulting trust which will arise in such circumstances has been described as 'the last resort to which the law has recourse when the draftsman has made a blunder or failed to dispose of that which he has set out to dispose of'.[15] In *Re Cochrane*[16] a

11. *Re Boyes* (1884) 26 Ch D 531.
12. [1967] 2 AC 291.
13. *Ibid.* at 329.
14. (1863) 14 Ir Ch R 523.
15. *Re Cochrane* [1955] Ch 309, 316.
16. [1955] Ch 309.

marriage settlement provided that assets were to be held on trust for the wife for life 'so long as she shall reside with [her husband]' and after her death for her husband and then for their issue as they should jointly appoint or in default of appointment at the age of 21, or in the case of daughters, on their marriage. The wife ceased to reside with her husband and her interest under the trust terminated. The income was thereafter paid to the husband until his death and the question then arose whether their children should become entitled to the income during the wife's lifetime. Harman J found that an omission had clearly been made by the draftsman of the settlement as there had been no provision to cover the events which had transpired. In the circumstances he held that a resulting trust should arise for the wife's lifetime.

It may often be difficult to distinguish a gift to a trustee on trust solely to carry out a specified purpose, the implication being that any remaining surplus will be held on a resulting trust, from a situation where a gift is made to a donee subject to the carrying out of some obligation in which case he will be permitted to keep whatever remains after this obligation has been fulfilled. Kekewich J commented in *Re West*[17] that '[i]t is impossible to say that because property is given to persons as trustees they therefore take no beneficial interest ... [n]evertheless, there is a presumption that a gift in trust is not a beneficial gift.' This question must be resolved by seeking to ascertain the true intentions of the donor but where the non-beneficial character of the gift is clear from the face of the trust instrument or will, it will be difficult to rebut the presumption of a trust.[18] A good example of a case falling into the latter category outlined above is *Re Foord*,[19] where a testator left his estate to his sister absolutely on trust to pay his widow an annuity. Sargant J held that the sister was beneficially entitled to the balance when the income of the estate exceeded the amount of the annuity and that no resulting trust arose.

A number of cases have dealt with the circumstances where property is given on trust for the maintenance or education of specified persons and the difficulties which arise when these purposes are fulfilled. Should the intended beneficiaries be permitted to keep the remaining trust property or should a resulting trust in favour of the donor arise once the stated objective has been achieved? Where the specified purposes can be regarded as merely constituting the testator's motive for making the gift, the donee will be permitted to retain the property, but this may be difficult to estab-

---

17. [1900] 1 Ch 84, 87.
18. *Re Rees' Will Trusts* [1950] Ch 204.
19. [1922] 2 Ch 519.

lish particularly where it is the donee's estate, rather than the donee personally, who stands to benefit. In *Re Trusts of the Abbott Fund*[20] contributions were made to a fund to be used for the maintenance of two distressed ladies. No provision had been made in relation to the disposal of the fund on the death of the survivor and Stirling J held that on her death the balance of the fund should be held on a resulting trust for the subscribers. This can be contrasted with *Re Andrew's Trust*,[21] where a fund was subscribed to by the friends of a deceased clergyman for the education of his children. Kekewich J held that when their formal education was complete, no resulting trust of the remaining balance should arise and that it should instead be divided equally amongst the children. He quoted with approval the following passage from the judgment of Wood VC in *Re Sanderson's Trusts*:[22]

> If a gross sum be given, or if the whole income of the property be given, and a special purpose be assigned for that gift, this Court always regards the gift as absolute, and the purpose merely as the motive of the gift, and therefore holds that the gift must take effect as to the whole sum or the whole income, as the case may be.

Kekewich J felt that he was entitled to construe 'education' in the broadest possible manner and even if a narrow interpretation were to be placed on the meaning of that word, it could be interpreted as being merely the 'motive of the gift' in the sense outlined in the passage above. This approach of treating the trust as being for the benefit of the beneficiaries generally with special reference to a particular purpose was followed in *Re Osoba*,[23] where a testator left property to his widow on trust to be used for her maintenance and 'for the training of my daughter up to university grade and for the maintenance of my aged mother'. The testator's mother predeceased him and his widow died some years later. When the daughter completed her university education the issue of whether the testator's children from a previous marriage could claim the residue on intestacy arose. Megarry VC set out the a number of general principles as follows:

> I think that you have to look at the persons intended to benefit, and be ready, if they can still benefit, to treat the stated method of benefit as merely indicating purpose, and no doubt, as indicating the

---

20. [1900] 2 Ch 326.
21. [1905] 2 Ch 48.
22. (1857) 3 K & J 497, 503.
23. [1978] 1 WLR 791 (ChD) and [1979] 1 WLR 247 (CA).

means of benefit which are to be in the forefront. In short, if a trust is constituted for the assistance of certain persons by certain stated means there is a sharp distinction between cases where the beneficiaries have died and cases where they are still living. If they are dead, the court is ready to hold that there is a resulting trust for the donors; for the major purpose of the trust, that of providing help and benefit for the beneficiaries comes to an end when the beneficiaries are all dead and are beyond earthly help, whether by the stated means or otherwise. But if the beneficiaries are still living, the major purpose of providing help and benefit for the beneficiaries can still be carried out even after the stated means have all been accomplished, and so the court will be ready to treat the stated means as being merely indicative and not restrictive.[24]

The Court of Appeal agreed that the testator's overriding intention was to provide for his wife and daughter and that the specified purposes should be merely regarded as an expression of his motives. In these circumstances no resulting trust arose and the beneficiaries took as joint tenants with the result that on her mother's death, the daughter became entitled to the whole of the residue.

It has been argued that there has been a certain lack of consistency in the case law in this area, although some distinguishing features can be identified. While in *Abbott* it was no longer possible to use the funds for the benefit of the beneficiaries, this was clearly not the case in *Andrews* and *Osoba*, where the beneficiaries were still alive. So while it would be difficult to distinguish between the motives of the subscribers in *Abbott* and *Andrews*, the results in these cases do seem to be justified by the surrounding circumstances.

A further difficulty may arise where a fund is comprised mainly of anonymous contributions. In *Re Gillingham Bus Disaster Fund*[25] donations were made to a fund set up to benefit those injured in an accident and to provide a memorial for those who had been killed. Some of this fund was derived from contributions made by known individuals but was comprised mainly of donations of an anonymous nature raised by street collections and other means. Harman J concluded that a resulting trust arose despite the obvious practical difficulties involved in drawing such a conclusion and that the Crown's claim to *bona vacantia* could not succeed merely because there were a number of donors whose identity could not

---

24. [1978] 1 WLR 791, 795-796.
25. [1958] Ch 300. See Atiyah (1958) 74 LQR 190.

be ascertained. He stated:

> The general principle must be that where money is held on trusts
> and the trusts declared do not exhaust the fund it will revert to the
> donor or settlor under what is called a resulting trust. The reasoning
> behind this is that the settlor or donor did not part with his money
> absolutely out and out but only *sub modo* to the intent that his wishes
> as declared by the declaration of trust should be carried into effect.[26]

This result was not followed in the later decision of *Re West Sussex Constabulary's Widows, Children & Benevolent (1930) Fund Trusts*,[27] in which
Goff J had to determine the manner of distribution of a fund made up
partly from the proceeds of entertainments and raffles, from collecting
boxes, and from donations and legacies. While Goff J concluded that the
gifts in the latter category were to be held on a resulting trust for the donors or their estates, he held that gifts in the first two categories went as
bona vacantia on the basis that they were absolute out and out gifts. While
the logic of the approach in *Gillingham* cannot really be faulted the practical result of such a finding is often wholly unsatisfactory and to this
extent the conclusion reached by Goff J may therefore be preferable.[28]

The Distribution of Surplus Funds on the Dissolution of
Unincorporated Associations[29]

Where surplus funds remain on the dissolution of an unincorporated association, some method of distributing these funds must be determined. In
Re Printers and Transferrers Amalgamated Trades Protection Society[30]
on the dissolution of a society formed to provide support for its members
and their families, surplus funds were distributed amongst the surviving
members in proportion to their contributions by way of a resulting trust.
This decision has been criticised on the basis that a proper application of
resulting trust principles would have ensured that such distribution would
not have been confined to the surviving members on the grounds that 'death

---

26. *Ibid.* at 310.
27. [1971] Ch 1.
28. Although to the extent that it involved the distribution of funds on the dissolution of
    a club or association, it is not in line with more recent authorities e.g. *Re Bucks
    Constabulary Widows' and Orphans' Fund Friendly Society (No. 2)* [1979] 1 WLR
    936, see *infra*.
29. For a recent article which addresses some of the issues raised in this area, see Matthews
    [1995] Conv 302.
30. [1899] 2 Ch 184.

does not deprive a man of his beneficial interest'.[31] A less convenient although more principled solution was accepted by Cohen J in *Re Trusts of Hobourn Aero Components Ltd's Air Raid Distress Fund*,[32] in which he held that on the dissolution of the association the assets should be distributed amongst all the members, past and present, in shares proportionate to their contributions.

More recent case law in England has tended to lay considerably more emphasis on the manner in which an association's assets are held prior to its dissolution. Where the funds are considered as being held on trust for the association's purposes, this will usually give rise to a resulting trust in the event of dissolution,[33] or where the donor effectively disclaims it, the assets will go to the Crown as *bona vacantia*.[34] Where on the other hand the donor has parted with his money on an absolute basis pursuant to a form of contract, the manner in which any surplus funds will be disposed of in the event of a dissolution will be governed by contract. This may either take the form of an express provision contained in the association's rules or in the absence of such a provision, in accordance with an implied term, usually to the effect that the surplus is to be divided equally amongst those individuals who are members at the time of the dissolution. In circumstances where an association may have been dissolved due to lack of members this will be impractical and the remaining assets will pass as *bona vacantia*.

The most important case in this area which seems to confirm that the modern trend is to favour a contractual approach is *Re Bucks. Constabulary Widows' and Orphans' Fund Friendly Society (No. 2)*,[35] which concerned the distribution of a fund established to provide benefits to the widows and orphans of deceased police officers and for the relief of members of the force during sickness or ill-health. When the Bucks. constabulary was amalgamated with others the issue of the proper distribution of the association's assets arose. Walton J held that the surplus funds should be distributed equally amongst the members of the association alive at the date of dissolution.[36] He also expressed the view that it is only where a

---

31. *Re Sick and Funeral Society of St John's Sunday School, Golcar* [1973] Ch 51, 59 *per* Megarry J.
32. [1946] Ch 86.
33. E.g. the category of donations and legacies in *West Sussex Constabulary's Widows Childrens & Benevolent (1930) Fund Trusts* [1971] Ch 1.
34. E.g. the category of the proceeds of collection boxes in *West Sussex Constabulary's Widows, Childrens & Benevolent (1930) Fund Trusts* [1971] Ch 1.
35. [1979] 1 WLR 936.
36. Contrast this with the approach taken in *Cunnack v. Edwards* [1896] 2 Ch 679 where it was held that the personal representatives of the members of an association were

club or association has become moribund that its assets should go as *bona vacantia*. This approach was followed in *Re GKN Bolts & Nuts Ltd (Automotive Division) Birmingham Works, Sports and Social Club*[37] and now seems to be generally recognised as the most practical way of resolving this question. However, it has not met with universal approval and in *Davis v. Richards & Wallington Industries Ltd,*[38] Scott J departed from the more recognised approach of analysing the manner in which the funds are held prior to dissolution and concluded that a resulting trust might still provide the correct solution in certain circumstances.[39]

The approach favoured in this jurisdiction seems to involve the rejection of the concept of a resulting trust in favour of a contractually based solution. However, there is still a lack of consensus on the issue of whether the distribution of surplus funds should be carried out on the basis of equal division or in accordance with the proportion of contributions made. In *Tierney v. Tough*[40] the manner of distribution of a fund established to provide benefits for the employees of the Grand Canal Company and their families had to be considered. O'Connor MR rejected the suitability of the resulting trust approach to the facts of the case before him in the following terms:

> As I understand that doctrine, it applies only to a case where the trusts or purposes to which a fund or property is dedicated do not exhaust the whole interest, whereupon such part of the fund or property as is not required for carrying out the trusts or the purposes of the settlor results, or, in other words, goes back to the settlor. Now, this principle would give back to the existing members only so much of the funds as represented their own contributions to it. . . . A resulting trust would have given the fund, so far as subscribed by deceased members, to their personal representatives, and not to other parties.[41]

He concluded instead that the assets were the property of the society which was composed of individual members and that the funds should be distrib-

---

not entitled to a share in the society's funds when it was dissolved after the death of the widow of the last surviving member on the basis that its members had received all that for which they had contracted. See also *West Sussex Constabulary's Widows, Childrens and Benevolent (1930) Fund Trusts* [1971] Ch 1.

37. [1982] 1 WLR 774.
38. [1990] 1 WLR 1511.
39. See Gardner [1992] Conv 41 for an excellent analysis of this decision.
40. [1914] 1 IR 142.
41. *Ibid.* at 155.

uted amongst the existing members in proportion to the contributions which they had made. In these circumstances he found that the fund could not be regarded as *bona vacantia* and that the Attorney General had no claim to the society's assets. While the basis for O'Connor MR's decision has been upheld as 'wholly convincing' by Walton J in *Re Bucks. Constabulary Widows' and Orphans' Fund Friendly Society (No. 2),*[42] the manner which he prescribed for distribution of the funds has not met with similar approval.[43] Another relevant authority is the decision of Johnston J in *Feeney v. MacManus,*[44] which concerned the dissolution of the General Post Office (Dublin) Dining Club which had a membership comprised of certain classes of post office officials. The club, which provided subsidized refreshments, ceased to function following the destruction of the GPO in 1916 and when the building was re-opened in 1929 a new club was formed with similar objectives and membership. The plaintiffs, who were the secretary and treasurer of the original club, sought directions from the court in relation to the distribution of its remaining property. It was held by Johnston J that the entire fund must be distributed in equal shares amongst the individuals who were members of the club at the time of its dissolution and the personal representatives of those who had died since that date. He concluded that it would be impossible to ascertain the proportions in which each of the members had subscribed to the club's funds and assets and that accordingly, distribution had to be on an equal basis.

This principle of equal distribution would appear to be firmly entrenched in England. In *Re Sick and Funeral Society of St John's Sunday School, Golcar*[45] Megarry J agreed that membership of a club or association is primarily a question of contract and that the sums paid by members cease to be their individual property and capable of forming the subject-matter of a resulting trust and that on dissolution the only interested persons should be the existing members of the club. However, he took a different view of the method of distribution and 'reject[ed] the basis of proportionate division in favour of equality, or division per capita.' Similarly in *Re Bucks.*

---

42. [1979] 1 WLR 936, 947. Although it could be argued that he decided simply that the inevitable consequence of following resulting trust principles would not yield the result desired, and that an approach which would allow him to distribute proportionately amongst existing members must therefore be arrived at.
43. Rickett [1980] CLJ 88, 116 suggests that it is 'an attempted half-way house which has no basis' and argues that once the manner in which the property was to be held was determined, division on the dissolution of the society ought to have been in accordance with that finding.
44. [1937] IR 23.
45. [1973] Ch 51.

Constabulary Widows' and Orphans' Fund Friendly Society (No. 2)[46]
Walton J accepted that provided that there is no other method of distribution prescribed by the terms of the contract, it should be on the basis of
equality amongst the existing members. Certainly this manner of distribution seems to be more in line with the principle of a contractual relationship which governs members' entitlements and it is likely that the basis of
division adopted by the High Court in *Feeney v. MacManus* will be applied in Ireland in the absence of any express provision requiring an alternative approach.

Quistclose Trusts

Considerable debate has surrounded the manner in which the so called
'Quistclose'[47] trust should be classified. While it may be considered to be
a form of express trust, the secondary trust which will arise in some circumstances can be classified as an automatically resulting trust and for
this reason it is convenient to deal with them at this point. Although there
has been no consideration given to the type of trust recognised in the
Quistclose case yet in this jurisdiction, trusts of this nature are likely to
assume increasing significance in the future and it is proposed to outline
the basic principles which relate to them.

While it is possible to identify significant differences between the concepts of a debt and a trust, they are not always mutually exclusive. As
Bingham J pointed out in *Neste Oy v. Lloyds Bank plc*[48] the existence of a
contractual obligation to pay a debt is not necessarily inconsistent with the
parallel existence of a trust in favour of the creditor. If a lender loans
money to a borrower subject to the conditions that it is to be kept in a
separate bank account and employed for a specified purpose, such an agreement may give rise to a trust.[49] A further question arises when, for whatever reason, the money cannot be used for the purpose laid down. It would
appear that in these circumstances, a primary purpose trust coupled with a
secondary resulting trust for the benefit of the lender will arise.[50] This
reasoning follows from the decision of the House of Lords in *Barclays*

---

46. [1979] 1 WLR 936.
47. Named after *Barclays Bank Ltd v. Quistclose Investments Ltd* [1970] AC 567.
48. [1983] 2 Lloyd's Rep 658, 663.
49. Where the money is used for the authorised purpose, the trust will determine and
    only the relationship of debtor/creditor, which involves personal liability, will re-
    main. However, where the borrower uses the money for an unauthorised purpose, the
    lender will be able to employ a proprietary tracing remedy.
50. See Rickett (1991) 107 LQR 608, 617.

Bank Ltd v. Quistclose Investments Ltd.[51] A company, R. Ltd, which was in serious financial difficulties, borrowed a sum of money from Quistclose for the purpose of paying a dividend to shareholders under an arrangement which spelt out that the money was only to be used for this purpose and which involved this money being paid into a separate bank account in Barclays bank, to whom R. Ltd was indebted. Before the dividend was paid, R. Ltd went into liquidation and the money in the account was claimed by both Quistclose and Barclays. The House of Lords held that the money had been paid into the account on trust for the purpose of paying the dividend and that since this purpose could not now be carried out, it was held on a resulting trust for Quistclose. As Lord Wilberforce said, the loan for the express purpose of ensuring the payment of the dividend gave rise 'to a relationship of a fiduciary character or trust, in favour, as a primary trust, of the creditors, and secondarily, if the primary trust fail[ed], of the third person',[52] namely the institution which had made the loan.

In such cases, it is not necessary that the term 'trust' is used provided the conditions outlined above, namely in relation to segregation of the funds and specifying the purpose for their use, have been complied with. This point was made clear by Lord MacDermott in the Northern Ireland decision of *Re McKeown*.[53] Here the applicant loaned a sum of money to McKeown, in whose favour an arbitration award had been made, so that the latter might pay the necessary fees and costs to enable him to recover the award. The loan was made on the condition that it would only be used for the purpose of paying these fees and costs and that the applicant would be paid out of the award. McKeown was adjudicated bankrupt before he received payment of the award and the applicant sought a declaration that the official assignee held the sum of the loan on trust for him. Lord MacDermott upheld the applicant's claim and did not appear to be deterred by the lack of the type of language usually associated with the creation of trusts. However, the words used must be sufficiently certain in nature and must show a sufficient intention to create a trust.[54]

The principle laid down in *Quistclose* was applied by the English Court of Appeal in *Re EVTR*[55] in a situation where the loan was made in order that a company might purchase new equipment rather than to ensure pay-

---

51. [1970] AC 567.
52. *Ibid.* at 580. This approach has been applied in other jurisdictions, e.g. in Australia (*Re Groom* (1977) 16 ALR 278) and New Zealand (by the High Court in *General Communications Ltd v. DFC New Zealand Ltd* [1990] 3 NZLR 406).
53. [1974] NI 226.
54. *Re Multi Guarantee Co. Ltd* [1987] BCLC 257.
55. [1987] BCLC 646.

ment of a debt. Dillon LJ concluded that: 'On *Quistclose* principles, a resulting trust in favour of the provider of the money arises when money is provided for a particular purpose only, and that purpose fails.'

It is important to point out that in the *Quistclose* case itself, the primary purpose of the trust was no longer capable of being carried out and the question of what the outcome will be where this obligation can still be fulfilled must be considered. Where a trust of this nature is created, a right to compel performance may also be vested in the 'beneficiaries' i.e. those contemplated as the ultimate recipients of the fund. This was the situation which arose in *Re Northern Development Holdings Ltd*[56] where funds were paid into a segregated account for the specific purpose of providing money for the unsecured creditors of a company which was in financial difficulties so that it might continue trading. When the company went into receivership, the question arose of who was entitled to the balance remaining in the account, the banks who had provided the funds, or the company's unsecured creditors. While as Millett[57] points out, Megarry VC might have distinguished the *Quistclose* decision on a number of grounds,[58] he held that the arrangement gave rise to a trust in that mould which might be enforced both by the banks and by the company and its unsecured creditors. This approach was followed by Peter Gibson J in *Carreras Rothmans Ltd v. Freeman Matthews Treasure Ltd,*[59] so considerable importance may attach to the question of whether the ultimate beneficiaries are in a position to enforce the obligation involved in the arrangement. Millett argues that the question of who can enforce a *Quistclose* trust should be governed by ascertaining the intention of the lender and suggests that it is only where the lender's intention is to benefit the party to whom the loan is made and not to benefit the ultimate recipient, except incidentally, that a resulting trust in the lender's favour will arise.

PRESUMED RESULTING TRUSTS

As a general principle, where the ownership of property is transferred to a grantee who gives no consideration, an inference arises that the grantee

---

56. Unreported, Chancery Division, 6 October 1978.
57. (1985) 101 LQR 269.
58. *Ibid.* at 278. He suggested that the distinctions were that the fund in *Northern Developments* was established to enable the company to continue trading which would necessarily involve it in incurring further liabilities and because the creditors were told of the existence, size and purpose of the fund, unlike in *Quistclose* where the contemplated recipients did not even know of its existence.
59. [1984] 3 WLR 1016.

holds the property by way of a resulting trust for the grantor. However, it must be stressed that is only a presumption which can be rebutted by evidence that a contrary result was intended[60] or by the presumption of advancement,[61] which involves the inference being drawn that a gift of property was intended rather than that it should be held on a resulting trust because of the relationship between the parties.[62]

Voluntary Conveyance or Transfer

Where the owner of property makes a voluntary transfer of it to another person, a presumption of a resulting trust arises unless there is sufficient evidence of a contrary intention to rebut the presumption[63] or the presumption of advancement dictates otherwise. The presumption of a resulting trust in these circumstances applies both to voluntary conveyances and transfers of personal property. The law relating to the transfer of freehold land is now affected by statute in England, so it is advisable to examine it separately.

Conveyance of Land

A voluntary conveyance of freehold land 'unto the grantee and his heirs' raised a resulting use to the grantor which was executed by the Statute of Uses, with the result that the legal estate reverted to the grantor. As Wylie states: 'Since the 1634 Statute a voluntary conveyance of land in Ireland without any uses expressed is ineffective and leaves the legal estate in the land in the grantor.'[64] If the gift of land was 'unto and to the use of the grantee and his heirs' this prevented a resulting use arising and the legal estate became effectively vested in the grantee. While there is no unanimity on this question, it is likely that the express reference to the use for the grantee rebuts the presumption that he holds it for the benefit of the grantor.

In England, the Law of Property Act 1925 repealed the Statute of Uses and section 60(3) provides that 'in a voluntary conveyance a resulting

---

60. *McEneaney v. Shevlin* [1912] 1 IR 32 & 278. This is the essence of the distinction between automatically and presumed resulting trusts. As Swadling points out (see 1996) 16 LS 110, 113) 'an automatic resulting trust cannot be rebutted by evidence of an intention to give'.
61. *Hepworth v. Hepworth* (1870) LR 11 Eq 10.
62. Considered *infra* pp. 160-169.
63. Swadling suggests (see (1996) 16 LS 110, 111) that an examination of the historical origins of the resulting trust reveals that '*any* evidence which is inconsistent with the presumption that the transferee is to be a trustee will suffice'.
64. *Irish Land Law* (3rd ed., 1997) p.545.

trust for the grantor shall not be implied merely by reason that the property is not expressed to be conveyed for the use or benefit of the grantee.' The effect of this subsection would appear to be that a voluntary conveyance of land takes effect as expressed unless there is evidence of a contrary intention, although it would still be advisable to make it clear that a gift was intended. Russell LJ has remarked in *Hodgson v. Marks*[65] that it is now a 'debatable question whether on a voluntary transfer of land by A to stranger B there is a presumption of a resulting trust' and it is pointed out in Hanbury and Martin[66] that where it is clear that no gift was intended the section does not prevent the implication of a resulting trust. The main difference between the law in England and in this jurisdiction would seem to be that in England, there will not be a presumption of a resulting trust merely because the transferor fails to state that a conveyance was for the benefit of the transferee, whereas in Ireland in these circumstances the inference is that a resulting trust will arise.

Transfer of Personalty
Where there is a voluntary transfer of personalty, the transferee is presumed to hold this property on a resulting trust for the transferor. This presumption will arise most often where there is a voluntary transfer into the joint names of the transferor and transferee but it may also be raised where it is made solely to the transferee.[67] In *Re Vinogradoff*[68] a testatrix had transferred an £800 war loan into the joint names of herself and her four year old granddaughter but continued to receive the dividends until her death. Farwell J held that after her death, the granddaughter held the loan on a resulting trust for the testatrix's estate. This decision illustrates well that presumed resulting trusts can often arise in circumstances where it is highly questionable whether this result would actually reflect the settlor's real intentions, if he had been given an opportunity to decide on the ultimate destination of the property concerned. The importance of the principle that this presumption is rebuttable, and to this extent only operates where no evidence to the contrary has been adduced, was adverted to by Lord Upjohn in *Vandervell v. IRC*[69] in the following terms:

> Where A transfers, or directs a trustee for him, to transfer the legal estate in property to B otherwise than for valuable consideration it

---

65. [1971] Ch 892, 933. See Sweeney (1979) 14 Ir Jur (ns) 282.
66. *Modern Equity* (15th ed., 1997) at p.244.
67. *Re Howes* (1905) 21 TLR 501; *Re Muller* [1953] NZLR 879.
68. [1935] WN 68.
69. [1967] 2 AC 291, 312.

is a question of the intention of A in making the transfer whether B was to take beneficially or on trust, and if the latter, on what trusts. If, as a matter of construction of the document transferring the legal estate, it is possible to discern A's intentions, that is an end of the matter and no extraneous evidence is admissible to correct and qualify his intentions so ascertained.

But if, as in this case (a common form share transfer) the document is silent, then there is said to arise a resulting trust in favour of A. But this is only a presumption and is easily rebutted.

This point is well illustrated in *Standing v. Bowring*,[70] where the plaintiff widow transferred stock into the joint names of herself and her godson, the defendant, having been warned that if she made the transfer she could not revoke it. It was held that the plaintiff could not claim a re-transfer on equitable grounds because she had not intended to make the defendant a mere trustee except in relation to the dividends payable on the stock. On the contrary, there was ample evidence to suggest that at the time of the transfer she intended to benefit the defendant and the presumption of a resulting trust was therefore rebutted. Cotton LJ stated:

> [T]he rule is well settled that where there is a transfer by a person into his own name jointly with that of a person who is not his child, or his adopted child, then there is *prima facie* a resulting trust for the transferor. But that is a presumption capable of being rebutted by shewing that at the time the transferor intended a benefit to the transferee.[71]

Joint Deposit Accounts[72]

One of the most common situations in which a transfer of property takes place into the joint names of the transferor and transferee is where a joint deposit account is opened. This is usually done in a manner which allows the transferor or depositor alone to retain dominion over the money in the account during his lifetime but which displays the intention that the balance should go to the other party should he survive him. Where such an arrangement is put in place the question arises whether the money which

---

70. (1885) 31 Ch D 282.
71. *Ibid.* at 287.
72. See generally Sheridan (1950-52) 9 NILQ 101; Montrose (1950-52) 9 NILQ 148; Delany (1957) 23 Ir Jur 31; Brady (1990) 12 DULJ (ns) 155 and Miller (1992) 6 Trust Law Int 57.

remains in the account on the depositor's death should be subject to a resulting trust in favour of his estate or whether it can be paid over to the other party. The approach traditionally followed was set out by Gordon J in *Doyle v. Byrne*[73] as follows:

> Where there is a transfer by a person into his own name jointly with that of a person who is not his child or adopted child, of money on deposit receipt there is, *prima facie*, a resulting trust to the transferor.

If this presumption is to be rebutted, the onus lies on the transferee to show that the transferor intended that the beneficial interest should pass to him.[74] The main policy argument against allowing the survivor or transferee to take a beneficial interest in circumstances where he has made no contribution to the monies in the account is that such an interest arguably passes as a form of testamentary disposition which has not complied with the formalities required by the Succession Act 1965. As we have seen above in relation to secret trusts, the courts in this jurisdiction have not always taken such a strict approach to this issue. It is ironic then that in the area of presumed resulting trusts, which are in theory supposed to give effect to a settlor or testator's intentions, the judiciary had until the recent Supreme Court decision in *Lynch v. Burke*[75] adopted a more restrictive approach to this policy question and often succeeded in arriving at a result which might be quite contrary to the transferor's actual intentions.

Although it was held in *Diver v. McCrea*[76] that no resulting trust arose even in circumstances where the depositer had kept control and dominion over the monies in a joint account during his lifetime, the Supreme Court in *Owens v. Greene*[77] declined to follow this approach. In that case, the deceased kept sums of money on deposit in the joint names of himself and a nephew, and of himself and a distant relative. He retained control over these funds during his lifetime but made it clear that he wished the money to go to his co-depositors in the event of his death. The Supreme Court held that these persons, who were volunteers, had failed to rebut the presumption of a resulting trust in favour of the deceased's personal representatives. Kennedy CJ stated the while it was open to the plaintiffs to seek to rebut the presumption of a resulting trust which arose in the cir-

---

73. (1922) 56 ILTR 125, 126-127.
74. *McEneaney v. Shevlin* [1912] 1 IR 32, 36 *per* Ross J; *Owens v. Greene* [1932] IR 225, 237 *per* Kennedy CJ.
75. [1995] 2 IR 159.
76. (1908) 42 ILTR 249.
77. [1932] IR 225.

cumstances this could only be done by establishing that it was the deceased's intention when putting the money in the accounts to give to the plaintiffs 'then and there and by that act, a right, that is to say an immediate present right to take the monies with which he associated their respective names by survivorship'.[78] It would not suffice to show a testamentary intention on the part of the deceased as a disposition of a testamentary nature could, in the opinion of the Chief Justice, only be made by will. Fitzgibbon J came to the same conclusion on the facts:

> In my opinion the plaintiffs have failed to establish any present intention on the part of [the deceased] to part with his property in, and absolute dominion over, the deposited money during his lifetime, and a disposition, to take effect only upon his death, if he should not have previously disposed of the money, cannot be effected except by a declaration of trust, which is admitted not to have been made by him.[79]

The reasoning in *Owens* was applied by Judge Sheridan in the Circuit Court decision of *Daniels v. Dunne*.[80] The deceased opened a joint account in the names of himself and the defendant. Although the words 'payable to either or survivor' appeared in the deposit account book, the customer history card stated that withdrawals were to be signed by the deceased only or his survivor. Judge Sheridan found that the deceased had retained in law total dominion over the money in the account until the time of his death and that *prima facie* the defendant held the monies in the account on a resulting trust in favour of the deceased's estate.

The most interesting recent case in this area is that of *Lynch v. Burke*[81] and both the High Court judgment of O'Hanlon J and that of O'Flaherty J in the Supreme Court include a useful analysis of the law in certain other common law jurisdictions in relation to the ownership of monies remaining in a joint deposit account on the death of the depositer. The Supreme Court decision is particularly noteworthy as it reversed the position taken by the courts in this jurisdiction for over six decades. Before examining the reasoning of the Supreme Court in more detail it is useful to explain how pressure to take such a step built up over the preceding years. In *Lynch* the deceased opened a joint account in the names of herself and the

---

78. *Ibid.* at 237-238.
79. *Ibid.* at 251-252.
80. (1990) 8 ILT 35 (Circuit Court, 2 February 1989).
81. [1990] 1 IR 1 (HC); [1995] 2 IR 159 (SC).

first named defendant, her niece. The latter had travelled from Scotland at
her aunt's request and both signed the necessary documentation for opening the account. All lodgments were made by the deceased and the account deposit book was endorsed payable to the deceased only or survivor.
The deceased bequeathed all her property to the plaintiff and O'Hanlon J
held that a resulting trust arose and that therefore the plaintiff was entitled
to the money remaining in the joint account. However, it is necessary to
examine in more detail precisely how O'Hanlon J arrived at this conclusion. He stated that as a general principle where money is deposited in a
joint account by a person who subsequently dies, there is an equitable
presumption of a resulting trust against the survivor in favour of the estate
of the deceased in respect of the beneficial interest in the monies remaining on deposit at the time of death. On the facts, O'Hanlon J held that the
deceased had intended that the first defendant would be entitled by right
of survivorship to the beneficial interest in this money and the equitable
presumption in favour of the deceased's estate was therefore rebutted. However, he felt obliged on the authority of the *Owens* decision to hold that the
transaction was an invalid gift and an unsuccessful attempt to make a testamentary disposition otherwise than by will. Despite this conclusion there
are definite signs in O'Hanlon J's judgment that he was unhappy with the
reasoning in the earlier Supreme Court decision. As he stated:

> I consider that in the present case I am bound to follow and apply
> [*Owens v. Greene*] but having regard to the fact that it is a decision
> which appears to conflict with the interpretation of this branch of
> the law in so many other common law jurisdictions it might well be
> a case where the Supreme Court would be disposed to review again
> the correctness of that decision, if a suitable opportunity arose for so
> doing.[82]

This statement was quoted with approval by Morris J in *AIB Finance Ltd
v. Sligo County Council,*[83] although once again the result in that case was
similar to that reached in *Owens v. Greene*. The deceased, a priest who
wished to benefit his home town in Co. Sligo, had lodged a sum of money
in a bank account in the joint names of himself and Sligo County Council
with the intention that the money should be used to carry out a specific
project under an urban renewal scheme. The priest died and the question
arose whether his executor or the county council was entitled to the mon-

---

82. *Ibid.* at 13.
83. [1995] 1 ILRM 81.

ies in the account. Although the mandate executed in favour of the bank contained a provision that these monies should be paid to the county council as survivor on the priest's death, there was evidence that the deceased had intended to and had in fact retained control over these funds during his lifetime. Morris J concluded that there was at most an incomplete gift and that the relationship of trustee and beneficiary had not existed as between the deceased and the county council. Therefore he found that a resulting trust in favour of the deceased's executor arose.

In the circumstances it was not necessary for Morris J to decide whether the reasoning in *Owens* was correct as there was insufficient evidence to rebut the presumption of a resulting trust in favour of the deceased's estate. Nevertheless it is interesting that he saw fit to expressly approve of O'Hanlon J's *dicta* in *Lynch* set out above[84] and this could be construed as evidence of the fact that the courts were increasingly dissatisfied with the *Owens* approach which was certainly out of line with the view taken in relation to this question in most other common law jurisdictions.

While some earlier Canadian cases had been decided on the basis of the approach laid down in *Owens*,[85] different reasoning was employed by the Supreme Court of Ontario in *Re Reid*[86] and by the High Court of Australia in *Russell v. Scott*.[87] In the latter case an elderly lady transferred money into an account in the joint names of herself and her nephew. Although Dixon and Evatt JJ found that she did not intend her nephew to benefit during her lifetime, they concluded that 'by placing the money in the joint names, the deceased did then and there and by that act give a present right of survivorship'. The court therefore interpreted her actions as giving the nephew an immediate beneficial interest which however, did not fall into possession until her death and which might be revoked up until that time. This approach, which involved regarding both parties upon the opening of the account as being jointly entitled at common law to a chose in action consisting of their contractual right against the bank which would accrue to the survivor, was a plausible alternative to the reasoning employed in *Owens* and avoided the difficulties inherent in regarding the transaction as a testamentary disposition, namely the need for compliance with the requisite statutory formalities.

O'Hanlon J in *Lynch* certainly seemed to favour this reasoning and

---

84. See *supra* n. 82.
85. *Hill v. Hill* (1904) 8 OLR 710; *Shortill v. Grannan* (1920) 55 DLR 416; *Larondeau v. Laurendeau* [1954] 4 DLR 293.
86. (1921) 50 OLR 595. See also *Re Aylward* [1955] 5 DLR 753.
87. (1936) 55 CLR 440.

Miller[88] suggested that the Supreme Court in *Owens* might not have ruled out reliance on such an approach by speaking in terms of rebutting the presumption of a resulting trust if the plaintiffs had been given 'then and there, a right, that is to say an immediate present right to take the moneys.'

The position in England would appear to be as set out in Halsbury as follows:

> [T]he fact that the transferor retains control during his lifetime over the property transferred into the joint names does not prevent the gift, even where it appears to be of a testamentary nature and not in conformity with the Wills Act 1837, from being an effective and complete gift *inter vivos* from the time of making, so as to vest the legal title to the property in the donee by survivorship on the death of the transferor.[89]

In *Young v. Sealey*,[90] Romer J, although he confessed that the reasoning in *Owens* appealed to him, concluded that the survivor should take free of a resulting trust in these circumstances, an approach which was followed in *Re Figgis*.[91]

So, by the time the Supreme Court was called upon to make a decision in *Lynch*, it was faced with persuasive arguments requiring it to re-examine the judgment of the former Supreme Court in *Owens*. While it could have been argued that the approach favoured in England and Australia and more latterly in Canada seemed to allow the making of so-called 'nuncupative wills' where there was no real justification for such a course of action, such as avoiding fraud, any policy argument against a more flexible approach was not easily reconcilable with the rationale of a resulting trust which might be said to depend on the implied intention of the donor.[92] It was certainly arguable that insistence on strict compliance with statutory provisions designed to prevent fraud was not necessary or even desirable where no danger of fraud would arise in bypassing their requirements, and where such an approach gave effect to a donor's real intentions about the disposition of his property on his death.

Delivering the judgment of the Supreme Court,[93] O'Flaherty J con-

---

88. (1992) 6 Trust Law Int 57, 59.
89. *Laws of England*, 4th edition, Volume 20 paragraph 40. As quoted by O'Hanlon J in *Lynch v. Burke* [1990] 1 IR 1, 13.
90. [1949] Ch 278.
91. [1969] 1 Ch 123.
92. See Brady (1990) 12 DULJ (ns) 155, 164-165.
93. [1995] 2 IR 159. See further Capper (1996) 47 NILQ 281; Breslin [1996] Comm LP 12; O'Doherty (1996) 14 ILT 167 and Mee (1996) 90 GILSI 70.

sidered the legal effect of opening a deposit account in joint names. He said that by her presence and signature, it was manifest that the first named defendant was a party to the contract from the outset and she must be entitled to claim as a party to the contract under its terms. He quoted with approval from the judgment of Dixon and Evatt JJ in *Russell v. Scott* and stated that since historically, the concept of a resulting trust was an invention of equity to defeat the misappropriation of property as a consequence of potentially fraudulent or improvident transactions, it would be paradoxical if the doctrine was allowed to defeat the clear intention of the donor as found by the trial judge. O'Flaherty J pointed out that in *Owens v. Greene,* the Supreme Court had been concerned to emphasize the importance of testamentary dispositions being required to comply with statutory requirements. He commented that if the arrangement in the case before him was not testamentary, which in his view it was not, these statutory requirements had no application. O'Flaherty J also stated that *Owens* had given cause for unease on a number of grounds and concluded that it was wrongly decided and should be overruled. He said that at law the defendant had a legal interest in the monies on deposit either by reason of the contractual relationship of the parties or in the alternative as a gift, which admittedly was not a completed gift in the conventional sense but was one which should be upheld as being a gift subject to a contingency, namely, the donor's death.

One cannot but agree with O'Flaherty J's conclusion that the result arrived at by the Supreme Court will introduce a measure of consistency into this area of the law, and as he stated 'restore.. equity to the high ground which it should properly occupy to ameliorate the harshness of common law rules on occasion rather than itself be an instrument of injustice'.[94] However, as Capper points out, there are conceptual difficulties with both the 'gift theory' and the 'contract theory' and as he comments, 'the underlying doctrinal principles remain very unclear'.[95] Capper is probably correct in suggesting that the 'contract theory' is preferable, and on this basis provided that the survivor has signed the necessary contractual documents and there is sufficient evidence of the donor's intention to rebut the presumption of a resulting trust, the outcome in similar cases in the future should be the same as in *Lynch.* So, while in some respects the manner in which this result was achieved was somewhat convoluted, it can be said with some degree of certainty that the Supreme Court judgment should

---

94. *Ibid.* at 168.
95. (1996) 47 NILQ 281, 293.

have laid to rest the rather paradoxical decision of *Owens v. Greene* once and for all.

Joint Bank Accounts of Husband and Wife

At this point it might be convenient to examine briefly the different principles which apply where joint bank accounts are opened in the names of a husband and wife, although the general principles in this area will be considered in more detail below under the heading 'The Presumption of Advancement'.[96] Dixon and Evatt JJ summarized the position as follows in *Russell v. Scott*:[97]

> [T]here is much authority to the effect that where a joint bank account is opened by husband and wife with the intention that the survivor shall take beneficially the balance at credit on the death of one of them that intention prevails, and, on the death of the husband, the wife takes the balance beneficially, although the deceased husband supplied all the money paid in and during his life the property was used exclusively for his own purposes.

So, the position would seem to be that where money is deposited in an account by one spouse in their joint names the presumption of a resulting trust in these circumstances may be rebutted by the presumption of advancement and *prima facie* the relationship between the parties will usually result in the survivor taking the balance remaining in the account beneficially.[98] So, in *Talbot v. Cody*,[99] where a man lodged sums of money in a number of accounts in the joint names of himself and his wife, it was held that his wife, who survived him, was beneficially entitled to these funds. Similarly, in *Colohan v. Condrin*,[100] it was held by O'Connor MR that the presumption that a wife should be beneficially entitled to monies in an account in these circumstances was not affected by the fact that the name of her husband's brother was also included on the deposit receipt. As he stated: 'It is well settled that if a deposit is made with a bank by a husband of his own money in the names of himself and his wife, there is a presumption that it is intended as an advancement in the event of her surviving her husband.'[101]

---

96. See *infra* pp. 160-169.
97. (1936) 55 CLR 440, 451.
98. *Re Young* (1885) 28 Ch D 705.
99. (1874) IR 10 Eq 138. See also *Re Hood* [1923] 1 IR 109.
100. [1914] 1 IR 89.
101. *Ibid.* at 94-95.

However, such a result should not always be assumed and one question which must be addressed is whether the account was opened merely for the parties' mutual convenience or whether it was intended as a means of making provision for the other spouse.[102] In certain circumstances the presumption that the surviving spouse was to benefit may be rebutted by showing that this was not the intention of the spouse who deposited the money, so in *Marshal v. Crutwell*[103] it was held that a wife was not beneficially entitled to monies remaining in a joint account arranged by her husband solely as a matter of convenience to enable her to sign cheques because of his failing health. Alternatively the depositing spouse may subsequently take some action which will effectively prevent the other from taking a beneficial interest, as in *M'Dowell v. McNeilly,*[104] where a husband endorsed a deposit receipt in favour of a third party who subsequently cashed it.

One related matter which will more usually be of importance where spouses separate is that where a husband and wife open a joint bank account with the intention of pooling their resources, the monies in this account will not be divided in accordance with their respective contributions but rather on an equal basis.[105] However either spouse can acquire sole beneficial ownership of assets purchased with monies from such a joint account.[106]

Purchase in the Name of Another

A variation of the principle considered above in relation to voluntary conveyances or transfers of property applies to such a situation. So, where a person provides the purchase money for property, whether real or personal, which is conveyed or transferred to another person or to himself and the other person jointly, it is presumed that the latter holds the property on a resulting trust for the person who provided the purchase money.[107]

---

102. *Re Figgis* [1969] 1 Ch 123.
103. (1875) LR 20 Eq 328.
104. [1917] 1 IR 117.
105. *Jones v. Maynard* [1951] Ch 572.
106. *Re Bishop* [1965] Ch 450, 456.
107. It was suggested by Pearce (see (1990) 41 NILQ 43) that the Statute of Uses might still have a role to play in this area and that the Act might execute the trust under which a person with no documentary title to property is held to have a beneficial interest by reason of a contribution to its acquisition. However, Mee argues convincingly against such a proposition (see (1996) 47 NILQ 367) pointing out that the doctrine of the purchase money resulting trust was developed by the courts after the enactment of the Statute of Uses and after the statute had been made a dead letter through the creation of trusts by means of a 'use upon a use'.

This principle was set out by Eyre CB in *Dyer v. Dyer*[108] as follows:

> The clear result of all the cases, without a single exception, is, that the trust of a legal estate ... whether taken in the names of the purchasers and others jointly, or in the names of others without that of the purchaser; whether in one name or several, whether jointly or *successive*, results to the man who advances the purchase money.

The operation of this principle is well illustrated by the decision of Pim J in *Re Slattery*.[109] A policy of insurance was taken out by Lawrence Slattery in the name and on the life of his brother. He paid the premiums on the policy and retained it in his possession and at no time did his brother have any interest in the policy or make any claim to it. When his brother died it was held that Lawrence Slattery was entitled to the monies payable on the policy; there was no evidence of any intention to make a gift of the interest under the policy to his brother and a resulting trust therefore arose.

The presumption of a resulting trust applies equally where two or more persons advance purchase money jointly but the property is conveyed or transferred to only one of them, in which case there will be a resulting trust in favour of the other party or parties proportionate to the extent of the contributions made.[110] This principle has proved to be extremely important in resolving disputes relating to the beneficial ownership of family property, which will be considered in detail below.[111]

However, it must be stressed that the presumption which arises in any of the above circumstances is liable to be rebutted, either by evidence that the purchaser intended to benefit the other party or because 'the purchaser is under a species of natural obligation to provide for the nominee',[112] known as the presumption of advancement. These two factors, which may lead to the rebuttal of the presumption of a resulting trust in the case of a voluntary conveyance or transfer, will now be considered.

Rebutting the Presumption of a Resulting Trust

Evidence of an Intention to Benefit
Where evidence establishes that the transferor or purchaser intended to

---

108. (1788) 2 Cox Eq Cas 92, 93.
109. [1917] 2 IR 278. See also *Re Scottish Equitable Life Assurance Society* [1902] 1 Ch 282 which concerned a similar factual situation and in which the *dicta* of Eyre CB in *Dyer* was cited with approval by Joyce J.
110. E.g. *McGillicuddy v. Joy* [1959] IR 189.
111. See *infra* pp. 176-195.
112. *Murless v. Franklin* (1818) 1 Swans 13, 17.

benefit the donee, no resulting trust will arise. This is well illustrated by
Standing v. Bowring,[113] where evidence showed that the plaintiff transferor
had intended to benefit her godson when she transferred stock into his
name. The judgment of the Court of Appeal also makes it clear that the
relevant time for establishing evidence of intention to make a gift is the
time of the transfer and once this is shown, a donor cannot subsequently
change his mind and withdraw this intention. Another illustration of this
principle is provided by the decision of *Fowkes v. Pascoe,*[114] where a Mrs
Baker made various purchases of stock in the joint names of herself and
the son of her daughter-in-law. After her death, the Court of Appeal upheld this individual's claim to be entitled to the stock on the basis that the
purchase had been intended as a gift and the presumption of a resulting
trust had therefore been rebutted. The general principle was well set out
by Mellish LJ:

> [A] man may make an investment of stock in the name of himself
> and some other person, although not a child or wife, yet in such a
> position to him as to make it extremely probable that the investment
> was intended as a gift. In such a case, although the rule of law, if
> there was evidence at all, would compel the Court to say that the
> presumption of trust must prevail, even if the Court might not be-
> lieve that the fact was in accordance with the presumption, yet, if
> there is evidence to rebut the presumption, then, in my opinion, the
> Court must go into the actual facts.[115]

Where Fraud or Illegality Exists
Where a trust is intentionally created for an illegal purpose, a resulting
trust in favour of the settlor or testator will not arise unless there is a failure to carry out this illegal purpose,[116] or where the direct consequence of
allowing the trust to proceed would lead to the perpetration of an unlawful
object, the defeat of a legal prohibition, or the protection of a fraud. This
latter principle was laid down by Lord Selborne in *Ayerst v. Jenkins,*[117]
where a settlor's personal representatives claimed that a resulting trust
arose in circumstances where a settlement had been founded on an illegal
consideration, namely the settlor's marriage to his deceased wife's sister,

---

113. (1885) 31 Ch D 282 considered above in the context of voluntary transfers. See also
     Dewar v. Dewar [1975] 1 WLR 1532 where the presumption was likewise rebutted
     by evidence of an intention to make a gift.
114. (1875) 10 Ch App 343.
115. *Ibid.* at pp. 352-353.
116. *Syme v. Hughes* (1870) LR 9 Eq 475.
117. (1873) LR 16 Eq 275.

which both parties knew to be illegal at that time. Lord Selborne refused the claim on the basis that a settlor was not entitled to relief in this form on the grounds of illegality of his own intention or purpose unless the direct result of the granting of such relief would be 'to effectuate an unlawful object or to defeat a legal prohibition or to protect a fraud.'[118]

It should be noted that where a transferor does not carry out the illegal purpose which was intended at the time of making the transfer, he may adduce evidence of his repudiated intention so as to recover the property.[119] This principle was confirmed by the decision of Hoffman J in *Sekhon v. Alissa*,[120] where a property was conveyed into the sole name of her daughter by a mother with the intention of avoiding liability to capital gains tax when the property was ultimately sold. Hoffman J held that as this unlawful purpose had not yet been carried out, the mother could rely on evidence of this purpose and found that the presumption of a resulting trust in the mother's favour had not been rebutted.[121]

It would appear that even where a transfer of property occurs for an illegal purpose, this will not prevent a resulting trust arising in favour of the transferee where the claim can be made without reliance on this unlawful purpose. This point is illustrated by the recent decision of the House of Lords in *Tinsley v. Milligan*.[122] Two women purchased a house in the plaintiff's sole name but on the understanding that they should be joint beneficial owners of the property in order to assist in the perpetration of a fraud on the Department of Social Security. When the parties quarrelled, the defendant disclosed the fraud to the department and the plaintiff moved out and brought proceedings against the defendant claiming possession and sole ownership of the property. The defendant counter-claimed and sought a declaration that the property was held on trust for the parties in equal shares. The majority of the House of Lords held that a party to an illegality can recover by virtue of a legal or equitable interest in property provided that he can establish his title without relying on his own illegality. In the circumstances it was held that the defendant had established a presumption of a resulting trust by showing that she had contributed to the purchase price of the house and that there was a common understanding between the parties that they owned it jointly. There was no need for her to

---

118. *Ibid.* at 283.
119. Although not where his illegal purpose has merely been frustrated by circumstances beyond his control; *Bigos v. Boustead* [1951] 1 All ER 92.
120. [1989] 2 FLR 94. See Kodilinye [1990] Conv 213.
121. A similar principle now operates in relation to rebutting the presumption of advancement. See *Tribe v. Tribe* [1996] Ch 107.
122. [1994] 1 AC 340.

establish the reason why the house had been conveyed solely into the plaintiff's name and it was held that there was no evidence to rebut the presumption of a resulting trust.

The Presumption of Advancement

The presumption of advancement arises where because of the relationship which exists between the parties, the donor or purchaser is under an obligation recognised in equity to provide for the person to whom the property is given.[123] Just as the presumption of a resulting trust can be rebutted by evidence showing that a gift was intended, so the presumption of advancement can be rebutted by evidence which establishes that the donor did not intend to benefit or make provision for the donee.[124] The manner in which these presumptions operate was summarised by Viscount Simonds in *Shephard v. Cartwright*:[125]

> The law is clear that on the one hand where a man purchases shares and they are registered in the name of a stranger there is a resulting trust in favour of the purchaser; on the other hand, if they are registered in the name of a child or one to whom the purchaser then stood *in loco parentis*, there is no such resulting trust, but a presumption of advancement. Equally it is clear that the presumption [of advancement] may be rebutted but should not . . . give way to slight circumstances.

It should be noted that the presumption of advancement has been regarded in various quarters in more recent times as being an outdated concept which can operate in an anomalous and arbitrary manner and which may be constitutionally suspect. As a result it is fair to say that in circumstances where it has traditionally been held to exist, it has become easier to rebut and where a relationship exists which does not give rise to the presumption on the basis of established principles, evidence which shows that a gift was intended will be readily accepted by a court. However, despite this erosion of traditional principles, it has recently been confirmed by the courts in this jurisdiction that the presumption has the status of an equitable doctrine rather than a mere rule of evidence[126] and must be recognised as

---

123. *Bennet v. Bennet* (1879) 10 Ch D 474, 476 *per* Jessel MR.
124. *Anson v. Anson* [1953] 1 QB 636; *Re Gooch* (1890) 62 LT 384. See further pp.169-175.
125. [1955] AC 431, 445.
126. *Per* Henchy J in *R.F. v. M.F.* [1995] 2 ILRM 572 and *per* O'Sullivan J in *Malone v. McQuaid* High Court 1996 No. 392 Sp, 28 May 1998.

such. Traditionally the presumption of advancement has operated in three types of relationship which will be examined in turn before consideration is given to the question of whether its ambit might be extended further.

Husband and Wife

The presumption of advancement arises where a husband transfers property to his wife or purchases it in her name.[127] However, traditionally where a wife bought property and put it in her husband's name, this did not give rise to the presumption of advancement and instead a resulting trust was presumed.[128] The general principle was set out by Malins VC in *Re Eykyn's Trusts*:[129] 'The law of this Court is perfectly settled that when a husband transfers money or other property into the name of his wife only, then the presumption is, that it is intended as a gift or advancement to the wife absolutely at once. ...' As we have seen above in the context of joint bank accounts, this principle has operated where a husband places money in a bank account in the joint names of himself and his wife.[130] It appears to apply even if the marriage is subsequently dissolved or declared voidable,[131] but not where the marriage is later declared void *ab initio*.[132] The presumption will apply as between engaged couples who subsequently marry,[133] but not to co-habitees.[134]

Lord Diplock in *Pettitt v. Pettitt*[135] expressed his view that the presumption was an anachronistic concept in the following terms:

> It would, in my view, be an abuse of the legal technique for ascertaining or imputing intention to apply to transactions between the post war generation of married couples 'presumptions' which are based upon inferences of fact which an earlier generation of judges drew as the most likely intentions of earlier generations of spouses belonging to the propertied classes of a different social era.

Certainly, in this jurisdiction, in view of the constitutional guarantee of equality, it would seem difficult to justify the continued existence of a

---

127. See e.g. *Irwin v. O'Connell* [1936] IR 44.
128. *Mercier v. Mercier* [1903] 2 Ch 98.
129. (1877) 6 Ch D 115, 118.
130. *Talbot v. Cody* (1874) IR 10 Eq 138; *Colohan v. Condrin* [1914] 1 IR 89, 94.
131. *Dunbar v. Dunbar* [1909] 2 Ch 639.
132. See *Re D'Altroy's Will Trusts* [1968] 1 WLR 120 which establishes this point in another context.
133. *Moate v. Moate* [1948] 2 All ER 486; *Ulrich v. Ulrich* [1968] 1 WLR 180.
134. *Calverley v. Green* (1984) 56 ALR 483.
135. [1970] AC 777, 824.

principle which undoubtedly seems to benefit a wife and not a husband. However, in *W. v. W.,*[136] although it was not strictly necessary for his decision, Finlay P took the opportunity to re-iterate that where a husband makes a contribution to the purchase of property in his wife's sole name, he will be presumed by a rebuttable presumption to have intended to advance his wife unless that presumption is rebutted.

In *J.C. v. J.H.C.*[137] Keane J held that a husband and wife should share the beneficial interest in property, which although conveyed to them both as joint tenants was purchased entirely out of monies provided by the husband. Keane J stated as follows:

> Where property is taken in the joint names of two or more persons, but the purchase money is advanced by one of them alone, the law presumes a resulting trust in favour of the person who advanced the purchase money. This presumption may however be rebutted; and in particular the circumstance of the person into whose name the property is conveyed being the wife of the person advancing the money may be sufficient to rebut the presumption under the doctrine of advancement.[138]

However, Keane J went on to refer to the remarks of Lord Diplock in *Gissing*, which cast doubt on the relevance of the presumption, and he appeared to base his decision on the fact that the evidence 'overwhelmingly' reinforced the presumption of advancement, which he said would arise had there been no other evidence as to the parties' intentions. Therefore, one could argue that Keane J appeared to regard the presumption of advancement as being relevant only where evidence to establish the parties' true intentions was lacking.

One of the most important authorities in the area is the Supreme Court decision of *R.F. v M.F.,*[139] which also concerned a dispute about ownership of property purchased by a husband in the parties' joint names. Henchy J appeared to accept the relevance of the presumption of advancement but went on to hold that it had been clearly rebutted in the circumstances of the case. The evidence established that the wife had refused to live in the house unless it was in their joint names and despite her promise to live there, which Henchy J considered to be an integral part of the arrangement, she had never done so.

---

136. [1981] ILRM 202, 204.
137. High Court 1982 No.4931P (Keane J) 4 August 1982.
138. *Ibid.* at p.3 of the unreported judgment.
139. [1995] 2 ILRM 572.

The most recent decision dealing with the application of the presumption of advancement in this context is that of O'Sullivan J in *Malone v. McQuaid*.[140] The defendant was the liquidator of a company in which the first and second named plaintiffs, a wife and husband respectively, were one-third shareholders. The defendant obtained a judgment against the husband and registered that judgment as a mortgage against the latter's alleged equitable interest in a property, which was not the family home. This house was registered in his wife's name and she was at the time negotiating a sale to a purchaser which subsequently fell through. In considering the plaintiffs' claim for damages against the defendant in relation to the loss of the sale, it became necessary for the court to establish whether the husband had an equitable interest in the house. O'Sullivan J accepted that assuming that the husband had provided some or all of the monies for the purchase of the house, 'whatever about the [husband's] obligation to provide [the house] for the benefit of his wife, he was clearly under an obligation to provide for his children'.[141] Accordingly he considered that he should apply the presumption of advancement unless it had been rebutted on the facts. O'Sullivan J pointed to the fact that there was some evidence that the husband had not intended to confer a beneficial interest on his wife and he had allegedly told a third party that he wanted to put the property in her name so that the tenants would not know that he owned the building. However, O'Sullivan J stated that the evidence which tended to rebut the presumption of advancement was of an indirect nature and he concluded that on the overall balance of the evidence it had not been rebutted and applied to the case before him. He therefore held that the entire beneficial interest in the property was vested in the wife, although he found that the registration of the judgment had not caused the abandonment of the sale and accordingly he refused to award damages against the defendant.

An examination of these decisions would suggest that the courts still tend to proceed on the basis that the presumption of advancement will *prima facie* apply where a husband transfers property to his wife or purchases it in her name. However, as the decision in *R.F. v M.F.* makes clear, the presumption can readily be rebutted by evidence establishing a contrary intention and in practice, it is only likely to directly influence the outcome of a case where there is little or no evidence to show what the parties' intentions in relation to ownership of the property actually were.

---

140. High Court 1996 No. 392 Sp, 28 May 1998.
141. *Ibid.* at p.18.

One further issue which can no longer be ignored is the lack of equality inherent in the principle that the presumption of advancement does not extend to circumstances where a wife purchases property in her husband's name. The point has recently been made by Hogan and Whyte[142] that 'the courts have ... identified a principle of equality of spouses within marriage implicit in Articles 41 and 42 which has sounded the death-knell for a number of common law rules reflecting a dominant role for the husband.' It is submitted that the presumption of advancement, albeit a creature of equity, cannot itself remain immune from constitutional developments over the last decade in this area of equality of spouses within marriage and the traditional principles referred to above must be regarded with a degree of caution.

Father and Child

Similarly, where a father purchases property in the name of his child or transfers it into the child's name, the presumption of advancement will apply. This is illustrated by the decision of *Hepworth v. Hepworth,*[143] where it was held that the voluntary transfer of stock into his son's name by a father operated as an absolute gift to the son. As Malins VC commented: 'The law is not doubtful that if this had been a transfer to a stranger it would have operated as a trust, but if a gift is made in favour of a child the presumption of law is that it is intended as an advancement or provision for the child'.[144] An important authority in this area is the judgment of Sullivan MR in *O'Brien v. Sheil.*[145] There a father lodged securities in a bank in the joint names of himself and his daughter which was held after his death to be an advancement in the daughter's favour, despite evidence which suggested that the father had subsequently intended the securities to be applied to different purposes. Sullivan MR stated that it was 'now settled law that a lodgment by a father in the joint names of himself and his child is as powerful and strong an indication of advancement as a lodgment in the name of the child alone'[146] and stressed that declarations made by the father which were subsequent to the advancement could not constitute evidence to rebut the presumption.[147]

---

142. Kelly, *The Irish Constitution* (3rd ed., 1994) p.713.
143. (1870) LR 11 Eq 10. See also *Crabb v. Crabb* (1834) 1 My & K 511; *Re Roberts* [1946] Ch 1; *B. v. B* (1976) 65 DLR (3d) 460.
144. *Ibid.* at 12.
145. (1873) IR 7 Eq 255.
146. *Ibid.* at 259.
147. See further *infra* pp. 169-175.

There have been conflicting views expressed on the question of the strength of the presumption of advancement in the case of a father/child relationship. It was suggested by Viscount Simonds in *Shepherd v. Cartwright*[148] that it should not 'give way to slight circumstances' and recently by O'Sullivan J in *Malone v. McQuaid*[149] that the presumption in such relationships is stronger than in the case of a husband and wife. However, the views of the Law Lords expressed in *Pettitt v. Pettitt*[150] would suggest that the presumption of advancement is no longer as strong as it was in any context and it has been acknowledged recently by the Court of Appeal in *McGrath v. Wallis*[151] in the context of a father/son relationship that the presumption may be rebutted by 'comparatively slight evidence'.

Persons in Loco Parentis to a Child

The presumption also applies where the donor or purchaser of property stands *in loco parentis* to the person in whose name this property is held or bought.[152] This principle was explained by Jessel MR in *Bennet v. Bennet*[153] in the following terms: 'nothing is better established than this, that as regards a child, a person not the father of the child may put himself in the position of one *in loco parentis*[154] to the child and so incur the obligation to make a provision for the child.' Jessel MR stressed that while the presumption of advancement applies to a father because he is under an obligation to provide for his child by virtue of the relationship between the parties, in the case of someone who stands *in loco parentis*, 'you must prove that he took upon himself the obligation.' This principle has been held to apply, *inter alia*, to the relationship between a father and an illegitimate child,[155] or his stepson.[156] It has been suggested in Hanbury & Martin[157] that the principle that the presumption of advancement did not extend to illegitimate children 'seems unaffected' by the provisions of the English Family Law Reform Act 1987 which to a large extent removed the disadvantages in terms of succession rights which affected the children of unmarried parents. If this is the case, it must be assumed that the provi-

---

148. [1955] AC 431, 445.
149. High Court 1996 No. 392 Sp, 28 May 1998.
150. [1970] AC 777, 815.
151. [1995] 2 FLR 114.
152. *Shepherd v. Cartwright* [1955] AC 431, 445.
153. (1879) 10 Ch D 474, 477.
154. Defined by Jessel MR as 'a person taking upon himself the duty of a father of a child to make provision for that child' (at 477).
155. *Soar v. Foster* (1858) 4 K & J 152.
156. *Re Paradise Motor Co.* [1968] 1 WLR 1125.
157. *Modern Equity* (15th ed.,1997) p.248, n.99.

sions of the Status of Children Act 1987 which effected similar reforms in this jurisdiction have not altered the position in relation to the operation of the presumption. In fact, this should have no practical effect, as such individuals would in all likelihood be deemed to come within the category of persons acting *in loco parentis* and would therefore in any event be affected by the presumption.

Does the Presumption Apply in other Circumstances?

The position in relation to gifts made by a mother to her child is still far from settled. The leading English authority of *Bennet v. Bennet*[158] is based on the reasoning that there is 'no moral legal obligation . . . no obligation according to the rules of equity . . . on a mother to provide for her child'.[159] More recent decisions there have tended to follow this approach[160] although there is also growing academic criticism of what is perceived to be an outdated view on this question.[161]

An analysis of decisions elsewhere in the common law world would suggest that the general trend is towards recognising that the relationship of mother and child does give rise to the presumption of advancement. While the authorities in Canada conflict on this point,[162] the courts in New Zealand[163] and Australia[164] seem to have come down in favour of the proposition that the presumption should apply to such relationships.

The position in this jurisdiction is somewhat unsatisfactory as there

---

158. [1879] 10 Ch D 474. See also *Re De Visme* (1863) 2 De GJ & S 17. However, note that the contrary conclusion was reached in *Sayre v. Hughes* (1868) LR 5 Eq 376.
159. *Per* Jessel MR at 478.
160. See *Sekhon v. Alissa* [1989] 2 FLR 94. However, note that in *Gross v. French* (1976) 238 EG 39 while the Court of Appeal failed to resolve the issue as a result of the finding by the court that even if the presumption of advancement did exist between a mother and daughter, it was rebutted on the facts of the case, the *dicta* of Scarman LJ suggested that the presumption should operate in such cases.
161. See Dowling [1996] Conv 274. Dowling suggests (at p.283) that the presumption should be 'updated to reflect the realities of life towards the beginning of the twenty-first century rather than left as a reminder of attitudes prevailing in the eighteenth'. Enonchong [1993] RLR 78, 84 points out that today's society has embraced the concept of equality of the sexes – he cites the decision of the House of Lords in *Barclays Bank plc v. O'Brien* [1994] 1 AC 180, 188 in support of this proposition - and says that it would be odd for the law to maintain a distinction which rests on a discredited concept.
162. *Re Dagle* (1990) 70 DLR (4th) 201 supports the position that the presumption applies, while *Mehta v. Canada Trust* (1993) 104 DLR (4th) 24 is evidence of the contrary view.
163. See *Re Brownlee* [1990] 3 NZLR 243.
164. *Dullow v. Dullow* (1985) 3 NSWLR 531; *Brown v. Brown* (1993) 31 NSWLR 582 and *Nelson v. Nelson* (1995) 132 ALR 133

have been no recent decisions in this area which might take account of changing perceptions of the parent/child relationship. In *Re Grimes*[165] Johnston J found that the presumption of advancement applied to a gift by a widowed mother to her son, and described the reasoning in *Bennet* as 'singularly unconvincing'. He went on to hold that even if the presumption did not apply, the former's intention to benefit the son in the circumstances of the case was sufficiently strong to rebut any presumption of a resulting trust. However a different conclusion was reached on this question by the Supreme Court in *McCabe v. Ulster Bank Ltd.*[166] The evidence surrounding the circumstances of the gift, which consisted of the lodgment by a widowed mother of sums in a bank account in the names of herself and her three daughters was in the words of Murnaghan J 'very meagre'. After an extensive review of the relevant authorities in the area both in this jurisdiction and in England, Murnaghan J concluded that the application of the presumption of advancement to the relationship between a mother and her child could not be based on any sound principle. He continued:

> I have come to the conclusion that the presumption must be based upon the obligation to make provision which a Court of Equity recognises in the case of a father, or of one who has assumed his obligation in this respect.
>
> In many cases of widowed mothers very slight circumstances may be sufficient to place the widow *in loco parentis*, i.e., of having assumed the father's obligation to provide. In such cases there will be a basis for the presumption, but in a case such as the present, where there are no circumstances to go upon save the mere relationship of mother and child, there is, in my opinion, no ground for an equitable presumption which will rebut a resulting trust.[167]

On the basis of the facts before the court, the Supreme Court concluded that there was insufficient evidence of the mother's intention to confer a benefit on her daughters to rebut the presumption of a resulting trust. On the one hand it is difficult to fault the reasoning of Murnaghan J having regard to the historical origins of the doctrine of advancement and if one were to follow his approach it is certainly true that in the majority of cases 'very slight circumstances' would suffice to establish that a widowed mother

---

165. [1937] IR 470.
166. [1939] IR 1.
167. *Ibid.* at 15.

had assumed the father's traditional obligation to provide for the child. However, it could also be said that the rationale which originally justified the imposition of the presumption as between father and child, namely that the former was under a moral obligation[168] to provide for the latter, is arguably today just as relevant to the position of a mother as to that of a father and it is difficult to justify a principle which continues to result in the drawing of such anomalous and arbitrary distinctions. Equally, if the courts in this jurisdiction were to apply the reasoning employed by the Supreme Court of South Australia in *Callaghan v. Callaghan,*[169] namely that the presumption of advancement is based on the relationship between the parties rather than on any obligation on the part of the transferor, it should make no difference whether the parent is a father or a mother.[170]

Keane[171] is correct in suggesting that it is also difficult to reconcile a reluctance to extend the presumption of advancement to mother/child relationships in the light of the position adopted by the Supreme Court in decisions such as *Re Tilson*[172] which stresses the concept of joint parental responsibility towards children. Finally, it can be said with a fair degree of certainty that even if the courts in this jurisdiction were to continue to draw such a theoretical distinction between the position of a mother and father in applying the presumption of advancement, it is likely that the evidence available to them in any particular case would suffice to ensure that any unjustified presumptions would be rebutted.

As pointed out above, there has been no evidence of a willingness on the part of the judiciary to extend the presumption of advancement to co-habitees, whether of different sexes,[173] or of the same sex.[174]

Finally, it should be noted that in the recent decision of *Fitzpatrick v. Criminal Assets Bureau,*[175] which concerned a dispute about whether a car seized by the first named defendant was in fact the property of an individual or of a company, the High Court refused to contemplate the extension of the presumption of advancement to a relationship of a commercial nature. As Shanley J stated:

---

168. See *Bennet v. Bennet* (1879) 10 Ch D 474.
169. unreported, 5 May 1995.
170. Although the language employed by O'Sullivan J in *Malone v. McQuaid* High Court 1996 No. 392 Sp, 28 May 1998 at p.18 would suggest that the rationale of obligation still subsists.
171. *Equity and the Law of Trusts in the Republic of Ireland* (1988) p.158. See further Kelly, *The Irish Constitution* (3rd ed., 1994, eds. Hogan and Whyte) p.713.
172. [1951] IR 1.
173. *Calverley v. Green* (1984) 155 CLR 242.
174. *Tinsley v. Milligan* [1994] 1 AC 340. See also Thornton [1993] CLJ 394, 395.
175. High Court 1997 No. 426 Sp, 27 February 1998.

I know of no decided case, and none was opened to me, which suggests that the relationships to which the presumption of advancement extend include those of a shareholder and the company in which he owns shares or the relationship between an individual and the company which he manages, controls or operates.[176]

Rebutting the Presumption of Advancement

As noted above, there has been some erosion of judicial confidence in the concept of the presumption of advancement due in part to the rather anomalous results which it may produce and to significant constitutional developments in the area of equality. In circumstances where the presumption has traditionally been held to exist, it has generally become easier to rebut[177] and where a relationship exists which does not give rise to the presumption on the basis of established principles, evidence which shows that a gift was intended will now be more readily accepted by a court. However, in addition to this general development, it is still important to note the circumstances in which the presumption has traditionally been rebutted.

Evidence that no Gift Intended
The presumption of advancement will be rebutted if evidence is adduced to show that no gift was intended by the donor or transferor. As Henchy J stated in *R.F. v. M.F.*:[178]

> If the relevant circumstances show that the paper result achieved by the conveyance conceals the real intention of the husband in entering into the transaction, so that the benefit contended for by the wife was not intended, the court will hold that the presumption of advancement has been rebutted.

In *Anson v. Anson*[179] a husband guaranteed his wife's bank account and was obliged to pay a sum of money to the bank on foot of this guarantee. It was held that the husband could recover this amount from the wife and

---

176. *Ibid.* at 28.
177. *Pettitt v. Pettitt* [1970] AC 777, 824 *per* Lord Diplock (quoted with approval by Keane J in *J.C. v. J.H.C.*, High Court, 1982 No.4931P, 4 August 1982). See also *McGrath v. Wallis* [1995] 2 FLR 114. However, there have also been examples of cases where the presumption has not been held to have been rebutted, see *Malone v. McQuaid* High Court 1996 No. 392 Sp (O'Sullivan J) 28 May 1998.
178. [1995] 2 ILRM 572, 577.
179. [1953] 1 QB 636. See also *Re Salisbury-Jones* [1938] 3 All ER 459.

that there was no presumption of advancement in a transaction of this nature. Pearson J stated that the husband had made it clear to his wife that his intention was not to relieve her of the debt, but to solve the immediate problem in which she found herself. Therefore it would appear that a transaction of this nature cannot be presumed to be an advancement unless the donor makes it clear to the donee at the time of making the guarantee that he does not expect to be reimbursed.

Where the relationship at issue is that of father and child it may be more difficult to identify with any degree of certainty the types of circumstances in which the presumption may be rebutted, particularly where the child is a minor as the father may be more likely to retain some element of control over the property.[180] However, it was held in *Re Gooch*[181] that where a father bought shares in a company purely to enable the son to become a director, the latter handing over the dividends received on these shares, and subsequently the share certificates, that the presumption of advancement had been rebutted. Similarly in *Warren v. Guerney*,[182] where a father arranged for a house to be conveyed into his daughter's name, it was held by the Court of Appeal that the presumption of advancement was rebutted by the fact that the father had retained the title deeds to the property,[183] and by the contemporaneous declarations made by him that it was not his intention that his daughter should be the sole beneficial owner of the house.

Nature of Evidence Admissible to Rebut Presumption
A further important question which must be considered is the type of evidence which will suffice to rebut the presumption of advancement. As Sullivan MR stated in *O'Brien v. Sheil*:[184] 'declarations of the [transferor], subsequent to the advancement, if they are not so connected with it as to be reasonably regarded as contemporaneous, cannot be evidence to rebut the presumption of advancement.' In that case, a memorandum found among a father's papers after his death was not admissible in evidence to rebut

---

180. See e.g. *Grey v. Grey* (1677) 2 Swans 594 where it was held that the fact that a son continued to allow his father receive the rents on a property was insufficient to rebut the presumption of advancement as it was 'an act of reverence and good manners' (at 600).
181. (1890) 62 LT 384.
182. [1944] 2 All ER 472.
183. It would appear that retention of title deeds alone might be insufficient to rebut the presumption.
184. (1873) IR 7 Eq 255. See also the decisions of *Fox v. Fox* (1863) 15 Ir Ch R 89 and *Sidmouth v. Sidmouth* (1840) 2 Beav 447 to which Sullivan MR referred.

the presumption of advancement in favour of his daughter in relation to a transfer of securities into their joint names during the father's lifetime.

The most important authority in this area is the decision of the House of Lords in *Shephard v. Cartwright.*[185] A father arranged for shares in certain private companies to be allotted to his children. He subsequently dealt with the shares, at one point crediting the profits of these dealings to a bank account in the children's names, but later appropriating these funds to his own purposes. After his death, the children succeeded in establishing that the shares registered in their names must be regarded as an advancement which had not been rebutted by their father's conduct. The House of Lords held that the father's conduct after allotting the shares could not go to prove that he had not intended to make an advancement to his children and laid down a number of important general principles in this regard. Viscount Simonds quoted with approval the following passage from *Snell's Equity:*[186]

> The acts and declarations of the parties before or at the time of the purchase, or so immediately after it as to constitute a part of the transaction, are admissible in evidence either for or against the party who did the act or made the declaration. . . . But subsequent declarations are admissible as evidence only against the party who made them, and not in his favour.

These principles would seem to mean that an act or declaration by a donor or transferor at the time of or prior to the transaction may be used by him to rebut the presumption while subsequent acts or declarations cannot be admitted to support his claim but may be used against him by the donee in order to support the application of the presumption. In addition, as pointed out by Oakley,[187] evidence of subsequent acts and declarations by the transferee can be admitted against him in order to enable the transferor to rebut the presumption of advancement. These principles were recently confirmed by the Supreme Court in *R.F. v. M. F.,*[188] where Henchy J stated as follows:

> The presumption of advancement . . . is, of course, rebuttable. For a rebuttal to be made out, it is for the husband to show, by reference to acts or statements before or around the transaction, that a beneficial

---

185. [1955] AC 431.
186. 24th ed., p. 153. Now see 29th ed., 1990, Baker and Langan, p.180.
187. Parker and Mellows, *The Modern Law of Trusts* (7th ed., 1998) p. 248.
188. [1995] 2 ILRM 572, 576-577.

interest was not intended to be conveyed in the circumstances relied on. As to subsequent acts or statements, the authorities show that they are admissible in evidence against the party making them, but not in his or her favour. Thus, subsequent acts or statements on the part of the wife are admissible in evidence to rebut the presumption of advancement.

Unlawful or Fraudulent Conduct

It would appear that the presumption of advancement cannot be rebutted by evidence that the transfer was made for a fraudulent or illegal purpose where this purpose has been wholly or partly carried out.[189] So, where for example, a father transfers land into his son's name with a view to achieving an unlawful purpose or where a husband puts property into his wife's name in order to evade the payment of taxes,[190] the transferor cannot adduce evidence of the improper purpose to rebut the presumption of advancement. In *Chettiar v. Chettiar*[191] a father transferred land into his son's name for an illegal purpose, namely to avoid certain regulations applying to the holding. The Privy Council concluded that the illegal purpose had been carried into effect and held that the father could not rely on evidence of this illegality to rebut the presumption of advancement in order to recover the land. It is not necessary to prove that the transferee was entirely unaware of the illegality in order to prevent the transferor relying on such rebuttal evidence. In *Gascoigne v. Gascoigne*[192] a man conveyed property into his wife's name to protect it from his creditors. It was held that he could not rely on this fact to rebut the presumption of advancement and that the wife could retain the property for her own benefit, notwithstanding the fact that she had been aware of the fraudulent purpose behind the transaction.

This principle has also been applied in Ireland. In *Parkes v. Parkes*[193] the defendant husband wanted to buy land and arranged for it to be con-

---

189. The decision of the English Court of Appeal in *Tribe v. Tribe* [1996] Ch 107 is to the effect that evidence of an illegal purpose can be relied upon where it has not been either wholly or partly carried into effect. This decision is considered in more detail *infra*. See also the *dicta* of Lord Denning MR in *Chettiar v. Chettiar* [1962] AC 294, 302. It should be noted at this point that the High Court of Australia has recently rejected this principle in *Nelson v. Nelson* (1995) 132 ALR 133 also considered below.
190. *Re Emery's Investment Trusts* [1959] Ch 410.
191. [1962] AC 294.
192. [1918] 1 KB 223. Equally, it is not necessary to establish that the transferor acted fraudulently, and his honest motives may even help to strengthen the presumption against him, see *Tinker v. Tinker* [1970] P 136.
193. [1980] ILRM 137.

veyed into his wife's name to obviate the need for Land Commission consent, which would have been necessary had he purchased the property in his own name as he was not an Irish citizen.[194] After the parties divorced, the husband registered an inhibition on the land and the wife instituted proceedings claiming that it had been wrongly registered. The husband counterclaimed that he was entitled to the beneficial ownership in the land and the wife put forward the argument that he should not be able to obtain relief in equity by setting up his own illegality or fraud. Costello J referred to *Gascoigne v. Gascoigne* and to *McEvoy v. Belfast Banking Co.,*[195] where a father had deposited money in his son's name to avoid death duties and stated:

> Just as the courts will not grant relief to a person who has allowed property to be placed in a wife's or son's name for the fraudulent purpose of defeating creditors ... or for the illegal purpose of evading liability to tax so it seems to me that the court should not grant relief to a purchaser who has placed property in his wife's name dishonestly and by means of an illegal act performed for the purpose of evading the law relating to the transfer of land.[196]

Therefore, the husband was not allowed to adduce evidence of his motives for conveying the land into his wife's name and could not rebut the presumption of advancement which operated in her favour.

However, it would appear that different considerations apply where the illegal purpose has not been carried out.[197] As Millett LJ stated in *Tribe v. Tribe*:[198] 'a person who has transferred property for an illegal purpose can nevertheless recover his property provided that he withdraws from the transaction before the illegal purpose has been wholly or partly performed.' This principle was applied specifically to a situation where

---

194. S.45 of the Land Act 1965 required that the consent of the Land Commission be obtained for the purchase of land to which the section applied by anyone other than a qualified person which means, *inter alia*, an Irish citizen.
195. [1934] NI 67.
196. [1980 ILRM 137, 144.
197. Note the comments of Denning MR in *Chettiar v. Chettiar* [1962] AC 294, 302 to the effect that 'if the fraudulent purpose had not been carried out there might well have been room for repentance and the father might have been allowed to have the land retransferred to him'.
198. [1996] Ch 107, 124. This is one of the exceptions to the general rule against relying on one's own illegality and is known as the doctrine of *locus poenitentiae*. See further Enonchong [1996] RLR 78.

the presumption of advancement applied in *Tribe*[199] in which the plaintiff had transferred shares in a family company to his son with a view to defrauding his creditors. The difficulties which might have led to claims being made against him were resolved and when the plaintiff sought to recover the shares from the defendant, the latter resisted his claim. The Court of Appeal held that the plaintiff transferor was entitled to adduce evidence of his intention to rebut the presumption of advancement in favour of his son, which he successfully did. Effectively this decision means that a plaintiff who has made a transfer of property to a person in whose favour the presumption of advancement arises can withdraw from the transaction before the illegal purpose has been wholly or partly carried out[200] and then recover the property by adducing evidence of his illegal purpose in order to rebut the presumption. However, as Millett LJ stressed the transferor 'must have withdrawn from the transaction while his dishonesty still lay in intention only. The law draws the line once the intention has been wholly or partly carried into effect.'[201] Millett LJ was of the view that while the withdrawal from the transaction must have been voluntary, genuine repentance in relation to the illegal purpose was unnecessary; as Nourse LJ stated, all that mattered was that no deception should have been practised on the plaintiff's creditors.

While it is likely that the courts in this jurisdiction will follow *Tribe,* it is less likely given the approach adopted by Costello J in *Parkes* that they would find that a transferor should be able to rely on an illegal purpose which has been carried into effect to rebut the presumption of advancement. However, it must be pointed out that the High Court of Australia has recently reached this conclusion in its decision in *Nelson v. Nelson*[202] which for the sake of completeness we should briefly consider. Mrs Nelson transferred a house into the names of her son and daughter so that she could obtain a subsidy for the purchase of a subsequent house. After the sale of the original house her daughter claimed a half-share in it and argued that Mrs Nelson could not adduce evidence of her illegal purpose in order to rebut the presumption of advancement.[203] However, the High Court of

---

199. See further Enonchong [1996] RLR 78; Pettitt (1996) 10 Trust Law Int 51; Virgo [1996] CLJ 23 and Rose (1996) 112 LQR 386.
200. Virgo argues in [1996] CLJ 23, 25 that in *Tribe* although nobody was actually deceived, the father had done all that he could to carry his illegal purpose into effect and that therefore the court should have concluded that his purpose had been partly carried out.
201. [1996] Ch 107, 133.
202. (1995) 132 ALR 133.
203. The court in Australia had already accepted that the presumption of advancement

Australia accepted evidence to rebut the presumption of advancement even though it was tainted with illegality and despite the fact that the illegal purpose had been carried into effect.[204] In reaching this conclusion the court effectively rejected the distinction drawn by the House of Lords in *Tinsley v. Milligan*[205] between cases where the presumption of advancement did or did not apply. As Lord Browne-Wilkinson had stated 'in cases where the presumption of advancement does not apply, a plaintiff can establish his equitable interest in the property without relying in any way on the underlying illegal transaction'.[206] However in cases where the presumption of advancement applies, in Lord Browne-Wilkinson's view 'in order to establish any claim, the plaintiff has himself to lead evidence sufficient to rebut the presumption of gift and in so doing will normally have to plead, and give evidence of, the underlying illegal purpose.'[207] This so called *Tinsley* distinction has been criticised by academics[208] and while the Court of Appeal in *Tribe* clearly felt bound to follow this reasoning, dissatisfaction at what is a rather arbitrary distinction is evident in particular in the judgment of Nourse LJ.[209] In the view of Dawson J in *Nelson,* the distinction had no basis in principle and was unjustifiable on policy grounds.[210] As he pointed out the distinction could not logically be based on the policy of discouraging the transfer of property for an illegal purpose 'because a knowledgeable transferor would choose a transferee other than one who could take advantage of the presumption of advancement'.[211]

It remains to be seen how the courts in this jurisdiction will react to such issues but in view of the persuasive reasoning employed by the High Court of Australia in *Nelson,* the conclusions arrived at in that case should not be lightly dismissed.

---

applies between a mother and her child. See *Dullow v. Dullow* (1985) 3 NSWLR 531; *Brown v. Brown* (1993) 31 NSWLR 582.

204. Rose has suggested (1996) 112 LQR 386, 388 that the rules which deny relief to a plaintiff who has been involved in illegality 'are crude and capricious, generally fail to discriminate between the relative demerits of the parties and may penalise a plaintiff disproportionately to the relevant wrongdoing'.

205. [1994] 1 AC 340.

206. *Ibid.* at 371-372.

207. *Ibid.* at 372. See also *Tribe v. Tribe* [1996] Ch 107, 117-118 *per* Nourse LJ.

208. See e.g. Enonchong (1995) 111 LQR 133 and [1996] RLR 78.

209. [1996] Ch 107, 118.

210. (1995) 132 CLR 133, 166.

211. *Ibid.* at 164.

Trusts of Family Property

Introduction

The circumstances which give rise to a resulting trust when property is voluntarily conveyed into the name of another or where it is purchased in another party's name have in general terms been outlined above. By far the most common application of these principles today occurs in relation to the question of ownership of the family home when cohabitees, or in certain limited circumstances, spouses separate and it is therefore useful to examine the case law in this area in some detail.

In the context of property disputes between spouses, section 12 of the Married Women's Status Act 1957 provided a statutory framework for the resolution of such issues, although it made no specific provision in relation to the principles to be applied in carrying out this function. Therefore until the enactment of the Judicial Separation and Family Law Reform Act 1989, equitable principles still governed the manner in which property disputes between spouses who separated were resolved. The 1989 Act provided a scheme for making property adjustment orders in the context of separation proceedings[212] and section 20(2) laid down specific factors which the court should have regard to in resolving these disputes.[213] This legislation was largely re-enacted in the Family Law Act 1995 and the provisions of section 16(2) of the latter Act replace those in section 20(2) of the earlier legislation. In addition, the Family Law (Divorce) Act 1996 has introduced a similar scheme for the making of property adjustment orders in the context of divorce proceedings.[214] Where this legislation applies, equitable principles need no longer be relied upon, but there are still a number of situations involving spouses where it may be necessary to determine ownership of matrimonial property in which the legislative provisions referred to above will not be relevant. In the first instance, where spouses decide to separate without obtaining a divorce or judicial separation or where they obtain a civil annulment, equitable principles will still govern any property dispute which may arise. Similarly, where one spouse dies,[215] or is adjudicated bankrupt,[216] or where a judgment

---

212. S. 15.
213. Note that the constitutionality of other provisions of this legislation was challenged unsuccessfully in *F. v. F.* [1994] 2 ILRM 401(HC); *F. v. Ireland* [1995] 2 ILRM 321(SC).
214. S.14 of the Act of 1996 provides that a court may make a property adjustment order on granting a decree of divorce or at any time thereafter and s.20 sets out the factors which the court should have regard to.
215. *E.N. v. R.N.* [1992] 2 IR 116.
216. *Wall v. Wall* High Court 1983 No. 402 Sp (Hamilton P)10 September 1986.

mortgage is registered against the interest of one spouse in a property,[217] it may be necessary to rely on equitable principles to determine the respective beneficial shares of the spouses. So, bearing in mind the limited circumstances in which equity still plays a role in resolving disputes concerning matrimonial property, it is useful to reiterate the following general principles.

Where a husband buys property in his wife's name or transfers it into her name, by virtue of the presumption of advancement, she will be regarded as the sole beneficial owner of the property provided that the presumption is not rebutted.[218] Where it is purchased solely by the husband but conveyed or transferred into their joint names, the same presumption of advancement will usually ensure that the parties are beneficially entitled as joint tenants.[219] However, where it is the wife who purchases the property and it is conveyed either solely into the husband's name or into their joint names, in the absence of rebutting evidence, the husband will hold any interest on a resulting trust for his wife. These situations are now relatively unusual in practice; more commonly the property will be purchased by way of a mortgage and both parties will effectively contribute to the instalments payable. However, it is quite common for a house to be conveyed solely into a husband or male partner's name in these circumstances and a question which has often arisen in practice is whether the wife or female partner should have any beneficial interest in the property arising from her contributions.

There are fundamental difficulties in employing the traditional concept of the purchase money resulting trust in these circumstances. In theory the beneficial interests of the parties should be assessed at the time the purchase occurs but such an assessment could not accommodate the practical reality of the situation which may involve the repayment of a mortgage loan over a period of years subsequent to the actual purchase. The Irish courts have tended to deal with this difficulty by treating mortgage repayments as the practical equivalent to paying the initial purchase price and as capable of giving rise to a proportionate beneficial interest under a resulting trust. An alternative approach suggested by Finlay P in *W. v. W.*[220] is to treat the repayment of the mortgage as the buying back of the equity of redemption from the mortgagee. As he stated:

[T]he fundamental principle underlying this rule of law is that the

---

217. See e.g *Malone v. McQuaid* High Court 1996 No. 392 Sp, 28 May 1998.
218. *Re Ekyn's Trusts* (1877) 6 Ch D 115, 118.
219. *J.C. v. J.H.C.*, High Court 1982 No. 4931P (Keane J) 4 August 1982.
220. [1981] ILRM 202.

redemption of any form of charge or mortgage on property in truth consists of the acquisition by the owner or mortgagor of an estate in the property with which he parted at the time of the creating of the mortgage or charge and ... there can be no distinction in principle between a contribution made to the acquisition of that interest and a contribution made to the acquisition of an interest in property by an original purchase.[221]

As a result it would appear that contributions towards the redemption of any mortgage over property, even if the money was not borrowed to purchase the property, can give rise to a resulting trust.[222] This latter approach in particular could give rise to serious anomalies[223] and the more straightforward former theory, although also technically flawed is less likely to lead to difficulties in its application.

While most of the case law in this jurisdiction in relation to the purchase money resulting trust deals with property disputes between spouses, the rationale behind such a trust as interpreted by the courts is that it should apply because of the circumstances in which the contributions are made, rather than because of the nature of the relationship between the parties. There was no suggestion made in either of the cases decided in this jurisdiction which related to cohabitees[224] that different principles should apply to property disputes between co-habiting partners as opposed to spouses. However, it should be borne in mind that unmarried cohabitees may not necessarily have the same intentions about sharing beneficial ownership in property as married couples and for this reason the presumption of a resulting trust will probably be more readily rebutted in such cases.

Subject to this caveat, it would appear that the principles established in case law are relevant today both in the limited circumstances set out above where matrimonial property issues between spouses are not governed by

---

221. *Ibid.* at 204-205. Quoted with approval by Finlay CJ in *E.N. v. R.N* [1992] 2 IR 116, 123.
222. As Mee points out in [1993] Conv 359, 363 this reasoning leads to the result that where a person contributes to the repayment of a loan he gains a share, not in what was purchased with the help of the loan, but in the security for the loan.
223. See further Mee [1993] Conv 359, 363. He points to the anomaly that a share will be gained by a woman who pays off a mortgage raised to finance improvements to a man's property, whereas a woman who pays for the same improvements in cash will not gain anything. In addition, Mee highlights the difficulty which would arise if someone repaid an unsecured loan which represents a portion of the purchase price of property. He argues that in such cases no trust could arise as there could be no question of buying back an estate transferred to the lender in the absence of any security for the loan.
224. *Power v. Conroy* [1980] ILRM 31 or *McGill v. S.* [1979] IR 238.

legislation and also to property disputes arising between cohabitees. The difficulties which have arisen in relation to deciding in what circumstances a beneficial interest may arise have largely centred on assessing the worth or suitability of the various types of contributions which can be made and it is proposed to examine these in turn.

Direct Contributions

It has been clearly established that where property is purchased in one spouse or partner's name but the other party has made direct contributions to the purchase price or the payment of instalments on the mortgage, the property will be held on a resulting trust to the extent of these contributions. The first signs that the concept of a trust would be employed by the courts to resolve disputes about the ownership of matrimonial property emerged from the decision of Kenny J in *Heavey v. Heavey*,[225] and subsequently in *C. v. C.*[226] he applied this reasoning in relation to the issue of direct contributions. The spouses purchased a family home in the husband's sole name although the wife made a direct contribution to the purchase price by paying the deposit and some of the mortgage repayments. When the parties' marriage broke down, the wife made an application pursuant to section 12 of the Married Women's Status Act 1957 claiming that she was entitled to half the beneficial interest in the house. Kenny J said that the correct approach was to apply the concept of a trust to the legal relationship which arises when a wife makes payments towards the purchase of a house or the repayment of mortgage instalments when the house is in the sole name of the husband. He continued by saying that when this is done, the husband then becomes a trustee for her of a share in the house proportionate to the size of her contributions. In view of the size of her contributions, Kenny J therefore granted a declaration that the wife was in the circumstances entitled to one-half of the beneficial interest in the family home.

The principle enunciated in *C. v. C.* was re-iterated in *W. v. W.*[227] by Finlay P in a comprehensive judgment in which he laid down a number of general principles. These included the following:

> Where a wife contributes by money to the purchase of property by her husband in his sole name in the absence of evidence of some inconsistent agreement or arrangement the court will decide that the

---

225. (1974) 111 ILTR 1.
226. [1976] IR 254.
227. [1981] ILRM 202, 204.

wife is entitled to an equitable interest in that property approximately proportionate to the extent of her contribution as against the total value of the property at the time the contribution was made.

The position was confirmed by Henchy J in the Supreme Court in *McC. v. McC.* [228] and it now seems indisputable in this jurisdiction that contributions of a direct nature towards the acquisition of the family home will give rise to an equitable interest in the absence of evidence of an agreement to the contrary.

The principle of proportionate interest which derives from the rationale behind the resulting trust has continued to be applied in this jurisdiction, and has ensured a degree of consistency in decision-making although perhaps at the expense of an element of flexibility which might be preferable in certain circumstances. In England where there has been uncertainty about whether contributions of a direct nature will give rise to a resulting or a constructive trust based on the parties' common intentions,[229] a claimant's share may be measured by reference to such intentions and may in some circumstances give rise to a share in excess of the actual financial contributions made.[230] Recently in *Midland Bank plc v. Cooke*[231] the Court of Appeal accepted that once a common intention has been established on the basis of direct financial contributions to the purchase price of property, the court should 'undertake a survey of the whole course of dealing between the parties relevant to their ownership and occupation of the property' and 'the scrutiny will not confine itself to the limited range of acts of direct contribution of the sort that are needed to found a beneficial interest in the first place'.[232] So, in this case although the wife's initial direct contribution had been only 6.4% of the value of the property,[233] the

228. [1986] ILRM 1, 2 *per* Henchy J.
229. In *Lloyds Bank plc v. Rosset* [1991] 1 AC 107, 133. Lord Bridge stated that 'direct contributions to the purchase price by the partner who is not the legal owner . . . will readily justify the inference necessary to the creation of a constructive trust.' However, contributions of a direct nature should under traditional principles give rise to a resulting trust. See further O'Hagan (1991) 42 NILQ 238, 244.
230. *Grant v. Edwards* [1968] Ch 638.
231. [1995] 4 All ER 562. See O'Hagan (1997) 60 MLR 420; Gardner (1996) 112 LQR 378; Oldham [1996] CLJ 194; Dixon [1997] Conv 66; Wragg [1996] Fam Law 298 and Pawlowski [1996] Fam Law 484.
232. *Ibid.* at 574. See also *Drake v. Whipp* [1996] 1 FLR 826 where the Court of Appeal found that the female partner's contribution to the actual expenditure on the property amounted to 19.4% of its value, but held on the basis of other contributions which she had made, that she was entitled to a one-third interest in it. See Dunn [1997] Conv 467.
233. A wedding gift of £1,100 was made jointly to Mrs Cooke and her husband by his parents and the court accepted that she had made a direct contribution to the pur-

Court of Appeal took into account 'the whole course of dealing between the parties' and held that she should be entitled to a one-half share in the house. As O'Hagan has commented: 'If a spouse or cohabitee contributes a proportionately trifling sum directly to the purchase of property, the initial direct contribution opens the door for the scrutiny of the relationship'.[234]

However, this difference in the approach adopted in England can in part be explained by the fact that the courts in that jurisdiction have recently taken a much more restrictive view of the circumstances in which contributions, if they are only of an indirect nature, can give rise to a trust.[235] To this extent by allowing contributions of a direct nature to trigger interests proportionately greater than those which might arise in this jurisdiction, the courts could be said to be merely seeking to avoid the hardship which might otherwise be caused by the application of such a stringent approach.

Indirect Contributions

The issue of whether contributions of a indirect nature, either to the purchase price of property or to mortgage repayments can give rise to a beneficial interest is one which was the subject-matter of considerable uncertainty for a time but now appears to be fairly settled in this jurisdiction. A substantial number of cases relating to this issue also came before the High Court in this jurisdiction in the late 1970s and early 1980s. Two distinct approaches can be identified, the first of which is well illustrated by the decision of Keane J in *M.G. v. R.D.*[236] The family home had been purchased in the sole name of the husband and all mortgage repayments and other expenses directly referable to the house were paid for by him. The wife used her salary to purchase items for the house and a car which was used by both parties but Keane J could find no evidence of an agreement of any kind that these outgoings should give her an interest in the property. He concluded that there must be evidence of a common intention that indirect contributions will give the contributor a share in the beneficial interest in property before the court would make such an order and in the circumstances of the case he dismissed the wife's claim. The alternative approach, and the one which has now found favour with the Supreme

---

chase price of the house in the form of her half of the gift. This conclusion was based on the reasoning of the Court of Appeal in *McHardy v. Warren* [1994] 2 FLR 338.

234. (1997) 60 MLR 420, 427.
235. See *infra Lloyds Bank plc v. Rosset* [1991] 1 AC 107.
236. High Court 1980 No. 423 Sp (Keane J) 28 April 1981. See also *McGill v. S.* [1979] IR 283; *S.D. v. B.D.* High Court 1981 No. 194 Sp (Murphy J) 19 March 1982; *B. v. B.* (MacKenzie J) High Court 22 April 1986.

Court, can be found in the judgment of Finlay P in *W. v. W.* [237] referred to above. The wife claimed a beneficial interest in the family farm on the basis of the fact that mortgages to which the property was subject had been paid off partly as a result of her contributions and she had also contributed to the carrying out of improvements to the property. Finlay P directed an issue to be tried as to the extent to which the wife had contributed to the repayment of the mortgages but rejected a claim to an equitable interest relating to improvements to which she had contributed after the property had been acquired. In relation to the issue of indirect contributions, he stated as follows:

> Where a wife contributes ... to a general family fund thus releasing her husband from an obligation which he otherwise would have permitting him to discharge liabilities out of that fund and permitting him to repay mortgage instalments, she will in the absence of proof of an inconsistent agreement or arrangement be entitled to an equitable share in the property which had been mortgaged and in respect of which the mortgage was redeemed approximately proportionate to her contribution to the mortgage repayments, to the value of the mortgage thus redeemed and to the total value of the property at the relevant time. [238]

This approach of assuming that the wife should be entitled to a beneficial interest proportionate to the extent of her indirect contributions 'in the absence of proof of an inconsistent agreement or arrangement' also found favour with the Supreme Court in *McC. v. McC.* [239] The wife had contributed to the cost of a previous family home and when it was sold this amount was put towards the cost of furniture in the new house, the purchase of which was financed by her husband's employers and secured by a mortgage. It was held by the Supreme Court that this original contribution was not applied to the purchase of the second house either directly or indirectly and had not been part of a general family fund. The court upheld the finding made by Costello J that the wife was only entitled to a one-third share in the furniture and fittings. However Henchy J made the following statement about the general effect of indirect contributions:

---

237. [1981] ILRM 202. See also *R. v. R.*, High Court 1978 No.574 Sp (McMahon J) 12 January 1979; *M.B. v. E.B.*, High Court 1979 No. 556 Sp (Barrington J) 19 February 1980; *C.R. v. D.R.* High Court 1983 No. 228 Sp (Lynch J) 5 April 1984, although on the facts the wife's claim did not succeed in this case.
238. *Ibid.* at 204.
239. [1986] ILRM 1.

When the wife's contribution has been indirect (such as contributing, by means of her earnings, to a general family fund) the court will in the absence of any express or implied agreement to the contrary, infer a trust in favour of the wife, on the grounds that she has to that extent relieved the husband of the financial burden he incurred in purchasing the house.[240]

Therefore, it would seem that where one partner makes an indirect contribution of a financial nature to the purchase of the property in a manner which can be identified as relieving the other party of a burden which he would otherwise bear in relation to these outgoings and thereby allows him to pay the mortgage instalments, this contribution will be recognised in the form of a proportionate beneficial interest. This is a sensible and pragmatic approach which recognises the reality that few spouses or partners will think of making any specific agreement about the effect which any contributions which they might make should have.[241] It is interesting to note that the Supreme Court's approach in *McC.* is diametrically opposed to the requirement laid down by Lord McDermott LCJ in the decision of the Northern Ireland Court of Appeal in *McFarlane v. McFarlane,*[242] where the Lord Chief Justice said that if an indirect contribution is to result in a wife acquiring a beneficial interest, it must be the subject of a proper arrangement between the spouses.

The law in England relating to the status of indirect contributions is at present considerably more restrictive than in this jurisdiction and while there are no signs of any move by the judiciary here towards such an approach it is nevertheless interesting to note these developments. A number of decisions of the English Court of Appeal in the late 1960s had established the so-called doctrine of 'family assets' described by Lord Denning MR in the Court of Appeal decision in *Gissing v. Gissing*[243] as follows:

Where a couple, by their joint efforts, get a house and furniture,

---

240. *Ibid.* at 2. This principle was accepted by Finlay CJ in *L. v. L.* [1992] 2 IR 77, 107-108 and by McGuinness J in *C.D. v. W.D.* High Court 1995 No. 587 Sp, 5 February 1997.

241. As was pointed out above, the same principles should in theory apply to contributions made by either spouses or cohabitees. Some consideration should perhaps be given to the fact that there is a greater likelihood in the case of unmarried couples that the legal owner did not intend his or her partner to derive an equitable interest in the property by making contributions to joint expenses. However, the present position would seem to be that unless there is evidence of an express or implied agreement to this effect, such contributions will be taken into account.

242. [1972] NI 59.

243. [1969] 2 Ch 85, 93.

intending it to be a continuing provision for them for their joint lives, it is the *prima facie* inference from their conduct that the house and furniture is a 'family asset' in which each is entitled to an equal share. It matters not in whose name it stands: or who pays for what: or who goes out to work and who stays at home. If they both contribute to it by their joint efforts, the *prima facie* inference is that it belongs to them both equally: at any rate when each makes a financial contribution which is substantial.

However, the validity of the doctrine of family assets was questioned by the House of Lords in *Pettitt v. Pettitt*[244] where it was held that section 17 of the Married Women's Property Act 1882 on which Lord Denning had relied, was purely procedural in nature and that the courts did not derive authority from it to transfer property rights from one spouse to another. So, by the time the *Gissing* case reached the House of Lords, the doctrine of family assets had been effectively discredited. While Lord Reid considered that there was no real reason to distinguish between direct and indirect contributions, a distinction which he felt in many cases would be 'unworkable', it was Lord Diplock's more restrictive attitude based on common intention which found favour with the English Court of Appeal during the 1980s.[245] A more flexible approach was adopted in the decision of *Grant v. Edwards*,[246] where a woman was held to be entitled to half the beneficial interest in a house in circumstances where she had made substantial contributions to the household expenses in excess of what would be expected as normal and without which, it was accepted, the defendant would not have been able to pay the mortgage instalments. The Court of Appeal held that in such circumstances, equity would infer a trust where although a house was purchased in the name of one party, there was a common intention that both parties should have a beneficial interest and the non-proprietary owner had acted to his detriment[247] on that intention.

---

244. [1970] AC 777. Essentially the House of Lords held that the effect of s.17 of the Married Women's Property Act 1882 was purely procedural and the courts had no jurisdiction under it to pass proprietary rights from one spouse to another. See further Brady (1984) 6 DULJ 1, 7-9.
245. See e.g. *Burns v. Burns* [1984] Ch 317 where it was held by the Court of Appeal that since the plaintiff had not made any substantial financial contribution to the acquisition of the house (although she had used her earnings to pay rates, telephone bills etc) the court could not impute a common intention that she should acquire a beneficial interest.
246. [1986] Ch 638.
247. The importance of this element of detriment was stressed by the Court of Appeal in *Midland Bank Ltd v. Dobson* [1986] 1 FLR 171.

However, the more recent decision of the House of Lords in *Lloyds Bank plc v. Rosset*,[248] although founded on the same principles of common intention and detriment was considerably more restrictive and seems to have set a fairly uncompromising precedent in this area. Lord Bridge stated that the fundamental question was whether, independently of any inference which might be drawn from the parties' conduct, there had been at any time prior to the acquisition of the house, or exceptionally at a later date, any agreement, arrangement or understanding reached between them that the property was to be shared beneficially. Such a finding of agreement could only be based on evidence of express discussions between the partners and once this was established it would be necessary for the partner asserting the claim to the beneficial interest to show that he had acted to his or her detriment or significantly altered his position in reliance on the agreement in such a manner as to give rise to a constructive trust.[249]

While such an approach could in limited circumstances result in a more extensive interest being granted to the contributing partner than the application of the straightforward Irish purchase money resulting trust, in the majority of cases it will lead to a more restrictive result and it can be criticised on a number of grounds. It is unclear why Lord Bridge saw fit to depart from the resulting trust approach even in the case of a direct contribution. In doing so, Lord Bridge has seemingly introduced the idea that any common intention must be founded on *express* agreement or representation, requirements which have traditionally not been associated with resulting trusts which are founded rather on the *presumed* intention of the parties. While the elements of common intention and detriment were well-established requirements in the case of indirect contributions, certainly in *Grant v. Edwards* the requisite intention was implied rather than being founded on express agreement. As O'Hagan[250] has commented Lord Bridge's requirement of express agreement or representation appears to flow from a confusion as to the nature of resulting and constructive trusts.

As the consideration of the recent decision of the Court of Appeal in *Midland Bank plc v. Cooke*[251] above shows, some of the rather harsh consequences of the decision of the House of Lords in *Lloyds Bank plc v. Rosset*, have been mitigated by a willingness to take into account contributions of an indirect nature even in the absence of evidence of express

---

248. [1991] 1 AC 107.
249. This approach has been applied in *Hammond v. Mitchell* [1991] 1 WLR 1127. See Lawson [1992] Conv 218.
250. (1991) 42 NILQ 238, 244.
251. [1995] 4 All ER 562. See *supra* 'Direct Contributions'.

agreement to do so provided that an initial direct contribution has been made. As we have seen such a payment may trigger an analysis of 'the whole course of dealing between the parties' and allow a broad range of other forms of contribution to be taken into account. However, as O'Hagan has pointed out where the contribution has only been indirect, no interest will arise under the *Lloyds Bank* principle in the absence of express discussions,[252] and this will be particularly unfair to claimants who have made very large indirect contributions towards the purchase of a property. For this reason, the approach adopted by the courts in this jurisdiction towards contributions of an indirect nature would seem to be fairer and more consistent.

Improvements to Property
In *W. v. W.*[253] Finlay P stated that where a wife expends monies or carries out work in the improvement of a property, the legal ownership of which is vested solely in the husband, she will not be entitled to an equitable share in this property by reason of such contributions unless she can establish that it was specifically agreed or that she was led to believe by virtue of the surrounding circumstances that she would be recompensed for it. In addition, he stressed that any claim which she might have was limited to a right to monetary compensation and could not give rise to any beneficial interest. This *dictum* was applied by Barron J in *N.A.D. v. T.D.*,[254] a case which shows the limitations of the device of the resulting trust in circumstances where a house is built on land which is solely the property of one partner. As Barron J commented:

> The circumstances in which a wife may contribute to the improvement of the property of her husband may obviously vary considerably between minor decorative improvements at the one end of the scale and payment for the erection of an entire dwelling-house at the other end. In each case, since the legal and beneficial ownership of the property was already vested in her husband he is entitled at law in the absence of a contrary agreement to take the entire benefit of the improvement.[255]

So, despite the fact that the plaintiff wife had contributed over one-third of the building costs of the family home, it was held that she was not entitled

252. (1997) 60 MLR 420, 427.
253. [1981] ILRM 202.
254. [1985] ILRM 153.
255. *Ibid.* at 162.

to any beneficial interest in the property. Barron J also considered the possible application of a constructive trust, which he said was a concept 'imposed by operation of law independent of intention in order to satisfy the demands of justice and good conscience'. However, he was satisfied that there was no evidence of any conduct on the husband's part which would make it inequitable for him to deny his wife's claim and he rejected the argument that she should have any share in the beneficial ownership of the family home.

A slightly less restrictive attitude was adopted by Finlay CJ in his recent judgment in *N. v. N.*,[256] in which the plaintiff widow claimed a beneficial interest in the family home on the basis of a number of different grounds. She had for a time applied her earnings from part time work towards family purposes and had managed bedsitter flats into which part of the house had been converted, the rental income from which was applied either directly or indirectly to the mortgage repayments. In addition, she claimed that her work in the home as a wife and mother should give her a beneficial interest, an argument which will be considered in more detail below. On the issue of improvements, Finlay CJ rejected the claim that the wife should have any additional percentage increase by virtue of her indirect contributions to a mortgage which was taken out to finance an extension to the property. He stated as follows:

> I do not consider as I indicated in my decision in *W.v.W.*, that a direct contribution, even in money's worth, to an improvement made on a family home by a wife, where the husband is the sole owner of it, can, in the absence of express or readily implied agreement, constitute a claim for a beneficial interest in it.[257]

So, while Finlay CJ's statement shows that some form of agreement is necessary if any claim in relation to improvements is to succeed, he at least seems to accept that provided evidence of such an agreement can be established, contributions can give rise to a beneficial interest rather than just an entitlement to monetary recompense. However, it must be pointed out that in the majority of cases it is unlikely that the partner claiming a share as a result of his or her contribution to improvements to the property will be able to provide evidence of the necessary agreement.

---

256. [1992] 2 IR 116.
257. *Ibid.* at 122. Contrast the position in England, where s.37 of the Matrimonial Proceedings and Property Act 1970 provides that a substantial contribution in money or money's worth to an improvement to property will give rise to a beneficial interest in the absence of evidence of any agreement to the contrary.

There is one situation according to Mee[258] in which a beneficial share may be obtained by a claimant because of contributions to improvements in the absence of an agreement to this effect. Mee suggests that on the basis of the reasoning of Finlay P in *W. v. W.*[259] and *E.N. v. R.N.,*[260] a partner who pays off a mortgage raised to finance improvements will gain a share but is of the view that an individual who pays for the same improvements in cash will be awarded nothing. This result is indeed anomalous and highlights the fact that consideration should be given to addressing the whole question of how to compensate partners who may contribute, often in a significant way, to improving property in which they have no legal ownership.

One possible solution is to allow claimants to rely on estoppel principles or alternatively to follow the 'common intention' analysis developed by the English courts. As we have seen this approach has led to a degree of inconsistency when applied to direct and indirect contributions but it does open up some possibilities in relation to contributions towards improvements, as the recent decision of the Court of Appeal in *Midland Bank plc v. Cooke*[261] shows. Provided that there is evidence of some initial direct contribution to the purchase price, the whole course of dealing between the parties will be scrutinised and the court will take into account 'all conduct which throws light on the question of what shares were intended'.[262]

Other Forms of Contribution
Traditionally the courts in this jurisdiction refused to accept that a partner's contribution by working in the home, whether in performing housework or looking after children, may give rise to a beneficial interest.[263] As Brady has commented[264] while the attitude of the Supreme Court in *McC.*

---

258. [1993] Conv 359.
259. [1981] ILRM 202.
260. [1992] 2 IR 116.
261. [1995] 4 All ER 562. Dixon points out ([1997] Conv 66, 72) that Mrs Cooke had made substantial improvements to the property and suggested that the case was a suitable one for an application under s.37 of the Matrimonial Proceedings and Property Act 1970 which allows a court to award a beneficial interest consequent upon spousal improvements to property which he says 'could have been used to generate a sizeable interest for Mrs Cooke without any violence to the principles of resulting or constructive trusts'. However, the operation of this section is subject to the existence of an 'express or implied agreement' between the parties and so is as limited in its application as the principle laid down by Finlay CJ in *E.N. v. R.N.* [1992] 2 IR 116.
262. *Ibid.* at 574.
263. *R.K. v. M.K.* High Court 1978 No. 330 Sp (Finlay P) 24 October 1978.
264. (1991) 42 NILQ 1, 9.

v. McC.[265] in relation to the issue of indirect contributions was evidence of a shift towards pragmatism, relief for a wife remained dependent on the fact that she has made a financial contribution to the acquisition of the property and no cognisance was taken of her work in the home. While this rather arbitrary approach was called into question by the High Court, the Supreme Court has to date declined to change its view on this issue.

In *B.L. v. M.L.*[266] the plaintiff wife had made no direct contributions to the purchase of the family home and her only indirect contribution was to its refurbishment and redecoration. However she spent most of her time running the household and looking after the children of the marriage. Barr J said that it was well settled that a wife's work in the home and in the care of her children did not amount to an indirect contribution entitling her to a beneficial interest in the family home, nor did work done by her in the maintenance or enhancement of the property. However, Barr J held that having regard to Article 41.2 of the Constitution, a woman who elected to adopt the full time role of wife and mother and was thus precluded from contributing directly or indirectly in money or money's worth from independent employment towards the acquisition by the husband of the family home and contents, should have her work in the home taken into account. In these circumstances Barr J held that the wife was entitled to a 50% beneficial interest in the family home and its contents.[267] However, in *E.N. v. R.N.*[268] Barron J said that while he could see the equity in recognising the contribution made by the plaintiff towards the welfare of the family, he did not see Article 41.2.2° as supporting her claim to a share in the family home and said that insofar as that provision might be construed as a guarantee of financial reward to mothers working in the home, it seemed to him that it must be construed as 'a guarantee of reward from outside the family rather than a re-distribution within the family'. Clearly in view of the differing opinions expressed by High Court judges on the issue, clarification was necessary and this came in the Supreme Court's decision in *L. v. L.*,[269] in which the appeal of the appellant husband from the decision of Barr J was allowed. Finlay CJ concluded that to allow the courts to extend the circumstances in which a wife may claim a beneficial interest in the family home to a situation where she has made no direct or indirect finan-

---

265. [1986] ILRM 1.
266. [1992] 2 IR 77.
267. This reasoning was approved *obiter* by Barrington J in *A.H. v. P.H.*, High Court 20 June 1989.
268. [1990] 1 IR 383. See also *J.F. v. B.F.* High Court (Lardner J) 21 December 1988.
269. [1992] 2 IR 77. See Jackson (1992) 14 DULJ (ns) 153.

cial contribution to the acquisition of the property or to a family fund but has performed the constitutionally preferred role of wife and mother in the home would not be to develop any principle known to the common law but rather would involve the creation of an entirely new right. As he said unless this result was 'clearly and unambiguously warranted by the Constitution or made necessary for the protection of a specified or unspecified right under it, it must constitute legislation and be a usurpation by the courts of the function of the legislature.'[270]

This reasoning was applied by the Supreme Court in the judgment which it delivered on the same day in *E.N. v. R.N.*[271] One further anomaly to emerge from this decision was that the court recognised that the wife's activities in managing the bedsitter flats were 'different from and not to be identified with the activities of a wife and mother in the home' and that the income earned from this enterprise which went directly or indirectly towards paying off the various mortgages taken out on the property should be recognised as a contribution which would give her a beneficial interest. Taking all the wife's contributions into account, the Supreme Court held that she was entitled to a half-share in the beneficial interest in the house. As Mee[272] has commented it is difficult to justify an approach which differentiates between unpaid work in the home which will not give rise to an interest and unpaid work in the legal owner's business which may be recognised.

Although the provisions of the Judicial Separation and Family Law Reform Act 1989 came into effect too late to assist the plaintiff in *L.* , that Act, the provisions of which were substantially re-enacted in the Family Law Act 1995, became relevant where the courts were called upon to make a property adjustment order on the granting of a decree of judicial separation. Section 16(1) of the Family Law Act 1995 now sets out the matters which the court is required to take into consideration in making certain orders including a property adjustment order and these include, by virtue of section 16(2)(f) 'contributions by looking after the home and caring for the family'. Section 20 of the Family Law (Divorce) Act 1996 sets out the same list of factors which the court is required to take into account in making, *inter alia*, property adjustment orders on the granting of a decree of divorce.

While the legislature has therefore now intervened to provide wider recognition of the contribution made by spouses who remain at home, the

---

270. *Ibid.* at 107.
271. [1992] 2 IR 116.
272. [1993] Conv 359, 366.

position of cohabitees in these circumstances remains far from satisfactory. One further point which is interesting to note about *L. v. L.*, is that McCarthy J referred to Article 41.2 and said that while the issue did not arise in the case before him, he wished to make it clear that he was not to be taken as holding that the guarantees provided for in that article were restricted to mothers of families based on the institution of marriage. However, having regard to the point made by Finlay CJ in *L.* that to follow the approach suggested by Barr J would be to develop existing law beyond the permissible limits of judicial interpretation, it is unlikely that McCarthy J's comment will hold out any hope for a cohabitee seeking to rely on any constitutional guarantee, which in any event would only extend to mothers.

As is the case in relation to contributions towards improvements, the English 'common intention' approach would, if applied in this jurisdiction, afford some protection to claimants and in *Grant v. Edwards*[273] Browne-Wilkinson VC accepted that 'labour or other unquantifiable actions' might be taken into account. However, as we have seen above, it would be necessary that the individual concerned had made some initial direct contribution to trigger the court's analysis of the 'whole course of dealing between the parties' or alternatively that there was evidence of some 'agreement, arrangement or understanding' that the contribution should be recognised as required by the House of Lords in *Lloyds Bank plc v. Rosset.*[274]

Possible Future Developments
As can be seen from the above summary of the manner in which recognition is or is not given to different forms of contribution to the purchase price of family property, the principles applied by both the English and Irish courts each have their respective advantages and disadvantages. The English principles have the advantage of flexibility; there is certainly merit in the 'broad brush' approach adopted by Waite LJ in *Midland Bank plc v. Cooke*[275] which allows consideration of 'all conduct which throws light on the question of what shares are intended'. In addition, it allows for quantification based on common intention rather than on the amount of the actual contributions made. However, the English approach also lacks consistency and can lead to arbitrary and unfair results e.g. where no direct contribution has been made and no evidence of express agreement can

---

273. [1968] Ch 638, 658.
274. [1991] 1 AC 107.
275. [1995] 4 All ER 562, 574.

be found, indirect contributions even on a large scale will be insufficient to establish a beneficial interest. It is difficult to justify the imposition of this stringent initial hurdle of direct contributions or express agreement on which evidence of common intention may be based and it is also fair to say that common intention is 'in most cases no more than a fiction'.[276] In addition, the detrimental reliance requirement set out by the House of Lords in *Lloyds Bank plc v. Rosset*[277] has been labelled problematic and inappropriate in the context of disputes between cohabitees,[278] and confusion about the nature of the trust concept being employed in such cases is not a sound basis for reasoned development of the law in this area in England.

The Irish approach on the other hand has the merit of consistency and comparative simplicity but is is also based on reasoning which is theoretically flawed to varying degrees and the limited nature of the contributions which are recognised as giving rise to a beneficial interest is a serious shortcoming. In particular the lack of recognition given to claimants in relation to contributions to improvements to property in the absence of an express or readily implied agreement that this should be the case and the unequivocal rejection of the principle that work in the home can give rise to a beneficial interest need to be addressed. As further judicial development of the resulting trust concept appears to have been ruled out by the Supreme Court's decision in *L. v. L.*, it would seem that if the rights of cohabitees in this area are to be extended by virtue of equitable principles then the possibility of other approaches must be explored.

The potential of the constructive trust as a device which will provide a remedy where 'justice and good conscience' demand it was explored by Barron J in *Murray v. Murray*.[279] The defendant was the legal owner of premises in respect of which he had paid the initial deposit; the remainder, approximately three-quarters of the price, was paid by way of a mortgage. The plaintiff, his nephew, had lived in the premises with his aunt, the defendant's sister, for many years and it was accepted by Barron J that the defendant had intended to transfer the house to his sister. While she was alive she paid the mortgage instalments and most of the outgoings on the property, although there was evidence that she had at one point refused to accept a transfer of the property. After her death the plaintiff claimed a

---

276. Riniker [1998] Conv 202, 207. Riniker suggests that in *Grant v. Edwards* the 'fictitious "common intention" was, in fact, no more than a reasonable expectation on the part of the party without legal title'. See also Glover and Todd (1996) 16 LS 325.
277. [1991] 1 AC 107.
278. Lawson (1996) 16 LS 218.
279. High Court 1993 No. 8582P (Barron J) 15 December 1995.

declaration that the entire beneficial ownership in the house was vested in his aunt at the date of her death and the defendant claimed the legal and beneficial ownership himself. The plaintiff claimed that the circumstances were such that it would be unconscionable for the defendant to rely on his legal title and he relied on the decision of *Hussey v. Palmer*[280] to support this claim. Barron J stated: 'It is I think quite clear that the law will impose a constructive trust in all circumstances where it would be unjust and unconscionable not to do so.' In his view *Hussey* was authority for the proposition that in certain circumstances where equity so required, 'a debt may be secured by the device of a constructive trust on the property created by the money involved'. He said that in the case before him the equity to create a constructive trust arose from the payment of monies which had resulted in the property being freed from the mortgage and the owner being relieved of other outgoings. Barron J concluded that the aunt was at the date of her death entitled to three-quarters of the beneficial interest in the property so the plaintiff, being her next of kin, was a tenant in common of the premises with the defendant.

It is interesting that the High Court decided not to seek to apply conventional purchase money resulting trust principles to this case. It is probably due to the uncertainty surrounding the issue of whether the plaintiff's aunt made her contributions intending that she would thereby acquire a beneficial interest in the property. Barron J pointed out that there was evidence of the fact that she had not wanted to take a transfer of the legal ownership of the property during her lifetime and so arguably the presumption of a resulting trust might have been rebutted in the circumstances if the court had sought to apply such reasoning. The question remains whether the constructive trust principles employed by the High Court could usefully be employed in other situations involving family property disputes where a claimant will not gain a beneficial share on the basis of traditional purchase money resulting trust principles. Mee suggests not and argues that a 'simple appeal to abstract notions of equity and fairness will not suffice'.[281] Given the almost universally unfavourable reaction to Lord Denning's new model constructive trust, to which Barron J's trust in *Murray* is undoubtedly related, this is probably an accurate prediction and it is likely that our courts will have to look elsewhere for more acceptable solutions.

It is interesting at this point to briefly consider the means employed

---

280. [1972] 1 WLR 1286.
281. (1996) 1 CPLJ 9, 13.

elsewhere in the common law world to resolve family property disputes.[282] The Canadian Supreme Court relies on the concept of 'unjust enrichment' and will intervene where there is 'an enrichment, a corresponding deprivation and the absence of any juristic reason for the enrichment'.[283] The Australian approach is founded on the concept of unconscionability and is based on the principles which might apply where a commercial joint venture is terminated.[284] In New Zealand the reasonable expectation principle is applied and where a claimant has contributed to the acquisition of the legal owner's property a constructive trust will be imposed on the basis that this must have been what the parties intended.[285] However, as Gardner points out, in all these jurisdictions there has tended to be 'a gap between the articulated doctrines and the manner in which cases are actually decided'.[286] He quite correctly asserts that all the doctrines make reference to the parties' own ideas but there is often little such thought on their part and in most jurisdictions 'the circle is squared by fabricating the necessary facts'.

Mee suggests that all these Commonwealth doctrines look to the parties' respective contributions to the wealth generated by the relationship rather than merely focussing on the financial contributions to the purchase of property which is the limitation inherent in the traditional purchase money resulting trust.[287] While none of these doctrines are ideal in themselves, Mee feels that it might be possible to develop a hybrid version which would share their broad scope but which would be founded on a principle consistent with the result which it generates. To achieve this, he suggests resorting to the concept of pooling, which already plays a significant role in the method employed in this jurisdiction, but instead to treat the relationship as an economic partnership and allow the courts to take into account 'all forms of contributions and all forms of wealth accumulation'.[288] However, Mee also identifies difficulties with such an 'ideal' doctrine and on balance would prefer a solution based on legislation. Indeed, given the Supreme Court's attitude in *L. v. L.* further judicial initia-

---

282. See Gardner (1993) 109 LQR 263 for an excellent summary of these approaches.
283. *Pettkus v. Becker* (1980) 117 DLR (3d) 257, 269 *per* Dickson J. See also *Sorochan v. Sorochan* (1986) 29 DLR (4th) 1.
284. See *Muschinski v. Dodds* (1985) 160 CLR 583 and *Baumgartner v. Baumgartner* (1987) 164 CLR 137.
285. *Lankow v. Rose* [1995] 1 NZLR 277. See also *Gillies v. Keogh* [1989] 2 NZLR 327.
286. (1993) 109 LQR 263, 279.
287. *The Property Rights of Cohabitees* (1999).
288. *Ibid.* at 309.

tives in this area are unlikely and it remains to be seen whether the legislature will be prepared to intervene further in what is undoubtedly a particularly problematic area.[289]

---

289. It should be noted that an attempt to pass legislation providing for automatic joint ownership of the matrimonial home proved unsuccessful. The Bill was declared unconstitutional by the Supreme Court in a reference under Article 26 of the Constitution in *Re Article 26 of the Constitution and the Matrimonial Home Bill 1993* [1994] 1 IR 350.

CHAPTER 8

Constructive Trusts

INTRODUCTION

A constructive trust is one which arises by operation of law and which comes into being as a result of conduct and irrespective of the intention of the parties. In general terms it can be described as a trust which is imposed by equity in order to satisfy the demands of 'justice and good conscience'[1] and to prevent a person deriving profit from fraudulent conduct or taking unfair advantage of a fiduciary position. As Deane J stated in the Australian decision of *Muschinski v. Dodds*:[2]

> Viewed in its modern context, the constructive trust can properly be described as a remedial institution which equity imposes regardless of actual or presumed agreement or intention (and subsequently protects) to preclude the retention or assertion of beneficial ownership of property to the extent that such retention or assertion would be contrary to equitable principle.

There can be some degree of overlap between the circumstances in which resulting and constructive trusts can arise[3] and from a practical perspective it makes little difference whether a trust is described as resulting or constructive as there is no requirement that the formalities which apply to express trusts be complied with in either case. In addition, it should be noted that the obligations and liabilities imposed on a constructive trustee will not necessarily be as extensive as those demanded of the trustee of an express trust and may tend to vary according to the nature of the circumstances giving rise to the imposition of the trust. It would appear that a constructive trust will take effect from the moment the conduct giving rise to the need for its imposition occurs,[4] which may be of crucial importance

---

1. *Hussey v. Palmer* [1972] 1 WLR 1286, 1290 *per* Denning MR.
2. (1985) 160 CLR 583, 614.
3. This can be seen primarily in relation to determining the beneficial interest in family property. See *infra* pp. 176-195.
4. *Re Sharpe (a Bankrupt)* [1980] 1 WLR 219, 225 *per* Browne-Wilkinson J.

when the trustee is liable to account for profits derived from the activities which led the court to impose the trust.

It is also important not to consider the imposition of a constructive trust in isolation; it must often be considered in conjunction with the proprietary remedy of tracing trust property or the personal remedy against a trustee for breach of trust. While these remedies may sometimes prove to be equally effective, where the constructive trustee is insolvent, it will be important to pursue a proprietary rather than a personal remedy which will ensure that the beneficiary ranks ahead of the trustee's general creditors.

The constructive trust is often regarded as a residual category which arises where fairness demands it, although it has also been said that equity's intervention in imposing such trusts 'must be based on principle; there must be some relationship between the relief granted and the circumstances which give rise to it.'[5] While it is possible to delimit several categories in which constructive trusts will arise, it would never be possible, nor indeed desirable, to define exhaustively the circumstances which might give rise to the imposition of such a trust. It is therefore proposed to examine the traditionally recognised categories in turn and then to consider where future developments in this area may lead.

ADVANTAGES GAINED BY PERSONS IN FIDUCIARY POSITIONS

General Principles

It is a fundamental principle that a trustee or other party in a fiduciary position will not be permitted to take advantage of his position to make a personal profit and any profit which he makes in this manner will be held by him as a constructive trustee for the benefit of the persons equitably entitled to the property. This principle was laid down as follows by Chatterton VC in *Gabbett v. Lawder*:[6]

> The fundamental position upon which the doctrine of constructive trusts proceeds is, that no person in a fiduciary capacity shall be

---

5. *Lonrho plc v. Fayed (No. 2)* [1992] 1 WLR 1, 9.
6. (1883) 11 LR Ir 295, 299. See also the *dicta* of Chatterton VC in *Kelly v. Kelly* (1874) 8 IR Eq 403, 406: 'It is the great principle that no person in a fiduciary position accepting any benefit attributable in any degree to that fiduciary position can be allowed to enjoy such benefit for himself.' See also *M'Cracken v. M'Clelland* (1877) IR 11 Eq 172, 176 and *Armstrong v. Armstrong* (1880) 7 LR Ir 207, 218 *per* Lord O'Hagan LC.

allowed to retain any advantage gained by him in his character as trustee. His *cestuis que trusts* are entitled to the benefit of any advantage so gained by him, to any addition or accretion to the trust estate which he may have acquired, and to all profit which he may have made by any dealing with it.

While it is not possible to provide an exhaustive definition of the categories of persons who occupy fiduciary positions, generally speaking such individuals can be distinguished from those who are merely bound by contractual obligations by the fact that those in the former category are obliged to act in a completely selfless manner. The most commonly encountered examples of fiduciary relationships are those existing between trustee and beneficiary, agent and principal, director and company and between partners, and although these categories are not closed, some limitations have been imposed on the extension of these obligations.[7] There has been a considerable divergence between the views expressed in England and in other common law jurisdictions on the question of the extent to which fiduciary obligations should be extended to commercial transactions. Certainly in England there are increasing signs of a reluctance on the part of the judiciary to impose the higher standards of conduct demanded by equity on transactions where the parties are dealing with each other at arm's length and on a relatively equal footing.[8] This attitude is exemplified by the following statement of Lord Mustill in the decision of the Privy Council in *Re Goldcorp Exchange*:[9]

> No doubt the fact that one person is placed in a particular position *vis-à-vis* another through the medium of a contract does not necessarily mean that he does not also owe fiduciary duties to that other by virtue of being in that position. But the essence of a fiduciary relationship is that it creates obligations of a different character from those deriving from the contract itself. Their Lordships have not heard in argument any submission which went beyond suggesting that by virtue of being a fiduciary the company was obliged honestly and conscientiously to do what it had by contract promised to do. Many commercial relationships involve just such a reliance by one party on the other, and to introduce the whole new dimension

---

7.   See e.g. *Tito v. Wadell (No. 2)* [1977] Ch 106; *Swain v. The Law Society* [1982] 3 WLR 261.
8.   See the comments of Mason (1994) 110 LQR 238, 245.
9.   [1995] 1 AC 74, 98.

into such relationships which would flow from giving them a fiduciary character would (as it seems to their Lordships) have adverse consequences far exceeding those foreseen by Atkin LJ in *Re Wait* [1927] 1 Ch 606.

While the vast majority of cases decided in this jurisdiction where a constructive trust has been held to arise due to a breach of fiduciary obligations have related to non-commercial transactions, this policy question is bound to have increased significance before our courts in the not too distant future, and it will be interesting to see whether the sentiments expressed by Lord Mustill will find favour here.

The Fiduciary Position of Trustees

The 'fundamental position' referred to above by Chatterton VC in *Gabbett v. Lawder*[10] applies strictly to trustees and personal representatives. These principles also apply to a varying degree to other categories of persons who act in a fiduciary capacity. It is not possible to state with certainty the extent to which these principles will apply to or be treated as irrebuttable presumptions of law in relation to such other categories and it is proposed to examine a number of situations which are relevant primarily, although not exclusively, to persons acting as trustees and personal representatives, and then to consider some of the circumstances in which liability will be imposed in the context of other types of fiduciaries.

Renewal of a Lease

A common situation which will give rise to the creation of a constructive trust is where a trustee of leasehold property obtains a renewal of the lease in his own name. It was circumstances such as these which led to the formulation of the so called rule in *Keech v. Sandford*,[11] which has formed the basis for the rather wider principle enunciated by Chatterton VC in *Gabett v. Lawder* above. In *Keech*, a trustee held a lease of the profits of Romford Market on trust for an infant. Before the expiration of the lease he applied for a renewal for the infant's benefit but the lessor refused to renew on the grounds that the infant could not enter into the usual covenants. The lessor indicated that he would be willing to give the trustee the lease instead and the latter accepted the renewal in his own name. It was held that despite the trustee's attempt to obtain a renewal for the infant's benefit, he must be regarded as holding the lease for the latter's benefit and was obliged to

---

10. (1883) 11 LR Ir 295.
11. (1726) Sel Cas T King 61.

pay over to the infant the profits which he received. King LC stated: 'This
may seem hard, that the trustee is the only person of all mankind who
might not have the lease; but it is very proper that the rule should be strictly
pursued'.[12]

This precise principle was outlined as follows by Chatterton VC in
Gabbett v. Lawder,[13] albeit in an *obiter* capacity:

> It has long been settled by a current of authorities that a trustee of a
> leasehold interest who obtains a renewal of the lease, whether by
> covenant or custom, or by the voluntary act of the reversioner, comes
> within this principle, and that he cannot hold the interest he so ac-
> quired for his own benefit, but as a constructive trustee of it for his
> *cestuis que trusts*.

In this context any advantage or profit derived by a trustee is deemed by
equity to be engrafted onto the property held on trust, a process known in
this jurisdiction as the doctrine of graft. The effect and ambit of this doctrine was discussed by Fitzgibbon LJ in *Dempsey v. Ward*[14] and it is clear
that it extends beyond trustees to other classes of individuals, with executors and administrators being specifically mentioned by Fitzgibbon LJ.
Under the rule in *Keech v. Sandford*, where a trustee or person in a fiduciary position surrenders an old lease with a view to obtaining a new one, he
will be held to be a constructive trustee, and this principle was illustrated
in the context of an executor by the decision of *M'Cracken v. M'Clelland*.[15]
There, an executor surrendered a holding which was subject to the Ulster
Custom while the old tenancy was still in existence and, in compliance
with the custom, was given a new tenancy on his own behalf. Chatterton
VC commented that he was at a loss to understand how the defendant, by
virtue of the position which he occupied as executor of the testator's estate, could contend that he was entitled to retain the benefit of the new
tenancy for himself and concluded that it was held on a constructive trust
for the estate.

The doctrine of graft was also applied in the context of an administrator of an estate in *Kelly v. Kelly*,[16] where a widow and administratrix of her
husband's estate continued in possession of land held on a tenancy from
year to year. The landlord determined the tenancy by serving a notice to

---

12. *Ibid.* at 62.
13. (1883) 11 LR Ir 295, 299.
14. [1899] 1 IR 463, 474-475.
15. (1877) IR 11 Eq 172. See also *Re Egan* [1906] 1 IR 320.
16. (1874) IR 8 Eq 403.

quit and the administratrix did not oppose this and was left in occupation at the same rent. It was held that while her conduct did not amount to fraud, the new tenancy was a graft on the old one and she was regarded as being in occupation of the premises as constructive trustee for the next of kin who would have been entitled to the original tenancy on her husband's death. Similarly, the doctrine of graft has been held to apply to the guardian of an infant,[17] and to a person managing the property of a lunatic.[18] A further category of persons to whom the doctrine applies is that of a limited owner, which is illustrated by the decision of the Irish Court of Appeal in *Re Brady's Estate*.[19] A testator bequeathed leasehold premises on trust to permit his wife to use and enjoy these for the remainder of the term so long as she should live and continue to be his widow. The widow, who did not remarry, remained on in beneficial possession of the lands for a period of three years after the expiry of the lease and then obtained a new lease of the premises in her own name. The Court of Appeal held that the widow was necessarily in the position of a limited owner only, in addition to being the executor and trustee under the will, and that the renewal of the lease which she obtained in her own name must be deemed to be a graft on the former one.

However, the doctrine of graft is not unlimited in its ambit;[20] although it was applied in *Hunter v. Allen*[21] to a case of tenants in common, Barton J commented that *Dempsey v. Ward*[22] was a useful decision in that 'it served to remind us that the frontiers of the doctrine of graft have in this country been reached; and that the doctrine should be cautiously applied.' In *Dempsey* it was held that there was no graft when the widow of a previous tenant of an expired lease obtained a new tenancy on her own behalf on the basis that there was nothing to connect these tenancies. Fitzgibbon LJ commented that 'to have a graft at all, there must still be life in the old stock'[23] and said that he entertained grave doubts about the extent to which the doctrine had been developed in this jurisdiction.

The crucial question which must be addressed in determining whether the new interest will be engrafted onto the old is whether the person obtaining the renewal occupies a fiduciary position. In the case of a trustee, there appears to be an almost irrebuttable presumption of a constructive

---

17. *Quinton v. Frith* (1868) IR 2 Eq 396, 494.
18. *Smyth v. Byrne* [1914] 1 IR 53.
19. [1920] 1 IR 170.
20. *Robinson v. Crosse & Blackwell Ltd* [1940] IR 56.
21. [1907] 1 IR 212.
22. [1899] 1 IR 463.
23. *Ibid.* at 474.

trust arising.[24] This has been confirmed by the following *dicta* of Chatterton VC in *Gabbett v. Lawder*:[25]

> Where a trustee obtains a renewal of a lease this Court will not allow the trustee to say that he did not obtain the additional interest as trustee, or that he procured it from personal favour to himself, or from the refusal of the landlord to deal with the *cestuis que trusts*, or for any similar reason. If his position could have caused or even contributed to his obtaining the advantage, it is in my opinion enough; and the Court will not undertake the difficult and often impossible task of investigating the motives of the parties to the transaction. If it results in either gain to the trustee or loss to the *cestuis que trusts*, the trustee is liable to hand over to them the one or make good the other.

However, as Romer LJ stated in *Re Biss,*[26] 'where the person renewing the lease does not clearly occupy a fiduciary position [he] is only held to be a constructive trustee of the renewed lease if, in respect of the old lease, he occupied some special position and owed, by virtue of that position, a duty towards the other persons interested,' and so the presumption of a constructive trust will ordinarily be rebuttable.[27] Where the person taking the renewal owes neither a fiduciary obligation nor a special duty, clearly no constructive trust will arise.[28]

Cretney[29] has commented that the distinction between persons who act in a fiduciary capacity and those who do not is a difficult one to draw and while he accepts that it may be justifiable to impose a special onus on trustees, asks 'why should it be contrary to public policy to allow a trustee to rebut a presumption of misbehaviour?' He argues that while it is quite acceptable that there should be a high onus on a trustee who has obtained a renewal of a lease which may only be discharged in rare cases, this does not justify the principle that the rule in *Keech v. Sandford* should be an absolute one. However as Oakley[30] has commented, although such a 'stringent penal rule' is difficult to justify in a modern context so far removed

---

24. *Re Biss* [1903] 2 Ch 40, 56 *per* Collins MR.
25. (1883) 11 LR Ir 295, 299-300.
26. [1903] 2 Ch 40, 61.
27. *Chan v. Zacharia* (1984) 154 CLR 178, 201-202 *per* Deane J.
28. *Robinson v. Crosse & Blackwell Ltd* [1940] IR 56, where Johnston J found that the defendants occupied neither a fiduciary nor 'quasi fiduciary' relationship. See also *Savage v. Dunningham* [1974] Ch 181.
29. (1969) 33 Conv 161.
30. Parker and Mellows, *The Modern Law of Trusts* (7th ed., 1998) p.308.

from the conditions which gave rise to it, there is no evidence of any retrenchment from this position by the judiciary either in England or in this jurisdiction.

Purchase of the Reversion in a Lease

The question of whether a trustee or other person in a fiduciary position may purchase the reversion of a lease held in trust or for his principal for his own benefit has been the subject of some controversy. Traditionally, the rule in *Keech v. Sandford* was applied in a limited way to such a purchase and a constructive trust would arise if the lease was renewable by contract or custom or where the trustee obtained the reversion by virtue of his position as lessee.[31] This principle was applied by the Irish Court of Appeal in *Gabbett v. Lawder,*[32] where the administrator of the estate of an intestate held lands under a lease as trustee. The fee simple reversion of these lands became vested in the Church Temporalities Commissioners who were authorized to sell it but before doing so they were bound to offer it to the lessee at a price to be named by them. The reversion was offered to the lessee who declined to buy it on the ground that the price was too high but he then bought it for himself at a public auction for a lower sum. It was held by the Irish Court of Appeal that in the circumstances the administrator became a constructive trustee of the reversion for the persons beneficially entitled to the personal estate of the deceased although he was entitled to the costs incurred by him in purchasing the reversion.

The authorities in England now appear to support the imposition of an absolute prohibition against the purchase of the reversion by a fiduciary irrespective of the circumstances in which this occurs and even where the fiduciary is not a trustee or personal representative. In *Protheroe v. Protheroe*[33] a husband held the leasehold interest in the family home, which it was agreed he held on trust for himself and his wife in equal shares. After the parties had separated, the husband bought the freehold reversion and it was held by the Court of Appeal that the wife was entitled equally with the husband to the proceeds of sale of the freehold. While it has been argued[34] that this conclusion was reached more as a result of a desire on the part of the court to do justice between the spouses rather than by way

---

31. See Cretney (1969) 33 Conv 161, 162. See also Jackson (1968) 31 MLR 707, 709. This seems to have been the position originally accepted in England, see *Randall v. Russell* (1817) 3 Mer 190; *Longton v. Wilsby* (1897) 76 LT 770 and see the *dicta* of Wilberforce J in *Phipps v. Boardman* [1964] 2 All ER 187, 201-202.
32. (1883) 11 LR Ir 295.
33. [1968] 1 All ER 1111.
34. Underhill & Hayton, *Law Relating to Trusts and Trustees* (15th ed., 1995) p.349.

of application of strict principles which should apply as between trustee and beneficiary, Lord Denning MR made the following general statement: 'There is a long established rule of equity from *Keech v. Sandford* downwards that if a trustee, who owns the leasehold, gets in the freehold, that freehold belongs to the trust and he cannot take the property for himself.'[35] This principle was followed without reference to the earlier authorities in this area in *Thompson's Trustee v. Heaton,*[36] where Pennycuick VC described Lord Denning's *dicta* as 'an application of the broad principle that a trustee must not make a profit out of the trust estate'.[37]

It is unlikely that the courts in this jurisdiction will take quite such a restrictive view of this position where a fiduciary purchases the reversion on a lease and it is probable that a trust will only arise in the circumstances outlined by Chatterton VC in *Gabbett v. Lawder* or where the fiduciary has clearly taken advantage of his position as lessee to obtain this benefit. However, having regard to the tenor of the authorities in the area, the onus will undoubtedly lie on the fiduciary to establish that he has not acted improperly, particularly where he occupies the position of trustee.

Competition with Trust Business

As we have seen above, a fundamental principle exists which prevents a trustee or other party in a fiduciary position from taking advantage of his position to make a personal profit and he will be required to hold any profit which he makes in this manner as a constructive trustee for the benefit of the persons equitably entitled to the property. In addition, a trustee must not place himself in a situation where his duty to the trust and his own personal interest may conflict,[38] in circumstances where he is likely to derive a profit by virtue of his fiduciary position. One situation which will obviously give rise to concern is where a trustee derives profits from a business which can be said to be in competition with any business carried on by the trust and this question was considered in detail by Chatterton VC in *Moore v. McGlynn.*[39] The testator who was a shopkeeper and postmaster bequeathed all his property to his brother and son to be held on

---

35. *Ibid.* at 1112.
36. [1974] 1 WLR 605.
37. *Ibid.* at 612. Jackson has criticised this decision on the grounds that in view of the categorisation laid down by Collins MR in *Re Biss* [1903] 2 Ch 40 of the types of relationships which will give rise to an irrebuttable presumption of a constructive trust arising, there should be at most a rebuttable presumption of a trust where a partner as opposed to a trustee obtains the reversion on a partnership lease. See (1975) 38 MLR 226.
38. *Re Jarvis* [1958] 1 WLR 815, 819 *per* Upjohn J.
39. [1894] 1 IR 74.

trust and managed by them for the benefit of his wife and children, and he directed that his brother should be entitled to a salary for managing the business. The brother was appointed postmaster and carried on this role in the same premises for a number of years. Subsequently, he set up his own business in the same town and opened the post office there. The question which had to be determined by the court was whether a trust could be imposed for the benefit of the testator's estate in relation to the new premises and business carried on by the testator's brother. Chatterton VC rejected this argument in the following terms: 'I am not prepared to hold that a trustee is guilty of a breach of trust in setting up for himself in a similar line of business in the neighbourhood, provided that he does not resort to deception, or solicitation of custom from persons dealing at the old shop'. However, he continued by saying:

> It is plain that the setting up a shop in a small town to a certain extent in rivalry with another must tend more or less to injure the business of any similar shop in the locality, and I think there would be an inconsistency between the duties of the defendant …as trustee and manager of the testator's business, and the necessary personal interest which he must take in his own. … I am of opinion that his new position disqualifies him from remaining any longer a trustee, and it would have been better for him to have procured his removal from the trusteeship before setting up for himself. He should not be continued in a position where his duties and his self interest may conflict.[40]

This rather lenient approach has met with some criticism and can be contrasted with the stricter view taken by Clauson J in *Re Thomson*,[41] where an injunction was granted restraining a trustee from carrying on a yacht brokerage business in the same town as that in which a similar business had been managed by him and his co-trustees on behalf of the trust. Clauson J said that having regard to the special nature of the business which he was pursuing, the defendant trustee would have been entering into engagements which would or might conflict with the interests of the beneficiaries as he would be obtaining commission for himself which might otherwise have been obtained on the beneficiaries' behalf. It can be argued that the decision in *Thomson* was influenced by the extremely specialized nature of the business in question, and Goff and Jones have commented that it is

---

40. *Ibid.* at 89-90.
41. [1930] 1 Ch 203.

doubtful whether there is an absolute rule against a trustee or executor carrying on a business in competition with his beneficiary.[42] Certainly it would seem unduly restrictive to impose a constructive trust where a trustee continues to carry on an existing business in competition with one to which he is subsequently appointed trustee. However, it is also doubtful whether it should be necessary to establish a motive of 'deception, or solicitation of custom' in order for a constructive trust to arise and it is arguable that the approach of Chatterton VC in *Moore* was unduly lenient and might not be followed.

Other Types of Fiduciary Relationships

Introduction
As Lord Herschell stated in *Bray v. Ford:*[43] 'It is an inflexible rule of a Court of Equity that a person in a fiduciary position ... is not, unless otherwise expressly provided, entitled to make a profit; he is not allowed to put himself in a position where his interest and duty conflict.' The rationale behind the imposition of a constructive trust in such circumstances was well summarised recently by McLachlin J delivering the judgment of the majority of the Supreme Court of Canada in *Soulos v. Korkontzilas*[44] in the following terms:

> The constructive trust imposed for breach of fiduciary relationship thus serves not only to do the justice between the parties that good conscience requires, but to hold fiduciaries and people in positions of trust to the high standards of trust and probity that commercial and other social institutions require if they are to function effectively.

Clearly where a fiduciary has been unjustly enriched at his principal's expense, the imposition of liability is fully justified. However, where the fiduciary has acted in an honest manner and the principal has not suffered any loss as a result of the former's conduct, the question of whether the fiduciary should be liable to account for any profit made is in principle less straightforward. The authorities would suggest that unjust enrichment is not a prerequisite for the imposition of liability and that a fiduciary will

---

42. *The Law of Restitution* (5th ed., 1998) p. 727.
43. [1896] AC 44, 51. Quoted with approval by Lindsay J in *Re Drexel Burnham Lambert UK Pension Plan* [1995] 1 WLR 32, 37. See also *Swain v. The Law Society* [1982] 1 WLR 17, 37 *per* Oliver J.
44. (1997) 147 DLR (4th) 214, 227.

be liable unless he acts with the knowledge and consent of his principal.[45] The extent of the rather restrictive approach taken by the courts in this area is well summarised by Jones:[46]

> Once a fiduciary is shown to be in breach of his duty of loyalty he must disgorge any benefit gained even though he acted honestly and in his principal's best interests, even though his principal could not otherwise have obtained the benefit, and even though the benefit was obtained through the use of the fiduciary's own assets and in consequence of his personal skill and judgment.

A number of academic commentators have questioned the fairness of such a rigid application of the principle in *Keech v. Sandford*, which Finn[47] has stated is applied 'in an arbitrary and technical fashion irrespective of any actual conflict of duty and interest, or of any actual misuse of a position of trust.' Similarly, Lowry[48] has questioned the correctness of applying a 'uniform set of inflexible rules to govern all fiduciaries irrespective of the particular circumstances in which they are operating', but the fact remains that the courts seem intent on continuing to apply the established principles in what may appear a rather arbitrary manner.[49]

Another question which must also be addressed is whether the opportunity for profit actually derived from the fiduciary relationship. In order to found liability it will be necessary to establish a connection between the fiduciary position and the profit made. Another important issue is the nature of the liability which should be imposed; the proprietary remedy of a constructive trust may have far-reaching consequences for third parties particularly where the fiduciary has insufficient funds to meet his creditors' demands and while there is no sign of an acceptance of such an approach by the judiciary in this area, it is possible that personal liability to account for any profits made might be a preferable form of remedy where a fiduciary has acted honestly and has not been unjustly enriched at his

---

45. This view is supported by the conclusion reached by the majority of the Supreme Court of Canada in *Soulos v. Korkontzilas* (1997) 147 DLR (4th) 214.
46. (1968) 84 LQR 472, 474.
47. *Fiduciary Obligations* (1977) p.261.
48. (1994) 45 NILQ 1, 2. Note also the comments of the English Law Commission in Consultation Paper No. 124 (1992) paragraph 2.4.2.
49. Although note the slightly more flexible approach adopted by Lindsay J in *Re Drexel Burnham Lambert UK Pension Plan* [1995] 1 WLR 32 where he held that the court had jurisdiction to give directions in relation to the winding up of a pension proposed by trustees who were themselves beneficiaries, notwithstanding this conflict between duty and interest.

principal's expense. Finally it should be borne in mind that 'there is more than one category of fiduciary relationship and the different categories possess different characteristics and attract different kinds of fiduciary obligation'.[50] Subject to this caveat, it is now proposed to examine some of the general principles which may apply in more detail, both in relation to the circumstances in which liability may be imposed and with reference to some specific types of fiduciary relationships.

The Liability of a Fiduciary to Account for Secret Commissions and Bribes
As a general principle, a fiduciary may not accept secret commissions or bribes arising out of a transaction in which he is acting on behalf of a principal without the knowledge and consent of his principal. An examination of the authorities in this area shows that the boundaries of the types of relationships which can be categorised as fiduciary are not clear and that such a classification may to an extent depend on the remedy which a court feels is justified in the circumstances of a case. For the purposes of imposing liability to account for any secret profits or commissions received, the interpretation placed on the term 'fiduciary' has always been a fairly liberal one. This is illustrated by the decision in *Reading v. Attorney-General*,[51] where a British Army sergeant was held to be liable to account to the Crown in relation to monies which he received for assisting in the smuggling of goods on the grounds that he had used his uniform and the privileges which attached to it to carry out these activities.

Traditionally, where a fiduciary receives a secret commission as a result of his position, he was liable as a constructive trustee of these monies. In *Williams v. Barton*[52] a trustee was employed by a stockbroking firm on terms which entitled him to half the commission earned by the firm on business introduced by him. His recommendation that the firm be used to value trust securities was followed and he was held liable to account to the trust as a constructive trustee in respect of the commission which he earned from this business. However, it was generally accepted on the authority of the decision of *Lister & Co. v. Stubbs*[53] that where a fiduciary received a bribe from a third party, although he was liable to account, he was not

---

50. *Per* Woolf MR in *Attorney General v. Blake* [1998] 1 All ER 833, 842. As Lord Browne-Wilkinson commented in *Henderson v. Merrett Syndicates Ltd* [1995] 2 AC 145, 206: 'the phrase "fiduciary duties" is a dangerous one, giving rise to a mistaken assumption that all fiduciaries owe the same duties in all circumstances'.
51. [1951] AC 507. See also *Attorney-General v. Goddard* (1929) 98 LJ KB 743.
52. [1927] 2 Ch 9.
53. (1890) 45 Ch D 1. Although note that there has been a certain amount of confusion about the precise *ratio* of the case, see Jacobs, *Law of Trusts in Australia* (5th ed.,

regarded as a constructive trustee of this sum.[54] Attempts were made to justify this position on the grounds that the use of the fiduciary position to exact a bribe in these circumstances did not deprive the beneficiary or principal of property which belonged or ought to have belonged to him.[55] The imposition of a personal as opposed to a proprietary remedy has important practical consequences; namely that the funds cannot be traced into property into which they might be converted and the beneficiary or principal cannot recover any profit made through the use of the money or acquire any preferential rights should the fiduciary become bankrupt. The rather anomalous result that a person who obtained a bribe might be merely obliged to account for its value, whereas a fiduciary who had earned a commission in good faith might be held to be a constructive trustee of this sum, was frequently criticised and it has been suggested that the cases of *Williams* and *Lister* should have been decided in the same way.[56] One view was that the imposition of a proprietary remedy should be confined to situations where a beneficiary has been deprived of property which he would otherwise have obtained. However, the alternative argument is that a constructive trust should have been imposed in both sets of circumstances on the grounds that a fiduciary should not be allowed to derive *any* advantage from acting in a manner contrary to his fiduciary obligations or from placing himself in a situation where his duties and personal interests might conflict.

While the questions have yet to be addressed by the courts in this jurisdiction, a recent decision of the Privy Council in *Attorney-General for Hong Kong v. Reid*[57] has gone some way towards resolving many of the anomalies which have developed in this area. While employed by the legal service of the government of Hong Kong in various capacities, ultimately as acting Director of Public Prosecutions, the first named respondent accepted bribes in breach of his fiduciary duty. He pleaded guilty to a number of bribery offences and was sentenced to eight years' imprisonment and ordered to pay a sum equivalent to the value of his assets which could only have been derived from bribes. These sums were not paid over and the Attorney-General for Hong Kong lodged caveats in New Zealand

---

1986, Meagher and Gummow) pp. 297-299 and Cope, *Constructive Trusts* (1992) pp.263-264.

54. See also *Metropolitan Bank v. Heiron* (1880) 5 Ex D 319.

55. Note that Millett has commented that the decision in *Lister* could not be supported 'as matter of policy, principle or authority' [1993] RLR 7, 29.

56. See Parker & Mellows, *The Modern Law of Trusts* (7th ed., 1998, Oakley) p.294; Millett [1993] RLR 7 and Oakley [1994] CLJ 31.

57. [1994] 1 AC 324. See also Oakley [1995] CLJ 377.

against the titles to properties in that jurisdiction which it was alleged had been purchased with monies received as bribes. The application of the Attorney-General for Hong Kong to renew the caveats was refused by the Court of Appeal of New Zealand but was allowed on appeal by the Privy Council. It was held that when a bribe is accepted by a fiduciary in breach of his duty, he holds that bribe on a constructive trust for the person to whom that duty is owed and to the extent to which they represented bribes received by the first respondent, the New Zealand properties were held in trust for the Crown. As Lord Templeman stated:

> The rule must be that property which a trustee obtains by use of knowledge acquired as trustee becomes trust property. The rule must, *a fortiori*, apply to a bribe accepted by a trustee for a guilty criminal purpose which injures the *cestui que trust*. The trustee is only one example of a fiduciary and the same rule applies to all other fiduciaries who accept bribes.[58]

Lord Templeman added that if the property representing the bribe decreases in value the fiduciary must pay the difference between that value and the initial amount of the bribe. If the property increases in value, the fiduciary is not entitled to any surplus in excess of the initial value of the bribe because he is not allowed by any means to make a profit out of a breach of duty. The decision of *Lister & Co. v. Stubbs* was rejected as being inconsistent with the principle that a fiduciary should not benefit from his own breach of duty and that he should account for the bribe as soon as he receives it.[59] Lord Templeman therefore concluded that: 'From these principles it would appear to follow that the bribe and the property from time to time representing the bribe are held on a constructive trust for the person injured.'[60]

This decision has been welcomed as it resolves the rather arbitrary inconsistency between the remedies imposed in circumstances where a fiduciary received a bribe and earned a commission.[61] However, while it may be reasonable that a fiduciary should not profit from a breach of duty

---

58. *Ibid.* at 332.
59. In *Attorney General v. Blake* [1996] 3 WLR 741, 750 Sir Richard Scott VC suggested that he would still be bound to follow *Lister & Co. v. Stubbs* but said that he was persuaded by the reasoning of Lord Templeman in *Reid* that *Lister* ought no longer to be regarded as good law. No reference to this point was made in the judgment of the Court of Appeal [1998] 1 All ER 833.
60. *Ibid.* at 336.
61. Oakley [1994] CLJ 31.

even if this means that the principal receives a windfall, it has been argued by Jones[62] that it is not so obvious that a windfall is justified where the contest is between creditors who have given value and a principal who has not. There is certainly merit in the argument that in circumstances where a recipient of a bribe is insolvent the imposition of a more limited form of remedy, such as a claim merely to secure the sum which represents the value of the bribe might be more equitable, given the enormous significance of proprietary remedies and their potential impact on creditors and third parties.

The Position of Agents

Where an agent puts himself in a position where his duty to his principal and his own interests may conflict and makes a profit out of his fiduciary position, he will be liable to account for this. Moore LJ summarised the nature of the fiduciary duty owed by an agent to his principal in *Sherrard v. Barron*[63] as follows:

> There is no dispute about the law, which is that an agent cannot without the knowledge of his principal make any profit for himself out of services rendered to his principal. Should he do so, he must account. It is equally settled law that it is the duty of the agent to make the fullest disclosure to his principal of all transactions in which the agent is making, directly or indirectly, a profit out of his principal. If this is done and the principal, expressly or by course of conduct, impliedly assents, the agent can retain his profit.

The requirement of disclosure and consent is strictly applied as can be seen from *Patten v. Hamilton*,[64] where an agent purchased a charge on his principal's estate at an undervalue and continued to collect the interest on the face value of the charge. It was held by the Irish Court of Appeal that in the absence of evidence that the principal had consented to the agent retaining the full benefit of the transaction, the agent should be treated as a trustee for the principal and the extra interest should be applied towards extinguishing the charge.

As Andrews LJ made it clear in *Sherrard v. Barron*, it is of paramount

---

62. [1994] Conv 156.
63. [1923] 1 IR 21, 24. Note also the *dicta* of James LJ in *Parker v. McKenna* (1874) 10 Ch App 96, 124 to the effect that 'no agent in the course of his agency, in the matter of his agency, can be allowed to make any profit without the knowledge and consent of his principal.' See also *Re Canadian Oil Works Corporation* (1875) 10 Ch App 593, 601 *per* Mellish LJ.
64. [1911] 1 IR 46. See the general principle set out by Cherry LJ at p.60.

importance in all transactions between agent and principal and between other parties who stand in a fiduciary relationship to one another that 'there should be nothing in the nature of underhand dealing.'[65] However, liability does not depend on any finding of fraud and applies equally even where it has not been shown that any advantage has been taken. It has also been established that it is irrelevant that the principal does not suffer any loss as a result of the agent's actions and in fact may have benefited, although in such circumstances, the agent may be entitled to remuneration for his endeavours. The best illustration of the rigour with which these principles have been applied is the decision of the House of Lords in *Boardman v. Phipps*.[66] Assets were held on trust for the benefit of a testator's children, the trustees being his widow, who was senile, his daughter and an accountant. The trust had a sizable minority shareholding in a textile company and with the consent of the two active trustees, Boardman, the trustees' solicitor, and one of the beneficiaries set about acquiring a majority shareholding in the company in order to make it more profitable. By purporting to act on behalf of the trust they obtained detailed information about the company and succeeded in gaining control of it, making a considerable profit as a result. The House of Lords held that Boardman and the beneficiary were liable to account to the trust for the profits which they had made, although it was held that they were entitled to payment for the work which they had carried out.

The majority view was that the defendants had placed themselves in a position in which their duty and self-interest might conflict and had abused their fiduciary position by utilizing information acquired in a fiduciary capacity. Lord Hodson and Lord Guest agreed that information could be characterized as trust property and found that since the defendants had made a profit out of using this information, they were liable to account for it. Lord Cohen felt that information was not property in the strict sense, and said that the mere use of knowledge which comes to an agent in the course of his agency does not necessarily make him liable,[67] but he will be required to account where, as in the case before him, he purported to act on behalf of the trust. Viscount Dilhorne and Lord Upjohn dissented, holding that the information obtained by the defendants when purporting to act as agents of the trust was not trust property and they found that in the circumstances there was no conflict between their private interests and their fiduciary duty to the trust.

---

65. [1923] 1 IR 21, 26.
66. [1967] 2 AC 46.
67. *Ibid.* at 102-103.

The distinction between the views expressed by the majority and minority members of the House of Lords is well summarized by Underhill and Hayton[68] as follows:

> The essential difference between the majority and the minority was that the majority favoured the traditional strict deterrent approach, so that (*non de minimis*) possibility of a conflict between private interest and fiduciary duty arising out of use of information received in a fiduciary capacity should give rise to constructive trusteeship of the shares purchased as a result of such information, whilst the minority favoured a liberal reasonable approach that only a real sensible possibility of a conflict should give rise to a constructive trusteeship of the shares and there was not such a real sensible possibility.

Certainly, the more liberal view has found favour with the courts in some other jurisdictions,[69] and the existence of the conflict of interest identified by the majority has been doubted by some commentators.[70] However, it has been argued that the majority view is preferable as it is more likely to protect the position of a principal or beneficiary who may be unaware of the agent's activities and in any event the agent can avoid liability if he obtains consent for the course of action which he intends to pursue before embarking upon it.

Finally, it is interesting to note that the majority of the Canadian Supreme Court has recently held in *Soulos v. Korkontzilas*[71] that an agent who acquires property from a third party in breach of his fiduciary obligations to his principal holds this property on a constructive trust despite the fact that the agent had not thereby realized any financial gain.[72] As McLachlin J stated: '[A] constructive trust is required in cases such as this to ensure that agents and others in positions of trust remain faithful to their duty of loyalty'.[73] In her view if the courts did not intervene by imposing a

---

68. *Law Relating to Trusts and Trustees* (15th ed., 1995) p. 360.
69. In Canada, see *Peso Silver Mines Ltd (NPL) v. Cropper* (1966) 58 DLR (2d) 1 and Australia, see *Consul Development Pty Ltd v. DPC Estates Pty Ltd* (1975) 5 ALR 231.
70. Jones (1968) 84 LQR 472.
71. (1997) 146 DLR (4th) 214. See further Smith (1997) Can Bar Rev 539; (1998) 114 LQR 14.
72. The view of the minority was that to impose a constructive trust where there had been no unjust enrichment would depart from settled principles, see the judgment of Sopinka J at p.236.
73. *Ibid.* at 231.

constructive trust in such circumstances the message which that would send out would be that agents might breach their fiduciary duties and the courts would do nothing unless the agent had made a profit. In the opinion of McLachlin J 'this will not do'; as she stated 'courts of equity have always been concerned to keep the person who acts on behalf of others to his ethical mark'.[74]

If the views of the majority of the House of Lords in *Boardman* and of the Supreme Court of Canada in *Soulos* are followed in this jurisdiction, it will lead to particularly strict standards being applied to the conduct of agents and a constructive trust will be imposed even where the principal has not sustained any loss as a result of the agent's actions or where the agent himself has not profited financially from any transaction entered into. It would seem likely that the view of the majority in *Boardman*, which is so firmly entrenched in England, will be followed here. Perhaps more uncertain is whether the slightly controversial principle of imposing a constructive trust in the absence of unjust enrichment will find favour with the courts in this jurisdiction.

The Position of Company Directors[75]
Company directors are treated as being fiduciaries insofar as they owe a duty to their company and they will not be permitted to place themselves in a position where their duty to the company and their personal interests will conflict or to derive a profit from their fiduciary relationship. As Swifen Eady J stated in *Transvaal Lands Co. v. New Belgium (Transvaal) Land & Development Co.*,[76] referring to the judgment of Lord Cranworth in *Aberdeen Railway Co. v. Blaikie*:[77] 'It was there decided that directors of a company have duties to discharge of a fiduciary nature towards their principal, and that it is a rule of universal application, that no one, having such duties to discharge, shall be allowed to enter into engagements in which he has, or can have, a personal interest conflicting, or which possibly may conflict, with the interests of those he is bound to protect.' This view has been echoed recently by Lightman J in *Neptune (Vehicle Washing Equipment) Ltd v. Fitzgerald*[78] where he stated that 'a director of a company owes a fiduciary duty to the company to act *bona fide* in the best interests of the company and to prefer its interests to his own where they conflict'.

---

74. *Ibid.* at 232.
75. See generally Sealy [1967] CLJ 83; Lowry (1994) 45 NILQ 1.
76. [1914] 2 Ch 488, 502.
77. (1854) 1 Macq 461.
78. [1996] Ch 274, 279.

While it has been argued that the rule in *Keech v. Sandford* should only apply to trustees in the strict sense, as Lowry[79] has noted, 'it has been taken to be of equal applicability to all types of fiduciaries including company directors, irrespective of the equity of a particular case.' There is no question that liability will be imposed where a director abuses his fiduciary position by diverting to himself a contract which could have been taken up on the company's behalf. So in *Cook v. Deeks*,[80] the Privy Council held that directors who had engaged in such conduct held the benefit of those contracts on a constructive trust for the benefit of the company. This principle was succinctly set out by Laskin J in *Canadian Aero Service Ltd v. O'Malley*:[81]

> A director or a senior officer ... is precluded from obtaining for himself, either secretly or without the approval of the company (which would have to be properly manifested upon full disclosure of the facts), any property or business advantage either belonging to the company or for which it has been negotiating; and especially is this so where the director or officer is a participant in the negotiations on behalf of the company.

Liability will also be imposed where the company itself was not in a position to take on a contract secured by a director where he takes advantage of his fiduciary position to achieve this. So in *Industrial Development Consultants v. Cooley*,[82] the defendant managing director of a company which provided construction consultancy services learnt in the course of negotiations on its behalf with a gas board that the board would not enter into an agreement with the company but that it would consider awarding the contract to him in a personal capacity. He secured a release from his employment by falsely claiming ill health and then entered into a contract with the board on his own behalf. Roskill J held that the defendant was a constructive trustee of the benefit of the contract and liable to account for the profits derived from it. As he stated: 'if the defendant is not required to account he will have made a large profit, as a result of having deliberately put himself into a position in which his duty to the plaintiffs who were employing him and his personal interests conflicted.'[83]

---

79. (1994) 45 NILQ 1, 2.
80. [1916] 1 AC 554.
81. (1974) 40 DLR (3d) 371, 382.
82. [1972] 1 WLR 443.
83. *Ibid.* at 453. However compare this finding with the decision of the Canadian Supreme Court in *Peso Silver Mines Ltd (NPL) v. Cropper* (1966) 58 DLR (2d) 1 where

In some cases this general principle that a director must not profit from his fiduciary relationship with the company has been inflexibly applied and if a director takes advantage of his position and makes a profit, the court will not look behind his motives for so doing.[84] So even where a director has acted in an honest and *bona fide* manner in what he believes are the best interests of the company, he will nevertheless be liable to account for any personal profit made as a result of his fiduciary relationship with the company. The harshness of this rule is well illustrated by the decision of the House of Lords in *Regal (Hastings) Ltd v. Gulliver.*[85] A company which owned a cinema formed a subsidiary to take up the lease of two additional cinemas so that they might be all sold as a going concern. The landlord insisted on the subsidiary company having a paid up share capital of 5,000 ordinary £1 shares and as the parent company had insufficient resources to subscribe for more than 2,000, the directors of the company agreed to take up the remainder. When the business was transferred to new controllers the directors made a personal profit on the transaction. The purchaser successfully brought an action in the company's name to account for this profit on the grounds that the directors had derived such profit by virtue of their office. Lord Russell stated:

> The rule of equity which insists on those, who by use of a fiduciary position make a profit, being liable to account for that profit, in no way depends on fraud, or absence of *bona fides*; or upon such questions or considerations as whether the profit would or should otherwise have gone to the plaintiff, or whether the profiteer was under a duty to obtain the source of the profit for the plaintiff, or whether he took a risk or acted as he did for the benefit of the plaintiff, or whether the plaintiff has in fact been damaged or benefited by his action. The liability arises from the mere fact of a profit having, in the stated circumstances, been made. The profiteer, however honest and well intentioned, cannot escape the risk of being called upon to account.[86]

This decision seems unduly harsh in that the directors had acted honestly and in the best interests of the company, particularly as the company itself could not have obtained the benefit of the transactions which ultimately

---

the court appeared to lay down the principle that it should not penalise a director in circumstances where he had acted in a *bona fide* manner and had taken up an opportunity which his company had been unable or unwilling to accept.

84. *Furs Ltd v. Tomkies* (1936) 54 CLR 583, 592 *per* Rich, Dixon and Evatt JJ.
85. [1967] 2 AC 134. (Initially reported at [1942] 1 All ER 378).
86. *Ibid.* at 144.

took place without the financial input of the directors. As Jones[87] has commented, while the policy issues in *Regal Hastings* were finely balanced the unquestioning adherence to the inexorable rule of equity by the House of Lords meant that these factors were never properly weighed against each other.

The fact that a director's liability to account for any profit made as a result of his fiduciary relationship with the company does not depend on *mala fides* but 'on the mere fact of a profit having been made' was recently restated by the House of Lords in *Guinness plc v. Saunders,*[88] in which the court had to consider the question of whether a director might be entitled to remuneration in circumstances where he had made a profit for the company. A committee of the board of directors of the plaintiff company had paid the second named defendant £5.2 million for his services in connection with a takeover bid being made by the plaintiff. Recovery of the money was claimed on the grounds that the second named defendant had received it in breach of his fiduciary duty as director in that he had not disclosed his interest in the agreement to the plaintiff company. The House of Lords agreed that he had failed to disclose his interest and ordered him to repay the money to the plaintiff. In relation to the second named defendant's claim for remuneration, it was argued that *Boardman v. Phipps* was authority for the proposition that in exceptional circumstances a court of equity might award remuneration to a trustee and that therefore it might make such payments to a director. However, Lord Goff concluded that the present case was 'very different' to *Boardman* and continued: 'Whether any such an allowance might ever be granted by a court of equity in the case of a director of a company, as opposed to a trustee, is a point which has yet to be decided. ... In any event I cannot see any possibility of such jurisdiction being exercised in the present case.'[89]

However, it is interesting to note that suggestions of a more flexible approach can be gleaned from a number of other recent decisions in England, albeit first instance decisions. It has been held in *Island Export Finance Ltd v. Umunna*[90] that a former director of a company might secure a contract to supply materials, supplied by the company on a previous occasion, in circumstances where the company was not actively seeking the new contract and where there was no connection between his resignation and the securing of this contract. Similarly in *Neptune (Vehicle Washing*

---

87. (1968) 84 LQR 472, 497.
88. [1990] 2 WLR 324. See Goulding [1990] Conv 296.
89. *Ibid.* at 342-343.
90. [1986] BCLC 460.

Equipment) Ltd v. Fitzgerald,[91] while Lightman J reiterated that where a director enters into an arrangement or transaction with himself or with a company in which he is interested, that arrangement may be set aside irrespective of whether the company has suffered as a result, he stated that it is a defence to such a claim that the company's shareholders have consented to the transaction or the articles of association allow it. The courts now appear to be taking a more pragmatic approach and recognising the practical reality that a director will inevitably acquire a general fund of knowledge in the course of carrying out his duties and that he cannot be expected to desist from all activities of a commercial nature on leaving his position or even to refrain from going into competition with the former company.[92]

While it can be argued that it is necessary to apply the relevant principles in this area in a rigid manner to deter those in positions of trust who might otherwise seek to take advantage of their positions, it is equally clear that an arbitrary application of the rule in *Keech v. Sandford* is not the answer and for this reason a more flexible approach in this area is to be welcomed.

THE LIABILITY OF STRANGERS AS CONSTRUCTIVE TRUSTEES

Introduction

Persons who are not appointed as trustees may nevertheless be liable to account to beneficiaries and be found to hold trust property as constructive trustees in certain circumstances, where they are found to possess the requisite degree of knowledge about the nature and consequences of their activities. So, where a stranger to the trust takes it upon himself to act as a trustee and subsequently commits a breach of trust, he will be liable for such a breach. In addition, a third party may incur liability where he receives or deals with trust property or where he assists in a fraudulent breach of trust in circumstances where the law is satisfied that he possesses a degree of knowledge[93] sufficient to justify the imposition of liability.

Before considering these principles in more detail, it is important to

---

91. [1996] Ch 274.
92. See *Balston Ltd v. Headlines Filters Ltd* [1990] FSR 385.
93. The question of the degree of knowledge required to impose liability in either of these circumstances is a very uncertain and complex one, which will be considered in detail below.

bear in mind that the imposition of constructive trusteeship on a stranger to a trust is not the only possible cause of action which may be pursued by a beneficiary where trust property is misappropriated. The alternatives are either a proprietary remedy at law or in equity to trace the trust property,[94] or a personal claim against the party responsible for effecting the breach of trust, either at law in the form of an action for money had and received, or in equity.[95] However, often the imposition of constructive trusteeship on a stranger may be the most useful form of remedy. In circumstances where a third party, increasingly a financial institution or professional, has assisted in a breach of trust, experience has shown that such defendants are far more likely to be in a position to meet any claim than the individual who was initially responsible for committing the breach of trust.[96] In addition, where the wrongdoing involves receipt or dealing with trust property, the imposition of constructive trusteeship may in many circumstances be a much more satisfactory remedy than pursuing a tracing claim. Obviously in some situations it will no longer be possible to trace the trust property and the imposition of a constructive trust may also allow for a more extensive form of recovery where there has been a reduction in the value of the trust property or an incidental profit made.

It is important to stress at this point that constructive trusteeship can only be imposed where the recipient or assister possesses the degree of knowledge necessary to justify the imposition of liability. It should therefore be borne in mind that while a beneficiary may be able to trace trust property into the hands of an innocent volunteer, the latter's liability will be confined to the return of the property or its proceeds while still in his possession, and a constructive trust with its additional proprietary consequences cannot be imposed in these circumstances.

There has been an ongoing debate about the circumstances in which liability should be imposed for knowing assistance in a breach of trust or knowing receipt of trust property. These issues will be examined in detail below under the respective headings of knowing assistance and knowing receipt but for the present it should be noted that it has been suggested that 'a person who has intermeddled by assisting in [a] breach [of trust] should be less exposed to liability than one who, with knowledge of the breach,

---

94. Considered *infra* Chapter 18.
95. As La Forest J pointed out in the Canadian Supreme Court decision of *Citadel General Assurance Co. v. Lloyds Bank Canada* (1997) 152 DLR (4th) 411, 438 'where more than one remedy is available on the facts, the plaintiff should be able to choose the one that is most advantageous'.
96. See Parker and Mellows, *The Modern Law of Trusts* (7th ed., 1998, Oakley) p.321.

has actually received the trust property to his or her benefit'.[97] It has been argued that while 'recipient liability is restitution-based, accessory liability is not'[98] and that given the fundamental distinction between the nature of liability in assistance and receipt cases, it makes sense to require a different threshold of knowledge for each category of liability.[99] Specifically it has been suggested that in knowing assistance cases, which are concerned with the furtherance of fraud, there should be a higher threshold of knowledge required of the stranger to the trust.[100] However, in knowing receipt cases, which are concerned with the receipt of trust property for the benefit of the recipient, it has been argued that there should be a lower threshold of knowledge required to found liability.

While there has been little case law in this area in Ireland, a wealth of authorities have emerged over recent years in other jurisdictions, particularly in England, Canada and New Zealand. This has been attributed in part to a growth in corporate fraud and to a greater willingness on the part of the judiciary to utilize equitable concepts in a commercial context. However uncertainty in relation to the principles to be applied is an increasing problem in this area of the law and the comment has recently been made that 'regrettably, the law does not yet exhibit the degree of certainty which the business community is entitled to expect'. In addition, it has been argued that advances in the law of restitution must necessarily lead to a fundamental reappraisal of the circumstances in which a stranger can be made liable for receiving trust property transferred in breach of trust.[101] To date, while some tentative steps towards such a 'fundamental reappraisal' have been taken in England,[102] there is still no sign of any wholesale departure on the part of the judiciary from the equitable principles relating to the imposition of constructive trusts which have developed over the years. While it remains to be seen whether the judiciary in Ireland will seek to take any radical steps in this area, it is probable that in the short term at least, they are more likely to follow the traditional principles laid down in England and for this reason it is proposed to examine this case

---

97. *Per* Smellie J in *Equiticorp Industries Group Ltd v. The Crown* [1996] 3 NZLR 586, 605.
98. *Royal Brunei Airlines Sdn Bhd v. Tan Kok Ming* [1995] 2 AC 378 at 386 *per* Lord Nicholls.
99. *Citadel General Assurance Co v. Lloyds Bank Canada* (1997) 152 DLR (4th) 411, 433 *per* La Forest J and *Gold v. Rosenberg* (1997) 152 DLR (4th) 385, 399 *per* Iacobucci J. See also *Agip Africa Ltd v. Jackson* [1990] Ch 265, 292 per Millett J.
100. *Ibid.* at 434.
101. Harpum in *Frontiers of Liability* (ed. Birks, 1993) Volume 1, p.9.
102. See e.g. *Lipkin Gorman v. Karpanale Ltd* [1991] 2 AC 548.

law in some detail before considering briefly some of the alternative options which may be pursued in the future.

Intermeddling in a Trust — the Trustee de son Tort

Where a person intermeddles in the affairs of a trust or performs acts characteristic of a trustee he will become a trustee de son tort i.e. because of his wrong.This principle was set out by Smith LJ in *Mara v. Browne*[103] as follows:

> [I]f one, not being a trustee and not having authority from a trustee, takes upon himself to intermeddle with trust matters or to do acts characteristic of the office of trustee he may thereby make himself what is called in law a trustee of his own wrong — i.e., a trustee de son tort, or as it is also termed, a constructive trustee.

In essence liability under this heading depends on the voluntary assumption of the obligations of trusteeship followed by actions which amount to a breach of trust. A stranger who purports to act as a trustee will be subject to all the liabilities usually imposed on an expressly appointed trustee and to the fiduciary obligations which preclude him from profiting from his position or from placing himself in a situation where his duty and interests may conflict.

In *Selangor United Rubber Estates Ltd v. Craddock (No. 3)*[104] Ungoed-Thomas J identified the following distinguishing features of a trustee de son tort: such persons do not claim to act in their own right but rather for the beneficiaries; their assumption to act is not of itself a ground of liability, except in the sense of liability to account for any failure in the duty so assumed, and their status as trustees precedes the occurrence which may be the subject of a claim against them. This can be contrasted with the situations which will be considered below where no trusteeship arises before, but only by reason of the action complained of, and where the trustees claim to act in their own right and not for the beneficiaries.

Assisting in the Misappropriation of Trust Property

It was accepted by Lord Selborne in *Barnes v. Addy*[105] that strangers will be made liable as constructive trustees where 'they assist with knowledge

---

103. [1896] 1 Ch 199, 209.
104. [1968] 1 WLR 1555, 1579.
105. (1874) LR 9 Ch App 244, 252.

in a dishonest and fraudulent design on the part of trustees'. A more recent formulation of what amounts to knowing assistance is set out by Lord Nicholls delivering the judgment of the Privy Council in *Royal Brunei Airlines Sdn Bhd v. Tan Kok Ming*[106] as follows: 'A liability in equity to make good resulting loss attaches to a person who dishonestly procures or assists in a breach of trust or fiduciary obligation'. This latter formulation focuses on the dishonesty of the person assisting in the breach of trust rather than requiring dishonesty on the part of the trustees as Lord Selborne's principle had done and it is likely that the Privy Council's interpretation will form the basis for future application of this principle.

There has tended to be a lack of uniformity in the terminology employed to describe the type of liability imposed in such circumstances. As Oakley[107] has suggested it might be more appropriate to regard these cases not as examples of the imposition of a constructive trust but rather as examples of the imposition of a distinct remedy in the form of liability to account in the same manner as a trustee. Blanchard J made a similar point in the recent decision of the New Zealand High Court in *Nimmo v. Westpac Banking Corporation*[108] as follows:

> [T]he term 'constructive trust' is misleading in this context, for what is involved is not the creation of a proprietary interest for a plaintiff over some asset of an assisting defendant, but rather the treatment of the assister as if that person were an actual or constructive trustee. The defendant is made to account as if a trust were imposed but there is actually no trust even of a constructive kind: the plaintiff is simply declared to be an unsecured creditor of the defendant for the sum for which the defendant is liable to account.

Despite the logic inherent in such an approach, an examination of the case law would suggest that strangers who assist in a fraudulent design amounting to a breach of trust will continue to be labelled as constructive trustees. In his judgment in *Baden v. Societe Generale pour Favoriser le Developpement du Commerce et de l'Industrie en France SA*[109] Peter Gibson J identified four elements which must be established if a case is to come within the category of 'knowing assistance'. These are (1) the existence of a trust; (2) the existence of a dishonest and fraudulent design; (3) the as-

---

106. [1995] 2 AC 378 at 392.
107. Parker and Mellows, *The Modern Law of Trusts* (7th ed., 1998) p. 325.
108. [1993] 3 NZLR 218, 226.
109. [1993] 1 WLR 509.

sistance by a stranger in that design; and (4) the knowledge of the stranger. The first and third of these requirements do not pose any real difficulties in terms of interpretation; while there may be a formal trust, this is not essential and it is sufficient if there is a fiduciary relationship between the purported trustee and the property of another person. However the second and fourth requirements have given rise to disputes of considerable complexity and it is necessary to examine them in some detail.

The Need for Fraudulent or Dishonest Conduct

The requirement of the existence of a fraudulent or dishonest design, which was set out by Lord Selborne in *Barnes v. Addy,*[110] meant that the conduct necessary to constitute a person as a constructive trustee under this heading had to be tainted with some kind of fraud or dishonesty. While Ungoed-Thomas J expressed the view in *Selangor United Rubber Estates Ltd v. Craddock (No. 3)*[111] that conduct which is morally reprehensible would suffice, this more flexible approach was rejected by the Court of Appeal in *Belmont Finance Corporation v. Williams Furniture Ltd,*[112] where the claim in relation to knowing assistance failed on the grounds, *inter alia*, that no sufficiently clear allegations of fraud or dishonesty had been established. Buckley LJ referred to the formulation of Lord Selborne in *Barnes* and said that to depart from it would introduce an undesirable degree of uncertainty into the law; as he said 'if dishonesty is not to be the criterion, what degree of unethical conduct is to be sufficient ?'[113] This view was echoed by Peter Gibson J in *Baden v. Societe Generale pour Favoriser le Developpement du Commerce et de l'Industrie en France SA*[114] where he stated that 'the relevant design ... must be dishonest and fraudulent'. The following statement of Scott LJ in the English Court of Appeal in *Polly Peck International plc v. Nadir (No. 2)*[115] seemed to have settled the matter:

> There is a general consensus of opinion that, if liability as constructive trustee is sought to be imposed ... on the basis that the defend-

---

110. (1874) LR 9 Ch App 244, 252.
111. [1968] 1 WLR 1555, 1591. Although note the subsequent comments of Sachs LJ in *Carl Zeiss Stiftung v. Herbert Smith & Co. (No. 2)* [1969] 2 Ch 276, 299.
112. [1979] Ch 250.
113. *Ibid.* at 267.
114. [1993] 1 WLR 509, 574. See also the comments of Millett J in *Agip (Africa) Ltd v. Jackson* [1990] Ch 265, 292.
115. [1992] 4 All ER 769, 777. Quoted with approval by Blanchard J in the New Zealand decision of *Nimmo v. Westpac Banking* [1993] 3 NZLR 218, 227.

ant has assisted in the misapplication of trust property (knowing assistance) 'something amounting to dishonesty or want of probity on the part of the defendant must be shown' (see *per* Vinelott J in *Eagle Trust plc v. SBC Securities Ltd* [1992] 4 All ER 488 at 499). Vinelott J described as 'settled law' the proposition that 'a stranger cannot be made liable for knowing assistance in a fraudulent breach of trust unless knowledge of the fraudulent design can be imputed to him. ...'(at 499). I respectfully agree.

One important issue referred to above which has led to considerable controversy recently is whether the breach of trust which is a prerequisite to accessory liability must itself be a dishonest and fraudulent breach of trust by the trustee or whether it suffices that the accessory himself has acted dishonestly. The Supreme Court of Canada considered this question in *Air Canada v. M. & L. Travel Ltd*[116] and Iacobucci J made it clear that 'generally there are good reasons for requiring participation in a fraudulent and dishonest breach of trust before imposing liability on agents of the trustees' and the issue seemed to be whether the breach of trust was itself fraudulent and dishonest rather than the accessory's actions.[117] However, the Privy Council has recently reached the opposite conclusion in *Royal Brunei Airlines Sdn Bhd v. Tan Kok Ming.*[118] As Lord Nicholls stated: 'In this regard dishonesty on the part of the third party would seem to be a sufficient basis for his liability, irrespective of the state of mind of the trustee who was in breach of trust.'[119] As he said it was difficult to see why, if a third party dishonestly assisted in a breach of trust, there should be a further prerequisite to his liability, namely that the trustee must also be shown to have been acting dishonestly.

The judgment of Lord Nicholls in *Royal Brunei Airlines* is also important in view of the consideration which he gave to the concept of dishonesty as the touchstone of accessory liability. He stated as follows:

> [I]n the context of the accessory liability principle acting dishonestly, or with a lack of probity, which is synonymous, means simply

---

116. (1993) 108 DLR (4th) 592, 617.
117. *Ibid.* at 618.
118. [1995] 2 AC 378. See also *Powell v. Thompson* [1991] 1 NZLR 597, 613. Harpum *Frontiers of Liability* (ed., Birks, 1993) Volume 1 p.13 has also recently suggested that 'there is no compelling reason why liability for knowing assistance should be confined to cases where the trustee's breach was fraudulent' and argues that the weight of authority is not so strong as to be an insuperable barrier to the adoption of a more flexible rule.
119. *Ibid.* at 385.

not acting as an honest person would in the circumstances. This is an objective standard. . . . Further, honesty and its counterpart dishonesty are mostly concerned with advertent conduct, not inadvertent conduct. Carelessness is not dishonesty. Thus for the most part dishonesty is to be equated with conscious impropriety. However, these subjective characteristics of honesty do not mean that individuals are free to set their own standards of honesty in particular circumstances. The standard of what constitutes honest conduct is not subjective. Honesty is not an optional scale, with higher or lower values according to the moral standards of each individual. If a person knowingly appropriates another's property, he will not escape a finding of dishonesty simply because he sees nothing wrong in such behaviour.[120]

The academic reaction to the approach adopted by the Privy Council in *Royal Brunei Airlines* has been overwhelmingly favourable,[121] and it has been welcomed as clarifying a number of uncertainties in this area in a purposeful manner. While there has to date been a surprising lack of reference to the Privy Council's decision in other common law countries, it would appear likely that the courts in this jurisdiction would follow it and apply the requirement that dishonesty or 'want of probity' on the part of the accessory must be shown.

The Knowledge Requirement
It is fair to say that the courts in England have been far from consistent in their attitude to this issue over the last few decades. Before examining the case law it might be useful to set out the various categories of knowledge identified by Peter Gibson J in *Baden v. Societe Generale pour Favoriser le Developpement du Commerce et de l'Industrie en France SA*, although considerable reservations have been expressed in relation to this categorisation,[122] and the Privy Council has recently suggested in *Royal Brunei Airlines Sdn Bhd v. Tan Kok Ming*[123] that 'the *Baden* scale of knowledge is

---

120. *Ibid.* at 389.
121. See Nolan [1995] CLJ 505; Harpum (1995) 111 LQR 545; Halliwell [1995] Conv 339; McCormack (1995) 9 Trust Law Int 102; Podzebenko (1996) 18 Syd Law Rev 234. However, Berg's reaction is less favourable, see (1996) 59 MLR 443.
122. See the comments of Millett J in *Agip (Africa) Ltd v. Jackson* [1990] Ch 265, 293 and of Knox J in *Cowan de Groot Properties v. Eagle Trust plc* [1992] 4 All ER 700, 761; and it has been described in *Nimmo v. Westpac Banking Ltd* [1993] 3 NZLR 218, 228 by Blanchard J as 'unhelpful and ... unrememberable'.
123. [1995] 2 AC 378.

best forgotten'. Nevertheless it has been employed in numerous decisions in this area over the last decade and it would be difficult to examine these without setting out the five categories of knowledge referred to by Peter Gibson J. These are as follows:

(i) actual knowledge;

(ii) wilfully shutting one's eyes to the obvious;

(iii) wilfully and recklessly failing to make such inquiries as an honest and reasonable man would make;

(iv) knowledge of circumstances which would indicate the facts to an honest and reasonable man;

(v) knowledge of circumstances which would put an honest and reasonable man on inquiry.

While many of the early authorities[124] restricted liability to a stranger who possessed knowledge in one of the first three categories outlined above, a number of first instance decisions in England from the late 1960s to the early 1980s did not follow this approach. In *Selangor United Rubber Estates Ltd v. Craddock (No. 3)*[125] a bank was held liable to account to the plaintiff company for acting in a dishonest manner to enable the company's assets to be used to purchase its own shares on the basis that the bank ought to have known that the payments were a dishonest application of the company's funds as its banker's draft was used to purchase the shares. Ungoed–Thomas J described the type of knowledge which was required as follows: 'knowledge of circumstances which would indicate to an honest reasonable man that such a design was being committed or would put him on inquiry, which the stranger failed to make, whether it was being committed.'[126] This reasoning was followed in *Karak Rubber Co. Ltd v. Burden (No. 2)*,[127] where it was held by Brightman J that a bank did not know but ought to have known that it was assisting in a dishonest plan to purchase a company's shares by means of its own assets and was therefore liable as a constructive trustee.[128]

---

124. E.g. *Barnes v. Addy* (1874) LR 9 Ch App 244; *Williams-Ashman v. Price* [1942] 1 Ch 219.
125. [1968] 1 WLR 1555.
126. *Ibid.* at 1590.
127. [1972] 1 WLR 602.
128. Brightman J quoted with approval the statement in *Selangor* in relation to the degree of knowledge required and found that a reasonable banker would have been put on inquiry which would in all probability have revealed the impropriety.(See p.1235.) See also *Baden v. Societe Generale* [1993] 3 WLR 509.

However, doubts were expressed about the unfair burden which such a requirement could place on innocent defendants and an alternative view, put forward by the Court of Appeal in *Carl Zeiss Stiftung v. Herbert Smith & Co. (No. 2)*,[129] where it was stressed that want of probity should be required to establish liability and the suggestion was made that constructive notice of the impropriety was insufficient, now seems to have come to the fore. One of the most important recent judgments in this area is that of Millett J in *Agip (Africa) Ltd v. Jackson*,[130] in which he confirmed that knowledge within the first three categories laid down in the *Baden* case is required. A senior officer in the plaintiff company fraudulently altered a payment order for £500,000 to a creditor by substituting the name of a company managed by the defendants which had been set up in order to launder the money. The money was credited to the company's bank account and following a series of transactions in which the money was transferred to various recipients, the company was wound up. The plaintiffs brought an action against the defendants to recover the money in which they claimed, *inter alia*, that the defendants were constructive trustees of the funds on the basis of knowing receipt and knowing assistance. Millett J held that none of the defendants could be held liable on the basis of knowingly receiving trust funds for their own benefit but that the defendants were liable under the heading of knowing assistance as 'they were at best indifferent to the possibility of fraud'. On the question of knowledge, Millett J said that constructive notice of the fraud is not sufficient to make a defendant liable and that 'the true distinction is between honesty and dishonesty'. Millett J continued:

> If a man does not draw the obvious inferences or make the obvious inquiries, the question is: why not? If it is because, however foolishly, he did not suspect wrongdoing or, having suspected it, had his suspicions allayed, however unreasonably, that is one thing. But if he did suspect wrongdoing yet failed to make inquiries because 'he did not want to know' (category (ii)) or because he regarded it as none of his business (category (iii)), that is quite another. Such conduct is dishonest, and those who are guilty of it cannot complain if, for the purpose of civil liability, they are treated as if they had actual knowledge.[131]

---

129. [1969] 2 Ch 276. Note also the comments of May LJ in *Lipkin Gorman v. Karpanale Ltd* [1989] 1 WLR 1340, 1355.
130. [1990] Ch 265. See Birks (1989) 105 LQR 528; Harpum [1990] CLJ 217 and Millett J (1991) 107 LQR 71.
131. *Ibid.* at 293.

This approach has also been advocated by May LJ in *Lipkin Gorman v. Karpanale Ltd*[132] in the following terms: 'there is at least strong persuasive authority for the proposition that nothing less than knowledge, as defined in one of the first three categories stated by Peter Gibson J in the *Baden* case, of an underlying dishonest design is sufficient to make a stranger a constructive trustee of the consequences of that design.'

The judgment of Fox LJ in the Court of Appeal in *Agip* temporarily confused the issue somewhat and he appeared to accept that all five categories of knowledge as set out in the *Baden* case were relevant.[133] However subsequently in *Eagle Trust plc v. SBC Securities Ltd,*[134] Vinelott J commented that it is implicit in Fox LJ's judgment in *Agip* that he accepted Millett J's conclusion that to establish liability for knowing assistance something amounting to dishonesty and want of probity must be shown.[135] In the view of Vinelott J: 'Constructive notice is not enough, though ... knowledge may be inferred in the absence of evidence by the defendant if such knowledge would have been imputed to an honest and reasonable man.'[136] The position as set out by Vinelott J has recently been confirmed by Scott LJ in the English Court of Appeal in *Polly Peck International plc v. Nadir (No. 2)*,[137] which concerned a claim that the plaintiff company's funds had been misappropriated by the defendant, its former chief executive. The court dismissed the plaintiff's claim for a Mareva injunction against the bank into which these funds had been transferred and Scott LJ approved the statement of Vinelott J that 'a stranger cannot be made liable for knowing assistance in a fraudulent breach of trust unless knowledge of the fraudulent design can be imputed to him'.

This approach to the question of the degree of knowledge required for the imposition of liability on grounds of knowing assistance is similar to that adopted in a number of recent decisions of the New Zealand High Court.[138] In *Marshall Futures Ltd v. Marshall*[139] Tipping J stated as follows:

---

132. [1989] 1 WLR 1340, 1355 although it was not necessary for the Court of Appeal to decide the issue.
133. The reasoning of the Court of Appeal has been criticised, see Harpum [1991] CLJ 409, 411.
134. [1993] 1 WLR 484.
135. *Ibid.* at 495.
136. *Ibid.* at 496.
137. [1992] 4 All ER 769.
138. Although note the *obiter* comments of Thomas J in *Powell v. Thompson* [1991] 1 NZLR 597, 615.
139. [1992] 1 NZLR 316, 326.

A person who is simply careless or unimaginative should not in my view be treated as having the requisite knowledge of the trustee's dishonesty and fraudulent design ... it is my view that the mind of the assistant must be shown to have been dishonest.

Wylie J took a similar view in *Equiticorp Industries Group Ltd v. Hawkins*,[140] where he concluded that while categories (i), (ii) and (iii) as laid down in the *Baden* case were relevant in determining whether or not a constructive trust was to be imposed in a case of knowing assistance, 'types (iv) and (v) not displaying a want of probity will not amount to unconscionable conduct and will not suffice.' The statements subsequently made by Cooke P in the New Zealand Court of Appeal in *Gathergood v. Blundell & Brown Ltd*[141] were open to more than one possible interpretation. However in *Nimmo v. Westpac Banking Corporation*,[142] Blanchard J commented that, while Cooke P's judgment might have been interpreted on a first reading as encompassing all five categories of knowledge within the *Baden* formulation, he was convinced that this was not the intention and that Cooke P was 'speaking only of a situation in which the assister had actual or Nelsonian knowledge, in which case the assistance rendered would be inherently dishonest'.[143] The Canadian Supreme Court recently spoke in substantially the same terms in its decision in *Air Canada v. M. & L. Travel Ltd.*[144] As Iacobucci J stated: 'The knowledge requirement for this type of liability is actual knowledge; recklessness or wilful blindness will also suffice'. This approach was approved, albeit in an *obiter* context, by La Forest J in the recent Supreme Court decision of *Citadel General Assurance Co. v. Lloyds Bank Canada*[145] where it was stated that in this context 'constructive knowledge will not suffice'.

One of the most important recent authorities on this point is the decision of the Privy Council in *Royal Brunei Airlines Sdn Bhd v. Tan Kok Ming*[146] where Lord Nicholls stated that '"knowingly" is better avoided as a defining ingredient of the principle'. He was of the view that framing the

---

140. [1991] 3 NZLR 700, 728.
141. [1992] 3 NZLR 643.
142. [1993] 3 NZLR 218.
143. *Ibid.* at 228. Although note that Blanchard J went on to say that he found the *Baden* test 'unhelpful and ... unrememberable'. See also the judgment of Grieg J in *Cigna Life Insurance New Zealand Ltd v. Westpac Securities Ltd* [1996] 1 NZLR 80, 87.
144. (1993) 108 DLR (4th) 592, 608.
145. (1997) 152 DLR (4th) 411, 421. See also *Gold v. Rosenberg* (1997) 152 DLR (4th) 365, 394 *per* Iacobucci J.
146. [1995] 2 AC 378. See Halliwell [1995] Conv 339. See also Ashe and Reid (1997) 4 Comm LP 188.

question in terms of 'knowledge' often leads to difficulties about the type of knowledge required and said that ' "knowingly" is inapt as a criterion when applied to the gradually darkening spectrum where the differences are of degree and not kind.'[147] However, Lord Nicholls said that when a court is called upon to decide whether a person is acting honestly, it will look at all the circumstances known to the third party at the time and to personal attributes such as his experience and intelligence. So if the concept of honesty is to be judged by objective standards, an accessory will not be able to escape liability by claiming that he did not 'know' that his actions were wrong.

Berg has questioned why the Privy Council saw fit to require dishonesty and reject the concept of 'knowingly' as a test of liability.[148] He points out as stated above that Lord Nicholls acknowledged that honesty has to be assessed in the light of what a person actually knew at the time.[149] In addition, he quite rightly asserts that the conclusion reached in the subsequent first instance decision of Rimer J in *Brinks Ltd v. Abu-Saleh (No. 3)*[150] shows that not only must it be established that the accessory was dishonest, but also that he knew or had reason to suspect that he was assisting a trustee in a manner contrary to the terms of the trust. So despite the clear desire of Lord Nicholls to move away from the use of knowledge as a means of determining liability in cases of knowing assistance, it is likely to remain with us in one form or another for some time to come.

Despite some divergence of opinion in the context of the terminology which should be employed, there is a certain degree of uniformity in terms of the ultimate result to be found in an examination of these recent English, New Zealand and Canadian authorities. It would therefore seem most unlikely that the courts in this jurisdiction would depart from these formulations of the dishonesty and the degree of knowledge necessary to provide the basis for a successful claim for knowing assistance.[151]

---

147. *Ibid.* at 391. In the view of Lord Nicholls the *Baden* scale of knowledge should be forgotten and as Halliwell has suggested this might be a particularly welcome development in the context of the proper role of equity in commercial transactions, see [1995] Conv 339, 343.
148. (1996) 59 MLR 443, 451. He argues that it appears that an accessory's liability for assisting in a breach of trust is now based on the same principles as the liability of a third party who induces a breach of contract and that liability for inducing a breach of contract depends not on dishonesty but on knowledge of the existence of the plaintiff's contract and an intention to interfere with its performance.
149. As Gardner points out (1996) 112 LQR 56, 67: 'It is doubtful then, that the new law of direct reference to a concept of dishonesty obviates any need for an exegesis upon cognisance'.
150. [1996] CLC 133. See Stevens [1996] Conv 447.
151. O'Dell has suggested in *Annual Review of Irish Law 1997* p.632 that the decision of

Knowing Receipt of and Inconsistent Dealing with Trust Property

General Principles

A recipient of property which has been misappropriated in breach of trust may be liable as a constructive trustee of this property provided that he possesses the necessary degree of knowledge of the breach of trust. Similarly, where a recipient of trust property deals with it in a manner which he knows to be inconsistent with the terms of the trust, he will be regarded as a constructive trustee of the property. This second category of liability covers situations in which the recipient might not be liable for 'receipt' as such, because he does not possess the requisite degree of knowledge, but subsequently deals with the property in a manner inconsistent with the trust after acquiring such knowledge. Millett J described these categories in his judgment in *Agip (Africa) Ltd v. Jackson*[152] as follows:

> [I]t is necessary to distinguish between two main classes of case under this heading.
>
> The first is concerned with the person who receives for his own benefit trust property transferred to him in breach of trust. He is liable as a constructive trustee if he received it with notice, actual or constructive, that it was trust property and that the transfer to him was a breach of trust; or if he received it without such notice but subsequently discovered the facts.
>
> The second and in my judgment distinct class of case is that of the person, usually an agent of the trustees, who receives the trust property lawfully and not for his own benefit but who then either misappropriates it or otherwise deals with it in a manner which is inconsistent with the trust. He is liable to account as a constructive trustee if he received the property knowing it to be such, though he will not necessarily be required in all circumstances to have known the exact terms of the trust.

McCracken J in *Taxback Ltd v. Revenue Commissioners* High Court 1996 No. 325 JR, 21 January 1997 'might well constitute the Irish adoption of the principle in *Tan*'. Although *Royal Brunei Airlines Sdn Bhd v. Tan Kok Ming* is referred to in the course of the judgment, it is submitted that there are no real grounds for O'Dell's assertion. The case concerned a dispute between the parties about the withholding by the Revenue Commissioners of refunds payable to the applicant VAT refunding agency. The Revenue contended on the authority of *Royal Brunei Airlines* that if they made payments to the applicant they might be assisting in the applicant's dishonesty and incur liability themselves. However, McCracken J rejected this argument and stated that unless they had statutory authority to withhold monies during an investigation of this type they must discharge their statutory obligations in relation to payment.

152. [1990] Ch 265, 291.

As Millett J pointed out, in either class of case outlined it is immaterial whether the breach of trust was fraudulent or not and the most controversial question associated with these categories of liability is the degree of knowledge required.

Before examining this question in more detail, it should be pointed out that the principles which apply in this area are still far from certain, and given their increasing use in a commercial context, this has become a cause for considerable concern. Furthermore there have recently been signs of a move away from equitable principles as a means of resolving questions of this nature.[153] The irony of such a development was not lost on Lord Nicholls as a recent comment shows:

> Whatever may ultimately emerge either from the courts or from the legislature, one point is clear. Traditionally equity has supplemented the common law, giving a remedy where the common law was rigid and harsh. With its emphasis on conscience and flexibility, equity went to the heart of the matter affording new rights, new remedies, new procedures. Now, ironically, part of the heartland of equity is itself under siege from the encroaching influence of the common law in the guise of restitution. A vigorous new force is at large.[154]

The Degree of Knowledge Required

There is a fundamental difference between the nature of liability in cases of knowing assistance and knowing receipt[155] and it has been argued that given this distinction, it makes sense to require a different threshold of knowledge for each category of liability.[156] It has been suggested that in cases of knowing receipt, which are concerned with the receipt of trust property for the benefit of the recipient, there should be a lower threshold of knowledge required than in cases of knowing assistance in order to found liability.[157] While the decision of the Privy Council in *Royal Brunei*

---

153. E.g. see the decision of the House of Lords in *Lipkin Gorman v. Karpanale Ltd* [1991] 2 AC 548.
154. Lord Nicholls 'Knowing Receipt: the Need for a New Landmark' in *Restitution: Past, Present and Future* ed. Cornish (1998) p.243.
155. As Iacobucci J stated in the Canadian Supreme Court decision of *Gold v. Rosenberg* (1997) 152 DLR (4th) 385, 396: 'participation in a fraud underlies liability in cases of knowing assistance; unjust enrichment is the essence of a claim in knowing receipt'.
156. *Citadel General Assurance Co v. Lloyds Bank Canada* (1997) 152 DLR (4th) 411, 433 *per* La Forest J and *Gold v. Rosenberg* (1997) 152 DLR (4th) 385, 396 *per* Iacobucci J. See also *Agip Africa Ltd v. Jackson* [1990] Ch 265, 292 *per* Millett J.
157. See the *dicta* of La Forest J in *Citadel General Assurance Co v. Lloyds Bank Canada*

Airlines Sdn Bhd v. Tan Kok Ming[158] provided the opportunity for a detailed analysis of the type of conduct or knowledge which would suffice to
establish liability in cases of knowing assistance, considerable controversy
still surrounds the question of the degree of knowledge required in cases
of knowing receipt and for this reason it is difficult to set out the relevant
principles in this area with any degree of certainty. It is proposed to trace
developments in a number of jurisdictions with a view to establishing the
attitude which the courts are likely to take in the future.

It was held by Buckley LJ in *Belmont Finance Corporation v. Williams
Furniture Ltd (No. 2)*,[159] that where a stranger to a trust receives trust
property with either actual or constructive knowledge of the breach of
trust, he will be regarded as a constructive trustee of this property. Liability was imposed in that case on the basis of a receipt of trust monies by a
company, the directors of which knew or ought to have known belonged to
the trust.[160]

However, subsequently in *Re Montagu's Settlement Trusts*,[161] Megarry
VC favoured the imposition of liability only in circumstances where the
recipient possessed actual knowledge of the breach of trust. The trustees
in that case had transferred certain chattels to a beneficiary (the tenth Duke
of Manchester) in breach of trust and he had disposed of a number of these
during his lifetime although his solicitor had been aware of the terms of
the settlement. After his death, the eleventh duke claimed that the tenth
duke was a constructive trustee of the chattels. Megarry VC held that while
the estate of the tenth duke was liable to return any remaining chattels or
their traceable proceeds, the duke himself was not liable as constructive
trustee as he had no actual knowledge that the chattels had been trust property transferred in breach of trust.

Megarry VC was of the view that the imposition of a constructive trust
should depend primarily on the actual knowledge of the recipient and not
on whether he is deemed to have constructive notice of the trust. He stated:

> I do not see why one of the touchstones for determining the burdens
> on property should be the same as that for deciding whether to im-
> pose a personal obligation on a man. The cold calculus of construc-
> tive and imputed notice does not seem to me to be an appropriate

---

(1997) 152 DLR (4th) 411, 434 to the effect that 'more is expected of the recipient,
who unlike the accessory, is necessarily enriched at the plaintiff's expense'.
158. [1995] 2 AC 378.
159. [1980] 1 All ER 393.
160. See also *Karak Rubber Co. Ltd v. Burden (No. 2)* [1972] 1 WLR 602.
161. [1987] Ch 264. See Hayton [1987] CLJ 395 and Harpum (1987) 50 MLR 217.

> instrument for deciding whether a man's conscience is sufficiently affected for it to be right to bind him by the obligations of a constructive trustee.[162]

Megarry VC held that in considering whether a constructive trust has arisen in the context of the knowing receipt of trust property, the basic question is whether the conscience of the recipient is sufficiently affected to justify the imposition of such a trust.[163] He stated that for this purpose, knowledge extends to the first three categories outlined in *Baden* for in such cases there is a want of probity which justifies the imposition of a constructive trust. A similar view was taken by Alliot J at first instance in *Lipkin Gorman v. Karpanale Ltd,*[164] in which liability for both knowing assistance and knowing receipt was at issue. A partner in the plaintiff firm of solicitors had withdrawn money mostly from the clients' account and lost it gambling at a club. The plaintiff firm brought an action against the club on the basis of knowing receipt and against their bank on the grounds of knowing assistance. The plaintiff failed to establish liability on the part of the club on this basis and the finding of liability against the bank was reversed on appeal to the Court of Appeal. The solicitors' appeal from the dismissal of their claim against the club was ultimately allowed by the House of Lords[165] but on a different basis. It was held that the innocent recipient of stolen money was obliged to pay an equivalent sum to the true owner where full consideration for it had not been given and where this party had been unjustly enriched at the expense of the true owner. Although the solicitors had no proprietary rights in the money in their bank account, at common law they were owners of a chose in action constituted by the indebtedness of the bank to them and could trace their property into its direct product, namely, the money drawn from the bank account by the gambler, and follow it into the hands of the club.

In *Agip Africa (Ltd) v. Jackson*[166] Millett J stated at one point in his judgment that a person who receives for his own benefit trust property transferred to him in breach of trust is liable as a constructive trustee if he received it 'with notice, actual or constructive' that it was trust property transferred in breach of trust. Later in his judgment he refers to the doubts expressed by Megarry VC in *Montagu* about whether constructive notice

---

162. *Ibid.* at 273.
163. This approach has recently been approved by Knox J in *Hillsdown Holdings plc v. Pensions Ombudsman* [1997] 1 All ER 862, 902-903.
164. [1987] 1 WLR 987.
165. [1991] 2 AC 548. See Birks [1991] LMCLQ 473; McKendrick (1992) 55 MLR 377.
166. [1990] Ch 265, 293.

is sufficient in relation to knowing receipt and appears to reserve the question of whether these doubts were well-founded. However, Gardner's suggestion that 'taken with Millett J's other remarks, this passage seems a reflection rather of courtesy towards a brother judge than of uncertainty on Millett J's part over his own view'[167] is probably accurate.

Subsequent decisions in England have failed to satisfactorily resolve this question. In *Polly Peck International plc v. Nadir (No. 2)*[168] Scott LJ suggested that the real question was whether the circumstances in which the transfers of trust monies were made should have made the recipient suspicious as to the propriety of what was being done. While he accepted that a defendant would be liable if he was shown to have wilfully and recklessly failed to make such inquiries as an honest and reasonable man would have made, Scott LJ expressed doubts about whether it would suffice if a defendant could be shown to have had knowledge of facts which would have put an honest and reasonable man on inquiry.

It has been argued that the principle of constructive notice imposes too high a burden in a commercial context and in *Eagle Trust plc v. SBC Securities Ltd*[169] Vinelott J distinguished between the type of knowledge which would be required to found liability in commercial and non-commercial[170] types of transactions. In relation to the former category he stated that in order to make a defendant liable as a constructive trustee, it must be shown that he knew in one of the senses set out in the first three categories identified in *Baden* that the property was misapplied trust property, or the circumstances must be such that, in the absence of any evidence or explanation by the defendant, that knowledge can be inferred.[171] In the view of Vinelott J this inference may be drawn 'if the circumstances are such that an honest and reasonable man would have inferred that the moneys were probably trust moneys and were being misapplied, and would either not have accepted them or would have kept them separate until he had satisfied himself that the payer was entitled to use them in discharge of the liability'.[172]

---

167. (1996) 112 LQR 64, 69-70.
168. [1992] 4 All ER 769.
169. [1993] 1 WLR 484.
170. Oakley suggests that for non-commercial transactions, Vinelott J appeared to favour the broader based view of liability for knowing receipt rather than that favoured by Megarry VC in *Re Montagu's Settlement Trusts*, see Parker and Mellows, *The Modern Law of Trusts* (7th ed., 1998, Oakley) p.345.
171. Vinelott J was of the opinion that a difference remains between inferred knowledge and notice and stated (at 494) that 'the term "notice" is often used in a sense or in contexts where the facts do not support the inference of knowledge'.
172. *Ibid.* at 506. See also the judgment of Knox J in *Cowan de Groot Properties Ltd v. Eagle Trust plc* [1992] 4 All ER 700, 759 although in the circumstances of the case, no liability arose.

However, it has been argued by Millett J that judges who have warned against extending constructive notice to commercial dealings 'were obviously referring to the doctrine in its strict conveyancing sense'.[173] Fox has suggested that this longstanding policy against extending constructive notice to commercial transactions[174] can be circumvented and that the same objections would not necessarily apply to an 'appropriately adjusted commercial standard of notice'.[175] In his view 'there are no compelling economic reasons why constructive notice, set at the proper commercial standard, should not become a basis of liability for knowing receipt arising out of a commercial transaction'. Certainly there have been decisions in other jurisdictions which have not displayed the same unwillingness to confine the basis of liability for knowing receipt in commercial cases to knowledge in the sense of the first three categories set out in *Baden*. In *Citadel General Assurance Co v. Lloyds Bank Canada*[176] the Canadian Supreme Court was willing to impose liability on a banker in respect of knowing receipt where he only possessed constructive knowledge of the breach of trust.

Indeed in one of the few authorities on the issue of knowing receipt in this jurisdiction, the Supreme Court appeared to be prepared to accept that constructive notice would suffice to ground liability even in a commercial context. In *Re Frederick Inns Ltd*,[177] payments were made by a group of associated companies to the Revenue Commissioners in the six months immediately preceding the commencement of the winding up of four of these companies out of the proceeds of sale of various licensed premises which had belonged to the companies. This sum was appropriated by the commissioners in reduction of the tax liabilities of not only the four companies involved in the proceedings but also those of six other companies in the group. The liquidator challenged these payments as being *ultra vires* insofar as they had effected an alienation of the companies' assets when they were insolvent. Lardner J held that the payments made by the companies which exceeded their liabilities and were intended to reduce the liabilities of the other companies in the same group were *ultra vires* on the grounds that each company was a separate entity. The commissioners' appeal was dismissed by the Supreme Court which held that no clause in the memoranda of association of any of the companies, properly construed,

---

173. *MacMillan Inc v. Bishopsgate Investment Trust plc (No. 3)* [1995] 1 WLR 978, 1000.
174. See *Manchester Trust v. Furness* [1895] 2 QB 539.
175. [1998] CLJ 391, 396.
176. (1997) 152 DLR (4th) 411.
177. [1994] 1 ILRM 387.

gave them power to pay the debts of an associate company and that the payments were therefore *ultra vires*. Blayney J held that the *ultra vires* payments constituted a misapplication by the directors of company funds in breach of their fiduciary duties. These monies had been received by the Revenue Commissioners with constructive knowledge of this breach as the memoranda of association of the four companies, which were documents of public record, revealed the absence of capacity. So, apart from the monies which the Revenue Commissioners had originally appropriated towards the discharge of the respective tax liabilities of the four companies involved in the proceedings, the payments were held by them on a constructive trust and had to be repaid to the official liquidator. The Supreme Court therefore ordered that the sums involved should be repaid by the Revenue Commissioners.

One disappointing aspect of the judgment from an academic perspective is the lack of consideration given to the question of the degree of knowledge required in a case of knowing receipt.[178] O'Dell has correctly asserted that the application of principle by Blayney J in *Re Frederick Inns Ltd* seemed to go even further than the fifth point on the *Baden* scale and he has commented that 'even if the *Baden* scale does not reach notice properly so-called, *Frederick Inns* certainly seems to'.[179]

The question of the degree of knowledge required to establish liability for knowing receipt has also been considered recently by the High Court in *Ulster Factors Ltd v. Entoglen Ltd*.[180] The first named defendant entered into a factoring agreement with the plaintiff whereby the first named defendant agreed to assign all its debts to the plaintiff by way of sale or assignment and the plaintiff agreed to make payment to or to the order of the first named defendant of a sum not exceeding the 'availability balance' as defined in the agreement. After the first named defendant went into liquidation, the plaintiff instituted proceedings against the company and its liquidator, the second named defendant, claiming the balance which it alleged was due to it. What remained at issue at the hearing of action was one payment made to a third party by the plaintiff which the liquidator claimed had not been properly paid. The defendants submitted that this payment was *ultra vires* the company and that it had been made without the company's authority. Laffoy J did not accept that the payment by the plaintiff was *ultra vires* the company. However, she went on to say that

---

178. O'Dell has commented that 'the requirement of knowledge as an ingredient was so easily satisfied that it was all but abandoned.' (See [1994] RLR 161).
179. *Annual Review of Irish Law 1997* p.644.
180. High Court 1992 No. 1060P (Laffoy J) 21 February 1997.

even if the liquidator had established that the payment was *ultra vires*, he had not made out any basis on which the plaintiff should be required in effect to make restitution for this payment. Laffoy J quoted with approval from the judgment of Blayney J in *Re Frederick Inns Ltd* in which he had applied the principle set out in *Belmont Finance Corporation Ltd v. Williams Furniture Ltd (No.2)*[181] and stated that 'what renders the recipient of or the dealer with funds which are being misapplied in breach of the fiduciary duties of the directors of a company liable as a constructive trustee is knowledge, actual or constructive, of the breach of trust'.[182] She found that the plaintiff did not have actual knowledge of any breach of duty and concluded that 'there was no obligation on the plaintiff to enquire as to the purpose for which any payment which the company requested the plaintiff to make to a third party was being made or to satisfy itself that the payment was *intra vires* the company and, even if the payment was *ultra vires*, constructive knowledge of a breach of trust cannot be imputed to the plaintiff for failure to make such inquiries'. Laffoy J also rejected the liquidator's contention that the payment was made without the company's authority and she held that the plaintiff was entitled to judgment in the amount claimed.

There seems little doubt that the judgment of the Supreme Court in *Re Frederick Inns* and the *dicta* of Laffoy J in *Ulster Factors* purport at the least to follow the principle laid down in *Belmont* that either actual or constructive knowledge suffices to establish liability for knowing receipt. Whether the approach adopted by the Supreme Court, which was effectively to accept that constructive notice suffices even in a commercial context, will be followed remains to be seen. Arguably it imposes an unnecessarily high onus on persons or bodies dealing with a company and it is interesting to note that the Supreme Court made no attempt to distinguish the standard required in relation to commercial and non-commercial transactions. While the argument put forward by Fox that there is no reason 'why constructive notice, set at the proper commercial standard, should not become a basis of liability for knowing receipt arising out of a commercial transaction' is a sound one, in the absence of a more detailed consideration of the knowledge/notice requirement in this jurisdiction, some doubt must still surround this question.[183]

---

181. [1980] 1 All ER 393.
182. *Ibid.* at 8.
183. It is interesting to note the divergence of opinion on the meaning of the term 'notice' between Vinelott J in *Eagle Trust plc v. SBC Securities Ltd* [1993] 1 WLR 484 and Millett J in *El Anjou v. Dollar Holdings plc* [1993] 3 All ER 717. While the approach of Vinelott J appears to assume that a reasonable person 'must always be-

It is interesting that there has also been a marked lack of consistency in other common law jurisdictions in relation to the circumstances in which liability will be imposed in cases of knowing receipt. In the New Zealand decision of *Marshall Futures Ltd v. Marshall*[184] Tipping J stated that in cases of knowing receipt 'where the person alleged to be a constructive trustee will usually have benefited personally from the breach of trust there are good policy reasons for allowing constructive knowledge in the form of categories (iv) and (v) to be sufficient to make him responsible'.[185] In the subsequent decision of *Equiticorp Industries Group v. The Crown*[186] Smellie J found that the defendant had either wilfully shut its eyes to the obvious or if not, had wilfully and recklessly failed to make the inquiries which a reasonable and honest commercial party would have made and therefore the need to make a decision about the knowledge of types (iv) and (v) on the *Baden* scale did not arise.The issue has also been considered in detail in two recent decisions of the Canadian Supreme Court. In *Citadel General Assurance Co .v. Lloyds Bank Canada*[187] La Forest J expressed the view that in cases of knowing receipt there should be a lower threshold of knowledge required of the stranger to the trust than in cases of knowing assistance. As he stated: 'More is expected of the recipient, who unlike the accessory, is necessarily enriched at the plaintiff's expense. Because the recipient is held to this higher standard, constructive knowledge (that is, knowledge of facts sufficient to put a reasonable person on notice or inquiry) will suffice as the basis for restitutionary liability.'[188] Similarly in *Gold v. Rosenberg*[189] Iacobucci J, albeit in a dissenting judg-

---

have as rigorously as he does in the land transfer context', Millett J accepts the idea that 'the reasonable person behaves differently in different contexts' (see Gardner (1996) 112 LQR 56, 62). Gardner believes that Millett J's approach is probably the better founded (at p. 63) and suggests that it is the formula to the effect that 'notice is a function of how the reasonable person would have behaved in the relevant circumstances . . . rather than the standards set in the land transfer cases, that truly defines notice'. It would certainly be useful if the courts in this jurisdiction were to consider this question and clarify what their understanding of 'notice' is, particularly in a commercial context.

184. [1992] 1 NZLR 316, 326.
185. A similar view was expressed by Wylie J in *Equiticorp Industries Group v. Hawkins* [1991] 3 NZLR 700, 728.
186. [1996] 3 NZLR 586.
187. (1997) 152 DLR (4th) 411. See Smith (1998) 114 LQR 394.
188. *Ibid.* at 434. See also *Carl B. Potter Ltd v. Mercantile Bank of Canada* (1980) 112 DLR (3d) 88; *Arthur Andersen Inc v. Toronto-Dominion Bank* (1994) 17 OR (3d) 363; *Glenko Enterprises Ltd v. Ernie Keller Contractors Ltd* (1996) 134 DLR (4th) 161.
189. (1997) 152 DLR (4th) 385.

ment,[190] stated that in cases of knowing receipt, a person need not have actual knowledge and that notice would suffice.

It has been argued that neither the restricted view of fault set out in *Re Montagu's Settlement Trusts*[191] nor the broader view of liability encompassing constructive knowledge provides a wholly satisfactory answer and that 'each will produce an unattractive result in some situations'.[192] There is arguably merit in Harpum's criticism of the approach of Megarry VC in *Re Montagu's Settlement Trusts*[193] that it ignores the restitutionary nature of the claim and in the viewpoint expressed by Thomas J in the New Zealand decision of *Powell v. Thompson*[194] that liability in the knowing receipt category is based on the concept of unjust enrichment, which is receipt-based and not fault-based. If one accepts this approach, it should therefore follow that the degree of knowledge possessed by the recipient should not be the decisive factor. There are signs of a movement towards acceptance of such a trend, both in the statement of the Privy Council in *Royal Brunei Airlines Sdn Bhd v. Tan Kok Ming*[195] that 'recipient liability is restitution-based' and in the view expressed by Budd J in *Dublin Corporation v. Ancient Guild of Incorporated Brick and Stone Layers and Allied Trades Union*[196] that an action in knowing receipt is 'restitutionary in character'. However, as the law stands at present in this jurisdiction, knowledge, or if the approach in *Re Frederick Inns* is followed, at least some form of notice, is still necessary before liability under the heading of knowing receipt can be imposed.[197]

---

190. The view of the majority was that the bank had not actually received the trust property. However, the minority found that there had been receipt and went on to consider whether the requisite degree of knowledge existed.
191. [1987] Ch 264.
192. *Per* Lord Nicholls 'Knowing Receipt: the Need for a New Landmark' in *Restitution: Past, Present and Future* ed. Cornish (1998) p.241.
193. [1987] Ch 264.
194. [1991] 1 NZLR 597, 607.
195. [1995] 2 AC 378, 386.
196. High Court 1991 No. 1556P (Budd J) 6 March 1996 at 51.
197. O'Dell has correctly suggested in *Annual Review of Irish Law 1997* at p. 644 that the approach adopted by the Supreme Court in *Re Frederick Inns* makes the traditional knowledge requirement very easy to satisfy. He continues: '[I]t is tantamount to emptying it of all content, and comes close to the imposition of strict liability. On this view, the express adoption of a restitutionary analysis would not work a large change in the law'. Indeed, while there is logic in such an argument, it is still unclear how favourably the courts in this jurisdiction would look upon it. O'Dell himself acknowledges that in this area 'academic discourse has raced well ahead of the caselaw, and might well be exploring routes which as the law develops may not even open up'. *Ibid.* at 645.

Possible Future Developments

It can be argued that in the light of the approach taken by the House of Lords in *Lipkin Gorman v. Karpanale Ltd*,[198] liability in this area might in future be decided in terms of common law principles in an action for money had and received, based on the concept of strict liability but subject to the defence of change of position. As Oakley[199] points out such a remedy possesses the distinct advantage that its imposition does not depend on the state of mind or degree of knowledge of the recipient. An interesting alternative theory has also recently been put forward by Lord Nicholls writing extra-judicially, who suggested that personal liability should be based on a combination of two separate principles.[200]

First, recipient liability should cover all third party recipients. This would be a principle of strict liability in that it would apply to every recipient with an impeachable title irrespective of fault, but it would be restitutionary in nature. It would be confined to restoring an unjust gain. Change of position would be available as a defence accordingly. Secondly, dishonest recipients should be personally liable to make good losses as well as accounting for benefits.

Harpum has welcomed this model for future development of the law as seeking to reconcile the views of those who consider that receipt-based liability should be founded on restitutionary principles and those who consider that it should be based upon equitable wrongdoing.[201] As he points out it would involve a move away from fault-based liability, which would be a welcome step in view of the present uncertainties in the area, but this would be balanced by the availability of the defences of change of position and *bona fide* purchase.

It is therefore possible that should the courts in this jurisdiction decide to follow such an approach or to develop an alternative of their own many of the issues addressed above may prove to be purely of academic interest in years to come. However, for the present, equitable principles are relevant and it is still necessary to distinguish between the circumstances giving rise to cases of knowing assistance and knowing receipt, not just because the former encompasses the requirement of a 'fraudulent and dishonest design' but because the degree of knowledge required to establish liability in the latter category is defined in broader terms.

---

198. [1991] 2 AC 548.
199. Parker and Mellows, *The Modern Law of Trusts* (7th ed., 1998) p.348.
200. 'Knowing Receipt: the Need for a New Landmark' in *Restitution: Past, Present and Future* ed. Cornish (1998) p.244.
201. 'Knowing Receipt: the Need for a New Landmark: Some Reflections' in *Restitution: Past, Present and Future* ed. Cornish (1998) p.248.

Liability of Agents of Trustees

An agent of a trustee will not be liable as a constructive trustee provided that in receiving trust property or in dealing with it, he has acted honestly and within the scope of his usual authority as an agent. So where he is acting in the capacity of agent, he will not be accountable to the beneficiaries, but only to his principal provided that he does not act outside the scope of his authority. This general rule was laid down by Lord Selborne in *Barnes v. Addy*[202] as follows:

> [S]trangers are not to be made constructive trustees merely because they act as the agents of trustees in transactions within their legal powers, transactions, perhaps of which a Court of Equity may disapprove, unless those agents receive and become chargeable with some part of the trust property, or unless they assist with knowledge in a dishonest and fraudulent design on the part of the trustees.

In that case solicitors advised against the appointment of a sole trustee although they prepared the documentation necessary for his appointment. When the trustee in question sold the trust property and misapplied the proceeds it was held that the solicitors could not be treated as constructive trustees as they had acted honestly in the course of their agency and had merely carried out the instructions of the trustees.

One of the most important recent authorities in this area is the decision of the Court of Appeal in *Carl Zeiss Stiftung v. Herbert Smith & Co. (No. 2)*,[203] where a solicitor who was given money by a client which the plaintiff claimed was held by the client on trust for the plaintiff was found not to be accountable for this money since there had been no want of probity on the solicitor's part. Edmund Davies LJ summarized his view of an agent's position as follows:

> A solicitor or other agent who receives money from his principal which belongs at law or in equity to a third party is not accountable as a constructive trustee to that third party unless he has been guilty of some wrongful act in relation to that money. ... To act 'wrongfully' he must be guilty of (i) knowingly participating in a breach of trust by his principal; or (ii) intermeddling with the trust property otherwise than merely as an agent and thereby becomes a trustee *de*

---

202. (1874) 9 Ch App 244, 251- 252.
203. [1969] 2 Ch 276.

son tort; or (iii) receiving or dealing with the money knowing that his principal has no right to pay it over or to instruct him to deal with it in the manner indicated; or (iv) some dishonest act relating to the money.[204]

It would appear that agents of trustees who are in receipt of trust property or who deal inconsistently with it, are to an extent regarded more favourably than a beneficial recipient of trust property and an agent's duty to inquire is less strictly interpreted.[205] This point is well illustrated by the decision of Kay J in *Williams v. Williams,*[206] where a solicitor disposed of lands which were subject to a settlement on the settlor's behalf in accordance with the latter's instructions. It was held that the solicitor was not liable to account since he neither knew of the settlement nor had wilfully shut his eyes to its existence although the facts disclosed that he should have been put on inquiry as to its existence. So where an agent acts honestly in following his principal's instructions, he will not be liable. This was confirmed by the judgment of Bennett J in *Williams-Ashman v. Price,*[207] where solicitors who had followed the instructions of a trustee in making an unauthorized loan and other investments were found not to be liable as constructive trustees as they had acted honestly on the trustee's instructions and had not intermeddled in the affairs of the trust.

However, where an agent receives trust property and, knowing that he is acting in breach of trust, deals with it in a manner inconsistent with its terms, he may be personally liable as a constructive trustee. This is evident from the decision of *Lee v. Sankey,*[208] where Bacon VC made it clear that where an agent receives trust monies and deals with them in a manner inconsistent with the trust of which he is aware, he is personally liable for the consequences. Solicitors who were employed by trustees to receive the proceeds of the sale of a testator's property and improperly paid over the money to only one of the two trustees, who dissipated the fund and subsequently died insolvent, were held liable to account to the beneficiaries in respect of the loss which had occurred.

---

204. *Ibid.* at 303-304.
205. *Carl Zeiss Stiftung v. Herbert Smith & Co. (No. 2)* [1969] 2 Ch 276, 297.
206. (1881) 17 Ch D 437.
207. [1942] Ch 219.
208. (1873) LR 15 Eq 204. See also *Soar v. Ashwell* [1893] 2 QB 390.

THE VENDOR AS CONSTRUCTIVE TRUSTEE

Traditionally it has been accepted that where a vendor enters into a specifically enforceable contract for sale,[209] equity regards him as a constructive trustee of the property which forms the subject-matter of the contract
until completion.[210] This is an example of the equitable doctrine of conversion and the purchaser is regarded as the owner of the property while
the vendor is looked upon as the owner of the purchase monies. Contracts
which are capable of being specifically enforced are predominantly contracts for the sale of land, as specific performance will only be granted
where a breach of contract cannot be adequately compensated by an award
of damages.[211]

The position in England was set out by Jessel MR in *Lysaght v.
Edwards*[212] in the following terms: 'The moment you have a valid contract
for sale the vendor becomes in equity a trustee for the purchaser of the
estate sold, and the beneficial ownership passes to the purchaser.' This
was also the position accepted by Henchy J in a minority judgment delivered in *Tempany v. Hynes*.[213] However the view of the majority[214] of the
Supreme Court as set out by Kenny J was as follows:

> [A] vendor who signs a contract with a purchaser for the sale of land
> becomes a trustee in the sense that he is bound to take reasonable
> care of the property until the sale is completed, but he becomes a
> trustee of the beneficial interest to the extent only to which the pur-
> chase price is paid. He is not a trustee of the beneficial interest merely
> because he signs a contract.[215]

---

209. Although note how this point has been modified by the view taken by the majority
     of the Supreme Court in *Tempany v. Hynes* [1976] IR 101 considered *infra*, to the
     effect that the beneficial interest only passes to the extent to which the purchase
     price is paid.
210. Once the purchase price has been paid in full, the vendor is then regarded as holding
     the property on a bare trust for the purchaser.
211. See further *infra* Chapter 14.
212. (1876) 2 Ch D 499, 506.
213. [1976] IR 101, 109. Henchy J stated: 'When a binding contract for the sale of land
     has been made, the law treats the beneficial ownership as having passed to the pur-
     chaser from the time the contract was made ... from then until the time of comple-
     tion, regardless of whether the purchase money has been paid or not, the vendor, in
     whom the legal estate is still vested, is treated for certain purposes as a trustee for
     the purchaser.' This also seems to be the view accepted in Australia, see *Legione v.
     Hateley* (1983) 57 ALJ 292 and *KLDE Pty Ltd v. Commissioner of Stamp Duties*
     (1984) 58 ALJR 545.
214. See the judgment of Kenny J, with whom O'Higgins CJ concurred.
215. *Ibid.* at 114.

The Law Reform Commission considered the issue of the interests of vendors and purchasers of land during the period between contract and completion in a report published in 1995[216] and concluded that the approach adopted by Henchy J in his minority judgment in *Tempany* was the 'only means by which the purchaser's interests prior to completion may be adequately protected'. The Commission therefore recommended the enactment of a statutory provision providing that when a binding contract for the sale of land has been entered into, the law should treat the beneficial ownership as having passed to the purchaser from the time the contract was made, subject to the condition that the sale is completed.

Once the beneficial interest passes, whether it is on contract as the Commission has recommended, or on payment of the purchase money, as the majority of the Supreme Court held in *Tempany*, the vendor is recognised as being a trustee of the property in the sense that he must take reasonable care of it. A vendor must maintain the property in a reasonable state of repair,[217] and will undoubtedly incur liability if he wilfully damages the property.[218] The obligation has been described by Lord Coleridge in *Clarke v. Ramuz*[219] as being 'to use reasonable care to preserve the property in a reasonable state of preservation and so far as may be, as it was when the contract was made.' In that case while the vendor remained in possession of property, a trespasser removed all the surface soil. It was held that the purchaser could maintain an action against the vendor for breach of trust by reason of the fact that he had taken no care to prevent the removal of the soil. However, it is only where the vendor acts in breach of his trust obligations or fails to take reasonable care that he can be made liable and any damage to the property which occurs without any fault on the part of the vendor is the responsibility of the purchaser. So when a purchaser enters into a specifically enforceable contract for sale, the risk of accidental damage to the property passes to him and he should insure against such risk.[220] As Jessel MR stated in *Lysaght v.*

---

216. LRC 49 -1995.
217. *Royal Bristol Permanent Building Society v. Bomash* (1887) 35 Ch D 390.
218. *Lysaght v. Edwards* (1876) 2 Ch D 499, 507.
219. [1891] 2 QB 456, 459-460.
220. This position was regarded as being unfair to purchasers and the Law Reform Commission pointed out in a report published in 1991 (LRC 39-1991) that it was unsatisfactory that the law as to the passing of risk did not accord with the reasonable expectations of the ordinary person. It recommended (at p.19) that the risk should instead pass to the purchaser 'in all situations where the purchaser goes into possession of the premises, or on completion of the purchase, whichever is the earlier'. Note the provisions of clause 43 of the Incorporated Law Society Standard Conditions of Sale (1991 Edition) the effect of which is to provide that the risk remains with the vendor until completion.

Edwards:[221]

> [If] anything happens to the estate between the time of the sale and
> the time of completion of the purchase it is at the risk of the pur-
> chaser. If it is a house that is sold, and the house is burnt down the
> purchaser loses the house. He must insure it himself if he wants to
> provide against such an accident.

This principle is well illustrated by the decision in *Rayner v. Preston*,[222]
where a vendor contracted with a purchaser for the sale of a house which
had been insured by the vendor against fire. After the date of the contract
but before completion, the property was damaged by fire and the vendor
received insurance money in respect of it. It was held that the purchaser
was not entitled as against the vendor to the benefit of the insurance money;
the risk had passed to the purchaser and it was therefore his responsibility
to ensure that the premises were insured.[223] This decision also illustrates
the qualified nature of the constructive trusteeship which arises in such
cases; while the vendor is a constructive trustee of the land, he is not trustee of anything substituted for the land such as insurance money paid to
him under his own insurance policy in relation to damage to the land caused
by fire. This point was made by Cotton LJ in *Rayner*, where he said that a
vendor was a trustee 'in a qualified sense only'.[224] This fact was also noted
by Lord Cairns in *Shaw v. Foster*[225] in the following terms:

> [T]he vendor, whom I have called the trustee, was not a mere dor-
> mant trustee, he was a trustee having a personal and substantial in-
> terest in the property, a right to protect that interest and an active
> right to assert that interest if anything should be done in derogation

---

221. (1876) 2 Ch D 499, 507. Although, see Thompson [1984] Conv 43. Note also that
    the Law Commission in England recommended that the risk should only pass on
    completion (See Law Commission Report No. 191 Paragraph 2.25 (1990)) and such
    a provision has also been incorporated in the Standard Conditions of Sale in that
    jurisdiction.
222. (1881) 18 Ch D 1. See also *Re Hamilton-Snowball's Conveyance* [1958] 2 WLR
    951.
223. Although note that this decision has been effectively overruled in England by the
    provisions of s.47 of the Law of Property Act 1925. See Wellings (1959) 23 Conv
    173, 174.
224. *Ibid.* at p.6.
225. (1872) LR 5 HL 321, 338. As Oakley comments 'the inevitable self interest of the
    vendor in the successful conclusion of the transaction does not sit very easily with
    his classification as a trustee.' (See Parker and Mellows, *The Modern Law of Trusts*
    (7th ed., 1998) p.376).

of it. The relation therefore, of trustee and *cestui que trust* subsisted, but subsisted subject to the paramount right of the vendor and trustee to protect his own interest as vendor of the property.

The qualified nature of the trust relationship existing between a vendor and purchaser in these circumstances is further illustrated by the fact that the vendor is entitled to keep the rents and profits of the land until completion and is under a duty to discharge all outgoings such as rates and taxes which may be payable in respect of the property until this date.[226] In addition, the vendor may retain possession of the land until the purchase price is paid and if the land is conveyed before this, he will have a lien on the land for the balance of the unpaid purchase money.[227]

The relationship which arises in these circumstances has been described as 'a highly self-interested modified form of trusteeship'[228] and some commentators have questioned whether the terms trustee and beneficiary should be used at all to describe the relationship between the vendor and the purchaser in such situations.[229] However it is also recognised that it is arguably too late to recast the nature of this relationship,[230] and the best approach is to regard the use of such terminology with a certain degree of caution.

THE MORTGAGEE AS CONSTRUCTIVE TRUSTEE

To a limited extent the liability of a mortgagee to a mortgagor has been described in terms of a trust relationship, although for a number of reasons the drawing of comparisons between the position of a mortgagee and trustee has been described as inappropriate. The strength of the trust analogy

---

226. *Re Highett and Bird's Contract* [1902] 2 Ch 214. However, it would appear that the purchaser is entitled to take the benefit and burden of any gains or losses of a capital nature accruing to the property.
227. *Mackreth v. Symmons* (1808) 15 Ves 329. This vendor's lien can be registered as a burden under s.69(1) of the Registration of Title Act 1964. Similarly the purchaser will have a lien on the land in respect of any purchase money paid prior to completion *Re Strong* [1940] IR 382.
228. Underhill and Hayton, *Law Relating to Trusts and Trustees* (15th ed., 1995) p. 399.
229. See Waters, *The Constructive Trust* (1964) where the opinion is expressed that until the purchase price is paid in full, the operation of a relationship of trustee and beneficiary is excluded by the fact that each party continues to guard their own position in a manner quite inconsistent with a trust relationship. Cope has commented in *Constructive Trusts* (1992) p.970 that the use of the term 'constructive trust' in the context of vendor and purchaser is an 'anomalous and inappropriate analogy'.
230. Hanbury and Martin, *Modern Equity* (15th ed., 1997) p. 314 and Cope, *Constructive Trusts* (1992) p. 970.

was never as strong in relation to mortgagees as it was in respect of vendors of property, particularly in view of the fact that a mortgagee did not usually enter into possession of the mortgaged property, while the vendor tended to remain in possession until completion. In addition, the mortgagee's natural desire to protect his own interests in the mortgage transaction and the trustee's obligation to act in the best interests of the beneficiaries were generally regarded as being incompatible.

However, traditionally where a mortgagee retained a surplus after exercising a power of sale over the mortgaged property, he held this on a constructive trust for whoever was entitled to the equity of redemption. This constructive trust was given statutory force and effectively superseded by section 21(3) of the Conveyancing Act 1881 which gave effect to previous practice.[231] Cope[232] suggests that one further aspect of the mortgagees's exercise of his power of sale may still give rise to a liability in equity to account as a constructive trustee, namely where a mortgagee purports to exercise this power in favour of himself without the fully informed consent of the mortgagor.

MUTUAL WILLS

Prerequisites for the Imposition of a Constructive Trust

Where two people, usually although not necessarily husband and wife, make an arrangement concerning the disposal of their property and execute mutual wills which are intended to be irrevocable and the survivor subsequently alters his will, his estate will be held by his personal representatives on a constructive trust to give effect to the arrangement provided for in the mutual wills.[233] However, before such a trust will arise, there must be evidence of an agreement to make mutual wills in substantially similar form and not to revoke them. As McPherson J stated in *Bigg v. Queensland Trustees Ltd*:[234] 'What matters is proof that the parties made an agreement to execute their wills in that form and that, expressly or by implication, they contracted not to revoke them.'

In determining whether the necessary agreement exists, the court will have regard to the terms of the wills but may also infer evidence of an

---

231. In England, this subsection has been replaced by s.105 of the Law of Property Act 1925.
232. *Constructive Trusts* (1992) p.976.
233. This principle can be traced to the decision of Lord Camden in *Dufour v. Pereira* (1769) 1 Dick 419. See generally Harper [1997] Conv 182, 188- 193.
234. [1990] 2 Qd R 11, 13. See Rickett (1991) 54 MLR 581.

agreement from the conduct of the parties and the surrounding circumstances. The mere fact that the wills were made simultaneously and in
substantially similar terms is not of itself sufficient proof that the parties
have entered into a legally binding agreement not to revoke them. This is
illustrated by the decision of Astbury J in *Re Oldham*,[235] where a husband
and wife executed mutual wills with similar provisions although there was
no evidence of any agreement that they should be irrevocable. After the
husband's death the wife remarried and made a new will. Astbury J upheld
the second will and stated that the fact that the two wills were made in
identical terms did not necessarily mean any agreement that they should
be irrevocable by the survivor.[236]

While the fact that the wills are made simultaneously and in the same
form is not *per se* proof of an agreement sufficient to justify the imposition of a constructive trust, it is a relevant factor to be taken into account in
determining whether an agreement exists. In *Re Cleaver*,[237] where a husband and wife made similar wills at the same time and subsequently altered them in the same manner, it was held that the trusts set out in these
wills would be enforced rather than those set out by the survivor, the wife,
in a will made subsequent to her husband's death. In the circumstances,
Nourse J was satisfied that there was sufficient evidence of an agreement
shown by the similarity of the provisions and the fact that the changes
were made simultaneously.

However, in *Re Goodchild*,[238] the most recent decision on this question, *Re Cleaver* was distinguished and the importance of having specific
evidence as to the testator's mutual intentions at the time of the execution
of the wills was stressed.[239] In this case the testator and his wife both
simultaneously executed wills in identical terms in favour of the first named
plaintiff, their only son. After her death, the testator married the defendant
and six weeks after making a new will in which he left his entire estate to
her, he died. The plaintiff brought an action seeking, *inter alia*, a declaration that after the death of his first wife, the testator held her estate on trust
for the plaintiff, and that after the testator's death, the defendant held his
estate similarly. Carnwarth J accepted that where there is a clear agree-

---

235. [1925] Ch 75.
236. *Ibid.* at p.88. See also *Birmingham v. Renfrew* (1937) 57 CLR 666, 675 *per* Latham
   CJ.
237. [1981] 1 WLR 939.
238. [1996] 1 WLR 694 (ChD); [1997] 1 WLR 1216 (CA). See Grattan [1997] Conv
   153; Richardson (1996) 10 Trust Law Int 88.
239. See also *Fisher v. Mansfield* [1997] 2 NZLR 230 where Heron J found that there
   was evidence of a mutual agreement between the parties at the time of the execution
   of the wills.

ment or other evidence that wills are intended to be mutually binding, the law will give effect to that intention by way of a 'floating trust' which becomes irrevocable after the death of the first testator and crystallises on the death of the second. However, he held that in the circumstances, the evidence fell short of establishing such an agreement between the testator and his first wife and the wills were not mutually binding. Carnwarth J stressed that the onus of proof lay on the plaintiff and said that there must be evidence of 'a specific agreement outside the wills not just some loose understanding or sense of moral obligation'.[240] He characterised *Re Cleaver* as an extreme example of the circumstances in which an agreement may be found on the basis of oral evidence but stated that in his view it did not provide any precedent for the case before him.[241]

The Court of Appeal upheld the conclusion that the wills were not mutually binding and affirmed the decision made by Carnwarth J. Legatt LJ also distinguished *Re Cleaver* in which he said there had been specific evidence as to the testator's mutual intentions at the time the wills were made, whereas in the case before him, he was satisfied that there was not. He was of the opinion that 'for the doctrine to apply there must be a contract' and stated that a key feature of the concept of mutual wills was the 'irrevocability of the mutual intentions'.[242] In his view what was missing in the case before him was evidence of a mutual intention that both wills should remain unaltered and that the survivor should be bound to leave the combined estates to his son.

The decision of the Court of Appeal would seem to mark a return to the stricter approach of Astbury J in *Re Oldham* and shows that the evidential difficulties facing a litigant who seeks to establish that the doctrine of mutual wills applies are not inconsiderable.[243]

The Time at which the Trust Arises

While some commentators have argued that the trust may arise either at the date of the agreement or at the time when the survivor dies, the correct

---

240. *Ibid.* at 706.
241. However, Carnwarth J went on to hold that the testator's wife's mistaken belief that the terms of the will were mutually binding imposed a moral obligation on him which justified the plaintiff's claim under the Inheritance (Provision for Family and Dependents) Act 1975 and that part of the estate which constituted her share should be available to meet the plaintiff's claim under the Act.
242. *Ibid.* at 1225.
243. Grattan has pointed out [1997] Conv 153, 159 that it has frequently been advocated that those seeking to execute mutual wills 'would be well advised to ensure that the agreement is recited in the body of the instruments'.

view would seem to be that it arises on the death of the first party to die. This means that the interest of a beneficiary will not lapse if he predeceases the survivor. In *Re Hagger*[244] a husband and wife made joint wills leaving a life interest in their property to the survivor and after that party's death on trust for sale for nine beneficiaries. One of these beneficiaries survived the wife, but predeceased the husband who left the property on different trusts. Clauson J held that the will operated as a trust from the date of the wife's death and that all the beneficiaries, including the one who had predeceased the husband, could claim their interests under the will.

Until recently it was unclear whether the trust only arose when the survivor received a benefit under the will of the first party to die.[245] As O'Hagan has pointed out, academic opinion favoured the requirement of benefit 'because to benefit under an agreement and afterwards renege on that same agreement is manifestly fraudulent'.[246] However, the decision of Morritt J in *Re Dale*[247] resolved this question by making it clear that a constructive trust can arise even where the survivor does not take any benefit from the will of the first testator. A husband and wife executed identical wills which both contained a bequest of their property in favour of their daughter and son in equal shares or to the survivor of them. Two months later the husband died and subsequently the wife made a new will in which she revoked all previous wills and bequeathed to the daughter the sum of £300, leaving the son the remainder of her property. The daughter claimed that the mutual wills had been made pursuant to a binding and irrevocable agreement and that the son held the estate of the mother as trustee for both of them in equal shares. The court had to consider as a preliminary issue the question of whether, for the doctrine of mutual wills to apply, it was necessary for the second testator to die to have obtained a personal financial benefit under the will of the first testator to die. In answering this question in the negative, Morritt J held that since the aim of the principle underlying the doctrine of mutual wills was to prevent fraud on the first testator to die, it was not confined to cases in which the surviving testator had benefited under the will of the first testator but extended to cases where the two testators had left their property to beneficiaries other than themselves.[248]

---

244. [1930] 2 Ch 190.
245. See Graham (1951) 15 Conv 28, 35-36.
246. (1994) 144 NLJ 1272.
247. [1994] Ch 31. See O'Hagan (1994) 144 NLJ 1272.
248. Note that Friel has commented (1996) 1 CPLJ 2,4 that where a survivor takes no benefit under a mutual will, the use of a constructive trust on property is 'inappro-

This approach has recently been confirmed by the decision of the Court of Appeal of British Columbia in *University of Manitoba v. Sanderson Estate*[249] in which it was held that the doctrine of mutual wills applied whether or not the survivor received a benefit under the will of the first to die.

Conclusions

Judicial and academic opinion has varied on the issue of the usefulness or otherwise of the doctrine of mutual wills. Morritt LJ recently described the doctrine as 'anomalous' in the course of his judgment in *Re Goodchild*[250] while Martin[251] has commented that 'the imposition by law of a trust in cases of mutual wills is a clumsy and inadequate way of dealing with a complicated problem' and can be regarded as being 'a kind of salvage operation'. In addition, Friel has suggested that there is an emerging judicial reluctance to use the device of the constructive trust to resolve 'what are inherently problems within the law of contract'.[252] However, O'Hagan[253] has stated that 'it is in this sphere that the constructive trust is seen in one of its most flexible forms' and the doctrine of mutual wills remains for the present a useful example of how a constructive trust will be imposed by equity to prevent unconscionable or fraudulent conduct.

FUTURE DEVELOPMENT OF THE CONSTRUCTIVE TRUST

Introduction – The Remedial Constructive Trust

Traditionally the courts in England and in this jurisdiction have labelled the constructive trust as a substantive institution although there have been some signs recently of a willingness to regard it more as a remedial concept. The institutional approach involves treating the constructive trust as a device which arises in certain defined situations e.g. where there has been a breach of fiduciary duty or the wrongful assumption of trust duties

---

priate and cannot be justified by legal theory'. Instead he suggests that a trust should be imposed not on the property but on the implementation of the contract between the parties.
249. (1998) 155 DLR (4th) 40.
250. [1997] 1 WLR 1216, 1230.
251. Hanbury and Martin, *Modern Equity* (15th ed., 1997), p. 311.
252. (1996) 1 CPLJ 2, 4.
253. (1994) 144 NLJ 1272.

by a stranger to the trust. The following explanation of a remedial constructive trust has been provided by Paciocco:[254]

> A plaintiff who requests a 'remedial constructive trust' seeks a declaration that he has a beneficial interest in specific property owned, or in the possession of, a defendant who has been unjustly enriched by that ownership or possession. If successful, the relief that the plaintiff obtains is proprietary in the sense that it gives the successful plaintiff rights in the specific property which are good, not only against the defendant, but also against most others, including and most especially, the general creditors of the defendant.

While Deane J in *Muschinski v. Dodds*[255] has commented that 'for the student of equity there can be no true dichotomy between the two notions' of 'institution' and 'remedy,' the question of whether there should be lines of demarcation between them has provoked considerable academic comment.[256] It is certainly fair to say that a difference is still perceived to exist between the traditional institutional trust which is so well-established in England and the newer breed of remedial constructive trust which has developed elsewhere in the common law world, particularly in Canada, as the following passage from the judgment of McLachlin J in the Canadian Supreme Court decision of *Soulos v. Korkontzilas*[257] illustrates:

> The situations which the judge may consider in deciding whether good conscience requires imposition of a constructive trust may be seen as falling into two general categories. The first category concerns property obtained by a wrongful act of the defendant, notably breach of fiduciary obligation or breach of duty of loyalty. The traditional English institutional trusts largely fall under but may not exhaust (at least in Canada) this category. The second category concerns situation where the defendant has not acted wrongfully in obtaining the property, but where he would be unjustly enriched to the plaintiff's detriment by being permitted to keep the property for himself.

---

254. (1989) 68 Can Bar Rev 315.
255. (1985) 160 CLR 583, 614.
256. See e.g. Gardner in *Frontiers of Liability* (ed., Birks, 1993) Volume 2 p. 186, 187-192; Cope, *Constructive Trusts* (1992) pp. 868-870. Sir Peter Millett has recently commented, writing extra-judicially, that 'while we still insist on the institutional character of the constructive trust, however, we undoubtedly use it as a remedial instrument.' (1998) 114 LQR 399.
257. (1997) 146 DLR (4th) 214, 227.

Slade LJ accepted in the English Court of Appeal decision of *Metall und Rohstoff AG v. Donaldson Lufkin & Jenrette*[258] that there is a 'good arguable case' for the existence of the remedial constructive trust in that jurisdiction and Lord Browne-Wilkinson has commented in *Westdeutsche Landesbank Girozentrale v. Islington LBC*[259] that 'the remedial constructive trust, if introduced into English law [might] provide a more satisfactory road forward'. However, Waters has expressed the view that in England 'the constructive trust continues to be seen as an institutional obligation attaching to property in certain specified circumstances'[260] and Sir Peter Millett has recently commented extra-judicially that the remedial constructive trust, which he says has taken root in the USA and Canada, is unlikely to do so in England or Australia.[261]

The reluctance to embrace the concept of the remedial constructive trust stems from two main sources. First as Millet made clear in *Lonrho plc v. Fayed (No. 2)*,[262] while equity must be flexible, its intervention must be based on principle and fears have been expressed that the development of this doctrine might lead to a form of 'palm tree justice'.[263] This argument was addressed by Deane J in *Muschinski v. Dodds*[264] in the following manner:

> The fact that the constructive trust remains predominantly remedial does not, however, mean that it represents a medium for the indulgence of idiosyncratic notions of fairness and justice. As an equitable remedy, it is available only when warranted by established equitable principles or by the legitimate processes of legal reasoning, by analogy, induction and deduction, from the starting point of a proper understanding of the conceptual foundation of such principles.

The other main concern about the imposition of a remedial constructive trust relates to the fundamental distinction between the effect of personal and proprietary rights in the context of insolvency. As Sir Peter Millett has

258. [1989] 3 WLR 563, 621.
259. [1996] AC 669, 715.
260. In Goldstein ed., *Equity and Contemporary Legal Developments* (1992) p.463.
261. (1998) 114 LQR 399. See also 'Restitution and Constructive Trusts' in *Restitution, Past Present and Future* (1998) p.199. See further Birks (1998) 12 Trust Law Int 202.
262. [1992] 1 WLR 1, 9.
263. See the dissenting judgments in the Canadian Supreme Court decision of *Pettkus v. Becker* (1980) 117 DLR (3d) 254.
264. (1985) 160 CLR 583, 615.

commented: 'The potential effect of a proprietary claim on creditors makes it unacceptable that rights of property should depend on vague and ill-defined notions of fairness'.[265]

As we shall see the judiciary in this jurisdiction have consistently failed to address directly the issue of whether the remedial constructive trust would be a welcome development here. While it would appear to have been applied in a number of cases[266] and there is some support for the use of the constructive trust as a remedy for unjust enrichment[267] such principles remain at an early stage of development. Before examining them in more detail it is proposed to trace how an earlier form of what is now recognised as the remedial constructive trust has fared and then to return to consider how it may develop in the future.

New Model Constructive Trusts

While it has generally been acknowledged throughout the common law world that the concept of 'justice' is too uncertain a basis on which to found a constructive trust which will create proprietary rights which may operate in a wider context than anticipated or required, Lord Denning pioneered just such a development in the English Court of Appeal in the late 1960s and early 1970s. In *Hussey v. Palmer*[268] Denning MR stated that a constructive trust would be imposed 'whenever justice and good conscience require it' and he subsequently described this extension of the existing law in *Eves v. Eves*[269] as 'a constructive trust of a new model'. These 'new model constructive trusts' were applied in a number of areas, particularly in relation to contractual licences and to family property but almost from the outset met with academic criticism. Oakley[270] commented that: 'It is unsatisfactory for a constructive trust to be imposed whenever the courts feel, on their own individual ideas of justice, that such a remedy will bring about the 'right' result' and Maudsley[271] said that it was possible to read into the decisions the principle that 'in cases in which the plaintiff ought

---

265. (1998) 114 LQR 399.
266. *Re Irish Shipping Ltd* [1986] ILRM 518; *H.K.N. Invest Oy v. Incotrade Pvt Ltd* [1993] 3 IR 152.
267. See the judgment of Budd J in *Dublin Corporation v. Ancient Guild of Incorporated Brick and Stone Layers and Allied Trade Union* High Court 1991 No. 1556P, 6 March 1996. Note that this judgment was reversed by the Supreme Court [1996] 1 IR 468 although Keane J did accept that a person can in certain circumstances be obliged to effect restitution of property where it would be unjust for him to retain it.
268. [1972] 1 WLR 1286, 1290.
269. [1975] 1 WLR 1338, 1341.
270. (1973) CLP 17, 39.
271. (1977) 28 NILQ 123.

to win, but has no legal doctrine or authority to support him, a constructive trust in his favour will do the trick.' Nevertheless it is interesting to note how this device was utilised in a manner which usually succeeded not only in providing a plaintiff with a remedy but also in creating proprietary rights which had a consequential effect on third parties.

For a number of years the new model constructive trust played an important role in determining the rights of contractual licensees in a series of cases which attracted considerable criticism. In *Binions v. Evans*[272] an employer consented to allowing the defendant, the widow of a former employee, to live rent-free in a cottage for the remainder of her life. The property was sold to the plaintiffs expressly subject to her interest at a lower price than would otherwise have been payable. The plaintiffs then purported to determine the tenancy and the Court of Appeal held that they could not do so. While Megaw and Stephenson LJJ found that the defendant was entitled to a tenancy for life, Lord Denning MR regarded her interest as a licence which was binding on the purchaser under a constructive trust. This approach was endorsed by the Court of Appeal in *DHN Food Distributors Ltd v. Tower Hamlets LBC,*[273] where a constructive trust was imposed by the court so as to enable it to make a finding that a contractual licensee had a sufficient interest to qualify for compensation in respect of land which had been compulsorily purchased.

However, the use of the constructive trust as a form of equitable remedy to do justice *inter partes* in order to protect the licensee's possession or occupation of the premises as against third parties was difficult to justify as they 'let in by the back door contractual licences as full equitable proprietary interests.'[274] As a result of the decision of the Court of Appeal in *Ashburn Anstalt v. Arnold,*[275] the ambit of the earlier judgments has been considerably restricted and Fox LJ made it clear that the court would not impose a constructive trust unless it was satisfied that the conscience of the owner of the land had been affected so that it would be inequitable to allow him to deny the claimant an interest. Therefore it was only in circumstances where a third party sought to renege on the undertaking to honour the licence that he would be liable as a constructive trustee and there was in the circumstances insufficient evidence to infer the existence

---

272. [1972] Ch 359. See Martin (1972) 36 Conv 266 and Hayton (1972) 36 Conv 277.
273. [1976] 1 WLR 852.
274. See Underhill & Hayton, *Law Relating to Trusts and Trustees* (14th ed., 1987) p. 328. Note that the passage was omitted from the 15th edition, published in 1995. See also Jacobs, *Law of Trusts in Australia* (5th ed., 1986, Meagher and Gummow) p.321.
275. [1988] 2 WLR 706.

of a constructive trust. It has been argued that the influence of the new model constructive trust in this area has now 'been almost wholly negated'[276] and in view of the rather arbitrary effect which its application has on property rights, it is unlikely to be rekindled in this jurisdiction.

The Attitude of the Irish Courts to the New Model Constructive Trust
Lord Denning's creation has met with some degree of limited approval in this jurisdiction, although recent authority suggests that a more precisely defined doctrine would be preferable.[277] In *N.A.D v. T.D.*[278] Barron J appeared to speak in similar terms to Lord Denning when he made the following statement:

> The constructive trust is imposed by operation of law independently of intention in order to satisfy the demands of justice and good conscience. Its imposition is dependent upon the conduct of the person upon whom the trust is imposed and prevents him from acting in breach of good faith. There is no fixed set of circumstances in which such a trust is imposed.

The case before Barron J concerned a claim relating to contributions allegedly made by the plaintiff towards the building of a house on a site bought in her husband's name. Barron J said that the essential prerequisite for the imposition of a constructive trust of the type under consideration was that there must be an element in the conduct of the person upon whom it is imposed which would make it inequitable for him to assert his legal rights. He concluded that there was no evidence of conduct on the part of the husband which would make it inequitable to deny the wife's claim and her claim to a share in the house therefore failed. So while Barron J spoke in general terms in language not dissimilar to that employed by Lord Denning, there was no real sign in his judgment of the flexibility which was the hallmark of this type of trust in England.

More recently in *H.K.N. Invest Oy v. Incotrade Pvt Ltd*[279] Costello J stated that a constructive trust will arise when the circumstances of the case are such as to render it inequitable for the legal owner of property to deny another's title to it and agreed that 'where a person . . . holds property in circumstances which in equity and good conscience should be held or

---

276. Parker & Mellows, *The Modern Law of Trusts* (7th ed., 1998, Oakley) p. 360.
277. See *Dublin Corporation v. Ancient Guild of Incorporated Brick and Stone Layers and Allied Trade Union* High Court 1991 No. 1556P (Budd J) 6 March 1996.
278. [1985] ILRM 153, 160.
279. [1993] 3 IR 152.

enjoyed by another he will be compelled to hold the property in trust for another'.[280] The case concerned a claim by the plaintiffs who had obtained judgment against the defendants, namely a company and the individuals responsible for conducting its affairs, and who sought to be allowed to complete execution of this judgment. In relation to monies received by way of commission on pre-incorporation contracts, Costello J held that although the individual defendants concerned might not have been fiduciaries at the time they received this commission, these funds were held on trust for the company and could not be the subject of a garnishee order. Costello J held that the monies received after incorporation were held by the individual defendants as fiduciaries on a constructive trust for the company and he made an order declaring that the liquidator was beneficially entitled to the proceeds of both sets of contracts as the assets of the company.

While arguably the result arrived at by Costello J was a just one in the circumstances of the case and ironically had the effect of strengthening the position of the general body of creditors, a class who often fare rather worse where a constructive trust is imposed,[281] it must be said that the reasoning is in some respects open to criticism. Principally, it is difficult to accept the fact that the individual defendants could be constructive trustees of funds which in theory belonged to a company which had not at the time come into existence. In addition, while the ready acceptance of the 'good conscience' approach by Costello J, reminiscent of Lord Denning's 'new model', as already stated achieved what would be considered by most to be a just result, it is not a development which will ease the task of those who seek to establish general principles in this area of the law.

There have been two further recent examples of constructive trusts being imposed because 'justice and good conscience' demand it. In *Murray v. Murray*,[282] considered above in the context of resulting trusts and family property,[283] the defendant, the plaintiff's nephew, had lived in a property belonging to the plaintiff — who had paid the initial deposit on it — for many years with his aunt, the defendant's sister, who during her lifetime had paid the mortgage instalments and most of the outgoings on the property. After her death the plaintiff, who was her next of kin, claimed that he was entitled to the beneficial interest in the property and argued that in the circumstances it would be unconscionable for the defendant to

---

280. *Ibid.* at 162.
281. See e.g. *Attorney-General for Hong Kong v. Reid* [1994] 1 AC 324 and Jones [1994] Conv 156.
282. High Court 1993 No. 8582P (Barron J) 5 December 1995.
283. See Chapter 7, pp. 176-195.

rely on his legal title. Barron J stated: 'It is I think quite clear that the law will impose a constructive trust in all circumstances where it would be unjust and unconscionable not to do so.' In his view *Hussey* was authority for the proposition that in certain circumstances where equity so required, 'a debt may be secured by the device of a constructive trust on the property created by the money involved'. He concluded that in the circumstances the plaintiff was entitled to three-quarters of the beneficial interest in the property and that he was a tenant in common of the premises with the defendant.

As noted earlier,[284] the lack of any evidence of the fact that the aunt intended to earn a beneficial interest for herself as a result of the contributions she had made seemed to preclude Barron J from finding that these contributions gave rise to a resulting trust and instead he turned to the more flexible constructive trust to provide a remedy. Mee is critical of this approach, stating that *Murray* shows the new model constructive trust in its worst light;[285] in his view the absence of intention should probably have precluded even a constructive trust arising, but its 'inherent vagueness' made it more plausible for Barron J to provide the plaintiff with a remedy.

Further detailed attention was given to the concept of the new model constructive trust in *Dublin Corporation v. Ancient Guild of Incorporated Brick and Stone Layers and Allied Trades Union*[286] although it should be noted that when the case came before the Supreme Court, the decision was reversed and the court did not find it necessary to explore the constructive trust issue.[287] The plaintiff corporation issued a compulsory purchase order which affected a hall owned by the defendants. An arbitrator made an award on the basis of the cost of reinstatement of the building and the defendants then substantially demolished the premises making reinstatement impractical. The plaintiff sought a declaration that the union held the sum awarded in trust for the reconstruction of the building and a mandatory injunction requiring the money to be applied for this purpose, or in the alternative, sought repayment of a sum which represented the difference between the figure awarded and that which would have represented the market value of the premises if reinstatement had not been envisaged. Budd J proceeded to examine the plaintiff's claim for restitution of part of the award on the basis of unjust enrichment. He also considered whether

---

284. See Chapter 7, pp. 192-193.
285. (1996) 1 CPLJ 9, 13.
286. High Court 1991 No. 1556P (Budd J) 6 March 1996.
287. *Sub nom Dublin Corporation v. Building and Allied Trade Union* [1996] 1 IR 468. See further O'Dell (1997) 113 LQR 245.

the sum awarded by the arbitrator was impressed with a trust for the plaintiff's benefit. Budd J rejected the contention that a resulting trust arose as he was satisfied that it was the intention of the corporation that the defendants should take the sum awarded beneficially.

In relation to the possibility of a constructive trust arising, the defendants sought to argue that no such trust could be inferred as monies which were not held on a constructive trust at the outset could not subsequently become impressed with such a trust at the behest of the donor on account of some event which occurred after the giving of the money. However, Budd J pointed to Denning MR's statement in *Hussey v. Palmer* to the effect that the trust may arise 'later on, as the circumstances require'. Budd J identified two types of constructive trust, one which arises where there is a fiduciary relationship and the other which arises because of the particular circumstances in which a person holds property. While this latter form of constructive trust has been described as arising 'whenever justice and good conscience require it', Budd J commented that the Irish courts have been cautious about adopting such a nebulous touchstone as 'justice and good conscience'. He stated that traditional doctrines of equity permit the imposition of a constructive trust to prevent a person from asserting or exercising a legal right in circumstances where this would amount to unconscionable conduct. In the view of Budd J 'a system of rules has been evolved which, on the whole, is both practical and just but which cannot claim scientific precision as a whole.' Accordingly he held that the extra money was paid to the defendant under a mistaken assumption and said that while the case was on the outer margins of the circumstances in which the law will imply a constructive trust, it seemed to him that there was strong justification for holding that a constructive trust had arisen.

On appeal to the Supreme Court, the defendants argued that by virtue of the doctrine of *res judicata,* the finality of the arbitration award could not be attacked and submitted that they had not at any stage represented that the hall would be reinstated.The Supreme Court allowed the defendants' appeal and held that the award was final and binding on both parties. Keane J accepted that in certain circumstances a person can be obliged to effect restitution where it would be unjust to retain the property but held that the doctrine of *res judicata* could not be significantly abridged by the invocation of the concept of unjust enrichment.

While Budd J accepted that a constructive trust should 'be imposed by operation of law and independent of the intention of the parties to satisfy the demands of justice and good conscience',[288] he also stressed that the

---

288. *Ibid.* at 119.

courts in this jurisdiction have been cautious about 'the nebulous touch-stone' of justice and good conscience and that the imposition of a constructive trust 'does not leave it open to the court to indulge random notions of what is fair and just as a matter of abstract morality'.[289] Budd J also made it clear that he was conscious of the far-reaching effect which the imposition of a constructive trust might have on third parties. For these reasons, it is fair to say that while Budd J undoubtedly favoured the use of the constructive trust as a remedy for unjust enrichment, it would appear that he was not endorsing the type of 'palm tree justice' with which Lord Denning's new model has often been associated.

Developments Elsewhere in the Common Law World
In Canada new model constructive trusts met with some degree of approval although in a 'much modified and more acceptable form'.[290] In *Rathwell v. Rathwell*[291] Dickson J approved of the *dicta* of Lord Denning in *Hussey v. Palmer,* but the formulation of the circumstances in which a constructive trust should be imposed depended on the concept of unjust enrichment. As he stated 'for the principle to succeed, the facts must display an enrichment, a corresponding deprivation, and the absence of any juristic reason . . . for the enrichment'.[292] This reasoning was further developed by Dickson J in *Pettkus v. Becker*[293] in which he stated that 'the principle of unjust enrichment lies at the heart of the constructive trust'. A recent summary of the position in Canada was put forward by McLachlin J in her judgment in *Soulos v. Korkontzilas*[294] in the following terms: 'The Canadian courts have never abandoned the principles of constructive trust developed in England. They have however, modified them. Most notably, Canadian courts in recent decades have developed the constructive trust as a remedy for unjust enrichment.'

However, the Canadian courts have also recognised the reality that 'the constructive trust does not lie at the heart of restitution'.[295] So, in *Sorochan v. Sorochan*[296] Dickson CJ stated that in determining whether unjust enrichment requires the imposition of the proprietary remedy of a construc-

---

289. *Ibid.* at 116.
290. Hodkinson [1983] Conv 420, 429.
291. [1978] 2 SCR 436.
292. *Ibid.* at 455.
293. (1980) 117 DLR (3d) 254, 273.
294. (1997) 146 DLR 214, 222. See Smith (1997) 76 Can Bar Rev 539.
295. *Per* La Forest J in *Lac Minerals Ltd v. International Corona Resources Ltd* (1989) 61 DLR (4th) 14, 48.
296. (1986) 29 DLR (4th) 1, 12.

tive trust, the court must address itself to the specific question of 'whether the claimant reasonably expected to receive an actual interest in property and whether the respondent was or reasonably ought to have been cognizant of that expectation.' Whatever approach is adopted it is important to bear in mind that 'there will be many cases where a plaintiff establishes a cause of action based upon the formula of unjust enrichment but where it will be unjust to remedy a breach of his rights with a remedial constructive trust order.'[297]

In New Zealand, Lord Denning's version of the constructive trust met with a rather hostile reaction almost immediately. In *Carly v. Farrell*[298] Mahon J commented as follows:

> I am being asked to apply a supposed rule of equity which is not only vague in its outline but which must disqualify itself from acceptance as a valid principle of jurisprudence by its total uncertainty of application and result. It cannot be sufficient to say that wide and varying notions of fairness and conscience shall be the legal determinant. No stable system of jurisprudence could permit a litigant's claim to justice to be consigned to the formless void of individual moral opinion. . . .

Similarly in *Avondale Printers and Stationers Ltd v. Haggie*[299] Mahon J doubted the correctness of *Hussey v. Palmer* and said that the reasoning which Lord Denning had developed was 'vindicated neither by principle nor authority'. However, more recently in *Lankow v. Rose*[300] Gault J stated that criticisms of Lord Denning's approach have been 'overstated' and in that decision the court confirmed that a constructive trust may be imposed based on the reasonable expectations of the parties.[301]

The new model constructive trust also met with limited success in Australia. In *Allen v. Snyder*[302] a majority of the Court of Appeal of New South Wales rejected it, commenting that 'the legitimacy of the new model is at least suspect: at best it is a mutant from which further breeding should

---

297. Paciocco (1989) 68 Can Bar Rev 315, 350.
298. [1975] 1 NZLR 356.
299. [1979] 2 NZLR 124.
300. [1995] 1 NZLR 277, 288.
301. See also *Gillies v. Keogh* [1989] 2 NZLR 327. Note also the *dicta* of Thomas J in *Powell v. Thompson* [1991] 1 NZLR 597 that 'the constructive trust has become a broad equitable remedy for reversing that which is inequitable or unconscionable'.
302. [1977] 2 NSWLR 685, 701.

be discouraged'. In *Muschinski v. Dodds*[303] Deane J commented that 'there is no place in the law of this country for the notion of a "constructive trust of a new model"' and while the Australian Chief Justice, Mason CJ, has conceded extra-judicially[304] that Lord Denning's creation may have been a 'shorthand version' of the type of remedial constructive trust now recognised in that jurisdiction, it is arguable that the latter owes little to earlier principles. It is therefore likely that henceforth the new model constructive trust, the underlying objective of which was to prevent a result which was 'inequitable' or contrary to the demands of good conscience, will no longer be applied in this rather flexible form.[305] In *Muschinski*, while Deane J rejected the argument that a constructive trust should be imposed based on broad notions of fairness or unjust enrichment, he found a more specific basis for the imposition of a trust, namely that equity would not permit a person to retain the benefit of property to the extent to which it would be unconscionable for him to do so. This approach was followed in *Baumgartner v. Baumgartner*[306] and the notion of unconscionability is now firmly established as the basis for the imposition of what might be termed a 'remedial constructive trust' in Australia.[307]

Possible Future Developments Relating to the Constructive Trust

In addition to the traditionally recognised circumstances which may give rise to a constructive trust, it now seems clear from developments in various parts of the common law world that unjust enrichment and unconscionable conduct can also lead to the imposition of such a trust. Unjust enrichment which is already a firmly established basis of liability in Canada,[308] presupposes '(1) receipt by the defendant of a benefit, (2) at the plaintiff's expense, (3) in such circumstances that it would be unjust to allow the defendant to retain the benefit'.[309] Although Lord Diplock in his

---

303. (1985) 160 CLR 583, 615. See also the comment of Glass JA in the New South Wales Court of Appeal in *Allen v. Snyder* [1977] 2 NSWLR 685, 694 that the new model constructive trust was 'without authoritative backing and contrary to principle and authority'.
304. (1994) 110 LQR 238, 250.
305. See Evans [1989] Conv 418.
306. (1987) 164 CLR 137.
307. Although note that Sir Peter Millett has recently suggested that such trusts are unlikely to take root in Australia, see (1998) 114 LQR 399.
308. *Pettkus v. Becker* (1980) 117 DLR (3d) 257; *Sorochan v. Sorochan* (1986) 29 DLR (4th) 1; *Soulos v. Korkontzilas* (1997) 146 DLR (4th) 214.
309. *B.P. Exploration Co. (Libya) Ltd v. Hunt (No. 2)* [1979] 1 WLR 783, 839. See also the formulation put forward by McLachlin J in *Soulos v. Korkontzilas* (1997) 146

judgment in *Orakpo v. Manson Investments Ltd*[310] denied that the principle was recognised in English law, there seems to be little doubt that the constructive trust will be employed as a remedy to prevent unjust enrichment.[311] In this jurisdiction, while the judgment of Finlay P in *Hickey & Co. v. Roches Stores (No. 1)*[312] did little to clarify whether the principle should be recognised as part of our jurisprudence, it seems to have been accepted by Henchy J in the Supreme Court decisions of *East Cork Foods Ltd v. O'Dwyer Steel Co. Ltd*[313] and *Murphy v. Attorney General*,[314] albeit in another context. While no express reference was made to the concept of unjust enrichment it seems to underlie the decision of Carroll J in *Re Irish Shipping Ltd*,[315] which concerned the imposition of a constructive trust. The former bankers of the company, Citibank, claimed a right of set off in respect of monies paid into the company's account in error by another bank, the Korean Exchange Bank. Carroll J held that Citibank was not entitled to claim such a right and that the money paid in error was subject to a constructive trust and could therefore be traced by the Korean bank. Carroll J quoted with approval the *dicta* of Vinson CJ in the American Supreme Court decision of *Healy v. Commissioner of Internal Revenue*[316] to the effect that a 'constructive trust is a fiction imposed as an equitable device for achieving justice'; therefore in the words of Carroll J 'it should not work an injustice'.[317] In addition, the judgment of Budd J in *Dublin Corporation v. Ancient Guild of Incorporated Brick and Stone Layers and Allied Trades Union*[318] clearly shows that he favoured the use of a constructive trust as a remedy for unjust enrichment.[319]

DLR (4th) 214, 222 '(1) the enrichment of the defendant; (2) the corresponding deprivation of the plaintiff; and (3) the absence of a juristic reason for the enrichment'.

310. [1978] AC 95, 104. Quoted by Murphy J in *Highland Finance Ireland Ltd v. Sacred Heart College of Agriculture Ltd* [1992] 1 IR 472, 477. See also the comments of Mahon J in the New Zealand decision of *Avondale Printers and Stationers Ltd v. Haggie* [1979] 2 NZLR 124, 148-155.

311. Note that unjust enrichment is recognised as a basis for actions at common law for money had and received. *Lipkin Gorman v. Karpanale Ltd* [1991] 2 AC 548; *Woolwich Equitable Building Society v. Inland Revenue Commissioners* [1992] 3 WLR 366 and *Re PMPA Garages Ltd (No. 2)* [1992] 1 IR 332.

312. High Court 1975 No. 1007P (Finlay P) 14 July 1976.

313. [1978] IR 103.

314. [1982] IR 241. See O'Dell (1993) 15 DULJ 27, 29-30.

315. [1986] ILRM 518.

316. (1953) 345 US 278. Also approved by Goulding J in the English case of *Chase Manhattan Bank NA v. Israel British Bank (London) Ltd* [1981] Ch 105.

317. [1986] ILRM 518, 522.

318. High Court 1991 No. 1556P (Budd J) 6 March 1996.

319. However, as O'Dell has pointed out (see (1993) 15 DULJ (ns) 27, 45) 'even if an action for restitution in equity is apt, the constructive trust is not the only remedy'.

As the Australian decisions considered above illustrate, it is clear that the need to remedy unconscionable conduct may also justify the imposition of a remedial constructive trust.[320] In *Reidy v. McGreevy*[321] Barron J appeared to accept that unconscionable behaviour could give rise to a constructive trust, although the matter before him merely concerned the preliminary issue of whether the plaintiff's claim was statute barred and his brief judgment contains no reasoning on this point.

It should be noted that the Chief Justice of Australia, Mason CJ, has identified one significant difference between the notions of unconscionable conduct and unjust enrichment. In his view:

> The former looks to the conduct of the person who takes unconscientious advantage of the person in the position of disadvantage and requires an assessment of that conduct whereas the latter looks to the expectations of the parties and inquires whether there was an enrichment, and corresponding deprivation, and the absence of any juristic reason for the enrichment.[322]

Whichever formula is employed as the basis on which liability should be imposed, clearly this post-Denning version of the remedial constructive trust is recognised as being a powerful form of remedy which should be applied only where the circumstances clearly warrant such a course of action,[323] and specifically only where the plaintiff has a higher claim in equity to the property in question than the general creditors of the proposed constructive trustee.[324] Any analysis of the circumstances justifying the imposition of a remedial constructive trust must include a consideration of the position of third parties, particularly unsecured creditors, who may be affected by this form of remedy and as Hayton has commented: 'too liberal an application of constructive trusts on property may greatly undermine property law and conveyancing practice'.[325] However, in the

---

320. *Muschinski v. Dodds* (1985) 160 CLR 583; *Baumgartner v. Baumgartner* (1987) 164 CLR 137.
321. High Court 1990 No. 11804P (Barron J) 19 March 1993. Note that O'Dell has commented (1993) 15 DULJ (ns) 27, 50 that 'equity can impose a remedial constructive trust in circumstances other than where the defendant has been unjustly enriched, if the defendant's conduct has nevertheless been unconscionable'.
322. (1994) 110 LQR 238, 251.
323. Rickett [1991] Conv 125 and see also Fridman (1992) 11 LS 304, 310.
324. Note the criticisms made by Jones [1994] Conv 156 of the decision of the Privy Council in *Attorney-General for Hong Kong v. Reid* [1994] 1 AC 324 in relation to the consequences of the imposition of a constructive trust on a fiduciary.
325. Underhill & Hayton, *Law Relating to Trusts and Trustees* (14th ed., 1987) p. 327. Note that the passage was omitted from the 15th edition, published in 1995.

last analysis the overriding preoccupation of judges and academic commentators alike is the perennial dilemma of choosing between 'predictability in the law and justice in the individual case' and the importance of steering a middle course 'between the extremes of inflexible rules and case-by-case "palm tree" justice'.[326]

The difficulties facing the courts in utilising the concept of the remedial constructive trust in a manner which will achieve this objective cannot be under estimated. However, it is submitted that the following statement of Deane J in *Muschinski v. Dodds*[327] comes close to summarising present attitudes towards the imposition of such trusts:

> The mere fact that it would be unjust or unfair in a situation of discord for the owner of a legal estate to assert his ownership against another provides, of itself, no mandate for a judicial declaration that the ownership in whole or in part lies, in equity, in that other: cf. *Hepworth v. Hepworth* (1963) 110 CLR 309, at pp. 317-318. Such equitable relief by way of constructive trust will only properly be available if applicable principles of the law of equity require that the person in whom the ownership of property is vested should hold it to the use or for the benefit of another. That is not to say that general notions of fairness and justice have become irrelevant to the content and application of equity. They remain relevant to the traditional equitable notion of unconscionable conduct which persists as an operative component of some fundamental rules or principles of modern equity.

---

326. *Peel v. Canada* (1992) 98 DLR (4th) 140, 164 *per* McLachlin.
327. (1985) 160 CLR 385, 616.

CHAPTER 9

Purpose Trusts

INTRODUCTION

As we have seen a private trust may be established in favour of specified or ascertainable individuals. In addition, a trust for purposes which are treated in law as charitable will be recognised as valid. The distinctive feature of such trusts is that they are regarded as being for the public benefit and are enforceable by the Attorney General. However, trusts for non-charitable purposes will not generally be regarded as valid as they are considered to lack the human beneficiaries necessary to secure their enforcement, to be too uncertain in nature, and will often offend the rules against perpetuities and inalienability. These potential difficulties do not prevent attempts being made to establish so called 'purpose trusts'; as Sheridan[1] has commented: 'distributors of largesse ... generally give because they want to, and not because giving can be accomplished with legal ease.' In certain limited circumstances purpose trusts have been recognised as valid, although these cases have tended to be regarded as 'concessions to human weakness or sentiment'[2] which 'ought not to be increased in number, nor indeed followed, except where the one is exactly like another'.[3] Therefore it is necessary first to consider the objections raised in relation to the enforcement of non-charitable purpose trusts and then to consider the limited exceptions to the general rule that they will not be enforced.

RATIONALE FOR POLICY OF NON-ENFORCEMENT OF PURPOSE TRUSTS

Enforceability — The Beneficiary Principle[4]

As stated above the Attorney General is charged with the responsibility of enforcing charitable trusts, and private trusts in favour of individuals can

---

1. (1953) 17 Conv 46.
2. *Re Astor's Settlement Trusts* [1952] Ch 534, 547 *per* Roxburgh J.
3. *Re Endacott* [1960] Ch 232, 251.
4. See generally McKay (1973) 37 Conv 420.

be enforced by the beneficiaries themselves. One of the principal objections to non-charitable purpose trusts is that there is no one who can ensure that the court will secure performance of the trust if this should become necessary. As Grant MR stated in *Morice v. Bishop of Durham*:[5] 'there must be somebody in whose favour the court can decree performance'. This principle was explained by Roxburgh J in *Re Astor's Settlement Trusts*[6] in the following terms: that a trustee would not be expected to be subject to an equitable obligation unless there was somebody who could enforce a correlative equitable right.

There seems little doubt about the relevance of the beneficiary principle in this jurisdiction, although some anomalous exceptions to the requirement that there should be human beneficiaries capable of enforcing the trust remain. These are largely confined to the categories of gifts for tombs and monuments and for specific animals which will be considered below, although occasionally decisions have been made which are difficult to justify and for this reason are unlikely to be followed. In *Re Gibbons*,[7] a testator directed that the residue of his estate should be disposed of by his executors, who were fellow priests 'to my best spiritual advantage, as conscience and sense of duty may direct'. While Barton J held that the bequest was not charitable in nature he found that it could be upheld as a valid private trust and rejected arguments that it was too indefinite and lacked the beneficiaries necessary for it to be so regarded. The rationale employed by Barton J in reaching this decision is far from clear and the decision could be said to fall within the category of 'troublesome, anomalous and aberrant cases' which Harman LJ suggested in *Re Endacott*[8] should not be added to.

It is important to note that the objection raised in this regard is not that the trust is for a purpose or object *per se* but rather that there is a lack of beneficiaries in whose favour the court can enforce the trust obligations.[9] Often it may be a matter of construction to determine whether a given trust

---

5.   (1804) 9 Ves 399. This principle was re-iterated by Lord Parker in *Bowman v. Secular Society Ltd* [1917] AC 406, 441 where he said that with the exception of charitable trusts 'a trust to be valid must be for the benefit of individuals'. See also *Re Wood* [1949] Ch 498, 501 *per* Harman J.
6.   [1952] Ch 534, 541.
7.   [1917] 1 IR 448.
8.   [1960] Ch 232, 251.
9.   *Re Denley's Trust Deed* [1969] 1 Ch 373, 383. Although note the comments of Barton J in *Re Gibbons* [1917] 1 IR 448, 453 in reply to such an argument that: 'The Court is not asked to compel enforcement of this trust. The executors are willing to carry it out; and I see no sufficient ground for refusing to allow them to effectuate, as they propose to do, the expressed intentions of the testator.'

is for the benefit of persons or purposes and what might appear at first glance as a purpose trust may be upheld as a discretionary trust for the benefit of individuals. So for example, a trust for the education of certain children might be construed as a trust of which these children are the beneficiaries, with the purpose of providing for their education being interpreted merely as an expression of motive for the gift.[10] This reasoning was developed by Goff J in *Re Denley's Trust Deed*[11] in a manner which resulted in the following principle being laid down:

> Where, then, the trust, though expressed as a purpose, is directly or indirectly for the benefit of an individual or individuals, it seems to me that it is in general outside the mischief of the beneficiary principle.

However, such a construction will not always be possible and Goff J stressed that there were limitations to the application of such a principle:

> I think that there may be a purpose or object trust, the carrying out of which would benefit an individual or individuals, where that benefit is so indirect or intangible or which is otherwise so framed as not to give those persons any *locus standi* to apply to the court to enforce the trust, in which case the beneficiary principle would, as it seems to me, apply to invalidate the trust, quite apart from any question of uncertainty or perpetuity.[12]

Therefore it would seem that a trust even if it is expressed in terms of a purpose may be valid and enforceable provided that it directly or indirectly confers a benefit on an ascertained or ascertainable individual or individuals and provided that it does not fall foul of the other objections to the enforcement of such trusts which will now be considered.

Enforceability — Clarity and Certainty

If non-charitable purpose trusts are to be recognised as valid they must be expressed in terms which are sufficiently clear and certain to enable a court to oversee their performance. So, for example in *Morice v. Bishop of Durham*,[13] a gift for 'such objects of benevolence and liberality as the

---

10. This type of approach can be found in *Re Andrew's Trust* [1905] 2 Ch 48; *Re Osoba* [1979] 1 WLR 247.
11. [1969] 1 Ch 373, 383-384.
12. *Ibid.* at 382-383.
13. (1804) 9 Ves 399.

Bishop of Durham in his own discretion shall most approve of' was considered to be too uncertain. As Grant MR stated: 'there can be no trust over the exercise of which this Court will not assume a control; for an uncontrollable power of disposition would be ownership, and not trust'.[14]

This principle is well illustrated by the decision in *Re Astor's Settlement Trusts*,[15] where an *inter vivos* settlement, expressly limited to the perpetuity period, provided that shares were to be held on trust for specified non- charitable objects including 'the establishment, maintenance and improvement of good understanding, sympathy and co-operation between nations' and 'the preservation of the independence and integrity of newspapers'. Roxburgh J held that the trusts fell foul of the beneficiary principle but he also made it clear that they would have failed as being too uncertain in nature. He stated:

> If (contrary to my view) an enumeration of purposes outside the realm of charities can take the place of an enumeration of beneficiaries, the purposes must, in my judgment, be stated in phrases which embody definite concepts and the means by which the trustees are to try to attain them must also be prescribed with a sufficient degree of certainty.[16]

The question of what will constitute a sufficient degree of certainty is itself not a issue altogether free from doubt. In *Re Gibbons*[17] Barton J described a direction that a gift should be applied to the best spiritual advantage of the testator, 'as conscience and sense of duty may direct' as 'wide' but 'not indefinite'. While Barton J may have been influenced by the willingness of the executors to carry out the testator's wishes in a manner which they were satisfied would comply with his intentions, a decision of this nature does little to clarify the approach which should be followed in this area.

It might be argued on the basis of *Re Thompson*[18] that there is authority to support the proposition that where the purposes or object of a trust are defined with sufficient clarity and certainty, a lack of human beneficiaries

---

14. *Ibid.* at 404-405. On appeal Lord Eldon stated as follows (1805) 10 Ves 522, 539: 'As it is a maxim, that the execution of a trust shall be under the control of the Court, it must be of such a nature, that it can be under that control; so that the administration of it can be reviewed by the Court.' See also *Chichester Diocesan Fund and Board of Finance v. Simpson* [1944] AC 341.
15. [1952] Ch 534. See Marshall (1953) 6 CLP 151.
16. *Ibid.* at 547.
17. [1917] IR 448.
18. [1934] Ch 342.

will not be fatal. There the testator gave a legacy of £1,000 to a friend to be applied towards the promotion and furtherance of fox hunting. Clauson J said that 'the object of the gift has been defined with sufficient clearness and is of a nature to which effect can be given'[19] and upheld its validity. However such a view appears to be directly in conflict with the principles laid down by Roxburgh J in *Re Astor's Settlement Trusts,*[20] and the better view would seem to be that unless the beneficiary principle can be overcome in the manner suggested by Goff J in *Re Denley's Trust Deed,*[21] the certainty of any purposes expressed will not cure the difficulty caused by the lack of beneficiaries. For this reason *Re Thompson* is perhaps best considered as a rather anomalous decision which is unlikely to be followed.

The Need for Compliance with the Rules against Perpetuities and Inalienability

While the first two objections to the enforcement of purpose trusts arise out of the principle that a trust for non-charitable purposes should fail if it cannot be properly controlled and if necessary administered by the court, this objection is based on considerations of public policy, which dictate that property should not be tied up for excessive periods of time. Essentially before a purpose trust will be enforced the court must be satisfied that its terms will not offend the rule against perpetuities and that the property included in the trust will not be rendered inalienable.[22] So even where a purpose trust might be interpreted as complying with the requirements of the beneficiary principle and as being sufficiently certain, it must be limited to the period of perpetuity[23] if it is to be valid.

It should be noted at this point that the terminology employed by judges in this area can be confusing. In this context what is at issue is essentially an application of the rule against inalienability or the rule against per-

---

19. *Ibid.* at 344. See also *Re Douglas* (1887) 35 Ch D 472, 486 *per* Cotton LJ.
20. [1952] Ch 534.
21. [1969] 1 Ch 373.
22. It was for this reason that numerous bequests for the saying of masses (now recognised as a valid charitable purpose, see *O'Hanlon v. Logue* [1906] 1 IR 247 and s.45(2) of the Charities Act 1961) were held to be void in the last century. See *Dillon v. Reilly* (1875) IR 10 Eq 152; *Beresford v. Jarvis* (1877) 11 ILTR 128; *M'Court v. Burnett* (1877) 11 ILTR 130; *Morrow v. M'Conville* (1883) 11 LR Ir 236 and *Small v. Torley* (1890) 25 LR Ir 388. Although note that the contrary conclusion was reached in *Phelan v. Slattery* (1887) 19 LR Ir 177 and *Reichenbach v. Quinn* (1888) 21 LR Ir 138.
23. The period of a life or lives in being plus 21 years or, if there is no life in being, a period of 21 years only.

petual trusts rather than the rule against perpetuities, although an examination of the authorities shows that judges tend to employ these phrases interchangeably.[24] The effect of the rule against inalienability is to render void a trust which comprises property which might remain inalienable beyond the perpetuity period and it is concerned with the duration of an interest which is already vested rather than with the time at which vesting occurs.[25]

Clearly one of the most important factors in determining whether a gift is void on these grounds will be whether the obligation involves merely the application of the income from the gift to the stated purpose. However, even where the application of the gift is not limited to income only and there is no direction that the capital be maintained indefinitely, it may still offend the rule against inalienability. This is illustrated by the decision of the Supreme Court in *Re Fossitt's Estate,*[26] where a bequest to the 'Orange Institution of Ireland' for the upkeep of a hall was held to be void for perpetuity, despite the fact that there was no evidence that the income alone was to be employed for this purpose. Fitzgibbon J stated:

> In my opinion it was the intention of the testator that the capital might be applied from time to time, if occasion should arise and the income of the fund was insufficient, towards the upkeep of the Hall, but I am satisfied that the testator contemplated the continued existence of the fund, in whole or in part, for an absolutely indefinite period, which might far exceed that fixed by law of a life or lives in being and twenty-one years after.[27]

Where a phrase such as 'so long as the law allows' or 'such period as the law permits' has been employed, a gift will be regarded as being valid for a period of 21 years. However, where no such qualification is included, a gift will be void unless it comes to a determination before the end of the perpetuity period. On the other hand, in some respects a fairly flexible attitude has been taken towards the need for compliance with the rule against inalienability and the courts have assumed that the requirements of the rule will be met where it appears that this is a reasonable interpretation of

---

24. E.g. *O'Byrne v. Davoren* [1994] 3 IR 373.
25. See Coughlan, *Property Law in Ireland* (2nd ed., 1998) p. 178.
26. [1934] IR 504. This can be compared to the decision of Haugh J in *Re Connor* [1960] IR 67, where a gift to a cemetery company for the upkeep of a family vault was upheld in circumstances where there was nothing to prevent the company 'resorting to the capital if and when, they think proper in their discretion to do so'.
27. *Ibid.* at 513.

a gift. So, in *Mussett v. Bingle*[28] where a testator gave a legacy of £300 to be applied in the erection of a monument to his wife's first husband and a further sum of £200, the interest on which was to be used for its maintenance, Hall VC upheld the validity of the former gift presumably on the assumption that the monument would be erected within the perpetuity period. The latter gift was clearly of a perpetual nature and therefore void.

EXCEPTIONAL CASES IN WHICH PURPOSE TRUSTS HAVE BEEN ENFORCED

Tombs and Monuments

At common law a trust for the erection of a tombstone or monument was not regarded as being charitable in nature. In this jurisdiction legislation has intervened in a limited way and section 50 of the Charities Act 1961 now provides that gifts for the maintenance or improvement of a 'tomb, vault, grave or ... tombstone' are deemed to be charitable gifts insofar as they do not exceed £60 a year in the case of income and £1,000 in any other case. However these monetary limits have not been increased in the years since the enactment of the legislation and in many cases gifts for such purposes will exceed these limits. In these circumstances a bequest for such a purpose will have to come within the rather anomalous exception which has developed at common law, the effect of which is that gifts for the erection of a tomb or monument or for its maintenance will be upheld as valid purpose trusts provided that they do not offend the rule against inalienability.

As illustrated by the decision of Hall VC in *Mussett v. Bingle*,[29] the courts appear to assume that directions of this nature will be carried out within the perpetuity period. However to come within this limited exception the trust must also be expressed with sufficient certainty to be carried out. In *Re Endacott*[30] a testator bequeathed his residuary estate valued at £20,000 to a specified parish council 'for the purpose of providing some useful memorial to myself'. The gift was held void by the Court of Appeal; Harman LJ stating 'I cannot think a case of this kind, the case of providing outside a church an unspecified and unidentified memorial, is

---

28. [1876] WN 170. See also *Re Filshie* [1939] NZLR 91.
29. [1876] WN 170. See also *Trimmer v. Danby* (1856) LJ Ch 424 where a bequest of £1,000 to erect a monument to the testator in St Paul's Cathedral was upheld.
30. [1960] Ch 232.

the kind of instance which should be allowed to add to those troublesome, anomalous and aberrant cases'.[31]

In circumstances where the statutory limits specified above have been exceeded, the issue of compliance with the rule against inalienability becomes of crucial importance in relation to gifts for the maintenance of graves and monuments, and if trusts of this nature are to be regarded as valid at common law they must be confined to the perpetuity period. *Mussett v. Bingle* illustrates that a gift for the maintenance of a monument without any words of qualification will be void and in *Toole v. Hamilton*[32] it was held by Porter MR that a bequest which was to be invested and the income thereof applied in maintaining an enclosure around a grave was also void. However, in *Pirbright v. Salwey*[33] a gift for the upkeep of a grave for so long as the law for the time being permitted was upheld as valid for a period of 21 years. Similarly, in *Re Hooper*[34] a testator bequeathed a sum of money to trustees to apply the income to the maintenance of family graves and monuments 'as far as they can legally do so'. Maugham J held that this trust was valid for a period of 21 years from the testator's death.

A number of devices can be employed to avoid the difficulty of complying with the rule against inalienability. Where a gift is given for the maintenance of an entire churchyard, this will be upheld as a valid charitable gift and so not subject to the rule,[35] and at common law this will provide an effective means of indirectly securing the maintenance of a particular grave or monument.[36] A further method appears to be to make a gift to a cemetery company, where one exists, to be applied for the maintenance of a grave or tomb.[37] In *Re Connor*[38] a bequest of £1,000 was made 'to the General Cemetery Company of Dublin to be applied for the maintenance and care of the family vault at Mount Jerome'. Haugh J said that the testatrix clearly bequeathed the money to the company with the sole limitation that it should be spent in the maintenance of the family vault

---

31.   *Ibid.* at 251.
32.   [1901] 1 IR 383. See also *Beresford v. Jarvis* (1877) 11 ILTR 128.
33.   [1896] WN 86.
34.   [1932] 1 Ch 38.
35.   *Re Vaughan* (1886) 33 Ch D 187.
36.   *Re Eighmie* [1935] Ch 524.
37.   Such an approach seems to have been justified in England in *Re Chardon* [1928] 1 Ch 464 on the basis that a determinable interest was not subject to the rule against perpetuities although by virtue of s.12 of the Perpetuities and Accumulations Act 1964 this is no longer the case. Note that s.1 of the Parish Councils and Burial Authorities (Miscellaneous Provisions) Act 1970 now authorises local and burial authorities to conclude agreements for the maintenance of graves for a period of up to 99 years.
38.   [1960] IR 67.

and concluded that there was nothing to prevent the company from resorting to the capital if and when it was found necessary to do so for the purposes outlined in the will. In the circumstances, he was satisfied that the gift was a valid non-charitable one which did not offend the rule against inalienability and which should therefore be enforced.

Animals

A gift to provide for the welfare of animals generally or for the care and maintenance of a class of animals is regarded as being charitable in law.[39] Gifts to provide for the care of specified animals while they are admittedly not of a charitable nature and would *prima facie* seem to fall foul of the beneficiary principle have been upheld as coming within the limited class of exceptions to the principle that non-charitable purpose trusts will not be enforced. In *Pettingall v. Pettingall*[40] a gift of £50 a year for the maintenance of the testator's favourite black mare was upheld as valid. In *Re Dean*[41] North J upheld a gift of £750 per annum for a period of 50 years for the care and maintenance of the testator's horses and hounds. He rejected the view that the court would not recognise the validity of a trust unless it is capable of being enforced by someone. In what has been recognised as a rather unsatisfactory judgment, North J then proceeded to virtually ignore the potential problem of violating the rule against inalienability and remarked that he would uphold a gift of this nature 'provided that it is not to last for too long a period'.[42] Such an approach to the perpetuity question is unlikely to be followed in England and has been rejected in this jurisdiction. In *Re Kelly*[43] a testator bequeathed a sum of money to be applied in the care and maintenance of his dogs with a gift over should any surplus remain on the death of the last dog. Meredith J upheld the gift as being valid for a period of 21 years following the testator's death, although it would have been technically void thereafter and the gift over was found to be void for remoteness. A number of points in his judgment are worth noting. It clearly emerges that only a human life can be used as a measuring life for the purpose of applying the rule against perpetuities. Meredith J expressed this point unequivocally in colourful language:

---

39. *Re Douglas* (1887) 35 Ch D 472; *Swifte v. AG* [1912] 1 IR 133; *Armstrong v. Reeves* (1890) 25 LR Ir 325. See further *infra* Chapter 10.
40. (1842) 11 LJ Ch 176.
41. (1889) 41 Ch D 552.
42. *Ibid.* at 557.
43. [1932] IR 255.

> If the lives of the dogs or other animals could be taken into account in reckoning the maximum period of 'lives in being and twenty-one years afterwards any contingent or executory interest might be properly limited, so as only to vest within the lives of specified carp, or tortoises, or other animals that might live for over a hundred years, and for twenty-one years afterwards, which of course is absurd. 'Lives' means human lives. It was suggested that the last of the dogs could in fact not outlive the testator by more than twenty-one years. I know nothing of that. The Court does not enter into the question of a dog's expectation of life. In point of fact neighbour's dogs and cats are unpleasantly long-lived; but I have no knowledge of their precise expectation of life ... there can be no doubt that 'lives' means lives of human beings, not of animals or trees in California.[44]

On the basis of this statement it would also appear that the court will not take judicial notice of the fact that certain animals will not live for a period of more than 21 years although authority in England suggests the contrary.[45] Meredith J rejected the suggestion that he should read into the will an implied limitation to a period of 21 years or 'so long as the law permits'. However he stressed that this did not prevent him from analysing a provision which was 'manifestly not good in its entirety' for the purpose of determining whether it included a severable part which did not offend the rule against perpetuities, which in the case before him, amounted to expenditure for a period of 21 years. Therefore, in the light of *Re Kelly* it can be said with a fair degree of certainty that in this jurisdiction purpose trusts for the care and maintenance of specified animals will be upheld for a period of 21 years provided that they are expressed with sufficient clarity. In the interests of certainty it is probably preferable that such trusts are clearly limited to a period of 21 years or 'so long as the law allows,' although if one accepts the approach of Meredith J such an omission will not be fatal.

Gifts to Unincorporated Associations[46]

An unincorporated association has been defined by Lawton LJ in *Conservative and Unionist Central Office v. Burrell*[47] as follows:

---

44. *Ibid.* at 260-261.
45. *Re Haines, The Times,* 7 November 1952. See Sheridan (1953) 17 Conv 46, 60.
46. See generally Rickett [1980] CLJ 88, 90-111.
47. [1982] 1 WLR 522, 525.

[T]wo or more persons bound together for one or more common purposes, not being business purposes, by mutual undertakings, each having mutual duties and obligations, in an organisation which has rules which identify in whom control of it and its funds rests and on what terms and which can be joined or left at will.

While a gift to a body corporate even for non-charitable purposes will be valid because such a body has a separate legal personality and therefore can enforce it, difficulties arise where it is sought to confer a gift of a non-charitable nature on an unincorporated association. An unincorporated association has no separate personality in law and is regarded as a collection of individuals and the potential difficulties which must be considered are that gifts of this nature may fall foul of the beneficiary principle or may contravene the rule against inalienability.

A number of different methods of conferring a benefit on unincorporated associations have been devised, the latter two of which have been recognised as essentially overcoming the potential problems referred to above.

A Gift by Way of Endowment for the Benefit of the Association

Where a gift is construed as an endowment for the benefit of the association, it will almost inevitably be found to be void as infringing the rule against inalienability. This point emerged from the decisions of the House of Lords in *Re Macaulay*[48] and of the Privy Council in *Leahy v. Attorney-General for New South Wales*.[49] However, if the wording of the gift is such that it satisfies the requirement of the rule against inalienability, the decision of Goff J in *Re Denley's Trust Deed*[50] would seem to confirm that the difficulties posed by the beneficiary principle can be overcome.

A Gift to the Members of the Association for the Time Being

A gift to an unincorporated association may be enforced if it is recognised as a gift to the members of the association alive at the time of the disposition, or in the case of a will, at the date of the testator's death. The beneficiary principle is satisfied as it is possible to ascertain who these members are and the rule against inalienability will not be infringed provided that the members are free to dispose of the property, both income and capital, at any time. This principle is explained as follows by Lovell:[51]

---

48. [1943] Ch 435n.
49. [1959] AC 457. Although note that on the facts of the case the gift was saved by the provisions of a New South Wales statute.
50. [1969] 1 Ch 373.
51. (1970) 34 Conv 77, 96.

In the context of trusts for unincorporated associations, it is submitted that the fact that the association can last forever is of no significance. ... Once there has been an effectual dedication to the purpose or enterprise, and provided that there is no restriction on the use of the capital, then there is no reason to argue that any principle of perpetuity is offended. Quite clearly the association may last for a period of time longer than the perpetuity period, but the property together with all other association assets is vested according to the trusts of the association and the latter can dissolve at any time if the members so wish it.

However it must be possible to construe the gift as being for the individual members of the association for the time being and as some of the authorities have shown such an interpretation is not always possible. So, in *Hogan v. Byrne*,[52] Christian J held that to put such a construction on the testator's bequest to 'monks named Christian Brothers' would be to defeat his real intention. He stated: 'If you do that you disappoint the testator's intentions. He intended that the land should be held by one body, and not that it should be divided into an indefinite number of parts each to belong to a different person.' As Christian LJ subsequently stated in *Stewart v. Green*,[53] sitting as Lord Justice of Appeal, two distinct interpretations of gifts of this nature are possible:

First a trust for the [individuals] who happened to compose the community at the moment of the testator's death in their natural capacities. Second, a trust for the community in its communal character, of whomsoever it should from time to time and for ever consist. The first would, of course, be good and effectual in law; and ... practically his purpose would be achieved. ... The other intent — that of giving to the community in a communal or quasi corporate character — would mean the *form* undoubtedly most accordant with the testator's ideas; but would labour under the disadvantage of being utterly incapable of legal realization; for as the community, as such, has no legal personality, it is incapable of taking in that character.

In the case before the court, counsel arguing in favour of the validity of the gift repudiated the first possible construction, relying instead on an argument based on its charitable nature which was not made out, and as a

---

52. (1863) 13 ICLR 166.
53. (1871) IR 5 Eq 470, 481.

result the bequest was declared void.[54] Similarly in *Morris v. M'Conville*,[55] Chatterton VC stressed that 'the court must act upon the intention of the testator as expressed in the words he has used'.[56] The Vice-Chancellor said that he found the terms of the testator's will impossible to reconcile with the theory of the gift in the case before him being to the individual members of a convent, and found that it was instead intended as a 'permanent contribution *de anno in annum* to the funds of the convent in its aggregate and quasi corporate capacity'[57] which he held to be void.

Despite such setbacks this approach of construing a gift to an association as being for the benefit of the members for the time being was successfully employed on a number of occasions towards the end of the last century particularly in the context of gifts to associations of a religious nature which were not considered at the time to be charitable in law. It was of particular importance in relation to gifts to contemplative religious orders, which were considered not to possess the necessary element of public benefit to qualify for charitable status. The decision of Gavan Duffy J in *Maguire v. Attorney General*[58] marked a change in judicial attitudes to the question of the public benefit inherent in gifts of this nature, and the provisions of section 45 of the Charities Act 1961 would now seem to confirm that gifts to contemplative religious orders are valid charitable gifts.[59] However the principles developed in these decisions are important and can be considered as being of general application.

In *Cocks v. Manners*[60] a gift to a contemplative order of nuns was treated as a gift to the superior of the community for the time being and in this manner was upheld on the basis that it did not infringe the rule against inalienability. This principle was applied in Ireland in *Re Delany's Estate*,[61] where a gift to a convent was upheld as being for the benefit of the nuns who comprised the community at the time of the testator's death. A

---

54. As Porter MR commented in *Bradshaw v. Jackman* (1887) 21 LR Ir 12, 22 the decision in *Stewart v. Green* might well have been different if counsel had insisted upon rather than repudiated the first of the two possible constructions of the will.
55. (1883) 11 LR Ir 236.
56. *Ibid.* at 247.
57. *Ibid.* at 250.
58. [1943] IR 238. Although note the decision of Overend J in *Re Keogh's Estate* [1945] IR 13.
59. S.45(1) provides: 'In determining whether or not a gift for the purpose of the advancement of religion is a valid charitable gift it shall be conclusively presumed that the purpose includes and will occasion public benefit.'
60. (1871) LR 12 Eq 574.
61. (1882) 9 LR Ir 226. See also *Re Wilkinson's Trusts* (1887) 19 LR Ir 531 and *Bradshaw v. Jackman* (1887) 21 LR Ir 12.

useful summary of this reasoning was set out in *Morrow v. M'Conville*,[62] although as noted above, it was not accepted as applying in the case before the court:

> [A] gift, not charitable, to a religious community, including not only the existing members, but also all persons who should be, or become thereafter members of it, during a period capable of extending beyond the legal limits prescribed by the rule against perpetuities is void; but ... if such gift, according to its true construction, is one to the individuals composing the community at the death of the testator, or some other time, within legal limits, appointed for ascertaining the class of such individuals, the gift is valid.[63]

The main consideration which must be taken into account by a court in applying this approach is that there must be nothing to indicate that any form of 'perpetual endowment' was contemplated and this was one of the major difficulties faced by Chatterton VC in *Morrow*, where the trust was clearly treated as being 'a continuing one'. This point was stressed by Overend J in his decision in *Re Keogh's Estate*,[64] where a testator made a bequest to the superioress for the time being of a convent and left the residue of his estate to the prior of an order, neither of which qualified as charitable gifts. Overend J was satisfied that there was nothing in the testator's will which suggested that he had contemplated that the money would be applied for a perpetual endowment and he upheld the gifts to the superioress and the prior to be used for the purposes of their orders.

This principle was applied in a different context in *Re Clarke*,[65] where a bequest was made to the Committee of the Corps of Comissionaires in London to aid in the purchase of a barracks or in any other way beneficial to the corps. Byrne J upheld the bequest as a valid gift to the members of the corps for the time being as they could at any time dispose of it. He stated:

> The test, or one test, appears to be, will the legacy when paid be subject to any trust which will prevent the existing members of the association from spending it as they please? If not, the gift is good. So also if the gift is to be construed as a gift to or for the benefit of the individual members of the association. On the other hand, if it

---

62. (1883) 11 LR Ir 236.
63. *Ibid.* at 246-247.
64. [1945] IR 13.
65. [1901] 2 Ch 110. See *Re Smith* [1914] 1 Ch 937.

appears that the legacy is one which by the terms of the gift, or which by reason of the constitution of the association in whose favour it is made, tends to a perpetuity, the gift is bad.[66]

The Supreme Court considered this issue in *Re Byrne,*[67] in which a testator left his residuary estate for the use and benefit of the Jesuit Order in Ireland. The majority of the Supreme Court[68] held that the work of the order, while largely charitable in nature, was not exclusively so and that it did not qualify as a charitable gift. As Murnaghan J stated if the testator meant his gift to enure for the benefit of 'a continuing body whose existence has not received legal recognition', it would fail. If on the other hand, his intention was to divide the money amongst individuals forming a class, there would be no legal objection to its validity. Murnaghan J re-iterated the point that 'the language of the testator must in each case be the guide' and upheld the bequest as a valid gift of a non-charitable nature for the benefit of an ascertainable class of persons.

The only real theoretical difficulty with such an approach is that any member who leaves the association can take his share with him unless he assigns it to the other members and a new member will have no share in the property. More recently in England an alternative theory has been developed which has found favour with the courts in that jurisdiction and which may well also prove to be the most suitable approach for the courts here to employ.

Property Held on Trust to be Applied in Accordance with the Contract Between the Members

This manner of construing a gift was summarised by Cross J as follows in *Neville Estates Ltd v. Madden*:[69]

> [I]t may be a gift to the existing members not as joint tenants, but subject to their respective contractual rights and liabilities towards one another as members of the association. In such a case a member cannot sever his share. It will accrue to the other members on his death or resignation, even though such members include persons who became members after the gift took effect. If this is the effect of

---

66. *Ibid.* at 114.
67. [1935] IR 782.
68. Murnaghan and Fitzgibbon JJ. Kennedy CJ dissented and held that the gift was charitable in nature.
69. [1962] Ch 832, 849. See Warburton [1985] Conv 318, 322-325.

the gift it will not be open to objection on the score of perpetuity or uncertainty unless there is something in its terms or circumstances or in the rules of the association which precludes the members at any given time from dividing the subject of the gift between them on the footing that they are solely entitled to it in equity.

This 'contract-holding theory' was applied by Brightman J in *Re Recher's Will Trusts,*[70] which concerned the validity of a gift to the 'London and Provincial Anti-Vivisection Society'. Brightman J concluded that it was not a gift to the members of the society at the date of the testator's death, nor an attempted gift to present and future members beneficially, nor a gift in trust for the purposes of the society. Instead he held that the legacy ought to be construed as a gift to the members beneficially as an accretion to their funds subject to the contract which they made between themselves. As he stated: 'In the absence of words which purport to impose a trust, the legacy is a gift to the members beneficially, not as joint tenants or as tenants in common so as to entitle each member to an immediate distributive share, but as an accretion to the funds which are the subject matter of the contract which the members have made *inter se*.'[71] A similar approach was applied by Oliver J in *Re Lipinski's Will Trusts,*[72] where a testator bequeathed half of his residuary estate to trustees to the 'Hull Judaeans (Maccabi) Association' in memory of his late wife to be used in the work of constructing new buildings for the association and/or improving them. Oliver J held the gift valid as an absolute gift to the members of the association beneficially as an accretion to its funds subject to the rules of the association. It was not open to objection on the grounds of perpetuity as Oliver J was satisfied that there was nothing in the will which suggested any intention to create a permanent endowment and he pointed out that the members could if they wished divide the gift between themselves. In this regard he distinguished the decision of the House of Lords in *Re Macaulay,*[73] where a gift was made for the 'maintenance and improvement' of a building on the grounds that in the case before him it was in his view quite evident that the association was free to spend the capital of the legacy if it chose to do so.

Essentially this contract holding theory involves the idea of property being held on trust to be applied in accordance with the contract existing

---

70. [1972] Ch 526.
71. *Ibid.* at 539.
72. [1976] Ch 235. See Widdows (1977) 41 Conv 179 and Gravells (1977) 40 MLR 231.
73. [1943] Ch 435n.

between the members contained in the rules of the association and it will satisfy the requirements of the rule against inalienability provided that the members are entitled to wind up the association and divide its property between them at any time. One clear advantage of this approach is that compliance with the beneficiary principle is not an issue as the property is held subject to the terms of a contract rather than on trust. In addition, a member who leaves the association or dies will lose his share in the property and any new member will automatically acquire one without the need for any formalities. However it is important to emphasise that the rules of the association must provide the necessary contractual element to the relationship between the members[74] and it is also necessary that the members have the requisite authority to divide the assets between themselves.[75]

Conclusion

While the categories of trusts for the erection and maintenance of tombs and monuments and for the care of animals seem to be accepted as enforceable provided that they do not offend the rule against inalienability, doubt remains about the validity of other forms of non-charitable purpose trusts. Provided that the certainty requirement is met it would appear that trusts for unincorporated associations can be enforced if one of the constructions outlined above is applied, and the reasoning of Goff J in *Re Denley's Trust Deed*[76] should ensure that difficulties raised by the need for compliance with the beneficiary principle and the rule against inalienability will effectively be overcome. As the cases make clear, if a construction is to be applied which will result in the gift being legally enforceable, it is important that such a construction can be ascertained from the words used by a donor or testator.[77] While recent decisions show a greater willingness to place a favourable construction on gifts of this nature, the warning given by the Court of Appeal in *Re Endacott*[78] that the categories of these 'anomalous' cases should not be extended should also be heeded.

In a general context the suggestion has been made that what might appear as an invalid purpose trust could be saved if it were construed as a power rather than a trust on the basis that there is no requirement that the beneficiary principle be satisfied in relation to powers. While this option

---

74. *Conservative and Unionist Central Office v. Burrell* [1982] 1 WLR 522, 525.
75. *Re Grant's Will Trusts* [1980] 1 WLR 360.
76. [1969] 1 Ch 373.
77. E.g. *Morrow v. M'Conville* (1883) 11 LR Ir 236, 247; *Re Byrne* [1935] IR 782, 818.
78. [1960] Ch 232.

has been explored,[79] it has been rejected on the basis that a valid power cannot 'be spelt out of an invalid trust'.[80]

From a practical perspective, where such advance planning is feasible, the incorporation of an association which a donor or testator wishes to benefit will undoubtedly provide a method of ensuring that the gift will be carried into effect. However, in the majority of cases, this will not be achieved and the courts will still be faced with the difficult policy question of whether to continue to extend the principle which allows for the enforcement of non-charitable purpose trusts in limited circumstances. While it could be argued that a refusal to enforce non-charitable purpose trusts should in theory at any rate lead to a greater preponderance of gifts of a charitable nature more likely to provide real benefit to the community, as Martin[81] comments 'capricious trusts are the rare ones'. She continues: 'The fact that they do exist is no reason for failing to establish a rational method of validating the useful ones.' Certainly the present approach is in many respects far from rational and lacks any real consistency. In the last analysis, in the absence of any legislative intervention in this area, we must continue to rely on the rather haphazard principles and devices developed at common law where it is sought to establish the validity of a non-charitable purpose trust.

---

79. By Harman J in *Re Shaw* [1957] 1 WLR 729, 746.
80. *IRC v. Broadway Cottages Trust* [1955] Ch 20, 36 *per* Jenkins LJ; *Re Shaw* [1957] 1 WLR 729, 746; *Re Endacott* [1960] Ch 232, 246.
81. Hanbury and Martin, *Modern Equity* (15th ed., 1997) p. 373.

CHAPTER 10

Charitable Trusts

INTRODUCTION

Advantages of Charitable Status

While as a general rule, subject to the exceptions examined above,[1] trusts for purposes rather than for the benefit of persons are invalid, charitable trusts which are considered to be for the public benefit are an exception to this principle. Charitable trusts are considered as being for the benefit of the public generally or at least for an appreciable section of it and for this reason have traditionally enjoyed a number of advantages over other types of trust.[2] Before examining in more detail the types of trusts which will qualify for such favourable treatment it is useful to set out briefly the advantages to be gained from establishing charitable status.

Charitable trusts do not depend on the existence of human beneficiaries to enforce them; they are considered to be of a public nature and as such are enforceable by the Attorney General.[3] The corollary of this proposition is that those individuals who might benefit from a trust considered to be legally charitable will not be recognised as having the right to enforce such trusts.[4]

A further advantage is that charitable trusts are not subject to the same requirements relating to certainty of objects which must be complied with if a private trust is to be considered valid.[5] Originally, provided that a trust could be identified as being exclusively[6] charitable in nature, such a trust

---

1. *Supra* Chapter 9.
2. As Mummery LJ has recently commented in the Court of Appeal decision in *Gaudiya Mission v. Brahmachary* [1997] 4 All ER 957, 963 'Under English law charity has always received special treatment. . . . It is, therefore, subject to special rules governing registration, administration, taxation and duration'. See also Warburton [1999] Conv 20, who states (at p. 29) that 'charitable trusts operate in a different legal, fiscal and social environment from family and commercial trusts'.
3. While the decision in *Re Denley's Trust Deed* [1969] 1 Ch 373 has made it possible for the beneficiary principle to be effectively by-passed in certain circumstances, a considerable number of purpose trusts will still fall foul of this principle.
4. *Re Belling* [1967] Ch 425.
5. See the *dicta* of Porter MR in *Re Brown* [1898] 1 IR 423, 427.
6. Note that s.49(1) of the Charities Act 1961 now provides as follows: 'Where any of

would be enforced even if the nature of these charitable objects was not expressly delimited.[7] In such circumstances a cy-près scheme[8] could be framed to ensure that the charitable intention of the donor or testator was given effect to. From a general perspective, charitable status is also desirable as it will facilitate the operation of cy-près jurisdiction should this become necessary. If a trust fails to qualify as charitable, this jurisdiction cannot be exercised and a bequest may fail, allowing a resulting trust to operate in favour of the donor or his estate. While resulting trusts are intended in theory to give effect to the unexpressed but presumed intention of the donor, this may not always be the case,[9] and it is certainly preferable to find a means of perpetuating the donor's charitable intention in as close a form as possible to that originally expressed by him.

Another crucial distinction is that charitable trusts may be perpetual in nature in so far as the rule against inalienability which has proved such a major stumbling block in any attempts to enforce non-charitable purpose trusts, does not apply to them. However, although charitable trusts may be of perpetual duration, they are subject to the rule against perpetuities to the extent that the initial vesting must be bound to take place within the relevant perpetuity period. This principle is subject to the limited exception that a gift over from one charity to another is not subject to the rule.[10]

Finally, it should be noted that charitable trusts also enjoy a number of significant fiscal immunities in terms of exemptions from liability to various forms of taxation. Sections 333 and 334 of the Income Tax Act 1967 grant exemptions from income tax under Schedules C, D and F in respect of income accruing to charitable bodies or trusts established for charitable

---

the purposes of a gift include, or could be deemed to include, both charitable and non-charitable objects, its terms shall be so construed or given effect as to exclude the non-charitable objects and the purpose shall, accordingly, be treated as charitable.'

7. *Re Koepplar's Will Trusts* [1986] Ch 423.
8. Where a gift is made to charity, it may be impossible to give effect to the intentions of the donor in the precise terms that he intended or it may be impractical or inconvenient to do so. The cy-près doctrine where it applies, allows for the making of a scheme for the application of such property for other charitable purposes as near as possible to those intended by the donor. This is considered in detail below.
9. E.g. *Re Vinogradoff* [1935] WN 68. See also the approach taken by the former Supreme Court in *Owens v. Greene* [1932] IR 225 in relation to the question of the beneficial ownership of money held in joint deposit accounts which persisted until it was reversed in the recent Supreme Court decision in *Lynch v. Burke* [1995] 2 IR 159.
10. *Christ's Hospital v. Grainger* (1849) 1 Mac & G 460; *Re Tyler* [1891] 3 Ch 252. Although clearly a gift over to a charity after a gift to an individual will be subject to the rule against perpetuities.

purposes to the extent that such income is applied for charitable purposes.[11] In addition, section 11(6) of the Corporation Tax Act 1976 provides for the carrying over of any exemptions which would apply under income tax provisions and section 79(3)(g) of the Act of 1976 also provides for a reduced rate of corporation tax to be applied to any company established 'solely for the advancement of religion or education' and which is precluded from distributing its profits to its members. Exemptions also apply in respect of capital taxes, and a capital gain which accrues to a charity is not chargeable to capital gains tax provided that it is applied for charitable purposes.[12] In addition, section 54(2) of the Capital Acquisitions Tax Act 1976 provides that a gift or inheritance taken for public or charitable purposes will be exempt from capital acquisitions tax provided that the Revenue Commissioners are satisfied that it has been or will be applied to such purposes.

The scope of the exemption from income tax provided by sections 333 and 334 of the Income Tax Act 1967 as amended has recently been considered by the High Court in *Revenue Commissioners v. Sisters of Charity of the Incarnate Word*.[13] The appellants contended that sections 333 and 334 applied to bodies or persons established for charitable purposes but only if they were established within the State and they claimed that the respondents in this case were not established within the State. The respondents claimed that there was no justification for giving the exemption provisions the confined interpretation contended for by the appellants and argued that even if the appellants' interpretation was correct, the charity was in fact established within the State through one of its branches. Geoghegan J accepted the conclusions reached by the Court of Appeal and the House of Lords in *Camille and Henry Dreyfus Foundation v. IRC*[14] in relation to the equivalent English provisions to the effect that a limited geographical meaning should be given to the expression 'established'. Geoghegan J then went on to consider whether the charity was in fact established in the State. He stated that 'a foreign charity with no activities base (for want of a better expression) in Ireland is not entitled to an exemption but a foreign

11. See further Judge, *Irish Income Tax* (1994) 18.023. Judge notes (18.025) that the use of income to meet the normal running expenses of a charity, including proper remuneration for its employees, has always been accepted as an application for charitable purposes.
12. S.22(1) of the Capital Gains Tax Act 1975. Subs.(2) provides that if such property subsequently ceases to be subject to charitable trusts any gain arising will be chargeable and will be calculated as if the property had been sold for its market value on that date.
13. [1998] 2 IR 553.
14. [1956] AC 39.

charity which does have such a base is entitled to it in respect of funds applied towards Irish charitable activities'. Geoghegan J concluded that having regard to the fact that the respondents owned and managed a nursing home in the State there was sufficient 'establishment' in Ireland to give rise to the exemption and he upheld the decision of the Circuit Court that the respondents were entitled to the benefit of the provisions of sections 333 and 334 of the Income Tax Act 1967 as amended.

In view of the extensive advantages enjoyed by charitable trusts, it has been argued that some limitation must be placed on their proliferation. While certain judicial statements show a tendency to adopt a benign attitude to this question,[15] the perceived benefit of undeserved fiscal immunity has proved a rather thorny issue over the years. An examination of the case law in England would suggest that this motive has led to a restrictive attitude being adopted to the wider question of whether certain trusts should qualify as being legally charitable.[16] For the present at least the concepts of fiscal immunity and charitable status continue to 'march hand in hand'[17] although, as Lord Cross has commented in *Dingle v. Turner*,[18] such a state of affairs is 'unfortunate' given that the question of whether a trust was so unlikely to benefit the public that it ought to be declared invalid and the question of whether it was likely to confer such substantial benefits to the community that it ought to enjoy fiscal immunity are, in his view, two distinct questions.[19] A better approach might be to do as the Radcliffe Commission[20] suggested and sever the connection, which would allow a more liberal approach to develop towards the question of the type of trusts which should qualify as being legally charitable unhindered by the baggage of perceived undeserved fiscal immunity. Arguably it is wrong that considerations such as the latter should influence judicial decisions about charitable status to too great an extent, but for the present such policy questions must continue to be borne in mind before embarking on an examination of the legal definition of charitable status.

---

15. *Weir v. Crum-Brown* [1908] AC 162, 167 *per* Lord Loreburn; *IRC v. McMullen* [1981] AC 1, 14 *per* Lord Hailsham.
16. See the comment of Lord Cross in *Dingle v. Turner* [1972] AC 601, 624 to the effect that such considerations 'pretty obviously influenced' the decisions of the courts in *Re Compton* [1945] Ch 123 and *Oppenheim v. Tobacco Securities Trust Co. Ltd* [1951] AC 297.
17. *Dingle v. Turner* [1972] AC 601, 624 *per* Lord Cross.
18. [1972] AC 601.
19. Note also the comments of Lord MacDermott in *Dingle v. Turner* [1972] AC 601, 614 who doubted whether consequential fiscal privileges had much relevance to the substantive question of whether a trust should be considered charitable in law. (A view shared by Viscount Dilhorne and Lord Hodson.)
20. Cmd. 9474. See Chapter 9, paragraphs 170 and 173.

Administration of Charities

While the Attorney General has the function of overseeing the enforcement of charities in Ireland and will be joined in any court proceedings brought in relation to such matters to ensure that the interests of charities are safeguarded, a statutory body ensures the proper administration of trusts on a day-to-day basis. This body, known as the Commissioners of Charitable Donations and Bequests, was initially established in Ireland in 1844. Its role is now governed by the provisions of Part II of the Charities Act 1961 and its jurisdiction and powers are set out in Chapter II of Part II of the Act of 1961 as amended by the Charities Act 1973. The commissioners, who shall be not more than eleven in number, are appointed by the government and hold office for life unless they retire or are removed from office.[21] They have power to advise charity trustees in relation to the administration of trusts[22] and can authorize the compromise of any proceedings brought by or against such trustees.[23] The commissioners may, with the consent of the Attorney General, sue for the recovery of any charitable gift which has been improperly withheld, concealed or misapplied,[24] and they have a general power to authorise or direct the institution of legal proceedings in relation to any charitable matter.[25] In addition, the commissioners have powers in relation to the investment of funds held on charitable trusts,[26] and as outlined below,[27] have also limited powers to frame a scheme applying property cy-près.[28] A further power, the exercise of which has recently been considered by the High Court is that contained in section 43 of the Charities Act 1961 as substituted by section 14 of the Charities Act 1973, by virtue of which the commissioners may appoint new trustees to a charity. In *Eastern Health Board v. Commissioners for Charitable Donations and Bequests*[29] an order was made by the commissioners pursuant to section 43 of the Charities Act 1961 as amended appointing new trustees of trusts established in respect of the Worth Library which had been housed in Dr Steeven's Hospital under the terms of a will which directed that the books concerned should not be removed from the room in the hospital in which they were kept. The hospital was closed in 1988 and

---

21. Ss. 7 and 8 of the Charities Act 1961.
22. S.21 of the Charities Act 1961.
23. S.22 of the Charities Act 1961.
24. S.23 of the Charities Act 1961.
25. S.25 of the Charities Act 1961.
26. S.32 of the Charities Act 1961 as substituted by s. 9 of the Charities Act 1973.
27. See *infra* p. 351 *et seq.*
28. S.29 of the Charities Act 1961 as amended by s.8 of the Act of 1973.
29. High Court 1991 No. 207 Sp (Denham J) 17 December 1991.

while the commissioners prepared a cy-près scheme, the books were temporarily housed in Trinity College Dublin. The plaintiff subsequently purchased the hospital and sought an order annulling the order of the commissioners appointing Trinity College and the director of the National Library to be trustees in place of the existing trustees. Denham J held that the appointment of the new trustees was not premature and had not prejudiced the plaintiff's position and stated that she was satisfied that it was the correct decision to move the books to Trinity College for safekeeping at the time when the hospital was being sold. She also rejected the claim that the commissioners had not complied with the procedures laid down by section 43 and held that the notice of the intention to appoint new trustees had been adequate.

Definition of Charity

Gavan Duffy J remarked in *Re Howley's Estate*[30] that '"charity" is in law an artificial conception, which during some 300 years, under the guidance of pedantic technicians, seems to have strayed rather far from the intelligent realm of plain common sense'. Whether such a colourful comment can be justified is open to debate but it is certainly arguable that the meaning of the term 'charity' in law bears no necessary relationship to a lay person's conception of the word.[31]

The first point to note is that no attempt has ever been made by the legislature, either here or in England, to actually define what is legally charitable. A list of charitable purposes was contained in legislation passed in both jurisdictions in the seventeenth century, although these statutes were never intended to define charitable objects in a legal sense but rather to enumerate a variety of purposes recognised as being legally charitable.[32] In addition, this list was never intended to be exhaustive and as Keane J has recently re-iterated in *Re Worth Library*,[33] a trust might be consid-

---

30. [1940] IR 109, 114.
31. See also the comments of Lord Sterndale MR in *Re Tetley* [1923] 1 Ch 258, 266.
32. As Lord Sugden LC commented in *Incorporated Society v. Richards* (1841) 4 Ir Eq R 177, 202: 'I consider that the object of the statute of Elizabeth was to remedy the abuses that then existed in the management of charitable property ...' and he accepted that the legislation in both jurisdictions was of similar effect. The comment has also been made by Lord Morton in *Royal College of Surgeons of England v. National Provincial Bank Ltd* [1952] AC 631, 650-651 that this was directed towards reforming abuses in the application of property devoted to charitable uses, rather than to defining the concept of a charity.
33. [1995] 2 IR 301, 333. See generally Delany (1994) 45 NILQ 364 and Brady (1994) 16 DULJ (ns) 153.

ered charitable if it fell within the 'spirit or intendment'[34] of the statute. While the Irish Statute of Charitable Uses 1634[35] was repealed by the Statute Law Revision Act (Ireland) 1878, it is nevertheless useful to set out the terms of the Preamble as the decisions given regarding its scope provide a useful insight into the question of what is legally charitable.[36]

> The erection, maintenance or support of any college, school, lecture in divinity, or in any of the liberal arts or sciences, or for the relief of any manner of poor, succourless, distressed or impotent persons, or for the building, re-edifying, or maintaining in repair of any church, college, school or hospital, or for the maintenance of any minister and preacher of the holy word of God, or for the erection, building, maintenance or repair of any bridges, causeyes, cashes, paces and highways within this realm, or for any other like lawful and charitable use and uses, warranted by the laws of this realm now established in force. ...

Although these words have provided a useful guide over the years, as Bright[37] has commented: its wording 'is clearly not tailored to current social problems.' Thomas J has recently stated in the decision of the New Zealand Court of Appeal in *Commissioner of Inland Revenue v. Medical Council of New Zealand*[38] that in applying the 'spirit and intendment' of the Preamble, it is important to be guided by principle rather than by a detailed analysis of decisions in particular cases, and it should be pointed out that judicial perceptions of what is charitable in law may have altered over the years.[39] Now a claim to charitable status is generally determined

---

34. See *Morice v. Bishop of Durham* (1804) 9 Ves 399, 405. This phrase has also been interpreted on occasion in a negative way to mean that a purpose might only be considered charitable if it fell within the 'spirit or intendment of the legislation'. See *Williams' Trustees v. IRC* [1947] AC 447, 455.
35. 10 Char 1, Sess. 3, c. 1. The English version, the Statute of Charitable Uses 1601, 43 Eliz. 1, c.4., preserved in subsequent legislation, was also finally repealed by the Charities Act 1960.
36. In the context of the English statute, see the comments of Lord Wilberforce in *Scottish Burial Reform and Cremation Society v. Glasgow City Corporation* [1968] AC 138, 154.
37. [1989] Conv 28, 31.
38. [1997] 2 NZLR 297, 314. See also the *dicta* of Sachs LJ in *Incorporated Council of Law Reporting for England and Wales v. Attorney General* [1972] Ch 73, 95.
39. Contrast for example *Re Hummeltenberg* [1923] 1 Ch 237 and *Funnell v. Stewart* [1996] 1 WLR 288. The former case, according to Fletcher (1996) 112 LQR 557 'tended to indicate that "faith healing" was not a charitable purpose'. By the time that the latter case was decided in 1996 it was accepted by the court that faith healing

by considering whether a particular purpose comes within one of the four broad categories identified by Lord Macnaghten in *Commissioners for Special Purposes of Income Tax v. Pemsel*,[40] which are as follows:

1. Trusts for the relief of poverty

2. Trusts for the advancement of education

3. Trusts for the advancement of religion

4. Trusts for other purposes beneficial to the community.

It is now generally accepted, both by textbook writers and by the judiciary, that trusts which are considered to be charitable in law fall into these four separate, although not necessarily mutually exclusive categories. While it has been recognised that this classification is one of convenience only and that there may be purposes which do not fit neatly into one or other of these categories,[41] or which fit into one or more categories at the same time,[42] it has nevertheless over the last century provided the basis on which the courts both in this jurisdiction and in England have approached the question of whether a trust should be accorded charitable status. Some consideration has been given in recent years in England to the question of providing further statutory guidance in this area.[43] Legislation enacted in England in 1993 provided that '"charity"[44] means any institution, corporate or not, which is established for charitable purposes and is subject to the control of the High Court'[45] and 'charitable purposes' was defined to

---

'had become a recognised activity of public benefit' (at 297) although as Hazel Williamson QC acknowledged 'this would not necessarily have been the case when *Re Hummeltenberg* was decided'. She held in the alternative that the purpose in any event qualified as charitable on the basis of the religious nature of the faith healing movement.

40. [1891] AC 531, 583. These categories were approved by Keane J in *Re Worth Library* [1995] 2 IR 301, 334. See also *In re Article 26 of the Constitution and the Employment Equality Bill 1996* [1997] 2 IR 321, 355.

41. *Scottish Burial Reform and Cremation Society Ltd v. Glasgow Corporation* [1968] AC 138, 154 *per* Lord Wilberforce.

42. See e.g. *Incorporated Council of Law Reporting for England and Wales v. Attorney General* [1972] Ch 73.

43. See the Report of the Committee on the Law and Practice Relating to Charities 1952 Cmd. 8710 (The Nathan Report) at paragraph 697. Note that the Committee on Charity Law and Voluntary Organizations 1976 (The Goodman Committee) suggested 'guidelines' which might be followed.

44. It was recently held by the English Court of Appeal in *Gaudiya Mission v. Brahmachary* [1997] 4 All ER 957 that the term 'charity' as contained in s.33 of the 1993 Act which deals with the taking of charity proceedings, did not include an institution established under the laws of another legal system.

45. S.96(1) of the Charities Act 1993.

mean 'purposes which are exclusively charitable according to the law of England and Wales'.[46] However, it is interesting that no attempt has been made in that jurisdiction to set out in legislation what is charitable in law or to define what constitutes 'charitable purposes'. In 'Charities : A Framework for the Future'[47] the view was expressed that 'the government consider that any attempt to define charity by any of [the suggested means] would be fraught with difficulty and might put at risk the flexibility of the present law which is both its greatest strength and its most valuable feature.'[48] This view would probably also prevail in this jurisdiction and there is considerable merit in Delany's comment that 'there is little to be gained by definitions, legislative or otherwise in charity matters. The social conscience of the judiciary working in the light of contemporary conditions will do more for the fair administration of charities than any definition.'[49]

The Macnaghten Classification and the Public Benefit Requirement

What this classification fails to make clear explicitly is that for a trust to be regarded as legally charitable, it must be of a public character and must contain some element of benefit to the public generally. An examination of the various judicial interpretations of the types of trust which are legally charitable show that there are in effect two hurdles to be overcome, first, an element of benefit, e.g. the relief of poverty and secondly, an element of *public* benefit.[50] Viscount Simonds commented in *IRC v. Baddeley*[51] that it is necessary to distinguish 'between a form of relief extended to the whole community, yet by its very nature advantageous only to a few and a form of relief accorded to a selected few out of a larger number equally willing and able to take advantage of it.' However, as Plowright[52] has pointed out, this type of formula has limitations if it is to be used as a practical criterion of assessment and is moreover not entirely accurate in defining the boundaries between private and charitable trusts.

---

46. S.97 of the Charities Act 1993.
47. 1989 Cmd. 694. See particularly paragraphs 2.07- 2.17.
48. *Ibid.* at paragraph 2.11. See also Mitchell (1999) 13 Trust Law Int 21.
49. *The Law Relating to Charities in Ireland* (1957) p.20. See also the comments of Sachs LJ in *Incorporated Council of Law Reporting for England and Wales v. Attorney General* [1972] Ch 73, 94.
50. In *Tudor on Charities*, Warburton (8th ed., 1995) at p.5 it is pointed out that this requirement may involve the consideration of two related questions viz. whether the purposes of the trust confer a benefit on the public or a section of the public and whether the class of persons eligible to benefit constitutes the public or a section of it.
51. [1955] AC 572, 592.
52. (1975) 39 Conv 183, 184.

This concept of public benefit varies considerably as between the different categories of charitable trusts;[53] in the case of trusts for the relief of poverty it has been greatly modified as a result of judicial intervention,[54] and in the Republic of Ireland in the case of trusts for the advancement of religion, section 45(1) of the Charities Act 1961 now provides that it shall be conclusively presumed that such a trust will occasion public benefit.[55] In addition, the requirement may differ as between different types of trusts in the fourth category and the point has even been made that it may seem anomalous to speak in terms of a public benefit requirement in this category as it is defined in terms of trusts for the benefit of the community.[56] It may appear therefore to be in some respects surprising that it is to this residual category that the most rigourous interpretation of the public benefit test has been applied.[57]

Perhaps due to the apparent latitude which this category allows for, the courts have traditionally taken a relatively strict view in interpreting what constitutes a trust for 'other purposes beneficial to the community'.[58] Greater flexibility towards this question can be seen in more recent deci-

---

53. See the statements of Lord Simonds in *Gilmour v. Coats* [1949] AC 426, 437, Lord Somervell in *IRC v. Baddeley* [1955] AC 572, 615 (see further Atiyah (1958) 21 MLR 138,139) and Carswell J in *Re Dunlop* [1984] NI 408, 425-426.

54. The so-called 'poor relations' trusts were recognised in a number of decisions handed down in the eighteenth century, see e.g. *Issac v. Defriez* (1754) Amb 595, and the modification of the public benefit requirement in this category is well recognised today, see *Gibson v. South American Stores (Gath & Chaves) Ltd* [1950] Ch 177; *Re Scarisbrick* [1951] Ch 622; *Dingle v. Turner* [1972] AC 601; *Re Cohen* [1973] 1 WLR 415.

55. See the recent *dicta* of Keane J in *Campaign to Separate Church and State Ltd v. Minister for Education* [1998] 2 ILRM 81, 83.

56. Hanbury & Martin, *Modern Equity* (15th ed., 1997) p.411.

57. See the comments of Babington LJ in *Trustees of the Londonderry Presbyterian Church House v. Commissioners of Inland Revenue* [1946] NI 178, 196; Lord Simonds in *Williams v. IRC* [1947] AC 447 and *IRC v. Baddeley* [1955] AC 572, 615 and of Lord Somervell in *IRC v. Baddeley* [1955] AC 572, 592 (although note the different conclusion reached by Lord Reid in *Baddeley* at pp. 612-613).

58. As Viscount Cave pointed out in *Attorney General v. National Provincial and Union Bank of England Ltd* [1924] AC 262, 265: 'Lord Macnaghten did not mean that all trusts beneficial to the community are charitable, but there are certain charitable trusts which fall within that category, and accordingly to argue that because a trust is for a purpose beneficial to the community it is therefore a charitable trust is to turn round his sentence and give it a different meaning. . . . It is not enough to say that a trust is for public purposes beneficial to the community or for the public welfare, you must also be show it to be a charitable trust.' See also the comments of Lindley LJ (pp.466-7) and Rigby LJ (p.476) in *Re Macduff* [1896] 2 Ch 451 and Andrews LJ in *Trustees of the Londonderry Presbyterian Church House v. Commissioners of Inland Revenue* [1946] NI 178, 187.

sions[59] but evidence of the more demanding approach can still be identified in terms of the application of the public benefit requirement to this category. On the other hand the courts have increasingly inferred that trusts falling within the other three categories will be 'assumed to be for the benefit of the community and therefore, charitable unless the contrary is shown'.[60] While this comment certainly reflects the position in relation to trusts falling within the first and third categories, trusts for the advancement of education have quite often not qualified as charitable trusts because of failure to satisfy the public benefit requirement. In England, the factors which will prevent the public benefit test being satisfied in the context of trusts for the advancement of education have extended beyond blood ties or a personal nexus to a 'nexus of contract',[61] and trusts for the education of persons, or relatives of persons, in common employment have been found not to be charitable in nature.[62]

THE MACNAGHTEN CLASSIFICATION

1. Trusts for the Relief of Poverty

The point has been made in *Tudor on Charities* that '"poor" is a relative term'[63] and the authorities have shown that it is not necessary for a class of persons to be destitute in order for a trust for their relief to qualify as charitable in nature. This point was made by Evershed MR in *Re Coulthurst*[64] as follows:

> It is quite clearly established that poverty does not mean destitution; it is a word of wide and somewhat indefinite import; it may not unfairly be paraphrased for present purposes as meaning persons

---

59. See e.g. the *dicta* of Lord Russell in *Incorporated Council for Law Reporting for England and Wales v. Attorney General* [1972] Ch 73, 88 where he suggested that if a purpose is beneficial to the community it is *prima facie* charitable in law.
60. *Per* Lord Simonds in *National Anti-Vivisection Society v. IRC* [1948] AC 31, 65. Quoted with approval by Keane J in *Re the Worth Library* [1995] 2 IR 301, 335.
61. Plowright (1975) 39 Conv 183, 185.
62. *Oppenheim v. Tobacco Securities Trust Co. Ltd* [1951] AC 297. See also *George Drexler Ofrex Foundation Trustees v. IRC* [1966] Ch 673 and *IRC v. Educational Grants Association Ltd* [1967] Ch 993. This approach was in line with the recommendations of the Goodman Committee Report on Charity Law and Voluntary Organisations (1976) paragraphs 38 and 50(b).
63. Warburton (8th ed., 1995) p. 29.
64. [1951] Ch 661, 665-6. See also *Re De Carteret* [1933] Ch 103, 108 *per* Maugham J.

who have to 'go short' in the ordinary acceptation of that term, due regard being had to their status in life and so forth.

There the Court of Appeal held that a trust for the benefit of the widows and children of deceased officers of a bank, who by reason of their financial circumstances were the most deserving, was a valid charitable trust. As Viscount Simonds commented in *IRC v. Baddeley*[65] 'there may be a good charity for the relief of persons who are not in grinding need or utter destitution' and a trust to provide for persons of limited or reduced means may come within the ambit of this category. So in *Re Gardom*,[66] a gift for the provision of a temporary residence for 'ladies of limited means' was held to be charitable. As Eve J commented, although such persons were not destitute, 'there are degrees of poverty less acute than abject poverty or destitution.'[67] However, there is often a fine line to be drawn between cases which will satisfy the requirement as being for the relief of poverty and those which will not. In *Re Sanders' Will Trusts*[68] Harman J held that a bequest to provide housing for the 'working classes' and their families resident in a certain district did not qualify, while in *Re Niyazi's Will Trusts*,[69] Megarry VC upheld as a valid charitable trust a gift 'for the construction of or as a contribution towards the cost of a working men's hostel' in the town of Famagusta in Cyprus. The most recent pronouncement on this issue would suggest that a more flexible attitude is now being taken towards the degree of poverty which must be established. In *Re Segelman deceased*[70] Chadwick J accepted that a gift to poor and needy members of a class of the testator's relatives was a valid charitable gift for the relief of poverty. He stated that the evidence suggested that 'most members of the class are comfortably off, in the sense that they are able to meet their day-to day expenses out of income, but not affluent' and that 'like many others in similar circumstances, they need a helping hand from time to time in order to overcome an unforeseen crisis'. Histed has commented that 'the court has come perilously close to implying that an occasional problem of expenditure exceeding income is sufficient to qualify a class member as "poor"'.[71] She states that even though this was presumably not the implication intended, she quite rightly suggests that 'the tone of the judgment

---

65. [1955] AC 572, 585.
66. [1914] 1 Ch 662.
67. *Ibid.* at 668.
68. [1954] Ch 265. The case was settled on appeal (see *The Times*, 22 July 1954).
69. [1978] 1 WLR 910.
70. [1996] Ch 171.
71. [1996] Conv 379, 386.

does suggest a more flexible approach to the poverty requirement than has obtained in earlier cases'.

A further limitation which should be noted is that the need which is to be relieved by the charitable gift must be attributable to the condition of the person to be benefited. This point was made by Peter Gibson J in *Joseph Rowntree Memorial Trust Housing Association Ltd v. Attorney General*[72] in the context of schemes to provide accommodation for disabled and elderly people, but it would have equal application to trusts for the poor and would seem to rule out any gift which does not go towards alleviating their condition of poverty. An earlier illustration of this principle was provided by Harman J in *Baddeley v. IRC*,[73] where he commented that a gift to amuse the poor would not relieve them and therefore would not be considered charitable. A further consideration is the fact that potential beneficiaries are young and therefore may not themselves have a means of support does not necessarily fulfil the poverty requirement. In *Browne v. King*[74] a gift to be applied for the benefit of the children of the tenantry of an estate under the age of twelve years did not qualify as charitable. As Porter MR stated: 'There is nothing to guide me in deciding that the gift is for children of poor persons, or persons in great need. The law imposes on parents the duty of supporting their children and there is nothing to satisfy me that the tenantry ... are not able to fulfil that obligation.'[75]

A gift of this kind may be expressed in either general or particular terms. So a gift to the poor in a general way will be upheld,[76] or a gift to the poor of a particular area,[77] or a particular religious denomination.[78] It has been established[79] that the fact that the recipients of the testator or donor's bounty are to be chosen by his executors or trustees does not present any difficulties. Similarly, in *Brett v. Attorney General*[80] it was held by the Supreme Court that a trust for 'such poor persons in the County of M. as the executor shall select and consider worthy of assistance' was charitable

---

72. [1983] Ch 159, 171 See also *Re Dunlop* [1984] NI 408, 414-416.
73. [1953] 1 WLR 84, 88. As he stated: 'Relief seems to connote need of some sort ... and not merely an amusement however healthy it is.'
74. (1885) 17 LR Ir 448.
75. *Ibid.* at 456.
76. *Attorney General v. Matthews* (1677) 2 Lev 167.
77. *Attorney General v. Exeter Corporation* (1826) 2 Russ 45.
78. *Attorney General v. Wansay* (1808) 15 Ves 231; *Dawson v. Small* (1874) LR 18 Eq 114; *Re Wall* (1889) 42 Ch D 510.
79. *Re Scarisbrick* [1951] Ch 622 and *Re Cohen* [1973] 1 WLR 415 where a trust 'for the maintenance and benefit of any relative of mine whom my trustees shall consider to be in special need' was upheld as charitable.
80. [1945] IR 526.

and that the power of selection conferred on the executor could not alter the essentially charitable nature of the gift.

It is important to distinguish a gift to specified poor individuals from a gift to a class of the poor. Trusts in the former category are not charitable in nature, while those in the latter are, even where this class is of limited scope. At this point it becomes necessary to consider the public benefit requirement in trusts for the relief of poverty in more detail and it is fair to say that the comment made by Martin[81] that the requirement in this category has been 'reduced ... almost to vanishing point' is an accurate one. This position has come about largely as a result of the development of the category of so called 'poor relations' trusts, whereby a donor or testator may create a valid charitable trust to benefit those of his relatives who are in straightened financial circumstances.[82] These cases are recognised as forming an exception to the general principle laid down by Lord Greene MR in *Re Compton*[83] that 'a gift under which the beneficiaries are defined by reference to a purely personal relationship to a named *propositus*, cannot on principle be a valid charitable gift.'

A justification for these types of trust has been suggested by Evershed MR in *Re Scarisbrick* in the following terms:

> The 'poor relations' cases may be justified on the basis that the relief of poverty is of so altruistic a character that the public element may necessarily be inferred thereby; or they may be accepted as a hallowed, if illogical, exception.[84]

An examination of the authorities suggests that the second rationale is the more likely and these types of trusts have come to be regarded as anomalous exceptions to the public benefit requirement which attaches to charitable trusts generally.[85] A good illustration of such a trust is provided in the *Scarisbrick*[86] case itself, where a trust to benefit such relations of the testatrix's son and daughters who in the opinion of the survivor of her children 'shall be in needy circumstances' was upheld as a valid charitable trust. Jenkins LJ, having set out the general requirement of public benefit in charitable trusts, continued as follows:

---

81. Hanbury and Martin, *Modern Equity* (15th ed., 1997) p.412.
82. See *Mahon v. Savage* (1803) 1 Sch & Lef 111.
83. [1945] Ch 123, 131.
84. *Re Scarisbrick* [1951] Ch 622, 639 and *Gibson v. South American Stores (Gath & Chaves) Ltd* [1950] Ch 177, 197 *per* Evershed MR.
85. See *Re Compton* [1945] Ch 123, 139 *per* Lord Greene MR.
86. [1951] Ch 622.

There is, however, an exception to the general rule, in that trusts or gifts for the relief of poverty have been held to be charitable even though they are limited in their application to some aggregate of individuals ascertained as above, and are, therefore, not trusts or gifts for the benefit of the public or a section thereof. The exception operates whether the personal tie is one of blood (as in the numerous so called 'poor relations' cases) or of contract, e.g., the relief of poverty amongst the members of a particular society ... or amongst employees of a particular company or their dependants.[87]

A further point which was made by the Court of Appeal in *Scarisbrick* is that no distinction should be drawn between trusts for the poor which are to have perpetual continuance and those which provide for immediate distribution amongst the recipients.[88] As Jenkins LJ stated: 'I see no sufficient ground in the authorities for holding that a gift for the benefit of poor relations qualifies as charitable only if it is perpetual in character.'[89]

Another recent example of a trust for poor relations being upheld is *Re Segelman deceased*[90] in which Chadwick J accepted that a gift to poor and needy members of a class of the testator's relatives, which was not to close until 21 years after his death, was a valid charitable gift for the relief of poverty and that it was not disqualified from being such by the restricted nature of the class. At the time of the hearing, there were 26 members of the class and Chadwick J stated that it was reasonable to assume that at the end of the period of 21 years from the testator's death, the class would be substantially larger. Chadwick J stated that *prima facie* a gift for the benefit of poor and needy persons is a gift for the relief of poverty and that such a gift is no less charitable because those whose poverty is to be relieved are confined to a particular class limited by ties of blood or employment. He quoted a statement from the judgment of Jenkins LJ in *Scarisbrick,* which had been approved by the House of Lords in *Dingle v. Turner,*[91] to the effect that the true question must be whether the gift was really for the relief of poverty amongst a class of persons or merely a gift to individuals,

---

87. *Ibid.* at 649.
88. In so doing the Court of Appeal reversed the finding of Roxburgh J at first instance in which he had held that the bequest was not charitable on the basis that a gift for immediate distribution lacked the necessary public character to render it charitable. (This finding was in the opinion of the Court of Appeal based on a mistaken interpretation of the decision of Grant MR in *Attorney General v. Price* (1810) 17 Ves 371).
89. *Ibid.* at 655.
90. [1996] Ch 171.
91. [1972] AC 601.

albeit with the relief of poverty amongst those individuals as the motive for the gift. Chadwick J continued by saying that the basis for disqualification as a charitable gift must be that the restricted nature of the class leads to the conclusion that the gift is really one to the individual members of a class. In his view the gift which he was required to consider was not of that character and had, in common with the gift in *Scarisbrick,* the feature that the class of those eligible to benefit was not closed on the testator's death but remained open for a further period of 21 years. Chadwick J stated that during that period issue of the named individuals born after the testator's death would become members of the class. In his opinion it was impossible to attribute to the testator an intention to make a gift to those after-born issue as such and his intention must therefore be taken to have been the relief of poverty amongst the class of which they would become members.

While Chadwick J did not address this point directly, the implication might be taken from his judgment that if the class of persons to benefit was confined to those of the testator's relatives living at the date of his death, the gift might have been construed as one to individual members of the class which would not qualify as being for the relief of poverty. Histed has commented that Chadwick J's opinion seemed to be that 'the more restricted the class, the more probable that the gift was one to individuals' and in her view the gift was saved by the inclusion of potential after-born issue.[92] She also expressed the view that the basis for the selection of the class appeared to depend not so much on the degree of relationship to the testator but on the possibility of future need and suggested that this factor also influenced the court's decision that the gift was a charitable one.

The relaxation of the public benefit requirement has been extended to other categories or classes of persons and so trusts for 'poor employees'[93] and 'poor members'[94] have also been recognised despite the existence of some personal nexus between the donor or testator and those whom he seeks to benefit. However the existence of the quality of poverty amongst those whom it is sought to benefit must be clear and trusts for employees have failed to qualify as charitable where this has not been evident.[95] So in *Re Cullimore's Trusts,*[96] a trust for the benefit and maintenance of the fami-

---

92. [1996] Conv 379, 385.
93. The validity of such trusts was recognised in England in *Re Gosling* (1900) 48 WR 300. See also *Gibson v. South American Stores (Gath & Chaves) Ltd* [1950] Ch 177.
94. *Spiller v. Maude* (1881) 32 Ch D 158n (members of mutual benefit society); *Re Young* [1955] 1 WLR 1269 (members of a social club).
95. See *Re Drummond* [1914] 2 Ch 90 where a trust to provide for the holiday expenses of employees in a department in a certain company was found not to be charitable. See also *Re Hobourn Aero Components Ltd's Air Raid Distress Fund* [1946] Ch 194.
96. (1891) 27 LR Ir 18.

lies of employees of a firm was found not to be charitable. As Porter MR stated: 'Mere kindness, generosity, or benevolence on the testator's part is not enough to constitute a charitable purpose; there must also be an element of poverty or need on the part of the object, or else the gift must be dedicated to some purpose, such as education, religion or the like which the law regards as charitable. There is nothing here to show that the persons whom the testator meant to benefit were to be poor persons.'[97]

However, the decision of the House of Lords in *Dingle v. Turner*[98] has clearly confirmed that trusts for the benefit of 'poor employees' will be recognised as valid charitable trusts. The testator directed trustees to apply the income of a fund for the purpose of paying pensions to poor employees of a firm who were 60 years of age and over, or who were at least 45 years of age and incapacitated from earning a living and the House of Lords upheld the gift as being a charitable trust. Lord Cross rejected the argument that the trust in the case before him should not be recognised as charitable despite the fact that the company was in some respects relatively small, employing around 600 people at the date of the testator's death. He stated:

> [T]he 'poor members' and 'poor employees' decisions were a natural development of the 'poor relations' decisions and to draw a distinction between different sorts of 'poverty' trusts would be quite illogical and could certainly not be said to be introducing 'greater harmony' into the law of charity. Moreover, though not as old as the 'poor relations' trusts, 'poor employees' trusts have been recognised as charities for many years; there are now a large number of such trusts in existence; and assuming, as one must, that they are properly administered in the sense that the benefits under them are only given to people who can fairly be said to be according to current standards, 'poor persons', to treat such trusts as charitable is not open to any practical objection.[99]

The principle laid down by Lord Cross is now well established and has been extended to include poor members of a profession. In *Re Denison*[100]

---

97. *Ibid.* at 24.
98. [1972] AC 601. The point is made in *Tudor on Charities* (Warburton (8th ed., 1995) p.35 that the decision not only removed any 'lingering doubts' about the validity of poor relations trusts but also confirmed the charitable nature of trusts for the relief of poverty amongst other classes of persons having a personal nexus in the form of a common employer.
99. *Ibid.* at 623.
100. (1974) 42 DLR (3d) 652.

the High Court of Ontario found that a bequest for the relief of 'impoverished or indigent members of the Law Society [of Upper Canada] and of their wives and widows and children' was charitable. While the extension of the exception to the public benefit requirement in cases of this nature has been criticised,[101] it is submitted that it is too firmly entrenched to be overturned at this stage, certainly in England, and it is most unlikely that the courts in this jurisdiction would see fit to depart from this position.

It should be noted that the preamble to the English Statute of Charitable Uses referred to 'the relief of aged, impotent and poor people'.[102] While it has been recognised that these purposes are to be construed in a disjunctive manner,[103] some textbook writers[104] and judges[105] have tended to consider them as being grouped under one heading. In the UK, trusts for the aged and the sick may still be characterised as falling into into the first rather than the fourth category in Lord Macnaghten's classification and some residual doubt remained until recently about whether the exception to the public benefit requirement could be extended to such trusts. This question seems to have been settled by Carswell J in *Re Dunlop*,[106] where he stated that the House of Lords in *Dingle v. Turner* intended to circumscribe the scope of the exception and 'to confine it to cases concerning the relief of actual poverty.'[107]

It can be argued that it is unrealistic to enforce the requirement that there should be no personal tie or nexus between a donor or testator and the class of individuals which he seeks to benefit in that a charitable gift will usually be motivated by such factors, and to strictly enforce it would not be practicable. This issue will be considered in more detail below, but for present purposes, it suffices to say that the requirement of public ben-

---

101. E.g. by the Report of the Goodman Committee on Charity Law and Voluntary Organisations, Chapter II, paragraph 37.
102. The version contained in the Statute of Charitable Uses (Ireland) 1634 referred to 'the relief ... of poor, succourless, distressed or impotent persons'.
103. *Joseph Rowntree Memorial Trust Housing Association Ltd v. Attorney General* [1983] Ch 159.
104. *Tudor on Charities*, Warburton (8th ed., 1995).
105. Lord Simonds in *Oppenheim v. Tobacco Securities Trust Co. Ltd* [1955] AC 297, 308.
106. [1984] NI 408. Considered in more detail *infra* p. 328.
107. *Ibid.* at 424. The judgment of Carswell J, considered in more detail below, would suggest that while potential beneficiaries of trusts for the aged and the sick must constitute 'a particular section of the community at large', a less strict public benefit test is applied to such categories than that which he suggested should apply to the fourth category.

efit has all but disappeared in the context of trusts for the relief of poverty.[108]

2. Trusts for the Advancement of Education

While trusts for the advancement of education in the formal sense have long been recognised as charitable in nature,[109] the concept of what is 'educational' in the sense of what will be recognised as legally charitable has been widened considerably over the last fifty years by a process of judicial interpretation. A gift for the advancement of education in a general manner will be recognised as charitable; so a bequest for 'educational ... purposes',[110] or a gift 'for the benefit, and advancement, and propagation of education and learning in every part of the world'[111] will be upheld. Similarly, a gift to schools,[112] or to colleges, either generally or to found a scholarship[113] will be recognised as charitable under this heading. In addition, more recent authorities have established that the ambit of trusts recognised as being for the advancement of education is not confined to those which are educational in the formal sense of the word.

In England it is possible to discern two distinct approaches to the question of what constitutes 'education'. A rather narrow view was taken by Harman J in *Re Shaw*,[114] which concerned a direction under the will of George Bernard Shaw that his trustees should use his residuary estate to provide for research, *inter alia*, into the advantages of reform of the alphabet. Harman J stated that 'if the object be merely the increase of knowledge that is not in itself a charitable object unless it be combined with teaching or education'.[115] He found that these latter elements were lacking in the case before him and also concluded that the objects were not beneficial to the community in a way regarded as charitable in law.

---

108. Although as Plowright comments (1975) 39 Conv 183, 187 'there are limits to the acceptable width of class even within this exception beyond which the court will not allow that the trust can properly be regarded as a charitable trust, but will conclude that it is nothing more than a private trust. It is this ... qualification that makes it unwise to assert that trusts for the relief of poverty form a complete exception to the requirement of public benefit.'
109. The Preamble to the Statute of Charitable Uses (Ireland) 1634 made reference to 'the erection, maintenance or support of any college, school, lecture in divinity, or on any of the liberal arts or sciences, the building, re-edifying, or maintaining in repair any college [or] school'.
110. *Re Ward* [1941] Ch 308.
111. *Whicker v. Hume* (1858) 7 HLC 124.
112. *Incorporated Society v. Richards* (1841) 4 Ir Eq R 177.
113. *R. v. Newman* (1684) 1 Lev 284.
114. [1957] 1 WLR 729.
115. *Ibid.* at 737. See also *Re Macduff* [1896] 2 Ch 451, 472-3 *per* Rigby LJ.

A more expansive interpretation of what should qualify as 'education' was put forward by Wilberforce J in *Re Hopkins' Will Trusts*,[116] where a gift to a society to be applied to the task of finding the Bacon-Shakespeare manuscripts was held to be a valid charitable trust. Wilberforce J stated:

> I think, therefore, that the word 'education' as used by Harman J in *Re Shaw* must be used in a wide sense, certainly extending beyond teaching, and that the requirement is that, in order to be charitable, research must either be of educational value to the researcher or must be directed as to lead to something which will pass into the store of educational material, or so as to improve the sum of communicable knowledge in an area which education may cover — education in this last context extending to the formation of literary taste and appreciation.[117]

Wilberforce J said that he would be unwilling to treat Harman J's words as meaning that the promotion of academic research is not a charitable purpose unless the researcher were engaged in teaching or education in the conventional sense. While he accepted that research of a purely private nature would not normally be educational, research of the character proposed in the case before him did not fall into this category as it was 'inherently inevitable and manifestly intended' that the results of such research should fall into the public domain. This point that education requires more than just the accumulation of knowledge and must involve some element of sharing or publication was reiterated by Buckley LJ in *Incorporated Council for Law Reporting for England and Wales v. Attorney General*.[118] The majority of the Court of Appeal found that the activities of the council fell within the second head of Lord Macnaghten's classification[119] and Buckley LJ commented in the course of his judgment that the concept of the advancement of education must extend 'to the improvement of a useful branch of human knowledge and its public dissemination'.[120]

In considering these divergent approaches in *Re Shaw* and *Re Hopkins* in *Re Worth Library*[121] Keane J commented that the views of Harman J in *Re Shaw* might not command universal acceptance today and that it was

---

116. [1965] Ch 669.
117. *Ibid.* at 680.
118. [1972] 1 Ch 73.
119. Sachs and Buckley LJJ. Russell LJ found that the purposes were charitable under the fourth head alone.
120. [1972] 1 Ch 73, 102.
121. [1995] 2 IR 301, 337.

possible that they would exclude from the legal definition of charity certain trusts for the encouragement of academic research which might reasonably be regarded as being for the public benefit. Keane J concluded by saying that if this was the likely interpretation of the views of Harman J, he would prefer those of Wilberforce J.

A closer examination of the judgment of Keane J in *Worth* confirms that he favours an interpretation at the liberal end of the spectrum. In this important decision, the High Court was called upon to decide whether to approve a cy-près scheme proposed by the trustees of the 'Worth Library' which consisted of a bequest of a large and valuable collection of books originally made in the eighteenth century to Dr Steevens' Hospital in Dublin. When the hospital was closed in 1988, the trustees of the library decided to transfer it temporarily to Trinity College, Dublin for safekeeping and appointed the college as trustees in their place.[122] The Eastern Health Board which had purchased the hospital premises that year took the view that the library should be returned to its original location and when the Attorney General gave his consent to the trustees' application to the High Court for an order framing a cy-près scheme,[123] the board was joined as a defendant to the proceedings. At the outset of legal arguments in the case, Keane J indicated to counsel for the various parties the fundamental issues which he felt required resolution, namely the question of whether the initial bequest of the Worth Library was in law a charitable trust, and if so, the type of charitable bequest which it represented. If this first question was answered in the affirmative, the court would then proceed to consider whether the conditions necessary for the exercise of its cy-près jurisdiction had been satisfied and decide what form of scheme should be approved. In considering the first submission of counsel on behalf of the plaintiff, that the initial bequest should qualify as being for the advancement of education, Keane J made the following general statement:

> [G]ifts for the advancement of education ... would embrace, not merely gifts to schools and universities and the endowment of university chairs and scholarships: 'education' has been given a broad meaning so as to encompass gifts for the establishment of theatres, art galleries and museums and the promotion of literature and music. In every case, however, the element of public benefit must be

---

122. The Attorney General took the view that an appropriately qualified independent person should also be appointed as a trustee and the Director of the National Library agreed to act in that capacity.
123. As he was required to do by s. 51(1) of the Irish Charities Act 1961.

present and, if the benefit extends to a section of the community only, that section must not be numerically negligible.[124]

Keane J rejected the argument that the trust might qualify as being one for the advancement of education on the basis of the lack of an element of public benefit but it is interesting to note that he stated that in any event a finding that the library was for educational purposes would involve 'some straining of the concept of "education" even beyond the liberal limits of the modern decisions,' given the insignificant portion of the library devoted to topics of medical interest.

A number of decisions have illustrated that the ambit of education for this purpose is not limited to education of the mind and extends to the physical education of those attending a school or college. So, in *IRC v. McMullen*[125] the House of Lords upheld as charitable under this heading a trust 'to organise or provide or assist in the organisation or provision of facilities which will enable and encourage pupils at schools and universities in any part of the United Kingdom to play association football and other games or sports and thereby to assist in ensuring that due attention is given to the physical education and development of their minds'.

Similarly, the concept of education has been found to extend to aesthetic education and to such purposes as the support of museums[126] and the promotion of an appreciation of art[127] and music.[128] As Vaisey J stated in *Re Shaw's Will Trusts*,[129] in upholding the validity of a gift for 'bringing the masterpieces of fine art within the reach of the people of Ireland of all classes in their own country,' he thought that 'education' included 'not only teaching, but the promotion and encouragement of those arts and graces of life which are after all, perhaps the finest and best part of the human character.'[130] In *Royal Choral Society v. IRC*[131] the English Court of Appeal upheld a trust to promote the performance of choral works. Lord Greene MR said that he disagreed with the narrow conception of education as meaning a teacher instructing a class and concluded that in his opinion 'a body of persons established for the purpose of raising the artistic state of the country ... is established for educational purposes.'[132]

---

124. *Ibid.* at 336.
125. [1981] AC 1. See also *Re Mariette* [1915] 2 Ch 284.
126. *British Museum v. White* (1826) 2 Sim & St 594.
127. *Re Shaw's Will Trusts* [1952] Ch 163.
128. *Re Delius* [1957] Ch 299.
129. [1952] Ch 163.
130. *Ibid.* at 172.
131. [1943] 2 All ER 101.
132. *Ibid.* at 105.

Gifts to professional bodies can qualify as being for the advancement of education provided that their objects are truly educational in nature rather than being the promotion of the status of the profession or the safeguarding of the welfare of its members. However, in practice such bodies and associations will frequently have ancillary objects which fall into the latter category. In *Miley v. Attorney General for Ireland*[133] the Irish Court of Appeal was required to determine whether a legacy to the Royal College of Surgeons in Ireland was one for 'charitable uses' within the meaning of section 16 of the Charitable Donations and Bequests Act 1844.[134] The court found that there were two main objects contemplated by the charter of the college, one being the promotion of the science of surgery, and the other being the regulation of the profession and the promotion of the interests of those practising it. The court concluded that the latter object was not a charitable one and that as the testatrix had not impressed her gift with a charitable purpose, the bequest should not be considered to be one for 'charitable uses' within the meaning of section 16 of the Act of 1844.

However, the courts in England have tended to take a more pragmatic approach to this issue by adopting reasoning well summarised by Greer LJ in *Geologists Association v. IRC*:[135]

> If you come to the conclusion, as you may in many cases, that one of the ways in which the public objects of an association can be served is by giving special advantages to the members of the association, then the association does not cease to be an association with a charitable object because incidentally and in order to carry out the charitable object it is both necessary and desirable to confer special benefits upon the members.

A similar principle was applied by the House of Lords in *Royal College of Surgeons of England v. National Provincial Bank Ltd.*[136] It was held that the main object of the college was the promotion and encouragement of

---

133. [1918] 1 IR 455.
134. S.16 (now repealed by the Charities Act 1961) rendered void gifts of land for charitable uses unless the instrument conferring the gift was executed at least three months prior to the death of the donor. The testatrix had died four days after the execution of her will and therefore the validity of her bequest, which would have been payable partly out of realty, would have been affected by the provisions of s.16 if it had been found to be charitable in nature.
135. (1928) 14 TC 271, 283. See also *Royal College of Nursing v. St Marylebone Borough Council* [1959] 1 WLR 1077, 1085.
136. [1952] AC 631.

the study and practice of surgery and that the professional protection of its members was ancillary to this overall objective and did not alter the charitable status of the college.

It can be said with a fair degree of certainty that the decision of the Irish Court of Appeal in *Miley* is now unlikely to be followed for a number of reasons. First, the surrounding circumstances of the case and the consequences of a finding of charitable status to the outcome must be borne in mind. Secondly, the court laid considerable emphasis on the earlier English decision in *Re Royal College of Surgeons of England,*[137] which was subsequently distinguished by the House of Lords in *Royal College of Surgeons of England v. National Provincial Bank Ltd*. In any event, legislation would seem to have resolved the question in a manner which should ensure that the decision in *Miley* would not now be followed. Section 49(1) of Charities Act 1961 provides that where the purposes of a gift include charitable and non-charitable objects, its terms will be construed so as to exclude the non-charitable objects. On this basis gifts such as that considered in *Miley* would probably be interpreted in such a way that they would be applied solely in furtherance of the charitable purposes of such a professional body.

The Element of Public Benefit

It is important to stress that a gift for the advancement of education will only qualify as charitable provided that it is for the benefit of the public generally or of an 'appreciably important class'[138] of the public. This principle was stressed in *Re Compton,*[139] in which the Court of Appeal held that a trust for the education of the descendants of three named individuals was not a valid charitable trust. As Lord Greene MR stated 'a gift under which the beneficiaries are defined by reference to a purely personal relationship to a named *propositus* cannot on principle be a valid charitable gift.'[140]

One of the most important English authorities in this area is the decision of the House of Lords in *Oppenheim v. Tobacco Securities Trust Co. Ltd,*[141] which concerned the validity of a trust set up to provide for the education of the children of employees or former employees of a tobacco

---

137. [1899] 1 QB 871.
138. *Verge v. Sommerville* [1924] AC 496, 499 *per* Lord Westbury.
139. [1945] Ch 123. See also *Re Hobourn Aero Components Ltd's Air Raid Distress Fund* [1946] Ch 86.
140. *Ibid.* at 131.
141. [1951] AC 297.

company or its subsidiaries. Despite the fact that the number of such employees exceeded 110,000 at the date of the settlement, it was held that the trust must fail as the distinguishing quality of the class of beneficiaries was a relationship with a named *propositus* and for this reason they could not constitute a section of the public. Lord Simonds stated as follows:

> These words 'section of the community' have no special sanctity, but they conveniently indicate first, that the possible (I emphasise the word 'possible') beneficiaries must not be numerically negligible, and secondly, that the quality which distinguishes them from other members of the community, so that they form by themselves a section of it, must be a quality which does not depend on their relationship to a particular individual.[142]

Lord MacDermott in his dissenting judgment considered that the '*Compton* test',[143] while it might often prove of value might equally, if a personal or impersonal relationship remained the criterion, prove to be 'a very arbitrary and artificial rule'. The reasoning of the majority in *Oppenheim* has not met with universal approval and the decision of Lord Cross in *Dingle v. Turner* shows an element of empathy with the views expressed by Lord MacDermott. In the view of Lord Cross the question of whether the beneficiaries under a trust constitute a section of the community is essentially one of degree and cannot of itself prove decisive in determining whether the trust is charitable in nature.[144] A further important reason for questioning the validity of the majority view in *Oppenheim* put forward by Lord Cross was his view that the decisions in both *Compton* and *Oppenheim* appeared to him to have been 'pretty obviously influenced by considerations of a perceived undeserved fiscal immunity which would be the result of a finding of charitable status.' Such concerns can also be seen to lie behind the comments made by Harman LJ in the course of his judgment in *IRC v. Educational Grants Association*[145] that 'it is an admirable thing that the children of employees should have a higher education, but I do not see why it should be at the expense of the taxpayer.' While this issue will be considered in more detail below, for the present it suffices to say that the

---

142. *Ibid.* at 306.
143. See *supra* n.140.
144. It is interesting to note that Lord Simonds in *Oppenheim* criticised the dissenting judgment of Lord MacDermott for the very reason that it made the question one of degree; an objection which Geoffrey Cross QC (later Lord Cross) writing in (1956) 72 LQR 189-190 said was not an objection which he believed to be very cogent.
145. [1967] Ch 993, 1013.

decision in *Oppenheim* should not be accepted unquestioningly as the basis for the decision may itself be reassessed in the future.

Despite these doubts, there is no evidence in any decisions made by the courts in this jurisdiction of a more relaxed attitude being applied towards this question of public benefit in the context of trusts for the advancement of education, although it should be pointed out that the authorities here have involved a considerably smaller number of potential beneficiaries than those considered in *Oppenheim*. In *Re McEnery*,[146] Gavan Duffy J concluded that a bequest to enable the nephews and nieces of the testator and their male descendants to obtain professions was too narrow in scope to be charitable and that the intention of the testator was to benefit specific individuals. As he stated: 'Courts of Equity generally have been consistently insistent on the public character of legal charity, importing a benefit to the community, or a section of the community. ...'[147]

When the question came before Keane J in *Re Worth Library*, he had no hesitation in finding that the trust could not qualify as being for the advancement of education as the library was clearly expressed to be for the use and benefit of three named office holders in the hospital alone. It is to an extent unfortunate that the question of whether a gift framed in slightly wider terms might have satisfied this requirement did not arise for consideration. Keane J nevertheless expressed some views on the issue which are of relevance, although he failed to clarify the position in any meaningful way. On the one hand, Keane J quoted with approval the statement of Lord Simonds in *National Anti-Vivisection Society v. I.R.C.*[148] to the effect that 'if the purpose is within one of the heads of charity forming the first three classes in [Lord Macnaghten's] ... classification ... the court will easily conclude that it is a charitable purpose' and stated that it has been accepted in England that gifts in the first three 'Pemsel' categories are presumed to be for the public benefit.[149] However he went on to comment that in the context of trusts for the advancement of education 'in every case ... the element of public benefit must be present and, if the benefit extends to a section of the community only, that section must not be numerically negligible.'[150]

Therefore it is fair to say that the question of the extent of the public benefit requirement is no closer to being resolved in this jurisdiction than

---

146. [1941] IR 323.
147. *Ibid.* at 326.
148. [1948] AC 31, 65.
149. A statement which is difficult to justify in the light of the decision of the House of Lords in *Oppenheim*.
150. [1995] 2 IR 301, 336.

it is in England, and while some support for a more lenient approach can be discerned from a portion of the judgment of Keane J in *Re Worth*, the overall effect of his decision is probably to maintain the *status quo* as it exists post-*Oppenheim*.

The effect of such an inflexible approach has been mitigated in both jurisdictions to a limited degree, by what are sometimes referred to as the 'founder's kin' decisions. So while a trust simply to educate a donor's relatives will not qualify as being charitable in nature,[151] a gift to an educational institution which contains a direction that preference be given to the 'founder's kin' may constitute a charitable trust. The effect of this principle was summarised in a general context as follows by Atiyah:[152]

> Where there is a charitable trust for the benefit of a section of the community the trust is not invalidated because the trustees are directed to give preference to certain beneficiaries who would not by themselves have constituted a section of the community.

This principle would seem to be supported by two English decisions, *Spencer v. All Soul's College*[153] and *Attorney General v. Sidney Sussex College*.[154] One example of a particularly liberal construction of this principle is the decision of O'Connor MR in *Re Lavelle*,[155] in which he upheld a bequest to a college which contained a direction that the income should be used to educate the testator's relatives there. While the facts of this case arguably fit within the 'founder's kin' exception established in the cases referred to above, the language employed by O'Connor MR should be treated with a degree of caution. In the course of his judgment he stated that 'gifts for the advancement of education are undoubtedly charitable and it has been decided that bequests for the education of the donor's descendants and kinsman are also charitable,' referring to the English authorities. This is misleading and as Lord Greene MR made clear in *Re Compton*,[156] for a gift to come within this limited exception, the primary object of the donor must be to endow a college for educational purposes and the preference afforded to his own family must be 'merely a method of giving effect to this intention'. This interpretation is supported by the

---

151. E.g. *Re McEnery* [1941] IR 323.
152. (1958) 21 MLR 138, 148.
153. (1762) Wilm 163.
154. (1869) LR 4 Ch App 722.
155. [1914] 1 IR 194.
156. [1945] Ch 123, 132.

dicta of Barton J in *Laverty v. Laverty*,[157] to the extent that he stated that in his opinion 'a valid charitable trust might be created for the advancement of education, with a preference for persons of a particular surname, either by the endowment of, or gift to, a school or college'.[158] He continued by saying *obiter* that such a trust might also be created by means of a gift to trustees, provided that it was sufficiently definite in nature. However, on the facts of the case before him, Barton J held that, having regard to the discretion vested in the trustees, a gift for the support and education in Ireland of Roman Catholic boys and men with specified surnames was not charitable in nature as it 'might have been intended to work, as a mere matter of private bounty'. On the basis that the comments of O'Connor MR in *Lavelle* do not seem to be supported by the authorities on which he placed reliance, and having regard to the fact that Barton J provided no justification for his *obiter* suggestion, there is a distinct possibility that the 'founder's kin' exception may still only be valid in this jurisdiction provided that the gift is expressed in the terms suggested by Lord Greene in *Re Compton*.

The principle to which Atiyah referred was given recognition by Upjohn J in *Re Koettgen's Will Trusts*,[159] where a trust established to further the commercial education of British born persons which included a direction that preference be given to employees of a particular firm, was upheld as charitable. However, subsequently in *Caffoor v. Commissioner of Income Tax, Columbo*,[160] the Privy Council showed a reluctance to adopt such an approach and found that the trust before them conferred such a priority on the donor's own relatives and descendants that 'the only fair way to describe [it was] as a family trust'.[161] Lord Radcliffe commented that *Koettegen* 'edges very near to being inconsistent with *Oppenheim*'[162] and Atiyah similarly comments that the decision of Upjohn J 'opens the way to serious evasion of the *Oppenheim* ruling'.[163] Often the result of such cases will turn on a matter of construction and the approach in *Koettgen* might well be embraced by the courts in this jurisdiction as a means of mitigating the severity of *Oppenheim* without giving consideration to the

---

157. [1907] 1 IR 9.
158. *Ibid.* at 13.
159. [1954] Ch 252.
160. [1961] AC 584.
161. *Ibid.* at 603.
162. *Ibid.* at 604. See also *IRC v. Educational Grants Association Ltd* [1967] Ch 993, 1010 *per* Denning MR.
163. (1958) 21 MLR 138, 148.

thorny question of the separation of the issues of fiscal immunity and charitable status which a full scale review of that decision might require.

3. Trusts for the Advancement of Religion

Introduction

Trusts purporting to fall into this category have always been numerous in this jurisdiction and the historical aspect of these trusts in particular has been well charted elsewhere.[164] More recently legislative intervention has helped to clarify what had been a most complex and uncertain area of the law which until comparatively recently was notable for the significant divergences which existed between the attitudes adopted in England and in this jurisdiction in relation to certain types of trusts which fall into this category.

The advancement of religion has been described by Lord Hanworth MR in *Keren Kayemeth Le Jisroel Ltd v. IRC*[165] as 'the promotion of spiritual teaching in a wide sense, and the maintenance of the doctrines on which it rests and the observances that serve to promote and manifest it. . . .' Certainly in England the judiciary has not tended to prefer one religion to another in determining the question of whether a trust falls into this category,[166] and as Cross J has commented: 'As between different religions, the law stands neutral, but it assumes that any religion is at least better than none'.[167] An examination of recent authorities would suggest that judicial attitudes are becoming increasingly flexible and that provided the religion in question is considered to be *bona fide*, the limited nature of its support or following will not preclude it from qualifying for charitable status.[168] The predominant view in other common law jurisdictions is that it is not necessary that a religion be monotheistic,[169] and it it remains to be seen whether the courts in this jurisdiction would take a similarly progressive approach. Certainly, Walsh J made it clear in *Quinn's Supermarket v. Attorney General*[170] that despite the references to the Christian nature of

---

164. Delany, *The Law Relating to Charities in Ireland* (1957) and Brady, *Religion and the Law of Charities in Ireland* (1976).
165. [1931] 2 KB 465, 477. See also the *dicta* of Donovan J in *United Grand Lodge of Ancient Free and Accepted Masons of England v. Holborn Borough Council* [1957] 1 WLR 1080, 1090.
166. See *Gilmour v. Coats* [1949] AC 426, 458-459 *per* Lord Reid.
167. *Neville Estates Ltd v. Madden* [1962] Ch 832, 853.
168. *Re Watson* [1973] 1 WLR 1472; *Centrepoint Community Growth Trust v. Commissioner of Inland Revenue* [1985] 1 NZLR 673.
169. Despite the views expressed by Lord Parker in *Bowman v. Secular Society* [1917] AC 406, 449.
170. [1972] IR 1, 23.

the State in Article 44 of the Constitution, religion is not confined to the Christian faith but it would be unwise to speculate unduly on the question of whether the courts in this jurisdiction would be prepared to stretch the meaning of 'religion' to the extent to which their counterparts elsewhere in the common law world have done.

Gifts in General Terms

A gift for 'religious purposes' has been held to be charitable on the basis that this will *prima facie* mean charitable purposes unless the context suggests otherwise. As O'Connor MR stated in *Arnott v. Arnott (No. 2)*,[171] it has been held that 'a gift for religious purposes and not more will be construed by the court as confined to such religious purposes as are in their nature charitable.' On the basis of this reasoning, it had been argued that a gift for 'charitable or religious purposes' should fail on the grounds that the use of the word 'charitable' shows that the word 'religious' means something distinct from charitable.[172] However, such an interpretation has been rejected in this jurisdiction and it was held by Barton J in *Re Salter*[173] that a gift framed in these terms will be charitable in nature. This can be distinguished from the wording employed in *Re Davidson*,[174] where a gift for 'charitable, religious or other societies, institutions, persons or objects' was found not to be charitable on the grounds that the words 'or other societies' would have enabled the trustees to apply the gift to societies or institutions which were neither charitable nor religious in character. A gift confined to a specified religion may also be charitable, so in *Copinger v. Crehane*,[175] a gift for 'the advancement and benefit of the Roman Catholic religion' was upheld as a valid charitable bequest on the grounds that its terms limited it strictly and exclusively to charitable purposes. The test in determining the validity of such bequests would appear to be that laid down by Grant MR in *Morice v. Bishop of Durham*,[176] which was summarised as follows by Chatterton VC in *Copinger*:[177] '[W]here the trustee is bound to apply the bequest to charitable purposes, the bequest shall not

---

171. [1906] 1 IR 127, 134. See also the *dicta* of Ross J in *Rickerby v. Nicholson* [1912] 1 IR 343, 347 that 'according to our law a bequest for a religious purpose is *prima facie* charitable'.
172. See *Rickerby v. Nicholson* [1912] 1 IR 343, 348. See also *Grimond v. Grimond* [1905] AC 124 which relates to an interpretation of Scots law.
173. [1911] 1 IR 289. See also *Rickerby v. Nicholson* [1912] 1 IR 343 and *Re Lloyd* (1893) 10 TLR 66.
174. [1909] 1 Ch 567.
175. (1877) LR 11 Eq 429.
176. (1804) 9 Ves 399.
177. (1877) LR 11 Eq 429, 431.

fail on account of the uncertainty of the object, but ... where there is a discretion to apply it to charitable purposes or to other purposes not charitable, and the trust is indefinite, the gift fails.'

The latter interpretation was placed on a bequest for 'such Roman Catholic purposes in the parish of Coleraine and elsewhere' as the trustees might deem proper by the Irish Court of Appeal in *MacLaughlin v. Campbell*,[178] and the gift was held to be void on the basis that it might be applied for a purpose other than a charitable one. The distinction is a fine one as the *dicta* of Fitzgibbon LJ makes clear:

> If the gift were made to 'the Church' e.g. the 'Church of Rome' or the 'Church of Ireland', I should think that it would import — at least *prima facie* — the operative institution which ministered religion and gave spiritual edification to its members; a gift in such terms would exclude objects which would be included in a gift for the 'purposes' of the individual members of a religious body.[179]

A bequest to 'the Christian Brethren' has been upheld as charitable,[180] as has a gift to 'foreign missions',[181] and 'to Presbyterian missions and orphans'.[182] However a gift for 'missionary purposes' was held by Sullivan MR in *Scott v. Brownrigg*[183] to be too vague and wide to be upheld, although it would appear that where there is sufficient evidence to connect the words 'purposes' or 'objects' with the preaching of religion, such a gift may be charitable.[184]

Gifts to Ecclesiastical Office Holders

It would appear that a gift for the benefit of the incumbent of an ecclesiastical office for the time being is charitable, whereas a gift for the particular individual who happens to hold that office at the time of the gift will not be. So, in *Gibson v. Representative Church Body*,[185] a bequest to the chaplain of the Rotunda chapel at the time of the testatrix's death and his successors was upheld as charitable. This can be contrasted with a separate

---

178. [1906] 1 IR 588.
179. *Ibid.* at 597.
180. *Re Brown* [1898] 1 IR 423.
181. *Dunne v. Duignan* [1908] 1 IR 228.
182. *Jackson v. Attorney General* [1917] 1 IR 332.
183. (1881) 9 LR Ir 246.
184. *Re Kenny* (1907) 97 LT 130 and *Re Rees* [1920] 2 Ch 59. See also *Jackson v. Attorney General* [1917] 1 IR 332, 335.
185. (1881) 9 LR Ir 1. See also *Robb v. Dorrian* (1877) IR 11 CL 292; *Re Corcoran* [1913] 1 IR 1.

gift in a codicil to the testatrix's will to the chaplain for his own personal use and with the decision of *Donnellan v. O'Neill*,[186] where a bequest to a cardinal absolutely for his own use and benefit was held to be a gift to the latter in his private capacity and not to be charitable in nature. The test was described by Kindersley VC in *Thornber v. Wilson*[187] as being 'whether the testator designates the individual as such, or as being the person who happens to fill the office'.

So, a gift to a minister for the time being or to a minister for the time being and his successors without more will be considered charitable in nature on the basis that the character of the office holder is such that it is inevitable that he will apply the gift for strictly charitable purposes. As Cozens-Hardy MR stated in *Re Davidson*,[188] while a court does not hold a trust charitable merely because the trustee has a religious office, 'if you find in a will words indicating that a distribution is to be made by persons in succession as holders of a particular religious or charitable office, that goes far to establish — and, it may be, goes sufficiently far to establish — the fact that the whole gift is charitable.' So, in *Reddy v. Fitzmaurice*[189] a residuary gift to a bishop for the time being and his successors without any further words of qualification was interpreted as being of a charitable nature. However, where additional words were attached to the gift which indicated the trusts on which the donee was to hold the property, the gift would fail at common law if the purposes could be construed as not being exclusively charitable ones.

A gift to an ecclesiastical office holder followed by words which did no more than confer a complete discretion on him or impose a specific limitation which fell within the scope of the charitable nature of his office would be charitable. This is illustrated by the decision of Joyce J in *Re Garrard*,[190] where a gift to the vicar and churchwardens for the time being of a certain parish 'to be applied by them in such manner as they shall in their sole discretion think fit' was upheld as a valid charitable gift. Similarly, in *Halpin v. Hannon*[191] a bequest to a named priest or his successor 'for such purposes in the diocese as he wishes' was found to be charitable. In the course of his judgment, after a consideration of some of the English authorities, Maguire CJ is reported as saying:

186. (1870) IR 5 Eq 523.
187. (1858) 4 Dr 350, 351. Quoted with approval by Barton J in *Re Corcoran* [1913] 1 IR 1, 6.
188. [1909] 1 Ch 567, 569. Quoted by Gavan Duffy J in *Re Howley* [1940] IR 109. See also the *dicta* of Black J in *Halpin v. Hannon* (1947) 82 ILTR 74, 77.
189. (1952) 86 ILTR 127.
190. [1907] 1 Ch 382. See also *Re Flinn* [1948] Ch 241 and *Re Rumball* [1956] Ch 105.
191. (1947) 82 ILTR 74.

> From these decisions it was clear that it was necessary to distinguish the case where a gift to the holder of a religious office was followed by words which made it clear that the gift might be applied to non-charitable purposes and that such was the testator's intention, and cases where later words do not clearly indicate an intention to widen a field of selection so as to include non-charitable objects. . . .[192]

However, where the words of qualification are wide enough to include purposes which might not be charitable in law, the position at common law was that the gift must fail, notwithstanding the charitable nature of the office generally. This proposition was established in a number of cases including *Dunne v. Byrne*,[193] where a residuary bequest to an archbishop and his successors to be applied wholly or in part as the archbishop might judge 'most conducive to the good of religion' in the diocese was held by the Privy Council to be void. Similarly, in *Farley v. Westminster Bank*,[194] the House of Lords held that a gift to the vicar and churchwardens of a parish for 'parish work' was too wide to be valid.

Therefore unless the gift was given in unqualified terms or on trusts which were unequivocally charitable in nature, the gift might fail. It is likely that the provisions of section 49 of the Charities Act 1961 which provides that 'where any of the purposes of a gift include, or could be deemed to include, both charitable and non-charitable objects, its terms shall be so construed or given effect as to exclude the non-charitable objects and the purpose shall, accordingly be treated as charitable' may now have resolved this problem of construction.

Gifts for the Celebration of Masses

As Delany[195] has commented: 'So much property is devoted to this type of gift in Ireland that it has become by far the most common object of benevolence.' Whether this statement is as accurate today is open to question, but gifts of this nature have led to an extensive amount of litigation over the last century. The charitable nature of such gifts was confirmed by section 45(2) of the Charities Act 1961, but it is an area which for a long time provoked considerable uncertainty and controversy.

Historically the legal principles applicable differed considerably be-

---

192. *Ibid.* at 75.
193. [1912] AC 407. See also *Re Davidson* [1909] 1 Ch 567.
194. [1939] AC 430. However note that this decision was distinguished by Romer J in *Re Simson* [1946] Ch 299.
195. *The Law Relating to Charities in Ireland* (1957) p. 53.

tween England and Ireland. The legality of such gifts was doubtful in England as a result of the interpretation placed on the Statute of Chantries 1547 but a majority of the House of Lords held in *Bourne v. Keane*[196] that gifts for the saying of masses were not illegal without holding that they were charitable bequests. Subsequently, in *Re Caus*,[197] Luxmoore J held that such gifts were charitable, although the findings of the House of Lords in *Gilmour v. Coats*[198] led to doubts being expressed about the validity of this decision. However, recently in *Re Hetherington*,[199] Browne-Wilkinson VC confirmed that a gift for the saying of masses is *prima facie* charitable since it is for a religious purpose and contained the necessary element of public benefit because in practice the masses would be celebrated in public. While he stressed that the celebration of a religious rite in private would not contain this essential public element, the Vice Chancellor made it clear that where either construction was possible, the gift was to be construed as one to be carried out only by charitable means, viz., celebrated in public.

In Ireland the Statute of Chantries never applied and the validity of a gift for the saying of masses was recognised by Lord Manners LC in *Commissioners of Charitable Donations and Bequests v. Walsh*,[200] a finding confirmed by the judgment of Blackburne MR in *Read v. Hodgins*.[201] However, the charitable nature of such gifts was examined in detail by the Court of Exchequer in *Attorney General v. Delaney*,[202] in which it was held that a bequest for masses to be said for the repose of the soul of the testatrix and her brother was not charitable on the basis that there was no stipulation that the masses be said in public. Palles CB commented that if the will had prescribed that the masses should be celebrated in public, he would have accepted them as being charitable. This reasoning suggested that the charitable nature of such gifts depended on whether a stipulation was made that they be said in public, although in a number of subsequent cases, gifts of this nature failed even where the inference was that they should be celebrated in public.[203] This misinterpretation of the judgment of Palles CB was particularly evident in the decision of *Kehoe v. Wilson*,[204]

---

196. [1919] AC 815.
197. [1934] Ch 162.
198. [1949] AC 426.
199. [1990] Ch 1. See Hopkins [1989] CLJ 373; Parry [1989] Conv 453.
200. (1828) 7 Ir Eq R 34n.
201. (1844) 7 Ir Eq R 17.
202. (1875) IR 10 CL 104.
203. *Beresford v. Jarvis* (1877) 11 ILTR 128; *M'Court v. Burnett* (1877) 11 ILTR 130.
204. (1880) 7 LR Ir 10. This decision was followed, albeit unwillingly, by Porter MR in *Perry v. Twomey* (1888) 21 LR Ir 480 although Chatterton VC subsequently pointed

where a bequest for masses 'to be celebrated in Ireland in a church open for public worship at the time of such celebration' was held not to be charitable. The view that where a gift contained a direction that the masses be celebrated in public such gifts should be regarded as charitable was however re-affirmed by the decision of the Irish Court of Appeal in *Attorney General v. Hall*.[205]

The question of the charitable nature of gifts for the saying of masses, whether in private or in public was finally resolved by the Irish Court of Appeal in *O'Hanlon v. Logue*.[206] A testatrix devised and bequeathed her property on certain trusts and then on trust to sell and invest the proceeds and pay the income thereof from time to time to the Roman Catholic Primate of Ireland for the time being for the celebration of masses for the repose of the souls of her late husband, her children and herself, the will containing no direction that these masses be said in public. The Court of Appeal upheld the charitable nature of the gift and made it clear that a bequest for the saying of masses, whether in public or not, constituted a valid charitable gift. In what was described by Brady[207] as 'a remarkable *volte face*' since his judgment in *Delaney*, Palles CB concluded that the view which he had expressed in the earlier case, that the only element of public benefit in the celebration of the mass is the edification of the congregation, was too narrow and failed to appreciate it 'as a gift from God'. This decision has been followed on a number of occasions,[208] and the issue was put beyond doubt by the enactment of section 45(2) of the Charities Act 1961, which reads as follows:

> For the avoidance of the difficulties which arise in giving effect to the intentions of donors of certain gifts for the purpose of the advancement of religion and in order not to frustrate those intentions and notwithstanding that certain gifts for the purpose aforesaid, including gifts for the celebration of Masses, whether in public or private, are valid charitable gifts, it is hereby enacted that a valid

---

out in *Healy v. Attorney General* [1902] 1 IR 342, that it was never his intention to depart from the view expressed by Palles CB in *Delaney's* case in relation to the validity of masses celebrated in public.

205. [1897] 2 IR 426.
206. [1906] 1 IR 247.
207. *Religion and the Law of Charities in Ireland* (1976) p. 81.
208. *Re Gibbons* [1917] 1 IR 448 and *Re Howley* [1940] IR 109, although Gavan Duffy J made some rather confusing remarks to the effect that a gift for masses, though charitable, might nonetheless fail if too remote. This suggestion would seem to be at odds with the charitable nature of the gift.

charitable gift for the purpose of the advancement of religion shall have effect and as respects it having effect, shall be construed in accordance with the laws, canons, ordinances and tenets of the religion concerned.

Gifts to Religious Orders

Historically there were a number of differences between gifts in favour of male religious orders and female ones. The effect of section 28 of the Roman Catholic Relief Act 1829 was that certain male religious orders such as the Jesuits were regarded as illegal, with the consequence that any gift to these orders was also tainted with illegality and void at law. These disabilities were not removed until the enactment of section 5 of the Government of Ireland Act 1920, which impliedly repealed them. The question of whether gifts to such orders could be considered charitable in nature arose in the case of *Re Byrne*,[209] where a testator directed that his residuary estate be given 'for the absolute use and benefit of the Jesuit Order in Ireland.' It was held by Johnston J that the bequest was not illegal but that it was not a charitable bequest and was void for uncertainty. On appeal, the majority of the Supreme Court held that the gift to the order was not a charitable legacy on the basis that the work of the order while largely charitable, was not exclusively so, although the gift was upheld as a valid gift of a non-charitable nature for the benefit of an ascertainable class of persons.[210] Kennedy CJ dissented, stating that bequests to religious institutions for religious purposes were *prima facie* charitable and concluded that the activities carried out by the Jesuits were clearly charitable in a legal sense.

While the disabilities imposed by the Roman Catholic Relief Act 1829 did not apply to religious orders of women,[211] gifts to such orders of a continuing nature might still fail at common law if the purposes of the order were not exclusively charitable. This problem was particularly evident in relation to contemplative orders on the grounds that they did not fulfil the necessary public benefit requirement. In these circumstances, the only possible solution was to uphold the gift on the basis that it was a valid gift for the benefit of those members of the community alive at the time of the testator's death. This point is well illustrated by the decision of Wickens VC in the English case of *Cocks v. Manners*,[212] which also proved

---

209. [1935] IR 782. See also *Re Keogh's Estate* [1945] IR 13.
210. See further *supra* Chapter 9. This result would now probably be avoided as a result of the operation of s.49 of the Charities Act 1961.
211. See s.37 of the Act of 1829.
212. (1871) LR 12 Eq 574.

to be of considerable importance in this jurisdiction. A testatrix directed that her property should be sold and after the payment of certain legacies that the proceeds should be distributed among certain specified religious institutions. Wickens VC held that a gift to the Sisters of Charity at a specified place payable to the superior for the time being was a good charitable gift. He considered that it was a 'voluntary association for the purpose of teaching the ignorant and nursing the sick' and said that it could not be distinguished in this respect from other types of voluntary associations performing charitable functions. However, the other bequest to a Dominican convent payable to the superior for the time being was not held to be charitable on the basis that the community had 'none of the requisites of a charitable institution' whether the word was used in its popular or legal sense. As Wickens VC commented: 'It is said ... that religious purposes are charitable, but that can only be true as to religious services tending directly or indirectly towards the instruction or the edification of the public'.[213] However, he held that this gift was valid as a good noncharitable gift, payable to the superior for the time being for the benefit of the existing members of the order, on the grounds that there was nothing to prevent them spending it as they pleased.

This finding that contemplative religious orders were not charitable in nature was applied in Ireland. As O'Connor MR stated in *Commissioners of Charitable Donations and Bequests v. McCartan*:[214]

> Monasteries of men and women are often, if not mostly, institutions, the members of which devote their lives exclusively to acts of piety such as pious meditation, prayer and self denial. Such institutions, however praiseworthy, are not charitable in the sense recognised by this Court.

In view of this approach the only way of establishing the validity of gifts to contemplative orders at that time was to apply the reasoning of Wickens VC in *Cocks v. Manners* and to interpret them as being to the community as it existed at the time of the testator's death, i.e. as a gift to the individual nuns of whom the community happened to consist at that time. This approach can be seen in *Re Wilkinson's Trusts*,[215] where the Irish Court of Appeal upheld a bequest to a superioress of a convent solely for the pur-

---

213. *Ibid.* at 585. See also the *dicta* of Fitzgibbon LJ in *Re Wilkinson's Trusts* (1857)19 LR Ir 531, 539.
214. [1917] 1 IR 388, 396.
215. (1887) 19 LR Ir 531. See also *Re Delany's Estate* (1882) 9 LR Ir 226; *Bradshaw v. Jackman* (1887) 21 LR Ir 12.

poses of the convent on this basis. However, as has been seen, it was not always possible to place such a construction on a gift and where it is interpreted as being a gift to those individuals who may successively become members of the community it will be void on the grounds of perpetuity.[216]

However, the view that contemplative religious orders did not provide some benefit to the community was questioned by Black J in *Munster and Leinster Bank Ltd v. Attorney General*,[217] and the issue arose directly before the High Court in the case of *Maguire v. Attorney General*.[218] The testatrix directed in her will that a sum of money be spent founding a convent 'of perpetual adoration' in a specified place or elsewhere as the trustees might determine. In the course of a detailed examination of the issues involved, Gavan Duffy J stated that it was a 'grave discredit to the law that there should, in this Catholic country, be any doubt about the validity of [such a bequest].'[219] He said that it had been assumed that the decision in *Cocks v. Manners* had decided as a matter of law that a testamentary gift to a contemplative order of nuns could not be charitable on the grounds that the public was not edified by the gift. However, Gavan Duffy J regarded it as a decision on a question of fact; that while at that time the public would not have been edified by private prayer unaccompanied by external works of charity, there was no reason for attributing the same outlook to public opinion in Ireland at the time when he was considering the case. As he stated: 'The finding, or assumption, in *Cocks v. Manners* that the convent of a contemplative community tended neither directly nor indirectly towards public edification has no scintilla of authority as a determinant of the actual position among us.'[220] Gavan Duffy J therefore upheld the gift as charitable by employing the reasoning of Palles CB in *O'Hanlon v. Logue*, without directly overruling *Cocks v. Manners*.[221]

Doubts were raised about the validity of the decision of Gavan Duffy J when the House of Lords held in *Gilmour v. Coats*[222] that a gift to a Carmelite priory which consisted of a community of cloistered nuns was

---

216. *Stewart v. Green* (1871) IR 5 Eq 470. See also *Morrow v. M'Conville* (1883) 11 LR Ir 236. See further *supra* Chapter 9.
217. [1940] IR 19, 30.
218. [1943] IR 238.
219. *Ibid.* at 244.
220. *Ibid.* at 248-249.
221. It is interesting to note that Brady, while acknowledging the provisions of Article 44.1.2 of the Constitution as it then existed, has commented that 'It is difficult to avoid the inference that while all recognised religions might now be equal before the law, the Roman Catholic religion, in Gavan Duffy J's view, was more equal than all the others.' *Religion and the Law of Charities in Ireland* (1976) p.92.
222. [1949] AC 426.

not charitable as it lacked the necessary element of public benefit. In addition, in *Re Keogh's Estate*,[223] in considering the validity of gifts to the superioress of a Carmelite convent and to the prior of an order of Carmelite fathers, Overend J said that whether or not these gifts could be supported as charitable gifts they could be upheld as valid gifts to the individuals comprising the communities in the manner laid down in *Re Wilkinson's Trusts*.[224] As a result of this uncertainty, legislation drafted in 1954 included a provision to confirm the charitable status of contemplative religious orders, although as Brady[225] points out, the legislation never progressed beyond its formal introduction in the Dáil.

The subsequent decision of Dixon J in *Bank of Ireland Trustee Co. Ltd v. Attorney General*[226] allayed these fears to an extent when he declined to follow the decision in *Gilmour* and held that a gift to be applied to the repair and/or improvement of a convent of a contemplative order of nuns was charitable. However, it was still felt that the matter should be put beyond doubt by legislation and section 45 (1) of the Charities Act 1961 now provides as follows:

> In determining whether or not a gift for the purpose of the advancement of religion is a valid charitable gift it shall be conclusively presumed that the purpose includes and will occasion public benefit.

Gifts for Churches and Other Miscellaneous Purposes

Gifts for the erection or maintenance of the fabric of a church building or its fixtures and fittings will be upheld as charitable. So a gift to a named church,[227] or to build a parsonage in connection with a church,[228] or for such purposes as the erection of a new altar and altar rails,[229] or the provision and maintenance of seating in a church will be regarded as valid.[230] It was held by O'Connor MR in *Re Greene*[231] that a gift 'for the decoration

---

223. [1945] IR 13.
224. (1887) 19 LR Ir 531.
225. *Religion and The Law of Charities in Ireland* (1976) p.92. See 184 *Dáil Debates* cols 555-557.
226. [1957] IR 257.
227. *Re Gare* [1952] Ch 80.
228. *Cresswell v. Cresswell* (1868) LR 6 Eq 69.
229. *Re Hawe* (1955) 93 ILTR 175. Although on the facts, the gift failed for remoteness it was contemplated as taking effect on the occurrence of events which might not necessarily occur within the perpetuity period.
230. *Re Raine* [1956] Ch 417.
231. [1914] 1 IR 305.

or improvement of the Roman Catholic Church of the Carmelite Fathers at Clarendon Street, in the City of Dublin' was charitable, although difficulties still existed at that time about gifts to benefit such purposes,[232] and in a number of earlier cases gifts for the repair and maintenance of churches belonging to monastic orders had been declared void.[233] O'Connor MR reasoned that the gift in the case before him was not a gift to a monastic community for its own purposes but rather was 'given for the decoration or improvement of a church whose purpose is public worship.'[234] Certainly today there would be no doubts about the legality or charitable nature of such gifts and they would undoubtedly be recognised as valid.

Similarly, gifts for the upkeep of a churchyard or cemetery will be regarded as charitable in nature,[235] whether it is open to persons of all denominations,[236] or possibly, as has been held in England, confined to those of a specific religion.[237] In *Re Quinn*[238] Budd J stated that he could see no real distinction between a gift for the repair and improvement of a church and for a churchyard and concluded that a gift given for the upkeep of a cemetery, open to persons of all denominations, was a gift for the advancement of religion. Even if this were not the case, Budd J was satisfied that the bequest would fall into the fourth category of Lord Macnaghten's classification, as being a gift for other purposes beneficial to the community.

Often this device of making a bequest for the upkeep of an entire churchyard is used as an indirect means of achieving an object of a more specific nature which might otherwise fail.[239] The general view is that gifts for the maintenance or repair of specific vaults or tombs if these are not part of the fabric of a church will not be regarded as charitable at common law. As we have seen above,[240] these may be upheld as valid purpose trusts provided they do not infringe the rule against inalienability or if they are of limited nature and fall within the statutory limits will be regarded as charitable by virtue of section 50 of the Charities Act 1961.[241]

---

232. See *supra* on gifts to male religious orders at p. 320.
233. *Kehoe v. Wilson* (1880) 7 LR Ir 10; *Liston v. Keegan* (1881) 9 LR Ir 539.
234. *Ibid.* at 319.
235. *Re Vaughan* (1886) 33 Ch D 187; *Re Pardoe* [1906] 2 Ch 184.
236. *Re Quinn* (1953) 88 ILTR 161.
237. *Re Manser* [1905] 1 Ch 68.
238. (1953) 88 ILTR 161.
239. E.g. *Re Eighmie* [1935] Ch 524. Although often where a gift is given for such a general purpose there will be no means of enforcing any specific direction regarding the upkeep of family graves or tombs. See the *dicta* of Budd J in *Re Quinn* (1953) 88 ILTR 161, 166 and *Re Manser* [1905] 1 Ch 68.
240. Chapter 9.
241. These limits are £60 per year in the case of income, or in any other case, £1,000.

The question of whether residences for priests, clergy and other persons connected with the church qualify as charitable is a difficult one to answer with accuracy, primarily because many of the cases in this area have arisen in the context of whether these premises should be exempt from rates. As Wylie[242] has commented 'the tests for exemption from rates on the ground of charity are much narrower than those for determining whether or not an object is otherwise charitable.' There is limited authority to support the proposition that gifts for the repair or upkeep of a residence of this nature may be charitable,[243] but the decisions made in a rating context would suggest otherwise. So in *Commissioner of Valuation v. O'Connell*,[244] Palles CB held that a house built by parishioners and used as a residence by a Roman Catholic priest was not exclusively used for charitable purposes so as to be exempt from rates. A similar finding was made in respect of a convent [245] and a basement portion of a church, used as a residence for a sexton on the grounds that it was a separate unit and not indispensably part of the fabric of the church.[246]

(4) Trusts for Other Purposes Beneficial to the Community

Introduction
This category can be described as the most difficult of Lord Macnaghten's classes of charitable trust to define and delimit, and embraces purposes which do not fall within any of the three categories already considered but which are nevertheless beneficial to the community in a way recognised by the law as charitable. The view was expressed by Lindley LJ in *Re MacDuff*[247] that Lord Macnaghten did not intend to lay down in *Pemsel's* case that every object of 'public general utility' must necessarily be charitable and this point was developed by Viscount Cave in *Attorney General v. National Provincial and Union Bank of England Ltd*[248] in the following terms:

> Lord Macnaghten did not mean that all trusts beneficial to the community are charitable, but that there were certain charitable trusts which fell within that category; and accordingly to argue that because a trust is for a purpose beneficial to the community it is there-

---

242. *Irish Land Law* (3rd ed., 1997) p.576. See also Brady (1968) 3 Ir Jur (ns) 215.
243. *Attorney General v. Bishop of Chester* (1785) 1 Bro CC 444.
244. [1906] 2 IR 479.
245. *Good Shepherd Nuns v. Commissioner of Valuation* [1930] IR 646.
246. *Mulholland v. Commissioner of Valuation* (1936) 70 ILTR 253.
247. [1896] 2 Ch 451, 466.
248. [1924] AC 262, 265. See also *Williams v. IRC* [1947] AC 447, 455 *per* Lord Simonds.

fore a charitable trust is to turn round his sentence and to give it a different meaning. So here it is not enough to say that the trust in question is for public purposes beneficial to the community or is for the public welfare; you must also show it to be a charitable trust.

A more flexible interpretation was placed on the *dicta* of Lord Macnaghten more recently by Russell LJ in *Incorporated Council for Law Reporting for England and Wales v. A.G.*,[249] where he suggested that in substance the position is that if a purpose is shown to be of sufficient benefit or utility to the community, it is *prima facie* charitable in law.[250] Here the Court of Appeal held unanimously that the purpose of providing law reports was charitable under the fourth head of Lord Macnaghten's classification; as Russell LJ commented such an object 'cannot be thought otherwise than beneficial to the community and of general public utility'.

However, the view expressed by Russell LJ has not met with universal approval and Dillon J subsequently commented in *Re South Place Ethical Society*[251] that it was not in line with earlier judicial statements[252] and that the approach to be adopted in considering whether something is within the fourth category 'is the approach of analogy from what is already stated in the preamble to the Statute of Elizabeth or from what has already been held to be charitable within the fourth category.'

Public Benefit

One of the primary difficulties in laying down guidelines as to the type of trust which may qualify under this heading is the perennial question of the necessary element of public benefit. A trust may appear to be one of general public utility but difficulties may arise when its application is confined to a limited group of persons. As we have seen above the test laid down by Viscount Simonds in *Oppenheim v. Tobacco Securities Trust Co. Ltd*[253] required that for a group of persons to constitute a 'section of the community', it must not be numerically negligible, and the quality which distinguishes these persons from other members of the community must

---

249. [1972] Ch 73.
250. As Gault J recently commented in *Commissioner of Inland Revenue v. Medical Council of New Zealand* [1997] 2 NZLR 297, 302 few institutions having objects of general public utility have been held not to be within the 'spirit and intendment' of the Preamble of the Statute of Charitable Uses Act 1601.
251. [1980] 1 WLR 1565, 1574.
252. Dillon J referred to the *dicta* of Lord Simonds in *Williams v. IRC* [1947] AC 447, 455.
253. [1951] AC 297, 306. See also the *dicta* of Lord Greene MR in *Re Compton* [1945] Ch 123, 131.

be one which does not depend on their relationship to a particular individual.

One view is that the application of the public benefit requirement to trusts falling within this fourth category should be more strictly enforced than in the other categories. This view is illustrated by a statement made by Babington LJ in *Trustees of the Londonderry Presbyterian Church House v. Commissioners of Inland Revenue* [254] to the effect that in this category 'there can be no charity until it is shown that the gift is to or for the benefit of the public or a section of the public'. Similar sentiments were expressed by Lord Somervell and Viscount Simonds in *IRC v. Baddeley*,[255] in which the majority of the House of Lords held that a trust to provide, *inter alia*, for recreational facilities for Methodists resident in a particular area of London did not fulfil the public benefit requirement and so was not a valid trust. Lord Somervell stated as follows:

> I cannot accept the principle submitted by the respondents that a section of the public sufficient to support a valid trust in one category must as a matter of law be sufficient to support a trust in any other category. I think that difficulties are apt to arise if one seeks to consider the class apart from the particular nature of the charitable purpose. They are, in my opinion, interdependent. There might well be a valid trust for the promotion of religion benefiting a very small class. It would not follow that a recreation ground for the exclusive use of the same class would be a valid charity. ...[256]

An alternative view was favoured by Lord Reid in his dissenting speech which is founded on the premise that the definition of the class of persons necessary to constitute a sufficient section of the community to satisfy the public benefit requirement should not vary from one category to the other.[257] Lord Reid rejected the suggestion that for example the members of one particular religion might constitute a 'section of the community' for one charitable purpose and yet be regarded merely as 'a fluctuating body of private individuals' for another charitable purpose.

An attempt to rationalize this whole question was made by Lord Cross in *Dingle v. Turner*,[258] where he stated as follows:

---

254. [1946] NI 178 196-197.
255. [1955] AC 572.
256. *Ibid.* at 615. See also the *dicta* of Viscount Simonds at 592.
257. See also the judgment of Andrews LCJ in *Trustees of the Londonderry Presbyterian Church House v. Commissioners of Inland Revenue* [1946] NI 178, 190.
258. [1972] AC 601. See also the dissenting judgment of Lord MacDermott in *Oppenheim v. Tobacco Securities Trust Co. Ltd* [1955] AC 297.

In truth, the question of whether or not the potential beneficiaries of a trust can fairly be said to constitute a section of the public is a question of degree and cannot be, by itself, decisive of the question whether the trust is a charity. Much must depend on the purpose of the trust. It may well be that, on the one hand, a trust to promote some purpose, *prima facie* charitable, will constitute a charity even though the class of potential beneficiaries might fairly be called a private class, and that on the other hand, a trust to promote another purpose, also *prima facie* charitable, will not constitute a charity even though the class of potential beneficiaries might seem to some people fairly describable as a section of the public.[259]

This approach has met with both academic[260] and judicial approval and as Carswell J stated in *Re Dunlop*,[261] if it is recognised that the manner in which the essential benefit to the public is effected varies as between the different categories of charity, it becomes easier to determine the existence of this element when examining a trust. Carswell J continued:

> The essence of the charitable nature [of trusts within Lord Macnaghten's fourth category] is that the beneficiaries should not be a private class, nor should any limitations be placed upon the gift which would prevent the public as a whole from enjoying the advantage which the donor intends to provide for the benefit of all of the public. It would be quite consonant with this concept that it should be more difficult for a trust under the fourth head to satisfy the requirements of public benefit, and that a bridge to be used only by Methodists should fail to qualify where a gift for the education of the children of members of that church might be a valid charity.[262]

In *Dunlop* Carswell J was required to consider the validity of a trust to found or assist in the founding of a home for 'Old Presbyterian Persons'. He held that the object was, subject to the satisfaction of the requirement of public benefit, a valid charitable gift for the relief of the aged as it relieved a need attributable to the condition of the persons to be benefited. Carswell J concluded that the public benefit requirement had been satisfied and that the gift could not be regarded as a private benefaction. The

---

259. *Ibid.* at 624. Quoted with approval by Gibson LJ in *Springhill Housing Action Committee v. Commissioner of Valuation* [1983] NI 184, 191.
260. See Jones [1974] CLJ 63, 65.
261. [1984] NI 408. See Dawson [1987] Conv 114.
262. *Ibid.* at 426.

fact that the people who would derive benefit from the trust were to be Presbyterians rather than any other denomination did not, in his view, negative the paramountcy of the public purpose of assistance for the aged.[263] In the opinion of Carswell J, the members of the Presbyterian Church were 'sufficiently defined and identifiable by a common quality of a public nature' and accordingly constituted a section of the public at large 'certainly for the purposes of a gift under Lord Macnaghten's first head'. It should be pointed out that in the UK the words aged, impotent and poor in the Preamble to the Statute of Charitable Uses have been read disjunctively and Carswell J had earlier expressed the view that the almost non-existent public benefit test in relation to trusts for poor relations and poor employees should not extend 'to the whole of Lord Macnaghten's first head' viz., trusts for the aged and impotent as well. However, the manner in which he stated his conclusion would suggest that the gift in the case before him probably qualified as a charitable trust under this first heading, to which a less strict public benefit test applied than that which he had suggested should be employed in relation to trusts falling into Lord Macnaghten's fourth category.

The extent of the public benefit requirement in this fourth category of charitable trusts has recently arisen in this jurisdiction in *Re Worth Library*,[264] in which Keane J considered two alternative submissions advanced by counsel for the plaintiff as to why the original gift should qualify as being within the fourth category of Lord Macnaghten's classification. While Keane J accepted that a gift for a library might be charitable in nature as being for the public benefit, he was satisfied that the relevant authorities had made it clear that such a gift was not charitable *per se*.[265] The bequest therefore failed to satisfy the public benefit requirement as it was to provide a library for the physician, surgeon and chaplain of the hospital 'who alone would have access to the room in which the library was housed'.[266] Keane J then proceeded to consider whether a gift of a library such as the one at issue which was expressed to be for the benefit of named office holders in the hospital only, could be regarded as being for the benefit of

---

263. It should be noted that by the time of the testator's death it was no longer practicable to use the properties envisaged by him for the purpose suggested and the court directed the preparation of a cy-près scheme.
264. [1995] 2 IR 301.
265. In this context, he referred to *Carne v. Long* (1860) 2 De GF & J 75 and *Re Prevost* [1930] 2 Ch 383.
266. Keane J concluded that the wording used by Dr Worth in directing that catalogues of the books contained in the library be compiled suggested that his primary concern was to ensure the security of the books rather than to facilitate scholars who might wish to peruse them.

the hospital generally and hence charitable.[267] Keane J rejected counsel's suggestion that the directions contained in the will regarding access to the books being restricted to named office holders was a precatory condition only, and concluded that these were directions 'which the testator wished to be complied with to the letter'.

Given the tenor of his approach to the whole question of public benefit, Keane J then reached a somewhat surprising conclusion. While the library itself would not have been of significant practical benefit to the office holders given the nature of the topics to which these books related, Keane J was of the view that the library itself 'in its beautiful setting would have provided a haven of quiet intellectual relaxation for the beneficiaries.'[268] He therefore concluded that the bequest of the library played a role in the advancement of the charity represented by the hospital and as such constituted a valid charitable bequest for the benefit of that institution within the fourth category of Lord Macnaghten's classification.

It is fair to say that this conclusion is certainly not in keeping with the general principles laid down by Carswell J in *Re Dunlop*, and that the result in that decision, as in *Worth*, was not altogether in keeping with the strictness of the public benefit requirement which it is theoretically necessary to overcome. One must question the reason why Keane J saw fit effectively to modify this stringent public benefit requirement in relation to trusts 'for other purposes beneficial to the community' in finding that the bequest in *Re Worth Library* was a valid charitable bequest for the benefit of the hospital. At this point the question might also be asked what is the rationale behind applying such a stringent public benefit requirement. The answer probably lies in the statement made by Lord Cross in the course of his judgment in *Dingle v. Turner*,[269] that 'in answering the question whether any given trust is a charitable trust, the courts ... cannot avoid having regard to the fiscal privileges accorded to charities'. As we have seen above, Lord Cross commented that the issues of validity and fiscal immunity were closely connected and he seemed to accept that the decisions in cases such as *Re Compton*[270] and *Oppenheim v. Tobacco Securities Trust Co. Ltd*[271]

---

267. It has been accepted that a gift for the benefit of a hospital is charitable in nature. See *Barrington's Hospital v. Commissioner of Valuation* [1957] IR 299; *Re McCarthy* [1958] IR 311; *Gleeson v. Attorney General*, High Court 1972 No. 2664 Sp (Kenny J) 6 April 1973.
268. *Ibid.* at 197.
269. [1972] AC 601, 624.
270. [1945] Ch 123.
271. [1951] AC 297.

were influenced by the fact that if the trusts at issue had been declared valid charitable trusts, they would have enjoyed a perceived 'undeserved fiscal immunity'.

Certainly it would appear that the overriding consideration in the mind of Keane J when deciding the question of the charitable status of the bequest in *Worth* seemed to be the desirability of finding it to be a charitable trust so that the court could apply the property cy-près rather than the issue of the fiscal privileges which would accompany such status. In view of the rather artificial straining of the traditional understanding of what is legally charitable which was necessary to reach such a result, a better approach might be the adoption of the solution proposed by the Radcliffe Commission,[272] namely to provide that only certain charities, which were clearly of obvious benefit to the public at large, should enjoy the fiscal privileges associated with charitable status.[273] On balance the suggestion of the Radcliffe Commission, if it were to avoid the distortion of the concept of public benefit in cases such as *Worth*, might lead to a more consistent application of principle. Even if one were to accept that the public benefit test in relation to trusts in the fourth 'Pemsel' category is no more stringent than in the others, it is difficult to justify the finding that a bequest for the benefit of three named office holders in a hospital could be of real benefit to the community generally. The 'charitable' nature of the bequest in a popular as opposed to a legal sense and the desirability of framing a cy-près scheme in the *Worth* case was never called into question and yet the fact that Keane J found it necessary to go through the motions of applying and ultimately satisfying the public benefit requirement illustrate the anomalies which the current legal position may create.

---

272. Cmnd 9474, Chapter 7. The Commission stated: 'In our view what is amiss in the present system is not the idea of giving income tax relief in respect of charity but the undue width of the range of what ranks as a charity for this purpose.' (Paragraph 170). 'We conclude ... that there would be no insuperable difficulty in producing a statutory definition of charity for tax purposes that would at any rate correspond more closely than the present with the accepted idea of what charity is.' (Paragraph 173)

273. Bright in [1989] Conv 28, 41 argued that 'the way ahead is to separate entitlement to fiscal privilege from entitlement to essential validity and charitable status'. It is also interesting to note that Brady, writing over 20 years ago, remarked that the effect of the comments of the Law Lords in *Dingle v. Turner* (referred to *supra* p. 240) might prompt legislation separating the fiscal and non-fiscal privileges consequent upon charitable status, but this has not occurred. See Brady (1976) 27 NILQ 198, 214. The alternative argument, expressed by the Newark Committee (Cmnd 396, paragraph 18) that such a separation would be 'manifestly inconvenient' must also be considered.

'For Other Purposes Beneficial to the Community' — an Objective or Subjective Test?

There has traditionally been a divergence in the position adopted by the judiciary in Ireland and England in relation to the test which should be applied by the courts in determining whether a purpose satisfies the requirement of being 'beneficial to the community' to the extent that it may be regarded as being charitable in law. The Irish authorities suggest that a subjective test should be applied and that due weight should be given to the donor's view of the charitable nature of his bequest provided that this purpose is not obviously illegal or immoral. However, the accepted view now in England and Northern Ireland is to adopt an objective test and allow the court to form an opinion on the issue based upon the evidence before it. Keane J remarked in *Re Worth Library* that as the objects under consideration in the case before him were such that an appreciable number of reasonable people would consider them to be charitable, it was not necessary for him to express any firm view on the divergence of opinion referred to above. However, it is interesting to note that the comments which he made would support the view that the court should give due weight to a donor's intentions in these circumstances.

The most important authority in the area in an Irish context is the decision of *Re Cranston*,[274] in which the Irish Court of Appeal was required to decide whether gifts for certain vegetarian societies were charitable in nature. The majority of the court upheld the conclusion reached by Porter MR that the objects of the societies could be said to be charitable within the legal sense of the term. Fitzgibbon LJ clearly believed that the view of the donor should be decisive in determining whether a gift fell within the category of 'other purposes beneficial to the community', provided that this purpose is not immoral nor illegal. He stated:

> What is the tribunal which is to decide whether the object is a beneficent one? It cannot be the individual mind of a judge, for he may disagree, *toto caelo*, from the testator as to what is or is not beneficial. On the other hand, it cannot be the *vox populi*, for charities have been upheld for the benefit of insignificant sects, and of peculiar people. It occurs to me that the answer must be — that the benefit must be one which *the founder* believes to be of public advantage, and his belief must be at least rational, and not contrary either to the general law of the land, or to thé principles of morality. A gift of

---

274. [1898] 1 IR 431.

such a character, dictated by benevolence, believed to be benefi-
cent, devoted to an appreciably important object, and neither *contra
bonos mores* nor *contra legem*, will in my opinion, be charitable in
the eye of the law, as settled by decisions which bind us. It is not for
us to say that these have gone too far.[275]

A similar view was taken by Barton J in *Shillington v. Portadown
UDC*,[276] who concluded that benefits which the testator wished to confer
on residents of his native town and its locality were 'such as he believed to
be of public advantage'. As, in his view, this belief was rational and not
illegal nor immoral, Barton J accepted that the bequest constituted a valid
charitable gift.

While this subjective approach was at one time favoured in England,[277]
it would now appear in that jurisdiction at any rate that the donor's intentions and beliefs as to the charitable nature of the bequest which he is
making are not factors which a court may take into consideration. This
view is well illustrated by the statements made by Russell J in *Re
Hummeltenberg*.[278] He referred to the views of the majority judges in the
Irish Court of Appeal in *Re Cranston*, and stated that although he agreed
with them insofar as they declared that the personal or private opinion of
the judge was immaterial, he disagreed with them to the extent that they
suggested that it was for the creator of the trust to determine whether the
purpose is beneficial to the public. In the view of Russell J 'the question
whether a gift is or may be operative for the public benefit is a question to
be answered by the court by forming an opinion upon the evidence before
it.'[279] This approach was endorsed by Lord Hanworth MR in *Re Grove-
Grady*,[280] where he said that the court must decide whether benefit to the

---

275. *Ibid.* at 446-447. Walker LJ also placed emphasis on the fact that the motive of the
donor in making the bequest was to benefit mankind generally. He did comment that
there may be cases in which the court might allow its own views to override those of
a donor, even where the gift was not illegal, immoral or contrary to public policy,
but he was satisfied that this was not such a case (p.450).
276. [1911] 1 IR 247. See also *Re Ni Brudair*, High Court 1976 No. 93 Sp (Gannon J) 5
February 1979.
277. *Re Foveaux* [1895] 2 Ch 501, 507.
278. [1923] 1 Ch 237.
279. *Ibid.* at 242. Cited with approval by Megaw J in *Re Lester* [1940] NI 92,103. See
also the *dicta* of Lord Simonds in *National Anti-Vivisection Society v. IRC* [1948]
AC 31, 65-66.
280. [1929] 1 Ch 557, 572. In this regard he cited with approval the statement made by
Holmes LJ in his dissenting judgment in *Re Cranston* that the issue 'does not depend on the view entertained by any individual — either by the judge who is to
decide the question, or by the person who makes the gift'.

community had been established and the courts in Northern Ireland have also adopted this objective approach.[281]

Although the views expressed by Keane J in *Re Worth Library* on this question were merely *obiter* and the objects put forward to the court, of the advancement of learning and of hospitals, would probably have been seen as being of benefit to the community irrespective of whether a subjective or objective approach had been applied, it is nevertheless of interest to note them because the same result will not always be arrived at by applying these divergent tests. Keane J stated:

> In every case, the intention of the testator is of paramount importance. If he intended to advance a charitable object recognised as such by the law, his gift will be a charitable gift. In the case of gifts which do not come within the first three categories, the fact that the testator's view as to the public utility of his favoured object — e.g. vegetarianism — is not shared by many people will not of itself prevent it from being, in the eyes of the law, a valid charitable object within the fourth category, provided it is not illegal, irrational or *contra bonos mores*.That, as I understand is the effect of the majority decision of the Irish Court of Appeal in *In re Cranston*.[282]

It is not difficult to envisage circumstances in which a donor's intentions and motives cannot be easily reconciled with those of the court, and public policy and an appreciation of what may be immoral are concepts which may undergo significant change over a period of time. This is aptly illustrated by changing judicial attitudes towards trusts created for the purpose of seeking to bring about the abolition of vivisection.[283]

While the courts in this jurisdiction are unlikely to take a liberal attitude towards the question of what types of trusts might be of an illegal or immoral nature, it would appear that they will continue to apply the *dicta* of Fitzgibbon LJ in *Re Cranston* and give due weight to a donor's intention in deciding the question of whether a trust is likely to benefit the community. This may yet prove to be of crucial importance if they are called upon to make a pronouncement on the charitable nature of bequests to organisations which an appreciable number of so called 'objective' members of society would not consider charitable. Clearly in such circum-

---

281. *Re Lester* [1940] NI 92, 101-105.
282. [1995] 2 IR 301, 335.
283. Considered in detail below, see *Armstrong v. Reeves* (1890) 25 LR Ir 325 and *National Anti-Vivisection Society v. IRC* [1948] AC 31.

stances, the divergence of view which Keane J rightly characterised as 'not material' in *Worth* might become highly relevant.

Specific Types of Trusts which may Qualify as being 'for Other Purposes Beneficial to the Community'

The range of trusts which may qualify under this heading is enormous and while it is not possible to classify them strictly under different headings, or to rule out the emergence of previously unrecognised heads of charity, by and large the types of trusts which will be enforced fall into one of a number of categories which will be considered below. One general point which was clarified by Lord Macnaghten in *Pemsel's*[284] case in a manner which seems to have met with subsequent judicial approval is that 'trusts [in this fourth category] are not the less charitable in the eye of the law, because incidentally they benefit the rich as well as the poor. ...' This approach was confirmed in this jurisdiction by the Irish Court of Appeal in *Re Cranston*.[285] So while it would appear that a trust which will benefit a category of persons under his fourth heading does not need to benefit the poor to the exclusion of the rich,[286] and the fact that rich and poor alike may benefit does not generally appear to be an issue,[287] a trust of this nature which will exclusively benefit the rich will not be charitable.[288]

Gifts for the Aged, the Disabled and the Sick

While the preamble to the English Statute of Charitable Uses refers to 'the relief of aged, impotent and poor people' the Irish statute specifically mentions 'the relief or maintenance of any manner of poor, succourless, distressed or impotent persons.' In the context of the English statute, it has been held that these words should be read disjunctively[289] and this approach now appears to be well established. In *Re Robinson*[290] Vaisey J upheld the validity of a bequest to 'old people over 65 years' in a certain

---

284. [1891] AC 531, 583.
285. [1898] 1 IR 431. See also *Barrington's Hospital v. Commissioner of Valuation* [1957] IR 299.
286. See *Keren Kayemeth le Jisroel Ltd v IRC* [1931] 2 KB 465, 492. Provided that the poor are not excluded from the ambit of the trust, *Re MacDuff* [1896] 2 Ch 451, 464 *per* Lindley LJ.
287. Although note the findings of Palles CB in *Clancy v. Commissioner of Valuation* [1911] 2 IR 173.
288. *Re MacDuff* [1896] 2 Ch 451, 471 *per* Rigby LJ.
289. *Joseph Rowntree Memorial Trust Hospital Association Ltd v. Attorney General* [1983] Ch 159, 171. As Peter Gibson J commented: 'It would be as absurd to require that the aged must be impotent or poor as it would be to require the impotent to be aged or poor, or the poor to be aged or impotent.' See also *Re Dunlop* [1984] NI 408, 414.
290. [1951] Ch 198.

district on the basis that 'old people over 65 years in a particular parish are a class of persons just as much objects of charity as the poor of the parish or the sick of the parish.'[291] Similarly, in *Re Glyn's Will Trusts*,[292] Danckwerts J confirmed that elderly people need not necessarily be poor to benefit from a charitable trust.

This issue does not arise in relation to the interpretation of the Irish statute as the words themselves are framed disjunctively.[293] Although some decisions appear to support the view that it is a sufficient charitable purpose simply to benefit the aged or the sick without more,[294] it is generally accepted that the trust must be for the relief of a need attributable to the condition of the persons to be benefited,[295] a point emphasized by Peter Gibson J in *Joseph Rowntree Memorial Trust Hospital Association Ltd v. Attorney General*,[296] in which a scheme to build self-contained dwellings for the elderly was found to be charitable in nature. Carswell J laid similar stress on the concept of 'relief' in *Re Dunlop*[297] in considering the charitable nature of a trust to the Presbyterian Residential Trust to found or help to found a home for 'Old Presbyterian persons'. Carswell J emphasized that the concept of relief and its connotation of meeting a need was in his view 'preferable to one which would admit as beneficiaries any aged persons, whatever may be the amount of their resources and irrespective of their needs arising from their condition of advancing years'.[298] He concluded that the gift was designed to serve the purpose of benefiting the public by providing accommodation for the relief of a class of persons requiring it by reason of their age and was therefore charitable in nature.

Similarly it has been held that gifts for the relief of the disabled or the sick will qualify under this fourth head of Lord Macnaghten's classification. In *Re Lewis*[299] a a bequest to 10 blind girls and 10 blind boys resident in a certain area was upheld by Roxburgh J who stressed that poverty was not an essential ingredient in order for the bequest to qualify as charitable in nature. A gift to the 'sick and wounded' has been found to be charita-

---

291. *Ibid.* at 201.
292. [1950] 2 All ER 1150n; [1950] 2 TLR 510.
293. *Barrington's Hospital v. Commissioner of Valuation* [1957] IR 299, 320 *per* Kingsmill Moore J. See also *Gleeson v. Attorney General*, High Court 1972 No.2664 Sp (Kenny J) 6 April 1973 at p. 11 of the unreported judgment and *Re Worth Library* [1995] 2 IR 301, 339.
294. E.g. *Re Robinson* [1951] Ch 198.
295. E.g. *Re Neal* (1966) 110 SJ 549; *Re Resch's Will Trusts* [1969] 1 AC 514.
296. [1983] Ch 159.
297. [1984] NI 408.
298. *Ibid.* at 414.
299. [1955] Ch 104. See also *Re Elliott* (1910) 102 LT 528.

ble[300] and in *Re Chaplin*[301] a gift 'to provide a home of rest that shall afford the means of physical and/or mental recuperation to persons in need of rest by reason of the stress and strain caused or partly caused by the conditions in which they ordinarily live and/or work' was accepted as being charitable as was a gift to a hospital to be applied for the purposes of a 'home of rest' for the nurses who worked there.[302]

In *Funnell v. Stewart*[303] the testatrix left her residuary estate to the first and second named defendants to further the spiritual work of a faith healing group. Her executors sought to determine whether the disposition created a valid charitable trust. Hazel Williamson QC was satisfied that the substance of the group's work was faith healing. She accepted that it was charitable, either on the basis that faith healing has become a recognised activity of public benefit (although she acknowledged that this might not necessarily have been the case when *Re Hummeltenberg* was decided), or on the basis that the religious nature of the faith healing movement renders this work a charitable purpose within which a sufficient element of public benefit is assumed so as to enable the charity to be recognised by law.

On the issue of religion and public /private services she stated that the gift was not prevented from being charitable by reason of the inclusion of the possibility of private services, 'which could clearly not themselves be charitable'.

A number of cases in this jurisdiction have established that gifts for the sick or to hospitals are charitable in nature. In *Re McCarthy's Will Trusts*[304] Budd J upheld as valid charitable gifts under this heading a bequest to a society which had as its principal object the care of the sick making pilgrimages to Lourdes and a bequest to a hospital at Lourdes which he described as being for the benefit of the sick and therefore 'clearly charitable'. The most important authority in this area is that of *Barrington's Hospital v. Commissioner of Valuation*,[305] in which the plaintiff hospital sought to challenge the changing of its exemption from rating valuation on the basis that its purposes were exclusively charitable in nature within the meaning of section 63 of the Poor Relief (Ireland) Act 1838. While Kingsmill Moore J accepted that 'charitable purposes' within the meaning of the section has a less extensive meaning than that given to those words in *Pemsel's* case,[306]

---

300. *Re Hillier* [1944] 1 All ER 480.
301. [1933] Ch 115.
302. *Re White's Will Trusts* [1951] 1 All ER 528.
303. [1996] 1 WLR 288.
304. [1958] IR 311.
305. [1957] IR 299.
306. *Ibid.* at 333.

his judgment nevertheless contains some important statements of general principle. He found that the term 'impotent' includes sick and injured persons and that 'a trust for the care of the sick or the maintenance of a hospital is a charity in the legal meaning of that term.'[307] The real issue which had to be resolved by the Supreme Court was whether the fact that the hospital admitted a number of fee-paying patients could alter this position. The court found that the presence in the hospital of a limited number of patients falling into this category did not detract from the charitable purpose of the institution and concluded that it was used exclusively for charitable purposes within the meaning of the section.[308] However, it is interesting to note that in the course of his judgment Kingsmill Moore J commented that 'if a hospital is being conducted exclusively for the well-to-do it ceases to be charitable'[309] and later in his judgment he modified this statement to read 'exclusively or predominantly'.[310]

In practice, the more important issue is probably the destination of any profits which may be derived from the hospital's activities and O'Daly J laid emphasis in *Barrington's* case on the fact that no private profit was derived from the premises by its occupiers. The non-profit making nature of a private hospital also proved to be of relevance in *Re Resch's Will Trusts*,[311] where a gift of the testator's residuary estate to a private non-profit making hospital was upheld as charitable despite the objection that it only provided for 'persons of means'. Lord Wilberforce confirmed that a hospital does not lose its charitable status 'because charges are made to the recipients of benefits' but stressed that a certain type of hospital might not qualify as charitable in nature, either because it 'is carried on commercially, i.e. with a view to making profits for private individuals, or that the benefits it provides are not for the public, or a sufficiently large section of the public to satisfy the necessary tests of public character.'[312] The destination of the profits derived from a private hospital also appeared to be of relevance in *Gleeson v. Attorney General*,[313] which concerned the charitable status of St Vincent's Private Hospital in Dublin which operated in

---

307. *Ibid.* at 321.
308. See also *Re Worth Library* [1995] 2 IR 301, 339-340. Although note the findings made by Palles CB in *Clancy v. Commissioner of Valuation* [1911] 2 IR 137 in relation to the charitable status of a hall where a majority of the persons using it paid for the use of the facilities.
309. [1957] IR 299, 322.
310. *Ibid.* at 334. Relying on *Governors of Royal Victoria Hospital v. Commissioner of Valuation* (1939) 73 ILTR 236.
311. [1969] 1 AC 514.
312. *Ibid.* at 540-541.
313. High Court 1972 No. 2664Sp (Kenny J) 6 April 1973.

conjunction with a public hospital. Kenny J stated that 'there is ... much to be said for the view that a private nursing home which charges fees and which is run in conjunction with a hospital and whose profits are applied for the purposes of the hospital is a legal charity'.[314] He reiterated that an institution does not cease to be charitable in nature because its activities benefit 'the rich as well as the poor' and concluded that the private hospital was a legally charitable institution.

Finally, it should be noted that a fairly flexible interpretation was placed by Keane J on the concept of a gift for the benefit of a hospital in *Re Worth Library*.[315] As noted above, Keane J concluded that the bequest of the library played a role in the advancement of the charity represented by the hospital by providing 'a haven of quiet intellectual relaxation' for the named office holders and as such constituted a valid charitable bequest for the benefit of that institution within the fourth category of Lord Macnaghten's classification. While Keane J commented that he did not feel that there was any ground for scepticism as to the capacity of Dr Worth's bequest to play a part in the advancement of the charity represented by the hospital, his conclusion is difficult to reconcile with his earlier attitude towards the public benefit question and undoubtedly extends present understanding of what might constitute a gift for the benefit of a hospital.

Gifts for Sporting and Recreational Purposes and for the Benefit of a Locality

In this context it may be necessary to draw a distinction between trusts to promote and encourage a particular sport or sports, which have traditionally not been regarded as charitable and trusts to provide facilities for recreational purposes, which will almost invariably be upheld. So in *Re Nottage*,[316] where a testator had sought to establish a trust to provide a prize for the most successful yacht of the season in order to encourage the sport of yacht racing, the Court of Appeal emphasised that a gift to encourage sport for its own sake was not in itself a charitable one. However a gift of this nature may be upheld where it is part of a more general charitable purpose such as improving the effectiveness of the armed forces. In *Re Gray*[317] a gift to a regimental fund for the promotion of sport[318] was

---

314. At p.11 of the unreported judgment.
315. [1995] 2 IR 301.
316. [1895] 2 Ch 649. See also *Re Patten* [1929] 2 Ch 276 (a gift to encourage the playing of cricket) and *Laing v. Commissioner of Stamp Duties* [1948] NZLR 154 (rowing, swimming and athletics).
317. 1925] Ch 362.
318. Limited to shooting, fishing, cricket, football and polo.

upheld on the basis that it would improve the efficiency of the army. As Romer J commented 'it is to be observed that the particular sports specified were all healthy outdoor sports, indulgence in which might reasonably be supposed to encourage physical efficiency.'[319] Similarly gifts to provide for the promotion of sport in a school,[320] or in educational institutions generally,[321] as we have seen will be regarded as being for the advancement of education.[322] The Goodman Committee[323] in England recommended that the encouragement of sport and recreation should in itself be recognised as a charitable object, provided that the requirement of benefit to the community is satisfied and in Canada it was held in *Re Laidlaw Foundation*[324] that the promotion of amateur athletic sports was charitable as it tended to both promote good health and advance education. It would appear that despite the earlier English authorities, trusts of this nature are likely to be upheld in this jurisdiction, particularly if they can be linked with the provision of recreational facilities.

The provision of recreational or leisure facilities such as parks[325] or playing fields[326] have been recognised as charitable objectives and in *Re Morgan*[327] a gift for 'a public recreation ground for amateur activities' for the benefit of a particular parish was upheld. The suggestion was made by Lord MacDermott LCJ in *Commissioner of Valuation v. Lurgan Borough Council*[328] that a distinction must be drawn between the provision of indoor and outdoor facilities and he commented that 'the law does not regard the mere provision of recreational facilities charitable unless they are provided in the open air on land dedicated to the use and enjoyment of the public.' However, this distinction is not supported by authority in this jurisdiction as an examination of the decision of a Divisional Court in *Clancy v. Commissioner of Valuation*[329] shows. The point at issue was whether a hall built with the object of 'promoting temperance among the poor and labouring classes of the town of Sligo and neighbouring districts' and used

---

319. *Ibid* at 365.
320. *Re Mariette* [1915] 2 Ch 284.
321. *IRC v. McMullen* [1981] AC 1.
322. See *supra* p. 306.
323. The Goodman Committee Report on Charity Law and Voluntary Organisations (1976).
324. (1984) 13 DLR (4th) 491.
325. *Brisbane City Council v. Attorney-General for Queensland* [1979] AC 411.
326. *Re Hadden* [1932] 1 Ch 133. The gift was for 'playing fields, parks, gymnasiums or other plans which will give recreation to an many people as possible'.
327. [1955] 1 WLR 738.
328. [1968] NI 104, 125.
329. [1911] 2 IR 173.

for such diverse activities as playing billiards and cards and taking baths, was used for exclusively charitable purposes. Persons using the hall were expected to pay an entrance fee; thereafter they were 'put on their honour' to make small contributions if they could afford to do so and the evidence established that more than half of the patrons made such contributions. Palles CB expressed the view that while the user of the hall might have been regarded as being exclusively charitable, the fact that its facilities were open to all, rich and poor alike posed a difficulty, and he concluded that its use by persons not falling within the ambit of the charitable purpose was not 'insignificant or insubstantial'. Gibson J found that the primary object of the institution was charitable as being 'for the moral and educational improvement of its visitors' but he agreed with the finding of Palles CB that its user was not exclusively charitable in nature. While the question was not expressly considered, it would appear that the court implicitly recognised that the provision of recreational facilities for the benefit of the public, whether outdoor or indoor, would be regarded as charitable.

A number of points should be noted about *Clancy's* case which would suggest its general value as a precedent is now limited. First, it was made in the context of a decision on rating, which as has been acknowledged,[330] often involves a more restrictive view of the concept of charitable status than might be employed in relation to a trust or gift. In addition, the fact that certain patrons of the hall paid for the use of the facilities should no longer appear to cause the same difficulty if one accepts by analogy the reasoning employed by the Supreme Court in the context of a hospital which took in fee-paying patients in *Barrington's Hospital v. Commissioner of Valuation*,[331] although it must be acknowledged that these individuals constituted a smaller percentage of the whole than the paying patrons in *Clancy*. A further consideration which would now be of relevance is the potential application to such cases of section 49 of the Charities Act 1961 which provides that where the purposes of a gift include charitable and non-charitable objects, its terms shall be construed so as to exclude the non-charitable objects.

It should also be noted that legislation has been introduced in England to regulate the status of trusts for recreational purposes, partly to restore the perceived *status quo* which was threatened by a number of restrictive decisions such as those of the House of Lords in *IRC v. Baddeley*[332] and by

---

330. *Barrington's Hospital v. Commissioner of Valuation* [1957] IR 299, 333.
331. [1957] IR 299.
332. [1955] AC 572.

the Court of Appeal in Northern Ireland in *Trustees of the Londonderry Presbyterian Church House v. IRC*.[333] Section 1 (1) of the Recreational Charities Act 1958 provides that subject to the provisions of the Act, 'it shall be and be deemed always to have been charitable to provide, or assist in the provision of facilities for recreation or other leisure time occupation if the facilities are provided in the interests of social welfare'. The latter requirement will be met if the facilities are provided 'with the object of improving the conditions of life' of those whom they are primarily intended[334] for and 'either (i) those persons have need of such facilities by reason of their youth, age, infirmity or disablement, poverty or social and economic circumstances or (ii) the facilities are to be available to the members or female members of the public at large.'[335] The meaning of these provisions was considered by the House of Lords recently in *Guild v. IRC*,[336] in which a testator left the residue of his estate to a town council for use in connection with the town's sport centre or for some similar purpose in connection with sport. The House of Lords held that on the true construction of section 1(2)(a) of the Recreational Charities Act 1958, facilities for recreation or other leisure time activities could be provided with the object of improving people's conditions of life notwithstanding that such people were not in a position of relative social disadvantage or suffering from some degree of deprivation. They concluded that the testator's bequest would come within the ambit of section 1(2) of the Act of 1958 and was therefore charitable in nature on the basis that people from all walks of life may have their condition of life improved by the provision of suitable recreational facilities. Similar legislation was introduced in Northern Ireland and was applied in *Springhill Housing Action Committee v. Commissioner of Valuation*,[337] in which a community centre in the Springhill estate in Belfast was found to be used wholly or mainly for charitable purposes. Gibson LJ stated that he was satisfied that the centre was occupied for a purpose which is normally charitable and the class of persons for whose benefit it was occupied, being the residents of a sizeable estate, was not so insignificant in number as to deprive it of its *prima facie* public character.

Trusts which make provision for the carrying out of public works or the provision of public facilities such as a village club and reading room in

---

333. [1946] NI 178.
334. S.1(2)(a).
335. S.1(2)(b).
336. [1992] 2 WLR 397.
337. [1983] NI 184.

a specified area,[338] are recognised as charitable. In addition gifts to a particular locality have traditionally been upheld provided they are of a general character or, where purposes are specified, where these are exclusively charitable in nature. A gift to a church council,[339] or to a town[340] will be upheld where the purposes are confined to general or public purposes beneficial to the community, although a gift to a parish to be applied to 'such public, benevolent or charitable purposes' as the trustees might think proper was construed disjunctively and was not regarded as charitable in nature.[341] An Irish decision which shows a more flexible approach is *Shillington v. Portadown UDC*,[342] where a gift to an urban council for the purpose of encouraging and providing 'means of healthy recreation' for the residents of an area was found to be charitable, aided by the application of a subjective test to the question of whether the trust was one beneficial to the community. As Barton J stated:

> The testator's purpose was a charitable or public purpose. He wished to benefit the residents of his native town and of its immediate neighbourhood. The benefits which he intended to confer on them were such as he believed to be of public advantage. That belief was rational and not contrary to the laws of the land or the principles of morality.[343]

This broader approach is to be welcomed and an application of the provisions of section 49 of the Charities Act 1961 would appear to ensure that trusts of this nature will be upheld in this jurisdiction.

Gifts for the Benefit of Animals

Gifts for the benefit of particular animals are not considered charitable, although as we have seen above,[344] they may be upheld if limited to the perpetuity period as an anomalous exception to the principle that purpose trusts will not be enforced. However, gifts for the welfare of animals generally or for a particular type of animal are recognised as charitable in law.

The rationale behind this finding has varied. In England, the motive of public utility appeared to underlie some of the early decisions in this area,[345]

---

338. *Re Scowcroft* [1898] 2 Ch 638.
339. *Re Norton's Will Trusts* [1948] 2 All ER 842.
340. *Re Allen* [1905] 2 Ch 400.
341. *Houston v. Burns* [1918] AC 337.
342. [1911] 1 IR 247.
343. *Ibid.* at 256-257.
344. See *supra* Chapter 9.
345. *London University v. Yarrow* (1857) 1 De G & J 72.

but more recently the idea that kindness towards animals tends to promote the morality of human beings seems to be fundamental to the reasoning employed. In *Re Wedgewood*[346] Swifen Eady LJ stated as follows:

> A gift for the benefit and protection of animals tends to promote and encourage kindness towards them, to discourage cruelty, and to ameliorate the condition of the brute creation, and thus to stimulate humane and generous sentiments in man towards the lower animals, and by these means promote feelings of humanity and morality generally, repress brutality and thus elevate the human race.

In an Irish context, there is evidence in the judgment of Chatterton VC in *Armstrong v. Reeves*[347] that the motive of safeguarding the welfare of the animals themselves might be sufficient to bring such trusts within the fourth heading of Lord Macnaghten's classification, although the approach in *Wedgewood* appears to have been taken by members of the Irish Court of Appeal in *Re Cranston*,[348] in which Holmes LJ commented: 'If it is beneficial to the community to promote virtue and to discourage vice, it must be beneficial to teach the duty of justice and fair treatment to the brute creation, and to repress one of the most revolting kinds of cruelty.'[349] Certainly in England the establishment of some benefit to human beings is of paramount importance as was stressed by Russell LJ in *Re Grove Grady*,[350] where he said that the validity of gifts in favour of animals depends on the question of whether they produce a benefit to mankind.

Whatever the rationale for enforcing trusts of this nature, a variety of different types of gifts have been upheld. These include trusts for the care of specific categories of domestic animals, for example, a gift to a 'Home for Lost Dogs',[351] to 'the Dublin Home for Starving and Forsaken Cats',[352] or 'for the welfare of cats and kittens needing care and attention'[353] have been upheld as charitable. Similarly gifts of a general nature for the pro-

---

346. [1915] 1 Ch 113, 122. See also the comments of Cozens-Hardy MR to the effect that a trust of this nature tends to 'promote public morality by checking the innate tendency to cruelty.' (at p.117)
347. (1890) 25 LR Ir 325.
348. [1898] 1 IR 431.
349. *Ibid.* at 457.
350. [1929] 1 Ch 557, 582. See also *National Anti-Vivisection Society v. IRC* [1948] AC 31, 45.
351. *Re Douglas* (1887) 35 Ch D 472.
352. *Swifte v. Attorney General* [1912] 1 IR 133.
353. *Re Moss* [1949] 1 All ER 495.

tection and benefit of animals,[354] or to a society which possesses such aims,[355] will be upheld, irrespective of whether its activities are confined to the protection of domestic animals or of animals useful to man.[356] In addition, a gift to institutions such as a sanctuary which provides refuge for sick and unwanted animals[357] will be regarded as charitable in nature. However, it is important that such institutions are not intended to be profit-making if they are to qualify for charitable status. As Russell LJ stated in *Re Satterthwaite's Will Trusts*:[358] '*prima facie*, an animal hospital is a charity, as being calculated to promote public morality by encouraging kindness, discouraging cruelty and stimulating humane sentiments to the benefit of mankind; but it lacks the quality of legal charity if it be carried on for private profit as a profession or occupation or trade.'

The object of promoting vegetarianism has been recognised as charitable and in *Re Cranston*[359] the Irish Court of Appeal upheld a gift to named vegetarian societies on the basis of a subjective test as to the element of public benefit which these involved.[360] Clearly the members of the Court of Appeal were not fully convinced of the benefit of such organisations but were satisfied that the testator clearly appreciated the benefit to be derived from their activities. As Fitzgibbon LJ commented:

> It is hard to see why the promotion of total abstinence from flesh should not be a 'charitable' object in the legal sense, if we are at liberty to recognise the promotion of total abstinence from intoxicants as charitable; moderation and temperance may be carried to excess, and though the benefits and drawbacks may differ in degree, they seem to be the same in kind. The motives of the promoters of teetotalism and of vegetarianism are equally unselfish, and equally benevolent, and the efforts of vegetarians, so far as I can form a judgment, seem less likely to do mischief than those of anti-vivisectionists, or even than those of the promulgators of the works of Joanna Southcote.[361]

---

354. *Re Wedgewood* [1915] 1 Ch 113. See also *Re Green's Will Trusts* [1985] 3 All ER 455.
355. *Armstrong v. Reeves* (1890) 25 LR Ir 325.
356. *Armstrong v. Reeves* (1890) 25 LR Ir 325, 341 *per* Chatterton VC.
357. *Re Murawski's Will Trusts* [1971] 1 WLR 707.
358. [1966] 1 WLR 277, 284.
359. [1898] 1 IR 431.
360. This finding that vegetarianism was a charitable object was applied in England by Joyce J in *Re Slatter* (1905) 21 TLR 295, without any reference to the different nature of the test employed in this jurisdiction.
361. *Ibid.* at 447.

In certain cases trusts which might appear to benefit animals have not been found to be charitable in nature. In *Re Grove-Grady*[362] a testatrix left her residuary estate on trust to found an animal benevolent society the objects of which included the provision of a refuge for the preservation of 'all animals, birds and other creatures not human'. The majority of the Court of Appeal held that the trust was not charitable as it lacked the necessary element of benefit to the community. Russell LJ stating that 'it is merely a trust to secure that all animals within the area shall be free from molestation or destruction by man. It is not a trust directed to ensure absence or diminution of pain or cruelty in the destruction of animal life.'[363] It is possible that such a decision would not be followed in this jurisdiction, particularly in view of the increased importance attached to preserving different species of wildlife,[364] or that alternatively such a trust might be upheld on the basis of its educational value.

Another category of trust which might be said to be of direct benefit to animals and which has met with differing judicial reaction over the last century is that of trusts which aim to abolish vivisection. In *Armstrong v. Reeves*[365] a legacy to the Society for the Abolition of Vivisection was held to be charitable on the grounds that the society was for the public benefit as it tended to correct and prevent cruelty to animals. Chatterton VC rejected the argument that there was something illegal in the nature of the society as one of its aims was to secure the suppression of vivisection by changing the law. In his view it was instead 'a society for the purpose of inducing the legislature by legitimate means, by bringing public opinion to bear, to make certain alterations in the law. ...'[366] A similar view was taken by Chitty J in *Re Foveaux*,[367] although more recently in England the House of Lords held in *National Anti-Vivisection Society v. IRC*[368] that the society was not entitled to income tax relief on the grounds that its object was not a charitable one. Faced with a finding of fact made in the lower court that the benefit to humanity in allowing vivisection outweighed the incidental suffering to animals, the House of Lords concluded that a trust which had been found to be detrimental to society could not be charitable merely because of the testator's opinion. The reasoning behind such a con-

---

362. [1929] 1 Ch 557.
363. *Ibid.* at 585.
364. Note the more recent decision of Holland J in *Attorney General of New South Wales v. Satwell* [1978] 2 NSWLR 200.
365. (1890) 25 LR Ir 325.
366. *Ibid.* at 339.
367. [1895] 2 Ch 501.
368. [1948] AC 31.

clusion would seem to be that while the protection of animals from cruelty is a charitable purpose, vivisection is a necessary element in medical research and its suppression could not therefore be considered to be beneficial to the community. This point is evident in the judgment of Buckley J in *Re Jenkins's Will Trusts*,[369] where he stated as follows:

> [T]he prohibiting of any forms of cruelty inherent in vivisection, however admirable that may be from an ethical point of view, is not a charitable activity in the contemplation of the law because the court cannot weigh the benefits to the community which result from using animals for vivisection and research against the benefits which would result to the community from preventing such practices.

Gifts for Political Purposes

It is well-established that trusts for the advancement of political purposes are not charitable and as a result gifts for the benefit of specific political parties will clearly not qualify for charitable status.[370] It is often not easy to distinguish trusts which will be accepted as being *bona fide* for the advancement of education from those which are merely disguised as being for such a purpose and are in fact designed to promote political purposes. In *Re Trusts of the Arthur McDougall Fund* [371] a trust for the teaching of political theory was accepted as being educational in nature and in *Re Koeppler's Will Trusts*[372] a bequest to fund the holding of conferences with political themes was also upheld. However, a more borderline case is *Re Scowcroft*[373] where a gift for the maintenance of a village club and reading room 'for the furtherance of Conservative principles and religious and mental improvement' was found to be charitable, the reasoning employed by Stirling J suggesting that he felt able to make this finding because the purposes of the trust were not predominantly political. A different conclusion was reached in *Re Hopkinson*,[374] where a trust for the advancement of adult education with particular reference to education in the Labour Par-

---

369. [1966] Ch 249, 255.
370. In relation to trusts to support a political party Hammond J has recently commented in the New Zealand decision of *Re Collier* [1998] 1 NZLR 81, 90 that the conclusion that trusts for their benefit are not charitable 'appears to be the agreed position throughout the common law world' and he has stated that he is not aware of any suggestion that any change to this position should be effected.
371. [1957] 1 WLR 81.
372. [1986] Ch 423.
373. [1898] 2 Ch 638.
374. [1949] 1 All ER 346. See also *Bonar Law Memorial Trust v. IRC* (1933) 49 TLR 220.

ty's doctrines was found not to be charitable. As Vaisey J commented: 'Political propaganda masquerading — I do not use that word in any sinister sense — as education is not education within the statute of Elizabeth. ... In other words it is not charitable.'[375] This reasoning was applied by Goulding J in *Re Bushnell*,[376] in which a bequest for 'the advancement and propagation of the teaching of socialised medicine' was found to have predominantly political rather than educational objectives and was therefore not charitable in nature. Often provided that the predominant motive for a trust is not political, it may be upheld and as Goulding J commented: 'The existence of some political motive is not necessarily fatal to a good charitable trust'.[377] An excellent summary of what appears to be the applicable principles is provided in *Tudor on Charities*[378] as follows:

> If ... a trust is predominantly political or propagandist, as where the furtherance of the principles of one particular party is, on the true construction of the trust instrument, the main object of the trust, then though it is worded in the terms of an educational trust, and there is provision for lectures and/or discussion classes which are in themselves of an educational character, but subsidiary to the main object, the trust will fail to qualify as a charitable trust for the advancement of education.

The principle that a trust which essentially has political objectives will not be regarded as charitable was confirmed in this jurisdiction in *Re Ní Brudair*,[379] where a gift for the benefit of republicans according to the objects of that movement as they were in the years 1919-1921 was found to be too vague and uncertain to constitute a valid charitable gift. Gannon J concluded that taking an overall view of the express directions of the testatrix and the 'latitude of apparent duty imposed on her trustees' he was satisfied that there was no charitable intention nor charitable gift in the legal sense in her will. He also commented that even if the testatrix had presented her trustees with the democratic programme of the Dáil of January 1919 by way of directions as to how the money was to be spent this was essentially a statement of broad political objectives and would not constitute a valid charitable trust.

---

375. *Ibid.* at 350.
376. [1975] 1 WLR 1596.
377. *Ibid.* at 1603. Approved by Slade J in *McGovern v. Attorney General* [1982] Ch 321, 343. See also *Re Scowcroft* [1898] 2 Ch 638.
378. (8th ed., 1995, Warburton) p. 51.
379. High Court 1976 No. 93 Sp (Gannon J) 5 February 1979.

Often trusts for the advancement of political purposes will involve advocating a change in the law and this latter objective provides one of the primary reasons why trusts of this nature will not be regarded as charitable.[380] Lord Parker laid down the reasons for this general principle in *Bowman v. Secular Society Ltd*[381] as follows:

> [A] trust for the attainment of political objects has always been held invalid, not because it is illegal, for everyone is at liberty to advocate or promote by any lawful means a change in the law, but because the court has no means of judging whether a proposed change in the law will or will not be for the public benefit, and therefore cannot say that a gift to secure the change is a charitable gift.

This principle was approved by Lord Simonds in *National Anti-Vivisection Society v. IRC*,[382] where it was held by the House of Lords that the main object of the society was political, namely the abolition of vivisection by means of an alteration in the law, and that for this reason it could not be considered as a body established for charitable purposes only. The *dicta* of Lord Parker in *Bowman* was analysed further by Slade J in *McGovern v. Attorney General*,[383] which concerned the question of whether a trust created by Amnesty International to achieve certain stated purposes could be registered as a charity. These purposes included the relief of needy persons who were or had been prisoners of conscience and their families, attempting to secure the release of such prisoners, procuring the abolition of torture or inhuman or degrading treatment or punishment, the promotion of research into the maintenance and observance of human rights and the dissemination of the results of such research. Slade J concluded that a trust the main objective of which was to secure a change in the laws of a foreign country could not be regarded as charitable because the court would have no means of knowing whether such a change would be for the public benefit and because of public policy considerations based on the risk of prejudicing relations between the countries concerned. Slade J laid down the following general principles:

(1) Even if it otherwise appears to fall within the spirit and intendment

---

380. As Hammond J recently stated in the New Zealand decision of *Re Collier* [1998] 1 NZLR 81, 89 'the conventional view in the British Commonwealth is that charitable trusts to change the law itself are invalid'.
381. [1917] AC 406, 442.
382. [1948] AC 31.
383. [1982] Ch 321. See Watkin [1982] Conv 387; Nobles (1982) 45 MLR 704.

of the preamble to the Statute of Elizabeth, a trust for political purposes falling within the spirit of Lord Parker's pronouncement in
Bowman's case, can never be regarded as being for the public benefit in the manner which the law regards as charitable.

(2) Trusts for political purposes falling within the spirit of this pronouncement include, *inter alia*, trusts of which a direct and principal purpose is either (i) to further the interests of a particular political
party; or (ii) to procure changes in the laws of this country; or (iii) to
procure changes in the law of a foreign country; or (iv) to procure a
reversal of government policy or of particular decisions of governmental authorities in this country; or (v) to procure a reversal of
government policy or of particular decisions of governmental authorities in a foreign country.[384]

One further point of importance to be derived from the judgment of
Slade J is his comment that if all the main objects of a trust are exclusively
charitable, the fact that the trustees may have incidental powers to employ
political means to further these objects will not deprive the trust of its
charitable status. This approach might allow for some qualification of Lord
Parker's *dicta* in *Bowman*, although it should be pointed out that its continued acceptance in England is bound to limit the possibilities of new
types of trusts qualifying for charitable status and as Hanbury and Martin
point out 'it is difficult to answer the criticism that organisations cam-
paigning for improvements in the law cannot be registered as charities,
while existing charities can and do campaign for and against change.'[385]
This point has been echoed by Hammond J in his judgment in the recent
decision of the New Zealand High Court in *Re Collier*[386] where he stated
'why is it that the law allows existing charities to make "political" statements; yet it impugns *ab initio* those which are proposed to be set up to
campaign for reform'. Clearly the notion that a 'coherent system of law
can scarcely admit that objects which are inconsistent with its own provisions are for the public welfare'[387] is being increasingly called into question and as Hammond J pointed out in *Re Collier* judges themselves often
make suggestions for changes in the law. For this reason groups and organisations which advocate reform of the law should not rule out the pos-

---

384. *Ibid.* at 340.
385. *Modern Equity* (15th ed., 1997) p.408.
386. [1998] 1 NZLR 81, 90.
387. *Per* Dixon J in *Royal North Shore Hospital of Sydney v. Attorney General for New
     South Wales* (1938) 60 CLR 396, 426.

sibility that they may qualify for charitable status in the future if such ideas take root.

CY-PRÈS JURISDICTION

Introduction

Where a gift is made to charity, it may be impossible or impracticable to give effect to the intentions of the donor in the precise terms which he intended. The cy-près doctrine where it applies, allows for the making of a scheme for the application of such property for other charitable purposes as near as possible to those intended by the donor. As Budd J stated in *Re Royal Kilmainham Hospital*:[388] 'The principle is applied where the method indicated by the donor of carrying out his charitable intentions becomes impracticable, or his intentions cannot be executed literally, most frequently owing to altered circumstances.' The rationale behind the operation of this doctrine is that provided a clear charitable intention is expressed, a gift should not be allowed to fail because the mode of effecting this intention, if specified, cannot be carried out, or no longer provides the most useful and effective manner of applying the bequest. From a practical perspective it will not be possible for a donor to forecast how circumstances affecting his gift will change over a period of time and this difficulty can be also said to underlie the cy-près doctrine. As Meredith J stated in *Governors of Erasmus Smith's Schools v. Attorney General*:[389]

> To apply without modification a charitable intention that is only expressed in relation to assumed facts and under different conditions is obviously not to carry out the real intention at all. It is on this principle that Courts of Law adapt the statement of a charitable intention to suit altered circumstances and conditions with a view to giving effect to the real intention. Donors cannot be expected to provide expressly for more than the world and the times with which they are familiar.

Therefore for a trust to attain charitable status is a most desirable aim, not

---

388. [1966] IR 451, 469.
389. (1931) 66 ILTR 57, 61. See also the *dicta* of Lord Eldon in *Moggridge v. Thackwell* (1803) 7 Ves 36, 69 as follows: 'If the testator has manifested a general intention to give to charity, the failure of the particular mode in which the charity is to be effectuated shall not destroy the charity; but if the substantial/general intention is charity, the law will substitute another mode of devoting the property to charitable purposes, though the formal intention as to the mode cannot be accomplished.'

only because of the advantages already considered, but also because it will facilitate the operation of cy-près jurisdiction should this become necessary. If a trust does not qualify as charitable, this jurisdiction cannot be exercised and a bequest may fail as contravening the rule against perpetuities, allowing a resulting trust to operate in favour of the donor or his representatives. Such resulting trusts will often not reflect the donor's wishes, and it is certainly preferable to find a means of perpetuating the donor's charitable intention in as close a form as possible to that originally expressed by him. An examination of the judgment of Keane J in *Re Worth Library*[390] would seem to confirm that as a prerequisite to the exercise of cy-près jurisdiction, a court must satisfy itself that the purpose for which the bequest was originally made was charitable. Despite the fact counsel were in agreement that the bequest in question was a charitable one, Keane J expressed the view that as the court was being invited to exercise its jurisdiction to approve a cy-près scheme, a jurisdiction which could only operate in relation to charitable bequests, he felt it necessary to investigate the issue of the charitable status of the original bequest fully. However, it is interesting to note that in another recent case of a similar nature, *Representative Church Body v. Attorney General*,[391] where O'Hanlon J was called upon to approve a cy-près application in relation to a collection of books in the Old Library of St. Canice's Cathedral, Kilkenny, he proceeded to grant the order sought without raising the question of the charitable nature of the bequest.

In practice, an important distinction must be drawn between circumstances where the gift fails *ab initio*, in which case the property can only be applied cy-près where the donor has manifested a general charitable intention and cases of subsequent failure where it is not necessary to show such an intention provided that the donor has made an absolute and perpetual gift to a particular charity. This distinction has been well summarised by Murray J in *Re Dunwoodie*[392] in the following terms:

> There is an important distinction between a charitable trust which is initially impossible or impracticable, i.e. impossible or impractica-

---

390. [1995] 2 IR 301.
391. [1988] IR 19. See further Osborough (1989) 24 Ir Jur (ns) 50.
392. [1977] NI 141, 145. This principle was expressed in a different manner by Budd J in *Re Royal Kilmainham Hospital* [1966] IR 451, 469 although the effect is the same. 'The cy-près principle is confined ... to cases where property is given with a general intention to charity with this exception, that where property is given absolutely and perpetually to charity for a particular purpose and has vested in the charity the fund can be applied cy-près irrespective of the donor's particular intention.' Quoted with approval by Keane J in *Re Worth Library* [1995] 2 IR 301, 341.

ble as at the death of the testator, and a charitable trust which becomes impossible or impracticable after his death. As regards the former type, the property involved will not be applied cy-près unless the court finds that the testator had a general charitable intention, but as regards the latter type — usually referred to as a case of supervening impossibility — the court will direct a cy-près application whether or not a general charitable intention on the part of the testator can be found in the relevant will.

Initial Failure of Charitable Purposes

In cases where the charitable purposes of a gift fail for one of the reasons which will be examined below, the doctrine of cy-près can be applied 'where, in form, the gift is given for a particular charitable purpose, but it is possible, taking the will as a whole, to say that, notwithstanding the form of the gift, the paramount intention, according to the true construction of the will, is to give the property in the first instance for a general charitable purpose rather than a particular charitable purpose. . . .'[393] Numerous attempts have been made by the judiciary to describe the meaning of the phrase 'general charitable intention'. In *Re Templemoyle Agricultural School*[394] Chatterton VC commented as follows:

> It does not mean merely an intention to give charity [sic] generally, without reference to any specified object, but it means an intention the substance of which is charitable, whether generally and without any specified object, in which case the Crown will prescribe the mode of effectuating it, or for an object more or less accurately specified, but with a mode of benefiting that object superadded, which cannot be lawfully or at all carried into execution, in which case the Court will carry out the substantial intention.

An alternative formulation was put forward by Kay J in *Re Taylor*:[395] 'if upon the whole scope and intent of the will you discern the paramount object of the testator was to benefit not a particular institution, but to effect a particular form of charity, independently of any special institution or mode, then, although he may have indicated the mode in which he de-

---

393. *Re Wilson* [1913] 1 Ch 314, 320-321 *per* Parker J. Quoted with approval by Budd J in *Munster and Leinster Bank Ltd v. Attorney General* (1954) 91 ILTR 34, 39.
394. (1869) IR 4 Eq 295, 301. It should be noted that this decision concerned a case of supervening failure, where arguably it was not necessary to establish a general charitable intent. See *infra.*
395. (1888) 58 LT 538, 543. See *Re Royal Kilmainham Hospital* [1966] IR 451, 469.

sires that to be carried out, you are to regard the primary paramount intention chiefly. . . .' A useful distinction was made by Dixon and Evatt JJ in *Attorney General for New South Wales v. Perpetual Trustee Co. Ltd*[396] between cases in which every element in the description of the trust is indispensable to its validity and operation and cases 'where a further and more general purpose is disclosed as the true and substantial object of the trust'.

While the view has been expressed that in seeking to ascertain whether a general charitable intention can be found in a will, the court should look only at the particular gift,[397] the position would seem to be that such an intention may be discerned from other gifts contained in the will.[398] This was made clear in *Re McGwire*[399] by Black J who stressed that 'a general charitable intention may be collected from the will as a whole'. It has also been suggested recently that because of a reluctance to establish a construction which will lead to intestacy, the courts may lean in favour of finding a general charitable intention.[400]

Whether a donor has displayed sufficient charitable intention is inevitably a question of construction of the relevant document;[401] clearly the more detailed the donor's directions, the less likely it will be that a general charitable intention can be discerned from the terms of the instrument. A number of recent decisions in England would appear to have widened considerably the scope of the concept of general charitable intention. In *Re Lysaght*[402] a testatrix made provision in her will for funds to be applied for medical studentships within the gift of the Royal College of Surgeons of England. One of the clauses provided that qualifying students must be male, British-born subjects, the sons of British-born doctors registered in the UK 'and not of the Jewish or Roman Catholic faith'. The college declined to accept the bequest in the terms set out in the will but expressed its willingness to do so provided the offending clause was deleted. It was held by Buckley J that to insist on enforcing the discriminatory provision would defeat the paramount intention of the testatrix, and a scheme was ordered which would enable implementation of the trust omitting the words

---

396. (1940) 63 CLR 209, 225. Quoted with approval by Murray J in *Re Stewart's Will Trusts* [1983] NI 283, 297.
397. *Mayor of Lyons v. Advocate-General of Bengal* (1876) 1 App Cas 91, 114.
398. *Re Satterthwaite's Will Trusts* [1966] 1 WLR 277, 286 *per* Russell LJ.
399. [1941] IR 33, 38.
400. *Per* Hammond J in *Re Collier* [1998] 1 NZLR 81, 95.
401. Dixon and Evatt JJ suggested in *Attorney General for New South Wales v. Perpetual Trustee Co. Ltd* (1940) 63 CLR 209, 226 that this question must be approached on the basis of the circumstances of the failure of the initial trust.
402. [1966] 1 Ch 191.

'and not of the Jewish or Roman Catholic faith'.[403] As Buckley J commented: 'A general charitable intention, then, may be said to be a paramount intention on the part of a donor to effect some charitable purpose which the court can find a method of putting into operation, notwithstanding that it is impracticable to give effect to some direction by the donor which is not an essential part of his true intention — not that is to say, part of his paramount intention.'[404] As Warburton[405] has commented this reasoning involves asking whether the impugned direction is essential to the donor's purpose and 'allows a far narrower and more detailed intention to amount to a "general" intention'. Although this more liberal approach will be beneficial in circumstances where a good charitable gift might otherwise fail, it is not so justifiable where it appears to defeat the real intention of a donor.

The former consideration applied in *Re Stewart's Will Trusts*,[406] in which a liberal approach to the concept of general charitable intention can also be discerned. The testator left the residue of his estate to a fund established by the Non-Subscribing Presbyterian Church of Ireland for the purpose of supplementing the income of ministers of that church and directed that the income from the residue of his estate should be used for the support of ministers whose congregations complied with certain conditions, one of which, relating to the use of unaltered and unabridged hymn books, was impossible to fulfil. Murray J ordered a cy-près scheme to remove this condition from the trust, holding that the paramount intention of the testator was to increase the salary of ministers of a Christian church. He stated that he could not see how it would be right to regard such an 'ill-considered' provision as an essential part of the charitable scheme particularly when the result of so doing would be to make the trust completely unworkable and frustrate the testator's paramount intention. This can be contrasted with a recent decision of the High Court in this jurisdiction which suggests that a more restrictive approach may be applied, although there was no discernible attempt to lay down any such general principle. In *Re Prescott*[407] a testatrix bequeathed her house to a Dublin parish of the 'Russian Orthodox Church abroad' and directed that if there were no members of that church living in Ireland that it should be sold and the proceeds

---

403. A similar approach was taken by Vinelott J in *Re Woodhams* [1981] 1 WLR 493 where a scheme to found music scholarships confined to orphans from named homes was altered to omit the latter restriction.
404. *Ibid.* at 202. Quoted with approval by Carswell J in *Re Currie* [1985] NI 299, 306.
405. [1981] Conv 231, 232.
406. [1983] NI 283.
407. [1990] 2 IR 342.

applied for the general purposes of the said church in England. At the time of the testatrix's death, the parish had ceased to exist and the executor applied to the court for directions as to the manner in which the proceeds of the sale of the house were to be distributed. MacKenzie J held that the gift of the house had lapsed as it was to a body which did not exist either at the time of making the will or at the death of the testatrix and the gift over being dependent on the validity of this gift also lapsed. While MacKenzie J accepted that there may be cases where a court can find a general charitable intention even in a case of a single gift,[408] he concluded that there was no indication that the testatrix had any intention other than to benefit the named institution in the case before him and he held that the doctrine of cy-près could not be applied. This appears to be a rather restrictive decision given the terms of the gift over in the testatrix's will and would certainly appear to be out of line with the English authorities in this area. On the whole it would be fair to say that the Irish courts have generally leaned in favour of a fairly flexible attitude to this issue.[409]

Initial impossibility in relation to a charitable trust may arise in any one of a number of circumstances. The gift may have been made to a non-existent institution and as Buckley J commented in *Re Davis*:[410] 'where you find a gift to a charitable institution which never existed, the Court, which always leans in favour of charity, is more ready to infer a general charitable intention than to infer the contrary.' While such an intention will not always be found in cases of non-existent institutions,[411] it would appear to be more difficult to establish in circumstances where the object once existed but ceased to do so before the gift took effect.[412] This point was made by Megarry VC in *Re Spence*,[413] where he commented that 'the court is far less ready to find [a general charitable] intention where the gift is to a body which existed at the date of the will but ceased to exist before the testator died, or as I have already held, where the gift is for a purpose

---

408. See e.g. *Biscoe v Jackson* (1887) 35 Ch D 460; *Re Currie* [1985] NI 299.
409. A general charitable intention was found in the following cases: *Daly v. Attorney General* (1860) 11 I C R 41; *Munster and Leinster Bank Ltd v. Attorney General* (1954) 91 ILTR 34; *Re Templemoyle Agricultural School* (1869) IR 4 Eq 295; *Re McGwire* [1941] IR 33; *Re Quinn* (1953) 88 ILTR 161; *Re Fitzgerald's Estate* (1957) 92 ILTR 192; *Re Currie* [1985] NI 299. Cases where no such intention was found include *Re Ffrench* [1941] IR 49n; *Attorney General for Northern Ireland v. Forde* [1932] NI 1; *McCormick v. Queen's University of Belfast* [1958] NI 1.
410. [1902] 1 Ch 876, 881. See e.g. *Daly v. Attorney General* (1860) 11 I C R 41.
411. *Re Goldschmidt* [1957] 1 WLR 524.
412. *Re Harwood* [1936] Ch 285, 287 *per* Farwell J. See also *Makeown v. Ardagh* (1876) IR 10 Eq 445, 452; *Re Prescott* [1990] 2 IR 342.
413. [1979] 1 Ch 483, 495.

which, though possible and practicable at the date of the will, has ceased
to be so before the testator's death.' Another reason for initial failure of a
gift is that the body or institution which the testator intended to benefit
may have been amalgamated with or absorbed into another institution by
the time the gift is to take effect. Such a gift may lapse if the court considers that on its true construction it is intended to have been for the originally specified purpose or institution alone.[414] However, it has been
established that where a named parish ceases to exist as a separate entity
and amalgamates with another, a gift to such a parish may be applied for
the purposes of the new unit.[415] Another common difficulty which arises
is that the institution may be misdescribed. As Chatterton VC commented
in *Re Geary's Trusts*:[416] 'The Court, however, will not allow a charitable
legacy to fail because of misdescription, but will endeavour to carry out
the testator's intention as nearly as possible.'

Finally, the possibility that the consent of the intended recipient to an
acceptance of the trust in its original terms may not be forthcoming must
be considered. In *Re Dunwoodie*[417] the testatrix bequeathed the residue of
her estate on trust for a particular Presbyterian Church with a direction
that the bequest should be used for the installation of bells at that church.
The committee of the church decided not to install the bells and the question arose whether the residuary bequest should devolve as on an intestacy
or be applied cy-près. Murray J held that the trust for the installation of the
bells must be treated as initially impossible to fulfil because the consent of
the relevant church authority which was essential to the fulfilment of the
trust had never been given. However, he was satisfied that the testatrix had
shown a general intention to further the general purposes of the particular
church and that the initial failure of trust in no way invalidated the general
trust for the church which remained perfectly good. In the circumstances,
he ordered that the property should be applied cy-près.

Subsequent Failure of Charitable Purposes

A gift may be capable of being carried out in the precise terms laid down
by the donor or testator at the time it takes effect but may subsequently fail
or become impossible or impracticable to enforce. In such circumstances,

---

414. *Re Rymer* [1895] 1 Ch 19.
415. *Corbally v. Representative Church Body* [1938] IR 35. See also *Re Bloomfield's
     Bequest* (1920) 54 ILTR 213 where a clergyman was found to be entitled to an
     endowment originally intended for the incumbent of a parish which had merged
     with his.
416. (1890) 25 LR Ir 171.
417. [1977] NI 141.

it is not necessary to establish a general charitable intention provided that the gift is given 'absolutely and perpetually to charity'. The material date for deciding the question of whether general charitable intention is necessary is therefore the date on which the trust comes into effect, which in the case of a will, is the date of the testator's death.[418] The effect of the distinction between initial and supervening impossibility was set out by Evershed MR in *Re Tacon*[419] as follows:

> It is well established that in the case of a gift to charity ... where no general charitable intention is present, then (1) if the charity has ceased to exist before the will comes into operation the gift lapses, but (2) if the charity is still in existence at the date mentioned, it is effective as a gift to the extent that the interests of the next-of-kin (or of whoever else take in default of the charitable interest taking effect) are for ever excluded, notwithstanding the later dissolution or disappearance of the charity.

One of the most important decisions establishing this principle in this jurisdiction is that of Budd J in *Re Royal Kilmainham Hospital*.[420] A hospital founded by Charles II in 1684 for the support and maintenance of old soldiers of his army and those of his successors gradually ceased to function after the setting up of the Irish Free State and the Irish government took over control of the lands and buildings. In 1961, the Royal Kilmainham Hospital Act was passed which provided, *inter alia*, for the settling of a scheme for some specified charitable purposes or purpose for the benefit of some classes of members of the defence forces. It was held by Budd J that since it was no longer possible to carry out the founder's intentions the available funds should be applied cy-près and he directed that they should be used to benefit organizations of former members of the defence forces and the British Army. Budd J stated as follows:

> There was no controversy as to the general principles applicable when charitable gifts, which have taken effect, subsequently fail for want of objects. If there is an absolute perpetual gift to a charity, even though the trusts declared are only for the accomplishment of a particular charitable purpose, the subject-matter is applicable cy-près upon failure of the trusts.[421]

---

418. *Re Wright* [1954] Ch 347.
419. [1958] Ch 447, 453.
420. [1966] IR 451.
421. *Ibid.* at 472.

Similarly, in *Re Worth Library*[422] Keane J found that the original bequest of the library in the will of Dr Worth was 'undoubtedly an absolute and perpetual gift' and for this reason could be applied cy-près when the hospital ceased to exist, notwithstanding his finding that no general charitable intention could be inferred on the facts before him.

In certain circumstances surplus funds may remain where a charitable purpose has been completed or where full provision has been made for its requirements and provided that it is an absolute and perpetual gift to charity, these funds may be applied cy-près. In *Trusts of the Rectory of St John*[423] a surplus remained after providing for the maintenance of the choir and choral service at a cathedral church in Cork City as required by the terms of a trust. Chatterton VC held that as part of these monies was not required for the literal fulfilment of the donor's intentions, some of the fund might be applied cy-près in the purchase of an organ for the church, a purpose which was essential for carrying that intention into effect.

Finally, it should be pointed out that there have been sporadic examples throughout the common law world of courts determining whether general charitable intent exists in cases of supervening failure,[424] although Picarda[425] has characterised such judgments as examples of the courts searching unnecessarily for such an intent and finding it. In the recent decision of the Newfoundland Court of Appeal in *Boy Scouts of Canada v. Doyle*,[426] which was a case of supervening failure, Marshall JA still went on to consider whether the requirement of general charitable intent was satisfied. However, he also considered the arguments in favour of dispensing with this latter requirement and concluded that whichever approach was followed, the conditions for cy-près were satisfied in the case before him. His judgment certainly cannot be taken as authority for the proposition that he was insisting on a requirement of general charitable intent even in cases of supervening impossibility or failure and the overwhelming weight of opinion is against such a proposition.[427]

---

422. [1995] 2 IR 301, 342.
423. (1869) IR 3 Eq 335.
424. E.g. *Re Templemoyle Agricultural School* (1869) IR 4 Eq 295 (Ireland); *Re North Devon and West Somerset Relief Fund Trusts* [1953] 1 WLR 1260 (England); *Parker v. Moseley* [1965] VR 580 (Australia); *Hay v. Murdoch* [1952] WN 145 where the House of Lords suggested that in Scotland a general charitable intent was required in all cases.
425. *The Law and Practice Relating to Charities* (2nd ed., 1995) p.299.
426. (1997) 149 DLR (4th) 22.
427. See e.g. the statement in *Tudor on Charities* by Warburton (8th ed., 1995) p.409 to the effect that 'the requirement of a general or paramount charitable intention is irrelevant in the case of a subsequent failure of a gift for charitable purposes'.

Legislative Reform of the Cy-près Doctrine

At common law this jurisdiction could only be exercised where it was impossible or impracticable to give effect to the wishes of a donor in the precise terms which he intended. However, the doctrine as it developed at common law was criticised as being too restrictive in nature and section 47 of the Irish Charities Act 1961 laid down much broader parameters for the exercise of this jurisdiction,[428] allowing a cy-près order to be made in circumstances where there were difficulties in implementing the original terms or where more effective use might be made of the trust property by framing an alternative scheme. It is helpful to set out in full the terms of section 47(1) which enumerates the circumstances in which a cy-près order may now be made.

> (1) Subject to subsection (2), the circumstances in which the original purposes of a charitable gift may be altered to allow the property given or part of it to be applied cy-près shall be as follows:—
>
>   (a) where the original purposes, in whole or in part—
>   (i)   have been as far as may be fulfilled; or
>   (ii) cannot be carried out, or cannot be carried out according to the directions given and to the spirit of the gift; or
>   (b) where the original purposes provide a use for part only of the property available by virtue of the gift; or
>   (c) where the property available by virtue of the gift and other property applicable for similar purposes can be more effectively used in conjunction, and to that end can suitably, regard being had to the spirit of the gift, be made applicable for common purposes; or
>   (d) where the original purposes were laid down by reference to an area which then was but has since ceased to be a unit for some other purpose, or by reference to a class of persons or to an area which has for any reason since ceased, either to be suitable, regard being had to the spirit of the gift, or to be practical in administering the gift; or
>   (e) where the original purposes, in whole or in part, have since they were laid down—
>   (i)   been adequately provided for by other means; or

---

428. See also s.13 of the Charities Act 1960 in England and s.22 of the Charities Act (Northern Ireland) 1964 which introduced similar reforms.

(ii) ceased as being useless or harmful to the community or for other reasons, to be in law charitable; or

(iii) ceased in any other way to provide a suitable and effective method of using the property available by virtue of the gift, regard being had to the spirit of the gift.

The provisions of section 47(1) have been applied in a number of cases. In *Re Royal Kilmainham Hospital* Budd J found that the original purposes of the gift could no longer be carried out according to the directions given and the spirit of the gift and that these original purposes had at least in part ceased to provide a suitable and effective method of using the property available. Subsection (1)(e)(iii) was again considered by O'Hanlon J in *Representative Church Body v. Attorney General*[429] in which the plaintiff sought a cy-près order under section 47 in relation to a collection of books kept in the Old Library attached to St Canice's Cathedral, Kilkenny. The plaintiff claimed ownership of the books and wished to sell them and apply the proceeds to the maintenance and repair of the cathedral. It was argued that the books were no longer used in the manner envisaged in the original bequests but the application was opposed by the Attorney General on the grounds that the collection was an important cultural asset for Kilkenny and that if it were sold there was no effective legal restriction on its exportation. O'Hanlon J held that the original purposes of the charitable gifts had ceased to provide a suitable or effective method of using the property available, regard being had to the spirit of the gift. He held further that it was permissible to alter the original purposes of the bequests and to allow the property to be applied cy-près and he made an order authorizing the sale of the collection by the plaintiff so that the proceeds might be applied to the repair and maintenance of the cathedral.

This decision provides a good illustration of how the original common law requirements in relation to the exercise of cy-près jurisdiction have now been relaxed. While it could be argued that section 47 was applied in an unduly lenient manner in this case, the requirement that the property be applied in conformity with the 'spirit of the gift' should ensure that due regard should be given to the wishes of a donor.

The equivalent English provision, section 13(1)(e)(iii) of the Charities Act 1993 has recently been considered by the Court of Appeal in *Varsani v. Jesani*.[430] A charitable trust had been established with the purpose of

---

429. [1988] IR 19. See further Osborough (1989) 24 Ir Jur (ns) 50. The equivalent provision in s.22 of the Charities Act (Northern Ireland) 1964 was applied in *Re Steele* [1976] NI 66.
430. [1999] 2 WLR 255.

promoting the faith of a particular Hindu sect and the charity's assets included a temple in London. Subsequently the members of the sect split
into two groups and this produced a situation in which neither group would
worship in the same temple as the other. Carnwarth J held that the court
had jurisdiction under section 13 of the Charities Act 1993 to make a regu-
latory scheme and ordered that the sect's assets be held on separate trusts
for the furtherance of the faith as practised by each group.

The minority group's appeal was dismissed by the Court of Appeal.[431]
Morritt LJ concluded that if the original purposes of the charity had led to
the impasse which in his view could not be resolved as a matter of faith,
then it was self-evident that the original purposes had ceased to be a suitable and effective method of using the available property. He concluded
that the spirit of the gift supported the submission that the court should
exercise the jurisdiction conferred on it by section 13(1)(e)(iii) of the 1993
Act by directing a scheme for the division of the property of the charity as
between the majority and minority groups. Chadwick LJ agreed that the
appeal should be dismissed for the reasons set out by Morritt LJ. In relation to the manner in which the spirit of the gift could be identified, he
stated as follows:

> The need to have regard to the spirit of the gift requires the court to
> look beyond the original purposes as defined by the objects speci-
> fied in the declaration of trust and to seek to identify the spirit in
> which the donors gave property upon trust for those purposes. That
> can be done, as it seems to me, with the assistance of the document
> as a whole and any relevant evidence as to the circumstances in
> which the gift was made.[432]

Section 47(2) of the 1961 Act provides that its provisions are not 'to affect
the conditions which must be satisfied in order that property given for
charitable purposes may be applied cy-près except insofar as these conditions require a failure of the original purposes'. Therefore the importance
of the distinction between initial and subsequent failure remains, to the
extent that general charitable intention must be established in the former
category, and the legislation has merely extended the circumstances in
which a cy-près application may successfully be brought.

Finally, it should be noted that the Commissioners of Charitable Donations and Bequests have jurisdiction to frame a cy-près scheme, initially

---

431. [1999] 2 WLR 255.
432. *Ibid.* at 270.

limited by the provisions of section 29 of the Charities Act 1961 to circumstances where the value of the charitable gift did not exceed £5,000, a figure extended by section 8 of the Charities Act 1973 to £25,000, and by section 52(a) of the Court and Court Officers Act 1995 to £250,000. In addition, it should be noted that section 52(c) of the Act of 1995 empowers the Minister for Justice to make orders from time to time varying this amount.

The Manner in Which Cy-près Jurisdiction Should be Exercised

As the word 'cy-près' suggests, in determining new purposes for which property should be applied, the court should seek to ensure that these purposes are as near as possible to those originally set out in the gift. In addition, as Keane J stated in *Re Worth Library*[433] it is also 'desirable that the original intentions of the testator should be adhered to so far as is possible', although as Keane J himself acknowledged, the difficulties in both ascertaining and giving effect to such intentions will be obvious where there has been a considerable lapse of time since the making of the initial gift. In the context of the facts in the case before him, he therefore stated that it would be futile to transport the donor in some form of time machine from the early eighteenth century to the present day and all that the court could do was 'to apply the gift as it might be applied by a late twentieth century equivalent of [the donor]'. In the circumstances, Keane J concluded that any cy-près scheme framed by the court must provide for the retention of the books and portraits which formed the subject-matter of the gift in their original setting, which after it ceased to be a hospital, became a health board headquarters.

Another recent example illustrating the importance of adhering to the original purposes as closely as possible is provided by the decision of Carroll J in *Doyle v. Attorney General.*[434] A fund was set up to benefit a child who suffered from a rare genetic skin disease and some of the money raised was used for her benefit. Following her death, the plaintiffs proposed the division of the funds between seven named charities which were institutions, all but one of which were located in the area in which the funds were raised, which treated the sick, the elderly and the handicapped. The scheme was opposed by the Attorney General on the grounds that many of the proposed beneficiaries were not as near as possible to the original purposes of the fund. Carroll J stated that the care of the elderly, the handicapped and the sick was not sufficiently close to the original

---

433. [1995] 2 IR 301, 343.
434. High Court 1993 No. 612 Sp (Carroll J) 22 February 1995.

purpose of the fund and said that she agreed with the submission that there should be some connection with the disease from which the original beneficiary had suffered, 'either by way of research, or treatment, or palliative care'. In her opinion, the requirement that regard should be had to the wishes of the trustees or other persons in charge of the property did not override the requirement that the application should be cy-près. Carroll J concluded that a proportion of the fund should be spent on a specialist clinic set up to treat sufferers from the disease and that a lesser proportion should be given to research into the disease, which was being carried out in a specified location on condition that the court could be provided with information as to what would constitute a meaningful contribution to research. Carroll J suggested that the plaintiffs might give their opinion as to the division of the fund as between these two purposes but added that if it was not possible to provide a meaningful sum for research, then the entire fund should go the specialist clinic.

Further light was thrown on the process of deciding how to apply property cy-près by the judgment of Marshall JA in the recent decision of the Newfoundland Court of Appeal in *Boy Scouts of Canada v. Doyle*.[435] The court had to determine how trust property should be applied cy-près when a particular boy scout troop in whose favour it had been established ceased to exist.[436] Marshall JA stated that the first step in the process required 'an examination of the trust settlement's general intent as a prelude to defining the mode which in substance will as nearly as possible execute the general charitable intent'.[437] He concluded that as the particular troop no longer existed, the trust should be applied for the benefit of the local scouting movement which was represented by the provincial council. In his view by making it possible for all scouting to benefit in place of one particular troop, the court could ensure that 'the general object will not be defeated but will continue to be executed in substance through the offices of the scouting movement'.[438]

Sign Manual Procedure

Where money or property is given to charity generally without provision being made for the appointment of trustees the government is considered

435. (1997) 149 DLR (4th) 22.
436. The Court accepted that there was no difficulty in holding that a trust for the benefit of a scouting troop fell within the parameters of the advancement of education and referred to the decision of Vaisey J in *Re Webber* [1954] 1 WLR 1500 on this point.
437. *Ibid.* at 79.
438. *Ibid.* at 81.

to be the trustee and is required to ensure the administration of the gift under the 'sign manual procedure'. In *Felan v. Russell*[439] property was bequeathed for 'pious purposes' and although it was accepted as being for charitable purposes, the trustee died before a scheme to apply the gift was settled. It was held that the gift vested in the Crown and that it should be disposed of under the sign manual procedure. Similarly, in *Merrins v. Attorney General*[440] Black J held that a gift in remainder to charity generally in relation to which no trustee had been appointed, should be applied at the 'will and pleasure' of the government.

---

439. (1842) 4 Ir Eq R 701. See also *Kane v. Cosgrave* (1873) IR 10 Eq 211.
440. (1945) 79 ILTR 121.

CHAPTER 11

Void and Voidable Trusts

A private trust may fail in circumstances where although it appears to be otherwise valid, it is in fact illegal or contrary to public policy. In such cases, where the trust is void, it is regarded as being invalid *ab initio* and never comes into effect. Alternatively, a trust may be voidable in certain circumstances; these trusts are not void *ab initio* and will remain in operation unless or until their validity is successfully challenged.

VOID TRUSTS

A trust may be void because it offends statutory provisions or the common law or because it may be contrary to public policy. Where a trust is declared void, the property which it was intended to include in it will be held on a resulting trust for the settlor or where such a trust arises under a will, it will lapse into the testator's residuary estate.

Where a trust involves the creation of a future interest it is subject to the rules against perpetuities and inalienability or perpetual duration. So, a trust will be void *ab initio* where it might vest outside the perpetuity period i.e. that of a life or lives in being plus a further period of 21 years allowing additionally for periods of gestation or where the property is tied to a specific purpose for a period of time in excess of the perpetuity period. These issues are considered in detail elsewhere and it is not proposed to consider them in this context.[1]

Conditions Precedent and Subsequent

Often the question of whether a trust is void relates to the issue of the validity of any condition to which the trust may be made subject and illegality often arises as a result of a condition imposed on what might otherwise be a valid gift. Such conditions fall into two categories; conditions precedent, which effectively preclude the trust from coming into effect

---

1.   Wylie, *Irish Land Law* (3rd ed.,1997) Chapter 5; Coughlan, *Property Law* (2nd ed., 1998) Chapter 10. On the rule against inalienability, see *infra* Chapter 10 in relation to purpose trusts.

unless and until the condition is fulfilled and conditions subsequent which do not prevent the gift vesting but render it liable to be divested if and when the condition is satisfied. Gifts which incorporate a void condition subsequent can still be enforced without the application of this condition,[2] whereas traditionally certain distinctions have to be made in the case of conditions precedent. Generally where a gift of realty is made dependent on a condition precedent which is found to be void, the gift will fail in its entirety.[3] In England a distinction was drawn in the case of gifts of personalty between situations where the condition was *malum in se* (intrinsically wrong in itself) as opposed to *malum prohibitum* (wrong in the eyes of the law).[4] In the former case, the gift would fail but in the latter case, the gift would be considered good and would pass unfettered by the terms of the invalid condition. This distinction was applied in that jurisdiction in cases such as *Re Piper,*[5] where a condition that children should not reside with their father was categorised as *malum prohibitum* with the result that the gift took effect free of the illegal condition. However, this principle was described as 'archaic' by Dixon J in *Re Blake*[6] who commented as follows: 'this is a curious and somewhat pedantic distinction to introduce in ascertaining the wishes of testators who, in the vast majority of cases, would be quite unaware of the existence of the distinction, and, even if they were aware of it, might be unable to obtain from lawyers any very precise idea of the nature and limits of the distinction.'[7] In the circumstances of the case, Dixon J found that the condition precedent which he was required to consider fell into neither category and concluded that the gift failed in its entirety. However, some doubt still surrounds the effect of an invalid condition precedent attached to a gift in this jurisdiction, particularly as Kenny J appears to have held subsequently in *Re Doyle*[8] that 'when a condition precedent attached to a gift is in violation of the donees's constitutional rights ... the donee takes the benefit of the gift without complying with the condition'.

---

2. *Duddy v. Gresham* (1878) 2 LR Ir 442.
3. *Re Turton* [1926] Ch 96.
4. See Delany (1955) 19 Conv 176.
5. [1946] 2 All ER 503.
6. [1955] IR 89.
7. *Ibid.* at 100. See the comments of Delany in (1955) 19 Conv 176, 177 that 'the distinction ... is both obsolete and inherently unsound' and 'can no longer be said to be based on any rational foundation — if indeed, it ever possessed one.'
8. High Court, 1972 (Kenny J). See Wylie, *Irish Land Law* (3rd ed., 1997) p. 555.

Trusts Contrary to Public Policy

Trusts which have as their object an illegal or immoral aim will be regarded as void on this ground. So trusts for such diverse objects as to provide for the payment of fines of convicted poachers[9] have been held to be void. Trusts in favour of future illegitimate children were considered to be void at common law as tending to promote immoral conduct[10] and were regarded as being contrary to public policy. However, this is no longer the case as a result of the intervention of statute and section 27(5) of the Status of Children Act 1987 repealed the common law rule which rendered trusts in favour of future illegitimate children void in relation to wills or settlements made after the commencement of the Act. Many trusts will be of doubtful validity because they contain conditions which may be vulnerable on public policy grounds and it is now proposed to examine some of these categories in greater detail.

1. Trusts in Restraint of Marriage
A condition in a trust which amounts to a general restraint on marriage is *prima facie* void.[11] However, it was made clear by Mellish LJ in *Allen v. Jackson*[12] that this principle does not apply to conditions which come into effect only upon a second marriage. It would also appear that in England at any rate, conditions which operate as a partial restraint on marriage, for example prohibiting marriage with certain classes of persons,[13] may be valid. Traditionally, a distinction has been drawn in that jurisdiction between a partial restraint imposed in relation to realty on the one hand and to personalty on the other hand. In the case of realty a partial restraint never appears to be regarded as invalid, whereas in respect of personalty, the condition is considered to be *in terrorem* only and invalid if there is no gift over on the happening of the marriage.[14]

In view of the fact that the right to marry has been recognised as an unspecified personal right which derives from Article 40.3 of the Constitution,[15] it is likely that even partial restraints on marriage would now be

9.   *Thrupp v. Collett* (1858) 26 Beav 125.
10. *Thompson v. Thomas* (1891) 27 LR Ir 457. As Keane comments in *Equity and the Law of Trusts in the Republic of Ireland* (1988) at p.192 it was doubtful whether this common law rule survived the enactment of the Constitution.
11. *Lloyd v. Lloyd* (1852) 2 Sim (NS) 255; *Re Hanlon* [1933] Ch 254.
12. (1875) 1 Ch D 399. See also the judgment of Ball C in *Duddy v. Gresham* (1878) 2 LR Ir 442.
13. *Perrin v. Lyon* (1807) 9 East 170.
14. *Duddy v. Gresham* (1878) 2 LR Ir 442; *Leong v. Cheye* [1955] AC 648, 660.
15. *Ryan v. Attorney General* [1965] IR 294, 313; *McGee v. Attorney General* [1974] IR

considered void in this jurisdiction and on the basis of the *dicta* of Kenny J in *Re Doyle* referred to above, it would appear that a donee would take the gift free from any such condition.

A corollary of this principle is that trusts made in contemplation of or which might encourage the future separation of a husband and wife are void. So, in *Re Johnson's Will Trusts*[16] a trust which cut down the testator's daughter's interest to a nominal amount so long as she was married and living with her husband was considered to be void on this basis. This decision can be distinguished from that in *Re Lovell,*[17] where the object of the trust was found to be to make provision for a woman during her separation until she might return to her husband or remarry and where the parties are already separated no objection should arise.[18] However, in view of the constitutional status of the institution of marriage in this jurisdiction, it is likely that a strict attitude will be taken by the courts here towards any trust which might have the effect of directly or indirectly weakening the marriage bond.

2. Trusts Tending to Interfere with Parental Duties

Trusts which seek to weaken the ties between parents and children by requiring that children reside apart from their parents have been held to be void as being contrary to public policy. So, in *Re Boulter*[19] a condition in a gift to the testator's grandchildren which provided that it should be forfeited if either or both of them should live with or be under the custody or control of their father was held to be void as being contrary to public policy and tending to encourage the separation of parents from their children. In addition, trusts which interfere with parental duties in relation to the upbringing of their children will also be considered void on policy grounds. In *Re Borwick*[20] a condition subsequent in a trust which provided that an interest should be forfeited if the beneficiary should before attaining the age of 21 'become a Roman Catholic or not be openly or avowedly Protestant' was found to be void as it interfered with the exercise of parental duty in relation to the religious upbringing of the child. Some doubt was

---

284, 301. Note also the comments of Gavan Duffy P in *Re McKenna* [1947] IR 277.

16. [1967] Ch 387. See also *Re Caborne* [1943] Ch 224. Although note the decision of *Re Thompson* [1939] 1 All ER 681 in which Bennett J came to the contrary conclusion.

17. [1920] 1 Ch 122.

18. *Wilson v. Wilson* (1848) 1 HLC 538.

19. [1922] 1 Ch 75. See also *Re Sandbrook* [1912] 2 Ch 471 and *Re Piper* [1946] 2 All ER 503 where the fact that the father was divorced did not affect the court's finding on this issue.

20. [1933] Ch 657. See also *Re Tegg* [1936] 2 All ER 878.

thrown on the validity of this approach by the decision of the House of Lords in *Blathwayt v. Baron Cawley*,[21] where a clause in a trust which provided for forfeiture of an interest if the beneficiary should become a Roman Catholic was upheld. The majority of the House of Lords acknowledged that such conditions would tend to influence or interfere with parental responsibilities but took the view that they should not be categorised as contrary to public policy.

The validity of this type of condition has been considered by the courts in this jurisdiction on a number of occasions. In *Re Burke's Estate*[22] Gavan Duffy P held that a condition in the testatrix's will that his nephew should be educated in a Roman Catholic school to be selected at the absolute discretion of the trustees, 'however well meaning from the standpoint of an anxious benefactor' was inoperative as it tended to override the rights and duties of parents in relation to the education of their children provided for in Article 42 of the Constitution. Perhaps the most important authority in this area is the judgment of Dixon J in *Re Blake*[23] in which he had to consider the validity of a trust in favour of the testator's grandchildren but subject to a condition that they be brought up as Roman Catholics. Dixon J referred to the relevant English authorities and to Article 42 of the Constitution and stated as follows:

> This Article puts the matter on a different and higher plane in this country, as the parental right and duty is declared and guaranteed by our fundamental law. Under it, the State 'guarantees to respect the inalienable right and duty of parents to provide, according to their means, for the religious and moral, intellectual, physical and social education of their children.' It is clear that any attempt to restrict or fetter that right would be contrary to the solemnly declared policy and conceptions of the community as a whole and therefore such as the Courts established under that Constitution could not and would not lend their aid to.[24]

The effect of such a finding was considered in detail by Dixon J. The distinction between a finding of invalidity in relation to conditions precedent and subsequent had been outlined as follows by Gavan Duffy P in *Re Burke's Estate*:[25]

---

21. [1976] AC 397.
22. [1951] IR 216.
23. [1955] IR 89.
24. *Ibid.* at 97.
25. [1951] IR 216, 224.

> The practical effect of the distinction is of the utmost importance: a
> gift made subject to a condition precedent fails altogether, as a rule,
> if the condition is found to be void, but if a gift is made subject to a
> condition subsequent which is found to be void or inapplicable, the
> condition disappears and the gift takes effect independently of the
> condition.

While Dixon J acknowledged that Gavan Duffy J had left open the possibility of there being an exception to the general rule in the case of conditions precedent, he concluded that the conditions in the case before him were void and unenforceable and that the gifts were dependent on their being carried out and were also void. Some doubt must be raised about such a conclusion in the light of the decision of Kenny J in *Re Doyle*, where it appears to have been stated that where a condition precedent to a gift is found to be in violation of the donee's constitutional rights the donee may take the benefit of the gift without complying with the condition. However, it should be pointed out that the condition in that case, which was found to be contrary to the provisions of Article 44.2.1 of the Constitution, was held in any event to be invalid on the grounds that it was impossible to perform.

VOIDABLE TRUSTS

Trusts falling within this category come into operation and will remain effective unless and until they are set aside in court proceedings. A trust may be voidable for a variety of reasons often because it comes into being as a result of mistake, misrepresentation, fraud, duress or undue influence. In addition a trust may be set aside where it amounts to an attempt to defraud a settlor's creditors or subsequent purchasers or where the settlor becomes bankrupt within a specified period of settling the property. In this context it is proposed to examine these latter situations, which are governed by specific statutory provisions in more detail.

Settlements Defrauding Creditors

In practice a person may often be tempted to settle property, usually on his family or close associates, in circumstances where he fears that his creditors may otherwise succeed in obtaining control over his assets. However, as Fitzgerald B commented in *Smith v. Tatton*:[26] 'A man must be honest

---

26. (1879) 6 LR Ir 32, 41. See also the comments of Jessel MR in *Re Butterworth* (1882)

before he is generous' and section 10 of the Conveyancing Act (Ireland) 1634[27] provides that any gift or conveyance of property, real or personal made for the purpose of delaying, hindering or defrauding creditors is 'void' as against such creditors, although this phrase has been interpreted as meaning 'voidable'.[28] Section 14 of the 1634 Act goes on to provide that this provision will not extend to conveyances *bona fide* made for good consideration[29] without notice of any fraud. The general object of this legislation was summarised by Palles CB in *Re Moroney*[30] as follows: 'The object of the statute was to protect the rights of creditors as against the property of their debtor. It was no part of its object to regulate the rights of creditors *inter se*, or to entitle them to an equal distribution of that property.' The extent of the fraudulent intent required by the statute is far from clear; in *Rose v. Greer*[31] Overend J stated that the class of fraud against which the statute is directed is 'one in which the debtor attempts to defeat his creditors by bogus or colourable transactions under which the debtor retains a benefit to himself'. While it was suggested by Pennycuick VC in *Lloyds Bank Ltd v. Marcan*[32] in the context of the then equivalent English provision,[33] that the word 'defraud' was not intended to be confined to cases involving actual deceit or dishonesty, Cairns LJ disagreed with this view when the matter was considered by the Court of Appeal[34] and said that fraud involves dishonesty, so that while deceit is not a necessary element, dishonest intention is required, at any rate when the conveyance is one for consideration.

However, the view expressed by Pennycuick VC seems to be more in accord with the position adopted in this jurisdiction. In *Re Moroney*[35] Palles CB appeared to accept that there might be cases falling within the ambit of

---

19 Ch D 588, 598: 'a man is not entitled to go into a hazardous business, and immediately before doing so, settle all his property voluntarily, the object being this: "if I succeed in business, I make a fortune for myself. If I fail, I leave my creditors unpaid. They will bear the loss".'

27.	10 Chas 1, sess. 2, c.3. (The original equivalent in England was 13 Eliz., c.5).
28.	*Re Eichholz* [1959] Ch 708.
29.	This requirement has been interpreted to mean valuable consideration including marriage consideration, but natural love and affection does not suffice, see *Re Rorke's Estate* (1865) 15 Ir Ch R 316.
30.	(1887) 21 LR Ir 27, 62. See also the comments of O'Connor MR in *National Bank Ltd v. Behan* [1913] 1 IR 512, 516, to the effect that 'the deed must be fraudulent in its conception or execution'.
31.	[1945] IR 503, 510.
32.	[1973] 1 WLR 339, 344.
33.	S.172 of the Law of Property Act 1925. Subsequently replaced by s.423 of the Insolvency Act 1986.
34.	[1973] 1 WLR 1387, 1391.
35.	(1887) 21 LR Ir 27.

the statute where no fraudulent intention actually exists in the settlor's mind but can be assumed as a matter of law from the consequences of his actions. At this point it is useful to set out the Chief Baron's comments in full:

> Therefore to bring a conveyance within the statute, first, it must be fraudulent; secondly, the class of fraud must be an intent to delay, hinder or defraud creditors. Whether a particular conveyance be within this description may depend upon an infinite variety of circumstances and considerations. One conveyance for instance, may be executed with the express intent and object in the mind of the party to defeat and delay his creditors, and from such an intent the law presumes the conveyance to be fraudulent, and does not require or allow such fraud to be deduced as an inference of fact. In other cases, no such intention actually exists in the mind of the grantor, but the necessary or probable result of his denuding himself of the property included in the conveyance, for the consideration, and under the circumstances actually existing, is to defeat or delay creditors, and in such a case, as stated by Mellish LJ in *Re Wood* LR 7 Ch App 302, the intent is, as a matter of law, assumed from the necessary or probable consequences of the act done.[36]

This view that it is not necessary to establish that the agreement was motivated by actual fraud provided that the necessary or probable result of the agreement was to defeat or delay creditors has recently been approved by Costello P in *McQuillan v. Maguire*.[37] A decree in favour of the plaintiffs against the first named defendant in relation to a building contract had been converted into a judgment mortgage over the latter's interest in a property. A month after the decree had been obtained, the second named defendant, who was the wife of the first named defendant, instituted proceedings under the Married Women's Status Act 1957 and an order was made by consent declaring that she was entitled to the entire beneficial interest in this premises. When the plaintiffs learnt of the order they instituted proceedings seeking a declaration that the first named defendant was at all material times the beneficial owner of the premises and that the judgment mortgage was well charged on that beneficial interest. The plaintiffs submitted that the order had been obtained by collusion and with the intention to defraud them and argued that it should be set aside in accord-

---

36. *Ibid.* at 61-62.
37. [1996] 1 ILRM 395.

ance with the provisions of the Conveyancing Act (Ireland) 1634. Costello P referred to *Re Moroney* and reiterated that the court did not have to find that the agreement had been motivated by actual fraud in order to set it aside. If it could be shown that the necessary or probable result of the agreement was to defeat or delay creditors, it could be avoided. He concluded that the agreement entered into between the defendants in the proceedings taken under the 1957 Act was void as it had the effect both of hindering and delaying the payment of a debt due by the first named defendant to the plaintiffs. He therefore held that the plaintiffs were entitled to a well charging order over the first named defendant's 50% of the premises on the basis that the wife had a 50% beneficial interest by virtue of contributions she had made to earlier family homes.

The onus would appear to be on the party alleging fraud,[38] particularly where it appears that the transfer or conveyance of the property was made in a *bona fide* manner for good consideration. The latter point emerges clearly from the decision of the High Court in *Bryce v. Fleming*.[39] The first named defendant assigned lands to the second named defendant at a price which reflected the estimate which the parties placed on the value of the lands. The plaintiff had three days previously obtained judgment against the first named defendant and was a creditor of his to nearly half the value of the lands in question. The second named defendant stated in evidence that she had paid the full value of the lands and that she had no knowledge of the judgment which had been obtained against the vendor. The Circuit Court judge declared the deed void as against the first named defendant's creditors on the grounds that he did not believe the evidence of the second named defendant that she had no knowledge of the fraudulent nature of the transaction. On appeal the plaintiff's action was dismissed on the basis that the assignment was for valuable consideration and the evidence of the plaintiff did not establish that there was any knowledge of fraud on the part of the second named defendant nor did it show that she had sought to acquire the land other than as a *bona fide* purchaser.

So, even where a conveyance is for valuable consideration, this fact alone will not suffice to prevent the application of section 10.[40] This point was developed by Palles CB in *Re Moroney*[41] in the following manner:

If, however, in such a case, the intent were not only to sell the prop-

---

38. *National Bank Ltd v. Behan* [1913] 1 IR 512, 516 *per* O'Connor MR.
39. [1930] IR 376.
40. *Cadogan v. Kennett* (1776) 2 Cowp 432, 434-435 *per* Lord Mansfield.
41. (1887) 21 LR Ir 27, 63.

erty, but forthwith to abscond with the proceeds, so as in effect to withdraw the property from the fund available for the creditors without providing an equivalent, I should entertain no doubt that in such a case there would be an intention to defraud creditors, which, if the purchaser had notice of, would avoid the sale, and which, whether he had notice or not, would be an act of bankruptcy by the vendor.

However, it will clearly be more difficult to impugn the validity of a deed made for valuable consideration; as Turner LJ stated in *Harman v. Richards:*[42] 'those who undertake to impeach for *mala fides* a deed which has been executed for valuable consideration, have, I think, a task of great difficulty to discharge'. As Johnston J made clear in *Bryce v. Fleming,*[43] where there is a *bona fide* purchase for valuable consideration it cannot be impeached unless the purchaser is shown to be privy to the vendor's intention.

A further point to note is that the mere fact that an individual with debts is selling property is not necessarily evidence that he intends to defeat his creditors rather than to obtain the means to satisfy these debts.[44] A *fortiori*, knowledge of such a fact will not be a sufficient ground for imputing to a purchaser knowledge of a fraudulent intention on the part of the vendor. From a practical perspective a sale of this nature often provides the means necessary to satisfy existing debts; while the property itself ceases to be available for the purpose of satisfaction, the consideration derived from the sale can be regarded as a 'substantial equivalent'.[45]

Some uncertainty surrounds the question of whether a settlement entered into with the intention of defrauding future creditors may come within the ambit of these provisions. In *Stileman v. Ashdown*[46] Lord Hardwicke accepted that this could be the case: 'It is not necessary that a man should actually be indebted at the time he enters into a voluntary settlement, to make it fraudulent; for, if a man does it with a view to his being indebted at a future time, it is equally fraudulent, and ought to be set aside.'

This principle was confirmed in this jurisdiction in *Murphy v. Abraham,*[47] where it was held by Smith MR that a voluntary deed in the

---

42. (1852) 10 Hare 81, 89. See also *Re Johnson* 20 Ch D 389, 393; *Bryce v. Fleming* [1930] IR 376, 379-380, 385.

43. [1930] IR 376.

44. *Bryce v. Fleming* [1930] IR 376, 380 *per* Johnston J.

45. *Re Moroney* (1887) 21 LR Ir 27, 63.

46. (1742) 2 Atk 477, 481 in relation to the initial equivalent English provision (13 Eliz, c.5). See also *Barling v. Bishopp* (1860) 29 Beav 417.

47. (1864) 15 Ir Ch R 371.

form of a post-nuptial settlement entered into by a trader prior to embarking upon a partnership arrangement was executed with a view to defrauding his future creditors and could be set aside. Subsequently, in *Smith v. Tatton*[48] Fitzgerald B concluded that there was no evidence of future indebtedness being in the contemplation of the grantor, although he seemed to accept that in principle at least, a deed might be impeached if this had been the case. He stated that there were two classes of cases in which a deed might be set aside on this ground, first where there were existing debts and secondly, where 'either by the provision of the deed or other circumstances, it is shown that future indebtedness was at least in the contemplation of the grantor, so as to point whatever other evidence there may be of fraud to future creditors.'[49] Doubt was cast on the validity of this principle by some of the *dicta* of the Irish Court of Appeal in *Re Kelleher*,[50] including the statement of Holmes LJ that once the debts of creditors existing at the date of a deed have been discharged, a later creditor cannot take advantage of what might have been relied on by previous creditors as an implied fraud on them. However, a closer reading of the decision would suggest that the decisive factor was the lack of any proof of an actual intention to defraud and it is likely that where such an intention can be established the principle laid down in *Murphy v. Abraham*[51] remains intact.

Finally, it appears to be well settled that merely preferring one creditor over another does not come within the mischief which the statute was designed to prevent[52] and that a debtor who gives a creditor security with the intention of preferring him to other creditors does not possess the necessary illegal intention.[53]

Voluntary Settlements to Defraud Purchasers

Section 1 of the Conveyancing Act (Ireland) 1634 provides that any voluntary conveyance made with the intention of defrauding subsequent purchasers is void (interpreted as meaning voidable), as against subsequent purchasers for value, and section 3 of the Act goes on to exclude *bona fide* conveyances for good consideration from the ambit of the section. The meaning of the term '*bona fide*' in this context was considered by Hamil-

---

48. (1879) 6 LR Ir 32.
49. *Ibid.* at 43.
50. [1911] 2 IR 1, 9.
51. (1864) 15 Ir Ch R 371.
52. *Glegg v. Bromley* [1912] 3 KB 474, 484 *per* Vaughan Williams LJ.
53. *Ibid.* at 492 *per* Parker J.

ton P in *Re O'Neill*,[54] who said that it must be taken to mean 'without notice of the intention to delay, hinder or defraud creditors of their lawful debts, rights and remedies.'

This legislation was interpreted strictly from the point of view of the person conveying the property and as Monahan CJ stated in *Gardiner v. Gardiner*:[55] 'from the fact of the deed being voluntary, we are justified in drawing the inference that the deed was made with intent to defraud purchasers.' The corresponding English enactment[56] was similarly interpreted,[57] and as Ronan LJ commented in *Re Moore*:[58] 'this principle plainly treated as fraudulent perfectly honest transactions, and was found, particularly in the case of settlements making provision for families, to operate very harshly and unjustly.' As a result, the Voluntary Conveyances Act 1893 was passed which provided in the words of O'Connor MR in *National Bank Ltd v. Behan*:[59] 'that no voluntary conveyance, if in fact made *bona fide* and without any fraudulent intent, should thereafter be deemed fraudulent or convinous within the meaning of the Act 10 Chas. 1, Sess. 2, c.3, by reason of any subsequent purchase for value.' However, it was held in *Behan* that despite these provisions, the onus of proving the *bona fides* of a voluntary settlement still lay on the person seeking to uphold it. O'Connor MR held that as infants were unable to prove affirmatively the *bona fides* of a voluntary conveyance of lands executed in their favour by their father, the conveyance was void as against a subsequent purchaser for value. He stated that in his view there could be no doubt as to the onus of proof under the Act of 1893 and that the words 'if *in fact* made *bona fide* and without any fraudulent intent' seemed to clearly place the onus on the party seeking the protection of the statute. This would seem to be an unduly restrictive approach and serious doubts about its validity were voiced by O'Brien LC in *Re Moore*.[60] Although he referred to the *Behan* decision and said that he would never overrule the judgment of the Master of the Rolls unless he considered that he was 'absolutely bound to reach a different conclusion', he went on to comment as follows:

> [O]rdinarily, I should have thought that the person on whom the onus of proof would lie under 27 Eliz. c.4, once the irrebuttable

---

54. [1989] IR 544.
55. (1861) 12 ICLR 565, 575.
56. 27 Eliz c.4.
57. *Doe v. Manning* (1807) 9 East 59.
58. [1918] 1 IR 169, 181.
59. [1913] 1 IR 512, 517.
60. [1918] 1 IR 169.

> presumption to which I have referred was swept away, was the person alleging fraud, just as under 13 Eliz., c.5, where an actual intent to defraud the grantor's creditors is alleged, the burden of proving such intent falls on the person alleging it.[61]

In view of the harsh and unjust operation of the earlier legislation to which Ronan LJ made reference this would certainly seem to be a fairer approach and while the decision of the Master of the Rolls in *Behan* was not formally overruled, it would seem likely that a court today would take such a step or that at the very least slight evidence indeed would suffice to establish that a transaction was *bona fide*.

Settlements by Bankrupts

Section 52 of the Bankruptcy (Ireland) Amendment Act 1872 which made provision for the setting aside in certain circumstances of settlements made by persons subsequently adjudicated bankrupt was repealed[62] and replaced by section 59 of the Bankruptcy Act 1988.[63] Section 59 now provides that any settlement of property,[64] not being a settlement before and in consideration of marriage, or made in favour of a purchaser or incumbrancer in good faith and for valuable consideration, shall be void as against the official assignee if the settlor is adjudicated bankrupt within two years of the date of the settlement and, if the settlor is adjudicated bankrupt within five years of the date of the settlement, shall be void unless the parties claiming under the settlement prove that the settlor was, at the time of making the settlement, able to pay all his debts without the aid of the property comprised in it and that the interest of the settlor in such property passed to the trustee of the settlement on its execution.

As in the case of the sections considered above, the reference to the settlement being void as against the official assignee has been interpreted as meaning voidable and therefore valid unless steps are taken to have it set aside.[65] There is no requirement to prove any fraudulent intent on the part of the settlor and it is the mere fact of him becoming bankrupt within the period of time laid down in the statute which brings the section into

---

61. *Ibid.* at 179.
62. By s.6, Second Schedule of the Bankruptcy Act 1988.
63. See generally Sanfey & Holohan, *Bankruptcy Law and Practice in Ireland* (1991) pp.121-124 and Forde, *Bankruptcy Law in Ireland* (1990) pp.130-134.
64. Defined in s.3 of the Act of 1988 to include real and personal property
65. *Per* Palles CB in *Re Doyle* (1891) Court of Appeal, unreported, quoted in Kiely, *The Principles of Equity as applied in Ireland* (1936) pp.70-71.

operation.[66] To secure protection against its provisions as Hamilton P commented in *Re O'Neill*:[67] 'it is necessary that the conveyance should be both for valuable consideration and *bona fide*' or that the settlement should be one in consideration of marriage.

In *Re O'Neill* the bankrupt conveyed his interest in premises to his daughter for slightly below the market value less than two years prior to being adjudicated bankrupt. The official assignee applied to have the conveyance set aside on the grounds that it had not been entered into *bona fide* and for valuable consideration. Hamilton P stated that the onus was on the official assignee to establish as a matter of probability that the conveyance was made with intent to delay, hinder or defraud creditors of their lawful debts, rights and remedies and that it was possible for the court to infer such intent from the circumstances of the case. In relation to the question of on whom the onus lay to establish that the conveyance was not made in good faith or for valuable consideration, Hamilton P stated that without deciding this question finally, he was prepared to deal with the particular case before him on the basis that the onus was on the official assignee to establish a lack of good faith on the part of the bankrupt's daughter. He concluded that while she must be regarded as a purchaser for valuable consideration, she did not purchase the premises in good faith as she must have been aware of her father's financial position and of the fact that the object of the transaction was to hinder, delay and defraud his creditors.

One further point to note about the judgment of Hamilton P in *Re O'Neill* is that he accepted as applying with equal validity to the Irish legislation the statement of Stirling J in *Mackintosh v. Pogose*[68] to the effect that to come within the saving clause in the section, it is sufficient that the purchaser acts in good faith and it is not necessary that both parties should have so acted.[69]

The other ground on which the application of the section may be avoided is where the settlement is made 'before and in consideration of marriage'. It was confirmed in *Re Campbell*[70] that this wording cannot extend to a post-nuptial settlement not made in pursuance of an ante-nuptial agreement. It has been held in England that for a settlement to be regarded as being in consideration of marriage, it must be made on the occasion of the marriage, must be conditioned only to take effect on the marriage taking place and it must be made by a person for the purpose of or with a view to

---

66. *Re Moore* (1897) 31 ILTR 5.
67. [1989] IR 544, 551.
68. [1895] 1 Ch 505, 509.
69. [1989] IR 544, 551.
70. (1878) 12 ILTR 163.

encouraging or facilitating the marriage.[71] In addition, it was held by the Irish Court of Appeal in *Re Downes*[72] that the exception in relation to settlements made before or in consideration of marriage is not confined to settlements made on the marriage of the settlor and in that case was held to extend to a settlement made on the marriage of the settlor's sister.

While section 59 of the Bankruptcy Act 1988 essentially reproduces the important features of section 52 of the Bankruptcy (Ireland) Amendment Act 1872, there are a number of important changes to note. Section 52 only applied to traders, a distinction which was criticised[73] and not retained in section 59. The ten-year period originally specified was reduced to five years in section 59(1) and the relevant date from which the two and five-year periods specified are to be calculated is now the date of adjudication of bankruptcy, whereas formerly it was reckoned from the date when an act of bankruptcy was committed.[74] In addition, the phrase 'and that the interest of the settlor in such property passed to the trustee of such settlement on the execution thereof' was included so that a settlement to take effect in the future would fall within the section. In addition, section 59(3) renders void as against the official assignee any transfer of property made in pursuance of a contract or covenant for the settlement of property acquired after its execution unless the payment or transfer comes within certain conditions set out in the subsection.[75]

---

71. *Rennell v. IRC* [1964] AC 173, 202 *per* Lord Cohen. See also *Re Densham* [1975] 1 WLR 1519, 1527 *per* Goff J in the context of equivalent English legislation.
72. [1898] 2 IR 635.
73. See Bankruptcy Law Committee Report (1972; Prl. 2714) ch.23.
74. *Re Mackey* [1915] 2 IR 347.
75. This subsection was inserted to meet the criticisms made in the Bankruptcy Law Committee Report (1972; Prl. 2714) chapter 23.10.1 (5).

CHAPTER 12

The Administration of Trusts

THE OFFICE OF TRUSTEE

Introduction

Wylie[1] has commented that 'the position of a trustee is an extremely exacting one and, all too frequently, a thankless one.' This statement is an accurate reflection of the view which might be expressed by many who agree to undertake such a role. Trustees are required to carry out duties and obligations which can often be of considerable complexity and in doing so are expected to display a high degree of honesty and integrity. Referring to the danger that the interests of innocent beneficiaries may be jeopardised by those appointed to safeguard them, Porter MR stated as follows in *Bank of Ireland v. Cogry Flax Spinning Co.*:[2]

> That is why it is so important to select an honourable and upright, as well as an intelligent and capable man for the office of trustee. If the selection is unfortunate, so may be the results.

Trustees are only entitled to payment for such endeavours if the trust instrument itself makes provision for remuneration and they are precluded from making any form of personal profit out of the affairs of the trust or as a result of placing themselves in a position where their own interests and those of the trust might conflict. By undertaking to act in this capacity, in addition to incurring the wrath of the beneficiaries should he fail to exercise his duties in a manner which they might consider appropriate, a trustee may also face the prospect of personal liability to account where he is found to have been in breach of duty.

In view of these considerations, it may reasonably be asked why any right-minded individual would ever agree to act as a trustee, and it is the onerous nature of the responsibilities which go with the office which is primarily responsible for the growth in the numbers of professional trus-

---

1. *Irish Land Law* (3rd ed., 1997) p. 595.
2. [1900] 1 IR 219, 236.

tees. Traditionally, trustees have fallen into two categories: non-professional trustees, who are often family members or close associates of the settlor or testator who agree to act out of a sense of duty and professional trustees, usually banks and financial institutions who undertake the role only in circumstances where suitable provision is made for their remuneration. Arguably it is preferable when creating a trust to ensure that a combination of these categories of trustees are appointed; it is often unwise to nominate only non-professional trustees,[3] for although they may and indeed should seek professional assistance where this is required, they may not always be aware of the circumstances in which this will be necessary.

Any person can be appointed a trustee in this jurisdiction, even a minor,[4] although in practice it is desirable to appoint a person who will be capable of carrying out the functions required of him. A corporation may act as a trustee provided that its memorandum and articles of association confer on it express authority to carry out this role. It is preferable that the trustees appointed reside in the jurisdiction but in special circumstances an exception may have to be made, and the court may even sanction the appointment of persons resident outside the jurisdiction where there is no practical alternative.[5] While a beneficiary or the close relative of a beneficiary[6] may be appointed a trustee, arguably this is undesirable in practice in view of the potential conflict of interest which might result. However, there may be difficulties in finding sufficient suitable persons who do not stand to benefit from the trust to act and it has also been argued that provided a beneficiary does not act as a sole trustee, it may even be preferable to appoint such a person as they will have an added incentive to ensure that the affairs of the trust are effectively and profitably conducted.

There is generally no minimum number of trustees necessary: one trustee will suffice except where statute requires otherwise,[7] although for practical reasons it is more desirable to have two or more. In this jurisdiction there is no upper limit on the number of trustees who may be appointed,[8] but for reasons of administrative workability it is obviously undesirable to

---

3. See e.g. *Turner v. Turner* [1984] Ch 100.
4. Although in England, s.20 of the Law of Property Act 1925 provides that the appointment of a minor to be a trustee of an express trust shall be void.
5. *Crofton v. Crofton* (1913) 47 ILTR 24.
6. *Re Jackson's Trusts* (1874) 8 ILTR 174.
7. Two trustees are required under s.39(1) of the Settled Land Act 1882 in order to give a receipt for capital money on a sale by a tenant for life unless the settlement authorises otherwise.
8. Note that in England, s.34 of the Trustee Act 1925 restricts the number of trustees in trusts of land to four.

have more than a reasonable number to facilitate the process of decision-making and to avoid the machinery of the trust becoming unwieldy.

Appointment of Trustees

The first trustees are ordinarily appointed by the settlor or testator in the trust instrument and where this is a will, the executors and trustees will often be the same persons. Where none are appointed or where those nominated predecease the testator or refuse to act, the court has jurisdiction to appoint trustees.[9] These trustees will hold as joint tenants, so where one or more dies, the survivors continue to act as trustees and on the death of a sole trustee, the trust property will vest in his personal representatives pending the appointment of new trustees.

As regards the appointment of new or additional trustees, this power of appointment may be exercised by persons nominated for that purpose in the trust instrument in the circumstances laid down in that document. Usually, this power will be framed so that it is exercisable whenever the persons nominated deem it necessary but where limitations are imposed these may be strictly construed. In *Re Wheeler*[10] a power to appoint a new trustee in circumstances where an existing trustee was 'incapable' of acting was held not to be exercisable where an incumbent became bankrupt on the grounds that while he might as a result have been deemed 'unfit' to act, this did not mean that he was 'incapable' of performing his duties. In addition to any express power contained in the trust instrument, a statutory power to appoint new trustees is contained in section 10 of the Trustee Act 1893. This statutory power must be exercised in writing and in practice it is desirable that it is exercised by deed to facilitate the application of section 12 of the Act of 1893 which makes provision for the vesting of trust property in new or continuing trustees. Section 10(1) provides that this power can be exercised by 'the person or persons nominated for the purpose of appointing new trustees by the instrument, if any, creating the trust, or if there is no such person or no such person able and willing to act, then the surviving or continuing trustees or trustee for the time being, or the personal representatives of the last surviving or continuing trustee'. This power can be exercised where a trustee:

(i) is dead, or

(ii) remains out of the jurisdiction for more than twelve months, or

---

9.   *Pollock v. Ennis* [1921] 1 IR 181.
10. [1896] 1 Ch 315.

(iii) desires to be discharged from his duties, or

(iv) refuses to act, or

(v) is unfit to act, or incapable of acting.

This power is confined to the appointment of replacements for original or substituted trustees, although where trustee(s) are being replaced the number may be increased. However, it should be noted that it does not confer a power to appoint additional trustees except in these circumstances and in this respect the law differs from that in Northern Ireland and England.[11]

In addition, section 25 of the Trustee Act 1893 confers a power on the court to appoint new or additional trustees whenever it is expedient to do so and would be 'inexpedient, difficult or impracticable so to do without the assistance of the court'. The procedure for bringing an application under section 25 is set out in Keane;[12] it must be brought by special summons grounded on affidavit if it is brought to the High Court,[13] or by petition grounded on affidavit if is made to the Circuit Court.[14]

Retirement of Trustees

A trustee may disclaim his appointment and refuse to take up the office at the outset and if he wishes to do this, to avoid any possible uncertainty he should preferably express his intention by deed.[15] However once a trustee has accepted the office and has failed to disclaim it within a reasonable time, he can only retire in specified circumstances. First, he can retire if there is an express clause in the trust instrument permitting him to do so or if he receives the consent of all the beneficiaries, provided that they are all *sui juris* and between them entitled to the entire beneficial interest in the trust property. In addition, statutory provision is made for retirement by virtue of section 11 of the Trustee Act 1893 which lays down that provided there will be at least two trustees left to administer the trust, a trustee may by deed declare that he wishes to retire and if his co-trustees consent by deed, he will be permitted to do so. Alternatively, an existing trustee may retire as a result of the exercise of the statutory power to appoint new trustees provided in section 10. In addition, a trustee may seek a court

---

11. See s.35 of the Trustee Act (NI) 1958 and s.36(6) of the Trustee Act 1925.
12. *Equity and the Law of Trusts in Ireland* (1988) pp.105-106.
13. Order 3 rule 11 of the Rules of Superior Courts 1986.
14. Order 48 rule 1 of the Rules of the Circuit Court 1950.
15. While disclaimer may be implied, in view of the limited circumstances in which a trustee may retire, it is preferable that an intention to disclaim should be unambiguously expressed.

order under section 25 of the 1893 Act which empowers the court to appoint new trustees for existing ones whenever it is expedient, difficult or impractical to do so without the court's assistance.

Removal of Trustees

A trustee may be removed from his office where express provision is made for this in the trust instrument or by the beneficiaries where they are *sui juris* and between them absolutely entitled to the trust property. In addition, a trustee may be removed where the court exercises the power conferred on it by section 25 of the Trustee Act 1893 to appoint a new trustee where an existing trustee refuses or is unfit to act. The court also has an inherent jurisdiction to remove trustees where they act dishonestly or incompetently or even where their conduct is deliberately obstructive. This point was confirmed by Murnaghan J in *Arnott v. Arnott*.[16] The defendant was removed from the position of trustee to which she had been appointed on the basis that the business, the subject-matter of the trust, was to be managed by the plaintiff in circumstances where her persistent non-cooperation rendered the trust virtually unworkable. Murnaghan J stated that the jurisdiction of the court to remove a trustee should be exercised if the welfare of the beneficiaries demanded it, even though no dishonesty or incompetence had been alleged or proved against the trustee in question. He said that the jurisdiction of the court was usually resorted to when a trustee has mismanaged a trust or has been proved dishonest or incompetent but the guiding principle to which all others must be subordinate was the welfare of the beneficiaries.

A further ground on which a court may exercise its inherent jurisdiction to remove a trustee is where there is a clear conflict of interest between the trustee's duty to the trust and his own personal interests. In *Moore v. McGlynn*[17] the defendant was discharged from further performance of the duties of trustee where he had set up a rival business in competition to that of which he was trustee for the benefit of the family of his deceased brother. Although Chatterton VC held that the new business should not be affected with a trust for the benefit of his brother's estate he was satisfied that it would be improper for the trustee to continue in a position where his personal interests and his duty to the trust might conflict. As he stated: 'his new position disqualifies him from remaining any longer a trustee, and it

---

16. (1924) 58 ILTR 145.
17. [1894] 1 IR 74. See also *Kirby v. Barden* High Court 1995 No. 769 Sp (Carroll J) 12 March 1999.

would have been better for him to have procured his removal from trusteeship before setting up for himself. He should not be continued in a position where his duties and his self-interest may conflict.'[18]

The fact that the primary issue which the court should have regard to in
deciding whether to order the removal of a trustee is the welfare of the
beneficiaries has recently been confirmed by Barron J in *Spencer v.
Kinsella*[19] in a judgment which although ultimately failing to resolve some
of the problems faced by the plaintiffs, did provide useful guidance in
relation to the circumstances in which a trustee may be removed from his
office. Showgrounds in Gorey were vested in trustees on trust so that they
might be used as a sports ground, park or pleasure ground subject to conditions as to payment or otherwise to be prescribed by the trustees. In
recent years the grounds had been used by a local football club and cours-
ing club and the land had also been used for the grazing of sheep. Complaints against the trustees were made by the football club which had spent
money on the repair and maintenance of the grounds, and it was alleged
that they were neglecting their duties and that the grounds were being
allowed to fall into a state of disrepair. The plaintiffs sought the removal
of the trustees on the basis that they had persistently refused to act when
called on to do so and submitted that the welfare of the beneficiaries required this course of action. They were supported in their claims by the
second named defendant but the remaining trustees submitted that they
had at all times acted in a *bona fide* manner and argued that the exercise of
their powers should not be interfered with by the court unless they had
acted *mala fide,* capriciously or outside the terms of the trust. Barron J
accepted that the existing situation could not be allowed to continue and
said that a reorganisation must take place, either with or without the assistance of the court. While he acknowledged that it was difficult to find local
people who had no affiliation with any organisation seeking to use the
grounds, he stated that 'in all cases of trust, it is a truism to say that no
trustee should allow his interest to conflict with his duty'. Barron J referred to the *Arnott* case and said that a trust is set up for the welfare of
beneficiaries and before determining whether or not any trustee should be
removed it is necessary to determine whether his continuation in office
will be detrimental to such welfare. He concluded that the welfare of the
beneficiaries was being affected by the difficulties which had been brought
to the court's attention and said that in view of the existing conflict of
interest some of the trustees who found themselves in such a position of

---

18. *Ibid.* at 90.
19. [1996] 2 ILRM 401.

conflict should step down and allow a general reorganisation to take place. Barron J stated that what was required was the appointment of trustees who were as far as possible impartial as between the various users of the grounds. However, he decided not to exercise the powers of the court at that time and to adjourn the matter for six months to enable the administration of the trust to be placed on a proper footing.[20]

Barron J's judgment is useful in that it confirms that the overriding principle to which the court must have regard in exercising its power to remove trustees is the welfare of the beneficiaries. Clearly the court can act where although there has been no breach of trust or actual misconduct, the conflict of interest existing amongst the trustees is such that the trust can no longer function effectively.[21] From a practical perspective conflict of interest can be as damaging to the welfare of the beneficiaries of a trust as actual misconduct and by placing the interests of the beneficiaries at the forefront of the matters to which the court should have regard, the decision of Barron J should ensure that sufficient attention is given to this point. His pragmatic approach is to be welcomed and it is submitted that while it is important that trustees seek to work together to resolve their differences it is also crucial that the court retains a power to intervene where the welfare of the beneficiaries is not being adequately protected.

THE DUTIES OF TRUSTEES

Duties on Appointment

The first duties of a trustee once appointed are to ascertain the nature and extent of the property comprised in the trust and to ensure that he under-

---

20. Hamilton CJ in the course of a Supreme Court judgment delivered on 13 January 1999 (Supreme Court 1996 No. 357) stated that the matter was re-entered before Barron J on 11 November 1996 and that the order which he made on that date recited that the court was informed that the issues between the parties had been resolved save as to the costs of the proceedings. In its judgment, the Supreme Court allowed an appeal brought by the sixth named defendant, the Minister for Agriculture, Food and Forestry in relation to the order for costs made against him by the trial judge.

21. It is interesting to contrast this approach with that recently adopted by the Supreme Court in *Dunne v. Heffernan* [1997] 3 IR 431 in relation to the removal of an executor pursuant to s.26(2) of the Succession Act 1965. Lynch J stated that an order removing an executor is a very serious step to take and that it is not justified because one of the beneficiaries appears to have felt frustrated and excluded from what he considered to be his legitimate concerns. In the view of Lynch J: 'It would require serious misconduct and/or serious special circumstances on the part of the [executor] to justify such a drastic step' (at p.443). See also *Flood v. Flood* High Court 1998 No. 376 Sp (Macken J) 14 May 1999.

stands the terms of the trust instrument. As Kekewich J stated in *Hallows v. Lloyd*:[22]

> I think that when persons are asked to become new trustees, they are bound to inquire of what the property consists that is proposed to be handed over to them, and what are the trusts. They ought also to look into the trust documents and papers to ascertain what notices appear among them of incumbrances and other matters affecting the trust.

It is essential that a trustee is aware from the outset of the precise nature of the powers conferred on him by the instrument e.g. in relation to investment, and he should seek legal advice if there is any reasonable doubt about the ambit of these powers.[23] A trustee must also ensure that the property which is subject to the trust is under his control and where necessary he must arrange for the property to be conveyed or transferred into the joint names of himself and his co-trustees. He must collect in any assets which are part of the trust and ensure that the trust fund is properly invested. In addition, a trustee should satisfy himself that there is no evidence of a breach of trust committed by a previous trustee which ought to be investigated or rectified. He must make all reasonable inquiries in this regard, and if the circumstances suggest that such a breach has occurred, he should take whatever steps may be necessary to remedy the breach, or he may find himself liable also.

Duty to Safeguard the Trust Assets

It is generally accepted that in relation to the management and administration of a trust, unpaid trustees are expected to use such due diligence and care as an ordinary prudent man would use in the management of his own affairs.[24] This obligation will be examined in more detail in the specific context of a trustee's duty of investment but in this section it is proposed to consider it in more general terms and also to consider the importance of preserving the trust assets, and the circumstances in which a trustee may be indemnified in relation to litigation.

---

22. (1888) 39 Ch D 686, 691.
23. In *Nestle v. National Westminster Bank plc* [1993] 1 WLR 1260, in which the plaintiff bank claimed to have had doubts about the precise scope of its investment powers, Dillon LJ stated (at p. 1265) that 'it was inexcusable that the bank took no step at any time to obtain legal advice as to the scope of its power'.
24. *Speight v. Gaunt* (1883) 9 App Cas 1, 19; *Re Lucking's Will Trusts* [1967] 3 All ER 726, 733.

The trustee's duty to safeguard trust assets has been interpreted as imposing fairly strict standards and would seem to require him to obtain payment of monies owing to the trust as soon as they become due. In *Re Brogden*[25] liability was imposed upon trustees of a marriage settlement who although they had taken reasonable steps to obtain payment of a sum due had stopped short of instituting proceedings because of the effect which they feared this would have on a family partnership. As Lopes LJ stated when a trust is owed money, the trustee is bound to demand payment and if this demand is not met within a reasonable time, he must 'take active measures to enforce its payment, and if necessary, . . . institute legal proceedings'.[26] He continued by saying that he knew of nothing which would excuse not taking action 'unless it be a well founded belief that such action on his part would result in failure and be fruitless, the burden of proving such well-founded belief lying on the trustee setting it up in his own exoneration'.

A trustee is bound to do the best he can from a financial point of view for the beneficiaries and this principle can in certain circumstances, particularly in relation to the sale of trust assets, require him to act in a manner which an ordinary prudent business man would not deem appropriate.[27] So, in *Buttle v. Saunders*[28] Wynn-Parry J stated that trustees 'have an overriding duty to obtain the best price which they can for their beneficiaries'. However, he went on to say that it would be an unfortunate simplification of the problem to state that the mere production of an increased offer at no matter how late a stage in the negotiations would impose an obligation upon a trustee to accept this offer, and stated that 'trustees have such a discretion in the matter as will allow them to act with proper prudence'. Wynn-Parry J therefore accepted that there might be cases where a trustee could properly refuse a higher offer and proceed with the lower one, although he was satisfied that this was not such a case and the tenor of his judgment undoubtedly suggests that it will be difficult for a trustee not to accept the best offer from a financial point of view irrespective of ethical or other considerations.

---

25. (1888) 38 Ch D 546.
26. *Ibid.* at 574. The decision in *Ward v. Ward* (1843) 2 HL Cas 777 would suggest that an exception to this principle exists where the taking of legal proceedings would impose financial hardship on a beneficiary.
27. As Templeman J stated in *Re Wyvern Developments Ltd* [1974] 1 WLR 1097, 1106 in relation to the obligations of a fiduciary, in this case an official receiver: 'He must do his best by his creditors and contributories. He is in a fiduciary capacity and cannot make moral gestures, nor can the court authorise him to do so.'
28. [1950] 2 All ER 193. See Bodkin [1950] Conv 228; Samuels [1975] Conv 177.

If a trustee believes that it is necessary to institute or defend litigation in order to safeguard the trust assets, he would be well advised to seek the approval of the court before determining what course of action to take. On the one hand as Lopes LJ stated in *Re Brogden*[29] where a debt is owed to the trust and has not been paid within a reasonable time the only thing which would excuse a trustee from not taking legal action would be a 'well-founded belief that such action on his part would result in failure and be fruitless'. On the other hand, there is also authority to the effect that a trustee can only be indemnified in relation to expenses properly incurred for the benefit of the trust and as Bowen LJ made in clear in *Re Beddoe*,[30] in this context the word 'properly' means 'reasonably as well as honestly incurred'. Bowen LJ went on to state as follows:

> While I agree that trustees ought not to be visited with personal loss on account of mere errors in judgment which fall short of negligence or unreasonableness, it is on the other hand essential to recollect that mere *bona fides* is not the test, and that it is no answer in the mouth of a trustee who has embarked in idle litigation to say that he honestly believed what his solicitor told him, if his solicitor has been wrong-headed and perverse.[31]

Similarly Lindley LJ stated that if a trustee brings or defends an action unsuccessfully and without the leave of the court, it is for him to show that the costs so incurred were 'properly' incurred and that while the fact that the trustee acted on counsel's opinion is a factor which ought to be in his favour, it will not provide him with indemnity.[32] The importance of acting on the basis of court authorisation if a trustee is to ensure that he will receive an indemnity has recently been reiterated by Lightman J in *Alsop Wilkinson v. Neary*.[33] He stated that a trustee's right to be indemnified extends in the case of a dispute with third parties to the costs of proceedings properly brought or defended for the benefit of the trust estate. However, Lightman J went on to say that '[v]iews may vary whether proceedings are properly brought or defended, and to avoid the risk of a challenge to

---

29. (1888) 38 Ch D 546.
30. [1892] 1 Ch 547. See also *Re England's Settlement Trusts* [1918] 1 Ch 24 where Eve J stated that the trustee's failure to obtain any sanction from the court was 'grievously aggravated by his deplorable conduct' in prosecuting an action in the names of himself and his co-trustee without any authority from the latter. In the circumstances the court held that the trustee was not entitled to his costs out of the trust estate.
31. *Ibid.* at 562.
32. *Ibid.* at 558. See also *Stott v. Milne* (1884) 25 Ch D 710.
33. [1996] 1 WLR 1220.

their entitlement to the indemnity . . . trustees are well advised to seek court authorisation before they sue or defend'. In his view provided trustees make full disclosure as to the strengths and weaknesses of their case, if they act as authorised by the court, their entitlement to an indemnity will be secure.

A further consideration which must be borne in mind where the trust fund is small and likely to be easily dissipated is that litigation is probably better avoided 'unless there is such a chance of success as to render it desirable in the interests of the estate that the necessary risk should be incurred'.[34] So in *Bradstock Trustee Services Ltd v. Nabarro Nathanson*[35] it was held that trustees had not failed in their duty to protect the trust estate when they discontinued litigation in circumstances where the trust fund was likely to have been exhausted in indemnifying them.

Duty to Invest

Trustees are under a duty to invest the trust property with a view to ensuring a steady income for the beneficiaries currently entitled to an interest while at the same time preserving the value of the capital for the benefit of those who may subsequently become entitled to an interest in the property.[36] Some important principles must be noted at the outset. A trustee is only permitted to invest in authorized securities and even where he adheres to this requirement, he must display impartiality and act with ordinary prudence in deciding which investments to make. So the fact that a form of investment is authorized by the trust instrument or by statute will not absolve a trustee from liability if he does not exercise the requisite degree of care in deciding which investments to make.

The question of whether an investment is authorized is governed in the first instance by the terms of the trust instrument, which will usually include an investment clause detailing the trustees' powers in this regard. Where a clause in the trust instrument expressly delimits the ambit of a trustee's power of investment, its provisions must be adhered to and investment in unauthorised securities will amount to a breach of trust.[37] However, in certain circumstances the court may sanction the overriding of express directions as to powers of investment where these are found to be in conflict with a settlor or testator's implied intentions. So, in *Re Lynch's*

---

34. *Per* Bowen LJ in *Re Beddoe* [1892] 1 Ch 547, 562.
35. [1995] 1 WLR 1405.
36. See *Stacey v. Branch* [1995] 2 ILRM 136, 142 *per* Murphy J.
37. *Rochfort v. Seaton* [1896] 1 IR 18; *Re Webber's Settlement Trusts* [1922] 1 IR 49.

Trusts[38] it was held by Johnston J that the court had jurisdiction to disregard a direction in a trust as to the lodgment of monies on deposit receipt and to direct these funds to be invested instead in suitable trustee securities. This finding was made as the predominant motive of the testator, as expressed in his will, was to make provision for the support and maintenance of his family and he concluded that the direction that the funds should remain on deposit receipt was subsidiary to this overall objective.

In the absence of an express investment clause, or subject to its terms, a trustee may invest the trust property in accordance with the statutory scheme laid down in Part I of the Trustee Act 1893 as amended by the Trustee (Authorized Investments) Act 1958. Section 3 of the Act of 1893 provides that this statutory power of investment is to be exercised according to the discretion of the trustees. Section 1 of the Act of 1958 as amended specifies what are authorised investments and section 2 of the 1958 Act empowers the Minister for Finance to vary this list. Until recently, the ambit of investments authorised by statute remained limited and was generally confined to investments such as Irish and British government securities, real securities, stock in semi-state bodies, debentures or debenture stock, in publicly quoted industrial and commercial companies registered in Ireland which met certain requirements, and in deposit accounts in specified financial institutions. More recently, the scope of authorised investments has been extended by statutory instrument and SI No. 28 of 1998 varies the list of investments set out in section 1 of the Act of 1958 by deleting those specified in the section and substituting those set out in the First Schedule to the order. These investments now include units or shares in certain unit trust or collective investment schemes, specified annuity and life assurance contracts and the equity of companies listed on the Irish Stock Exchange and other recognised exchanges which meet certain financial requirements. One interesting innovation is clause 4 of the Second Schedule of the order which provides that where any part of the trust fund is invested in equities, the trustee shall review those investments at intervals of not more than six months.[39]

It is now quite common to authorize trustees to invest in such a manner as they think fit and in *Re Harari's Settlement Trusts*[40] a clause in a trust which gave trustees power to invest 'in or upon such investments as to them may seem fit' was held by Jenkins J to mean that the trustees should be empowered to invest in any investments which they honestly thought

---

38. [1931] IR 517.
39. See SI No. 327 of 1990, SI No. 75 of 1992 and SI No. 28 of 1998.
40. [1949] 1 All ER 430.

were desirable. Jenkins J said that to hold otherwise would be to read words into the settlement which were not there and stated that he saw no reason to impose any restriction on the plain and ordinary meaning of the words employed.

A power to invest in 'real securities' covers investment in mortgages of land,[41] but not in its purchase.[42] It should be noted that such a power does not authorise trustees to lend trust funds on the security of a judgment mortgage.[43] In addition, in relation to the investment in mortgages of land, Smith MR stressed in *Smithwick v. Smithwick*[44] that 'it may be that a trustee lending on a second mortgage should exercise greater caution than if there was no prior encumbrance. . . .' A degree of statutory protection is afforded to trustees who lend funds on the security of any property by section 8 of the Trustee Act 1893 which provides that no liability shall arise 'by reason only of the proportion borne by the amount of the loan to the value of the property at the time when the loan was made' provided that certain conditions laid down in the section are met.

It is important to stress that even where a trustee does not stray outside the ambit of investments authorised either by the terms of the trust or by statute, he must nevertheless observe certain standards in carrying out his duties in this regard. As O'Connor MR pointed out in *Re O'Connor*:[45] 'however unlimited the power of investment may be, the trustee remains subject to the jurisdiction of the court. The trustee has no power to act dishonestly, negligently or in breach of trust to invest on insufficient security'. O'Connor MR continued by saying that subject to the power of the court to compel a dishonest or grossly incompetent trustee to account, it is in the power of the settlor or testator to place funds in the hands of the trustee to be invested in the fullest sense of the word and it was held in the instant case that a clause which permitted the trustees to invest in property 'as they think most desirable, but not in British funds' authorized them to invest in freehold land in Ireland and England.

The standard of care and prudence which must be employed by a trustee in exercising his powers of investment has been considered by the courts on numerous occasions, although it has not always been expressed in a consistent manner. In *Learoyd v. Whiteley*[46] Lindley LJ stated in the

---

41. This extends to mortgages of certain leasehold land, see s.5(1) of the Trustee Act 1893.
42. *Robinson v. Robinson* (1877) IR 10 Eq 189.
43. *Johnston v. Lloyd* (1844) 7 Ir Eq R 252.
44. (1861) 12 Ir Ch R 181, 196.
45. [1913] 1 IR 69, 75-76.
46. (1886) 33 Ch D 347, 355.

Court of Appeal that a trustee would have to take not only such care as a prudent man would take if he had only himself to consider but the care that an ordinary prudent man would take if he were making investments for the benefit of those for whom he felt morally bound to provide.[47] When the matter reached the House of Lords, Lord Watson spoke along the same lines and stated that 'business men of ordinary prudence may, and frequently do, select investments which are more or less of a speculative character; but it is the duty of a trustee to confine himself to the class of investments which are permitted by the trust, and likewise to avoid all investments of that class which are attended with hazard'.[48]

These statements would suggest that the degree of care which a trustee might exercise in relation to the investment of his own money may be insufficient; a greater duty of care is required. However, despite the fact that these principles were apparently quoted with approval by Brightman J in *Bartlett v. Barclays Bank Trust Co. Ltd,*[49] a more flexible approach seems to have been approved in that case, at any rate as regards non-professional trustees. The defendant bank was trustee of a trust, the only assets of which were nearly all the shares in a family property company. It was thought that funds might be more readily raised to pay taxes due on the death of the life tenants if the company went public and that a public issue would be more successful if the company was also involved in property development. One speculative purchase resulted in large losses to the trust fund, and the plaintiff beneficiaries succeeded in their claim against the bank for breach of trust. Brightman J stated as follows:

> The cases establish that it is the duty of a trustee to conduct the business of the trust with the same care as an ordinary prudent man of business would extend towards his own affairs. . . . That does not mean that the trustee is bound to avoid all risk and in effect act as an insurer of the trust fund. . . . The distinction is between a prudent degree of risk on the one hand, and hazard on the other. Nor must the

---

47.   In interpreting this obligation, Thomas J has recently commented in a decision of the New Zealand High Court in *Jones v. AMP Perpetual Trustee Co. NZ Ltd* [1994] 1 NZLR 690, 706 that: 'This duty includes the duty to seek advice on matters which the trustee may not understand, such as the making of investments, and in receiving that advice to act with the same degree of prudence. It is not enough to act in good faith and with sincerity. Consequently, although a trustee may take advice on investments, he or she is not bound to accept and act on that advice. They must, in addition to being honest and sincere in relation to the advice which is received, continue to act as an ordinary prudent person would act.'
48.   (1887) 12 App Cas 727, 733.
49.   [1980] Ch 515.

court be astute to fix liability upon a trustee who has committed no more than an error of judgment, from which no business man, however prudent can expect to be immune.[50]

A further important principle which was confirmed by Brightman J was that in his opinion a higher duty of care is expected of a professional trustee, such as a trust corporation which carries on the specialized business of trust management. This point had been made *obiter* by Harman J in *Re Waterman's Will Trusts*,[51] where he stated that a paid trustee is expected to exercise a higher standard of diligence and knowledge than an unpaid trustee. Brightman J concluded that a professional corporate trustee is liable for breach of trust if loss is caused to the trust fund because it neglects to exercise the special care and skill which it professes to have. He held that the bank had wrongfully and in breach of trust neglected to ensure that it received an adequate flow of information concerning the activities of the boards of the companies concerned and that it had failed in its duty whether it is judged by the standard of the prudent man of business or of the skilled trust corporation.[52]

The application of the standard of 'an ordinary prudent man of business' had more disturbing consequences from the point of view of the beneficiary in *Nestle v. National Westminster Bank plc.*[53] By virtue of the terms of a settlement made in 1922 the defendant bank, the successor to the original trustee, was given wide powers to invest in equities. However, the bank never obtained legal advice about the scope of its powers of investment and assumed that these were narrower than they in fact were. The plaintiff, the remainder beneficiary, contended that the trust fund which was worth approximately £269,000 when she became absolutely entitled in 1986 should have been worth well over £1 million by then if the fund had been properly invested. Hoffman J rejected the plaintiff's claim and concluded that the bank had acted conscientiously, fairly and carefully throughout its administration of the trust. The Court of Appeal dismissed the plaintiff's appeal and concluded that the plaintiff had not succeeded in establishing that she had suffered loss. Legatt LJ stated that it had not been established that a prudent trustee, knowing the true scope of the power of investment and having conducted regular reviews, which the bank had not done, would have invested the fund in such a manner that it would have

50. *Ibid.* at 531.
51. [1952] 2 All ER 1054, 1055.
52. [1980] Ch 515, 535.
53. [1993] 1 WLR 1260.

been worth more than it was when the plaintiff became entitled to it.[54] The Court of Appeal applied the traditional test; as Legatt LJ stated: 'the essence of the bank's duty was to take such steps as a prudent businessman would have taken to maintain and increase the value of the trust fund. Unless it failed to do so, it was not in breach of trust.'[55]

Although the Court of Appeal did not find the bank liable, the judges did not agree with the trial judge's conclusion that the bank had acted conscientiously and as Legatt LJ commented: 'No testator, in the light of this example, would choose this bank for the effective management of his investment.'[56] Kenny[57] has rightly commented that it is a sad reflection on the present state of trust law that a bank which 'no testator ... would choose ... for the effective management of his investment' should be found not to be liable for mismanagement of the trust. The law in this area in England at any rate would seem to unduly favour the position of the trustee.[58] As Doyle[59] has commented there is no reported case in which a trustee has been found liable for a breach of trust arising from investment within the ambit of that authorized by the trust instrument or the general law where the trust capital has simply continued to erode as a result and he concludes that 'the burden of proof facing potentially litigious beneficiaries is prohibitively high.' Certainly in the case of professional trustees, the reasoning which surfaced in *Bartlett* of applying a stricter standard might be developed further to avoid a result such as that arrived at in *Nestle*.

The extent of the duty imposed on a trustee in relation to investment of trust property has recently been considered in this jurisdiction by Murphy J in *Stacey v. Branch*.[60] The plaintiff beneficiary brought a claim against the defendant trustee alleging a breach of trust on the grounds that the latter had not managed a trust property with the necessary degree of care and claimed specifically that if this house had been let over a period of 14

---

54. Similarly Staughton LJ stated that it must be shown that the bank's failure to appreciate the scope of its powers or to conduct periodic reviews led it to make decisions which it should not have made or to fail to make decisions which it should have made, and that loss thereby resulted.
55. *Ibid.* at 1283.
56. *Ibid.* at 1284. See Martin (1992) 142 NLJ 1279.
57. [1993] Conv 63, 67.
58. Watt and Stauch have commented [1998] Conv 352, 361 that the reasoning of the Court of Appeal in *Nestle* showed an 'erroneous conflation of the quite distinct processes of determining breach of trust and determining the lass caused by that breach'. In their view, the effect of this has been 'to leave the English courts unduly reluctant to review the exercise of investment discretions, no matter how imprudently discharged'.
59. (1991) 5 Trust Law Int 138, 142.
60. [1995] 2 ILRM 136. See Buttimore (1996) 14 ILT (ns) 48.

years rather than maintained by a caretaker, it would have yielded a substantial rental income. The trust deed conferred on the defendant the power to deal with this property 'as he in his absolute discretion shall think fit' pending the attainment of 21 years by the plaintiff. Murphy J made it clear that words such as 'absolute discretion' would not necessarily relieve a trustee from his duty to exercise reasonable care and prudence. However, he was satisfied that the defendant's decision to place the caretaker in occupation of the premises was one made *bona fide* in the exercise of his discretion and he dismissed the plaintiff's claim. Murphy J also gave some consideration to the nature of a trustee's duty of investment in general terms and it is worth setting this *dicta* out in full.

> What is the nature of the duty imposed on a trustee? A trustee must, of course, invest trust funds in the securities authorised by the settlement or by statute. To invest in any other securities would be of itself a breach of trust; but, even with regard to those securities which are permissible, the trustee must take such care as a reasonably cautious man would take having regard not only to the interest of those who are entitled to the income but to the interest of those who will take in the future. In exercising his discretion a trustee must act honestly and must use as much diligence as a prudent man of business would exercise in dealing with his own private affairs; in selecting an investment he must take as much care as a prudent man would take in making an investment for the benefit of persons for whom he felt morally bound to provide. Businessmen of ordinary prudence may, and frequently do, select investments which are more or less of a speculative character; but it is the duty of a trustee to confine himself not only to the class of investments which are permitted by the settlement or by statute, but to avoid all such investments of that class as are attended with hazard.[61]

This statement which requires a trustee in selecting investments to exercise the care which a prudent man would take in making an investment for the benefit of persons for whom he felt morally obliged to provide imposes a relatively stringent standard on trustees. However, it can also be said that the degree of care which a prudent man would exercise in these circumstances has altered over the years;[62] as Panckhurst J has recently

---

61. *Ibid.* at 142.
62. There is certainly some evidence of a more pragmatic approach to the question of the degree of risk which a trustee may take in making investment decisions elsewhere in the common law world. As Thomas J stated in *Jones v. AMP Perpetual Trustee Com-*

commented in the New Zealand decision of *Re Mulligan*[63] 'prudence provides a flexible standard, one which will change with economic conditions and in the light of contemporary thinking and understanding'. Dillon LJ made a similar comment in the course of his judgment in *Nestle v. National Westminster Bank plc*[64] to the effect that '[t]rustees should not be reckless with trust money but what a prudent man should do at any time depends on the economic and financial conditions at that time — not on what judges of the past, however eminent, held to be prudent in the conditions of 50 or 100 years before'.[65] Therefore there is probably merit in Curran's[66] suggestion that 'it could certainly be argued that some speculative investment e.g. hedging and support of an overall portfolio policy would be perfectly acceptable today'.

Finally, it should be stressed that where the default on the part of the trustees, as in *Nestle* and *Stacey*, is due to lack of initiative rather than to speculative investment decisions, it would still seem to be extremely difficult for a beneficiary to succeed in establishing a breach of trust on the part of the trustee.

Another question which arises in relation to investment is the extent to which trustees are entitled to take into account non-financial considerations in making investment decisions. In *Cowan v. Scargill*[67] it was made clear that trustees should not be influenced in their choice of investment by such considerations. A mineworker's pension fund was managed by ten trustees, five of whom were members of the National Union of Mineworkers. These five trustees refused to agree to a revised investment plan put forward on the basis, *inter alia*, that it contemplated increased overseas investment and investment in forms of energy such as oil and gas which were in competition with coal. It was held by Megarry VC that these trustees were in breach of duty in refusing to concur in the adoption of this investment plan. Megarry VC stated:

> Trustees may have strongly held social or political views. They may
> be firmly opposed to any investment in South Africa or other coun-

---

pany *NZ Ltd* [1994] 1 NZLR 690, 707: 'Neither prophecy or prescience is expected of trustees and their performance must be judged, not by hindsight, but by facts which existed at the time of the occurrence'. Similarly in *Re Mulligan* [1998] 1 NZLR 481, 501 Panckhurst J stated that 'a trustee is neither a surety, nor an insurer of the fund for which he is responsible'.

63. [1998] 1 NZLR 481, 500.
64. [1993] 1 WLR 1260.
65. *Ibid.* at 1268.
66. (1996) 90 GILSI 340.
67. [1985] Ch 270.

tries, or they may be opposed to any form of investment in companies concerned with alcohol, tobacco and armaments or many other things. In the conduct of their own affairs, of course, they are free to abstain from making any such investments. Yet under a trust, if investments of this type would be more beneficial to the beneficiaries than other investments, the trustees must not refrain from making the investments by reason of the views that they hold.[68]

It should be noted that Megarry VC seemed to accept that trustees might pursue an ethical investment policy provided that the financial implications of doing so were equally beneficial from the point of view of the beneficiaries.[69] Lord Nicholls, writing extra-judicially, has also accepted this point in the following terms:

> The range of sound investments available to trustees is so extensive that very frequently there is scope for trustees to give effect to moral considerations, either by positively preferring certain investments or negatively avoiding others, without thereby prejudicing beneficiaries' financial interests.[70]

The question of the extent to which trustees may pursue an ethical investment policy is clearly even more relevant in relation to charitable trusts and this issue has recently been considered by Nicholls VC in *Harries v. Church Commissioners*.[71] The plaintiffs sought declarations that the commissioners were obliged to have regard to the object of promoting the Christian faith and not to act in a manner which would be incompatible with that object when managing the assets of which they were trustees. The plaintiffs contended that the commissioners in making investment decisions attached overriding importance to financial considerations and that they were only prepared to take non-financial considerations into account to the extent that they did not significantly jeopardise or interfere with accepted investment principles. It was held by Nicholls VC in refusing the declarations sought that it was axiomatic that charity trustees were

---

68. *Ibid.* at 287-288.
69. Megarry VC also pointed out that he was not suggesting that the benefit of the beneficiaries meant solely their financial benefit and said that if they hold strong views on certain moral and ethical issues, it might not be for their benefit to know that they were obtaining financial returns from sources which they would not consider morally acceptable. However, Megarry VC stressed that in his view cases in which such considerations might arise would be 'very rare'.
70. (1995) 9 Trust Law Int 71, 75.
71. [1992] 1 WLR 1241. See Buttimore (1995) 13 ILT (ns) 141.

concerned to further the purposes of the trust of which they had accepted the office of trustee. When property was held by trustees for the purpose of generating money, *prima facie* the purposes of the trust were best served by the trustees seeking to obtain the best return which was consistent with commercial prudence and in most cases the best interests of the charity required that the trustee's choice of investments be made solely on the basis of well-established investment criteria. The circumstances in which charity trustees were bound or entitled to make a financially disadvantageous investment decision for ethical considerations were extremely limited and there was no evidence that such circumstances existed in the case before the court. Nicholls VC stated as follows:

> The law is not so cynical as to require trustees to behave in a fashion which would bring them or their charity into disrepute. ... On the other hand, trustees must act prudently. They must not use property held by them for investment purposes as a means for making moral statements at the expense of the charity of which they are trustees.[72]

The approach adopted in *Cowan* can be justified on the basis that if the criteria of the most sound decision from a financial point of view is qualified in any way, the court will lose the means of judging investment decisions on the basis of an objective standard and will instead move into the realm of a purely subjective one. However the judgment of Nicholls VC in *Harries* has been criticised by Nobles,[73] who argues that the investment policy of charitable trusts, like the manner in which they distribute funds, should be governed by the charitable purposes which they purport to further. He argues that: 'If trustees cannot make, or cannot be allowed to make, controversial moral judgments on the extent to which their investments give effect to their charity's purposes then they should not be able to make the same judgments when giving away its property. Conversely, if they can be trusted to make these judgments when giving away the charity's property, they can be trusted to make its investments on the same basis.'[74] There is an undeniable logic to this argument, but in practice it may prove far from easy to implement and oversee such an approach.

Duty to Maintain Equality Between Beneficiaries

A trustee is obliged to balance what may often be the competing interests

---

72. *Ibid.* at 1247.
73. [1992] Conv 115.
74. *Ibid.* at 118.

of a life tenant and remainderman in relation to the trust property. As Panckhurst J stated in the decision of the New Zealand High Court in *Re Mulligan*:[75] 'It is elementary that a trustee must act with strict impartiality and endeavour to maintain a balance between the interests of life tenant and remaindermen. Put another way, a trustee must be even-handed as between income and capital beneficiaries.' Hoffmann J also acknowledged the importance of ensuring that a trustee acts in a fair manner in making investment decisions which may have different consequences for different classes of beneficiaries in the course of his judgment at first instance in *Nestle v. National Westminster Bank plc.*[76] However, he stressed that trustees must have a wide discretion in this regard and stated that he preferred the formulation that a trustee must act fairly rather than one which required strict equality between tenant for life and remainderman. As he stated: 'It would be an inhuman law which required trustees to adhere to some mechanical rule for preserving the real value of capital when the tenant for life was the testator's widow who had fallen upon hard times and the remainderman was young and well off'.[77]

It should be noted that in seeking to ensure that a fair result is achieved, a trustee may be obliged to convert certain types of trust investment into an alternative form and this in turn may necessitate apportionment of the beneficiaries' interests.

Duty to Convert Trust Property

This duty arises specifically in two situations, first where there is an express trust for sale an obligation is imposed on a trustee to sell the property as soon as practicable. It should be noted that a mere power to sell the trust property is not sufficient to give rise to such an obligation to convert.[78] In addition, a duty to convert may arise under what is known as the rule in *Howe v. Earl of Dartmouth*,[79] which effectively provides that where residuary personalty is settled by will in favour of persons who are to enjoy it in succession, subject to a contrary provision in the will, all assets of a wasting, future or reversionary nature or which consist of unauthorized securities should be converted into property of a permanent or income bearing character.[80]

---

75. [1998] 1 NZLR 481, 501.
76. Chancery Division, 29 June 1988.
77. At p.5 of the unreported judgment.
78. *Re Pitcairn* [1896] 2 Ch 199.
79. (1802) 7 Ves 137.
80. See *Hinves v. Hinves* (1844) 3 Hare 609, 611.

The effect of the rule was summarised by Walker LC in *Re Harris*[81] as follows:

> The general rule is, that where there is a general residuary bequest of personal estate, including chattels real, to be enjoyed by persons in succession, the Court puts upon the bequest the interpretation that the persons indicated are to enjoy the same thing in succession, and converts the property as the only means of giving effect to that intention.

The rule only applies to a residuary bequest in a will, not to a specific bequest nor where there is an *inter vivos* settlement on the basis that the settlor was assumed to have had an accurate idea of the state of the assets when he created the trust.[82] In addition, the application of the rule will be excluded where the will provides otherwise or where it was clearly the testator's intention that the property should be enjoyed *in specie*. The latter finding was made by Meredith J in *Re Abbott*[83] where he held that the testator had contemplated the trustees retaining the bulk of the property and must be presumed to have intended the tenants for life to enjoy it in the form in which it was left. In the circumstances, Meredith J was satisfied that the rule in *Howe v. Earl of Dartmouth* was excluded by virtue of the language employed by the testator himself. This can be compared with the decision in *Re Harris*,[84] where the Irish Court of Appeal found insufficient evidence of intention on the part of the testatrix that the property should be enjoyed *in specie*. Walker LC stated that the rule must be applied unless, 'upon the fair construction of the will, you find a sufficient indication of intention that it is not to be applied'[85] and he held that the burden should be on the person seeking to exclude its application.

The purpose of the rule was in theory to benefit the remainderman and prevent the tenant for life from enjoying the benefit of unauthorized or wasting securities to the detriment of the former. However, today investment in certain unauthorized securities such as 'equities' will be more likely to benefit the remainderman due to the likelihood of high capital appreciation and ironically he may often be worse off where the rule is applied. The apportionment rules were considered by the Law Commis-

---

81. [1907] 1 IR 32, 35.
82. *Re Van Straubenzee* [1901] 2 Ch 779.
83. [1934] IR 189. See also *Alcock v. Soper* (1833) 2 My & K 699; *Re Sewell's Estate* (1870) LR 11 Eq 80 and *Re Fisher* [1943] Ch 377.
84. [1907] 1 IR 32. See also *Re Berry* [1962] Ch 97.
85. *Ibid.* at 35.

sion in England in a report published in 1982[86] and it was acknowledged that in practice the rules of apportionment are almost always excluded in well-drafted settlements. It is worth quoting some of the comments contained in the report in relation to the existing rules which are just as relevant to the position in this jurisdiction.

> It is quite clear that in present day investment conditions the rules both of conversion and apportionment pending conversion have little if any relevance. When they do apply they require, in effect, the sale of equities, other than those authorised by the Trustee Investment Act 1961, and re-investment in gilt-edged securities. At a time when investment in equities may be the only way in which the capital value of the fund can in fact be maintained the traditional theory that re-investment is necessary to protect those interested in the capital no longer holds good. Conversely, the yield on fixed interest investments is now such as to provide the tenant for life with an income which is as high as and may be higher than the average yield on unauthorised equities.[87]

Duty to Apportion

Where Duty to Convert Arises
Where a duty to convert arises in either of the above situations, in the absence of any indication that the tenant for life is to enjoy the income until the conversion is effected, a duty also arises to apportion the original property between the tenant for life and the remainderman pending conversion. Where the assets are of a wasting, hazardous or otherwise unauthorised nature, this is presumed to benefit the tenant for life at the expense of the remainderman as this property may produce a high level of income to the detriment of its capital value. In making any apportionment, the trustee should ensure that the beneficiary currently in possession only receives income equivalent to the current yield on authorised investments and that any additional monies should be added to the trust capital.

In assessing when the capital should be valued for the purpose of calculating this yield, a distinction must be drawn between situations where there is a power to postpone conversion and cases where there is no such power. In the former case, the date of valuation is considered to be the date of the testator's death and in the latter case, if no sale is effected in the meantime a date one year after his death is employed.[88] This principle is

---

86. The Powers and Duties of Trustees (23rd Report) Cmnd 8733.
87. *Ibid.* paragraph 3.31.
88. This distinction is illustrated in *Brown v. Gellatly* (1867) LR 2 Ch App 751.

adopted on the basis that the testator's personal representatives are deemed to have an 'executor's year' in which to effect the administration of the estate. Whichever date is deemed to be the valuation date, the tenant for life is entitled to interest on the value of the assets at that date from the date of death until the date of the actual conversion.

The opposite problem to that referred to above in relation to wasting or hazardous securities arises in the context of future, reversionary or other non-income bearing assets. In the latter case, the life tenant will obtain no benefit from these types of security until the interest falls into possession and it may be necessary to sell such property and re-invest it in securities which will ensure a more equitable division as between the life tenant and the remainderman. The question of determining the manner of such apportionment is calculated in accordance with the rule in *Re Earl of Chesterfield's Trusts*.[89] The effect of this rule is well summarised by Wylie.[90]

The trustees should calculate what sums invested at 4% interest at the date of the testator's death, accumulating at compound interest at that rate with yearly rests, would, after deduction of income tax at the standard or basic rate, produce the actual sum raised by sale of the future or reversionary interest. The sum so calculated should be treated as the capital and the difference between it and the sum received from the sale of future or reversionary interest should be paid to the tenant for life as income.

Keane[91] has suggested that there is no reason why the rate payable on judgment debts, currently fixed at 8%,[92] should not apply in this jurisdiction in relation to the application of this principle. It should also be noted that this rule will not apply where the settlor or testator manifests a contrary intention.

Duty to Apportion in Other Circumstances
A duty to apportion may arise in other circumstances, some of which will now be considered.

(a) *Under the Rule in Allhusen v. Whittel*[93]
The purpose of this rule is to achieve equity between the tenant for life and remainderman in relation to the payment of debts and other duties due out of an estate. Often debts will not be paid for a considerable period after the

---

89. (1883) 24 Ch D 643.
90. *Irish Land Law* (3rd ed., 1997) pp. 638-639.
91. *Equity and the Law of Trusts in the Republic of Ireland* (1988) p.114.
92. Reduced from 11% by the Courts Act 1981 (Interest on Judgment Debts) Order 1989 (SI No.12 of 1989).
93. (1867) LR 4 Eq 295.

death of a testator and in the meantime the tenant for life will continue to enjoy the income from the estate, including that portion which is owed to creditors. The effect of the rule is to charge the tenant for life with interest on the monies subsequently used to meet whatever debts may be payable out of the estate and so put him in the same position as if these debts had actually been paid at the time of the testator's death. The manner in which this apportionment is achieved is set out in *The Modern Law of Trusts* as follows:[94] 'the rule requires a calculation of the average income of the estate from the date of death to the date of payment, taken net after the deduction of income tax at the basic rate.' It is important to note that the application of this rule may be excluded where the contrary intention is expressed by the testator.[95]

(b) *Under the Rule in Re Atkinson*[96]

This rule governs the manner in which an apportionment is made where an authorised mortgage security is sold and the proceeds received are insufficient to satisfy the amounts of the outstanding principal and interest in full. By virtue of the rule, these proceeds are apportioned between the tenant for life and the remainderman in the proportion which the amount due for arrears bears to the amount due in respect of the principal.[97] The circumstances in which the rule applies are still uncertain. It has been held that it applies to monies due under a holding of debenture stock,[98] but not to arrears of dividends on preference shares.[99]

(c) *Where Repairs or Improvements are Carried Out*

Where repairs are effected to trust property which are necessitated by ordinary wear and tear and which can be considered merely as maintenance, the cost of such work should come out of the income of the trust and must be borne by the tenant for life.[100] However, where work can be regarded as effecting a permanent improvement to property it is considered that the cost should be deducted from the trust capital,[101] and therefore this will have a greater effect on the interest of the remainderman.

---

94. Parker and Mellows (7th ed., 1995, Oakley) at p. 583. See also *Corbett v. Commissioners of Inland Revenue* [1938] 1 KB 567, 584-585 *per* Romer LJ.
95. *Re McEuen* [1913] 2 Ch 704.
96. [1904] 2 Ch 160.
97. See also *Stewart v. Kingsale* [1902] 1 IR 496.
98. *Re Walker's Settlement Trusts* [1936] Ch 280.
99. *Re Sale* [1913] 2 Ch 697.
100. *Re Kingham* [1897] 1 IR 170; *Re Waldron and Bogue's Contract* [1904] 1 IR 240.
101. *Brereton v. Day* [1895] 1 IR 518.

(d) *Purchase or Sale of Shares Cum Dividend*

As a general rule, there will be no apportionment in relation to shares purchased or sold just before or after the payment of a dividend and the entire amount received is deemed to be capital. This may prove to be unjust, e.g. where shares are sold just before the dividend is declared the price reflects the amount which will be paid although if they had been retained until the payment was actually made the amount of the dividend would have been treated as income. This principle of non-apportionment may therefore be inequitable and it has been held that where it gives rise to a 'glaring injustice'[102] it may not be applied.

(e) *Distribution of Accumulated Profits in the Form of Bonus Shares*

It was decided by the House of Lords in *Bouch v. Sproule*[103] that such shares should be treated as capital except where a company has no power under its articles of association to create new shares in this manner, in which case they will be treated as income.

(f) *Distribution of Capital Profit*

Where a company makes a capital profit and distributes it in the form of a cash bonus or capital dividend, it is regarded as a distribution of income to which the tenant for life is entitled.[104] So, in *Re Meagher*,[105] where a company decided to allot stock to its shareholders in the form of a 'special capital profits dividend', it was held by Kingsmill Moore J that it should be treated as income and paid to the tenant for life.

Duty to Distribute

A trustee is under an obligation to ascertain the identity of those who are entitled under the trust instrument and to take the necessary steps to ensure that the trust property is distributed in accordance with its terms. In England, section 27 of the Trustee Act 1925 as amended provides that trustees may advertise for potential beneficiaries and provided that certain requirements specified in the section are complied with, they may proceed to distribute the trust property amongst the beneficiaries whose identity is known to them. There is no equivalent statutory power in this jurisdiction, although section 49(2) of the Succession Act 1965 lays down a procedure

---

102. *Re MacLaren's Settlement Trusts* [1951] 2 All ER 414, 420.
103. (1887) 12 App Cas 385. See also *Re Carson* [1915] 1 IR 321; *Hill v. Permanent Trustee Co. of New South Wales* [1930] AC 720, 730-732.
104. *Re Sechiari* [1950] 1 All ER 417; *Re Kleinwort's Settlements* [1951] Ch 860.
105. [1951] IR 100.

whereby personal representatives of a deceased person may advertise for claimants and may distribute the estate amongst those who have lodged claims within the period specified. While trustees have no statutory power to assist them in carrying out this task, it would seem to be good practice for them to follow a similar course where doubts arise as to the identity of those entitled under the terms of a trust.

A beneficiary who is underpaid or who receives no payment at all has a right of action against the trustees for breach of trust, although the trustee in turn will have a right of recovery against any person who has been overpaid or paid in error. There is authority in England to support the proposition that where a trustee who is also a beneficiary underpays himself, he has no remedy but this has been criticised and it is unlikely that such a harsh principle would be followed in this jurisdiction.

Where a reasonable doubt exists about the respective claims of the beneficiaries a trustee may apply to the court for directions and will be protected from liability in this regard provided he follows these directions.[106] Such an application may be brought before the High Court by special summons grounded on affidavit and it is prudent for a trustee to take such a course of action where legitimate doubt exists about the manner in which the trust assets should be distributed.

In circumstances where the whereabouts or continued existence of a beneficiary is unknown, the court may authorise distribution of the trust property to proceed after a specified period of time. Such an order is known as a 'Benjamin order' and may be made after a period of seven years on the authority of the decision of Joyce J in *Re Benjamin*.[107] The testator's son disappeared in 1892 and under the will of his father, who died the following year, he was entitled to a share in the latter's estate if he survived the testator. Joyce J concluded that the son must be presumed dead and the court gave the trustees liberty to distribute his share on the basis that he had predeceased the testator.

The principles laid down in *Re Benjamin* were applied in *Re Green's Will Trusts*.[108] The testatrix's son went missing in 1943 while on a wartime bombing raid and was certified by the Air Ministry as presumed dead. She bequeathed the residue of her estate to trustees for her son's benefit and directed that if he had not come forward to claim the property by the year 2020 the trustees were to establish a charitable foundation for the benefit of cruelly treated animals. The court gave the executors liberty to deal

---

106. *Re Londonderry's Settlements* [1965] Ch 918.
107. [1902] 1 Ch 723.
108. [1985] 3 All ER 455.

with the estate on the basis that the son had predeceased the testatrix and made a Benjamin order, the effect of which was to enable the charity to enjoy the testatrix's estate as from the date of her death. This decision has been criticised by Luxton[109] on the grounds that such an order was contrary to the intention of the testatrix. However, from the point of view of the trustees, bringing an application to court is undoubtedly the most prudent course of action in such cases and while the order made may not always accurately reflect the wishes of a testator, it will at least have the advantage of absolving them from any personal liability.

Duty to Keep Accounts and Provide Information

A trustee is obliged to keep clear and accurate accounts of the trust property and a beneficiary is entitled to inspect these accounts although in theory if he wants a copy of them he must pay for them. This obligation to keep accounts arises independently of any question that a breach of duty may have occurred as was made clear by Chatterton VC in *Moore v. McGlynn*,[110] where he pointed out that the obligation arises merely by virtue of the relationship of trustee and beneficiary. It is not strictly necessary for a trustee to have these accounts audited although it may be prudent where the complexity of the trust demands it and it would usually be wise for a trustee to obtain professional assistance in this area where he does not possess the relevant expertise himself.

It has also been established that a beneficiary is entitled to inspect documents relating to the assets of the trust,[111] although it would seem that beneficiaries should only be permitted to have access to information relating to their interest in the trust property, so, for example, a remainderman would only be entitled to information relevant to capital transactions. The obligation on trustees to provide information is well-established,[112] and the extent of the entitlement was set out as follows in *The Law Relating to Trusts and Trustees*[113] and quoted with approval by Kenny J in *Chaine-Nickson v. Bank of Ireland*:[114]

> When a beneficiary has a vested interest in a trust fund so that he has a right to payment of the income, the trustees must at all reasonable times at his request give him full and accurate information as to

---

109. [1986] Conv 138.
110. [1894] 1 IR 74, 86.
111. *O'Rourke v. Darbishire* [1920] AC 581, 626 *per* Lord Wrenbury.
112. *Low v. Bouverie* [1891] 3 Ch 82, 99 *per* Lindley LJ.
113. Underhill (11th ed., 1959) p.401. (Now see 15th ed., 1995, Hayton).
114. [1976] IR 393, 396.

the amount and state of the trust property and permit him or his solicitor, to inspect the accounts and vouchers and other documents relating to the trust.

There was some doubt about whether this entitlement extended to beneficiaries under a discretionary trust but this was resolved by Kenny J in *Chaine-Nickson*. The plaintiff was one of a number of potential beneficiaries under a settlement of property vested in the defendants as trustees on discretionary trusts. The plaintiff sought an order directing the defendants to give him particulars with regard to matters relating to the administration of the trust. The defendants argued that in the case of a discretionary trust, none of the potential beneficiaries were entitled as of right to any information relating to the management of the trust. As Kenny J pointed out the logical result of this argument was that the trustees were not under an obligation to account to anyone in relation to their actions, a proposition he could not accept. He therefore concluded as follows:

> Legal principle and the one relevant authority [*Moore v. McGlynn*] establish that a potential beneficiary under a discretionary trust is entitled to copies of the trust accounts and to details of the investments representing the trust funds.[115]

However, it would appear on the authority of the decision of the English Court of Appeal in *Re Londonderry's Settlement*,[116] that trustees exercising a discretionary power are not bound to disclose to the beneficiaries the reasons which motivate them in reaching a decision as to the manner in which the trust property should be distributed. The trustees of a discretionary family trust decided to distribute the capital of the trust. The defendant, a daughter of the settlor, was dissatisfied with the provision made for her and her children and sought access to the minutes of the trustees' meetings, documents prepared for the meetings and correspondence entered into between those involved in the administration of the trust. The trustees only supplied her with copies of the intended appointments of capital and copies of the trust accounts, and sought clarification from the court in relation to the extent of their duty of disclosure. The Court of Appeal held that the trustees were not under an obligation to disclose the reasons for their decisions on the basis that they could not otherwise properly exercise their confidential role. As Danckwerts LJ stated:

---

115. *Ibid.* at 399. See also *Re Murphy's Settlements* [1998] 3 All ER 1, 9.
116. [1965] Ch 918.

> It seems to me that where trustees are given discretionary trusts which involve a decision upon matters between beneficiaries, viewing the merits and other rights to benefit under such a trust, the trustees are given a confidential role and they cannot properly exercise that confidential role if at any moment there is likely to be an investigation for the purpose of seeing whether they have exercised their discretion in the best possible manner.[117]

However, Danckwerts LJ continued by saying that this position might be otherwise if a case were made of lack of *bona fides* and it has been suggested that a beneficiary determined to discover the grounds on which a trustee's discretion has been exercised might do so by instituting litigation alleging that this discretion has been exercised *mala fides* and then obtaining an order for discovery.[118] The result in *Re Londonderry's Settlement* has been criticised on the grounds that it allows the trustees to be effectively unaccountable in the exercise of their decision making functions in relation to the distribution of the assets of a discretionary trust.[119] There is some considerable merit in the principle that trustees in these circumstances should disclose at least in outline, the reasons which have motivated them in coming to their decisions if only to avoid unnecessary allegations of bad faith but it remains to be seen how the courts in this jurisdiction will deal with these conflicting arguments.

Duty Not to Profit from the Trust

It is a well-established rule that a person who occupies a fiduciary position is not entitled to make a profit from that position unless expressly authorised to do so, or to place himself in a situation where his interest and duty may conflict.[120] As we have seen above,[121] this principle is strictly applied to the relationship between a trustee and beneficiary and a trustee is not entitled to retain any financial benefit which he has gained as a result of his fiduciary position. This point was reiterated by Lord O'Hagan C in *Armstrong v. Armstrong*:[122]

> I think it is plain that a trustee, so making a commodity of his position, and gaining a profit which but for it he would not have secured,

---

117. *Ibid.* at 935-936.
118. Megarry (1965) 81 LQR 192, 196.
119. See also *infra* p. 440.
120. *Bray v. Ford* [1896] AC 44, 51 *per* Lord Herschell. See also *Re Drexel Burnham Lambert UK Pension Plan* [1995] 1 WLR 32, 37 *per* Lindsay J.
121. See *supra* Chapter 8.
122. (1880) 7 LR Ir 207, 218.

must be held, on general principles and for the safety of *cestuis que trusts*, to retain that profit for the benefit of the trust estate.

In addition, the operation of this principle can be seen in relation to the issue of charging fees for work done on behalf of the trust and also arises where a trustee attempts to purchase trust property.

Remuneration and Expenses

As a general principle, a trustee is not entitled to remuneration for work carried out by him in his capacity as trustee.[123] This principle has been applied even where a trustee has expended considerable time and energy in performing the duties imposed upon him by the trust instrument.[124] However, it is not without exceptions and as Lord Normand commented in *Dale v. IRC*,[125] it does not mean 'that reward for services is repugnant to the fiduciary duty, but that he who has the duty shall not take any secret remuneration or any financial benefit not authorised by the law, or by his contract, or by the trust deed under which he acts, as the case may be.' Clearly where the trust instrument itself makes provision for remuneration, this will be paid and if a settlor or testator wishes to appoint a professional trustee, it is essential that satisfactory provision be made in this regard. Although such clauses are often strictly construed,[126] much will depend on the precise wording employed. It has recently been held in England that provided the instrument expressly authorises it, a trustee may employ a company which he controls to provide services for the trust and the company may be paid for such services.[127]

In addition, the court has an inherent jurisdiction to order that a trustee be remunerated for his services where no provision for payment has been made in the trust instrument or to allow a trustee to receive payment in excess of what was originally laid down or agreed. So, in *Re Duke of Norfolk's Settlement Trusts*[128] the Court of Appeal agreed to increase the rate of remuneration authorised by the settlor. It would appear that such payment will only be ordered by the court in fairly exceptional cases where the trustee's efforts have resulted in considerable profit accruing to the trust, as in *Boardman v. Phipps*,[129] where remuneration on a generous scale

123. *Re Ormsby* (1809) 1 Ba & B 189-90.
124. *Barrett v. Hartley* (1886) LR 2 Eq 789.
125. [1954] AC 11, 27.
126. *Re Gee* [1948] Ch 284, 292 *per* Harman J.
127. *Re Orwell's Will Trusts* [1982] 1 WLR 1337.
128. [1982] Ch 61, 78 *per* Fox LJ.
129. [1967] 2 AC 46.

was permitted in recognition of the results achieved, even though these had been effected in breach of trust.

A further exception to the general principle of no remuneration will also be made where a trustee makes an arrangement to this effect with all the beneficiaries, provided that they are *sui juris*. Where they are not all of full age and capacity, such as where some of the beneficiaries may be minors or as yet unborn, application must be made to the court to authorise any payment.

The position of a trustee who is also a solicitor gives rise to some difficulties. As a general rule such a person is not entitled to charge for his services and it has even be suggested that if he were, it might encourage the institution of unnecessary litigation.[130] However where a solicitor/trustee acts for himself and his co-trustees in litigation relating to the trust and the costs of his so acting do not exceed the costs which would have been incurred had he acted for his co-trustees only, he is entitled to be paid these costs. This principle is known as the rule in *Cradock v. Piper*[131] and has been applied in this jurisdiction in *Re Smith's Estate*.[132]

A trustee is entitled to be reimbursed for expenses properly incurred in the administration and management of the trust. This principle was set out as follows by Chatterton VC in *Courtney v. Rumley*:[133]

> The principle upon which this Court acts in reference to the allowance of expenses to trustees is, that the trust property shall reimburse them all the charges and expenses incurred in the execution of the trust, and in this the Court will always deal liberally with a trustee acting *bona fide*. But when the costs or expenses claimed have been incurred through the misconduct or negligence of the trustee, he will not be allowed them.

This principle is given statutory confirmation by section 24 of the Trustee Act 1893 which provides that a trustee 'may reimburse himself, or pay or discharge out of the trust premises all expenses incurred in or about the execution of his trusts or powers.' As Chatterton VC made clear in *Courtney v. Rumley*, the fact that a trustee proves unsuccessful in litigation will not prevent him from being reimbursed provided that he is acting in good faith.[134]

---

130. *New v. Jones* (1883) 1 Mac & G 685n.
131. (1850) 1 Mac & G 664.
132. [1894] 1 IR 60.
133. (1871) IR 6 Eq 99, 106.
134. *Graham v. McCashin* [1901] 1 IR 404.

Purchase of Trust Property

Subject to strictly limited exceptions, it is an established principle that a trustee may not purchase trust property from himself and his co-trustees because if this were permitted the trustee would effectively be both vendor and purchaser. This rule, sometimes referred to as the 'self-dealing rule' was summarised as follows by Megarry VC in *Tito v. Wadell (No. 2)*:[135] 'The self-dealing rule is (to put it very shortly) that if a trustee sells the trust property to himself, the sale is voidable by any beneficiary *ex debito justitiae*, however fair the transaction.' Thus any sale is voidable at the option of a beneficiary, who should take steps to have the transaction set aside within a reasonable time.[136] As Lord Kingsdown stated in *Smith v. Kay*,[137] in a portion of his judgment quoted with approval by Napier CS in *King v. Anderson*,[138] in the case of the trustee/beneficiary relationship, 'the Court presumes confidence put and influence exerted'. Therefore there appears to be an almost irrebuttable presumption in such cases that undue influence has been exercised and it is unlikely to be sufficient to establish that the trustee was acting honestly and that the price paid was a fair one. Equally, it has been established that the right of the beneficiaries to have a transaction of this nature set aside does not depend on the fact that the trustee has made a profit.[139] The strict manner in which the self-dealing rule is applied is well illustrated by the decision of the Privy Council in *Wright v. Morgan*.[140] Property was left to two trustees on trust for sale to only one of them. This trustee assigned his right to the other who retired from his office and then purchased the property at a price fixed by independent valuers. The Privy Council held that this sale must be set aside as only a sale to the other trustee had been authorised by the terms of the will.

As a general principle this rule cannot be evaded by selling the trust property to a relative or associate of the trustee or to a company controlled by him; at the very least in such circumstances the transaction will be closely scrutinised by the court to ensure that it is not merely a colourable device to preclude the application of the self-dealing rule. It would also appear that the principle applies where a trustee has recently retired,[141] although not where he has retired a considerable time before purchasing the trust property.[142]

135. [1977] Ch 106, 241.
136. *Webb v. Rorke* (1806) 2 Sch & Lef 661, 672 *per* Lord Redesdale.
137. (1859) 7 HLC 750, 779.
138. (1874) IR 8 Eq 625, 628.
139. *Ex p. Lacey* (1802) 6 Ves 625.
140. [1926] AC 788.
141. *Wright v. Morgan* [1926] AC 788.
142. *Re Boles & British Land Company's Contract* [1902] 1 Ch 244.

There are three main exceptions to the principle that a trustee may not purchase trust property from himself and his co-trustees. First, he may do so where the trust instrument expressly permits this,[143] although any such authorisation will be strictly construed. Secondly, the court may sanction a purchase in a suitable case or thirdly the beneficiaries may consent provided that they are *sui juris* and all agree to this course of action. In addition, there are borderline cases where the court may feel that it is inappropriate to apply the self-dealing rule, as in *Holder v. Holder.*[144] There one of the executors of a will, who had renounced his executorship soon after his appointment and had taken little part in the administration of the estate prior to doing so, purchased trust property at an auction for a price above the reserve fixed by an independent valuer. The Court of Appeal declined to set aside the sale on the application of one of the beneficiaries. However, it would be fair to say that the circumstances of this case were exceptional and it would be incorrect to assume that this decision marks the beginning of any general trend towards a watering down of the self-dealing rule.[145]

However a less strict approach has always been adopted by the courts where a trustee purchases property from a beneficiary rather than from the trust itself, sometimes referred to as the 'fair-dealing rule'.[146] While a presumption of undue influence will arise because of the nature of the relationship, this is rebuttable and the onus lies on the trustee to show that the transaction should be upheld.[147] Megarry VC laid down this principle in *Tito v. Wadell (No. 2)* in the following terms:[148]

> [I]f a trustee purchases the beneficial interest of any of his beneficiaries, the transaction is not voidable *ex debito justitiae*, but can be set aside unless the trustee can show that he has taken no advantage of his position and has made full disclosure to the beneficiary, and that the transaction is fair and honest.

---

143. *Sargeant v. National Westminster Bank plc* (1990) 61 P & CR 518.
144. [1968] Ch 353.
145. See e.g. *Re Thompson's Settlement* [1985] 3 WLR 486, 497 *per* Vinelott J.
146. See generally Nolan 'Conflicts of Interest, Unjust Enrichment and Wrongdoing' in *Restitution, Past Present and Future* ed. Cornish (1998) . As Nolan states at p.95 a fiduciary faced with an action under the fair-dealing rule as opposed to the self-dealing rule can successfully defend the action by showing that he acted with 'objective' fairness.
147. *Thomson v. Eastwood* (1877) 2 App Cas 215, 236 *per* Lord Cairns.
148. [1977] Ch 106, 241.

Similarly, in *Coles v. Trecothick*[149] Lord Eldon commented that a trustee may buy from a beneficiary provided that 'there is a distinct and clear contract, ascertained to be such after a jealous and scrupulous examination of all the circumstances' and provided that there is no evidence of fraud, concealment or of advantage being taken by the trustee of information acquired by him as a result of his position.

In such circumstances where a trustee is seeking to establish that he gave full value for the property, it will obviously be desirable that an independent valuation is obtained. In addition, in order to establish that a trustee did not take unfair advantage of the beneficiary, it may be advantageous to prove that independent legal advice has been given, although it has been established that a lack of such advice or an independent valuation will not necessarily prove fatal from the point of view of the trustee. In *Provincial Bank of Ireland v. McKeever*[150] it was stated by Black J that where a trustee takes a voluntary benefit from a beneficiary there is a presumption that the benefit was obtained by undue influence. However, he also made it clear that this presumption may be rebutted, irrespective of whether the beneficiary has had independent advice, if it is shown that the transfer was the result of the free exercise of an independent will. This point was also made by Costello J in *Smyth v. Smyth*.[151] The deceased gave a life interest in a field to his brother, who was one of the trustees of his will, and the remainder interest to his nephew. The nephew agreed to sell this interest to his uncle and subsequently sought to have the sale set aside on the grounds of undue influence and on the basis that as trustee the defendant should not have purchased the plaintiff's interest in this manner. Costello J confirmed that the onus of proving the *bona fides* of the transaction lay on the defendant and said that he was required to examine the surrounding circumstances 'with very great care' with a view to ascertaining whether any unfair advantage had been taken by the defendant. Costello J held that the price paid by the defendant was in fact a fair one and that the defendant had not sought to take advantage of his position as trustee or to influence the plaintiff's decision to sell. He further concluded that the defendant was not under any obligation to ensure that the plaintiff received independent legal advice nor was he under a duty to procure an independent valuation as in his view both the defendant and his solicitor were correct in their assessment that the price agreed was a fair one.

---

149. (1804) 9 Ves 234, 247.
150. [1941] IR 471.
151. High Court 1975 No. 4369P (Costello J) 22 November 1978.

Duty Not to Delegate[152]

The general principle in relation to delegation by a trustee of his powers and functions was summarised by Lord Langdale MR in *Turner v. Corney*[153] as follows:

> [T]rustees who take on themselves the management of property for the benefit of others have no right to shift their duty on other persons; and if they employ an agent, they remain subject to the responsibility towards their *cestuis que trust*, for whom they have undertaken the duty.

The rationale behind the principle of non-delegation of a trustee's duties is that the office is viewed as one where confidence is placed in the abilities of the particular individual appointed and it is therefore expected that he should personally look after the interests of the beneficiaries. So, in *Re O'Flanagan and Ryan's Contract*,[154] where a testator appointed his wife as trustee of property to hold for herself and their children, it was held by Porter MR that she had no power to delegate this role.

However, the principle of *delegatus not potest delegare* cannot be applied inflexibly to the position of trustees and it has long been recognised that a trustee may delegate in situations of 'legal necessity' or 'moral necessity'.[155] Provision may be made for delegation in the trust instrument, and provided that the delegation does not exceed what is authorised it will be permissible. In addition, it has been recognised that the proper administration of a trust would not be practicable if a trustee was not free to delegate the performance of certain functions to professional agents, such as solicitors and brokers. So, a trustee may employ a qualified professional person as his agent where the exercise of his office demands that these services be obtained and as Wylie[156] has commented, it may even in certain circumstances amount to a breach of trust not to delegate.

The general principle is that where an ordinary prudent man of business would employ an agent to act on his behalf, a trustee will be entitled to delegate his functions and will not be liable for the default of an agent

---

152. See Jones (1959) 22 MLR 381, 381-385.
153. (1841) 5 Beav 515, 517.
154. [1905] 1 IR 280. See also *Carr v. Connor* (1929) 63 ILTR 185, 189 where Fitzgibbon J commented that a trustee is 'bound to exercise his own judgement'.
155. *Ex p. Belchier* (1754) Amb 218.
156. *Irish Land Law* (3rd ed., 1997) p. 610.

employed in these circumstances.[157] In *Speight v. Gaunt*[158] the defendant trustee had employed a broker at the request of the beneficiaries to purchase stock. When the broker absconded with the monies provided for the purchase, the beneficiaries sought to make the defendant liable for breach of trust. It was held by the Court of Appeal and confirmed by the House of Lords that the defendant had acted prudently as a reasonable man of business would have acted in employing a broker to act in these circumstances and that he was not liable.

A number of further points should be noted about the circumstances in which a trustee may delegate to an agent. First, a trustee must exercise his own discretion in appointing an agent, he cannot delegate the making of this choice.[159] So, in *Fry v. Tapson*[160] trustees did not exercise their own judgment in relation to the appointment of a valuer appointed to advise them in a transaction where money was lent on a mortgage, but instead relied on the recommendation of their solicitor. This individual was in fact an agent of the mortgagor and when loss subsequently occurred, it was held that the trustees were liable as they had not made the decision in relation to who should be appointed themselves. It is also important to note that an agent should not be entrusted with responsibilities not normally undertaken by that class of agent[161] so, for example, a solicitor should not be employed to carry out work which should properly be within the remit of a broker's functions.[162]

In addition, even where an agent is properly appointed in the circumstances, a trustee must still exercise a reasonable degree of supervision over the agent's activities.[163] Some indemnity is provided by the provisions of section 24 of the Trustee Act 1893 which provides that a trustee shall be liable only for his own acts and defaults and not for those of any other trustee or banker or broker unless any loss occurs as a result of 'wil-

---

157. *Speight v. Gaunt* (1883) 22 Ch D 727, 739-740 *per* Lindley LJ; *Fry v. Tapson* (1884) 28 Ch D 268, 280.
158. (1883) 22 Ch D 727.
159. *Re Weall* (1889) 42 Ch D 674. Kekewich J pointed out that 'a trustee is bound to exercise discretion in the choice of his agents' but went on to state that provided he selects properly qualified persons he cannot be made responsible for their intelligence or honesty.
160. (1884) 28 Ch D 268. See also *Speight v. Gaunt* (1883) 22 Ch D 727, 756 *per* Lindley LJ.
161. Trustees must ensure that they select persons who are 'properly qualified' to carry out the function at issue. *Per* Kekewich J in *Re Weall* (1889) 42 Ch D 674, 678.
162. *Rowland v. Witherden* (1851) 3 McN & G 568.
163. In terms of the degree of supervision required in such circumstances, trustees are expected to exercise the 'ordinary prudence which a man uses in his own affairs'; *Mendes v. Guedalla* (1862) 2 J & H 259, 277 *per* Page Wood VC.

ful default' on his part. The meaning of the latter term was considered by Lindley LJ in *Re Chapman*[164] where he commented that 'trustees acting honestly, with ordinary prudence and within the limits of their trust, are not liable for mere errors of judgment'.

A further relevant statutory exemption is provided by section 17 of the Trustee Act 1893 which lays down that a solicitor may be entrusted with the receipt of purchase money deriving from the sale of trust property and either a solicitor or banker may receive insurance monies. The validity of the power of delegation is dependent in the former case on the solicitor having custody of a deed containing a receipt for the money and in the latter case on the solicitor or banker having the insurance policy with a receipt signed by the trustees. The effect of the section is that in these defined circumstances, a trustee will not be liable merely because he has delegated his functions although subsection (3) goes on to provide that liability may be imposed where the trustees allow the monies received to remain in the hands of or under the control of the solicitor or broker for a period longer than is reasonably necessary.

It should also be noted that section 23 of the Trustee Act 1925 has widened considerably the power to delegate in England; as Maugham J commented in *Re Vickery*:[165] 'it revolutionises the position of a trustee or an executor so far as regards the employment of agents' and it has been suggested on the basis of this decision that provided the trustee acts with subjective good faith in the appointment of an agent, he will not incur liability.[166] However, this proposition has often been called into question,[167] and in 1982 the Law Reform Committee recommended that 'a trustee who has delegated some of his responsibilities should be expected to keep a check on the actions of his agent'.[168] From a general perspective the Committee's recommendations were quite restrictive in nature and in a Law Commission Consultation Paper on Trustees' Powers and Duties published in 1997 it was stated that the fundamental changes which had occurred since the publication of the earlier report required 'a substantial widening of trustees' delegation powers'.[169] The Commission provisionally recommended that subject to the expression of a contrary intention in the trust

---

164. [1896] 2 Ch 763, 776.

165. [1931] 1 Ch 572, 581.

166. This was the effect of the *dicta* of Hoffman J in *Steel v. Wellcome Custodian Trustees Ltd* [1988] 1 WLR 167, 174 . See also Ham (1995) 9 Trust Law Int 21, 24.

167. See e.g. Jones (1959) 22 MLR 381; Stannard [1979] Conv 345.

168. 23rd Report on the Powers and Duties of Trustees (1982) Cmnd 8733 paragraph 4.11.

169. Consultation Paper No. 146 paragraph 6.11.

instrument, trustees 'should have authority to delegate to agents their powers to administer the trust, including their power of investment and management'[170] but should not generally have authority to distribute the income or capital of the trust. However, the Commission also suggested that trustees should review any delegation of their functions at regular intervals and exercise adequate supervisory functions in relation to the delegation of their powers of management. The Commission has yet to express a firm view on the question of what standard of care should be expected of trustees in relation to their powers of delegation but has suggested a formula either along the lines of acting with the care of an ordinary prudent person of business or with the care and diligence which can reasonably be expected having regard to the nature of the trust and the skills of the trustees.[171]

It is submitted that the Law Commission's proposals are to be welcomed for two distinct reasons. First, the existing rules as to the standard of care required of trustees when delegating are unclear and unsatisfactory. Secondly, as Kenny has commented 'delegation of some or all of the acts of trusteeship is an inevitable consequence of modern trusteeship'[172] and trustees cannot be expected to carry out all the tasks associated with the management of the trust.[173] The same criticisms could also be levelled at the law as it exists in this jurisdiction and, as will be discussed below, some reform of the law in this area is clearly necessary to reflect the realities of modern trusts.

THE POWERS OF TRUSTEES

Introduction

Before the intervention of statute in this area, where a trust instrument was being drafted it was necessary to ensure that sufficient powers were conferred on the trustees by the instrument to enable them to carry out their duties in the manner envisaged by the settlor or testator. The Trustee Act 1893 now confers a number of basic powers on trustees but this legislation

---

170. *Ibid.* paragraph 6.26.
171. *Ibid.* paragraph 6.55.
172. [1997] Conv 372, 373.
173. Statute increasingly provided for delegation in specified circumstances in England, e.g. s.34 of the Pensions Act 1995 recognises the need to delegate in relation to the management of pension funds and s.9 of the Trusts of Land and Appointment of Trustees Act 1996 empowers trustees to appoint a beneficiary as attorney to carry out their functions in relation to land (see further Clements (1998) 61 MLR 56).

was only intended to augment the powers conferred by the trust instrument, which will often still determine the precise extent of the trustees' powers. It is now proposed to examine some of the more important statutory powers conferred on trustees but it should be borne in mind that in the final analysis the terms of the instrument itself are still of overriding importance.

Power of Sale and to Give Receipts

A trustee may be authorised to sell trust property by virtue of an express power contained in a trust instrument or alternatively such a power may be implied e.g. in circumstances where the rule in *Howe v. Earl of Dartmouth*[174] applies. The only other circumstances in which a trustee may sell trust property is where he is authorised to do so by the court or where a power of sale is conferred on him by statute.

Where a trustee holds property on trust for sale or with a power of sale, statutory powers are conferred on him in relation to the conduct of the sale by section 13 of the Trustee Act 1893. The section provides that subject to a contrary intention being expressed in the trust instrument, a trustee is empowered to sell the trust property in whole or in part and either by public auction or by private contract subject to such conditions as he thinks fit.

The overriding duty of a trustee selling trust property is to obtain the best price for the beneficiaries,[175] although it should be noted that section 14 of the Trustee Act 1893 provides that a sale may not be impeached by a beneficiary on the grounds that any of the conditions of sale were unduly depreciatory unless it appears that the consideration for the sale was thereby rendered inadequate. In such cases, the position of the purchaser is also protected unless it appears that he was acting in collusion with the trustee at the time the contract for sale was concluded.[176]

A further relevant power is contained in section 15 of the Act of 1893 which provides that a trustee who is either a vendor or purchaser may sell or buy trust property without excluding the application of section 2 of the Vendor and Purchaser Act 1874.

A statutory power is conferred on trustees by section 20 of the Trustee Act 1893 to give receipts and it provides that a written receipt by a trustee for the money, securities or property sold is a sufficient discharge to the

---

174. (1802) 7 Ves 137. See *supra* pp. 401-402.
175. *Buttle v. Saunders* [1950] 2 All ER 193, 195. See also *Re Cooper and Allen's Contract for Sale to Harlech* (1876) 4 Ch D 802, 815 *per* Jessel MR.
176. S.14(2) of the Act of 1893.

person paying and effectively exonerates him from being answerable for any loss or misapplication of the property.

Power of Maintenance

Express provision can be and often is made in the trust instrument empowering the trustees to apply the income of the trust property for an infant's benefit.[177] Statutory powers of maintenance are also conferred on trustees by section 43 of the Conveyancing Act 1881 which empowers them to use trust income towards the maintenance or education of infant beneficiaries in certain circumstances. In situations where this power is exercisable, trustees may pay maintenance to an infant's parent or guardian or otherwise apply the income for the maintenance, education or benefit of an infant. Section 43 can be applied where property is held on trust for an infant beneficiary for life or for any greater interest, whether absolutely or contingently on attaining the age of 18 or on the occurrence of any event before attaining that age. However, if the vesting of the interest is contingent on reaching a greater age or on the happening of some future event, the statutory power cannot be employed.

A further limitation on this statutory power is that it only applies where the trust property 'carries the intermediate income' i.e. the income which arises between the time of the coming into effect of the trust and the time the infant attains his majority, or the contingency occurs. As a general principle, a future or contingent gift will not be regarded as carrying the intermediate income which could be applied for maintenance except where it is a gift of residuary personalty, as in such cases the income can go to no-one except the residuary legatee. However, other types of future or contingent legacies will only carry the intermediate income in limited circumstances, as set out by Ker.[178] First, they will be regarded as carrying the income where the testator was the parent of or *in loco parentis* to the infant beneficiary, except where the contingency is the attaining of some age greater than the age of majority,[179] or where the testator has provided another fund out of which the infant is to be maintained. So, in *Re Ferguson*[180] it was held by O'Connor MR that a contingent specific bequest carried the intermediate income as the testator was *in loco parentis* and had made no alternative provision for the maintenance of the legatee before the bequest vested. The second exception is where the testator has

---

177. E.g. *Russell v. Russell* [1903] 1 IR 168.
178. (1953) 17 Conv 273, 276-278.
179. *Re Abrahams* [1911] 1 Ch 108.
180. (1915) 49 ILTR 110.

manifested an intention that the infant is to be maintained as in *Re Church-ill*,[181] where the testatrix had given a legacy to her grand-nephew and directed that any part of it should be paid towards his advancement in life or otherwise for his benefit. The third exception is where the testator segregates a fund for the legatee and is set out in the following terms by Chatterton VC in *Johnston v. O'Neill*:[182]

> It is, no doubt, the general rule that general legacies payable at a future day, even though vested, do not carry interest before the day of payment, except legacies given to a child by a parent, or a person *in loco parentis*. But to this general rule there are exceptions, one of which is, that where a fund is directed to be presently separated from the general personal estate for the purpose of providing for the future payment of certain legacies, it carries the interest accruing up to the time of payment, to the legatees, with the capital sum. In such cases, the rule that the interest follows the capital prevails, and the legatee gets his legacy with its interim accretions.

A statutory power to permit the court to make payments of income or capital is conferred by section 11 of the Guardianship of Infants Act 1964 which provides that an application may be brought by the guardian of the infant where such a payment is necessary for his maintenance or education. In addition, the court also has an inherent jurisdiction to make an order sanctioning the use of capital by trustees for the maintenance of infants where they have no other means of support.[183] In *Re O'Neill*[184] Maguire P directed that a payment be made out of the trust capital for the maintenance and education of the testator's children, although he made it clear that it was a jurisdiction which should only be exercised where it was really necessary. He stated:

> I must be satisfied that such a course is not only beneficial but necessary to the welfare of the minors. ... The jurisdiction to make an advance out of capital is not to be exercised lightly. Where a minor is actually destitute the way is clear, but where the minors, as here, are not destitute, the question of the existence of a sufficient element of necessity becomes a difficult problem.[185]

---

181. [1909] 2 Ch 431.
182. (1879) 3 LR Ir 476, 480-481.
183. *Robison v. Killey* (1862) 30 Beav 520, 521.
184. [1943] IR 562.
185. *Ibid.* at 564-565.

Power of Advancement

While 'maintenance' usually refers to the payment of income for the benefit of infant beneficiaries, the term 'advancement' is used to describe payments made out of the trust capital to a beneficiary before he becomes entitled to an interest under the trust. Traditionally, 'the word "advancement" meant ... the establishment in life of the beneficiary who was the object of the power or at any rate some step that would contribute to the furtherance of his establishment'.[186] A power to make advancements out of capital may be expressly conferred by the trust instrument.[187] In addition, as seen above, a statutory power exists under section 11 of the Guardianship of Infants Act 1964 whereby the court can sanction capital payments for the support of an infant beneficiary where an application is made by the infant's guardian.

Power to Compound Liabilities

By virtue of section 21 of the Trustee Act 1893, trustees may 'compromise, compound, abandon, submit to arbitration or otherwise settle' any debt or claim without being responsible for any loss occasioned by any act done by him in this regard in good faith. As Overend J stated in *Re Boyle*[188] in relation to this power, which is also conferred on executors and administrators: 'There is no question that an executor has power to compromise even a doubtful claim, if he *bona fide* believes it to be in the interest of the estate.'

Power to Insure

While trustees originally had no power to insure unless this was conferred by the trust instrument, section 18 of the Trustee Act 1893 provides that they may insure trust property 'against loss or damage by fire' to an amount not exceeding three-quarters of the full value of the property. In addition, section 18(2) provides that this power does not apply to any building or property which the trustees are bound to convey absolutely to any beneficiary on being requested to do so.

It is in some respects surprising that trustees are not under an obligation to insure trust property in view of their general duty to safeguard the assets of the trust and it is interesting to note that the English Law Reform Committee recommended that they should be placed under a duty to in-

---

186. *Pilkington v. IRC* [1964] AC 612, 634.
187. *McMahon v. Gaussen* [1896] 1 IR 143; *L'Estrange v. L'Estrange* [1902] 1 IR 467.
188. [1947] IR 61, 69.

sure against any risk in circumstances where a prudent man of business would take this step.[189]

LIABILITY OF TRUSTEES FOR BREACH OF TRUST

Extent and Measure of Liability

A trustee will be found to be acting in breach of trust if he fails to perform the duties required of him or if he acts in an unauthorized manner. A breach may occur in a variety of circumstances such as where trust monies are invested in unauthorised investments, where a trustee fails to distribute the trust estate to the beneficiaries in the correct proportions, or where he fails to exercise a proper degree of supervision over the management of the trust by his co-trustees. However, it will be necessary for the beneficiaries to establish conduct which in the opinion of the court amounts to a breach of trust.[190]

Where a trustee fails to comply with the duties imposed on him by the trust instrument he is liable to make good the loss to the trust estate or where he makes an unauthorised profit for himself, even if this does not cause loss to the trust, he must account for it. As a general rule, a trustee is liable only in respect of the breaches of trust which he has himself committed and not those committed by his co-trustees, so liability is personal and not vicarious.[191] However, this indemnity will not apply where his conduct amounts to wilful default on his part, and inactivity on the part of a trustee in circumstances where he ought to have intervened can often be regarded as sufficient grounds for imposing liability.

A trustee is not liable for breaches of trust committed before his appointment unless there is evidence indicating such a breach which requires him to investigate further. It is therefore important that on appointment a trustee takes whatever steps are necessary to ensure that the trust affairs are in order and investigates anything which causes him suspicion. When a trustee retires from a trust he remains liable for breaches committed by him during his term of office and his estate remains liable after his death. Where a breach occurs shortly after his retirement he will be liable if he retired in order to facilitate a breach of trust which he foresaw would take

---

189. 23rd Report, Cmnd 8733, paragraph 4.33.
190. See *Carr v. Connor* (1929) ILTR 185 where Fitzgibbon J concluded at p.191 that 'the plaintiffs had failed to prove that the defendant was guilty even of an error of judgment still less of any wilful default.'
191. *Townley v. Sherborne* (1634) J Bridg 35, 37.

place or if he contemplated at the time that a breach of trust would be effected and decided to retire to avoid direct involvement. This issue was considered by Kekewich J in *Head v. Gould*,[192] where he held that to make a retiring trustee liable for a breach of trust committed by his successor it must be proved that the breach committed was not merely the outcome of the retirement and new appointment but was contemplated by the former trustee when the retirement took place; as he said the former trustees 'must be proved to have been guilty as accessories before the fact of the impropriety actually perpetrated.'[193]

The measure of a trustee's liability where an unlawful profit has been made as a result of his breach of trust is that he should account for the profit.[194] It should be noted that the Privy Council has recently held that where such an unlawful profit has been made, a plaintiff is entitled either to an account of the profits made by the defendant in breach of his fiduciary obligations or to damages for the loss suffered by the plaintiff by reason of the breach; the plaintiff must make an election between these remedies.[195]

In other cases where there has been a breach of trust or fiduciary duty, the measure of a trustee's liability is the loss caused to the trust estate either directly or indirectly. Where the breach consists of a trustee making an unauthorized investment, the measure of damages will be the loss incurred by the trust in selling this investment if this is the course of action agreed on by the beneficiaries. Where trustees improperly retain an unauthorized investment, they will be liable for the difference between the price which the property would have fetched if sold at the proper time and the price actually received for it. This point is well illustrated by the decision of Romilly MR in *Fry v. Fry*.[196] A testator had directed that an inn should be sold 'as soon as convenient' after his death. The trustees refused an initial offer of £900 and nine years after the testator's death, the value of the property was greatly depreciated by the opening of a railway which deprived it of its coach traffic. The inn still remained unsold some 26 years after the testator's death. The estates of the trustees who had died in the interim were held liable for the difference between the original offer of

---

192. [1898] 2 Ch 250.
193. *Ibid.* at 274.
194. As the Privy Council made clear in *Attorney General for Hong Kong v. Reid* [1994] 1 AC 324 in such circumstances if assets are bought with trust monies, any increase in their value will be held on a constructive trust for the trust, whereas if they decrease in value the trustee will be personally liable in relation to such loss.
195. *Tang Man Sit v. Capacious Investments Ltd* [1996] 1 AC 514.
196. (1859) 27 Beav 144.

£900 and the amount of the proceeds of the sale which the court directed should take place.

Where trustees improperly sell an authorised investment they may be liable either to account for the proceeds of sale or to repurchase the investment at its value at the date of the judgment.[197] In addition, where the trustees pay out trust funds to the wrong person, they will be liable to make good this amount so that the correct beneficiary can be paid.[198]

The principles relating to equitable compensation where loss has been caused as a result of a breach of trust or fiduciary duty have recently been considered in some detail by the House of Lords in *Target Holdings Ltd v. Redferns*.[199] As Lord Browne-Wilkinson commented:

> Equitable compensation for breach of trust is designed to achieve exactly what the word compensation suggests: to make good a loss in fact suffered by the beneficiaries and which, using hindsight and common sense, can be seen to have been caused by the breach.[200]

Lord Browne-Wilkinson stated that the equitable rules of compensation for breach of trust have largely been developed in relation to so-called traditional trusts, where the only way to properly protect the rights of the beneficiaries is to restore to the trust fund what ought to be in it. In such cases, he said that the basic rule is that 'a trustee in breach of trust must restore or pay to the trust estate either the assets which have been lost to the estate by reason of the breach or compensation for such loss'.[201] However, Lord Browne-Wilkinson stressed that there does have to be some causal connection between the breach of trust and the loss to the trust estate for which the compensation is recoverable. So, as the decision of the House of Lords made clear, a trustee will not be required to compensate for loss which would have occurred in any event even if there had been no breach of trust.[202]

Lord Browne-Wilkinson then went on to consider what the position would be where, at the time of the bringing of an action claiming compensation for breach of trust, those trusts had come to an end. In such circum-

---

197. *Re Bell's Indenture* [1980] 1 WLR 1217.
198. See *Target Holdings Ltd v. Redferns* [1996] 1 AC 421.
199. [1996] 1 AC 421.
200. *Ibid.* at 439.
201. *Ibid.* at 434.
202. This so-called stringent test of causation or measure of loss has recently been applied by the Court of Appeal in *Swindle v. Harrison* [1997] 4 All ER 705 in the context of breach of fiduciary duty.

stances, he stated, the court will not order restitution to be made to the trust estate, but rather will direct that payment of compensation be made directly to the beneficiaries. In such cases the measure of compensation will be the same, i.e. 'the difference between what the beneficiary has in fact received and the amount he would have received but for the breach of trust'.[203]

Another question which must be addressed is the date at which the actual loss to the trust should be assessed. Traditionally, it was accepted that the loss should be ascertained at the date proceedings commenced,[204] but Vinelott J disputed this in *Re Bell's Indenture*,[205] where he stated that the loss should be ascertained instead at the date of judgment. Further confusion was caused when it was stated in *Jaffray v. Marshall*[206] that the trustees were liable to pay compensation at the highest intermediate value of the property between the date of the breach and the date of judgment. However, as a result of the consideration given by the House of Lords to this issue in *Target Holdings Ltd v. Redferns*[207] it now seems clear that liability is to be assessed at the date of judgment. As Lord Browne-Wilkinson stated:

> [T]he fact that there is an accrued cause of action as soon as the breach is committed does not in my judgment mean that the quantum of compensation payable is ultimately fixed as at the date when the breach occurred. The quantum is fixed at the date of the judgment at which date, according to the circumstances then pertaining, the compensation is assessed at the figure than necessary to put the trust estate or the beneficiary back into the position it would have been in had there been no breach.[208]

Finally, it should be noted that where a trustee is under an obligation to replace trust funds, he is charged with interest on the sum due. At common law this figure was 4% but the minimum rate now payable is 8% as prescribed by the Courts Act 1981 (Interest on Judgment Debts) Order 1989.[209]

---

203. [1996] 1 AC 421, 435. See also *Swindle v. Harrison* [1997] 4 All ER 705, 717.
204. *Re Massingberd* (1890) 63 LT 296.
205. [1980] 1 WLR 1217, 1233.
206. [1993] 1 WLR 1285.
207. [1996] 1 AC 421. See Ulph (1995) 9 Trust Law Int 86; Nolan [1996] LMCLQ 161; Rickett (1996) 112 LQR 27; Capper [1997] Conv 14.
208. Ibid. at 437.
209. SI No. 12 of 1989.

Liability of Trustees Inter Se

Where two or more trustees are involved in a breach of trust, liability is joint and several, so each is liable in respect of the whole loss although all may not have been equally blameworthy.[210] In such circumstances, a decree against all the trustees involved may be enforced against one or more of them,[211] and those against whom execution is levied may claim contribution from the other trustees involved in the breach of trust. The effect of the operation of this principle is that while all the trustees may not be equally blameworthy, they may still be held to be equally liable. The fact that this is arguably not always fair in practice is well illustrated by the decision of the Court of Appeal in *Bahin v. Hughes.*[212] A testator gave a legacy to his three daughters on trust to pay the income to the plaintiff for life and after her death to her children. One of the daughters and the husband of another effected an unauthorized investment in leasehold property and when this security proved insufficient, the plaintiff sought to impose liability on all the trustees. The Court of Appeal held that they were jointly and severally liable and all equally responsible for indemnifying the beneficiaries. In the opinion of the court, the money had been lost just as much as a result of the default of the inactive trustees as by the innocent though erroneous action of their co-trustee. Cotton LJ remarked:

> It would be laying down a wrong rule to hold that where one trustee acts honestly, though erroneously, the other trustee is to be held entitled to indemnity who by doing nothing neglects his duty more than the acting trustee.[213]

It has been accepted that in limited circumstances where a breach of trust has occurred, a trustee may escape liability or may be entitled to indemnity from a co-trustee. Where one trustee acts in a fraudulent manner he alone will be liable. In certain other circumstances, a trustee will be entitled to indemnity from his co-trustee against his own liability. So, where one trustee alone receives the benefit of a breach of trust or where the

---

210. As Panckhurst J stated recently in the decision of the New Zealand High Court in *Re Mulligan* [1998] 1 NZLR 481, 502 'it is elementary that a duty of diligence rests on each trustee' and that 'the starting point is that where a breach of trust has been committed, the trustees are jointly and severally liable to the beneficiaries for any loss caused by the breach' (at 511).
211. *Fletcher v. Green* (1864) 33 Beav 426, 430.
212. (1886) 31 Ch D 390.
213. *Ibid.* at 396. Note that the provisions of the Civil Liability Act 1961 apply to a breach of trust. See the definition of 'wrong' in s.2 and see also Part III Chapter 1 of the Act on the liability of concurrent wrongdoers.

breach reflects the fault of one trustee in his area of particular expertise indemnity may follow.[214] Similarly, where one trustee has exercised a controlling influence over the others which has effectively prevented his co-trustees from exercising independent judgment. This type of influence may be found to exist, e.g. where there is one professional trustee such as a solicitor although Kekewich J stressed in *Head v. Gould*[215] that there is no rule that 'a man is bound to indemnify his co-trustee against loss merely because he [is] a solicitor.' Certainly in that case where the co-trustee had been shown to be an active participant and not merely to have acted on the solicitor's advice, no indemnity could be obtained. Finally, where a trustee is also a beneficiary and has participated in a breach of trust, he must indemnify his co-trustees to the extent of his beneficial interest.[216]

Protection of Trustees from Personal Liability

A trustee who has committed a breach of trust may escape personal liability if he can establish certain circumstances. First, where the beneficiary has instigated, participated in or even consented to the breach of trust, the trustee will not be liable for any breach which occurs. Some of the factors which may influence the court in deciding whether the beneficiary's conduct will be such as to afford protection to the trustee were considered by Wilberforce J at first instance in *Re Pauling's Settlement Trusts*,[217] where he stated as follows:

> The court has to consider all the circumstances in which the concurrence of the *cestui que trust* was given with a view to seeing whether it is fair and equitable that, having given his concurrence, he should afterwards turn round and sue the trustees; that, subject to this, it is not necessary that he should know what he is concurring in is a breach of trust, provided that he fully understands what he is concurring in, and that it is not necessary that he should himself have directly benefited by the breach of trust.

A similar view has recently been expressed by Laskin JA, delivering the judgment of the Ontario Court of Appeal in *Gold v. Rosenberg*,[218] to the effect that in order for a beneficiary's consent to be valid, he must be

---

214. *Per* Panckhurst J in *Re Mulligan* [1998] 1 NZLR 481, 502.
215. [1898] 2 Ch 250, 265.
216. *Chillingworth v. Chambers* [1896] 1 Ch 685.
217. [1962] 1 WLR 86, 108. Approved by the Court of Appeal in *Holder v. Holder* [1968] Ch 353.
218. (1995) 129 DLR (4th) 152, 157.

capable of giving approval and must understand what is being approved. However, Laskin JA agreed that it was not necessary for the trustee to show that the beneficiary knew that the act or omission in question constituted a breach of trust.

A good example of a case in which a breach of trust was committed at the instigation of a beneficiary is *French v. Graham*.[219] Two trustees, one of whom was a solicitor, lent trust funds at the request of the tenant for life of a settlement on a security which proved totally inadequate. The non-professional trustee stood in the opinion of Brady LC in the 'ordinary position of a trustee who has been induced to commit a breach of trust at the request of one of his *cestuis que trust*' and was entitled to be indemnified by the tenant for life in respect of his liability for breach of trust. However, the Lord Chancellor was satisfied that the tenant for life had relied on the trustee solicitor advising him in the transaction in his professional capacity and as the latter had made no sufficient investigation of the title of the property involved, he was not entitled to be indemnified by the tenant for life.

The decision of a beneficiary to participate in or consent to a breach of trust will only usually[220] be relevant in this context where he is of full age and capacity and his participation or consent must have been freely given with full knowledge of the surrounding facts and circumstances. As Wilmer LJ stated in *Re Pauling's Settlement Trusts*[221] if the trustee can establish 'a valid request or consent by the beneficiary'[222] to an advance made in breach of trust, that will provide the trustee with a good defence against any claim by the beneficiary. In *Pauling* the trustees of a marriage settlement made a number of advancements to the children of the marriage with their mother's consent and although nominally paid to the children this money was applied to family purposes. The children subsequently brought an action claiming that these sums had been improperly paid out and the trustees relied on the consent and acquiescence of the advanced beneficiaries. However in the view of the Court of Appeal this was not effective to absolve the trustees from liability in every case and it was held that some of the payments to the beneficiaries had constituted breaches of trust for which the trustees were liable.[223]

---

219. (1860) 10 Ir Ch R 522. See also *Rutherfoord v. Maziere* (1862) 13 Ir Ch R 204.
220. However in *Overton v. Banister* (1844) 3 Hare 503 the court refused to allow an infant who had fraudulently misrepresented her age to succeed in arguing that any assent was ineffective.
221. [1964] Ch 303.
222. *Ibid.* at 335.
223. Note that a statutory defence is now provided in England by s. 61 of the Trustee Act 1925 where the trustees have acted honestly and reasonably.

The court has an inherent jurisdiction where a beneficiary has been instrumental in effecting a breach of trust to require the beneficiary to indemnify the trustee in respect of the latter's liability to make good any loss incurred.[224] This principle was reiterated by Chitty J in *Sawyer v. Sawyer*[225] in the following terms:

> [E]ach person at whose instance the trustees have committed a breach of trust is liable to recoup the subject of that breach of trust to the trustees ... it must be shown that the breach of trust was committed at the instance and request of the *cestuis que trust*. I make no distinction between instance and request, but it must be shown clearly that the breach of trust was instigated by them and that they were acting and moving parties to it.

However the proposition that 'a *cestui que trust* is bound to make good to the trustee every loss occasioned by an investment made with his privity' was rejected by Brady LC in *Browne v. Maunsell*,[226] and it would appear that where a beneficiary has merely consented to the breach of trust, his beneficial interest can only be impounded in this way where he has obtained a personal benefit from the breach. This power to impound a beneficiary's interest has now been given statutory authority by section 45 of the Trustee Act 1893 which provides that where it can be established that a beneficiary has instigated or requested or consented in writing to a breach of trust, the court may order that the interest of the beneficiary should be impounded with a view to indemnifying the trustee. This power will not normally be exercised in favour of the trustee unless it can be established that the beneficiary was aware at the time that the conduct which he instigated or consented to amounted to a breach of trust.

Even where a beneficiary is not involved prior to the breach being committed, a trustee may still be protected from liability where the beneficiary subsequently acquiesces in the breach or executes a release absolving the trustee from liability. As Lord Eldon stated in *Walker v. Symonds*:[227] 'either concurrence in the act or acquiescence without original concurrence will release the trustees' but he went on to state that this is only a general rule and that the court must investigate the circumstances which induced the concurrence or acquiescence. For acquiescence to be effec-

---

224. *Keays v. Lane* (1869) IR 3 Eq 1.
225. (1883) 28 Ch D 595, 598. Quoted with approval by Johnston J in *Anketill Jones v. Fitzgerald* (1930) 65 ILTR 185, 191.
226. (1856) 5 Ir Ch R 351.
227. (1818) 3 Swans 1, 64. See also *Re McKenna's Estate* (1861) 13 Ir Ch R 239.

tive in this context, the beneficiary must be *sui juris* and have consented freely to the trustee's actions will full knowledge of the surrounding facts and circumstances and it appears that the onus lies on the party alleging acquiescence to prove facts from which the beneficiary's consent can be inferred.[228]

Similarly a release even of an informal nature may be effective to absolve a trustee from liability,[229] but it is essential that the beneficiary executed such a release with full knowledge of the facts and of the consequences of his actions.[230] Westbury LC summarised the position in *Farrant v. Blanchford*[231] as follows:

> Where a breach of trust has been committed, from which a trustee alleges that he has been released, it is incumbent on him to show that such release was given by the *cestui que trust* deliberately and advisedly with full knowledge of all the circumstances, and of his own rights and claims against the trustee. ...

Finally, it should be noted that a trustee may be protected from an action for breach of trust by virtue of the provisions of the Statute of Limitations 1957. Section 2(2) provides that no action may be brought after six years from the date on which the cause of action accrued. However, section 44 goes on to provide that this limitation period will not apply where the claim is founded on any fraud or fraudulent breach of trust to which the trustee was party or where the claim is to recover trust property or the proceeds of trust property retained by the trustee and converted to his use.

VARIATION OF TRUSTS

As a general principle a trustee must administer a trust according to the terms laid down in the trust instrument and any deviation will constitute a breach of trust.[232] Therefore a court will not, except in limited circumstances which will be considered below, sanction the performance of acts

---

228. *Life Association of Scotland v. Siddal* (1861) 3 De G F & J 58, 77.
229. *Ghost v. Waller* (1846) 9 Beav 497.
230. *Thompson v. Eastwood* (1877) 2 App Cas 215.
231. (1863) 1 De G J & Sm 107, 119.
232. As Marshall JA has recently commented in the decision of the Newfoundland Court of Appeal in *Boy Scouts of Canada v. Doyle* (1997) 149 DLR (4th) 22, 63: 'It is, therefore, a basic tenet of law that, in the absence of authorization conferred upon them in the trust settlement, trustees may not appropriate to themselves the right to vary the terms of the trust settled upon them, or assume powers that have not been conferred upon them'.

by the trustees which are not authorised by the trust instrument and it will not generally be possible to alter or vary the terms of a trust once it becomes effective.

The question of variation in the terms of a trust instrument after it has come into operation is one which has assumed increasing importance especially in view of the need to adapt the terms of trusts to meet changing taxation requirements. As Lord Denning MR commented in *Re Weston's Settlements*:[233] 'Nearly every variation that has come before the court has tax avoidance for its principal object'. In addition, it may be necessary or in any event highly desirable to alter the original terms of a trust for a variety of other reasons and the courts must attempt to steer a path between giving effect to the intentions of a testator or settlor expressed in the trust instrument and seeking to envisage how these individuals might have wished the instrument to be altered in the light of changed circumstances.

Variation of the Terms of a Trust Without Court Approval

In certain situations the terms of the trust may be varied without court approval. Where the beneficiaries are all of full age and capacity and together are absolutely entitled to the trust property, they may terminate the trust and require that it be distributed in accordance with their directions, a principle sometimes referred to as the rule in *Saunders v. Vautier*,[234] although the decision in that case is expressed in slightly narrower terms.[235] There the testator bequeathed stock on trust to accumulate the dividends until a beneficiary attained the age of 25 and directed that the capital and the accumulated dividends should then be transferred to the beneficiary. When the latter reached the age of 21, he successfully claimed that he was entitled to call for the immediate transfer of the entire fund.

In practice this principle has been interpreted as meaning that any one or more adult beneficiaries who are of sound mind and entitled to the whole beneficial interest under a trust, can direct the trustees to transfer the trust property to them and put an end to the trust.

A further situation in which the terms of the trust may be varied without the sanction of the court is where an express power of advancement contained in the trust instrument is exercised by the trustees in order to secure a capital advance to the remainderman.

---

233. [1969] 1 Ch 223, 245.
234. (1841) Cr & Ph 240.
235. See *Wharton v. Masterman* [1895] AC 186, 198 *per* Lord Davey.

Variation of the Terms of a Trust With Court Approval

As a general principle a court will not permit trustees to deviate from the terms of a trust in performing their duties, although variation of a trust scheme may be sanctioned by the court in certain limited circumstances.[236] The need for court approval to vary the terms of a trust arises where there are unborn or minor beneficiaries who cannot consent to a variation which might be desirable[237] e.g. from the point of view of reducing liability to taxation.

Emergency or Salvage Jurisdiction

The court has an inherent power to sanction variation of a trust instrument in cases of necessity to avoid the destruction of or ensure the preservation of trust property e.g. to effect essential repairs to a building to save it from collapse. This 'emergency or salvage' jurisdiction may be exercised where some crisis unforeseen by the settlor or testator has arisen and it is necessary for the trustees to vary the terms of the trust so as to enable them to take action where the consent of the beneficiaries cannot be obtained, often because they are not yet in existence or are under a disability. The most common reason for invoking this jurisdiction is to authorize the sale or mortgage of trust property for the purpose of effecting essential repairs to it. This principle was set out as follows by Gavan Duffy J in *Re Johnson's Settlement*:[238]

> Where trustees are not trustees for sale and have no power of sale or management, and where the limitations are equitable, I hold that the Court can as a last resort if no other way is open, apply the principle of salvage in order to sanction the expenditure out of capital of the money necessary for doing such repairs, constituting permanent improvements, as are essential to the preservation of the settled property.

In *Re Johnson's Settlement* the court authorized the trustee to mortgage

---

236. *Chapman v. Chapman* [1954] AC 429, 445 *per* Lord Simonds LC. See also *per* Lord Asquith at 469.
237. As Huband JA has recently commented in delivering the judgment of the Manitoba Court of Appeal in *Teichman v. Teichman Estate* (1996) 134 DLR (4th) 155, 157 in relation to the rule in *Saunders v. Vautier* 'unanimity [is] required, except that the court could consent on behalf of the beneficiaries who were minors or otherwise lacked capacity or who were as yet unborn, so long as the arrangement was for the benefit of those beneficiaries'.
238. [1944] IR 529, 533-534. See also *Bank of Ireland v. Geoghegan* [1955-56] Ir Jur Rep 7.

settled lands for the purpose of raising money to effect repairs and in *Neill v. Neill*[239] Kenny J sanctioned the further mortgaging of a sheep farm over which the trust held a mortgage to raise funds for the continued running of the farm in a time of crisis. The ambit of this salvage jurisdiction has been extended to other types of emergency situations and perhaps the high watermark of this jurisdiction is the decision of the English Court of Appeal in *Re New*[240] where the court authorized trustees to concur in a shareholders' scheme for the reconstruction of a company where the evidence showed that the scheme would be greatly to the advantage of all the parties involved. Romer LJ said that while as a rule the court has no jurisdiction to give sanction to the performance by trustees of acts not authorized by the terms of the trust it can intervene where the trustees have been embarrassed by an emergency. However, he stressed that: 'Of course, the jurisdiction is one to be exercised with great caution, and the Court will take care not to strain its powers.'[241] This decision has been criticised as being too liberal and it did not signify any general move to broaden the jurisdiction of the court in this area; as Kekewich J subsequently commented in *Re Tollemache*:[242] while the decision of the Court of Appeal was useful, 'it [did] not purport to enlarge the jurisdiction of the court'.

To Effect a Compromise of a Dispute

The court also has authority to sanction a variation in the terms of a trust in order to effect a compromise of disputes as between the claims of various beneficiaries. Before the decision of the House of Lords in *Chapman v. Chapman*,[243] the courts had accepted a fairly wide definition of the word 'compromise'. However, it was held by the majority of the House of Lords in *Chapman* that there must be a genuine dispute for this jurisdiction to be brought into effect and not merely a desire to alter the terms of the original trust. Lord Cohen dissented as Lord Denning MR had done in the Court of Appeal and held that the jurisdiction of the court in this context extended to effecting a compromise in a wide sense between the tenant for life and the remainderman. Partly as a result of this decision, legislation was introduced in England in the form of the Variation of Trusts Act 1958 which provides that a court may, if it thinks fit approve an arrangement varying or revoking a trust or enlarging the powers of the trustees on the applica-

---

239. [1904] 1 IR 513.
240. [1901] 2 Ch 534.
241. *Ibid.* at 545.
242. [1903] 1 Ch 457, 465.
243. [1954] AC 429.

tion of defined classes of beneficiaries or potential beneficiaries.[244] It remains to be seen whether, in the absence of similar legislation in this jurisdiction, our courts would adopt the more flexible approach of the minority in *Chapman*.

To Permit the Payment of Maintenance

Maintenance may be paid by virtue of the statutory power in section 43 of the Conveyancing Act 1881 or the court may permit maintenance to be paid out of interest directed to be accumulated.[245] A variation of this nature will be authorized on the grounds that a settlor or testator would not have intended the beneficiaries to be left without reasonable means. So, in *Re Collins*[246] a testator directed that the income of his real and personal property should be accumulated for 21 years and gave the accumulated property to his sister for life with remainder to her sons and their children. The court held that an annual sum be paid out of the income of the personal estate for the maintenance and education of the sister's sons. Pearson J stated as follows:

> Where a testator has made provision for a family ... but has postponed the enjoyment, either for a particular purpose or generally for the increase of the estate, it is assumed that he did not intend these children should be left unprovided for or in a state of such moderate means that they should not be educated properly for the position and fortune which he designs them to have. . . .[247]

LIKELY FUTURE DEVELOPMENTS IN RELATION TO THE ADMINISTRATION OF TRUSTS

Lord Nicholls writing extra-judicially has commented that '[t]imes change

---

244. As Mummery LJ has recently stated in the decision of the Court of Appeal in *Goulding v. James* [1997] 2 All ER 239, although the jurisdiction provided for in the Act has been invoked 'thousands of times' there have been 'remarkably few reported cases on its construction'. In *Goulding,* the court approved an arrangement varying the terms of a trust which was undoubtedly for the benefit of unborn beneficiaries although extrinsic evidence had been given to the effect that this variation would run contrary to the testatrix's original intentions See further Luxton (1997) 60 MLR 719.
245. See *supra* pp. 421-422.
246. (1886) 32 Ch D 229.
247. *Ibid.* at 232.

and with them the problems confronting trustees'.[248] The Law Commission in England has also recently pointed out that 'trusteeship is an increasingly specialised task that often requires professional skills that . . . trustees may not have'.[249] As the range of choices in relation to investment of trust funds has increased, so have the difficulties inherent in the management of trust investments which is becoming an increasingly technical area requiring specialist expertise. However, as was noted above, the circumstances in which a trustee may delegate have not kept pace with such developments, with the result that a trustee may find himself trying to make investment decisions which he lacks the knowledge to make in a fully informed way.

Partly as a result of such factors, increasing numbers of professionals are being appointed to act as trustees. This in itself leads to difficulties and as Kenny has recently commented 'Equity's rules are unsuited to modern professional trusts'.[250] As she points out no professional trustee would act unless paid for doing so and despite this fact trusts are still governed 'by rules derived from a social era when trustees were generously donating their time and skill to the administration of another's property'. Undoubtedly the tasks performed by professional trustees require considerable skill and experience for which they are well remunerated and as Kenny suggests, in view of this, beneficiaries of modern trusts should be regarded as clients entitled to a high level of service and standard of professionalism.

There have been suggestions made in the context of a trustee's duty to invest to the effect that a higher standard of care is expected of a professional trustee. So in *Re Waterman's Will Trusts*[251] Harman J stated *obiter* that a higher standard of diligence and knowledge is required and this was confirmed by Brightman J in *Bartlett v. Barclays Bank Trust Co. Ltd*[252] who said that a greater duty of care is owed by a professional trustee such as a trust corporation which carries on the specialised business of trust

---

248. (1995) 9 Trust Law Int 71. As Legatt LJ commented in *Nestle v. National Westminster Bank plc* [1993] 1 WLR 1260, 1281: '[I]n Victorian times . . . little was demanded of a trustee beyond the safeguarding of the trust fund by refraining from improvident investment. This process was no doubt also intended to save beneficiaries from trouble and anxiety, or what is now called "hassle"'.

249. Consultation Paper No. 146 on Trustees' Powers and Duties (1997) paragraph 1.1. The Commission commented that as a result of changes both in the way in which financial markets operate and the purposes for which trusts are now employed, the present law is no longer always adequate to enable trustees to administer a trust to the best advantage of the beneficiaries or the objects of the trust'.

250. (1996) 146 NLJ 348.

251. [1952] 2 All ER 1054, 1055.

252. [1980] Ch 515.

management. However, in *Nestle v. National Westminster Bank plc*,[253] while
the defendant was a professional institution, Legatt LJ merely stated that
'the essence of the bank's duty was to take such steps as a prudent businessman would have taken to maintain and increase the value of the trust
fund'.[254] When one considers the skill which a professional trustee professes to have and the fact that such a trustee will be financially rewarded,
often quite substantially, for acting in this capacity, the reluctance of the
Court of Appeal to impose a higher standard is surprising.

There have been some signs to indicate that the judiciary are aware
that traditional principles developed in the context of family trusts are no
longer adequate or suitable to deal with modern commercial trusts. The
most useful statement to this effect is contained in the speech of Lord
Browne-Wilkinson in *Target Holdings Ltd v. Redferns*[255] in the following
terms:

> [I]n my judgment it is in any event wrong to lift wholesale the de-
> tailed rules developed in the context of traditional trusts and then
> seek to apply them to trusts of a quite different kind. In the modern
> world the trust has become a valuable device in commercial and
> financial dealings. The fundamental principles of equity apply as
> much to such trusts as they do to the traditional trusts in relation to
> which those principles were originally formulated. But in my judg-
> ment, it is important, if the trust is not to be rendered commercially
> useless, to distinguish between the basic principles of trust law and
> those specialist rules developed in relation to traditional trusts which
> are applicable only to such trusts and the rationale of which has no
> application to trusts of a quite different kind.

As Nolan has commented, drawing a distinction between different types
of trusts might be justifiable in principle as it recognises that the relationship between trustee and beneficiary and therefore their correlative rights
can vary widely from one context to another.[256] On the other hand Ulph
argues that the unity of trust principles is already under threat due to the
wide variety of contexts in which these principles operate and suggests
that the approach in *Target* strains this unity even further.[257] Finally it
should be noted that while the House of Lords concluded that traditional

---

253. [1993] 1 WLR 1260.
254. *Ibid.* at 1283.
255. [1996] 1 AC 421, 435.
256. [1996] LMCLQ 161, 163.
257. (1995) 9 Trust Law Int 86, 88.

principles should not apply to the case before them, as Capper points out the *dicta* of Lord Browne-Wilkinson offers little real insight into how the rules relating to commercial trusts should differ from those applicable to traditional trusts.[258]

One distinct area in which the established principles relating to the administration of trusts are clearly of doubtful utility is in relation to pension trusts. However, even in this context there has been considerable judicial debate in England about the efficacy of developing new principles which will take into account the different nature of such trusts. In *McDonald v. Horn*[259] Hoffmann LJ acknowledged that 'pension funds are a special form of trust' and in *Mettoy Pension Trustees Ltd v. Evans*[260] Warner J pointed out that beneficiaries under a pension scheme are not volunteers and said that in construing the trust instrument it was important to bear in mind the origin of the beneficiaries' rights under it. However, in *Cowan v. Scargill*[261] Megarry VC stated that he could 'see no reason for holding that different principles apply to pension fund trusts from those which apply to other trusts'. This point was reiterated by Rattee J in *Wilson v. Law Debenture Trust Corporation plc*[262] where he commented that 'in general the principles applicable to private trusts as a matter of trust law apply equally to pension schemes'. In *Wilson* counsel for the plaintiffs submitted that in the case of a pension scheme, in the absence of express provision to the contrary, a trustee should be bound to give reasons for the exercise of the discretion conferred upon him as it would seem unreasonable that members of the scheme who had bought their interests could not see whether the trustee had exercised his discretion properly. However, Rattee J rejected this argument in the following terms:

> It would in my judgment be wrong in principle to hold that the long-established principles of trust law as to the exercise by trustees of discretions conferred on them by their trust instruments, in the context of which parties to a pension scheme such as the present entered into those schemes, no longer apply to them and that the trustees are under more onerous obligations to account to their beneficiaries than they could have appreciated when appointed, on the basis of the relevant trust law as it has stood for so long.[263]

258. [1997] Conv 14, 22.
259. [1995] 1 All ER 961, 973.
260. [1990] 1 WLR 1587, 1618.
261. [1985] Ch 270, 290.
262. [1995] 2 All ER 337, 347.
263. *Ibid.* at 348.

Despite the rather restrictive terms of this judgment, it can be argued that the proposition put forward by counsel for the plaintiffs seemed eminently reasonable in the context of a pension scheme in which the 'beneficiaries' were individuals who had paid for their interest in the trust. The decision of the Court of Appeal in *Re Londonderry's Settlement*[264] to the effect that trustees are not obliged to disclose to the beneficiaries their reasons for acting seems out of touch with the commercial realities of modern pension trusts and it is likely that this question will be revisited. It should be noted that in England, section 35 of the Pensions Act 1996 now requires pension fund trustees to disclose their investment policy and this move towards greater accountability is clearly a desirable step.

Finally it is submitted that any piecemeal attempts at reform which can be effected by judicial decisions are likely to be insufficient to properly address the substantial practical difficulties facing trustees required to ad-minister modern trusts. Furthermore it is clearly necessary to introduce a greater degree of accountability for the benefit of beneficiaries of certain types of trusts who are not volunteers and who are effectively paying for the trustees' services; as Kenny has argued such individuals should be regarded as 'clients, entitled to a high level of service'.[265] While there is some merit in the argument that for the sake of certainty the same princi-ples should apply to all types of trust, it is submitted that such a view must yield to the reality that modern trusts are now called upon to fulfil many diverse functions. For this reason comprehensive legislation addressing these issues would clearly be desirable.

---

264. [1965] Ch 918.
265. (1996) 146 NLJ 348.

CHAPTER 13

Injunctions

INTRODUCTION

At common law the usual remedy where a plaintiff succeeded in his action was an award of damages; this form of relief was often inadequate or inappropriate and equity supplemented the legal remedies available by developing alternative types of remedy such as the injunction. An injunction is an order restraining the person to whom it is directed from carrying out a specified act or requiring him to perform such an act; it is a most flexible and versatile form of remedy and is used with increasing frequency today.

The injunction developed initially as a means of doing justice in cases where the traditional common law remedy of damages could not achieve such an aim. As the Court of Chancery grew in stature, the device of the injunction was even employed to restrain the enforcement of the judgments of the common law courts. This led to a bitter dispute between the two systems, a dispute which was resolved by the then king, James I, following the *Earl of Oxford's case*[1] in favour of the Court of Chancery. A distinction has been drawn between the grant of equitable injunctions in the so-called 'exclusive jurisdiction', i.e. in circumstances where it is sought to protect an equitable right, for example the right of a beneficiary under a trust, and the grant of injunctions in the 'auxiliary jurisdiction' where the remedy is used to protect a legal right. Over a period of time this auxiliary jurisdiction became widely used and eventually power was given to the common law courts themselves to grant injunctions by the Common Law Procedure (Ireland) Act 1856.[2] Around this time jurisdiction was also given to the Court of Chancery to award damages in addition to or in lieu of an injunction by the Chancery Amendment Act 1858, known as Lord Cairns' Act, and from a procedural point of view the two systems grew even closer together. The enactment of the Judicature (Ireland) Act 1877 effectively

---

1. (1615) 1 Rep Ch 1.
2. The suggestion was made in the context of the equivalent English legislation, the Common Law Procedure Act 1854, that it resulted in the common law courts having more extensive jurisdiction in this area than the Court of Chancery; *Quartz Hill Consolidated Gold Mining Co. v. Beall* (1882) 20 Ch D 501, 509 *per* Baggallay LJ.

brought about a fusion of procedure and section 28(8) provided that the court was empowered to grant interlocutory relief 'whenever it was just and convenient to do so'. Debate has raged ever since, particularly in England, over the question of whether the Judicature Act and its successors effected any enlargement of the court's power to grant an injunction. In *Moore v. Attorney General*[3] Murnaghan J expressed the view that the Act 'extends the principles upon which jurisdiction was formerly exercised by the Court of Chancery' and Jessel MR commented in *Beddow v. Beddow*[4] that the courts now had unlimited power to grant an injunction whenever it was just and convenient to do so. However, the better view would seem to be that the legislation did not confer any additional jurisdiction on the court; as Brett LJ commented in *North London Railway Co. v. Great Northern Railway Co.*:[5] 'if no court had the power of issuing an injunction before the Judicature Act, no part of the High Court has power to issue an injunction now'. This view has been accepted by the House of Lords in England,[6] and despite the comment of Murnaghan J in *Moore* it would seem to be the logical conclusion to reach.

Injunctions may be classified in a number of ways, first as between those which impose negative and positive obligations. The most common form of injunction falls into the former category and is known as a prohibitory injunction, namely one which restrains the performance or continuance of a wrongful act. The latter form of order is known as a mandatory injunction and has the effect of requiring the performance of an act. A further classification can be made between interim and interlocutory injunctions on the one hand and perpetual injunctions on the other hand. The former are granted prior to the trial of an action; an interim injunction is obtained for a limited period and will have effect only until further order and is often, although not invariably sought on an *ex parte* basis.[7] An interlocutory injunction will have effect until the final hearing of the action takes place and its purpose is to maintain the *status quo* between the par-

---

3. [1927] IR 569, 580. See also the *dicta* of Chatterton VC in *Cork Corporation v. Rooney* (1881) 17 LR Ir 191, 200.
4. (1878) 9 Ch D 89, 93. See also *Argyll v. Argyll* [1967] Ch 302.
5. (1883) 11 QBD 30, 36-37. See also *Day v. Brownrigg* (1878) 10 Ch D 294, 307 *per* James LJ.
6. *Gouriet v. Union of Post Office Workers* [1978] AC 435; *The Siskina* [1979] AC 210; *South Carolina Insurance Co. v. Assurance Maatschappij 'de Zeven Provincien' NV* [1987] AC 24.
7. Where a matter is particularly urgent a plaintiff may apply for such an order on an *ex parte* basis and such an order will generally continue until the next motion day when the defendant will have the opportunity of putting his side of the case.

ties as far as possible until the final determination of the issues in dispute by the court.

A perpetual injunction on the other hand will only be granted at the trial of the action where a plaintiff has established a right and the actual or threatened infringement of that right by the defendant. In practice, the order amounts to a final determination of the issues in dispute by the court although it does not mean that the injunction will necessarily last perpetually as its name suggests.

Finally a distinction should be drawn between *quia timet* injunctions which are granted in respect of wrongs which are merely threatened or apprehended and other forms of injunction which are designed to prevent the continuance of a wrong or to guard against its repetition.

THE PRINCIPLES GOVERNING THE GRANT OF INJUNCTIONS

General Principles Governing the Grant of Perpetual Injunctions

Introduction
An injunction will only be granted to protect a right of the plaintiff whether a legal right deriving from the common law, an equitable right (e.g. the right of a beneficiary under a trust), a constitutional right, or a right deriving from a specific statutory power. The plaintiff must establish a sufficient interest in the protection of this right,[8] and an injunction will not issue to remedy mere inconvenience or where the interference with the plaintiff's rights is trivial. Traditionally it was thought that the grant of an injunction was limited to circumstances where a proprietary right had been infringed or threatened but this is certainly no longer the general rule. As Spry[9] has commented 'any attempt to found the jurisdiction to grant injunctions exclusively on the existence of property or proprietary rights is not justified'.

A further cardinal principle which must be borne in mind is that injunctions, like other forms of equitable remedy are discretionary in nature. So while a plaintiff may establish the infringement of a right and a *prima facie* entitlement to relief he may still be denied this relief on discretionary grounds. However, this discretion cannot be exercised in an arbitrary manner but rather in accordance with well established principles which have

---

8. *Maxwell v. Hogg* (1867) 2 Ch App 307, 311 *per* Turner LJ.
9. *Equitable Remedies* (5th ed., 1997) p. 340.

been considered in detail by the courts. This principle was laid down by Evershed MR in *Pride of Derby and Derbyshire Angling Association Ltd v. British Celanese Ltd*:[10]

> It is, I think, well settled that if A proves that his proprietary rights are being wrongfully interfered with by B, and that B intends to continue his wrong, then A is *prima facie* entitled to an injunction, and he will be deprived of that remedy only if special circumstances exist, including the circumstance that damages are an adequate remedy for the wrong that he has suffered.

It is now proposed to examine the operation of some of these discretionary factors in practice. It should be pointed out that many cases never progress beyond the interlocutory stage and in general the same discretionary principles operate irrespective of whether a perpetual or interlocutory order is being sought. The specific factors relevant to the grant of interlocutory relief will be considered in detail below.

The Inadequacy or Inappropriateness of Damages as a Remedy
Historically, the main reason for the intervention of the Court of Chancery was the inadequacy or inappropriateness of damages or other remedies at common law. Therefore in the context of the grant of an injunction, a plaintiff was required to satisfy the court that the right which he sought to protect was of such a nature that an award of damages would not leave him in all respects in as good a position as if he had obtained enforcement of this right. As Lindley LJ stated in *London and Blackwell Railway Co. v. Cross*:[11] '*prima facie* you do not obtain injunctions to restrain actionable wrongs, for which damages are the proper remedy'. This principle still operates today, although arguably in a slightly more modified form and no injunction will be granted where an injury can be properly compensated in monetary terms but will only issue e.g to restrain a continuing nuisance or the breach of a negative contract. However the trend in modern cases has been to move away from the traditional question of asking 'are damages an adequate remedy?' to 'is it just, in all the circumstances, that a plaintiff should be confined to his remedy in damages?'.[12]

It will often be considered just to confine a plaintiff to an award of damages where the wrongdoing of which he complains has ceased and is

---

10. [1953] Ch 149, 181.
11. (1886) 31 Ch D 354, 369.
12. *Evans Marshall & Co. Ltd v. Bertola SA* [1973] 1 WLR 349, 379 *per* Sachs LJ.

not likely to re-occur, and where his loss is quantifiable. However a question which has often arisen, particularly in the context of interlocutory applications, is the extent to which difficulties in quantifying a plaintiff's loss may make damages an inadequate form of relief. In *Yeates v. Minister for Posts and Telegraphs*[13] Kenny J commented that 'an injunction is granted before the hearing of an action only when damages will not be an adequate remedy or when the assessment of damages will be extremely difficult'. This issue of difficulty in the quantification of damages was recently considered by the Supreme Court in *Curust Financial Services Ltd v. Loewe-Lack-Werk Otto Loewe GmbH*,[14] where Finlay CJ stressed that: 'Difficulty, as opposed to complete impossibility, in the assessment of ... damages should not, in my view, be a ground for characterizing the awarding of damages as an inadequate remedy.' In the circumstances the Supreme Court was satisfied that the quantum of damages could be assessed and that no interlocutory injunction should be granted. Clearly where wrongdoing is likely to continue into the future it may not be feasible to attempt to assess the measure of damages necessary to compensate a plaintiff and in such circumstances the grant of an injunction will often prove to be the only just remedy.

The Conduct of the Parties

The discretionary considerations which are taken into account by a court in deciding whether to grant an injunction relate not only to the nature of the right which a plaintiff seeks to enforce and to the potential consequences of the decision to grant or refuse relief, but may also include factors relating to the conduct of the person invoking the jurisdiction of the court, and to a lesser extent, the conduct of the defendant. In this regard, two of the maxims considered earlier are relevant, namely 'he who comes to equity must come with clean hands' and 'he who seeks equity must do equity'.[15] While these maxims should be treated with caution, they do reflect the general principles which operate in relation to a plaintiff's conduct.

Where an injunction is sought by a plaintiff in furtherance of the perpetration of fraud, a court will not hesitate to refuse relief but conduct falling far short of fraud may also disentitle a plaintiff to an equitable

---

13. [1978] ILRM 22, 24.
14. [1994] 1 IR 450, 469. Quoted with approval by Kelly J in *Fitzpatrick v. Garda Commissioner* High Court 1996 No. 121 JR, 16 October 1996 at p.14. See also the comments of Hamilton J in *Reno Engrais et Produits Chemiques SA v. Irish Agricultural Wholesale Society Ltd* [1976-77] ILRM 179, 184 and of Keane J in *Oblique Financial Services Ltd v. The Promise Production Co. Ltd* [1994] 1 ILRM 74, 79.
15. See *supra* Chapter 2.

remedy. The effect of the maxim 'he who comes to equity must come with clean hands'[16] is such that where a plaintiff who has been guilty of some impropriety or disreputable conduct seeks relief in the form of an equitable remedy, it may be refused by the court on discretionary grounds.[17] However, the court will decline to intervene on the basis of the 'clean hands' principle[18] unless there is a sufficient connection between the inequitable conduct and the subject matter of the dispute. As Scrutton LJ commented in *Moody v. Cox*:[19]

> Equity will not apply the principle about clean hands unless the depravity, the dirt in question on the hand, has an immediate and necessary relation to the equity sued for.

This proposition is well illustrated by *Argyll v. Argyll*,[20] where it was held by Ungoed-Thomas J that the alleged immorality of the plaintiff's conduct which had led to divorce did not deprive her of her entitlement to an injunction to restrain a breach of confidence by her husband. As Ungoed-Thomas J stated 'A person coming to equity for relief ... must come with clean hands, but the cleanliness required is to be judged in relation to the relief that is sought.'[21] The so called 'clean hands' principle has been applied in a wide variety of situations where an injunction has been sought e.g. where the plaintiff's conduct has been 'unfair and unreasonable',[22]

---

16. For a statement of this general principle, see *Dering v. Earl of Winchelsea* (1787) 1 Cox 318, 319-320 where Eyre LCB stated: 'a man must come into a Court of Equity with clean hands; but when this is said, it does not mean a general depravity; it must have an immediate and necessary relation to the equity sued for; it must be a depravity in a legal as well as in the moral sense'. See also *Tinker v. Tinker* [1970] P 136, 143 *per* Salmon LJ.

17. See *Overton v. Banister* (1844) 3 Hare 503; *Gascoigne v. Gascoigne* [1918] 1 KB 223; *McEvoy v. Belfast Banking Co. Ltd* [1934] NI 67; *Smelter Corporation of Ireland Ltd v. O'Driscoll* [1977] IR 305 and *Parkes v. Parkes* [1980] ILRM 137. The latter case illustrated the proposition that a plaintiff may be refused equitable relief where his conduct in relation to the transaction at issue has been less than honest even where this conduct has not directly prejudiced the defendant.

18. See generally Pettit [1990] Conv 416. Pettit suggests (at p.424) that unclean hands seems to be a 'last resort defence' to be invoked where none of the so-called nominate defences are applicable but where it would be unconscionable for the plaintiff to be granted relief by the court.

19. [1917] 2 Ch 71, 87-88. The plaintiff's claim for rescission of a contract succeeded despite the fact that he had given a bribe to the vendor's solicitor, although admittedly in an unconnected matter.

20. [1967] Ch 302.

21. *Ibid.* at 332.

22. *Shell UK Ltd. v. Lostock Garage Ltd* [1976] 1 WLR 1187, 1199 *per* Lord Denning MR.

where he has sought to safeguard his rights by 'deplorable means'[23], where he has committed a breach of covenant,[24] or where he has attempted to mislead the court.[25]

This principle has recently been referred to by the Supreme Court in *Curust Financial Services Ltd v. Loewe-Lack-Werk Otto Loewe GmbH,*[26] in which the court had to consider whether the alleged breach by the plaintiff of an exclusive licensing agreement, consisting of its sub-contracting the manufacture of a product without the prior written consent of the first named defendant, should disentitle it to relief. As a general principle, Finlay CJ accepted that the court has a discretion, where it is satisfied that a person has come to court otherwise than with 'clean hands', to refuse equitable relief in the form of an injunction on that ground alone. However, he continued by saying that 'it seems to me that this phrase must of necessity involve an element of turpitude and cannot necessarily be equated with a mere breach of contract.'[27] Finlay CJ made reference to the fact that what might be established as a breach by the plaintiff of the agreement not to sub-contract, namely the entering into an arrangement with a third party for this purpose, might also be established as having been provoked by a wrongful repudiation on the part of the first named defendant of its own contractual obligations under the licensing agreement. He therefore concluded that it would be unreasonable that such conduct should disentitle the plaintiff to an injunction to which it would otherwise be entitled and this would suggest that the Supreme Court appears willing to take on board the flexible approach adopted in England in recent years towards the application of the 'clean hands' principle.

The application of the maxim 'he who seeks equity must do equity' can be seen where the court will decline to grant an injunction to a party who e.g. seeks to enforce contractual rights while at the same time refusing to perform his own contractual obligations or to give an assurance that he will do so in the future. This proposition is well illustrated by the decision of the Court of Appeal in *Chappell v. Times Newspapers,*[28] which concerned a dispute which had arisen between unions and employers in the printing industry. Following selective industrial action, the employers threatened to terminate their employees' contracts unless normal production was resumed. The plaintiffs, who were individual union members who

---

23. *Hubbard v. Vosper* [1972] 2 QB 84, 101 *per* Megaw LJ.
24. *Litvinoff v. Kent* (1918) 34 TLR 298.
25. *Armstrong v. Sheppard & Short Ltd* [1959] 2 QB 384, 397.
26. [1994] 1 IR 450, 468.
27. *Ibid.* at 467.
28. [1975] 1 WLR 482.

had not personally been involved in any industrial action, sought an interim injunction to restrain their respective employers from terminating their contracts of employment, although they refused to give the undertakings sought by the employers not to engage in disruptive activities. The Court of Appeal refused to grant an interim injunction on the grounds that the plaintiffs had failed to establish that they themselves intended to act equitably by abiding by the terms of their contracts of employment. As Lord Denning MR said 'it has long been settled both at common law and in equity that in a contract where each has to do his part concurrently with the other, then if one party seeks relief, he must be ready and willing to do his part in it.'[29]

The issue of the influence which the conduct of the defendant may have on the decision of a court to grant or withhold relief of this nature is one which has been considered less frequently. In *News Datacom Ltd v. Lyons*[30] in which the plaintiff sought an interlocutory injunction to restrain an alleged breach of copyright in software used to decode satellite television signals, Flood J said that the the mere fact that the conduct of one of the parties, in this case the defendant, might be questionable as a matter of ethics or morality was not a reason to grant relief in the absence of any other accepted grounds for making the order sought.

Laches and Acquiescence

The court may also refuse to grant an injunction on the grounds of laches or acquiescence. The defence of laches is said by Spry[31] to arise if two conditions are satisfied:

> [F]irst, there must be unreasonable delay on the part of the plaintiff in the commencement or prosecution of proceedings, and secondly, in view of the nature and consequences of that delay it must be unjust in all the circumstances to grant the specific relief that is in question, whether absolutely or on appropriate terms or conditions.

The length of the delay will be judged from the time the plaintiff had sufficient knowledge of the facts giving rise to the claim or where he had a reasonable suspicion of the infringement of his rights. Delay by itself is unlikely to bar a claim for equitable relief but when coupled with other circumstances, often relating to the conduct of the plaintiff, it may be suf-

---

29. *Ibid.* at 502.
30. [1994] 1 ILRM 450.
31. *Equitable Remedies* (5th ed., 1997) p. 431.

ficient to lead to an equitable remedy being refused. Clearly once a plaintiff is appraised of the facts which would lead him to seek the intervention of the court he should proceed without undue delay and should not wait until the eleventh hour before bringing proceedings. This point was stressed by O'Hanlon J in *Lennon v. Ganly*,[32] in which he refused the plaintiff an injunction restraining the defendants from embarking on a rugby tour to South Africa, because, *inter alia* he had delayed until just before the tour was due to commence and because a considerable period of time had elapsed since news of it had first been announced. However, the courts will take a realistic view of what will constitute undue delay and unless it is of appreciable length or some serious prejudice has been suffered by reason of it, it will not be a bar to relief.[33]

The view was expressed by Budd J in *Cahill v. Irish Motor Traders' Association*[34] that delay by itself will not disentitle a plaintiff to an injunction to protect a legal as opposed to an equitable right unless the claim is barred by statute. This view would also seem to prevail in Australia where Deane J commented in *Orr v. Ford*[35] that 'Laches is an equitable defence and is not available in answer to a legal claim'. However the Court of Appeal in *Habib Bank Ltd v. Habib Bank AG Zurich*[36] drew no distinction between legal and equitable rights in this context and made it clear that the defence of laches can apply whenever an injunction is sought. Whether this view would now find favour in Ireland remains to be seen, but it is likely that there will be a move towards the approach adopted in *Habib* in this jurisdiction also.

It would appear that a shorter period of inactivity will defeat a claim for an interlocutory injunction than is required to defeat an action for a perpetual injunction. This reflects the fact that while the refusal of an injunction at the interlocutory stage does not preclude the plaintiff from ultimately obtaining the relief which he seeks, refusal at the trial stage will finally dispose of his claim. In *Howard v. Commissioners of Public Works in Ireland*,[37] which involved a claim for an interlocutory injunction to restrain the respondents from proceeding with development work on a pro-

---

32. [1981] ILRM 84.
33. See e.g. *An Post v. Irish Permanent plc* [1995] 1 ILRM 336 where Kinlen J found that any delay in bringing an application for interlocutory relief was insufficient to influence the decision to grant relief. See also *Irish Shell Ltd v. Elm Motors Ltd* [1984] IR 200, 216 and *Carrigaline Community Television v. Minister for Transport* [1994] 2 IR 359.
34. [1966] IR 430, 449.
35. (1989) 167 CLR 316, 340 *per* Oliver LJ .
36. [1981] 1WLR 1265, 1285.
37. High Court 1992 No. 331JR (O'Hanlon J) 3 December 1992.

posed visitor centre and national park in the Burren, O'Hanlon J placed emphasis *inter alia* on the conduct of the parties. He concluded that the application should be refused because he believed that the balance of convenience lay in favour of allowing the work to proceed and because the applicants had delayed unduly in seeking the relief while the respondents had behaved in an 'irreproachable manner'.

Further consideration was given to the relevance of delay in the context of an application for an interlocutory injunction in *Newport Association Football Club Ltd v. Football Association of Wales Ltd.*[38] The plaintiffs, Welsh football clubs, sought an interlocutory injunction allowing them to play their home matches in Wales the following season as their revenue had decreased substantially as a result of sanctions preventing them playing there imposed by the defendant association when they decided to participate instead in a league organised by the English Football Association. Jacob J commented that normally a party who has delayed for two years or more before applying for an interlocutory injunction will be refused it on grounds of delay as the final trial could have taken place by that time and the *status quo* is likely to have changed. However, Jacob J was satisfied that notwithstanding these points the case before him was a wholly exceptional one and stated that if the injunction was not granted, there was a real risk that the plaintiffs would simply cease to exist. In addition, he adverted to the fact that this was not a case where the plaintiffs had been standing by for two years; during that time they had been actively seeking a solution to the problem and a reversal of the defendant's decision. Jacob J therefore concluded that while he took the delay into account, it was not enough to persuade him to withhold the injunction which he proposed to grant.

Acquiescence is described as arising in the following circumstances by Spry:[39] 'first, there must, on the part of the plaintiff, be an assent or lying by in relation to the acts of another person; and secondly, in view of the assent or lying by and consequent acts it must be unjust in all the circumstances to grant the specific relief that is in question.' Similarly, in *Archbold v. Scully*[40] Lord Wensleydale said: 'if a party, who could object, lies by and knowingly permits another to incur an expense in doing an act under the belief that it would not be objected to, and so a kind of permission may be said to be given to another to alter his condition, he may be said to acquiesce.' The operation of the principle of acquiescence as a

---

38. [1995] 2 All ER 87.
39. *Equitable Remedies* (5th ed., 1997) p. 440.
40. (1861) 9 HLC 360, 383.

defence to a claim for an injunction can best be explained by reference to a number of examples. In *Sayers v. Collyer*[41] the plaintiff failed to obtain an injunction to restrain the use of a house as a beer shop in breach of covenant as he had been aware of this breach for a number of years and had even bought beer there himself. As Baggallay LJ commented 'I can hardly imagine a stronger case of acquiescence than this.'[42] A good example of a case in which acquiescence barred a claim for an injunction but not a remedy in damages is the decision of the Court of Appeal in *Shaw v. Applegate.*[43] The defendant purchased property and covenanted not to use it as an amusement arcade and the vendor subsequently assigned the benefit of the covenant to the plaintiffs. Three years after the defendant had started to install amusement machines the plaintiff sought an injunction to restrain the breach of covenant. The Court of Appeal held that to deprive the possessor of a legal right of that right on the ground of his acquiescence the situation must have been such that it would be dishonest or unconscionable to seek to enforce it. Since the plaintiffs had been confused about whether the defendants' activities constituted a breach of covenant, it could not be said that the plaintiffs would be acting dishonestly or unconscionably in seeking to enforce their rights under the contract when they did. However, in view of the goodwill built up by the defendant over a period of years and the expenditure incurred by him, the court held that the appropriate remedy was damages and not an injunction.

Effect on Third Parties

There have been judicial statements made suggesting that the courts in deciding whether to grant an injunction should have regard to the surrounding circumstances and to the rights of those who may be peripherally involved,[44] and that an injunction should not be granted where this will have the effect of 'very materially injuring the rights of third parties'.[45] However, Spry[46] has stated that 'it is not generally appropriate that specific private rights should be denied in order to give rise to an indefinite advantage to the general public' and this view has tended to prevail. The question was considered by the Supreme Court in *Bellew v. Cement Ltd,*[47]

41. (1884) 28 Ch D 103.
42. *Ibid.* at 107.
43. [1977] 1 WLR 970.
44. *Wood v. Sutcliffe* (1851) 2 Sim (NS) 163, 165.
45. *Hartlepool Gas & Water Co. v. West Hartlepool Harbour & Rly Co.* (1865) 12 LT 366, 368.
46. *Equitable Remedies* (5th ed., 1997) p. 402.
47. [1948] IR 61.

in which the majority of the court concluded that the general public convenience should not be taken into account in weighing up whether to grant relief in the form of an injunction. The plaintiffs sought an interlocutory injunction to restrain the defendants, who were the sole manufacturers of cement in the State, from carrying out blasting operations in a quarry which it was alleged constituted a nuisance. The defendants argued that in view of the importance of the defendants' products to the building industry and having regard to the fact that because of the impending long vacation blasting operations would have to cease for several months, an injunction should not be granted. It was held by the Supreme Court in granting the order sought that the plaintiff had made out a *prima facie* case[48] of nuisance and that the court was not entitled to take the public convenience into consideration when dealing with the rights of private parties. As Maguire CJ stated: 'This matter is a dispute between private parties and I think that the court should be concerned, only, to see that the rights of the parties are safeguarded.'[49] Black J dissented and stated that while the concept of public convenience cannot justify the refusal of a remedy for a nuisance, it is a different matter to say that it cannot, or ought not to, affect the way in which a nuisance should be dealt with.[50]

In England there have been conflicting authorities on this question, but the most recent decision would seem to support the view of the majority in *Bellew*. In *Miller v. Jackson*[51] the owner of a house situated beside a cricket ground sought an injunction to prevent the club continuing with its activities which involved a risk of injury from cricket balls landing on the property. While two members of the Court of Appeal agreed that these activities constituted a nuisance, Cumming-Bruce LJ agreed with the view of Lord Denning MR that an injunction should not be granted in these circumstances and that the plaintiff should be confined to a remedy in damages. In his view 'a court of equity must seek to strike a fair balance between the right of the plaintiffs to have quiet enjoyment of their house and garden without exposure to cricket balls occasionally falling like thunderbolts from the heavens, and the opportunity of the inhabitants of the village in which they live to continue to enjoy the manly sport which constitutes a

---

48. This was the accepted test in relation to the granting of an interlocutory injunction at the time. It has now been replaced by the requirement of establishing that there is a fair question to be tried. See *infra* p. 467.
49. *Ibid.* at 64.
50. Note that in *Wall v. Feely*, High Court 1983 No. 7014P (Costello J) 26 October 1983, Costello J appeared to take the public convenience into account albeit to the limited extent of considering how this would affect the defendant local authority, although it did not ultimately influence his decision.
51. [1977] QB 966.

summer recreation for adults and young persons, including one would hope and expect, the plaintiff's son.'[52] This view was unanimously disapproved of several years later by a differently constituted Court of Appeal in *Kennaway v. Thompson.*[53] The plaintiff sought an injunction to restrain a nuisance which consisted of excessive noise caused by power boat racing on a lake in the vicinity of her house. The Court of Appeal granted an injunction which greatly restricted the club's activities on the grounds that the public interest in allowing the racing to continue uninterrupted could not prevail over the plaintiff's entitlement to enjoy her home free from the tortious interference which this racing caused.

While the view expressed by the Supreme Court in *Bellew* and the Court of Appeal in *Kennaway* would seem to be the correct one, there has been some evidence of a tendency to look beyond the rights of the parties actually involved in an action in assessing whether to grant an injunction, particularly at the interlocutory stage. In *Howard v. Commissioners for Public Works,*[54] the applicants sought an interlocutory injunction to restrain the respondents from proceeding with development work on a proposed interpretative centre in the Burren. O'Hanlon J concluded that the evidence was sufficient to satisfy him that major disruption of a very serious kind would occur if the project were to be brought to a standstill. He said that he had no doubt that the financial loss would be very substantial, that the respondents might find themselves facing serious liabilities for breach of contract and that many people would lose their employment. In addition, O'Hanlon J was of the view that the loss and damage which would be sustained by the applicants if the interlocutory relief were refused did not fall within the category of what he could regard as irreparable damage and he concluded that the interlocutory order should be refused. While other factors, such as the conduct of the parties was also referred to, it is difficult to avoid the conclusion that O'Hanlon J was influenced at least in part by the wider public convenience which involved primarily the employment prospects of those working on the project in deciding to refuse the relief sought.

The question of whether the court could take into account the wider question of public convenience was raised again recently in *An Post v. Irish Permanent plc,*[55] but Kinlen J said that he would express no view on the matter at the interlocutory stage as it was one more properly to be determined at trial.

---

52. *Ibid.* at 988.
53. [1981] QB 88.
54. High Court 1992 No.331JR (O'Hanlon J) 3 December 1992.
55. [1995] 1 ILRM 336, 349.

A related question is whether the activities of third parties should have any effect on the decision of a court to grant or refuse an injunction. Arguably this should not be a factor and the court should confine itself to an examination of the issues which affect the parties directly involved, although the approach adopted by Keane J in *Phonographic Performance (Ireland) Ltd v. Chariot Inns*[56] suggests that this will not always be the case. The plaintiff sought an interlocutory injunction restraining the defendants from permitting certain sound recordings from being played in public when the defendant refused to pay an amount claimed by the plaintiff by way of 'equitable remuneration' within the meaning of the Copyright Act 1963. Keane J concluded that there were 'unquestionably serious issues at stake between the parties involving difficult questions of law' and held that as more damage would be caused by refusing than by granting an injunction the order sought should be granted. However, in the course of his judgment, Keane J made reference to the fact that if the interlocutory injunction was refused and the plaintiff was ultimately successful, large sums would have to be recovered from other operators who might follow the defendants' example and refuse to pay and said that it was unlikely, given the number of businesses involved, that all these sums would be recovered. While the conclusion reached by Keane J was probably correct in the circumstances, as Coughlan[57] has pointed out, the question should arguably have been decided solely by reference to the infringement of the plaintiff's rights allegedly committed by that defendant and the defendant could hardly be held accountable for the activities of independent third parties.

Jurisdiction to Award Damages under Lord Cairns' Act

While originally the Court of Chancery had no jurisdiction to award damages, the Chancery Amendment Act 1858 (Lord Cairns' Act) authorized the court in all cases where it had jurisdiction to grant an injunction or an order of specific performance to award damages either in addition to or in substitution for the other remedies. This power to award damages in equity declined in significance after the enactment of the Judicature Act which conferred jurisdiction on the courts to make an award of damages in any case where this could have been done previously by the common law courts. However, it is still necessary to rely on Lord Cairns' Act in circumstances where no entitlement to damages lies at common law; e.g. where the right

---

56. High Court 1992 No. 4673P (Keane J) 7 October 1992.
57. [1993] EIPR D-10.

in question is equitable in nature, or where a breach of the plaintiff's rights has not yet occurred and is merely anticipated.[58] The discretion granted by Lord Cairns' Act is similar to that exercised since the enactment of the Judicature Act to make an award of damages in lieu of granting an injunction and it does not seem necessary to draw any distinction in relation to the general principles involved.

An attempt to lay down a 'good working rule' in relation to the principles governing the award of damages in lieu of an injunction under Lord Cairns' Act was made by Smith LJ in *Shelfer v. City of London Electric Lighting Co.*[59] An electric lighting company caused considerable discomfort and annoyance to the lessee of premises by carrying out excavation work. At first instance Kekewich J held that while the defendants had created a continuing nuisance, damages should be the only remedy, although the Court of Appeal allowed the plaintiff's appeal against the refusal of an injunction. Smith LJ laid down the general principle that damages should only be awarded in lieu of an injunction or specific performance in the following circumstances:[60]

(1) If the injury to the plaintiff's legal rights is small,
(2) And is one which is capable of being estimated in money,
(3) And is one which can be adequately compensated by a small money payment,
(4) And the case is one in which it would be oppressive to the defendant to grant an injunction. ...

Smith LJ continued by saying that even where these four principles are satisfied, an injunction may still be awarded if the defendant has acted in reckless disregard of the plaintiff's rights. A further point stressed by Lindley LJ which is of particular importance is that the court in exercising this jurisdiction will not allow a wrong to continue simply because the wrongdoer is able and willing to pay for the injury he may inflict.

The application of the *Shelfer* principles did not meet with universal approval in England, so, in *Fishenden v. Higgs & Hill Ltd*[61] Hanworth MR said that they were for guidance only and Romer LJ made it clear that if one of the four requirements was not fulfilled, it did not mean that an injunction must be granted. The Court of Appeal, while upholding a find-

---

58. *Johnson v. Agnew* [1980] AC 367, 400.
59. [1895] 1 Ch 287.
60. *Ibid.* at 322-323.
61. (1935) 153 LT 128.

ing of nuisance with regard to interference with a right to light, held that in the circumstances damages were a sufficient remedy. However, more recently these principles were accepted in *Kennaway v. Thompson*,[62] where the plaintiff sought an injunction to restrain power boat racing on a lake near her house. The Court of Appeal held that the principles in *Shelfer's* case applied and awarded her an injunction limiting the racing activities on the grounds that the injury to the plaintiff was not small or capable of estimation in monetary terms nor could the sum, awarded by the High Court judge who had decided to award damages in lieu, be considered a small payment. Lawton LJ said that he considered that *Shelfer's* case was binding on him and stressed that in cases of continuing nuisance the jurisdiction to award damages in lieu should only be exercised in very exceptional circumstances.

The leading Irish authority in this area is *Patterson v. Murphy*,[63] in which the plaintiffs sought damages and an injunction arising out of alleged acts of nuisance caused by blasting and quarrying activities carried on by the defendants in a field adjoining their house. Costello J found that these activities did constitute acts of nuisance and held that the plaintiffs were entitled to an injunction. He said that the infringement of their rights was most serious; the injury which they had suffered and would continue to suffer if the nuisance were allowed to continue had been and would be considerable and he was satisfied that damages would not adequately compensate them. Costello J laid down a number of 'well established principles' on which the court exercises its discretion in deciding whether to grant an injunction and it is worth setting them out in full.

> 1. When an infringement of the plaintiffs' right and a threatened further infringement to a material extent has been established, the plaintiff is *prima facie* entitled to an injunction. There may be circumstances, however, depriving the plaintiff of this *prima facie* right but generally speaking the plaintiff will only be deprived of an injunction in very exceptional circumstances.
>
> 2. If the injury to the plaintiffs' rights is small, and is one capable of being estimated in money, and is one which can be adequately compensated by a small money payment and if the case is one in which it would be oppressive to the defendant to grant an injunction, then

---

62. [1981] QB 88. See also *Jaggard v. Sawyer* [1995] 1 WLR 269, 277-278 *per* Bingham MR.
63. [1978] ILRM 85, 99-100.

these are circumstances in which damages in lieu of an injunction may be granted.

3. The conduct of the plaintiff may be such as to disentitle him to an injunction. The conduct of the defendant may be such as to disentitle him from seeking the substitution of damages for an injunction.

4. The mere fact that a wrong-doer is able and willing to pay for the injury he has inflicted is not a ground for substituting damages.

Costello J distinguished the decision of Gannon J in *Halpin v. Tara Mines Ltd,*[64] in which the plaintiffs had been refused an injunction and awarded damages in respect of a nuisance caused by the defendant's prospecting activities. While he found that these activities had amounted to a nuisance, Gannon J was satisfied that the defendant had modified its operations and improved its working practices to such an extent by the time of the trial of the action that the court should decline to grant an injunction.

While the point made by Lindley LJ in *Shelfer* that a court will not allow a wrong to continue simply because the wrongdoer is able and willing to pay for the injury he may inflict is an important one, where the wrongdoing is unintentional and the plaintiff has suffered no loss in its trading position, a remedy in damages may meet the justice of the situation. In *Falcon Travel Ltd v. Owners Abroad Group plc* [65] the plaintiff, a retail travel agent in the Wicklow and Dublin areas sought an injunction against the defendants who had opened an office in this country on the grounds of alleged passing off. Due to the similarity in the companies' names confusion arose and there was bad publicity for the plaintiff on one occasion although in general their turnover increased because of the confusion. Murphy J accepted that while the defendant was aware of the plaintiff's business, he was satisfied that it had not intended to exploit its reputation or business. While it did not appear that the plaintiff's business had suffered, Murphy J accepted that the plaintiff had suffered damage in that its reputation had become submerged into that of the defendant and he concluded that the tort of passing off had been established. Although he said that an injunction would ordinarily be the most suitable means of protecting the plaintiff's property rights, he took into account the fact that the wrongdoing was unintentional and that the plaintiff had suffered no loss in its trading position as well as the fact that an injunction would involve the defendant in enormous expense. In view of these factors,

---

64. [1976-77] ILRM 28.
65. [1991] 1 IR 175.

Murphy J decided to exercise his discretion to award damages in lieu of an injunction, calculated with a view to organizing an advertising campaign to make it clear to the public that the plaintiff and defendant were separate businesses.

The Measure of Damages Under Lord Cairns' Act

The question of the measure of damages which can be awarded under Lord Cairns' Act is one which has provoked considerable uncertainty in England and this controversy is not one which the courts in this jurisdiction have directly addressed. In *Johnson v. Agnew*[66] the House of Lords held that there was no difference in the measure of damages which could be awarded under Lord Cairns' Act and at common law, Lord Wilberforce stating that the Act 'does not provide for the assessment of damages on any new basis'.[67] However, no reference was made by the House of Lords in *Johnson* to the earlier decision of Brightman J in *Wrotham Park Estate Co. v. Parkside Homes Ltd*[68] in which he had considered the measure of damages to be awarded in equity in lieu of an injunction for breach of a restrictive covenant. As the plaintiff had sustained no loss, any damages which would have been awarded at common law would have been purely nominal,[69] but Brightman J concluded that a 'just substitute' for the injunction sought would be the sum which the plaintiff might have obtained in return for modifying the covenant.

Ingman has suggested that Brightman J's conclusion in *Wrotham Park* may have resulted from a misunderstanding as to what Lord Cairns' Act was intended to achieve.[70] In his view the primary object of the legislation was a purely procedural one and he asserts that it was 'never intended to change the substantive law so as to permit a court of equity to award damages on a different basis from that recognised at common law in a case where damages were available both in equity and at law.'[71] However it should be pointed out that in *Wrotham Park* damages would not have been available at law and for this reason, the decision may still be defended on its own facts.

---

66. [1980] AC 367.
67. *Ibid.* at 400.
68. [1974] 1 WLR 798. It should be noted that *Wrotham Park* appears to have been approved by the Court of Appeal in *Stoke-on-Trent City Council v. W. & J. Wass Ltd* [1988] 1 WLR 1406 in which the House of Lords decision in *Johnson* was not referred to.
69. Although it should be stressed that on the facts of this case, as a restrictive covenant was involved, damages could only be awarded under Lord Cairns' Act.
70. [1994] Conv 110.
71. *Ibid.* at 120.

Subsequently in *Surrey County Council v. Bredero Homes Ltd*,[72] in which the plaintiff only sought common law damages as the grant of an injunction had become impossible before proceedings were issued, the Court of Appeal expressed different views on the earlier decisions. Dillon LJ stated that in his opinion the award of significant damages in *Wrotham Park* was inconsistent with *Johnson* and said that the conclusion of Brightman J involved the assumption that Lord Cairns' Act had effected a substantive and not merely a procedural change in the law, a finding which ran contrary to what had been stated by the House of Lords. However, the majority of the Court of Appeal on an *obiter* basis expressed the view that the conclusion reached in *Wrotham Park* was a fair and just one in the circumstances.

More recently the Court of Appeal in *Jaggard v. Sawyer*[73] have addressed the question of whether it is possible to reconcile the earlier decisions. The Court of Appeal concluded that the trial judge had been correct to apply the *Wrotham Park* approach to the assessment of damages to compensate the plaintiff for a continuing breach of her rights, and it was clearly of significance to this decision that the damages included compensation for future injury. Millett LJ adverted to this fact when he stated that 'when the court awards damages in substitution for an injunction, it seeks to compensate the plaintiff for loss arising from future wrongs that is to say, loss for which the common law does not provide a remedy'. He also rightly pointed out that in *Johnson v. Agnew* the plaintiff was claiming damages for loss occasioned by a single, once-off, past breach of contract. He continued as follows:

> In my view Lord Wilberforce's statement [in *Johnson v. Agnew*] that the measure of damages is the same whether damages are recoverable at common law or under the Act must be taken to be limited to the case where they are recoverable in respect of the same cause of action. It cannot sensibly have any application where the claim at common law is in respect of a past trespass or breach of covenant and that under the Act is in respect of future trespasses or continuing breaches of covenant.[74]

Millett LJ's analysis is certainly appealing as if it is accurate, it would

---

72. [1993] 1 WLR 1361.
73. [1995] 1 WLR 269. See also Ingman [1995] Conv 141.
74. *Ibid.* at 291. It is interesting to note that while Millett LJ characterised the *Wrotham Park* decision as one concerning a single past breach of covenant(at 291), Bingham MR considered it to involve a 'continuing invasion' of the plaintiff's rights (at 281).

provide clarification of how these principles should be applied in the future, but it has been criticised in some quarters as being 'unsatisfactory'.[75] A useful summary of how the law seems to be in England at present is put forward in the following terms by Ingman.[76]

> [T]he position after *Jaggard* appears to be that if damages are available only under the statute they will be measured on the *Wrotham Park* basis (as in *Jaggard*). Where the statutory jurisdiction cannot be invoked (as in *Bredero Homes*) damages will continue to be measured on common law principles. If on the facts, both common law and statutory damages are available (as in *Johnson v. Agnew*) their measure (according to Millett LJ at least) will be the same under both jurisdictions.

However, as Ingman also points out, whether Millett LJ's interpretation of *Johnson* is correct, or whether *Wrotham Park* was in fact overruled by it, is a question which will ultimately be for the House of Lords to decide. In view of the uncertainty remaining in this area even in the wake of *Jaggard*, judicial clarification would certainly be welcome and until this is forthcoming it is difficult to predict how the courts in this jurisdiction will deal with the issues involved.

Principles Governing the Grant of Mandatory Injunctions

While a prohibitory injunction requires a defendant to refrain from doing certain acts, a mandatory injunction is one which compels a defendant to carry out an obligation or to perform a specified act. Traditionally, the courts were reluctant to grant an injunction of a mandatory nature and during the last century it was not uncommon to frame an injunction in terms which were prohibitory in form even though the order was mandatory in substance. This trend was reversed by the decision of *Jackson v. Normanby Brick Co.*[77] and now where a mandatory order is called for it will be framed in this form.

Mandatory injunctions can be classified into two types, restorative and enforcing. The former type which is granted more frequently requires the party to whom it is directed to put right the consequences of his actions, e.g. by removing an offending structure. The enforcing mandatory injunction on the other hand requires the performance of some positive obliga-

---

75. Goodhart [1996] RLR 3, 7.
76. [1995] Conv 141, 148.
77. [1899] 1 Ch 438.

tion, often of a continuing nature. To succeed in obtaining a mandatory order, particularly of the latter kind, it must be possible to specify with a sufficient degree of particularity precisely what action is required to comply with its terms and it must be quite clear 'what the person against whom the injunction or order is made is required to do or to refrain from doing.'[78] Maugham LJ laid down this requirement in *Fishenden v. Higgs and Hill Ltd*[79] in the following terms:

> I think a mandatory injunction, except in very exceptional circumstances, ought to be granted in such terms that the person against whom it is granted ought to know exactly what he has to do.

This statement was quoted with approval by Murphy J in *Bula Ltd v. Tara Mines Ltd (No.2)*,[80] in which he refused to grant mandatory interlocutory injunctions, *inter alia*, because in his opinion, if granted in the terms sought, the orders would not be certain enough in their terms to enable it to be ascertained whether the defendants were complying with the injunctions granted by the court.

In theory there appears to be no difference between the principles which apply to the granting of a mandatory and prohibitory injunction at the trial of an action[81] and it has been said that care and caution must be exercised by a judge in either case and that no greater degree of caution is required in deciding to grant a mandatory order.[82] However, it must be recognised that in practical terms, the making of a mandatory order will usually impose an additional degree of hardship or expense on a defendant and such factors may often influence a judge in deciding how to exercise his discretion. One English authority which suggests that an additional degree of caution is required in the context of mandatory orders is the decision of the House of Lords in *Redland Bricks Ltd v. Morris*.[83] Land owned by the respondents, who carried on the business of strawberry farming, was affected by subsidence caused by quarrying work undertaken by the appellant on adjoining property. It was estimated that the cost of remedying the subsidence would be wholly disproportionate to the value of the land af-

---

78. *Attorney-General v. Staffordshire County Council* [1905] 1 Ch 336, 342.
79. (1935) 153 LT 128, 142. See also *Redland Bricks Ltd v. Morris* [1970] AC 652, 666 where Lord Upjohn stated that the defendant must know what he has to do as a matter of fact not as matter of law. However note the comments of Staughton LJ in *Channel Tunnel Group Ltd v. Balfour Beatty Construction* [1992] QB 656, 678.
80. [1987] IR 95, 104 .
81. *Davies v. Gas Light & Coke Co.* [1909] 1 Ch 248, 259 *per* Warrington J.
82. *Smith v. Smith* (1875) LR 20 Eq 500, 504 *per* Jessel MR.
83. [1970] AC 652.

fected. The respondents were awarded damages and both prohibitory and mandatory injunctions to restrain further excavation, but the House of Lords, placing emphasis on the disproportionate cost of remedial work, allowed the appeal against the grant of a mandatory injunction. Lord Upjohn stated:

> A mandatory injunction can only be granted where the plaintiff shows a very strong probability upon the facts that grave damage will accrue to him in the future ... It is jurisdiction to be exercised sparingly and with caution but, in the proper case, unhesitatingly.[84]

It was the view of Lord Upjohn that unlike in the case of a prohibitory injunction, the cost of the works which the defendant would be required to carry out must be taken into account except where the defendant has acted quite unreasonably. Where, as in the case before him, the defendant had acted reasonably, although wrongly, the cost of remedying his actions was a factor which should be taken into account. While these latter principles seem reasonable, Lord Upjohn's insistence on establishing a 'very strong probability ... of grave damage' has been criticised and it has been said that this view cannot be accepted without qualification.[85] Spry suggests the following alternative that 'whenever an injury to the plaintiff is shown, being an injury that might, before it took place, have been enjoined by a prohibitory injunction if the court thought fit, a mandatory injunction may be granted unless consequent prejudice to the defendant is so disproportionate that the course is unjust in all the circumstances'.[86]

While there may be no difference in theory between the principles which govern the grant of prohibitory and mandatory injunctions at trial, different considerations apply to the granting of mandatory as opposed to prohibitory injunctions of an interlocutory nature.[87] At the very least a plaintiff must show strong evidence of continuing or imminent prejudice before a court will make an order of this nature. In *Shepherd Homes Ltd v. Sandham*[88] Megarry J made it clear that the court is far more reluctant to grant a mandatory injunction than a prohibitory injunction and said that the 'case has to be unusually strong and clear before a mandatory injunc-

---

84. *Ibid.* at 665.
85. Spry, *Equitable Remedies* (5th ed., 1997) p. 547. See also Meagher, Gummow and Lehane, *Equity Doctrines and Remedies* (3rd ed., 1992) p.617 where they comment that the decision 'scintillates with dubious propositions'.
86. *Equitable Remedies* (5th ed., 1997) p. 547.
87. *Irish Shell Ltd v. Elm Motors* [1984] IR 200, 217 *per* Costello J.
88. [1971] Ch 340. See also *Locabail International Finance Ltd v. Agroexport* [1986] 1 WLR 657.

tion will be granted'[89] and the court must 'feel a high degree of assurance that at the trial it will appear that the injunction was rightly granted.'[90] Megarry J himself acknowledged that it was not possible to 'draw firm lines or impose any rigid classification' in this area and a more flexible approach was adopted subsequently by Hoffman J in *Films Rover International Ltd v. Cannon Film Sales Ltd*,[91] where he said that the 'high degree of assurance' test does not have to be satisfied in every case before an interlocutory injunction of a mandatory nature may be granted. Hoffman J pointed out that in an exceptional case, withholding such an injunction would carry with it a higher risk of injustice than granting it, even where the court cannot feel a high degree of assurance about the plaintiff's likelihood of succeeding at the trial.[92]

There is still a degree of uncertainty in this jurisdiction about the test which should be applied in the context of mandatory interlocutory injunctions.[93] In *Bula Ltd v. Tara Mines Ltd (No.2)*[94] Murphy J said that while he agreed with much of what had been said by Megarry J in *Shepherd Homes Ltd v. Sandham*, he would be reluctant to accept the proposition that the granting or withholding of a mandatory interlocutory injunction should be related to or dependent on the strength of the applicant's case. This approach is in line with that adopted by the Supreme Court in *Campus Oil Ltd v. Minister for Industry and Energy (No.2)*,[95] in which O'Higgins CJ made it clear that the likelihood of success at trial should not be a factor in the granting of interlocutory relief generally although he did go on to say that such relief will only issue in mandatory form in exceptional cases, such as that before the court. The trend in most other recent cases has been to emphasize the fact that mandatory interlocutory injunctions will only issue in very limited circumstances and reference has been made to the likelihood of a plaintiff succeeding at trial. In *Boyhan v. Tribunal of Inquiry into the Beef Industry*[96] Denham J declined to grant an interlocutory injunction of a mandatory nature in favour of the United Farmers Association directing that they should be granted full legal representation before

---

89. *Ibid.* at 349.
90. *Ibid.* at 351.
91. [1987] 1 WLR 670.
92. *Ibid.* at 680.
93. Note that where relief of an interlocutory nature is required, a plaintiff may seek an interlocutory mandatory injunction requiring it to specifically perform an agreement, see *Beshoff Brothers Ltd v. Select Service Partner Ireland Ltd* High Court 1998 No. 8102 P (O'Sullivan J) 28 July 1998.
94. [1987] IR 95.
95. [1983] IR 88.
96. [1992] ILRM 545. See also *O'Dea v. O'Briain* [1992] ILRM 364.

the beef tribunal as she was satisfied that the limited representation granted to it by the tribunal was sufficient in the circumstances. In the course of her judgment Denham J described a mandatory injunction as a 'powerful instrument' and said that in seeking 'this exceptional form of relief ... it is up to the plaintiffs to establish a strong and clear case — so that the court can feel a degree of assurance that at a trial of the action a similar injunction would be granted.'[97] In *Boyle v. An Post*,[98] while Lardner J decided to grant a mandatory order of an interlocutory nature directing An Post to pay the plaintiffs their wages after the payroll computer had to be shut down following the suspension of a number of staff, he stated that it was 'an exceptional case where one can say with assurance that at the hearing of the substantive action the plaintiffs are bound to succeed.'[99]

However, it should be noted that a much less restrictive approach was favoured by Carroll J in her judgment in *A. & N. Pharmacy Ltd v. United Drug Wholesale Ltd.*[100] The plaintiff, which had set up a new pharmacy in Limerick, sought a mandatory interlocutory injunction compelling the defendant, a wholesaler in its area, to supply it with non-generic pharmaceutical products. As a result of the refusal of the defendant and other major wholesalers to supply the plaintiff, it had been forced to import products from abroad at anti-competitive prices. Carroll J held that there was a serious issue to be tried and that the balance of convenience favoured the plaintiff; in other words the ordinary test which it is accepted applies to interlocutory injunctions of a prohibitory nature had been satisfied. She found that it was likely that damages would not be an adequate remedy because the plaintiff would be forced out of business if it could not obtain the supplies it required and decided to grant a mandatory injunction of an interlocutory nature compelling the defendant to supply the plaintiff on a cash on delivery basis. This seems far from the requirement of a 'strong and clear' case contemplated in the earlier decisions and Carroll J seemed content to apply the less restrictive test favoured in the context of interlocutory injunctions of a prohibitory nature. It is however, unlikely that this decision is indicative of a general trend towards a less restrictive approach in this area and it is probable that the courts will continue to be much less willing to grant interlocutory injunctions of a mandatory rather than a prohibitory nature.

---

97. *Ibid.* at 556.
98. [1992] 2 IR 437.
99. *Ibid.* at 442.
100. [1996] 2 ILRM 46.

Principles Governing the Grant of Interlocutory Injunctions

The essential aim of an interlocutory injunction is to preserve the *status quo* existing between the parties to an action until the trial of the issues in dispute can take place and it will have effect until the final determination of the rights of the parties by the court. The rationale behind the grant of such injunctions is primarily the need to protect the rights of a plaintiff by preserving the circumstances which exist at the time he institutes proceedings to prevent him suffering irreparable prejudice by reason of the delay which must necessarily occur between the institution of proceedings and the trial of the action. O'Higgins CJ summarised these principles as follows in *Campus Oil Ltd v. Minister for Industry & Energy (No.2)*:[101]

> Interlocutory relief is granted to an applicant where what he complains of is continuing and is causing him harm or injury which may be irreparable in the sense that it may not be possible to compensate him fairly or properly by an award of damages. Such relief is given because a period must necessarily elapse before the action can come for trial and for the purpose of keeping matters *in statu quo* until the hearing.

In practice the courts grant far more injunctions of an interlocutory than a perpetual nature as many disputes are resolved after the interlocutory stage and do not proceed to trial for various other reasons.[102] In certain circumstances, where the parties consent, the court may even treat the application for an interlocutory order as the trial of the action. While this procedure will inevitably lead to a more expeditious resolution of the issues to be determined, it will only be a suitable course to take where there is no dispute about the facts as an interlocutory hearing is conducted on the basis of affidavit evidence alone.

A further important preliminary point to note is that where an interlocutory injunction is sought, a plaintiff will almost invariably be required to give an undertaking as to damages and the court will have to be satisfied as to the plaintiff's ability to honour such an undertaking should this become necessary.[103] It would appear that the giving of an undertaking will only be dispensed with in 'special circumstances',[104] and it was stressed by Budd J in *Keenan v. CIE*[105] that such an undertaking is a *sine qua non*

---

101. [1983] IR 88, 105.
102. *Fellowes & Son v. Fisher* [1976] QB 122, 129 *per* Lord Denning MR.
103. *Brigid Foley Ltd v. Ellott* [1982] RPC 433, 435-436 *per* Megarry VC.
104. *Attorney-General v. Albany Hotel Co.* [1896] 2 Ch 696, 700 *per* North J.
105. (1963) 97 ILTR 54.

where a mandatory interlocutory injunction is sought. While it is required for the defendant's benefit to ensure that he can be recompensed if it is subsequently shown that no interlocutory order should have been made, it is given to the court and accordingly non-compliance with any undertaking given will constitute a contempt of court.

In principle a court may grant an injunction of an interlocutory nature whenever it is 'just and convenient so to do'[106] and it has been stressed that the remedy 'should be kept flexible and discretionary. ... and must not be made the subject of strict rules.'[107] However, in practice recognised guidelines have generally been applied by the courts in deciding whether to grant or refuse this form of relief. It has recently been acknowledged[108] that there is 'no significant difference' between the principles which apply to the granting or withholding of interlocutory injunctions in this jurisdiction and in England, with the proviso that in this jurisdiction a court cannot by its order abridge or in any way diminish the constitutional rights enjoyed by any of the parties to the action.

Traditionally, a plaintiff would be granted an interlocutory injunction only if he could establish a *'prima facie* case' i.e. a probability that he would succeed in his claim at the hearing of the action, and the effect of this requirement was that a plaintiff had to show that it was more likely than not that he would succeed. This test was accepted by the House of Lords in *J.T. Stratford and Sons v. Lindley*[109] and by the majority of the Supreme Court in *Esso Petroleum Co. (Ireland) Ltd v. Fogarty.*[110] However there was evidence of a different approach being suggested in some cases based on whether there was a fair or substantial question to be decided[111] and the *prima facie* test was criticized on the basis that it led to confusion as to the object sought to be achieved by this form of relief.

It was finally rejected by the House of Lords in 1975 in favour of a less rigid requirement in the landmark decision of *American Cyanamid Co. v. Ethicon Ltd.*[112] The plaintiff sought and obtained an interlocutory injunc-

---

106. Order 50 rule 6 of the Rules of the Superior Courts 1986.
107. *Hubbard v. Vosper* [1972] 2 QB 84, 96 *per* Denning MR.
108. *Oblique Financial Services Ltd v. The Promise Production Co Ltd* [1994] 1 ILRM 74, 76-77.
109. [1965] AC 269, 338 *per* Lord Upjohn.
110. [1965] IR 531, 538 *per* O Dálaigh CJ.
111. *Educational Co. of Ireland Ltd v. Fitzpatrick* [1961] IR 323, 337 *per* Lavery J and *Esso Petroleum Co. (Ireland) Ltd. v. Fogarty* [1965] IR 531, 541 *per* Walsh J.
112. [1975] AC 396. This test met with approval in a number of other common law jurisdictions, see further Kerr (1983) Ir Jur (ns) 34 at 39, footnote 25. It is still generally applied in England, apart from in a number of exceptional cases. However, it should be noted that Laddie J has recently suggested in *Series 5 Software v.*

tion to restrain the defendant from marketing surgical products in alleged infringement of the plaintiff's patent. The modified test propounded by Lord Diplock required a plaintiff to show that the claim was not frivolous or vexatious, in other words that there was 'a serious question to be tried', and where this was established, the court had to go on to consider the balance of convenience which involved assessing the probable implications for both parties should the relief sought be granted or refused. Lord Diplock stated that: 'It is no part of the court's function at this stage of the litigation to try to resolve conflicts of evidence on affidavit as to facts on which the claims of either party may ultimately depend nor to decide difficult questions of law which call for detailed argument and mature considerations. These are matters to be dealt with at the trial'.[113]

Although an assessment of where the balance of convenience lay involved consideration of a number of factors, the most important of these was recognised as being the question of the adequacy of damages. The court was required to consider first, whether if no interlocutory order was made and the plaintiff were to succeed at the trial in establishing an entitlement to a permanent injunction, he would be adequately compensated by an award of damages. The court also had to consider whether the defendant would be adequately compensated by an award of damages if the decision went against him at the interlocutory stage but he was ultimately successful at the trial.

If there was doubt as to the adequacy of the respective remedies in damages, the court was required to consider other factors, such as the taking of whatever measures would be necessary to preserve the status quo. The concept of the *status quo* was considered by Lord Diplock in *Garden Cottage Foods Ltd v. Milk Marketing Board*[114] where he said that 'the relevant *status quo* ... is the state of affairs existing during the period immediately proceeding the issue of the writ claiming the permanent in-

---

Clarke [1996] 1 All ER 853, 865 that 'Lord Diplock did not intend . . . to exclude consideration of the strength of the cases in most applications for interlocutory relief.' He continued as follows: 'It appears to me that what is intended is that the court should not attempt to resolve difficult issues of fact or law on an application for interlocutory relief. If, on the other hand, the court is able to come to a view as to the strength of the parties' case on the credible evidence, then it can do so. . . . If it is apparent from that material that one party's case is much stronger than the other's then that is a matter the court should not ignore. To suggest otherwise would be to exclude from consideration an important factor and such exclusion would fly in the face of the flexibility advocated earlier in *American Cyanamid*.'

113. *Ibid.* at 407. Quoted with approval by McCarthy J in *Irish Shell Ltd v. Elm Motors Ltd* [1984] IR 200, 224 and by Blayney J in *Ferris v. Ward* Supreme Court 1995 Nos. 333 & 334, 7 November 1995.

114. [1984] AC 130, 140.

junction or, if there be unreasonable delay between the issue of the writ and the motion for an interlocutory injunction, the period immediately preceding the motion.' This interpretation is arguably correct although it has not always been strictly followed. In *Bayzana Ltd v. Galligan*[115] the plaintiff sought an injunction restraining the defendants from picketing a factory premises which it had bought with notice of the dispute. The majority of the Supreme Court concluded that there was a fair question to be tried and was satisfied that the balance of convenience favoured the plaintiff employers. However, McCarthy J in his dissenting judgment pointed out that in this instance the *status quo* to be preserved was that pertaining when the plaintiff became involved in the matter when it was aware of the dispute and of the picket and upheld the order of Hamilton P which merely restricted the number of pickets.

As McCracken J has recently commented in *Private Research Ltd v. Brosnan*:[116] 'Weighing heavily in favour of the plaintiff is the general rule that, where possible, the court should strive to maintain the *status quo*. However, this is only one element in considering the balance of convenience and there is no absolute rule that the *status quo* must be maintained'. In some cases, the balance of convenience will lie in favour of refusing an interlocutory injunction, notwithstanding that this may result in the alteration of the parties' respective positions. An example of this is the decision of McCracken J in *B. & S. Ltd v. Irish Auto Trader Ltd*[117] in which he refused to grant an injunction restraining the defendant from publishing, printing and distributing its magazine 'Auto Trader' in Ireland despite the plaintiff's claim that the tort of passing off had been established. McCracken J held that in view of the fact, *inter alia*, that the defendant had acted in a *bona fide* manner and that there was unlikely to be confusion between the parties' magazines, he was satisfied that the balance of convenience lay in refusing the relief sought notwithstanding that this altered the *status quo*.

While these *Cyanamid* principles met with a mixed reception in this jurisdiction in the years immediately following the decision of the House of Lords,[118] they were approved in *Campus Oil Ltd. v. Minister for Indus-*

---

115. [1987] IR 238.
116. [1996] 1 ILRM 27, 32.
117. [1995] 2 ILRM 152.
118. See Kerr, *op. cit.* at 39-40. Note that in *TMG Group Ltd v. Al Babtain Trading and Contracting Co* [1982] ILRM 343, 353, Keane J stated that 'insofar as the decision of the House of Lords in *American Cyanamid Co. v. Ethicon Ltd* suggests the application of different principles to applications of this nature, it does not represent the law in this country'. While they were applied at first with some reluctance by the Court of Appeal in *Hubbard v. Pitt* [1976] QB 142 and *Fellowes & Son v. Fisher* [1976] QB 122 they are now generally accepted in England.

try and Energy (No.2)[119] and have been applied since in numerous decisions.[120] The plaintiff claimed a declaration that the obligation imposed on it by statutory instrument to buy a specified portion of its petroleum oil supplies from a State-owned refinery was contrary to Articles 30 and 31 of the EEC Treaty. The issue was referred to the European Court of Justice and the defendants sought an interlocutory injunction compelling the plaintiff to comply with the terms of the order pending determination of the plaintiff's claim at the trial of the action. It was held by Keane J in granting an interlocutory injunction that the probability of success at the trial was not the proper test to be applied by the court in deciding whether to grant such an injunction. Instead an applicant must establish that there is a fair question to be determined and that the balance of convenience lay on the side of granting the injunction. This finding was upheld by the Supreme Court and O'Higgins CJ stated as follows:

> In my view, the test to be applied is whether a fair *bona fide* question has been raised by the person seeking the relief. If such a question has been raised, it is not for the Court to determine that question on an interlocutory application; that remains to be decided at the trial. Once a fair question has been raised ... then the Court should consider the other matters which are appropriate to the exercise of its discretion to grant interlocutory relief. In this regard, I note the view expressed by Lord Diplock in *American Cyanamid Co. v. Ethicon Ltd*. I merely say that I entirely agree with what he said.[121]

These principles were re-iterated and applied by the Supreme Court in *Westman Holdings Ltd v McCormack*,[122] in which the plaintiff sought an injunction to prevent the defendants, who had been employed by a company from which the plaintiff had bought a business, from picketing their premises. It was held by the Supreme Court that an interlocutory injunction granted to the plaintiffs should continue until the trial of the action. Finlay CJ said that while the loss which would be suffered by the plaintiff if it was refused an injunction but subsequently succeeded in establishing that the picketing was unlawful would be exclusively pecuniary loss, the

---

119. [1983] IR 88. See also *Irish Shell Ltd v. Elm Motors Ltd* [1984] IR 200.
120. Some recent examples include *Connolly v. Byrne* Supreme Court 1997 No. 13, 23 January 1997; *D.G.S. Retail v. PC World* High Court 1997 No. 13388P (Laffoy J) 13 January 1998; *Clane Hospital Ltd v. VHI* High Court 1998 No. 3740P (Quirke J) 22 May 1998.
121. *Ibid.* at 107.
122. [1992] 1 IR 151.

combination of the inability on the part of some of the defendants to pay damages and the potential immunity from liability of the trade union, made it improbable that the plaintiff would, if refused an injunction, be able to obtain compensation. In addition, he found that the undertaking which the plaintiff must give in order to obtain the interlocutory injunction would be an adequate method of compensating the defendants in respect of any loss of wages which they might suffer and only their right to picket would remain uncompensated.

The following useful summary of the principles which the court should adhere to when considering applications for interlocutory relief is set out in the recent judgment of Quirke J in *Clane Hospital Ltd v. Voluntary Health Insurance Board*,[123] in which the plaintiffs sought an interlocutory injunction restraining the defendants from replacing their scheme of charges for medical services. He stated that the court should adopt the following sequence of issues for consideration:[124]

1. Whether or not the applicant has raised a fair, substantial[125] *bona fide* question for determination.

2. Whether, if the applicant were to succeed at the trial in establishing his right to a permanent injunction, he could be adequately compensated by an award of damages.

3. Whether, if the respondent were to be successful at the trial, he could be adequately compensated under the applicant's undertaking as to damages for any loss which he would have sustained by reason of the grant of interlocutory relief.

4. If either party or both have, by way of evidence, raised a real and substantial doubt as to the adequacy of the respective remedies in damages available to either party, then where does the 'balance of convenience' lie?

5. In some instances are there any 'special factors' (usually technical in nature) which may influence the exercise of discretion and the grant of the relief sought?

---

123. High Court 1998 No. 3740P (Quirke J) 22 May 1998.
124. *Ibid.* at 10.
125. On the same page of his judgment, Quirke J spoke in terms of the plaintiff establishing 'a fair *bona fide* question' and it is unlikely that he was deliberately seeking to make the test harder to satisfy by inserting the word 'substantial'. However, in view of the fact that the latter term did not appear in either the *American Cyanamid* or *Campus Oil* decisions, it is probably better omitted.

Quirke J concluded that the plaintiffs had raised a fair, substantial and *bona fide* question for determination, but he was satisfied that if the plaintiffs succeeded at the trial in establishing their right to a permanent injunction, they could be adequately compensated by an award of damages and in the circumstances, he decided to refuse the relief sought by the plaintiffs.

To date there have been no signs of any real attempt on the part of the judiciary in this jurisdiction to depart from the *American Cyanamid* and *Campus Oil guidelines*,[126] apart from in the exceptional cases considered below, although it is possible to identify cases where more colourful language has been employed. In *News Datacom Ltd v. Lyons*,[127] despite his apparent acceptance of the test in *Campus Oil*, namely, that a person seeking the grant of an interlocutory injunction must show that there is a fair question to be tried, Flood J stated that to raise a fair question to be tried in cases of breach of copyright the plaintiff must tender some positive evidence 'which at minimum gives rise to an implication that copying has taken place and which rescues the court from the doldrums of unadulterated speculation though falling far short of an established probability'. In the circumstances, Flood J refused to grant an interlocutory injunction to restrain the defendants from infringing the plaintiff's copyright in the software and smart cards used to decode scrambled satellite television signals.

At this point it should be reiterated that an interlocutory injunction, like any other type of equitable remedy is a discretionary form of relief and while the so-called '*Cyanamid* principles' have provided the basis for the exercise of the courts' jurisdiction in this area for some time, they should be regarded as guidelines[128] rather than rules which must be strictly adhered to. As Gray[129] has pointed out insofar as Lord Diplock's formulation suggests that an applicant faces a series of hurdles and that once he has surmounted them he is guaranteed success, it is unfortunate. As she states, this approach goes beyond the provision of assistance to a judge in the exercise of his discretion and in fact amounts to a significant restriction of discretion.

Lord Diplock himself acknowledged that there may be special factors which should be taken into consideration in individual cases, although the

---

126. Although note the *dicta* of O'Flaherty J in *Curust Financial Services Ltd v. Loewe-Lack-Werk Otto Loewe GmbH* [1994] 1 IR 450, 472.
127. [1994] 1 ILRM 450.
128. *Cayne v. Global Natural Resources plc* [1984] 1 All ER 225, 237 *per* May LJ. See also *Cambridge Nutrition Ltd v. British Broadcasting Corporation* [1990] 3 All ER 523, 535.
129. [1981] CLJ 307, 313.

fact that a trial is likely to take place within a short space of time is not one of them. This point was made by Kinlen J in the course of his judgment in *An Post v. Irish Permanent plc*,[130] in which the plaintiff sought an interlocutory injunction to restrain alleged passing off in relation to the use of the term 'savings certificate' by the defendant to describe a financial savings product which it was issuing in competition with the plaintiff. Kinlen J granted an interlocutory injunction as he found that there was a serious question to be tried and that the balance of convenience favoured the granting of the order and rejected the argument that the fact the matter was likely to be tried quickly was an important consideration.[131]

Circumstances in which a Departure from Cyanamid Guidelines Justified
It is now acknowledged that departure from the *Cyanamid* principles is justified in certain circumstances.[132] The most obvious of these is where the parties agree that the hearing of the interlocutory application will constitute the trial of the action. Other exceptions have developed and while it would not be wise to attempt to set these out in an exhaustive manner, the following situations have been recognised.

(i) Where there is no Arguable Defence to the Plaintiff's Claim
This principle is almost self-explanatory and as Scott J made clear in *Official Custodian for Charities v. Mackey*,[133] the *Cyanamid* principles are not applicable in a case where there is no arguable defence as there will clearly be no serious question to be tried in such a case. So e.g. where a plaintiff has clear title and the defendant's trespass is indisputable, the balance of convenience will play no part in the court's decision and the plaintiff may obtain an interlocutory injunction to restrain the trespass, even where it has caused no damage.[134] This principle has recently been confirmed by Keane J in *Keating & Co. Ltd v. Jervis Shopping Centre Ltd*[135] where he stated that: 'It is clear that a landowner, whose title is not in issue, is *prima facie* entitled to an injunction to restrain a trespass and . . . this is also the case where the claim is for an interlocutory injunction only'.[136] However, as Keane J pointed out this principle is subject to the following qualifica-

---

130. [1995] 1 ILRM 336.
131. Note that the case was settled prior to trial with the defendant giving an undertaking that it would not sell products bearing the name 'savings certificates'.
132. As Kelly J pointed out in *Reynolds v. Malocco* [1999] 1 ILRM 289, 294 'these principles have a wide but not a universal application'.
133. [1985] Ch 168, 187.
134. *Patel v. W.H. Smith (Eziot) Ltd* [1987] 1 WLR 853.
135. High Court 1995 No. 9606P (Keane J) 1 March 1996.
136. *Ibid.* at p.9.

tion, set out by Balcombe LJ in the Court of Appeal decision in *Patel v. W.H. Smith (Eziot) Ltd*[137] as follows: 'However, the defendant may put in evidence to seek to establish that he has a right to do what would otherwise be a trespass. Then the court must consider the application of the principle set out in *American Cyanamid Co. v. Ethicon Ltd* in relation to the grant or refusal of an interlocutory injunction'. In the *Keating* case, Keane J stated that it was clear that the defendants were asserting a right to operate a crane in the airspace above the plaintiff's premises. In his opinion there was a serious question to be tried as to whether they had such a right and it followed that the plaintiff would not be entitled to an interlocutory injunction unless it could satisfy the court that damages would not be an adequate remedy. Keane J concluded that the plaintiff had not established that damages would be an inadequate remedy and decided for this and other reasons to refuse the injunction sought.

(ii) Where an Interlocutory Injunction is Sought in the Context of a Trade Dispute

The conclusions reached by the Supreme Court in both *Bayzana Ltd v. Galligan*[138] and *Westman Holdings Ltd v. McCormack*[139] made it clear that the common law position clearly favoured the employer where proceedings were brought seeking to restrain picketing by means of an interlocutory injunction. An employer could usually establish that the balance of convenience favoured the preservation of the *status quo* pending the trial of the action and the courts were often influenced by the potential inability on the part of some of the defendants to pay damages. In addition, they placed little emphasis on the loss of the defendants' right to picket, stressing instead that that they could if necessary be subsequently compensated in respect of any loss of wages which they might suffer.[140]

Attempts have been made to redress this imbalance by means of legislation and section 19 of the Industrial Relations Act 1990 has qualified the effect of common law principles in the context of trade disputes. The effect of section 19(2) would appear to be that once a plaintiff establishes an entitlement to an interlocutory injunction by showing that there is a fair

---

137. [1987] 1 WLR 853, 859.
138. [1987] IR 238.
139. [1992] 1 IR 151.
140. As Keane J commented in *Nolan Transport (Oaklands) Ltd v. Halligan* High Court 1993 No.1008P, 22 March 1994 it was common knowledge that the use by employers of the procedure of seeking an interlocutory injunction 'meant that the use of what were otherwise legitimate methods sanctioned by law by trade unions of advancing their interests were effectively neutralised by the way in which the law operated'.

question to be tried, the court must consider whether the defendants can establish a fair case that they were acting in furtherance or contemplation of a trade dispute. If they can, the injunction will not be granted; if they cannot, the court will go on to consider as it does at common law, whether the balance of convenience favours the grant of an injunction.[141] This statutory provision can only be availed of by defendants where they have complied with the formalities laid down in the statute in relation to such matters as the holding of secret ballots and the giving of adequate strike notice and the consequence of failing to abide by such procedures is that the new restrictions on an employer's ability to obtain an interlocutory injunction do not apply.[142]

This point is well illustrated by the two recent decisions in which those involved in industrial action were unable to rely on the provisions of section 19 as they had failed to comply fully with the requirements contained in the Act. In *Nolan Transport (Oaklands) Ltd v. Halligan*[143] which concerned an application to restrain picketing, Keane J had to consider whether the defendants could invoke the statutory protection afforded to them by the section. He stated as follows:

> [I]t seems to me as a matter of first impression that the onus must be on the person resisting the injunction to establish that the provisions of section 14 of the Industrial Relations Act 1990 have been complied with, which seems to me to be crucial to the operation of the section. If the section has been complied with, then the Oireachtas goes on to provide for this unusual and special situation where the court must apply particular considerations to the granting of an interlocutory injunction, considerations which otherwise would not apply. Before a trade union is afforded the protection of section 19 of the Industrial Relations Act and, conversely, an employer is deprived of the protection that he would normally have at common law in relation to the obtaining of an interlocutory injunction in circumstances where his business is or could be affected, I would take the view that the court must be satisfied on the evidence before it that section 14 has been complied with.

In the case before him, Keane J said that he was satisfied that there was no evidence of sufficient weight to indicate that section 14 had been com-

---

141. See Kerr (1990) ICLSA 90/19-33.
142. See Kerr [1993] ELR xi.
143. High Court 1993 No.1008P (Keane J) 22 March 1994.

plied with and and therefore the defendants could not rely on section 19(2) of the Act. He then went on to consider the application on the basis of the principles normally applicable to the granting of an interlocutory injunction and concluded that an injunction should be granted restraining the defendants from picketing other than in a peaceful manner.[144]

A similarly strict approach to the application of section 19(2) of the 1990 Act has been taken both by the High Court and the Supreme Court in *G. & T. Crampton Ltd v. Building and Allied Trades Union,*[145] in which the plaintiff sought an interlocutory injunction to restrain the defendants from picketing its premises. The plaintiff argued that a precondition to the operation of section 19(2) of the Industrial Relations Act 1990 had not been complied with as there had been no effective secret ballot held sufficient to comply with the requirements of section 14 of the Act. Laffoy J granted the interlocutory injunction sought and the defendants appealed. The Supreme Court was satisfied that the trial judge had been entitled to come to the conclusion that a condition precedent to the implementation of section 19 had not been established and upheld the conclusions which she had reached in deciding the matter on the basis of the principles set out in the *Campus Oil* case, namely that a fair question had been raised, that damages would be an inadequate remedy and that the balance of convenience lay in favour of granting the injunction.

A number of points should be made in relation to these decisions and their consequences. First, as Purcell has commented 'it is quite clear that the courts require a rigid application and strict adherence to the rules of the trade union introduced pursuant to section 14 [of the 1990 Act]'.[146] In addition, it is clear from the judgment of Keane J in *Nolan Transport* that the onus is on the person resisting the injunction to show that the secret ballot procedure has been properly complied with.[147] For this reason trade unions should take care to ensure that they have not only complied with the necessary statutory requirements but that they will be in a position to establish this to the court. In both cases the court seemed satisfied that a fair case had been made out that the defendants were acting in contempla-

---

144. Keane J said that the dispute had been in existence for 'a very considerable time' and observed that the court's jurisdiction had only been invoked relatively late in the proceedings. Accordingly he said that he was not satisfied that it would be reasonable to restrain the defendants from picketing altogether and stated that provided the picketing remained peaceful, as the defendants claimed that it was, they would not in any way be affected by the granting of the injunction.
145. [1998] 1 ILRM 431.
146. (1998) Bar Review 239, 242.
147. See also the judgment of Laffoy J in *G. & T. Crampton Ltd v. Building and Allied Trades Union* High Court 1997 No. 7727P, 20 November 1997.

tion or furtherance of a trade dispute and it should not be difficult for defendants engaged in legitimate industrial action to establish this point. Given the obvious advantage from the point of view of defendants of being able to rely on the provisions of section 19(2), some lessons should be learned from the strict approach taken by the court towards the application of the legislation. Finally, it remains to be seen whether in a case where compliance with the statutory requirements has been established, it will appear that the balance may have swung too far in favour of employees.

(iii) Where an Interlocutory Injunction is Sought in Proceedings for Defamation

It would appear that a more onerous task faces a plaintiff seeking an interlocutory injunction to restrain publication of alleged defamatory matter, partly because of a traditional reluctance on the part of the courts to interfere unduly with an individual's right to freedom of expression,[148] a right given constitutional protection in this jurisdiction.[149] A further reason for such caution is that while a statement might appear defamatory, a defendant may intend to plead a variety of defences at the trial, including those of fair comment and justification,[150] or he may seek to establish that he is protected by privilege. The general principle was laid down by Lord Esher MR in *Bonnard v. Perryman*[151] in the following terms:

> [T]he subject matter of an action for defamation is so special as to require exceptional caution in exercising the jurisdiction to interfere by injunction before the trial of an action to prevent an anticipated wrong....Until it is clear that an alleged libel is untrue, it is not clear that any right at all has been infringed; and the importance of leaving free speech unfettered is a strong reason in cases of libel for dealing most cautiously and warily with the granting of interim injunctions.

The issue was considered by the Supreme Court in *Sinclair v. Gogarty*,[152] where Sullivan CJ stated that 'an interlocutory injunction should only be granted in the clearest cases where any jury would say that the matter complained of was libellous, and where if the jury did not so find, the

---

148. *Femis-Bank (Anguilla) Ltd v. Lazar* [1991] Ch 391.
149. Article 40.6.1.i of the Irish Constitution 1937.
150. *Gallagher v. Tuohy* (1924) 58 ILTR 134. However, note the comments of O'Connor J in *Cullen v. Stanley* [1926] IR 73, 85 in this regard.
151. [1891] 2 Ch 269, 284.
152. [1937] IR 377, 384.

court would set aside the verdict as unreasonable.' The Supreme Court held that imputations made in relation to the plaintiffs were clearly so defamatory that an injunction should be granted to prevent the continued sale of a book which contained these statements.

This question was also considered in *Connolly v. RTE.*[153] The plaintiff sought an interlocutory injunction to restrain further broadcasts by the defendant of material which she alleged was defamatory of her. The plaintiff claimed that if there was an issue to be tried and damages were not an adequate remedy, the balance of convenience should determine the question of whether to grant relief. The defendant argued that the principles laid down in *Campus Oil* did not apply and that the established law in cases of alleged defamation was that injunctions were 'very rarely granted'. Carroll J stated that there was no reason why both of these principles could not be applied and said that 'in considering the balance of convenience, the court must take into account the right to freedom of expression balanced against the plaintiff's right to a good name in the light of the law on injunctive relief in defamation cases.'[154] She concluded that while she was satisfied that there was an issue to be tried and that damages would not be an adequate remedy, the balance of convenience was in favour of not granting an injunction and said that it was preferable that the alleged libel should be tried by a jury. While Carroll J did not expressly agree with the defendant's contention that injunctions should rarely issue in such cases, it is implicit in the conclusion which she reached that it will be extremely difficult to establish that the balance of convenience favours the granting of interlocutory relief in defamation cases.

The principles laid down in *Bonnard v. Perryman* have recently been applied in England by the majority of the Court of Appeal in *Holley v. Smyth*[155] where it was held that the courts' discretion to grant an interlocutory injunction would not ordinarily be exercised to restrain a libel where the defendant had a defence or claimed justification unless the plaintiff had proved that the libel was plainly untrue. Auld LJ stated as follows:

> The courts' power to grant interlocutory relief to restrain a libel is discretionary . . . but is is a discretion that must be exercised with great caution.
>
> The discretion to grant such relief is guided by the statutory constraint in section 37(1) of the Supreme Court Act 1981 that it should

---

153. [1991] 2 IR 446.
154. *Ibid.* at 448.
155. [1998] 2 WLR 742.

be exercised only where 'it appears to the court to be just and convenient to do so'.

Where there is a defence or claim of justification the discretion is further guided by the rule in *Bonnard v. Perryman* that it is not normally just or convenient to grant relief unless the plaintiff has proved that the libel is plainly untrue.[156]

Sir Christopher Slade LJ stressed that 'neither the would be libeller's motive nor the manner in which he threatens publication nor the potential damage to the plaintiff is normally a basis for making an exception to the rule'[157] although he accepted that the court may be left with a residual discretion not to apply the rule in *Bonnard* in exceptional circumstances, one being where it is satisfied that the defamatory statement is clearly untrue.

The most recent decision in this area is that of Kelly J in *Reynolds v. Malocco*.[158] It contains a most useful summary of the principles to be applied where an interlocutory injunction is sought in defamation proceedings and in particular clarifies the effect which a plea of justification should have in this context. The plaintiff sought an interlocutory injunction to restrain the defendants from publishing an article about him which he alleged defamed him in two respects. He contended that the words in the article in the natural and ordinary meaning or by innuendo alleged, first, that he permitted the sale of drugs in his nightclub premises and was benefiting therefrom and secondly, that he was a homosexual. The first named defendant contended in relation to the first complaint that the words did not bear the meaning ascribed to them and argued that if they did, he would plead justification at the trial and asserted in relation to the second complaint that the words did not bear the meaning contended for. Kelly J referred to the *American Cyanamid / Campus Oil* principles and stated that they have a 'wide but not universal application' and that in 'a small number of cases special rules which are not encompassed by these principles apply'. He continued as follows:

> A plaintiff in an action such as this, in order to obtain an interlocutory injunction must show not merely that he has raised a serious issue concerning the words complained of but that there is no doubt that they are defamatory. Furthermore, if the defendant intends to

---

156. *Ibid.* at 756-757.
157. *Ibid.* at 761.
158. [1999] 1 ILRM 289.

plead justification or any other recognised defence, normally an injunction of this type will be refused.

The jurisdiction to grant interlocutory injunctions to restrain publication of defamatory statements has been described as one 'of a delicate nature' which 'ought only to be exercised in the clearest cases'(see the judgment of Lord Esher MR in *Coulson v. Coulson* (1887) 3 TLR 846).[159]

Kelly J explained that the reason for the court's reluctance to grant interlocutory injunctions in cases of this nature is grounded in the importance attached to the right of free speech, a right now fortified by Article 10 of the European Convention for the Protection of Human Rights and Fundamental Freedoms. In his view he had to first ascertain whether the plaintiff's complaints were made out with the degree of clarity required so as to enable him to conclude that the words complained of were undoubtedly defamatory and if so, he then had to consider whether, in the light of the defendant's stated intention to plead justification in relation to the first allegation, an injunction could be granted. The reason why he had to consider the latter aspect of the case was because of the principle laid down in *Bonnard v. Perryman* and approved by the Supreme Court in *Sinclair v. Gogarty* to the effect that where a defendant in a libel action intends to plead justification, a court will not grant an interlocutory injunction to restrain publication of the statement complained of. The question then arose whether a bald statement of intent to plead justification was sufficient to debar a plaintiff who might otherwise be entitled to an injunction from such relief and in this regard Kelly J approved of the approach of the Supreme Court in *Cullen v. Stanley*[160] which allowed the court to examine the evidence adduced by the defendant in support of the justification plea so as to ascertain whether it had any substance or prospect of success. He did not think that 'a rule which permits a defendant to in effect oust the ability of this Court to intervene by way of injunction in an appropriate case by the simple expedient of expressing an intention to plead justification at the trial of the action is consistent with the obligations imposed on the court under the Constitution'.[161]

Applying these principles to the first complaint, Kelly J concluded that the innuendo to the effect contended for by the plaintiff was clear and stated that in the absence of a successful plea of justification a jury would

---

159. *Ibid.* at 294-295.
160. [1926] IR 73.
161. *Ibid.* at 297.

say that the matter complained of was libellous, a verdict which he did not believe that the Supreme Court would set aside as unreasonable. In relation to the question of a plea of justification he was satisfied that the first named defendant's averment did not go anywhere near demonstrating the existence of an arguable prospect of making out the defence. With regard to the second allegation, he also concluded that a jury would be entitled to find in the plaintiff's favour and it did not appear to him that such a verdict could be regarded as perverse. As there was no plea of justification in relation to this complaint, it followed that in his view the plaintiff had made out a sufficiently strong case to satisfy the test required for the grant of an interlocutory injunction. However, Kelly J pointed out that it did not automatically follow that an injunction should be granted as such relief was of a discretionary nature. He repeated that the jurisdiction was 'of a delicate nature' and that the court must be circumspect to ensure that it does not necessarily interfere with the right to freedom of expression and stated that he did not want to set out in a hard and fast manner the factors which the court should take into account in the exercise of its discretion. In his view it was sufficient if he identified one issue of particular importance which had influenced the exercise of his discretion in the case before him and this was that it was unlikely that the plaintiff would be able to recover any damages from the defendants if the interlocutory injunction was refused but he later succeeded at the trial. In these circumstances Kelly J was satisfied that his discretion must be exercised in favour of granting an interlocutory injunction rather than refusing it.

It is submitted that the approach adopted by Kelly J is an eminently reasonable one and his attitude towards the effect of a plea of justification would seem fairer than the alternative view which involves accepting that a bald statement of intent to plead justification would be sufficient to debar a plaintiff who might otherwise have been entitled to an injunction to such relief. His judgment also seems to achieve a reasonable balance between safeguarding the right to free speech by confirming that injunctive relief should only be granted in the clearest cases and ensuring that a plaintiff is not left without any remedy at all where the words complained of appear to be clearly defamatory.

(iv) Where an Interlocutory Injunction is Sought to Restrain the Presentation of a Petition for the Winding Up of a Company
This exception has been accepted in England for some time,[162] and the approach taken there has recently been followed by the High Court

---

162. *Bryanston Finance Ltd v. De Vries (No.2)* [1976] Ch 63.

in this jurisdiction. In *Truck and Machinery Sales Ltd v. Marubeni Komatsu Ltd*[163] the plaintiff sought an injunction to restrain the defendant from presenting a petition to wind the company up. Counsel for the plaintiff sought to rely on the *Campus Oil* principles and argued that the plaintiff had raised a serious question as to whether the sum claimed was due and owing by it and that the balance of convenience lay in favour of restraining the petition until the hearing of the action. Counsel for the defendant argued that in order to obtain such relief, the plaintiff would have to establish that the presentation of the petition was an abuse of process and that it was bound to fail or at least, that there was an alternative remedy available. Keane J stated that he was satisfied that the jurisdiction to restrain the presentation of a petition to wind up a company is one which should only be exercised with great caution. He referred to the principles set out by the Court of Appeal in *Bryanston Finance Ltd v. De Vries (No.2)*[164] and in *Coulson Sanderson & Ward v. Ward*[165] and said that he was satisfied that this was the approach which should also be adopted in this jurisdiction. He continued as follows:

> The constitutional right of recourse to the courts should not be inhibited, save in exceptional circumstances, and this applies as much to the presentation of a petition for the winding up of a company by a person with the appropriate *locus standi* as it does to any other form of proceedings. The undoubted power of the courts to restrain proceedings which are an abuse of process is one which should not be lightly exercised. In the context of winding-up petitions, I have no doubt that it should be exercised only where the plaintiff company has established at least a *prima facie* case that its presentation would constitute an abuse of process. In many cases, a *prima facie* case will be established where the plaintiff company adduces evidence which satisfies the court that the petition is bound to fail, or at the least, that there is a suitable alternative remedy. It would not be appropriate to apply the principles laid down by the Supreme Court in *Campus Oil Ltd v. Minister for Industry and Energy (No.2)* in cases of this nature where it is the creditors' right to have recourse

---

163. High Court 1995 No. 6928P (Keane J) 23 February 1996.
164. [1976] Ch 63.
165. [1986] 2 BCLC 99. As Slade LJ had commented: '[T]he court should not, on the hearing of an interlocutory motion, interfere with what would otherwise appear to be the legitimate presentation of a winding up petition by someone qualified to present it unless the evidence before it is sufficient to establish *prima facie* that the plaintiff company will succeed in establishing that the proceedings sought to be restrained would constitute an abuse.'

to the courts, rather than any right of the plaintiff company, which is under threat.[166]

Keane J concluded that the plaintiff company had failed to establish a *prima facie* case that the presentation of the petition would be an abuse of process or that it would be bound to fail. In addition, there was no alternative remedy open to the defendant and he held that the injunction sought should be refused.

(v) Where the Trial of the Action is Unlikely

It is now well-established that as a pre-requisite for the application of the guidelines in *Cyanamid* it must be shown that a trial is in fact likely to take place. This principle was laid down in England by Lord Diplock in the decision of *N.W.L. Ltd v. Woods*,[167] where he stressed that Cyanamid was not dealing with a case where the grant or refusal of an injunction would in effect dispose of the action finally in favour of whichever party was successful, and that where these circumstances exist an important additional element must be brought into the assessment of the balance of convenience. He continued as follows:

> Where ... the grant or refusal of the interlocutory injunction will have the practical effect of putting an end to the action because the harm that will have been already caused to the losing party by its grant or refusal is complete and of a kind for which money cannot constitute any worthwhile recompense, the degree of likelihood that the plaintiff would have succeeded in establishing his right to an injunction if the action had gone to trial is a factor to be brought into the balance by the judge in weighing the risks that injustice may result from his deciding the application one way rather than the other.[168]

This approach has been followed by the Court of Appeal in England in a number of cases. In *Cayne v. Global Natural Resources plc*[169] the plaintiff shareholders sought an interlocutory injunction to restrain the defendant company from implementing a merger agreement and proceeding with the allotment of shares prior to the company's impending annual general meeting. If the injunction was granted the balance of power in the company

---

166. At pp. 20-21 of the unreported judgment.
167. [1979] 1 WLR 1294.
168. *Ibid.* at 1307.
169. [1984] 1 All ER 225.

would remain the same until after the crucial vote was taken and the plaintiffs would therefore obtain the result which they sought; on the other hand if the injunction was refused the votes of the new shareholders would ensure that the plan of the incumbent directors succeeded. As Kerr LJ commented 'the practical realities ... are that, if the plaintiffs succeed in obtaining an injunction, they will never take this case to trial'. May LJ stated that in a case such as that before the court where the grant or refusal of an injunction will effectively dispose of the action in favour of the successful party, the 'balance of the risk of doing an injustice' better described the process involved. The Court of Appeal concluded that in these circumstances it would not be appropriate to apply the *Cyanamid* guidelines which were based on the assumption that a proper trial would determine the issues at a later stage and instead justice required that the defendant should be entitled to dispute the plaintiff's claim at the trial of the action and if an injunction would preclude this it should not be granted at an interlocutory stage. A similar finding was made by the Court of Appeal in *Cambridge Nutrition Ltd v. British Broadcasting Corporation*,[170] in which the plaintiff sought an injunction to prevent the broadcast of a TV programme about low calorie diets which focused particularly on its activities, claiming that the BBC had undertaken not to broadcast the programme until after an official report on the subject had been published. The nature of the programme was such that it was only suitable for transmission in its existing form before publication of the report and the defendant resisted the plaintiff's claim. The Court of Appeal re-iterated that where the decision on an application for an interlocutory injunction was the equivalent of giving final judgment the court should not grant the order merely because the plaintiff was able to show a good arguable case and the balance of convenience lay in favour of granting an injunction. Instead the court should assess the relative strength of each party's case before deciding whether the injunction should be granted. Kerr LJ stressed that the *Cyanamid* principles were no more than a set of useful guidelines and 'must never be used as a rule of thumb, let alone as a strait-jacket'.[171] He concluded that the case before him was not an appropriate one for the application of these guidelines 'because the crucial issues between the parties do not depend on a trial, but solely or mainly on the grant or refusal of the interlocutory relief.'

More recently, in *Lansing Linde Ltd v. Kerr*[172] the Court of Appeal

---

170. [1990] 3 All ER 523.
171. *Ibid.* at 535.
172. [1991] 1 WLR 251.

confirmed that a trial judge may properly take into account a plaintiff's prospects of success at trial where the grant or refusal of interlocutory relief will effectively determine the matter. In this case the plaintiff company sought an interlocutory injunction to enforce a clause in the defendant's contract of employment which stipulated that he would not work for any of its competitors for a period of 12 months after termination of his employment with the company. The defendant who occupied a senior position in the company had given six months' notice and a month later accepted the position of managing director of a competitor. It was held by the Court of Appeal that the trial judge had properly taken into account the plaintiff's prospects of success at the trial, having regard to the fact that it would not be possible to hold a trial before the period for which the plaintiff claimed to be entitled to an injunction had expired, or substantially expired, and that in those circumstances in was not enough to decide merely that there was a serious issue to be tried.

Recently an unsuccessful attempt was made in *Symonds Cider and English Wine Co. Ltd v. Showerings (Ireland) Ltd*[173] to further extend the list of situations in which the *Cyanamid* principles should not be applied to all passing off actions on the grounds that in such cases the outcome of the interlocutory proceedings often determines the final outcome of the action. The plaintiff instituted proceedings alleging trade mark infringement and passing off against the defendant and sought an interlocutory injunction restraining the defendant from selling its cider under the mark 'Golden Scrumpy' in cans so similar to their own. It was submitted on the plaintiff's behalf that the principles by which the court should be guided in determining the application for interlocutory injunctions were those set out by the House of Lords in *American Cyanamid* as adopted by the Supreme Court in *Campus Oil*. However, counsel for the defendant submitted that the *American Cyanamid* guidelines had been significantly refined particularly in the field of intellectual property. He pointed to the fact that in a passing off action such as this, the outcome of the interlocutory proceedings often determined the final outcome of the action and submitted that in such circumstances the court is justified in considering the substantive case. Laffoy J rejected this contention and said that having regard to the decision of the Supreme Court in *Westman Holdings Ltd v. McCormack*[174] – which applied the *Cyanamid* principles – it was not open to her, assuming that the plaintiff established that there was a fair and *bona fide* question to be tried, to express any view on the strength of the

---

173. [1997] 1 ILRM 481.
174. [1992] 1 IR 151.

contending submissions. She concluded that she was satisfied that the plaintiff had shown that there were fair issues to be tried but that the balance of convenience lay in favour of refusing the interlocutory relief.

The approach adopted by Laffoy J would seem to suggest that the courts in this jurisdiction are still anxious to adhere to the *American Cyanamid / Campus Oil* guidelines unless there is good reason for departing from them. Laffoy J certainly showed a reluctance to extend the list of recognised exceptions to an entire class of proceedings, namely intellectual property disputes, although undoubtedly there may be individual cases falling under this heading in which the facts may warrant the conclusion being reached that the trial of the action is unlikely to take place and that a wider consideration of the merits of both parties' cases is therefore justified.

Whether Special Considerations Apply where the Presumption of Constitutionality is Involved

This question has been considered in a number of decisions which deal with such issues as seeking to restrain the ratification of a treaty or the implementation of legislative provisions and an application to prohibit the exercise of a statutory power. In *Crotty v. An Taoiseach*[175] the plaintiff sought an interlocutory injunction to restrain the defendants from ratifying the Single European Act, a treaty which introduced a number of changes to the treaties establishing the European Communities, and also sought to challenge the constitutionality of the European Communities (Amendment) Act 1986. In delivering his judgment on the application for interlocutory relief, Barrington J stated that he must endeavour to follow the procedure laid down in *Campus Oil*, but added that the issues raised before him were of a constitutional nature 'in relation to which weight must be given to the presumption of constitutionality'. He stated that subject to this consideration, he had to direct his mind to whether the applicant had raised a fair question of law although he said that it appeared to him to be proper to attach a greater significance to the term a 'fair question of law' in the case before him than would be attached to that term in private litigation because of the existence of the presumption of constitutionality, which attaches to legislation and a similar presumption in favour of executive acts of the government. Applying these considerations, Barrington J was satisfied that the plaintiff had raised a number of fair and substantial issues for the court to decide and he concluded that the balance of convenience lay in favour of granting the injunction sought rather than refusing it.

---

175. [1987] IR 713.

In *Pesca Valentia Ltd v. Minister for Fisheries and Forestry*[176] the plaintiff sought an interlocutory injunction restraining the defendants from enforcing a term in a licence granted pursuant to the Fisheries (Consolidation) Act 1959 as amended which required that three-quarters of the crew of a trawler should be of Irish nationality. The Supreme Court had to consider whether any special principles applied to an application for an interlocutory injunction to prohibit the exercise of a statutory power presumed to be constitutional. Finlay CJ stated that he was satisfied that the presumption of constitutionality which applied to the legislation was material in relation to the determination by the court of whether the plaintiff had established a fair question to be tried at the hearing of the action. In addition, he was satisfied that the consequence arising from the making of an interlocutory injunction of preventing the executive from carrying out powers vested in it by a statute enjoying the presumption of constitutionality was a matter for consideration in assessing where the balance of convenience lay. However Finlay CJ stated that he was not satisfied that 'there is any special principle applicable to an application for an interlocutory injunction of this kind'. The Supreme Court dismissed the defendants' appeal against the grant of an interlocutory injunction, but varied the terms of the order.

A similar view has recently been expressed by Kelly J in *Controller of Patents, Designs and Trademarks v. Ireland*[177] in which a slightly different issue arose. The plaintiff sought, *inter alia*, an order restraining the defendant minister from implementing or bringing into operation sections 4 and 5 of the Intellectual Property (Miscellaneous Provisions) Act 1988 until further order of the court. Counsel for the defendants argued that where relief of this nature is sought it is not sufficient to establish that there is a serious issue to be tried and submitted that a stronger case than that had to be shown. The principal basis for this assertion was the fact that the legislation carried with it a presumption of constitutionality, but having referred to the *dicta* of Finlay CJ in *Pesca Valentia*, Kelly J stated that it seemed to him that the mere existence of the presumption of constitutionality in favour of the impugned legislation did not mean that new or different rules should be applied to the application. Instead he was of the view that he must weigh the presumption of constitutionality in the balance when deciding the question of whether a serious issue to be tried had been established and also in deciding where the balance of convenience lay. Applying these principles to the facts of the case before him, Kelly J

---

176. [1985] IR 193.
177. High Court 1998 No. 8283P (Kelly J) 31 July 1998.

concluded that the plaintiff had not established that there were any serious issues to be tried and said that in any event the balance of convenience would lie in favour of refusing the relief sought.

So, it would appear that the courts are of the view that no special principles are to be applied to applications for interlocutory injunctions where issues relating to the presumption of constitutionality are involved. However, it is also clear that at the very least this presumption must be weighed in the balance when deciding the question of whether a serious issue to be tried has been established. Whether Barrington J intended any more by his comment in *Crotty* that he would attach a greater significance to the term a 'fair question of law' in such cases has not been clarified and clearly some further judicial consideration of the issues involved would be welcome.

Principles Governing the Grant of Quia Timet Injunctions

While an injunction will generally issue on the basis of an infringement of a plaintiff's rights, an order known as a *quia timet* injunction may also be granted before any injury or damage has actually been sustained, in circumstances where the injury to the plaintiff is merely threatened or apprehended. As Lord Upjohn stated in *Redland Bricks Ltd v. Morris*:[178] 'to prevent the jurisdiction of the courts being stultified equity has invented the *quia timet* action, that is an action for an injunction to prevent an apprehended legal wrong, though none has occurred at present, and the suppliant for such an injunction is without any remedy at law.' This jurisdiction is preventative in nature and will be exercised either where a person threatens and intends to do an unlawful act, in which case the order is generally prohibitory in nature or where the plaintiff's rights have already been infringed and he alleges that this infringement will be repeated, in which case a mandatory injunction is the most likely remedy.[179]

Spry[180] suggests that the same general equitable principles are applied whether or not there has been a breach of the plaintiff's rights or merely a threatened violation of these rights: 'It may properly be said that wherever a court with equitable jurisdiction might enjoin an act if that act had been commenced, it may, in the exercise of its discretion, enjoin the act although it has not yet commenced, provided that its imminence is sufficiently clearly established in order to justify intervention in all the

---

178. [1970] AC 652, 664.
179. *Proctor v. Bayley* (1889) 42 Ch D 390, 398 *per* Cotton LJ; *Redland Bricks Ltd v. Morris* [1970] AC 652, 665 *per* Lord Upjohn.
180. *Equitable Remedies* (5th ed., 1997) p. 378.

circumstances'. However, as he points out, the fact that no breach has as yet occurred is of relevance as it may be more difficult to establish that there is a sufficient risk of future injury to justify the immediate grant of an injunction.[181] Therefore it is important to consider how likely it is that injury will in fact occur and how severe the apprehended damage is required to be before a *quia timet* injunction will be granted. It is insufficient for a plaintiff merely to state that he harbours fears in this regard;[182] in the words of Chitty J in *Attorney-General v. Manchester Corporation:*[183] 'he must show a strong case of probability that the apprehended mischief will, in fact, arise.'

The onus of proof which lies on a plaintiff seeking a *quia timet* injunction has been considered in this jurisdiction on a number of occasions. In *Attorney General (Boswell) v. Rathmines and Pembroke Joint Hospital Board*[184] the plaintiff sought an injunction to restrain the defendant from building a smallpox hospital in a Dublin suburb. While there was conflicting expert evidence about the suitability of the site and the risk of the spread of disease, an injunction was refused on the ground that no real danger had been proved. Chatterton VC spoke in terms of having to establish 'a reasonable, well-grounded apprehension ... [of] substantial damage' and Holmes LJ warned against accepting 'as a measure of danger, the fears of the timid and unreasonable'. However it was the statement of Fitzgibbon LJ which has been most frequently referred to and he stated:

> To sustain the injunction, the law requires proof by the plaintiff of a well-founded apprehension of injury — proof of actual and real danger — a strong probability, almost amounting to moral certainty, that if the Hospital be established, it will be an actionable nuisance.[185]

---

181. See e.g. *McGrane v. Louth County Council*, High Court 1983 No.28F (O'Hanlon J) 9 December 1983 where a *quia timet* injunction sought by the plaintiff to restrain the defendants from developing a rubbish dump was refused.
182. *Attorney-General for Dominion of Canada v. Ritchie Contracting & Supply Co.* [1919] AC 999, 1005 *per* Lord Dunedin.
183. [1893] 2 Ch 87, 92. See also *Litchfield-Speer v. Queen Anne's Gate Syndicate (No. 2) Ltd* [1919] 1 Ch 407, 412 where Lawrence J spoke of the plaintiff proving 'that he will certainly sustain substantial damage'.
184. [1904] 1 IR 161. See also *Attorney-General v. Nottingham Corporation* [1904] 1 Ch 673.
185. *Ibid.* at 171. This test seems to have been accepted by Finlay P in *C. & A. Modes v. C. & A. (Waterford) Ltd* [1976] IR 198 where he said that if the action before him was to be equated with an application for a *quia timet* injunction, which he did not necessarily so decide, the standard of proof laid down by Fitzgibbon LJ was the correct one. In the Supreme Court, Henchy J agreed that there were sufficient grounds for the conclusion that this onus of proof had been discharged in the circumstances,

This passage was quoted with approval by Judge Fawsitt in the Circuit Court decision of *Radford v. Wexford Corporation*,[186] where the plaintiffs failed in their application for a *quia timet* injunction to restrain the defendants from further proceeding with the construction of a public lavatory on a site adjoining the main street of Wexford town as they had not established a 'strong probability that the apprehended mischiefs will in fact arise'.

The slightly less stringent test of 'reasonable probability' was applied by Meredith J in *Independent Newspapers Ltd v. Irish Press Ltd*,[187] in which the plaintiff company sought to restrain the defendant from publishing and passing off a newspaper with a title in which it claimed the property and goodwill. It was held by Meredith J that the plaintiff has failed to establish that damage would occur as it had not been able to show that the goodwill in the title was still an 'attractive force' and he refused to grant the injunction sought. Meredith J examined the onus which must be satisfied before a court would grant a *quia timet* injunction and said that it would not do so 'unless it is satisfied that there is a reasonable probability that what is threatened to be done is calculated in the ordinary course of events, or according to the ordinary course of business, to cause damage to the plaintiff'.[188] Subsequently, in *Whelan v. Madigan*[189] Kenny J spoke in terms of a establishing a 'probability' simpliciter and granted a *quia timet* injunction to restrain the defendant from interfering with the plaintiffs' quiet enjoyment of their flats.

In view of the lack of consensus in relation to the degree of probability of injury required before a court will grant a *quia timet* injunction, perhaps the suggestion made by Russell LJ in *Hooper v. Rogers*[190] has much to commend it. He stated that 'the degree of probability of future injury is not an absolute standard: what is to be aimed at is justice between the parties having regard to all the relevant circumstances'.[191] In addition, it should be stated that the degree of probability of injury is not the only factor which should influence the court and the greater the damage or prejudice likely to be caused, the more justifiable the court's intervention will be.

---

but concluded that he was satisfied that what the plaintiffs claimed was not a *quia timet* injunction.
186. (1954) 89 ILTR 184.
187. [1932] IR 615.
188. *Ibid.* at 631.
189. [1978] ILRM 136.
190. [1975] Ch 43.
191. *Ibid.* at 50.

Detailed consideration was given to the circumstances in which a *quia timet* injunction should be granted in the recent judgment of Geoghegan J in *Szabo v. ESAT Digiphone Ltd.*[192] The plaintiffs, who were schoolchildren attending a national school, sought *quia timet* injunctions to restrain the erection and operation of a mobile phone base station in the grounds of a garda station located beside their school. Geoghegan J referred to the test employed in *Attorney-General v. Manchester Corporation*, namely that the plaintiff must show 'a strong case of probability that the apprehended mischief will, in fact, arise' and stated that he was inclined to think that it went too far, although he did say that for a *quia timet* injunction to be granted, there would have to be 'a proven substantial risk of danger',[193] a view which he said was supported by the decision of the Irish Court of Appeal in the *Boswell* case. In that case, Walker LJ had also expressed the opinion that where there was conflicting expert evidence, the judge himself could not form a view as an expert and if the conflict left him in doubt, he could not in a *quia timet* action decide that the case for the plaintiff had been made out.

Geoghegan J then went on to consider the correct principles to be applied in relation to applications for interlocutory *quia timet* injunctions and said that he would adopt the treatment of the subject in *Spry on Equitable Remedies*,[194] in which the author made it clear that there is no difference in the legal principles to be applied to interlocutory *quia timet* injunctions and any other kind of interlocutory injunction. However, as Spry pointed out in his consideration of *quia timet* injunctions in general, it should not be thought that it is never material that no breach of the applicant's rights has taken place at the time of the hearing of the application and if no breach has taken place, it may be more difficult to establish, as a matter of evidence, that there is a sufficient risk of a future injury to justify the immediate grant of an injunction. Geoghegan J concluded that it was highly improbable at the very least that any injury would ensue to the children before the hearing of the action and in these circumstances he did not think that it would be just or reasonable to grant a *quia timet* injunction.

It is interesting to note that the notion of applying the *Campus Oil* guidelines has been canvassed in two recent cases dealing with *quia timet* injunctions. In *Szabo* Geoghegan J said that he doubted whether their application was appropriate in a case such as that before him, but this was

---

192. [1998] 2 ILRM 102.
193. *Ibid.* at 110.
194. 4th ed., p.459 Now see 5th ed., 1997.

because he said there was something distasteful about balancing the convenience of the defendant in being able to carry on its business against alleged dangers to the health of the plaintiffs. In *National Irish Bank Ltd v. RTE*[195] Shanley J stated that he was deciding the interlocutory application before him on the basis of the principles in *Campus Oil*, rather than on the basis of the test laid down in *Boswell*, even though the application was of a *quia timet* nature. He explained that he was doing so because he was dealing with a situation where the defendant had actually conceded that its aim was to publish confidential information belonging to the plaintiff and in his view in such a case, the *Campus Oil* principles were 'a more appropriate guide than the more stringent burden' that the test in *Boswell* would impose.

However, it would appear that even if the courts no longer insist upon the test of 'a proven substantial risk of danger' being satisfied in every case in which a *quia timet* injunction is sought, it will nevertheless remain more difficult to obtain an injunction of this nature, not least because, as Spry has pointed out, if no wrongdoing has yet occurred, it will be more difficult to establish, as a matter of evidence, that there is a sufficient risk of a future injury to justify the grant of an injunction.

Finally, it should be pointed out that before a *quia timet* injunction will be granted against a defendant, it is important to establish that it is the defendant himself who has threatened to carry out the action in question. So, in *Celsteel Ltd v. Alton House Holdings Ltd*[196] the Court of Appeal set aside an injunction granted against a lessor, and left in place the injunction granted against the lessee, who was the party actually threatening to erect the car wash to which the plaintiff objected.

SPECIFIC CIRCUMSTANCES IN WHICH AN INJUNCTION WILL BE GRANTED

To Restrain a Breach of Contract

While the usual method of enforcing a positive obligation in a contract is by an order of specific performance, an injunction may be granted to restrain the breach of a negative undertaking contained therein. It was sug-

---

195. High Court 1998 No. 1306 P (Shanley J) 6 March 1998. Note that the Supreme Court upheld the refusal of an interlocutory injunction restraining the defendant from publishing information which the plaintiff asserted was confidential, see [1998] 2 ILRM 196.
196. [1986] 1 WLR 512.

gested by Lord Cairns in *Doherty v. Allman*[197] that an injunction will issue to secure enforcement of a negative contractual obligation almost as a matter of course. He stated as follows:

> If parties, for valuable consideration, with their eyes open, contract that a particular thing shall not be done, all that a Court of Equity has to do is to say, by way of injunction, that which the parties have already said by way of covenant, that the thing shall not be done; and in such case the injunction does nothing more than give the sanction of the process of the Court to that which already is the contract between the parties. It is not then a question of the balance of convenience or inconvenience, or the amount of damage or of injury — it is the specific performance, by the Court, of that negative bargain which the parties have made, with their eyes open, between themselves.

However, it has been said that this statement is 'the starting point, not a summation of equity's attitude to negative stipulations'[198] and it must not be read without some qualification. In England it has been stated that it must be applied in the light of the surrounding circumstances of each case,[199] and wider discretionary considerations have been taken into account where an order of a mandatory nature has been sought. In *Shepherd Homes Ltd v. Sandham*[200] the plaintiff sought a mandatory injunction to compel the defendant to pull down a fence erected in breach of covenant. It was held by Megarry J in refusing the injunction that the court would exercise its discretion to withhold an injunction more readily if it were mandatory than if it were prohibitory and that even a blameless plaintiff could not as of right claim to enforce a negative covenant by means of a mandatory injunction. He commented that 'the enforcement of a negative covenant at the trial by a mandatory injunction is far more a matter of judicial discretion and not of right than in the case of a prohibitory injunction'[201] and said that the statement of Lord Cairns although it *prima facie* applies to mandatory injunctions, does not apply in its full width and is tempered by judicial

---

197. (1878) 3 App Cas 709, 720.
198. Meagher, Gummow and Lehane, *Equity Doctrines and Remedies* (3rd ed., 1992) p.568.
199. *Shaw v. Applegate* [1977] 1 WLR 970, 975 *per* Buckley LJ.
200. [1971] Ch 340. See also *Wrotham Park Estate Co. Ltd v. Parkside Homes Ltd* [1974] 1 WLR 798.
201. *Ibid.* at 351. See also *Sharp v. Harrison* [1922] 1 Ch 502, 512 *per* Astbury J and *Charrington v. Simons & Co. Ltd* [1970] 1 WLR 725, 730.

discretion. This approach is in line with that put forward by Spry[202] who points out that it is clear that in proceedings for specific performance to enforce the performance of positive obligations in a contract, considerations of hardship and other discretionary factors are relevant and may induce the court to refuse relief, so there is no reason in principle why the same considerations should not apply to proceedings to enforce contractual rights by injunction.

Where an interlocutory injunction is sought to restrain the breach of a negative covenant, there are conflicting authorities on the question of whether an injunction should issue as a matter of course. It has been held in England in *Hampstead & Suburban Properties Ltd v. Diomedous*[203] that the principle in *Doherty v. Allman* should apply where there is a 'plain and uncontested breach of a clear covenant.'[204] It seems to have also been accepted by the Supreme Court in *Dublin Port and Docks Board v. Britannia Dredging Co. Ltd*,[205] in which the plaintiff sought an interlocutory injunction restraining the defendant from removing dredging equipment from a site where it had undertaken to carry out work. The court held that as the defendant had agreed to this negative term and as it was satisfied that a breach of the covenant was imminent, an interlocutory injunction should be granted. O Dálaigh CJ concluded that the principle in *Doherty v. Allman* was accordingly applicable and said that the court was not concerned to examine either the balance of convenience or the amount of damage. In the circumstances where the parties had entered into a negative covenant, it was the duty of the court to hold the defendants to their bargain pending the trial.[206]

However, subsequently in *TMG Group Ltd v. Al Babtain Trading and Contracting Co.*[207] Keane J distinguished the facts of the case before him from those in *Dublin Port and Docks Board* and stated as follows:

> The circumstances of the present case are wholly different: the defendants strenuously contend that neither of the transactions which the company proposes to enter into will constitute a breach of their contractual obligations under the shareholders' agreement. I do not

---

202. *Equitable Remedies* (5th ed., 1997) p. 586.
203. [1969] 1 Ch 248.
204. *Ibid.* at 259 *per* Megarry J. Although note the comments of Ungoed-Thomas J in *Texaco Ltd v. Mulberry Filling Station Ltd* [1972] 1 WLR 814, 831.
205. [1968] IR 136.
206. *Ibid.* at 147. Applied by Costello J in *Irish Shell Ltd v. Elm Motors Ltd* [1984] IR 200, 216.
207. [1982] ILRM 349.

think that Ó Dálaigh CJ in the passages to which I have referred, was laying down any general principle that, in all cases where the plaintiff establishes a *prima facie* case of a breach of a negative stipulation in a contract, the court could disregard any question of the balance of convenience as between the parties. His observations were clearly confined to a case where one party to a contract was proposing to act in breach of a negative contract (and indeed to repudiate the whole contract) in circumstances where the court was not satisfied on the evidence that they were entitled so to do.[208]

Subsequently in *Irish Shell Ltd v. Elm Motors Ltd*[209] McCarthy J endorsed these views and said that save in the most exceptional circumstances, the determination of an application for an interlocutory injunction lies solely on a consideration of the questions of whether a fair case has been made out and where the balance of convenience lies. This question has recently been addressed again by the Supreme Court in *Premier Dairies Ltd v. Doyle*.[210] Delivering judgment in the High Court, Kinlen J held that the defendants, who had entered into distribution agreements with the plaintiff to deliver its products, should be held to the terms of the negative covenant contained in the agreements preventing them from competing with the plaintiff and he stated that the decision of the Supreme Court in *Britannia Dredging Co. Ltd* governed the case.[211] However, the defendants appealed against this order arguing, *inter alia,* that the clause in question was contrary to sections 4 and 5 of the Competition Act 1991. O'Flaherty J dismissed the appeal but it is interesting to note the comment which he made about the *Doherty v. Allman/Britannia Dredging* principle. He was satisfied that if there had been no other factors in the case he would have held that it came 'four square within the *Britannia Dredging* decision'. However, O'Flaherty J stated that as there was scope for an argument to be made as to the applicability of the Competition Act 1991 which he described as 'a rather complex piece of legislation which, so far, has not been judicially mined to any extent', it was not in his view appropriate to apply the *Britannia Dredging* principle to the case. O'Flaherty J accordingly went on to consider whether there was a fair case to be tried, which he was satisfied that there was and to consider where the balance of convenience lay. While he disagreed with Kinlen J about the applicability

---

208. *Ibid.* at 353.
209. [1984] IR 200.
210. [1996] 1 ILRM 363.
211. High Court 1995 No. 7008P (Kinlen J) 29 September 1995.

of the *Britannia Dredging* principle, O'Flaherty J was satisfied that the former's conclusion that the balance of convenience favoured the plaintiffs was correct and for this reason affirmed his decision to grant the interlocutory relief sought. On balance the comments of McCarthy J in *Irish Shell Ltd*, referred to above, seem to reflect current practice and it is likely that *Britannia Dredging* may be interpreted as being confined to its own specific facts.

The jurisdiction of the courts to grant an injunction is wider than its jurisdiction to grant specific performance, and often a positive obligation in a contract may not be specifically enforceable.[212] It is therefore often of practical significance that even where a contract contains no express negative stipulation it may be possible to imply a negative undertaking which can be enforced by the grant of an injunction. As Lord Selborne stated in *Wolverhampton and Walsall Railway Co. v. London and North-Western Railway Co.*[213] in such circumstances, the courts should look to the substance and not merely the form of the agreement and this approach has generally although not universally[214] been followed.[215] In *Catt v. Tourle*,[216] where a publican agreed to procure all his beer supplies from a specified source an injunction was granted restraining him from obtaining these supplies elsewhere. Similarly in *Metropolitan Electric Supply Co. v. Ginder*[217] the defendant agreed to take all his electricity requirements from the plaintiff for a specified period. The court construed the contract as an undertaking not to obtain electricity from another supplier and granted an injunction to restrain the defendant from doing so. This principle has also been applied in this jurisdiction in *Irish Shell Ltd v. Elm Motors Ltd*,[218] where injunctions were granted to compel the defendant to comply with the terms of covenants in a lease. As Costello J stated once it was established that these covenants were enforceable it did not matter that they were expressed in the form of a positive rather than a negative obligation.

---

212. The courts have traditionally displayed a reluctance to grant specific performance of part only of a contract. See *Ryan v. Mutual Tontine Westminster Chambers Association* [1893] 1 Ch 116, 125.
213. (1873) LR 16 Eq 433, 440.
214. See *Mortimer v. Beckett* [1920] 1 Ch 571 where Russell J laid emphasis on the positive form of the agreement in declining to grant an injunction.
215. See e.g. in relation to covenants affecting the use of land, *Tulk v. Moxhay* (1848) 2 Ph 774.
216. (1869) LR 4 Ch App 654.
217. [1901] 2 Ch 799. See also *James Jones & Sons Ltd v. Earl of Tankerville* [1909] 2 Ch 440.
218. [1984] IR 200.

Particular Considerations which Apply to Contracts for Personal Services
As stated above this remedy may be of importance where the positive obligation in the contract is not specifically enforceable, although in certain
circumstances, particularly in the context of contracts for personal services, it is accepted that an injunction should not be granted by the court
where this would indirectly provide for specific performance of the positive terms of the contract. As Kenny J stated in *Yeates v. Minister for Posts
and Telegraphs*[219] in the context of an application for an injunction which
if granted would have indirectly amounted to specific performance, 'it is
settled law that the courts never specifically enforce a contract for personal services'. Despite this principle on occasion the courts have permitted the issue of an injunction to restrain a negative undertaking in a contract
for personal services which may indirectly cause the contract to be performed; as O'Flaherty J stated in *Capital Radio Productions Ltd v. Radio
2000 Ltd*[220] 'while a person cannot be forced to work against his will for
someone he can, if in breach of contract, be *prevented* from working for
anyone else.' This principle is well illustrated by the decision of Lord St
Leonards in *Lumley v. Wagner*.[221] The defendant undertook to sing at the
plaintiff's theatre for a specified period and not to perform elsewhere during this time. Subsequently, the defendant agreed another contract for a
larger fee with a third party and the plaintiff sought an injunction to restrain her from singing for this person. Lord St Leonards held that the
plaintiff was entitled to an injunction to restrain the breach of the negative
stipulation in the contract. The decision has been criticized on the basis
that it amounted to the equivalent of ordering specific performance of the
original contract, although as Lord St Leonards pointed out, the defendant
could not have been compelled to fulfil this obligation. This approach was
followed in *Warner Brothers Pictures, Incorporated v. Nelson*,[222] in which
the defendant, Mrs Nelson, better known as the actress Bette Davis, agreed
to act for a studio for a period of five years and undertook not to act for any
other party during this time or to engage in any other occupation without
the written consent of the studio. The plaintiff sought to enforce the obligation not to act for anyone other than itself and Branson J granted an
injunction to restrain her from breaching this undertaking. He stated that
where a contract of personal service contains negative covenants, the enforcement of which will not amount either to a decree of specific perform-

219. [1978] ILRM 22, 24.
220. Supreme Court 1998 No.128 & 129, 26 May 1998.
221. (1852) 1 De G M & G 604.
222. [1937] 1 KB 209.

ance of the positive covenants of the contract or to a decree under which the defendant must remain idle or perform the positive covenants, the court will enforce those negative covenants subject to the consideration that an injunction is a discretionary remedy and the court in an order of this nature may limit the terms of the injunction to what it considers reasonable in the circumstances. While an injunction covering all the negative covenants in the contract would have forced the defendant to perform her contract or to remain idle, that objection was removed by the limited form in which the order was sought. Branson J rejected the argument that the order made amounted to an indirect form of specific performance and said that while the plaintiff might be tempted to perform the contract in view of the fact that alternative work would be considerably less lucrative, she would not be driven to do so.

A related question is whether an employer can be compelled to continue to employ an employee and this issue was considered in *Page One Records Ltd v. Britton.*[223] The plaintiffs had contracted with a group of musicians known as 'the Troggs' that they would act as their manager for a period of five years and the group agreed not to employ anyone else during this time. When the plaintiffs sought an injunction to prevent the employment of another manager the court refused to grant an injunction on the basis that as a practical matter it would force the group to continue to employ the plaintiffs. Stamp J said that it would be tantamount to ordering specific performance of a contract of personal services and it would be wrong to put pressure on the defendants to continue to employ someone in a fiduciary capacity in whom they had lost confidence.

The approach adopted by Stamp J is in many respects preferable to that of Branson J in that it was unrealistic to expect the defendants in either case to give up their chosen careers and the alternative was that they would find themselves compelled to perform a contract of personal services. The Court of Appeal in England has recently confirmed this point and has reasserted the view that an injunction should not be granted if its indirect effect would be to compel performance of a contract for personal services. In *Warren v. Mendy*[224] a boxer agreed that he would not be managed by anyone except the plaintiff for a three-year period but subsequently entered into a management agreement with the defendant. The plaintiff sought an injunction to restrain the defendant from inducing a breach of contract and from acting for the boxer. The effect of such an injunction would have been to restrain the boxer from performing services for the defendant and

---

223. [1968] 1 WLR 157.
224. [1989] 1 WLR 853. See McClean [1990] CLJ 28.

would arguably have compelled him to perform his agreement with the plaintiff and the Court of Appeal held that no injunction should be granted. Nourse LJ commented that Branson J's approach in *Warner Brothers Pictures, Incorporated v. Nelson* was 'extraordinarily unrealistic' and stated as follows:

> [T]he following general principles are applicable to the grant or refusal of an injunction to enforce performance of the servant's negative obligations in a contract for personal services inseparable from the exercise of some special skill or talent. In such a case the court ought not to enforce the performance of the negative obligations if their enforcement will effectively compel the servant to perform his positive obligations under the contract. Compulsion is a question to be decided on the facts of each case, with a realistic regard for the probable reaction of an injunction on the psychological and material, and sometimes the physical, need of the servant to maintain the skill or talent. The longer the term for which the injunction is sought, the more readily will compulsion be inferred. ... An injunction will less readily be granted where there are obligations of mutual trust and confidence, more especially where the servant's trust in the master may have been betrayed or his confidence in him has genuinely gone.[225]

McCutcheon has stated that 'the practical consequence of *Warren v. Mendy* is to make it highly improbable that negative injunctions will be granted in sports cases, at least where the contract is for anything other than a short duration'[226] and has expressed the view that the approach of the English courts may be too lenient. In contrast he points out that the North American courts have placed a greater emphasis on ensuring that contracts of this nature are honoured and that individuals do not renege on their commitments simply because a more lucrative opportunity is presented to them.[227] There is clearly merit in his argument that 'if contractual obligations are to be taken seriously it is to be expected that the law would lean towards their enforcement rather than minimising the consequences of their breach to the wrongdoer' and it will be interesting to see whether the approach adopted in North America will ultimately be taken on board either in England or in this jurisdiction.

---

225. *Ibid.* at 867.
226. (1997) 17 LS 65, 74.
227. See e.g. *Washington Capitols Basketball Club Inc. v. Barry* (1969) 304 F Supp 1193; *Cincinnati Bangals Inc v. Bergey* (1974) 453 F Supp 129.

A limited exception to the general principle that employer and employee should not be forced to work together has been recognised where a relationship of mutual trust and confidence still exists between them. This is illustrated by the decision of the Court of Appeal in *Hill v. C.A. Parsons & Co. Ltd*,[228] where an injunction was granted against an employer to restrain an alleged wrongful dismissal after the employer had reluctantly been forced to terminate the contract of employment of an engineer who had refused to join a trade union. While arguably this amounted to indirect specific performance of a service contract, the majority of the court justified its decision on the basis that a relationship of mutual trust and confidence still existed between the parties. The employer in this case clearly still had confidence in his employee and had only acted in response to pressure from the trade union. This decision can be contrasted with that of the Irish High Court in *Yeates v. Minister for Posts and Telegraphs*,[229] in which the plaintiff civil servants, who had been suspended from their positions without pay when they refused to pass a picket placed on the premises in which they worked, sought interlocutory injunctions restoring them to their positions and giving them the right to remuneration. In this instance the employer clearly had lost confidence in the employees and had consciously wanted to suspend them. Kenny J refused the injunctions sought on the grounds, *inter alia*, that to restore the plaintiffs to their former positions would amount to specific performance of a contract for personal services which the court would not order on principle.

A subsequent decision which is out of line with those just considered is *Irani v. Southampton and South-West Hampshire Health Authority*,[230] in which Warner J granted an injunction to restrain the dismissal of an employee in circumstances where there were irreconcilable differences between him and a consultant but no complaints of professional incompetence. This result is less justifiable in that unlike in *Hill*, the employer actively sought the employee's dismissal and it is far from clear whether such an approach would be followed.[231] The better approach would seem to be that it is only in circumstances where the employer still retains trust and confidence in the employee that any order which will have the effect of obliging the parties to continue working together should be made.

---

228. [1972] Ch 305. See also *Powell v. London Borough of Brent* [1987] IRLR 466 and *Robb v. Hammersmith* [1991] ICR 514.
229. [1978] ILRM 22.
230. [1985] IRLR 203.
231. See Madden (1985) 3 ILT (ns) 134.

Rather conflicting signals on this issue have been sent out in the most recent judgment delivered in this area, by Laffoy J in *Courtney v. Radio 2000 Ltd.*[232] The plaintiff radio presenter had been informed in writing that his employment with the defendant was to terminate forthwith and sought a number of reliefs, including an injunction restraining the defendant from implementing his purported dismissal until the trial of the action and an order requiring the defendant to reinstate the plaintiff to his position pending the trial. The defendant submitted that the plaintiff was employed to present live broadcasts and given that trust and confidence no longer existed on its part, it would be inappropriate for the court to grant the reliefs sought. Laffoy J agreed that it would not be appropriate to make an order requiring the defendant to reinstate the plaintiff but decided that the balance of convenience lay in favour of granting an injunction restraining the defendant from implementing the purported dismissal until the trial of the action. She stated as follows: 'I consider that employment as a broadcaster, which is a high profile occupation, is in a special category and that the plaintiff might possibly establish at the trial of the action that this is one of the exceptional circumstances in which an injunction is the appropriate remedy in an employer and employee dispute. However, I express no view whatsoever on this issue'. It should be pointed out that, given the fact that a relationship of trust and confidence no longer existed between the parties it would be surprising if a court deemed it appropriate to grant a permanent injunction in such circumstances.

To Restrain the Commission or Continuance of a Tort

As Hanbury and Martin[233] make clear, equity plays no part in determining whether a tort has been committed or threatened; that is purely a question of law but once this is established, a court may in its discretion grant or withhold an injunction on the basis of equitable principles.

Equity will commonly intervene and grant an injunction in the case of nuisance which is usually of a continuing nature and the remedy of an injunction will be the most appropriate form of remedy in the circumstances.[234] In relation to acts of public nuisance, i.e. acts or omissions which cause damage to the public generally, proceedings for an injunction may only be brought by the Attorney General either on his own motion or at the relation of an individual unless the individual can establish that he

---

232. High Court 1997 No. 7903P (Laffoy J) 22 July 1997.
233. *Modern Equity* (15th ed., 1997) p.791.
234. See e.g. *Bellew v. Cement Ltd* [1948] IR 61; *Patterson v. Murphy* [1978] ILRM 85.

has suffered some special damage or that a private right of his has been infringed.[235]

An injunction is often sought to prevent a threatened or continued trespass to land, although if the trespass is of a trivial nature and involves no appreciable injury to the plaintiff,[236] an order will not be granted. Injunctions are also sought with increasing frequency in relation to alleged passing off,[237] and in the area of industrial relations. As noted above, the common law principles relating to the grant of an interlocutory injunction clearly favoured the employer where proceedings were brought seeking to restrain picketing by means of an interlocutory injunction and it remains to be seen whether the provisions of section 19 of the Industrial Relations Act 1990 will adequately redress this imbalance.[238]

The circumstances in which an injunction may be granted to restrain alleged defamation are difficult to define with precision, although as noted the traditional reluctance on the part of the courts to interfere unduly with an individual's right to freedom of expression has been reflected in the rather onerous burden facing potential plaintiffs.[239]

To Restrain a Breach of Constitutional Rights

It is a well established principle that damages will lie in respect of a breach of constitutional rights,[240] and that the amount of such an award may vary from exemplary damages where the State has deliberately and without justification infringed a person's constitutional rights[241] to a purely nominal sum where the breach has caused no real damage.[242] However, it has also been recognised that an injunction will lie to restrain unconstitutional activities, such as in *Murtagh Properties v. Cleary*[243] where an injunction was granted by Kenny J to restrain the picketing of a licensed premises on the basis that it amounted to unlawful interference with the constitutional

---

235. *Boyce v. Paddington Borough Council* [1903] 1 Ch 109, 113 *per* Buckley J.
236. *Fielden v. Cox* (1906) 22 TLR 411; *Llandudno Urban District Council v. Woods* [1899] 2 Ch 705.
237. See e.g. *Independent Newspapers Ltd v. Irish Press Ltd* [1932] IR 615; *C.& A. Modes v. C. & A* (Waterford) Ltd [1976] IR 198; *Three Stripe International Ltd v. Charles O'Neill & Co. Ltd* [1989] ILRM 124; *An Post v. Irish Permanent plc* [1995] 1 ILRM 336.
238. See *supra* pp. 473-476.
239. See *supra* pp. 476-480. *Sinclair v. Gogarty* [1937] IR 377, 384; *Connolly v. RTE* [1991] 2 IR 446 and *Reynolds v. Malocco* [1999] 1 ILRM 289.
240. See e.g. *Meskell v. CIE* [1973] IR 121; *Hayes v. Ireland* [1987] ILRM 651.
241. *Kennedy v. Ireland* [1987] IR 587.
242. *Kearney v. Ireland* [1986] IR 116.
243. [1972] IR 330.

right of the employees who worked there to earn their livelihood. This approach was followed by O'Hanlon J in *Parsons v. Kavanagh*,[244] in which the plaintiff, who operated a passenger bus service on a route pursuant to a statutory licence, sought an injunction to prevent the defendants operating a bus service without a licence on the same route. O'Hanlon held that having regard to the plaintiff's constitutional right to earn a livelihood, which carried with it the entitlement to be protected against any unlawful activity on the part of another person which materially infringed that right, the plaintiff was entitled to the injunction sought.

One area which has provoked a considerable amount of case law in this regard is Article 40.3.3 of the Constitution which provides that 'the State acknowledges the right to life of the unborn and, with due regard to the equal right to life of the mother, guarantees in its laws to respect, and as far as practicable, by its laws to defend and vindicate that right'. In *Attorney General (SPUC) v. Open Door Counselling*[245] Hamilton P granted an order restraining the defendants from assisting pregnant women within the jurisdiction to travel abroad to obtain abortions by providing information relating to clinics where abortions are carried out or by referring them to such clinics. As he stated 'the courts will provide a procedure for the enforcement and protection of personal rights and the power of the courts in this regard does not depend on legislation. The public interest and the common good require that personal rights be respected, vindicated and protected.'[246] The Supreme Court rejected the defendants' appeal and Finlay CJ commented that the Attorney General, in whose name the proceedings had been brought, was an especially appropriate person to invoke the jurisdiction of the court to defend and vindicate the constitutional right in question. Further proceedings were taken in the case of *SPUC v. Grogan*,[247] in which the plaintiff sought an interlocutory injunction restraining the defendants from distributing certain information in relation to abortion services available outside the State. The Supreme Court allowed the plaintiff's appeal against the decision of Carroll J to refer questions of interpretation to the European Court of Justice without making any order in relation to the grant of the injunction. Finlay CJ said that the application for an interlocutory injunction consisted of an application to restrain an activity which had clearly been declared by the Supreme Court to be unconstitu-

---

244. [1990] ILRM 560.
245. [1988] IR 593.
246. *Ibid.* at 606.
247. [1989] IR 753.

tional and laid down the following principles which in his view should apply in such cases. He stated:

> [I]t is clearly quite inappropriate to approach the exercise of the discretion to grant or refuse an interlocutory injunction, upon the basis of a supposed *status quo ante* consisting of activities which are constitutionally forbidden acts. The true principle which falls to be considered in this case in relation to the exercise of that discretion is the unqualified existence of the relevant provisions of the Constitution at the time of the application for an injunction which, in my view, having regard to the constitutional law applicable, replaces the ordinary concept of *status quo ante* arising in interlocutory cases. With regard to the issue of the balance of convenience, I am satisfied that where an injunction is sought to protect a constitutional right, that the only matter which could properly be capable of being weighed in a balance against the granting of such protection would be another competing constitutional right.[248]

Finlay CJ concluded that where the right sought to be protected is that of life, there could be no question of an entitlement in European Community law, as a corollary to the right to travel to avail of services, counterbalancing as a matter of convenience the necessity for an interlocutory injunction.

This line of reasoning was further developed in the controversial decision of *Attorney General v. X.*,[249] in which Costello J granted an injunction restraining the defendant and her parents from leaving the jurisdiction for a period of nine months or from arranging a termination of pregnancy, an order which was subsequently set aside on appeal by the Supreme Court.

To Protect Public Rights

An injunction may issue to restrain activities which are detrimental to the public generally. As a general rule such an injunction may only be sought successfully by the Attorney General, either acting on his own initiative, or at the relation of another who seeks to prevent infringement of a right. As an exception to this general principle, an individual may seek an injunction to restrain interference with a public right if this interference also amounts to an infringement of a private right or would cause special dam-

---

248. *Ibid.* at 765.
249. [1992] 1 IR 1.

age to this individual.[250] However the traditional principles in this area were thrown into some doubt by a number of decisions of the Supreme Court in the late 1980s such as *Crotty v. An Taoiseach*,[251] in which the plaintiff successfully sought an injunction to prevent the State ratifying the Single European Act, a treaty which introduced a number of signifi-cant changes to the treaties establishing the European Communities. In *SPUC v. Coogan*[252] the Supreme Court held that the Attorney General did not have an exclusive right to commence proceedings seeking to secure compliance with the provisions of Article 40.3.3° of the Constitution and that any citizen showing a *bona fide* interest and concern in its enforce-ment might do so. The Supreme Court held that the plaintiff, who was not in the position of an officious or meddlesome intervenient in the matter, had sufficient *locus standi* to maintain an action against individuals whom it claimed were acting in a manner contrary to Article 40.3.3° without being required to act in relator proceedings.

A question which has provoked considerable debate is whether an in-junction may be sought to restrain the infringement of a public right even where a statutory remedy exists, in particular where the activity also con-stitutes a criminal offence. While the use of an injunction to restrain a breach of the criminal law has been described as a remedy of last resort,[253] it would appear that the Attorney General, in his role as guardian of the rights of the public, may obtain such a remedy. It has been stressed that an injunction will only be granted in these circumstances where the statutory remedy is inadequate and it has been established in England that an indi-vidual may not take such an action in the absence of interference with private rights or special damage. So, in *Gouriet v. Union of Post Office Workers*[254] the plaintiff failed to obtain an injunction to restrain a threat-ened boycott of postal communications between the UK and South Africa which amounted to a breach of the Post Office Act 1953 when the Attor-ney General declined to bring a relator action.

This issue has been considered in this jurisdiction on a number of oc-casions and in *Attorney General (O'Duffy) v. Appleton*[255] the Attorney General was granted an injunction in a relator action in which it was sought to restrain the activities of a company formed for fraudulent purposes con-

---

250. *Lonrho v. Shell Petroleum Co Ltd* (No.2) [1982] AC 173.
251. [1987] IR 713.
252. [1989] IR 734.
253. *Waverly BC v. Hilden* [1988] 1 WLR 246, 265 *per* Scott J.
254. [1978] AC 435.
255. [1907] 1 IR 252.

trary to the Dentists Act 1878. The most important decision in this area is that of Costello J in *Attorney General v. Paperlink*,[256] in which an injunction was sought to restrain the defendants from operating a courier service in breach of the statutory power of the minister under the Post Office Act 1908. Costello J accepted as correct the statement of Professor Casey[257] to the effect that 'it is possible for [the Attorney General] to obtain an injunction to restrain someone from acting in breach of a statutory provision even where his action constitutes an offence,' and also the following statement of Lord Denning MR in *Attorney General v. Chaudray*:[258]

> Whenever parliament has enacted a law and given a particular remedy for the breach of it, such remedy being in an inferior court, nevertheless the High Court always has reserve power to enforce the law so enacted by way of an injunction or declaration or other suitable remedy. The High Court has a jurisdiction to ensure obedience to the law whenever it is just and convenient to do so.

In the course of his judgment, Costello J laid down a number of important principles. He confirmed that the Attorney General has the right to seek an injunction to restrain a breach of statute, even where the statute prescribes alternative remedies including criminal sanctions. Costello J stressed that such a jurisdiction should only be exercised in exceptional circumstances and said that the court must consider the adequacy of the alternative remedy but conceded that the fact that a criminal prosecution had not been brought did not in itself preclude the court from granting an injunction. Costello J was satisfied that there were exceptional circumstances justifying the granting of an injunction in the case before him and in answer to the defendant's argument stressed that the court was not trying a criminal charge but was merely exercising 'a distinct and different jurisdiction in civil proceedings'.

MAREVA INJUNCTIONS[259]

Traditionally, the courts would not grant an injunction to restrain a defendant from dealing with or dissipating his assets prior to the trial of an

---

256. [1984] ILRM 373.
257. *The Office of the Attorney General in Ireland* (1980) p.149.
258. [1971] 1 WLR 1614, 1624.
259. See generally Capper, *Mareva Injunctions* (1988) and Courtney, *Mareva Injunctions and Related Interlocutory Orders* (1998).

action.[260] However, a number of decisions of the English Court of Appeal in the mid-1970s resulted in a change in this position and now a 'Mareva' injunction may be granted to prevent a defendant from removing assets from the jurisdiction or from disposing of them within the jurisdiction in a manner likely to frustrate the plaintiff's proceedings. More recently it has been accepted that an injunction of this nature may even extend to assets held outside the jurisdiction on a worldwide basis.[261]

The genesis of Mareva injunctions can be traced to the decision of the English Court of Appeal in *Nippon Yusen Kaisha v. Karageorgis*,[262] in which Denning MR stated that 'it seems to me that the time has come when we should revise our practice'. The plaintiff shipowners let a number of ships to charterers who defaulted after initially making some payments. Believing that the defendants had certain funds in London banks which would be sent out of the jurisdiction, the plaintiff sought an injunction to prevent this happening. The Court of Appeal held that where there is a strong *prima facie* case that a plaintiff is entitled to money from a defendant within the jurisdiction and the plaintiff has reason to believe that the defendant may remove these assets from the jurisdiction, the court may grant an interlocutory injunction on an *ex parte* basis restraining the defendant from disposing of these assets. This principle was confirmed several weeks later in *Mareva Compania Naviera SA v. International Bulkcarriers SA*,[263] the decision which gave its name to the form of injunction granted in these cases.

A Mareva injunction is interlocutory in nature and its usual purpose is to prevent the dissipation or removal of assets before the trial of an action, although it may be granted to prevent a defendant disposing of assets after the trial has taken place to avoid execution of a judgment. As Kerr LJ stated in *Z. Ltd v. A-Z and AA-LL*[264] the jurisdiction to grant such injunctions is of general application and the courts are loathe to lay down any limitation in relation to the nature or subject-matter of proceedings in which they can be sought, although they tend to be employed predominantly in the commercial sphere. While in theory an order of an unlimited nature can be made, this will often be unnecessary and will inflict disproportionate hardship on a defendant, so in practice a limited order is usually granted

---

260. *Lister & Co. v. Stubbs* (1890) 45 Ch D 1.
261. *Babanaft International Co, SA v. Bassatne* [1990] Ch 13; *Deutsche Bank Atkiengesellschaft v. Murtagh* [1995] 1 ILRM 381 and *Bennett Enterprises Ltd v. Lipton* [1999] 1 ILRM 81.
262. [1975] 1 WLR 1093, 1095.
263. [1975] 2 Lloyd's Rep 509.
264. [1982] QB 558, 584.

which will at least allow retention of sufficient funds to provide for living expenses, or in the case of a company, the costs of its day-to-day running.

A number of guidelines for determining whether a Mareva injunction should be granted were laid down by Lord Denning MR in *Third Chandris Shipping Corporation v. Unimarine SA*[265] as follows:

> (i) The plaintiff should make full and frank disclosure of all matters in his knowledge which are material for the judge to know. ...
> (ii) The plaintiff should give particulars of his claim against the defendant, stating the ground of his claim and the amount thereof, and fairly stating the grounds made against it by the defendant.
> (iii) The plaintiff should give some grounds for believing that the defendant has assets here. ...
> (iv) The plaintiff should give some grounds for believing that there is a risk of assets being removed before the judgment or award is satisfied. ...
> (v) The plaintiff must, of course, give an undertaking in damages — in case he fails in his claim or the injunction turns out to be unjustified.

A Mareva injunction will usually be sought on an *ex parte* basis and the plaintiff will be required to divulge all material facts to the court and failure to make sufficient disclosure may result in the Mareva injunction being subsequently discharged.[266] As Donaldson LJ commented in *Bank Mellat v. Nikpour*:[267]

> The rule requiring full disclosure seems to me to be one of the most fundamental importance, particularly in the context of the Draconian remedy of the Mareva injunction. It is in effect, together with the Anton Piller order, one of the law's two 'nuclear' weapons. If access to such a weapon is obtained without the fullest and frankest disclosure, I have no doubt at all that it should be revoked.

Although a Mareva injunction is a form of interlocutory injunction, it has been argued that the strength of the plaintiff's case is more important in Mareva proceedings than where other types of interlocutory order are sought,[268] and there is authority in England to the effect that 'a "good

---

265. [1979] QB 645, 668-669.
266. See *The Assios* [1979] 1 Lloyd's Rep 331 and *Bank Mellat v. Nikpour* [1985] FSR 87.
267. [1985] FSR 87, 92.
268. See Capper, *Mareva Injunctions* (1988) p. 34

arguable case" is no doubt the minimum which the plaintiff must show in order to cross. ... the "threshold" for the exercise of the jurisdiction.'[269] This standard also seemed to be required by McWilliam J in *Fleming v. Ranks (Ireland) Ltd*,[270] although he declined to grant a Mareva injunction on the basis of the facts before him.

The standard of proof required has been considered again by the High Court in two recent cases. In *Moloney v. Laurib Investments Ltd*,[271] in which the plaintiff sought a Mareva injunction pending the trial of her action for damages for personal injuries against the defendant, Lynch J concluded that the plaintiff had a 'stateable case' against the defendant company and said that it was not appropriate that he should seek to establish anything more regarding the issue of liability at the hearing of the application. However in the circumstances Lynch J doubted that the grant of the order sought would improve the plaintiff's prospects of enforcing a judgment in her favour, and having regard to his findings that the grant of such an injunction would cause very serious loss to the defendant which could not be made good if the company were ultimately successful and also bearing in mind the probable prejudice to the rights of its *bona fide* creditors, Lynch J declined to grant the relief sought.

This question was given more extensive consideration by Murphy J in *Countyglen v. Carway*,[272] who stressed that it would be wrong to require a plaintiff seeking a Mareva injunction to establish as a probability that his claim would succeed. The applicant company brought proceedings against the respondents seeking various orders including a declaration that they had been guilty of fraud and/or conspiracy to defraud, breach of trust and breach of duty and orders pursuant to section 12 of the Companies Act 1990 directing the respondents to repay sums which they had allegedly unlawfully and wrongfully removed from the company. The High Court granted an interim Mareva injunction and the issue of whether to grant an interlocutory order and ancillary relief then came before the court. Murphy J stated that he doubted that there was any significant difference between the expressions 'good arguable case' and 'substantial question to be tried', but he said that if such a distinction could be drawn he would prefer the latter formulation. He confirmed that the 'probability test' had been rejected by the Supreme Court in *Campus Oil* and stated 'in my view, it would be entirely inappropriate for the court on an interlocutory applica-

---

269. *The Niedersachsen* [1984] 1 All ER 398, 415.
270. [1983] ILRM 541, 546.
271. High Court 1993 No. 3189P (Lynch J) 20 July 1993.
272. [1995] 1 ILRM 481.

tion to review such of the evidence as is available to it and attempt to forecast the outcome of the proceedings as a matter of probability or likelihood. What can and should be done is to determine that there is a fair and serious question to be tried.'[273] Murphy J stated that it was in relation to the risk of the defendant's assets being dissipated in advance of any judgment and also with regard to the general balance of convenience that considerations different from those pertaining in relation to conventional injunctions arose. On the basis of the evidence available to the court, Murphy J concluded that the proper inference to draw was that the defendants did have assets within the jurisdiction, that there was a real risk that these assets would be dissipated and that the defendants were not apprehensive of any real inconvenience to them as a result of a Mareva being granted and he made the order sought.

It is interesting to note that in the recent case of *O'Mahony v. Horgan*,[274] which will be considered in more detail below, the Supreme Court seemed to favour the 'good arguable case' test. While Capper[275] suggests that it may be more difficult to establish this than that there is a serious or substantial question to be tried, he also says that the differences between the two tests should not be exaggerated.[276] In any event, as we will see, it is the other aspects of the proofs required to establish an entitlement to a Mareva injunction which clearly differentiate such applications from those in which an ordinary interlocutory injunction is sought.

A consideration of the balance of convenience between the parties will necessarily involve the weighing up of different factors to those which will normally be of relevance where an interlocutory injunction is sought. In the first instance, the plaintiff will not usually be seeking an injunction at trial, but rather an award of damages which the Mareva order is designed to safeguard. Similarly the question of the adequacy of damages as a remedy, which is often of considerable importance in deciding where the balance of convenience lies, will not be a factor. Instead the court will be required to weigh up the plaintiff's claim for relief against the likelihood of undue hardship or inconvenience being caused to the defendant. Finally, it should be borne in mind that a Mareva injunction, like any other form of equitable remedy is granted on the basis of equitable principles and at the discretion of the court and will not be made in favour of a plaintiff whose conduct has been questionable in nature.[277]

---

273. *Ibid.* at 487.
274. [1996] 1 ILRM 161.
275. (1995) 17 DULJ (ns) 110.
276. *Ibid.* at 114.
277. *The Assios* [1979] 1 Lloyd's Rep 331, 334 *per* Shaw LJ.

Before a court will be satisfied that there is a real risk that a defendant is likely to frustrate the court's judgment by disposing of his assets, it will generally be necessary to establish either that they will be removed from the jurisdiction or that they will be dissipated within the jurisdiction.[277] Different considerations obviously apply in relation to an extra-territorial Mareva which will be considered below. In relation to the risk of removal of assets from the jurisdiction, the defendant's domicile and place of residence or business may be of significance. In *Powerscourt Estates Ltd v. Gallagher*,[278] in which McWilliam J granted a Mareva injunction against the defendants, the fact that they were directors of a group of companies many of which were located outside the jurisdiction was relevant as this would have facilitated the removal of assets from the jurisdiction of the Irish courts.

One of the most important issues which must be addressed in the context of Mareva injunctions is the extent to which it is necessary to adduce evidence that the defendant's intention is to frustrate the judgment of the court. This issue was considered by McWilliam J in *Fleming v. Ranks (Ireland) Ltd.*[279] A union issued strike notice and the first defendant announced that its mills would have to close. The plaintiff employees sought a Mareva injunction restraining the defendants from dealing with their assets so as to reduce their value below a certain level. McWilliam J stated as follows:

> I am of opinion that, to justify such an injunction, the anticipated disposal of a defendant's assets must be for the purpose of preventing a plaintiff from recovering damages and not merely for the purpose of carrying on a business or discharging lawful debts.[280]

McWilliam J concluded that the balance of convenience clearly favoured the defendants, both on account of the perishable nature of the goods which they sought to dispose of and having regard to the fact that any undertaking in damages given by the plaintiffs would be of little value. Subsequently, in *Powerscourt*, McWilliam J echoed this view when he stated that a Mareva injunction may be granted where 'it appears to the court that

---

277. See *Larkins v. National Union of Mineworkers* [1985] IR 671, 694.
278. [1984] ILRM 123. See Capper, *op. cit.*, p.40.
279. [1983] ILRM 541.
280. *Ibid.* at 546. Murphy J also drew attention to this point in *Countyglen plc v. Carway* [1995] 1 ILRM 481, 488 and said that McWilliam J had declined to make the order sought in the *Ranks* case as he accepted that there had been no intention of disposing of assets with a view to evading any obligation to the plaintiff.

dispositions are likely to be made for the purpose of preventing a plaintiff from recovering the amount of his award, as distinct from conducting the normal business or personal affairs of the defendant'.[281]

This issue has also recently been addressed by the Supreme Court in *O'Mahony v. Horgan*.[282] The plaintiff had been appointed liquidator of a company of which the respondents were directors. Murphy J granted an interlocutory injunction to restrain the second named respondent from disposing of or dissipating a sum of money payable under an insurance policy. The Supreme Court allowed the appeal of the second named respondent. It held that before a plaintiff will be entitled to a Mareva injunction, he must establish that there is a likelihood that the defendant's assets will be dissipated with the intention that they would not be available to meet any decree ultimately made in the proceedings and found that this intention had not been established in the case before the court. Hamilton CJ stated that:

> [T]he cases establish that there must be an intention on the part of the defendant to dispose of his assets with a view to evading his obligation to the plaintiff and to frustrate the anticipated order of the court. It is not sufficient to establish that the assets are likely to be dissipated in the ordinary course of business or in the payment of lawful debts.[283]

Commenting on this decision, Courtney[284] has stated that the Supreme Court has clarified the fact that an applicant for a Mareva injunction must adduce specific evidence of 'the requisite intention' and he is of the view that this requirement will be given greater emphasis in the future. This view would certainly seem to be borne out by two recent High Court decisions. In *Production Association Minsk Tractor Works v. Saenko*[285] McCracken J quoted the above passage from *O'Mahony* and stated that he did not think that there was any evidence before him to establish an intention on the part of the defendants to dispose of assets with a view to evading their obligations to the plaintiff or frustrating the anticipated order of the court. He stressed that a Mareva injunction is 'an extremely drastic remedy' and concluded that in his view the plaintiffs had not satisfied the

---

281. [1984] ILRM 123, 126.
282. [1996] 1 ILRM 161.
283. *Ibid.* at 167-168. Quoted with approval by O'Sullivan J in *Bennett Enterprises Inc. v. Lipton* [1999] 1 ILRM 81, 89. See also *Aerospares Ltd v. Thompson* High Court 1998 No. 13568P (Kearns J) 13 January 1999, p.4.
284. (1996) 3 Comm LP 3, 8.
285. High Court 1998 No. 869P (McCracken J) 25 February 1998.

criteria necessary to succeed in their application. Similarly in *OBA Enterprises Ltd v. TMC Trading International Ltd*[286] Laffoy J quoted the same passage from *O'Mahony* and concluded that in her view the plaintiffs had not adduced evidence to show or entitle her to infer that the defendant was likely to dissipate its assets with the intention of evading its obligations, if any, to the plaintiffs.

In contrast, the approach of the English courts has tended to focus on the effect of the defendant's actions rather than on his intention. In *The Niedersachsen*[287] Kerr LJ accepted that no 'nefarious intent' was required and said that the plaintiff need only establish a real risk that a judgment in his favour would remain unsatisfied.[288] As Capper[289] has pointed out, it may be unrealistic to expect a plaintiff to be in a position to adduce evidence of a defendant's intentions in this regard in making an *ex parte* application and a more flexible approach may be necessary when a Mareva is sought on this basis, as will usually be the case in practice. In a recent comment on the *O'Mahony* case Capper has reiterated this point stating that 'while the approach in the Irish cases reduces the risk of abuses of the Mareva jurisdiction it is unrealistic and unfair, especially on an *ex parte* application, to require plaintiffs to show that the defendant *intends* by the disposal of assets to defeat any judgment the plaintiff may obtain'.[290] Capper's suggestion 'that an intention may be inferred from the risk that assets will be disposed of for no good reason'[291] would seem to mitigate the harshness of this evidential requirement and it would seem fair to suggest that provided all the other procedural hurdles have been overcome, this requirement should be applied in a relatively flexible manner. Certainly a more pragmatic approach towards this question has been taken by O'Sullivan J in the recent High Court decision in *Bennett Enterprises Inc. v. Lipton,*[292] discussed in more detail below in the context of extra-territorial Mareva injunctions. He stressed that if any dissipation of assets were to occur in the ordinary course of business, this of itself would not justify the granting of a Mareva injunction and that the anticipated dissipation must be for the purpose of the defendant evading his obligation to the plaintiff. He then went on to state as follows:

---

286. High Court 1998 No.12535P (Laffoy J) 27 November 1998. See Courtney (1999) 6 Comm LP 39.
287. [1984] 1 All ER 398.
288. See also *Derby & Co. Ltd v. Weldon (Nos 3 & 4)* [1990] Ch 65, 76.
289. *Mareva Injunctions* (1988) p.48.
290. (1995) 17 DULJ (ns) 110, 117.
291. *Ibid.* at 119.
292. [1999] 1 ILRM 81. See Courtney (1999) 6 Comm LP 39.

Equally, however, I consider that direct evidence of an intention to evade will rarely be available at the interlocutory stage. I consider it is legitimate for me to consider all the circumstances in relation to the case and I do not consider that this approach is in any way prohibited by or at variance with the principles set out in the Supreme Court judgment in *O'Mahony v. Horgan.*[293]

Initially the Mareva injunction evolved as a remedy against foreign-based defendants who possessed assets within the jurisdiction of the court and while it was thought at one time that such injunctions could only issue against such foreign-based defendants, this limitation has been eroded by the courts.[294] So in both *Fleming v. Ranks (Ireland) Ltd*[295] and *Powerscourt Estates v. Gallagher*[296] McWilliam J accepted that the types of cases in which Mareva injunctions may be granted are not confined to those where the defendant is resident outside the State.

A Mareva injunction operates in *personam*[297] to restrain the defendant from dealing with the assets to which the order relates and it gives no proprietary right over these assets nor priority over other creditors. Therefore the rights of a third party with an interest in an asset will not be prejudiced and it was held by the English Court of Appeal in *Cretanor Maritime Co. Ltd v. Irish Marine Management Ltd*[298] that the plaintiff was not entitled to a Mareva injunction in relation to funds owed by the defendant where a debenture holder had appointed a receiver over those funds. However, once a third party has been notified of an injunction, he will be restrained from dealing with assets in a manner contrary to its terms otherwise he may be in contempt of court. It is therefore in the plaintiff's interest to notify any third parties such as banks who may be holding assets belonging to the defendant of the terms of the order as soon as it is made.

An issue which has arisen in both England and this jurisdiction and ultimately been resolved by legislation in both countries is the question of whether an application for a Mareva injunction can be regarded as an independent cause of action and so granted in aid of proceedings commenced in another jurisdiction. This question was answered in the negative both

---

293. *Ibid.* at 89.
294. See e.g. *A.J Bekhor & Co Ltd v. Bilton* [1981] QB 923.
295. [1983] ILRM 541, 546.
296. [1984] ILRM 123.
297. Although note the rather ambiguous comments to the contrary of Lord Denning MR in *Z. Ltd v. A-Z and AA-LL* [1982] QB 558, 573.
298. [1978] 1 WLR 966.

by the House of Lords in *The Siskina*[299] and by the Supreme Court in *Caudron v. Air Zaire.*[300] In the latter case, the plaintiffs who were the ex-employees and dependants of ex-employees of the defendant sought a Mareva injunction to prevent the removal of a plane belonging to the defendant from the jurisdiction. The Supreme Court discharged the injunction granted by the High Court on the basis that a Mareva injunction could not be claimed as primary relief in the action but only as an ancillary order. Article 24 of the Brussels Convention on Jurisdiction and Enforcement of Judgments in Civil and Commercial Matters now permits the courts of a contracting state to grant relief by way of a Mareva injunction in aid of proceedings under the convention pending before the courts of another contracting state. Section 11 of the Jurisdiction of Courts and Enforcement of Judgments (European Communities) Act 1988 makes provision to this effect, so the effect of the *Caudron* decision has been reversed in this regard.

One of the most significant developments in relation to Mareva injunctions in recent years has been the willingness of the courts to make such orders in respect of assets outside the jurisdiction on a worldwide basis.[301] Originally Mareva injunctions were of a more limited nature and as Dillon LJ commented in *Ashtiani v. Kashi*[302] 'the basis of the jurisdiction, as it seems to me, is clearly limited to the assets within the jurisdiction of this court'. The reasons for this practice were far from compelling,[303] and in a series of decisions on the late 1980s, the English Court of Appeal extended the scope of Mareva injunctions to cover worldwide assets. In *Babanaft International Co. SA v. Bassatne*[304] such an order was granted against the defendants who held assets in a number of foreign jurisdictions as well as England and against whom judgment in the sum of $15 million had been obtained. Kerr LJ concluded that 'in appropriate cases, though they may well be rare, there is nothing to preclude our courts from granting Mareva type injunctions against defendants which extend to their assets outside the jurisdiction.'[305] However, he stressed that unqualified Mareva injunctions covering assets abroad can never be justified as they involve an exorbitant assertion of jurisdiction of an *in rem* nature over

---

299. [1979] AC 210. Reversed by s.25 of the Civil Jurisdiction and Judgments Act 1982. See *Balkanbank v. Taher* [1994] 4 All ER 239.
300. [1986] ILRM 10.
301. See generally Capper (1991) 54 MLR 329.
302. [1987] QB 888, 899.
303. See Collins (1989) 105 LQR 262, 269.
304. [1990] Ch 13.
305. *Ibid.* at 28.

third parties outside the jurisdiction of the court. It was therefore necessary to restrict such injunctions so as to bind only the defendant personally and to include a limiting proviso which made it clear that the order did not affect third parties.

Extra-territorial Mareva injunctions are more likely to be granted after judgment has been obtained as the risk that such an order will be made in favour of a party who is wrongly asserting a cause of action is removed and it has been stressed that pre-judgment orders will be granted on a worldwide basis less readily than after trial.[306] In *Republic of Haiti v. Duvalier*[307] the Court of Appeal granted a pre-trial Mareva against the assets of the defendants on a worldwide basis although Staughton LJ stressed that the cases in which it would be appropriate to grant such an injunction were 'rare — if not very rare indeed'.[308] The other notable feature of this decision is that the limiting proviso was extended to the effect that the order should not affect any third parties unless and to the extent that it is enforced by the courts of the state in which the defendants' assets are located. Similarly in *Derby & Co. Ltd v. Weldon*[309] the Court of Appeal granted a worldwide Mareva injunction prior to judgment in view of the large sums of money involved, the insufficiency of assets within the jurisdiction, the existence of foreign assets and the finding that there was a real risk that they would be dissipated before the trial. A point made by the Court of Appeal and subsequently reiterated by it in *Derby & Co. Ltd v. Weldon (Nos. 3 & 4)*[310] is that a Mareva injunction should be limited to assets within the jurisdiction of the court if these are sufficient to meet the plaintiff's claim. However, there will often be insufficient domestic assets or even none at all and the court stressed in the latter case that this will not be a bar to obtaining an order on a worldwide basis. A further attempt was made by the Court of Appeal in *Derby & Co. Ltd v. Weldon (Nos. 3 & 4)* to clarify the position of third parties by putting forward a modified version of what has become known as the '*Babanaft* proviso'.[311] This new version of the proviso abolishes what was seen as the rather artificial distinction drawn between legal and juridicial persons and gives the order extra-territorial effect over persons who are subject to the jurisdiction of the court making the order and who have been given written notice of it and who are

---

306. *Babanaft International Co. SA v. Bassatne* [1990] Ch 13, 40 *per* Neill LJ and *Republic of Haiti v. Duvalier* [1990] QB 202, 214 *per* Staughton LJ.
307. [1990] QB 202.
308. *Ibid.* at 215.
309. [1990] Ch 48.
310. [1990] Ch 65.
311. *Ibid.* at 84.

in a position to 'prevent acts or omissions outside the jurisdiction of this court which assist in the breach of the terms of this order'.

The fact that Mareva injunctions may be made on a worldwide basis has recently been confirmed by the Irish High Court in *Deutsche Bank Atkiengesellchaft v. Murtagh*.[312] The plaintiff sought an order restraining the defendants from dealing with extra-territorial assets. Costello J was satisfied that 'the court has jurisdiction to restrain the dissipation of extra-territorial assets where such an order is warranted by the facts'. He said that it was well-established in England that a Mareva injunction may extend to foreign assets and that he believed the Irish courts had similar powers to avoid frustration of subsequent orders. It should be noted that the order made a month later by Murphy J *Countyglen v. Carway*[313] was confined to assets of the defendants within the jurisdiction, but this was the extent of the order sought by the plaintiffs. His comment that a Mareva injunction should be restricted to assets within the jurisdiction of the court must be viewed as purely *obiter* and it is unlikely that such an approach will be followed in view of the unequivocal approval given by Costello J to orders of an extra-territorial nature. This is borne out by the approach adopted recently by O'Sullivan J in *Bennett Enterprises Ltd v. Lipton*.[314] The plaintiffs instituted proceedings against the defendants for breach of contract and sought, *inter alia*, an interlocutory injunction restraining the defendants from reducing the monies in certain trust funds below a stated sum. O'Sullivan J stated that it was clear that the defendants had no assets within the jurisdiction but said that he did not consider that the plaintiffs' alleged failure to establish that there were assets within the jurisdiction was necessarily fatal to their application. On the contrary, he said that he could see the logic in the observation of Donaldson MR in *Derby v. Weldon (Nos. 3 & 4)* to the effect that the fewer the assets within the jurisdiction the greater the necessity for taking protective measures in relation to those outside it. O'Sullivan J also pointed out that in *Babanaft* Kerr LJ had stated that 'some situations, which are nowadays by no means uncommon, cry out — as a matter of justice to plaintiffs — for disclosure orders and Mareva type injunctions covering foreign assets of defendants even before judgment.'[315] The plaintiffs accepted that any order which the court might make would be subject to the '*Babanaft* proviso' and O'Sullivan J concluded that he would make an interlocutory order as sought by the plain-

---

312. [1995] 1 ILRM 381.
313. [1995] 1 ILRM 481.
314. [1999] 1 ILRM 81. See Courtney (1999) 6 Comm LP 39.
315. [1990] 1 Ch 13, 33.

tiffs and stated that he would discuss with counsel the precise form of the order.

A further important aspect of Mareva jurisdiction which has particular relevance in the context of worldwide orders, is the power to make ancillary orders, for example requiring disclosure of the defendant's assets. This was adverted to by Ackner LJ in *Bekhor & Co. v. Bilton*,[316] where he stated that the court has power to make 'all such ancillary orders as appear to the court to be just and convenient, to ensure the exercise of the Mareva jurisdiction is effective to achieve its purpose'. Costello J also referred to this power to make ancillary orders in *Deutsche Bank Atkiengesellchaft v. Murtagh* and said that in a suitable case the court will grant a disclosure order requiring the defendant to swear an affidavit in relation to assets outside the jurisdiction. It is certainly in the context of worldwide orders that ancillary powers take on the greatest significance and it may even prove to be of more significant practical importance than the Mareva injunction itself. As Collins[317] has pointed out if proper disclosure is made in relation to the defendant's foreign assets, the plaintiff will be able to seek an attachment order in relation to these assets in the relevant foreign jurisdiction. The Court of Appeal has recently re-emphasised the importance of disclosure orders in *Gruppo Torras SA v. Sheikh Fahad Mohammad Al-Sabah*.[318] The plaintiff obtained a Mareva injunction against the defendant together with an ancillary order requiring him to disclose the nature and extent of his assets both in England and abroad. The court rejected the defendant's application to have the disclosure order discharged and reaffirmed the importance of orders of this nature. As Steyn LJ commented without such ancillary powers, the Mareva injunction itself 'would be relatively toothless procedure in the fight against rampant transnational fraud'.

In the final analysis the effectiveness of Mareva injunctions, particularly those of an extra-territorial nature will depend on the extent to which the courts can guarantee their observance. It appears to have been accepted that it would be wrong in principle for the courts in one jurisdiction 'to impose or attempt to impose obligations on persons not before the court in respect of acts to be done by them abroad regarding property outside the jurisdiction' on the basis that this would amount to an attempt to claim an 'exorbitant' extra-territorial authority.[319] However defendants and in particular third parties will often be outside the jurisdiction of the court which

---

316. [1981] QB 923, 940.
317. (1989) 105 LQR 262, 297.
318. 16 February 1994; (1994) 144 NLJ 932.
319. *Babanaft International Co. SA v. Bassatne* [1990] Ch 13, 44 *per* Nicholls LJ. See also the judgment of Neill LJ at 40.

has made the Mareva injunction and so not amenable to control by that court. As Collins[320] has commented:

> In practice the remedy is likely to be most effective where the defendant is an individual present within the jurisdiction (or a company with offices within the jurisdiction) or if the defendant has a real interest in defending the substance of the English action or (as the case may be) in appealing the English judgment. It is possible that these are the only cases in which the remedy will be effective, and this may be regarded as a cynical but realistic, conclusion.

The far-reaching and often draconian nature of Mareva injunctions is more readily recognised today than when the jurisdiction was first exercised.[321] However, as against this, the sophisticated fraudulent endeavours which can often extend into numerous different jurisdictions are also becoming increasingly difficult to control. There have been some signs in a recent decision of the English Court of Appeal that the judiciary are more willing at present to recognise the former consideration than the latter. In *Polly Peck International plc v. Nadir (No. 2)*,[322] while Millett J found that the plaintiff had shown an arguable case of liability and granted a Mareva injunction, the Court of Appeal concluded that the balance of convenience was against its continuance and discharged the order. Scott LJ stressed that the court will not grant a Mareva injunction before any liability has been established if the injunction would interfere with the normal course of the defendant's business particularly if the cause of action which was sought to be protected, as in the case before him, was no more than speculative. In his view to grant a Mareva injunction in these circumstances would be 'not simply wrong in principle but positively unfair'.[323] Zuckerman[324] has commented that the approach of the Court of Appeal in *Polly Peck* restores the Mareva jurisdiction to its true basis as a measure against abuse rather than a form of security for the plaintiff. There appeared to be signs in the judgment of Lynch J in *Moloney v. Laurib Investments Ltd*[325] of a willingness to have regard to such considerations in that

---

320. (1989) 105 LQR 262, 296.
321. See e.g. the comments of Hamilton CJ in *O'Mahony v. Horgan* [1996] 1 ILRM 161, 166 and of McCracken J in *Production Association Minsk Tractor Works v. Saenko* High Court 1998 No. 869P (McCracken J) 25 February 1998 at p.5 to the effect that a Mareva injunction is 'an extremely drastic remedy'.
322. [1992] 4 All ER 769.
323. *Ibid.* at 784.
324. (1992) 108 LQR 559, 561.
325. High Court 1993 No. 3189P (Lynch J) 20 July 1993.

he appeared to place emphasis on the fact that the grant of the injunction sought would interfere with the normal course of the defendant's business and that it would cause serious loss which could not subsequently be made good if the defendant were ultimately successful. Signs of a more cautious approach are also evident in the Supreme Court decision of *O'Mahony v. Horgan;*[326] as O'Flaherty J commented: 'it needs to be emphasised that the Mareva injunction is a very powerful remedy which if improperly invoked will bring about an injustice, something that it was designed to prevent'. While it is arguable that the requirement of establishing an intention on the defendant's part to dispose of his assets with a view to evading his obligation to the plaintiff and to frustrate the anticipated order of the court imposes too great a burden on plaintiffs, the rationale behind such a requirement is understandable given the potentially far-reaching consequences of granting a Mareva injunction. What is clearly required in such cases is a careful balancing of the rights of both plaintiffs and defendants if this powerful legal weapon is not to be abused.

ANTON PILLER ORDERS

Anton Piller orders were developed as a means of dealing with cases where there is a serious risk that a defendant may destroy or otherwise dispose of material in his possession which may be of vital importance to the plaintiff if he is to establish his claim at a trial.[327] An Anton Piller order requires the defendant to consent to a plaintiff, attended by his solicitor, entering his premises to inspect and if necessary take away any documents or articles specified in the order. As Scott J commented in *Columbia Pictures Incorporated v. Robinson;*[328] 'Anton Piller orders are used to prevent a defendant, when warned of impending litigation, from destroying all documentary evidence in his possession, which might, were it available, support the plaintiff's cause of action.' Where appropriate an order may include directions that the defendant should provide discovery of documents or answer specified interrogatories. Such an order is obtained on an *ex parte* basis and applications are often heard *in camera*[329] as secrecy will be of

---

326. [1996] 1 ILRM 161, 170.
327. As Paperny J commented recently in the decision of the Alberta Court of Queen's Bench in *Capitanescu v. Universal Weld Overlays Inc* (1996) 141 DLR (4th) 751, 757: 'The primary aim of such an order is to preserve evidence to ensure that the pending civil action is not frustrated through lack of evidence'.
328. [1987] Ch 38, 71.
329. S.45(1) of the Courts (Supplemental Provisions) Act 1961 makes provision for this.

the essence if the order is to have the required effect and if the defendant is forewarned he will in all likelihood take steps to frustrate the plaintiff's intentions.[330] This remedy is of particular use in the context of the misappropriation of intellectual property, particularly in the areas of infringement of copyright and patents and in relation to the exploitation of trade secrets.

The practice of making orders of this nature developed in England in the mid 1970s,[331] and the jurisdiction to do so was confirmed by the Court of Appeal in *Anton Piller KG v. Manufacturing Processes Ltd*,[332] the decision which gave its name to the form of order. The plaintiffs claimed that the defendants were selling confidential information to their competitors which they had obtained in their capacity as selling agents for the plaintiff's electrical equipment and sought access to documents on the defendant's premises. The Court of Appeal made an *ex parte* order permitting the plaintiffs to enter the defendant's premises to inspect, remove or make copies of documents relating to the equipment. Lord Denning MR stated as follows:

> It seems to me that such an order can be made by a judge *ex parte*, but it should only be made where it is essential that the plaintiff should have inspection so that justice can be done between the parties: and when, if the defendant were forewarned, there is a grave danger that vital evidence will be destroyed, that papers will be burnt or lost or hidden, or taken beyond the jurisdiction, and so the ends of justice be defeated: and when the inspection would do no real harm to the defendant or his case.[333]

In addition, Omrod LJ laid down three 'essential pre-conditions' which must be satisfied before an order of this nature will be granted; namely that the plaintiff must have an extremely strong *prima facie* case, the potential or actual damage must be very serious for the plaintiff and there must be clear evidence that the defendant has incriminating documents or articles in its possession and there must be a real possibility that these will be destroyed before any application inter partes can be made.

As Omrod LJ made clear in his judgment, the order operates *in personam* against the defendant and requires him to consent to its execution. While

---

330. See the comments of Templeman LJ in *Rank Film Distributors Ltd v. Video Information Centre* [1982] AC 380, 418.
331. The first reported decision was in *EMI Ltd v. Pandit* [1975] 1WLR 302.
332. [1976] Ch 55, 61.
333. *Ibid.* at 61.

it is not equivalent to a search warrant and cannot be enforced by the plaintiff without the defendant's consent,[334] failure to comply with the order will constitute contempt of court. The terms of an order will usually require that in executing it, the plaintiff or his representatives should afford the defendant the opportunity of obtaining legal advice provided that this is done forthwith. In assessing whether delay in complying with the terms of an order will constitute contempt, the courts may take a relatively lenient view, as in *Bhimji v. Chatwani*,[335] in which Scott J stressed that something more than 'a mere technical breach of the obligation to allow entry forthwith' must be shown.

One issue which has provoked controversy is the extent to which a defendant should be penalised for failing to comply with an Anton Piller which is subsequently set aside. In *Hallmark Cards Inc. v. Image Arts Ltd*[336] Buckley LJ stated that while a defendant who refuses to comply with the terms of an order pending his application to have it set aside is technically in contempt of court, he did not believe that such a defendant should be liable to any penalties if the order was subsequently discharged. However, in *Wardle Fabrics Ltd v. G. Myristis Ltd*[337] Goulding J stressed that disobedience of an order constituted contempt even if it was later set aside and in the case before him required the defendants to meet the cost of the plaintiff's motion for contempt on an indemnity basis. While it cannot be disputed that failure to comply with the terms of an Anton Piller order in whatever circumstances technically amounts to contempt of court and should not be condoned, it is submitted that the courts should be slow to impose penalties where the order is subsequently set aside in view of the potential for abuse inherent in this far-reaching and often draconian form of relief.

In view of this potential for abuse, a plaintiff will be required to make certain undertakings to the court before an Anton Piller order will be granted and as Browne-Wilkinson VC commented in *Tate Access Floors v. Boswell*,[338] failure to observe these undertakings 'should not be tolerated'. In view of the *ex parte* nature of the application, the plaintiff will be re-

---

334. As Lord Denning MR stated in *Anton Piller KG v. Manufacturing Processes Ltd* [1976] Ch 55, 61 if the defendants refuse the plaintiff permission to enter premises, the plaintiff must not force his way in but should bring this fact to the attention of the court.
335. [1991] 1 WLR 989, 1003.
336. [1977] FSR 150, 153. See also the judgment of Lord Donaldson MR in *WEA Records Ltd v. Visions Channel 4 Ltd* [1983] 1 WLR 721.
337. [1984] FSR 263.
338. [1991] Ch 512.

quired to make full and frank disclosure of all material facts to the court and failure to do so may result in the order being discharged and a finding of liability in damages being made against the plaintiff. As with other forms of order of an interlocutory nature, the plaintiff will be required to give an undertaking in damages and where he has acted improperly, either in the manner in which he has made his application or has executed the order, the court will not hesitate to enforce this undertaking or to award both compensatory and aggravated damages. This point is illustrated by the judgment of Scott J in *Columbia Picture Industries v. Robinson*[339] in which the plaintiffs brought proceedings against the defendants for breach of copyright relating to an alleged video piracy operation. The plaintiffs obtained an Anton Piller order but failed to disclose all material facts in making their application and in executing it removed items not included in its terms. The defendants then brought a motion seeking to have the order set aside and Scott J found that the plaintiffs and their solicitors had failed to make full and frank disclosure of all material matters to the court and had acted oppressively and in abuse of their powers in executing the order. He made a finding that no purpose would be served by setting aside the order as it had already been executed but held that the plaintiffs were liable in damages to the defendants who had ceased trading as a result. Scott J was clearly acutely aware of the potential for abuse inherent in Anton Piller orders as can be seen from the following extract from his judgment:

> [A] decision whether or not an Anton Piller order should be granted requires a balance to be struck between the plaintiff's need that the remedies allowed by the civil law for the breach of his rights should be attainable and the requirement of justice that a defendant should not be deprived of his property without being heard. What I have heard in the present case has disposed me to think that the practice of the court has allowed the balance to swing much too far in favour of plaintiffs and that Anton Piller orders have been too readily granted and with insufficient safeguards for respondents.
>
> The draconian and essentially unfair nature of Anton Piller orders from the point of view of respondents against whom they are made requires, in my view, that they be so drawn as to extend no further than the minimum extent necessary to achieve the purpose for which they are granted, namely the preservation of documents or articles which might otherwise be destroyed or concealed.[340]

---

339. [1987] Ch 38.
340. *Ibid.* at 76.

The views of Scott J were subsequently echoed by Hoffman J in *Lock International plc v. Beswick*[341] in which the latter stressed that there must be proportionality between the perceived threat to the plaintiff's rights and the remedy granted.

Capper has recently commented on the options facing a defendant when confronted with an Anton Piller order which he believes should not have been granted.[342] First, he may refuse to allow the order to be executed until he has had an opportunity to apply to the court for its discharge. This may be a potentially dangerous course of action as the defendant's refusal to comply with the order immediately constitutes contempt of court, although if the application to discharge the order is successful this is not likely to be viewed seriously. The second alternative is to apply for the order to be discharged after it has been executed, which is what happened in the *Columbia* case. However, as Capper points out, this is often of questionable value as the damage will already have been done, and the defendant will usually simply be seeking to force the plaintiff to comply with his undertaking in damages. The third option, which can be pursued where a plaintiff fails to serve a statement of claim or otherwise proceed with the action after the execution of an order, is for a defendant to apply for dismissal of the plaintiff's action. This option was recently followed by the plaintiffs in the Northern Irish case of *Group 4 Securitas (Northern Ireland) Ltd v. McIldowney*[343] which was decided by Girvan J. The defendant succeeded in obtaining a dismissal of the plaintiffs' action following the execution of an Anton Piller order even though the plaintiffs were only two weeks late in delivering their statement of claim. Nothing of substance had been found as a result of the execution of the order and as Capper has commented 'in giving the plaintiffs precious little indulgence, Girvan J was clearly (and rightly it is submitted) influenced by a desire to warn practitioners and litigants against using the draconian remedy of the Anton Piller order in this way'.[344]

Another factor which has tended to swing the balance back in favour of defendants in recent years has been the increasingly frequency with which the privilege against self-incrimination has been invoked. This issue was considered by the House of Lords in *Rank Film Distributors Ltd v. Video Information Centre*,[345] in which it was held that a defendant could invoke

---

341. [1989] 1 WLR 1268, 1281.
342. (1998) 49 NILQ 210.
343. [1997] NIJB 23.
344. *Ibid.* at 212.
345. [1982] AC 380.

this privilege to resist the making of an Anton Piller order. The appellants believed that unauthorised persons had pirated copies of their films and were selling videos of them and sought relief including Anton Piller orders which required the respondents, *inter alia*, to disclose certain information relating to these video cassettes. It was held by the House of Lords that disclosure of the information sought by the appellants would tend to expose the respondents to a charge of conspiracy to defraud and that there was no way in which the court could compel disclosure while at the same time protecting the respondents from the consequences of self-incrimination.[346]

Lord Russell pointed out in the course of his judgment that because the privilege against self-incrimination could largely deprive the owner of copyright of his right to the protection of his property, legislation in this area would be desirable. This privilege was withdrawn in England by section 72 of the Supreme Court Act 1981 in proceedings to obtain disclosure of information relating to the infringement of rights in the area of intellectual property which provided that matters disclosed would not be admissible in evidence against the defendant in proceedings against him for a related offence.[347] However the privilege can still be invoked in other forms of action and as the decision of Browne-Wilkinson VC in *Tate Access Floors v. Boswell*[348] shows it can still provide a most effective weapon in a defendant's fight against the application of Anton Piller orders. In *Tate*, the plaintiffs alleged that the individual defendants who had formerly been senior employees of theirs had in the course of their employment fraudulently obtained large sums from the plaintiffs and had created the defendant companies specifically for the purpose of fraudulently invoicing the

---

346. In the area of copyright infringement, film companies have generally tended to choose the alternative method of informing the gardaí of their suspicions of video piracy, which is a criminal offence. If satisfied that a genuine complaint has been made, the gardaí can seek a warrant to search for infringing material under s.27 of the Copyright Act 1963 as amended by s.2 of the Copyright (Amendment) Act 1987. In practice, such a procedure is regarded as being preferable to seeking an Anton Piller order as it does not involve the copyright owner in any expense and entry can be enforced. In addition, in most video piracy cases, the defendant is unlikely to be in a position to pay damages even if the plaintiff succeeds in a civil action, and a criminal prosecution is perceived to be a more effective means of closing down the operation.

347. See also s.434 (5) of the Companies Act 1985, s.291 of the Insolvency Act 1986 and s. 2 of the Criminal Justice Act 1987 in England. As Lord Templeman commented in *A.T. & T. Istel Ltd v. Tully* [1993] AC 45, 55: 'Parliament has thus recognised the unsatisfactory results of the common law privilege against self-incrimination and has been willing to abrogate or modify that privilege'.

348. [1991] Ch 512.

plaintiffs. The individual defendants had then allegedly authorized payments to the invoicing companies for their own benefit. The plaintiffs were granted worldwide Mareva injunctions against all the defendants and Anton Piller orders compelling the defendants to disclose their assets and permitting the plaintiffs to enter premises to search and seize relevant documents. The defendants sought to have these orders set aside and while Browne-Wilkinson VC refused to discharge the Mareva injunctions, he did set aside the Anton Piller orders against the individual defendants. He held that the privilege against self-incrimination could properly be invoked in a case involving discovery in a fraud action where as in the case before him, on the facts alleged by the plaintiff there was a real risk that a defendant might be prosecuted for conspiracy in the jurisdiction and the documents and information sought by the order might be incriminating.[349] Browne-Wilkinson VC stated that it has not been wholly clear from the decision in *Rank Film* whether it had been held that the privilege against self-incrimination applied to the search and seizure aspects of an Anton Piller order. However, he confirmed that in the case before him, the privilege applied both to those parts of the order which required the defendants to produce and verify information and that part which required them to permit the plaintiffs to search their premises and seize material.

There have been signs of a growing judicial awareness in England of the 'profoundly unsatisfactory'[350] nature of this privilege and in *A.T. & T. Istel Ltd v. Tully*[351] the House of Lords while acknowledging that it could only be altered by parliament, found that there was no reason to allow a defendant in civil proceedings to rely on it, thus depriving a plaintiff of his rights, where the defendant's position could be adequately safeguarded by other means. In addition, it can be seen from the decision in *IBM (UK) Ltd v. Prima Data International Ltd*[352] that a plaintiff may avoid the difficulties which emerge from *Rank Films* and *Tate* where an Anton Piller order contains a proviso which clearly safeguards a defendant's right to claim the privilege and if the order is not executed until he has been told of this right and expressly declines to claim it. However in proceedings which do not come within the ambit of the statutory exceptions the risk that a defendant may be able to invoke successfully the privilege against self-in-

---

349. It was accepted that there was no real risk of the corporate defendants which were overseas companies being prosecuted for conspiracy in England and it was held that the individual defendants could not object to the order made against the companies as there was no privilege against self-incrimination by a third party.
350. *A.T. & T. Istel Ltd v. Tully* [1993] AC 45, 53 *per* Lord Templeman.
351. [1993] AC 45.
352. [1994] 1 WLR 719.

crimination to frustrate the plaintiff's attempts to safeguard evidence to support his claim will remain.[353] This problem is even more marked in this jurisdiction where the common law privilege against self-incrimination remains unaffected by legislation cutting down its effect. While there have been no reported cases involving Anton Piller orders heard before our courts, it is only a question of time before this jurisdiction begins to be invoked with increasing frequency and legislative intervention to at least curtail the common law privilege may well be necessary if these orders are to be effective.

In an English context, Dockray and Laddie[354] have suggested that unless the ambit of section 72 is extended Anton Piller jurisdiction will to a large extent become incapable of being exercised and comment that in their view something more than 'limited legislative tinkering'[355] is required. They quite rightly comment that if legislation in this area is introduced it should also tackle the thorny question of potential abuse of this jurisdiction by plaintiffs and it would certainly appear that the 'inherently oppressive'[356] nature of the order is now more readily acknowledged by the judiciary. It is interesting to note that reference was made to some of their suggestions by Nicholls VC in *Universal Thermosensors Ltd v. Hibben.*[357] While the issues in the case relating to the oppressive manner in which an Anton Piller order granted to the plaintiff had been settled during the course of the trial of the action, Nicholls VC clearly felt that the procedure lent itself 'too readily to abuse' and laid down a number of safeguards in relation to the execution of Anton Piller orders which he felt should be observed. In his view such orders should only be executed during working hours and if executed at a private house and where it is at all likely that a woman may be in the house alone, the solicitor serving the order must be, or must be accompanied by, a woman.[358] He also suggested that unless seriously impracticable, a detailed list of items removed from the premises should be prepared which the defendant should be given an opportunity to check at the time and that the order should not be executed at business premises in the absence of a responsible company representative unless

---

353. See *A.T & T. Istel v. Tully* [1993] AC 45.
354. (1990) 106 LQR 601.
355. *Ibid.* at 603.
356. *Bhimji v. Chatwani* [1991] 1 WLR 989, 1002 *per* Scott J.
357. [1992] 1 WLR 840.
358. Note that in Ireland there may be constitutional difficulties in executing an Anton Piller order at a private house in view of Article 40.5 of the Constitution which provides that: 'The dwelling of every citizen is inviolable and shall not be forcibly entered save in accordance with law.'

there is good reason for so doing. Nicholls VC also recommended that, pursuing the suggestion made by Dockray and Laddie, judges should give serious consideration to the desirability of providing that the order should be served and its execution supervised by an experienced solicitor familiar with the workings of such orders other than a member of the firm of solicitors acting for the plaintiff and that a summary *inter partes* review of the manner in which the order is executed should then be conducted by the court. He concluded by saying that 'if plaintiffs wish to take advantage of this truly draconian type of order, they must be prepared to pay for the safeguards which experience has shown are necessary if the interests of defendants are fairly to be protected.'[359]

Whether these suggestions will be taken up in England remains to be seen, although as Davenport[360] has commented they should 'if followed ... go far towards correcting some of the more undesirable features of the manner in which this draconian order has been put into effect.' In view of the lack of case law in this area in Ireland, the judiciary will probably have to appraise themselves of some of the difficulties associated with this form of order at first hand before many of these essentially useful suggestions are likely to be taken up.

---

359. *Ibid.* at 861.
360. (1992) 108 LQR 555.

CHAPTER 14

Specific Performance

GENERAL PRINCIPLES

Where a court makes an order for specific performance, a party to a contract is compelled to carry out his contractual obligations.[1] As with the equitable remedy of the injunction, this remedy was developed by the Court of Chancery to provide relief where common law remedies were inadequate or inappropriate and is based on the principle that a person should be entitled to have that which he has contracted for rather than merely an award of damages. If a claim for specific performance is to be entertained, it is essential to prove that a valid and enforceable contract exists between the parties[2] for which consideration has been provided. The terms of this contract must also be sufficiently certain before a court will decree performance and the onus lies on the plaintiff to establish this.[3] At one time it was felt that the expression 'specific performance' presupposed the existence of an executory as opposed to an executed agreement.[4] However, the Privy Council has made it clear[5] that there is no reason why the 'equitable right to specific relief' should be governed by any different considerations in relation to executed as opposed to executory agreements and the distinction would not appear to be of practical significance in this jurisdiction.[6]

Specific performance of a contract will not be granted where the plaintiff has an adequate remedy at common law; as Lord Selborne stated in

---

1. See generally Farrell, *The Irish Law of Specific Performance* (1994) for a comprehensive examination of all aspects of this remedy. See also Jones and Goodhart, *Specific Performance* (2nd ed., 1996).
2. *Holohan v. Ardmayle Estates*, Supreme Court 1966 No. 60, 1 May 1967 *per* Walsh J at p.4.
3. *Williams v. Kenneally* (1912) 46 ILTR 292, 294 *per* Barton J.
4. *Wolverhampton and Walsall Rly Co. v. London & North-Western Railway Co.* (1873) LR 16 Eq 433, 439 *per* Lord Selborne LC.
5. *Australian Hardwoods Pty Ltd v. Commissioner for Railways* [1961] 1 All ER 737, 743 *per* Lord Radcliffe.
6. Keane, *Equity and the Law of Trusts in the Republic of Ireland* (1988) p. 244 and Farrell, *The Irish Law of Specific Performance* (1994) p.3.

Wilson v. Northampton and Banbury Junction Railway Co.:[7] 'The court gives specific performance instead of damages, only when it can by that means do more perfect and complete justice.' It has come to be recognised that a more 'complete' form of relief can be afforded to a plaintiff by granting a decree for specific performance in certain types of situations e.g. in relation to a contract for the sale of land and that equally some forms of contract such as those that might involve a degree of supervision do not easily lend themselves to this type of remedy.

The Discretionary Nature of the Remedy

Like all equitable remedies, specific performance is granted only on a discretionary basis. The exercise of this discretion must not be arbitrary or capricious[8] and is 'governed as far as possible by fixed rules and principles'.[9] This view has been echoed in numerous cases and as Romilly MR pointed out in *Haywood v. Cope*[10] 'what one person may consider fair another person may consider very unfair' and there must be some settled principles upon which to determine how this discretion is to be exercised. These points were well summarised as follows by Black LJ in *Conlon v. Murray*:[11]

> The remedy of specific performance still retains the character of an equitable remedy. It is not granted as of right but is a discretionary remedy which may be withheld in cases of a type where the court, having regard to the conduct of the parties and all the circumstances of the case considers in its discretion that the remedy ought not to be granted. This discretion is not, of course, the arbitrary discretion of the individual judge but is a discretion to be exercised on the principles which have been worked out in a multitude of decided cases.

Despite his clear acceptance of the proposition that the discretion to grant

---

7. (1874) 9 Ch App 279, 284.
8. *Smelter Corporation v. O'Driscoll* [1977] IR 305, 310-311.
9. *Lamare v. Dixon* (1873) LR 6 HL 414, 423.
10. (1858) 25 Beav 140, 151.
11. [1958] NI 17, 25. See also the *dicta* of Haugh J in *Nolan v. Graves* [1946] IR 376, 391 where he emphasised that the jurisdiction to grant specific performance must be exercised with discretion and care and the recent *dicta* of Lord Hoffmann in *Co-Operative Insurance Co. Ltd v. Argyll Stores (Holdings) Ltd* [1998] AC 1, 16 to the effect that the grant or refusal of specific performance remains a matter for the judge's discretion and that while there are no binding rules governing the exercise of this discretion, this does not mean that there cannot be settled principles to guide the court.

or withhold the remedy of specific performance must be exercised in accordance with settled principles, Black LJ rejected the suggestion that the types of cases in which the remedy will be refused should be categorised in any rigid manner.

Before examining in more detail some of the categories of contract which may be specifically enforced by the court, it is worth considering a few general principles which are observed in deciding whether to grant relief. First, the courts have traditionally been loathe to grant specific performance of contracts which would require supervision, principally contracts to build and repair and contracts for services. While it has been accepted in both types of situation that this is not an inflexible rule,[12] it has certainly proved to be a relevant factor when a court in determining whether specific performance will lie.[13] Secondly, it is well accepted that an order of this nature will not be granted where to make it would be futile, e.g. if a plaintiff seeks specific performance of a lease for a term that has already expired,[14] or even where the lease is determinable by the defendant. Also for this reason, specific performance of a partnership agreement determinable at will will not be granted as it would not place the plaintiff in a more beneficial position. Similarly, in *Tito v. Wadell (No. 2)*[15] Megarry VC declined to make the order of specific performance sought by the plaintiff to replant specified portions of an island with particular crops as it was highly unlikely that they would grow successfully and because of problems relating to access, harvesting them would be difficult if not impossible. He concluded that he did not think that 'the court ever should, in its discretion, make an order which it is convinced would be an order of futility and waste'.[16]

Damages in Lieu of or in Addition to Specific Performance

Section 2 of the Chancery Amendment Act 1858, better known as Lord Cairns' Act, conferred power on the Court of Chancery to award damages either in addition to or in substitution for specific performance. Since the enactment of the Judicature (Ireland) Act 1877 jurisdiction has been conferred on the courts to make an award of damages in any case where this could have been done previously under common law, and often where it is

---

12. *Lift Manufacturers Ltd v. Irish Life Assurance Co. Ltd* [1979] ILRM 277, 280; *Hill v. C.A.Parsons & Co. Ltd* [1972] Ch 305.
13. See further *infra* pp. 540-546.
14. *Walters v. Northern Coal Mining Co.* (1855) 5 De GM & G 629, 639.
15. [1977] Ch 106. See particularly pp.326-327.
16. *Ibid.* at 327.

felt that an order of specific performance is not a suitable remedy in the circumstances, a plaintiff will have a claim for damages at common law. However it is in situations where a plaintiff may have no legal remedy that the jurisdiction conferred by Lord Cairns' Act is of such significance, e.g. where a contract for the sale of land has not been evidenced in writing as required by the Statute of Frauds but may be enforceable in equity because there have been acts of part performance.[17] In order for a court to exercise this jurisdiction, there must be present 'all those ingredients which would enable the Court, if it thought fit, to exercise this power and decree specific performance'.[18] It is important to stress that damages may not be granted in equity where there is no valid contract which could be specifically enforced but are usually awarded where the court decides that on discretionary grounds, damages are a more appropriate form of relief. As Finlay CJ observed in *O'Neill v. Ryan (No. 3)*[19] there may well be cases where the courts will decide 'it is not fair to specifically perform this contract; we will award damages instead.' So where delay has occurred, insufficient to establish the defence of laches, a plaintiff may be confined to a remedy in damages on discretionary grounds.[20] Equally where specific performance is no longer possible where e.g. another agreement is accorded priority over that which a plaintiff seeks to enforce, damages will be the appropriate remedy.[21]

The House of Lords has laid down in *Johnson v. Agnew*[22] that damages under Lord Cairns' Act should be assessed on the same basis as that which applies at common law and despite some earlier decisions which supported the contrary view,[23] this approach seems to be the preferred one. Finally it should be noted that damages may also be awarded in addition to an order of specific performance and this jurisdiction may be exercised whenever the court believes it to be necessary to do so.[24]

---

17. See *infra* pp. 533-538.
18. *Ferguson v. Wilson* (1866) 2 Ch App 77, 91 *per* Cairns LJ.
19. [1992] 1 IR 166, 196.
20. *White v. McCooey* [1976-77] ILRM 72 and *Lark Developments Ltd v. Dublin Corporation*, High Court 1992 No. 2888 P (Murphy J) 10 February 1993 at pp.14-15.
21. *O'Connor v. McCarthy* [1982] IR 161, 178 *per* Costello J.
22. [1980] AC 367.
23. See *Wroth v. Tyler* [1974] Ch 30.
24. *Grant v. Dawkins* [1973] 3 All ER 897. See also *Duggan v. Allied Irish Building Society* High Court 1974 No 2302 P (Finlay P) 4 March 1976 at p.16.

SPECIFIC PERFORMANCE OF PARTICULAR TYPES
OF CONTRACT

Contracts for the Sale of Land

An order for specific performance is often sought in relation to contracts
for the sale of land. While it cannot be said that a plaintiff is entitled to a
decree in these circumstances because of the discretionary nature of the
remedy, in practice an order will usually be granted provided that a valid
contract which complies with the necessary statutory formalities exists,
and it has been stated that the onus lies on the defendant to establish why
the remedy should be refused in such cases.[25] It is generally accepted that
land is unique and will have a special value to a purchaser and that he
cannot be adequately compensated by an award of damages which would
enable him to buy other property instead.[26]

It is important to emphasise that in order to seek successfully an order
of specific performance of a contract for the sale of land, it is necessary to
comply with certain requirements. In the first instance there must be a
valid contract made for consideration. Once this is established, there must
be compliance with section 2 of the Statute of Frauds (Ireland) 1695 which
requires that there be a note or memorandum in writing of the contract
signed by the person to be charged or by someone authorised by him to do
so, or there must be some good reason why equity will not insist on compliance e.g. where to insist on compliance would facilitate a fraud or where
sufficient acts of part performance can be established.[27] However as
Farrell[28] points out the initial question must be whether there is a valid
contract as if there is not, the question of a sufficient note or memorandum
does not arise.[29] As Ross J stated in *Lord Bellew's Estate*[30] the purpose of

---

25. *McCrystal v. O'Kane* [1986] NI 123, 132; *Broughton v. Snook* [1938] Ch 505, 513.
26. There is authority in Canada to support the view that where land is bought for invest-
    ment or resale that an award of damages would provide adequate compensation, see
    Jones and Goodhart (2nd ed., 1996) p. 130, n. 8. However authority in Australia,
    Pianta v. National Finance and Trustees Ltd (1964) 38 ALJR 232 and the dissenting
    judgment of Sir Garfield Barwick in *Loan Investment Corporation of Australasia v.
    Bonner* [1970] NZLR 724, 745, supports the view that the motive of the purchaser
    should be irrelevant to the question of whether specific performance should be granted.
    See also [1984] Conv 130.
27. It is necessary for the defendant to plead absence of writing, and technically speak-
    ing if he does not, it cannot act as a bar to specific performance.
28. *The Irish Law of Specific Performance* (1994) at p. 109.
29. As in *Boyle v. Lee* [1992] 1 IR 555.
30. [1921] IR 174, 176. See also the *dicta* of Finlay P in *Doherty v. Gallagher* High
    Court 1973 No. 2830P, 9 June 1975 at p. 14.

the statutory requirement is to guard against fraud and provide for a 'definite kind of proof' before the agreement can be enforced. To comply with these requirements the note or memorandum must be in writing and contain all the essential terms of the agreement such as a description from which the property can be readily identified and the purchase price. In addition as Keane J made clear in *Mulhall v. Haren*[31] it must contain a recognition, express or implied, of the existence of the oral contract sought to be enforced. A recent example of a case in which these requirements were satisfied is *Aga Khan v. Firestone*,[32] in which Morris J ordered specific performance of the agreement entered into by the first named plaintiff and the defendants on the basis that there was a sufficient note of the oral agreement to satisfy the requirements of section 2 of the Statute of Frauds, as it recognised the existence of the oral contract and contained all the essential terms of the agreement. Similarly in *Kavanagh v. Delicato*,[33] Carroll J accepted that a letter with a map annexed to it, referring to the property, the parties, the purchase price and the closing date and signed by an auctioneer with the vendor's consent, which was sent to the plaintiff purchasers' solicitors constituted a sufficient note or memorandum of the agreement to satisfy the requirements of the statute.

Often where an oral agreement is reached between parties, there may be no sufficient note or memorandum to satisfy the requirements of the Statute of Frauds and equity is faced with the dilemma of insisting on strict compliance with the formalities and allowing alternative evidence of the agreement in order to prevent the perpetration of a fraud. It is a well-established principle that a statute may not be used as an instrument of fraud and in the exercise of this equitable jurisdiction, the courts will prevent a defendant from relying on non-compliance with the statutory formalities where to do so would amount to fraud. Equally, a plaintiff may be able to obtain specific performance in the absence of a sufficient note or memorandum of an agreement by invoking the equitable doctrine of part performance which allows a plaintiff to rely on his own actions as evidence of the existence of an agreement. The rationale behind the operation of this doctrine was set out by Chatterton VC in *Hope v. Lord Cloncurry*[34] where he stated as follows:

> The principle upon which the rule in cases of part performance was engrafted on the Statute of Frauds is, that it would be a fraud on the

---

31. [1981] IR 364, 391. See also *Kelly v. Park Hall School* [1979] IR 340, 352.
32. [1992] ILRM 31. See also *McCarter & Co. Ltd v Roughan* [1986] ILRM 447.
33. High Court 1989 No. 7536P (Carroll J) 20 January 1996.
34. (1874) IR 8 Eq 555, 557.

part of the person who had entered into an agreement by parol for a lease or sale, to turn around and say that it did not legally exist.

Similarly in *Lowry v. Reid*[35] Andrews LJ stated that the issue is 'whether the plaintiff has an equity arising from part performance which is so affixed upon the conscience of the defendant that it would amount to a fraud on his part to take advantage of the fact that the contract is not in writing.' The right to relief rests not so much on the contract as on what has been done in pursuance of it. There a mother undertook to make a will leaving her son two farms and thereby induced him to sell his farm to his brother. She made a will in those terms but subsequently revoked it leaving the plaintiff son with only a life interest. It was held that he was entitled to specific performance and that there were acts of part performance sufficient to take the case out of the reach of the statute.

It would appear, despite some suggestions to the contrary,[36] that the doctrine of part performance applies to all cases in which a court would entertain a claim for specific performance if the contract had been in writing and is not confined to agreements for the sale of land[37] and this point would seem to have been confirmed in this jurisdiction by Palles CB in *Crowley v. O'Sullivan*.[38] However, in practice the vast majority of cases in which the doctrine will be relied on concern contracts for the sale of land.

This point was made by the House of Lords in *Maddison v. Alderson*[39] that 'the acts relied upon as part performance must be unequivocally, and in their own nature, referable to some such agreement as that alleged.' A less strict requirement set out in *Fry on Specific Performance*[40] and approved by Andrews LJ in *Lowry v. Reid*[41] is that 'the operation of acts of part performance seems only to require that the acts in question be such as must be referred to some contract, and may be referred to the alleged one'. This view appears to have been accepted by the majority of the House of Lords in *Steadman v. Steadman*[42] where it was suggested that it would be sufficient if the acts of part performance in question were, on the balance of probabilities, referable to some contract and not inconsistent with the contract in fact entered into. This question was also considered by Keane

---

35. [1927] NI 142, 154-155. See also the *dicta* of Lord Redesdale in *Bond v. Hopkins* (1802) 1 Sch & Lef 413, 433.
36. *Britain v. Rossiter* (1879) 11 QBD 123.
37. *McManus v. Cooke* (1887) 35 Ch D 681, 697 *per* Kay J.
38. [1900] 2 IR 478, 489-92. See also *Lowry v. Reid* [1927] NI 142, 157.
39. (1883) 8 App Cas 467.
40. (6th ed., 1921), p.278.
41. [1927] NI 142, 159.
42. [1976] AC 536.

J in *Silver Wraith Ltd v. Siúicre Éireann Cpt*[43] where he stated *obiter* that the acts should be 'unequivocally referable to the type of contract alleged'.[44] It has also recently been addressed by the Supreme Court in *Mackie v. Wilde*[45] in which Barron J gave detailed consideration to the circumstances in which the doctrine of part performance operates. In his view '[w]hat is required is that the acts relied upon as being acts of part performance be such that on examination of the contract which has been found to have been concluded and to which they are alleged to refer show an intention to perform that contract'.

In *Mackie* the plaintiff and the first named defendant were the owners of a joint fishery on rivers in Co. Donegal. The original rules for the operation of the fishery had been laid down in an indenture but the plaintiff was dissatisfied with the arrangements relating to the number of people who could fish on the rivers and the parties met with a view to reaching agreement about the number of annual licences and daily tickets which would be issued. Subsequently correspondence took place between the parties in which the plaintiff sought to obtain the defendant's written agreement to the limiting of the number of licences for the fishery. The plaintiff then instituted proceedings claiming that there was a binding agreement that each party would be limited to the granting of 25 annual licences and submitted that there had been part performance on foot of the agreement. Costello P held that a concluded agreement to this effect had been reached and that an additional term relating to the number of day tickets which could be granted had also been agreed upon. He therefore ordered that the first named defendant be restrained from issuing more than 25 annual licences and ten day tickets and this finding was appealed to the Supreme Court. The defendants submitted that the trial judge had been incorrect in finding that there had been a concluded agreement and that there were no sufficient acts of part performance to make the agreement enforceable. Barron J accepted the first submission and concluded that there had not been a concluded agreement reached. It remained for him to consider whether there had been sufficient acts of part performance. He quoted extensively from the speech of Lord Simon in *Steadman v. Steadman* and from those of Lord O'Hagan and the Earl of Selborne LC in *Maddison v. Alderson* in relation to the nature of the doctrine and the acts which could be relied upon to constitute part performance. Barron J stated that ultimately the court is seeking to ensure that a defendant is not, in relying

43. High Court 1987 No. 6178 P (Keane J) 8 June 1989 at p.12.
44. See Farrell, *op. cit.* pp. 138-140 for a more detailed consideration of this question.
45. [1998] 2 IR 578.

upon statute, 'breaking faith' with the plaintiff. He stated that the doctrine of part performance is based on three things; the acts on the part of the plaintiff which are said to have been in part performance of the concluded agreement, the involvement of the defendant with respect to such acts and the oral agreement itself. Barron J stated that ultimately what is essential is that:

(1) there was a concluded oral contract;
(2) the plaintiff acted in such way which showed an intention to perform that contract;
(3) the defendant induced such acts or stood by while they were being performed; and
(4) it would be unconscionable and a breach of good faith to allow the defendant to rely on the terms of the Statute of Frauds to prevent performance of the contract.[46]

Barron J stated that it is more logical to find out what the parties had agreed since in the absence of a concluded agreement there is no point in seeking to find acts of part performance. As noted above he stated that the doctrine requires that the acts relied upon as being acts of part performance should be such that on an examination of the contract which has been found to have been concluded and to which they are alleged to refer, they show an intention to perform the contract. He also said that in the earlier cases it had been assumed that the acts of part performance must necessarily relate to and affect land and nothing which he had said should be taken to suggest a modification of that position. Barron J continued by saying that the detriment to the plaintiff must be the result of what the plaintiff does with the defendant standing by and not detriment to the plaintiff as a result of what the defendant does with the plaintiff standing by. Barron J concluded that there was nothing in what was alleged which would in any way be a breaking of faith by the defendant with the plaintiff for the defendant to plead the Statute of Frauds. He therefore held that even if there had been a concluded oral agreement as claimed, there were no acts on the part of the plaintiff which showed an intention to perform the alleged contract.

As Spry[47] has stated it should also be emphasised that 'an act of part performance must be judged, not in the abstract, but in the light of all the material circumstances, in order to establish whether it is sufficiently unequivocal'. The acts upon which a plaintiff seeks to rely in establishing

---

46. *Ibid.* at 587.
47. *The Principles of Equitable Remedies* (5th ed., 1997) p. 280.

part performance must be his own acts and not those of the defendant, although often an action such as the taking and giving of possession of land may be attributable to both parties. This is one of the most common acts of part performance in practice, and another common example particularly in relation to an agreement for a lease is the carrying out of improvements or alterations to property.[48] In *Starling Securities Ltd v. Woods*[49] McWilliam J held that entry onto land and the demolition of buildings thereon constituted sufficient acts of part performance.

While traditionally payment of purchase money was not a sufficient act of part performance,[50] this view must now be re-assessed in the light of the approach followed by the majority of the House of Lords in *Steadman v. Steadman*.[51] As Lord Reid stated: 'to make a general rule that payment of money can never be part performance would seem to me to defeat the whole purpose of the doctrine and I do not think that we are compelled by authority to do that.'[52] There the House of Lords held that payment of arrears of maintenance by a husband to his wife and the incurring of other costs such as those involved in the sending of a transfer agreement to her were sufficient acts of part performance of an agreement of a compromise reached between the parties whereby she would sell him her interest in the family home. Subsequently, McWilliam J in his judgment in *Howlin v. Thomas F. Power (Dublin) Ltd*[53] said that he could not disagree with the reasoning of the majority in *Steadman* but stressed that the application of the doctrine was still confined to cases where it would be fraudulent or inequitable for a defendant to rely on the statute.

Finally, it should be noted that in England, it would appear that the equitable doctrine of part performance is no longer recognised and section 2(1) of the Law of Property (Miscellaneous Provisions) Act 1989 now provides that contracts for the sale of land must be in writing. Some slight doubt on this issue remains as a result of the *dicta* of Neill LJ in *Singh v. Beggs*[54] in which he stated that the doctrine is an equitable one and 'it may be that in certain circumstances [it] could be relied on'.[55] However, as

---

48. *Rawlinson v. Ames* [1925] Ch 96.
49. High Court 1975 No. 4044P 24 May 1977.
50. *Clinam v Cooke* (1802) 1 Sch & Lef 22, 40-41; *Maddison v. Alderson* (1883) 8 App Cas 467, 478-9.
51. [1976] AC 536.
52. *Ibid.* at 541.
53. High Court 1977 No.736P (McWilliam J) 5 May 1978.
54. (1996) 71 P & CR 120.
55. *Ibid.* at 122. However, Neill LJ went on to reject the claim that the plaintiff's conduct could amount to part performance.

Swann[56] has pointed out it has generally been assumed that section 2 succeeded in giving effect to the policy of abolishing the doctrine of part performance;[57] as he comments 'the doctrine had become uncertain and confused and its abolition was a deliberate policy choice'.[58]

Before leaving this area, it is worth noting that specific performance may also be granted in relation to the assignment of a leasehold interest, or in relation to an option to purchase or re-purchase land. While traditionally specific performance of a lease of property for a short period or of a contractual licence to occupy land would not be granted, this would seem to no longer be the case. So in *Verrall v. Great Yarmouth Borough Council*[59] the Court of Appeal granted specific performance of a contractual licence allowing the National Front to hold its annual conference in the defendant's hall.

Contracts for the Sale of Personal Property or to Pay Money

As a general principle a court will not exercise its discretion to award specific performance where damages would be an adequate remedy. Therefore as a rule specific performance will not be granted in relation to a contract for the sale of goods because a breach of such a contract will usually be adequately remedied by an award of damages. However it is important to stress that specific performance will not be refused merely because the object at the centre of the dispute is a chattel,[60] and where the item in question is of 'unusual beauty, rarity and distinction'[61] an order to enforce the contract specifically may be made. Often goods will fall into this category because of their rarity or antiquity, as for example, an Adam door in a house.[62]

A further question which it has been suggested a court should ask itself is whether the object in question is of 'peculiar and practically unique value'[63] to the individual concerned. This involves a more subjective approach which may not always be followed and perhaps a better test would be to ask whether an award of damages would 'place the disappointed

---

56. [1997] Conv 293.
57. See e.g. *Firstpost Homes Ltd v. Johnson* [1995] 1 WLR 1567, 1571.
58. *Ibid.* at 295.
59. [1981] QB 202.
60. *Falcke v. Gray* (1859) 4 Drew 651, 657-658.
61. *Ibid.* at 658.
62. *Phillips v. Lamdin* [1949] 2 KB 33.
63. *Behnke v. Bede Shipping Co. Ltd* [1927] 1 KB 649, 661.

buyer or seller in as good a position as delivery of the article or receipt of the price'.[64]

There is certainly authority to suggest that specific performance will be refused where the subject matter of the contract is an 'ordinary article ... of commerce and of no special value or interest'. This point was made by McCardie J in *Cohen v. Roche*[65] in which he refused to order specific performance of a contract to deliver up eight Hepplewaite chairs and held that the plaintiff's remedy should be confined to damages for breach of contract. McCardie J also appeared to lay emphasis on the fact that the chairs were bought by the plaintiff 'in the ordinary way of his trade for the purpose of ordinary resale at a profit'.[66] While arguably this fact may be relevant as it will often suggest that an alternative to the item or items contracted for may be readily available, this will not always be the case and the question of whether the goods at issue are freely available elsewhere would seem to be a better test. While this approach was not accepted by the Court of Appeal in *Societe des Industries Metallurgiques SA v. Bronx Engineering Co. Ltd,*[67] in which an order of specific performance was refused despite the urgent need for the object in question and the likely delay in procuring an alternative, it is submitted that if the question of the adequacy of damages is properly applied, the availability of the goods should be of primary concern. This approach was followed by Goulding J in *Sky Petroleum Ltd v. VIP Petroleum Ltd*[68] albeit in the context of the grant of an injunction, where he granted an interlocutory injunction to restrain the defendant from withholding supplies of petrol from the plaintiff at a time when these were limited and the plaintiff would have had little chance of finding an alternative supplier.

It should be noted that section 52 of the Sale of Goods Act 1893 confers a discretion on a court to order specific performance of a contract for the sale of goods provided these are 'specific' or 'ascertained'. It was suggested by Lord Hanworth MR in *Re Wait*[69] that the section adds nothing to the equitable jurisdiction of the courts in this area and an examination of the case law would tend to confirm this view. Certainly in *Sky Petroleum Ltd v. VIP Petroleum Ltd* Goulding J granted what amounted in substance to an order that a contract be specifically performed in respect of a commodity which might have been said to have been neither specific nor as-

---

64. *Dougan v. Ley* (1946) 71 CLR 142, 150 *per* Dixon J.
65. [1927] 1 KB 169, 181.
66. *Ibid.* at 179.
67. [1975] 1 Lloyd's Rep 465.
68. [1974] 1 WLR 576.
69. [1927] 1 Ch 606.

certained and the statutory power would seem to be in some respects less flexible than the equitable discretion which exists in this context.

The concept of free availability is also relevant in relation to contracts for the sale of shares or other securities. It would seem to be accepted on the authority of the *dicta* of Shadwell VC in *Duncuft v. Albrecht*[70] that a contract for the purchase of shares which 'are not always to be had in the market' and are therefore not readily obtainable may be specifically enforced. However this principle does not apply if 'anyone can go and buy them'[71] and damages will clearly be an adequate remedy where the purchaser can easily obtain the same amount of identical shares or securities elsewhere. One qualification to this principle is that even where the shares are freely available on the market, specific performance may be granted where the contract is for the sale of a quantity of shares which would give a controlling interest in a company,[72] or where it concerns a substantial holding which may alter the outcome of a takeover battle.[73]

As a general principle a contract to pay or lend money cannot be specifically enforced as damages will provide an adequate remedy.[74] However, where the contract is for the payment of an annuity or other periodic amount, or where the contract requires the payment of a sum to a third party,[75] specific performance may be ordered.[76]

Contracts Requiring Supervision

Traditionally, the courts have been most unwilling to order specific performance of a contract which would require supervision on an ongoing basis; as Dixon J stated in *J.C. Williamson Ltd v. Lukey and Mulholland:*[77] 'specific performance is inapplicable when the continued supervision of the Court is necessary in order to ensure the fulfilment of the contract'. This principle could be said to underlie the courts' traditional reluctance

---

70. (1841) 12 Sim 189, 199.
71. *Re Schwabacher* (1908) 98 LT 127, 128 *per* Parker J.
72. *Dobell v. Cowichan Copper Co. Ltd* (1967) 65 DLR (2d) 440.
73. *Pernod Ricard Comrie plc v. FII (Fyffes) plc* High Court 1988 No. 8388 P (Costello J) 21 October 1988 and Supreme Court 1988 No. 345, 11 November 1988.
74. *Loan Investment Corporation of Australasia Pty Ltd v. Bonner* [1970] NZLR 724.
75. While there is some doubt about whether a contract to pay a lump sum to a third party as opposed to a periodic payment would be specifically enforced, the better view is that it should, as the plaintiff in these circumstances is liable to recover only nominal damages.
76. *Beswick v. Beswick* [1966] Ch 538.
77. (1931) 45 CLR 282, 297-298. Quoted by Lord Hoffman in *Co-Operative Insurance Society Ltd v. Argyll Stores (Holdings) Ltd* [1998] AC 1, 12.

to order specific performance of a contract to carry on a business,[78] and is also a significant factor where it is sought to enforce contracts to build and repair and for services.

One of the main authorities illustrating equity's dislike of granting specific performance of contracts requiring supervision is the decision of the Court of Appeal in *Ryan v. Mutual Tontine Westminster Chambers Association*.[79] The lease of a flat in a block of flats contained a covenant to the effect that the lessors should provide a porter who was 'constantly in attendance'. The lessors appointed a person who was frequently absent but the plaintiffs failed in their action for specific performance of the covenant on the basis that it would require 'constant superintendence by the court'.[80] More recent authorities would suggest that the difficulty of supervising the enforcement of contracts of this nature should not be a bar to specific performance but merely one of the factors to be taken into account in determining whether relief should be granted and a modification of the traditional position can be seen in the decision of Mervyn Davies J in *Posner v. Scott-Lewis*.[81] The defendants owned a block of flats and the terms of the lease between them and the tenants contained a covenant that they would employ a resident porter. The person employed as a porter ceased to be resident in the building and the plaintiff tenants brought an action for specific performance of the covenant. Mervyn Davies J agreed that the arrangements which had been made were insufficient to ensure compliance with the clause in the lease and held that there had been a breach of covenant. He stated that the requirement that the defendants employ a resident porter required little superintendence and decided to grant an order of specific performance in the circumstances. Mervyn Davies J listed the factors which in his opinion should be considered in deciding whether specific performance should be granted in such cases. First, it must be asked whether there is a sufficient definition of what has to be done in order to comply with the order of the court.[82] Secondly, the question of whether enforcing compliance would involve superintendence by the court to an unacceptable degree must be addressed, and thirdly, the prejudices or hardships which would be suffered by the parties if the order is made or not made must be considered. Therefore it would appear that

---

78. *Co-Operative Insurance Society Ltd v. Argyll Stores (Holdings) Ltd* [1998] AC 1.
79. [1893] 1 Ch 116.
80. *Ibid.* at 123 *per* Lord Esher.
81. [1987] Ch 25.
82. See also the *dicta* of Megarry VC in *Tito v. Wadell (No. 2)* [1977] Ch 106, 322 to the effect that 'the real question is whether there is a sufficient definition of what has to be done in order to comply with the order of the court'.

where the terms of the obligation are sufficiently precisely defined and specific performance would seem to be the fairest remedy in the circumstances, it may be granted provided the order would not require an unacceptable degree of superintendence.

The issue of enforcing contracts which would require constant supervision has recently been examined in detail by the House of Lords in *Co-Operative Insurance Society Ltd v. Argyll Stores (Holdings) Ltd.*[83] The plaintiff landlord sought specific performance of a covenant in a lease requiring the defendant, which was the anchor tenant in a shopping centre, to keep its supermarket premises open for retail trade during usual business hours for the duration of the lease. The trial judge refused to order specific performance on the basis that there was a settled practice that an order which would require a defendant to run a business would not be made but the majority of the Court of Appeal ordered that the covenant be specifically performed. Leggatt and Roch LJJ were satisfied that the contract defined the tenant's obligations with sufficient precision to enable it to know what was required to comply with the order and seemed heavily influenced by the fact that the defendant had acted 'with gross commercial cynicism'.[84] Millett LJ who dissented, was satisfied that the existence of a practice not to grant specific performance in such circumstances was beyond dispute and also pointed to the fact that to compel a defendant to carry on a business which it considered was not commercially viable would be to expose it to 'potentially large, unquantifiable and unlimited losses which may be out of all proportion to the loss which his breach of contract has caused to the plaintiff'.[85] The House of Lords allowed the defendant's appeal and reversed the decision of the Court of Appeal to grant specific performance of the covenant in the lease. Lord Hoffmann referred to the fact that the 'settled and invariable practice'[86] not to order a person to carry on a business had never been examined by the House of Lords[87] and proceeded to examine the rationale underlying it in some detail. He stated that the practice is not entirely dependant on damages being an adequate remedy[88] and that the most frequent reason given is that such orders would

83. [1998] AC 1. See further Jones [1997] CLJ 488; Phang (1998) 61 MLR 421; McMeel (1998) 114 LQR 43; Tettenborn [1998] Conv 23; Luxton [1998] Conv 396.
84. [1996] Ch 286, 295 *per* Legatt LJ.
85. *Ibid.* at 304.
86. Per Slade J in *Braddon Towers Ltd v. International Stores Ltd* [1987] 1 EGLR 209, 213.
87. Phang has commented (1998) 61 MLR 421, 423 that the principle is 'so well entrenched . . . that it is seldom analysed and instead, is often repeated almost as a ritual incantation'.
88. McMeel has commented (1998) 114 LQR 43, 45 that both the dissenting judgment

require constant supervision by the court. Lord Hoffmann pointed out that there has been some misunderstanding about what is meant by continued superintendence; supervision would in practice take the form of rulings by the courts and he said that it was the possibility of the court having to give an indefinite series of rulings in order to ensure the execution of the order which has been regarded as so undesirable. This was because the only means available to the court to enforce its order was punishment for contempt and this weapon was often so powerful as to be unsuitable as an instrument for resolving such disputes. Lord Hoffmann went on to distinguish between orders which require a defendant to carry on an activity such as running a business and orders which require him to achieve a result and said that the possibility of repeated applications for rulings on compliance which arises in the former case does not exist to anything like the same extent in the latter. A further objection, which would apply in either case, is the likelihood of imprecision in the terms of the order and if the terms cannot be precisely drawn, the possibility of wasteful litigation over compliance is increased. The fact that the terms of a contractual obligation are sufficiently definite to escape being void for uncertainty or to found a claim for damages does not necessarily mean that they will be sufficiently precise to be capable of being specifically enforced. A final point, which would be relevant to an order requiring a defendant to carry on a business, is that which was emphasised by Millett LJ, namely that it may cause injustice by allowing the plaintiff to enrich himself at the defendant's expense and the loss which the defendant may suffer through having to comply with the order may be far greater than the plaintiff would suffer from the contract being broken. He therefore concluded that: 'The cumulative effect of these various reasons, none of which would necessarily be sufficient on its own, seems to me to show that the settled practice is based upon sound sense'.[89] Lord Hoffmann stressed that the grant or refusal of specific performance remains a matter for the judge's discretion and that while there were no binding rules, this does not mean that there could not be settled principles which the courts would apply in all but exceptional circumstances. However, he pointed out that he could envisage cases of gross breach of personal faith, or attempts to use the threat of

---

of Millett LJ and the speech of Lord Hoffmann make it clear that the true test is one of 'appropriateness of relief' and that the adequacy of damages is only one factor to be brought into account. Similarly Jones has stated [1997] CLJ 490 that 'the formula of "adequacy of damages" is a chameleon one; specific performance should be granted if it is the more appropriate remedy'.

89. *Ibid.* at 16.

non-performance as blackmail, in which the needs of justice would override all the considerations which support the settled practice.

Academic reaction to the decision of the House of Lords has been mixed; while Jones concludes that 'on balance, the conclusion . . . is more to be welcomed than deplored'[90] Tettenborn has characterised it as 'an unfortunate failure to liberalise the rules of specific performance' and has expressed the view that it sits ill with the idea that it should be the function of the courts to ensure as far as possible that contracts should be performed rather than broken. As Phang has commented the concept of constant supervision continues to constitute a major obstacle to the grant of specific performance in the context of continuous acts such as the running of a business.[91] However, as we shall see, in the context of obligations to achieve a result which is what contracts to build or repair will often entail, lack of precision in the terms of the obligation has been the major stumbling block.

Contracts to Build or Repair
By their nature building contracts will often be of an intricate and indefinite nature involving the performance of a variety of different obligations. As Porter MR noted in *Rushbrooke v. O'Sullivan*,[92] the attitude of courts of equity towards their enforcement has not always been consistent, but the predominant view has traditionally been that they should rarely be enforced particularly as their uncertain nature would make it difficult for a court to determine whether any order made has been complied with. In addition, it is often argued that damages will be an adequate remedy where another builder can be found to carry out the work. In practice the likelihood of obtaining specific performance has tended to hinge on two main issues; primarily the certainty of the terms of the contract and to a lesser extent, the degree of supervision which an order for specific performance would require.[93] One of the most important decisions in this area is that of the Court of Appeal in *Wolverhampton Corporation v. Emmons*,[94] where Romer LJ laid down the principle that a court would order specific performance of a building contract if three conditions were satisfied. First, the work in question must be defined with sufficient precision in the contract; secondly, the plaintiff must have a substantial interest in the performance of the contract and damages must not be an adequate remedy

---

90. [1997] CLJ 488, 491.
91. (1998) 61 MLR 421, 432.
92. [1908] 1 IR 232, 234.
93. See the comments of Goff LJ in *Price v. Strange* [1978] Ch 337, 359.
94. [1901] 1 KB 515, 525.

and thirdly the defendant must have 'by the contract obtained possession of the land on which the work is contracted to be done'. The plaintiff corporation sold land, which was part of a scheme for street improvement, to the defendant who agreed to build houses on the land. The court ordered specific performance of the covenant to build on the basis that the conditions outlined above were satisfied and held that the defendant's interest in having the contract specifically performed was such that it was not capable of being compensated by damages.

The first of these principles formed the basis of the court's decision in *Rushbrooke v. O'Sullivan*[95] in which Porter MR concluded that 'the exact nature of the work to be done [had] not been so specifically defined or ascertained as to justify a decree for specific performance'.[96] Similarly in *Redland Bricks Ltd v. Morris*[97] Lord Upjohn commented that 'the court must be careful to see that the defendant knows exactly in fact what he has to do and this means not as a matter of law but as a matter of fact, so that in carrying out an order he can give his contractors the proper instructions'. It has been stated that this requirement of sufficient definition does not mean that the contract must be so specific that it leaves no room for doubt,[98] and Spry[99] has suggested that the requirement should be that 'the obligations in question must be at least so clear that it will be possible for the court at any later application, upon the proper presentation of evidence, to determine whether the acts of the parties do or do not amount to due performance.' Provided the extent of the works which must be carried out to comply with the contract can be deduced from the evidence, it would seem that the courts have at times been willing to decree specific performance.[100]

The third requirement as laid down by Romer LJ has been qualified to a degree by Farwell J in *Carpenters Estates Ltd v. Davies*,[101] where the latter stated that it was not essential that the defendant had obtained possession of the land by virtue of the contract at issue provided that he is 'in possession of the land on which the work is contracted to be done'. In this case the court granted specific performance of a covenant entered into by the defendant to lay sewers on her land as she was in possession of this

---

95. [1908] 1 IR 232.
96. *Ibid.* at 237.
97. [1970] AC 652, 666.
98. *Molyneux v. Richard* [1906] 1 Ch 34, 42 *per* Kekewich J.
99. *The Principles of Equitable Remedies* (5th ed., 1997) p. 115.
100. *Todd & Co. v. Midland Great Western Rly of Ireland Co.* (1881) 9 LR Ir 85.
101. [1940] Ch 160.

land and the plaintiffs could not proceed to build houses on the land which she had sold them without these works being carried out.

Clearly where the defendant is in possession of the lands specific performance may often be the preferred option as the plaintiff could not employ another builder without committing a trespass. While his qualification of Romer LJ's requirement would seem quite acceptable, Farwell J appeared to go on to suggest that the mere fact that the defendant does not have possession of the land on which the work is contracted to be carried out should not necessarily be a complete bar to relief in the form of specific performance.[102] This statement is definitely questionable for as Farwell J himself acknowledged,[103] if the defendant is not in possession of the land, it may be impossible for him to carry out the works.

The requirements laid down in *Wolverhampton Corporation v. Emmons* were applied to a situation in which a tenant sought to enforce a landlord's covenant to repair in *Jeune v. Queens Cross Properties Ltd.*[104] Tenants alleged that their landlord was in breach of a covenant to repair by failing to reinstate a balcony at the front of the property after it had partially collapsed. It was accepted by Pennycuick VC that the court had a power which should be carefully exercised to make an order against a landlord to do specific work under a covenant to repair and an order of specific performance was granted in the circumstances.

Finally it should be stressed that despite the result in cases such as *Wolverhampton* and *Jeune*, it should not be assumed that orders which require a defendant to achieve a result as opposed to those which require him to carry on an activity will necessarily be enforced by specific performance. In the last analysis as Lord Hoffmann commented in *Co-Operative Insurance Society Ltd v. Argyll Stores (Holdings) Ltd* the grant or refusal of specific performance remains a matter for the judge's discretion and the level of precision which must be present if an obligation is to be enforced is difficult to predict with accuracy.

Contracts for Services

As a general principle, contracts which involve the performance of personal services will not be specifically enforced.[105] This is due partly to the fact that the courts would often be required to exercise a degree of super-

---

102. *Ibid.* at 165.
103. *Ibid.* at 164-165.
104. [1974] Ch 97.
105. As McCutcheon has commented (1997) 17 LS 65, 66 there is a 'near universal reluctance' to order performance of a contract for personal services.

vision in relation to any order made[106] and partly because of a reluctance on the part of the judiciary as a matter of policy to compel individuals to work together in circumstances where the relationship of trust and confidence between them no longer exists. As stated above, McWilliam J accepted in the course of his judgment in *Lift Manufacturers Ltd v. Irish Life Assurance Co. Ltd*[107] that the principle that specific performance will not be granted of a contract for services is not a rigid one and he acknowledged that where there does not seem to be any reason for the court to supervise performance of the contract, this argument against enforcement cannot apply. However it is generally accepted that from a policy perspective it is undesirable to force parties to fulfil obligations arising under contracts for the provision of services and as an examination of the relevant authorities in this area will show, it is usually only where a relationship of mutual trust still exists between the parties that the courts will be willing to grant specific performance, or where circumstances require it, an injunction.[108]

These issues were examined in some detail by Megarry J in his judgment in *C.H. Giles & Co. v Morris*,[109] where he commented that the so-called rule that contracts for personal services or involving the continuous performance of services will not be specifically enforced is plainly not absolute and without exception. He continued:

> I do not think that it should be assumed that as soon as any element of personal service or continuous services can be discerned in a contract the court will, without more, refuse specific performance. ... As is so often the case in equity, the matter is one of balance of advantage and disadvantage in relation to the particular obligations in question; and the fact that the balance will usually lie on one side does not turn this probability into a rule.[110]

---

106. See *supra Ryan v. Mutual Tontine Westminster Chambers Association* [1893] 2 Ch 116 and *Posner v. Scott Lewis* [1987] Ch 25.
107. [1979] ILRM 277.
108. See *supra* Chapter 13.
109. [1972] 1 WLR 307.
110. *Ibid.* at 318. Quoted with approval by Goff LJ in *Price v. Strange* [1978] Ch 337, 359-360. As McCutcheon has commented (1997) 17 LS 65, 67 Megarry J's judgment displays a 'willingness to depart from the traditional rule and to order performance where problems of superintendence would not arise and where the possibilities of evasion are not such as to render the order vain'. However, he points out that the efforts of Megarry J have not provided a base from which a general jurisdiction to order performance in such circumstances has been developed.

The *Giles* case concerned the issue of specific performance of a service agreement and the question arose whether the presence in the contract of a term in relation to the appointment of a third party prevented the court decreeing specific performance of the agreement. Megarry J accepted that there was a distinction between an order to perform a contract for services and an order to procure the execution of such a contract and held that on the facts, the contract was specifically enforceable. As Megarry J said specific performance may be granted of an agreement to execute an instrument even if the obligations which that instrument creates would not be specifically enforced.

In relation to contracts of employment, the policy arguments against enforcement are strong where a relationship of mutual trust and confidence no longer exists between the parties. However, as the decision of the Court of Appeal in *Hill v. C.A. Parsons & Co. Ltd*[111] illustrates, in exceptional cases where such a relationship still subsists, the courts will enforce a contract of employment, in this instance by the grant of an injunction. In this case, the court granted an injunction restraining the dismissal of an employee where his employer had been coerced by a trade union into taking such a course of action when the employee refused to join the union and where the employer still retained confidence in the employee's ability to do his job.

DEFENCES TO AN ACTION FOR SPECIFIC PERFORMANCE

Introduction

Having considered some of the types of cases in which a court will grant specific performance, it is now necessary to examine the various defences which may be put forward where a claim for specific performance is made. It is important to point out that while some of these defences may provide an absolute bar to relief (e.g. the fact that the contract is an illegal one) the majority are of a discretionary nature and will often be merely one of a number of factors which the court will be required to consider in deciding whether to grant relief. In addition, it is necessary to draw a distinction between two types of cases; first, those where even if the defence is successfully established the validity of the contract itself remains unaffected and where the defendant may still be liable in damages (e.g. where the

---

111. [1972] Ch 305.

defence of hardship is raised). These cases should be distinguished from those where the defence (e.g. mistake or misrepresentation) is sufficient to secure rescission of the contract.

Before examining these defences under various headings it is also necessary to stress that the types of cases in which specific performance will be refused do not fall into 'rigid categories'[112] and the following examination is not intended to be exhaustive.

Lack of Mutuality

It has traditionally been accepted that a court would not grant specific performance at the suit of one party when it could not do so at the suit of the other and that in order to obtain a decree of specific performance, the contract had to be mutually enforceable. This point was summarised in the following manner by O'Connor LJ in *O'Regan v. White:*[113]

> Generally speaking, at any rate, it would not be even-handed justice to compel specific performance against the one party, where the same remedy would not be available against the other party in respect of matters to be by him performed under the contract.

The operation of this principle can be seen in relation to the situation in which an infant seeks to enforce specifically a contract into which he has entered. So, in *Flight v. Bolland*[114] a minor failed to obtain a decree of specific performance of a contract because such a decree could not be obtained against him. As Leach MR commented: 'It is a general principle of courts of equity to interpose only where the remedy is mutual.'

One question which has provoked considerable controversy is whether the question of mutuality is to be determined at the time the contract is entered into or at the date of the judgment. The former approach was favoured by Fry[115] and by Meredith J in *Murphy v. Harrington,*[116] who stated

---

112. *Conlon v. Murray* [1958] NI 17, 26.
113. [1919] 2 IR 339, 393. See also his statement at p.392 that 'equity will not aid one party to an agreement to have *in specie* that for which he bargained unless it can likewise aid (if necessary) the other party to have *in specie* that for which he bargained'.
114. (1828) 4 Russ 298.
115. *Specific Performance* (6th ed., 1921) p. 219. 'A contract to be specifically enforced by the Court must, as a general rule, be mutual — that is to say, such that it might, *at the time it was entered into,* have been enforced by either of the parties against the other of them' (emphasis added).
116. [1927] IR 339, 344. See *Bayley v. Shoesmith's Contract* (1918) 87 LJ Ch 626.

that in relation to the issue of mutuality 'the material point in time to be considered is the time when the contract was entered into.' However, this point of view did not meet with the universal approval either of academic commentators,[117] or of members of the judiciary,[118] and the question was considered again by the English Court of Appeal in *Price v. Strange*.[119] The plaintiff and the defendant agreed that the former should carry out certain repairs to the defendant's property in return for a new underlease. When the plaintiff had completed half the work, the defendant refused to allow him to continue and repudiated the agreement. The plaintiff sought specific performance of the agreement which was refused by the trial judge on the grounds that the contract was not capable of mutual enforcement at the time it was entered into.

However, the Court of Appeal did not agree with this conclusion. Buckley LJ stressed that the time at which the mutual availability of specific performance must be considered is the time of judgment and said that the correct principle is that 'the court will not compel a defendant to perform his obligations specifically if it cannot at the same time ensure that any unperformed obligations of the plaintiff will be specifically performed, unless perhaps, damages would be an adequate remedy to the defendant for any default on the plaintiff's part.'[120] However, perhaps the most important principle to emerge from the decision of the Court of Appeal is that a lack of mutuality does not result in the court being without jurisdiction to entertain a claim for specific performance but is rather a matter to be taken into account in deciding whether to exercise its discretion in favour of granting the remedy. In this case, the Court of Appeal held that specific performance of the agreement should be granted subject to the defendant being recompensed for any repair work carried out by her and concluded that in any event the defendant had waived any defence of want of mutuality by allowing the plaintiff to start the repair work and in accepting the increased rent payable under the new underlease.

Misrepresentation

The fact that a contract was induced by reason of a misrepresentation will usually be a defence in an action for specific performance. Certainly any misrepresentation which justifies rescission will suffice and specific per-

---

117. Langdell (1887-88) 1 Harv LR 104; Saunders (1903) 19 LQR 341.
118. See the judgment of O'Connor LJ in *O'Regan v. White* [1919] 2 IR 339, 395.
119. [1978] Ch 337.
120. *Ibid.* at 367-368.

formance may even be refused where there is no right to rescind. This point was made by Jessel MR in *Re Banister*[121] where he stated as follows:

> I apprehend that the considerations which induce a Court to rescind any contract and the considerations which induce a Court of Equity to decline to enforce specific performance of a contract are by no means the same. It may well be that there is not sufficient to induce the Court to rescind the contract but still sufficient to prevent the Court enforcing it.

This point was reiterated by Lindley LJ in *Re Terry and White's Contract*,[122] where he said that 'a less serious misleading' of the defendant is sufficient to provide a defence in an action for specific performance than would be required to justify rescission. In practice successfully raising the defence of misrepresentation where specific performance is sought will be of less benefit to a defendant as he may still be liable in damages to the plaintiff whereas if rescission of the contract is granted this will not be an option.

In some cases while a defendant in a specific performance action may have had good grounds for rescission this right may have been lost for one reason or another,[123] and in these circumstances the misrepresentation should almost invariably still provide a good defence.

Misrepresentation will only provide a defence to specific performance where it has induced the defendant to enter into the contract and he has been prejudiced as a result, although it may not be necessary to prove that the misrepresentation provided the sole motivation for the defendants' decision to enter into the agreement. It seems to have been accepted that even an innocent misrepresentation may suffice in this regard; as Brett LJ stated in *Re Banister*:[124] 'if there be a misrepresentation of facts however innocently made, the court of equity will not enforce the performance of the contract.' However, it would be fair to say that where the facts would never have warranted rescission or where the representation relates merely to a matter of opinion, a degree of caution should be exercised. Often where the misrepresentation can be classed as innocent in nature the question of whether it can provide a valid defence will depend on whether the court can find evidence of fundamental unfairness in the transaction. This

---

121. (1879) 12 Ch D 131, 142.
122. (1886) 32 Ch D 14, 29.
123. E.g. as a result of the doctrine of laches or because the parties cannot be restored to their original positions.
124. (1879) 12 Ch D 131, 147.

point can be deduced from the decision of the Supreme Court in *Smelter Corporation v. O'Driscoll*[125] in which the plaintiff claimed an order of specific performance in relation to a contract for the sale of lands. The plaintiff's agent had told the defendant in the course of negotiations that if she did not agree to sell, the local authority would acquire the lands compulsorily and although the agent believed this statement to be true, it was actually without foundation. The Supreme Court held that while the plaintiff's agent had acted in a *bona fide* manner, by reason of the misrepresentation of the facts by the agent, the defendant had been under a 'fundamental misapprehension' as to the true position. O'Higgins CJ concluded that in these circumstances there was a fundamental unfairness in the transaction and that it would be unjust to grant a decree of specific performance. The general principles in this area are well summarised by Spry[126] as follows:

> If the defendant has entered into the material contract, or has elected not to rescind, in reliance on misleading statements or actions of the plaintiff, specific performance is refused either if circumstances of unfairness render it unreasonable to grant relief (and here it is generally of importance whether the plaintiff knew or ought to have known that his statements or actions might be relied upon) or if in view of the error or misunderstanding of the defendant and the hardship that may be suffered by him it is unreasonable to grant relief (and here it may be less important, though it is usually relevant, whether the plaintiff knew or ought to have known that his statements or acts would be relied upon), or if in view of both of these considerations it is unreasonable to grant relief.

A final point which should be made is that 'misrepresentation may arise as much from suppression of the material facts as from mis-stating them.' This point emerges from the judgment of Smith MR in *Geoghegan v. Connolly*,[127] where he found that there had been such a suppression of the facts in the particulars of sale of property as to disentitle the plaintiff to a decree of specific performance.

Mistake

In certain circumstances, mistake will constitute a defence to an action for specific performance. In determining whether specific performance should

---

125. [1977] IR 305.
126. *The Principles of Equitable Remedies* (5th ed., 1997) p. 162.
127. (1859) 8 Ir Ch R 598, 609.

be refused on this ground, the court will often be primarily influenced by unfairness or hardship caused by any misapprehension or mistake on the part of the defendant as to the nature of the contractual obligations.

The mistake may be of such proportions that it prevents a valid contract coming into existence at all; in these circumstances clearly no order of specific performance can be made. However, it is also necessary to consider the types of mistake, which although they do not prevent the contract being initially effective, may be of such a nature that a court will in the exercise of its discretion refuse to grant specific performance. Therefore specific performance may be refused where the mistake is not such as to render the contract void at law, or even where there is no right to rescind in equity. In other words, as we have seen above in the context of misrepresentation, a less serious mistake is sufficient to provide a defence in an action for specific performance than would be required to justify rescission.

There will also be types of mistake which are neither serious enough to justify rescission nor to provide a good defence in an action for specific performance. This can be seen from an examination of the decision of Murphy J in *Ferguson v. Merchant Banking Ltd*[128] in which the plaintiff claimed specific performance of a contract for the sale of land. The defendant company was being wound up and the official liquidator contested the plaintiff's right to have the contract performed. It was claimed that the agreement between the parties was for the sale of specified residential estates and ancillary lands and that it was never intended that a vacant site with development potential should be included in the sale. The defendant sought rescission of the contract or rectification thereof to give effect to what it argued was the true intention of the parties. While Murphy J accepted that a mistake had been made in that the official liquidator had not intended to dispose of the property with development potential, he found that there had not been a fundamental error nor an absence of agreement on any fundamental term. He concluded that whether the matter was viewed as one of fundamental mistake or absence of consensus, the defendant was not entitled to deprive the plaintiff of the benefit of the contract which he had entered into and in the circumstances held that he was entitled to an order of specific performance and the defendant's counter-claim was rejected.

Where a defendant seeks to rely on mistake as a defence, often a crucial question will be whether the plaintiff contributed in any way to the

---

128. [1993] ILRM 136.

misapprehension or misunderstanding. Certainly where the plaintiff is aware
of the mistake and seeks to take advantage of it a court will not grant
specific performance in his favour. In *Webster v. Cecil*[129] a vendor offered
property for sale for £1,250 instead of £2,250 as he had intended and the
purchaser accepted the offer knowing that the former had made a mistake.
Specific performance of the sale was refused on the basis that the mistake
had been clearly proved and the defendant had immediately given notice
of it. Romilly MR therefore concluded that the court would not compel the
defendant to sell property for much less than its real value. On the other
hand, where the mistake is solely that of the defendant and the plaintiff has
in no way contributed to it, the courts are unlikely to refuse specific performance. This point is illustrated by the decision in *Tamplin v. James*[130]
where property was offered for sale by reference to plans which correctly
described the area of the site. The defendant did not look at the plans and
mistakenly assumed that a piece of land behind the premises was included
in the sale and agreed to buy on this basis. The plaintiff was granted a
decree of specific performance when the defendant failed to complete the
purchase. As James LJ stated: 'for the most part the cases where a defendant has escaped on the ground of a mistake not contributed to by the plaintiff have been cases where a hardship amounting to an injustice would
have been inflicted upon him by holding him to his bargain, and it was
unreasonable to hold him to it. ... If a man makes a mistake of this kind
without any reasonable excuse he ought to be held to his bargain.'[131]

This statement was quoted with approval by Costello J in *O'Neill v.
Ryan (No. 3)*[132] in a judgment which confirms the point that where a plaintiff has in no way contributed to the mistake it would not be unjust or
unreasonable to require the defendant to carry out his contractual obligations. The plaintiff had instituted various proceedings against a number of
defendants including an action under section 205 of the Companies Act
1963, claiming oppression and seeking damages for wrongful dismissal,
fraud, misrepresentation and conspiracy. He claimed that the respondents
in the section 205 proceedings had offered to buy his shares in the company at a stipulated price and to pay his costs and sought specific performance of this agreement. The defendants resisted the claim contending that
the agreement relied on had been entered into by mistake and that they had
intended this offer to settle to apply to more than just the section 205

---

129. (1861) 30 Beav 62.
130. (1880) 15 Ch D 215.
131. *Ibid.* at 221.
132. [1992] 1 IR 166, 192.

action and submitted that as the parties had not been *ad idem* there was no contract in existence which could be specifically enforced. Costello J said that he had to balance the hardship which the defendants contended they would suffer against the hardship which the plaintiff would be subject to if the contract was not specifically enforced. He held that a valid enforceable agreement had come into existence, that the plaintiff had in no way contributed to the situation which had arisen and concluded that the plaintiff was entitled to an order of specific performance.

While it would appear that even where the plaintiff has contributed to the mistake in an unintentional manner the defence may succeed,[133] it remains difficult to lay down any definite principles in relation to a situation where the plaintiff bears no responsibility for the mistake which has occurred. While specific performance has on occasion been refused where the mistake made is entirely attributable to the defendant,[134] the better view would seem to be that in such cases there must be other circumstances which would make it 'highly unreasonable' to decree performance of the contractual obligations. This approach is well set out by Lord Macnaghten in *Stewart v. Kennedy*[135] in which he acknowledged that while a court may refuse specific performance in cases of mistake not caused or contributed to by the plaintiff, it has acted in this manner because it would not be reasonable to compel the defendant to carry out his obligations.

In the last analysis perhaps the most realistic formula is that put forward by James LJ in *Tamplin v. James*[136] of whether a 'hardship amounting to an injustice' would be caused to the defendant by not allowing him to resist a decree for specific performance on the basis of the mistake which has occurred. Spry[137] has captured the essence of the cases where the mistake may not be sufficiently grave to justify rescission and yet may be serious enough to persuade the court to refuse to decree performance. In his view it is necessary rather than regarding the mistake or misapprehension as an independent discretionary factor, instead to treat it as a matter which, together with other considerations such as hardship or unfairness, may make it inequitable to grant specific performance of a contract.

Hardship

In the exercise of its discretion, a court may decide to refuse to order spe-

---

133. *Denny v. Hancock* (1870) 6 Ch App 1.
134. *Malins v. Freeman* (1837) 2 Keen 25.
135. (1890) 15 App Cas 75, 105.
136. (1880) 15 Ch D 215.
137. *The Principles of Equitable Remedies* (5th ed., 1997) p. 157.

cific performance of a contract where to do so would inflict unnecessary hardship on the defendant, even where the plaintiff is not responsible for this. This fact was acknowledged by Budd J in his judgment in *Lavan v. Walsh*, [138] where he said that it is well-established that a court 'will not enforce the specific performance of a contract the result of which would be to impose great hardship on either of the parties to it.' [139] However it was conceded by counsel in that case that the question of hardship should generally be judged at the time the contract is entered into and as Budd J commented proof of subsequent hardship would have to be 'strong and above suspicion'. This issue was further considered by the Supreme Court in *Roberts v. O'Neill*, [140] in which the plaintiff claimed specific performance of a contract for the sale of a licensed premises. The defendants claimed that to grant specific performance of the contract with the plaintiff would be to impose unreasonable hardship on them because of the large increase in the value of the property since the date of the contract. McCarthy J acknowledged that hardship might provide a good defence to an action for specific performance where an existing hardship was not known at the date of the contract. However, he clearly felt that subsequent hardship should operate as a defence only in exceptional cases:

> While recognising that there may be cases in which hardship arising after the date of the contract is such that to decree specific performance would result in great injury, there must be few such cases and, in my view, they should not include ordinarily cases of hardship resulting from inflation alone. To permit as an ordinary rule a defence of subsequent hardship, would be to add a further hazard to the already trouble strewn area of the law of contracts for the sale of land. [141]

In the circumstances the Supreme Court decided to grant a decree of specific performance and concluded that it was not a case in which the court should intervene to deny this remedy to a contracting party to what was 'at the time, a perfectly fair and proper transaction'.

However, it is clear from both the *Lavan* and *Roberts* cases that where a serious injustice would otherwise result, supervening hardship may in an exceptional case provide a defence. A good example of the type of cir-

---

138. [1964] IR 87.
139. *Ibid.* at 102.
140. [1983] IR 47.
141. *Ibid.* at 64.

cumstances which might warrant such a conclusion is provided by *Patel v. Ali,*[142] in which the claim of a purchaser of a house to an order of specific performance against the vendor was resisted on the grounds of hardship. After the parties had entered into the contract the vendor became seriously ill, necessitating the amputation of her leg. To compound her difficulties she gave birth to a second child and her husband who had been adjudicated bankrupt was sent to prison for a time. Evidence was adduced that she relied greatly on the help of neighbours and of members of her family living nearby to cope with looking after the household and that to enforce specifically the contract for sale would cause undue hardship. Goulding J acknowledged that 'the court has sometimes refused specific performance because of a change of circumstances supervening after the making of the contract and not in any way attributable to the plaintiff'[143] and refused to grant an order in these circumstances and instead awarded damages to the purchaser.

Clearly in deciding whether to exercise its discretion on this basis, the court must balance the hardship which the defendant contends he would suffer against the hardship which the plaintiff would sustain if the contract were not specifically enforced,[144] which may for example relate to the likelihood that the plaintiff may not be able to recover damages to compensate him for the defendant's wrongdoing.

The predominant view is that hardship which may be caused to third parties as a result of a decision to grant specific performance is a factor which may be taken into account by a court.[145] So, in *Conlon v. Murray*[146] Black LJ seems to have attached some weight at least to the fact that if the vendor's executors were compelled to proceed with a contract for the sale of her farm, her brother would have had nowhere to live. Whether hardship which may be suffered by the public generally will be relevant is less easy to predict but in either case the weight which a court will attach to it will depend largely on the probable extent of the hardship or prejudice which will ensue.

Closely related to the issue of the potential hardship which may be caused to the defendant are general considerations of unfairness which are more likely to concern the manner in which the plaintiff has behaved. So

---

142. [1984] Ch 283.
143. *Ibid.* at 287.
144. *O'Neill v. Ryan (No. 3)* [1992] 1 IR 166, 192. See also *Beshoff Brothers Ltd v. Select Service Partner Ireland Ltd* High Court 1998 No. 8102P (O'Sullivan J) 28 July 1998.
145. Although note the comments of Issacs J in *Gall v. Mitchell* (1924) 35 CLR 222, 230.
146. [1958] NI 17.

where the plaintiff has acted in an unconscionable manner so as to take advantage of the weakness of a defendant's position, specific performance may be refused. A good illustration of the operation of this principle is the decision of the Northern Ireland Court of Appeal in *Conlon v. Murray* to which reference has just been made. The plaintiff brought an action for specific performance of a contract for the sale of a farm against the vendor which was continued against her executors after her death. The vendor was an elderly lady who had agreed to the sale in a distressed state without taking any time for reflection and without the benefit of independent advice. While Black LJ acknowledged that specific performance of a contract will not be refused on the sole ground that one of the parties had not received legal advice, he stated that in view of the 'extraordinary and unexplained haste' with which the transaction had been rushed through, the court should hesitate to decree specific performance. He said that it is well-established that there is a class of case in which a contract may be of such a nature that the court will not order it to be rescinded, but at the same time looking at the substantial justice of the case, will not order that it be specifically performed. In the circumstances in the exercise of its discretion, the Court of Appeal refused to grant specific performance. This result can be contrasted with that arrived at by Murray J in *McCrystal v. O'Kane*[147] in which *Conlon* was distinguished and suggestions that the plaintiff had taken unfair advantage of the defendant in concluding an agreement for the sale of land rejected.

Laches

As a general principle, a plaintiff who delays unreasonably in bringing proceedings for specific performance may fail to obtain the relief which he seeks where by reason of his delay it would be inequitable to grant the remedy sought. It is important to stress that delay alone will probably be insufficient without some further element of prejudice and it will be necessary to show circumstances which when considered in conjunction with the delay would render the granting of a decree for specific performance unjust.

It is clear from the judgment of O'Connor J in *Guerin v. Heffernan*[148] that where a plaintiff intends to seek relief in the form of specific performance he is bound to proceed without delay; as he said: 'A man who sleeps on his rights does not find favour in a court of equity.'[149] There the defend-

---

147. [1986] NI 123.
148. [1925] 1 IR 57.
149. *Ibid.* at 68.

ant sought to repudiate a contract for the purchase of a farm and the plaintiff, after threatening to institute proceedings against him, did nothing for a period of over a year. O'Connor J concluded that during the intervening time the defendant might well have assumed that the plaintiff had abandoned his rights under the contract and had accepted the defendant's repudiation and held that on this basis the plaintiff was not entitled to relief in the form of specific performance.

It is difficult to lay down reliable guidelines about the length of delay which may disentitle a plaintiff to relief as the question is often governed by other factors such as the conduct of the parties. However, Spry[150] has stated that 'the general rule is that in order to establish that the delay of the plaintiff has been excessive it must appear that, in all the material circumstances, a reasonably assiduous person would have proceeded with substantially greater speed or diligence.' In *Lazard Brothers & Co. Ltd v. Fairfield Properties Co. (Mayfair) Ltd*[151] the plaintiff failed to issue proceedings for specific performance until over two years had passed since the contract had been concluded. Megarry VC said that if specific performance was to be regarded as a prize 'to be awarded by equity to the zealous and denied to the indolent' the plaintiff might not succeed, but this was not the case and in the absence of any evidence of any other prejudice or circumstances which would make it unjust to grant relief, he made the order sought.

Usually, unless the parties have stipulated otherwise, time will not be of the essence to a contract in equity so a plaintiff may still be entitled to an order for specific performance even after the date for performance of the contractual obligations has passed, although he might still be liable for damages for breach of contract for failing to complete on time. However, where the court finds that time is of the essence a plaintiff will not be entitled to relief in the form of an order for specific performance in these circumstances.

Impossibility and Frustration

A court will not make an order of specific performance compelling a party to a contract to perform his obligations where it will not be possible for him to comply with the order which the court proposes to make; as Brewster LC stated in *Sheppard v. Murphy:*[152] 'a Court of Equity cannot compel him to do that which is impossible'. This point has recently been reiterated

---

150. *The Principles of Equitable Remedies* (5th ed., 1997) pp. 227-228.
151. (1987) 121 SJ 793.
152. (1868) IR 2 Eq 544, 557.

by Murphy J in *Neville & Sons Ltd v. Guardian Builders Ltd,*[153] where he commented that 'if a contract is discharged by impossibility then clearly no court could compel its performance'. However, as Brewster LC also made clear in *Sheppard*, a party cannot take steps to make performance of his contractual obligations impossible and then seek to rely on this as a defence.

A contract may be rendered impossible to perform by reason of frustration and the circumstances in which this may occur have recently been considered by the Supreme Court in *Neville & Sons Ltd v. Guardian Builders Ltd.*[154] The plaintiff and defendant entered into an agreement whereby the plaintiff contracted to build houses on a site owned by the defendant. It was accepted that the only effective means of access to the site would be by the construction of a new roadway which involved the acquisition of a strip of land owned by the county council. Difficulties arose in acquiring this land; the plaintiff sought specific performance of the agreement and the defendant contended that by reason of the difficulties which had arisen in relation to access to the site performance of the contract had been rendered impossible or possible only in circumstances so different from those contemplated that both parties were relieved from further performance. Murphy J accepted that performance of the contract had been frustrated by intervening circumstances and held that the plaintiffs were not entitled to specific performance, although this decision was reversed by the Supreme Court. In the course of his judgment Blayney J quoted with approval[155] from the speech of Lord Simon in *National Carriers Ltd v. Panalpina (Northern) Ltd*[156] as follows:

> Frustration of a contract takes place when there supervenes an event (without default of either party and for which the contract makes no sufficient provision) which so significantly changes the nature (not merely the expense or onerousness) of the outstanding contractual rights and/or obligations from what the parties could reasonably have contemplated at the time of its execution that it would be unjust to hold them to the literal sense of its stipulations in the new circumstances; in such case the law declares both parties to be discharged from further performance.

---

153. [1990] ILRM 601, 616. Reversed by the Supreme Court [1995] 1 ILRM 1.
154. [1995] 1 ILRM 1.
155. *Ibid.* at 7.
156. [1981] AC 675, 700. See also the judgment of Kenny J in *Browne v. Mulligan* [1976-77] ILRM 327, 332-333 in relation to the possible basis for the doctrine of frustration.

Blayney J concluded that what had transpired could not be termed a supervening event which significantly changed the nature of the defendant's obligations and while it made performance of the contract more onerous, he was satisfied that the defence of frustration should fail.

Finally, it would appear that a party cannot rely on the doctrine of frustration to provide a defence where the contract has been frustrated by an event which he anticipated or should have anticipated.[157]

---

157. *McGuill v. Aer Lingus Teo*, High Court 1981 No. 2238 (McWilliam J) 3 October 1983 at pp.13-14.

CHAPTER 15

Rectification

INTRODUCTION

Rectification is a discretionary equitable remedy which allows for the correction of an instrument which has failed to record the actual intentions of the parties to a contract. This jurisdiction allows the court to rectify documents, such as deeds, in order to make them correspond with the pre-existing agreement of the parties. For example, in the case of a contract for the sale of land, where a deed did not reflect the agreement of the parties, equity would allow rectification so as to ensure that the final instrument gave proper effect to the prior contract. This jurisdiction is viewed as an exception to the parol evidence rule that oral evidence will not suffice to alter a written document.

It is important to stress that this does not constitute rectification of the contract, but only of the writing recording the contract. This point is well summarised in the following *dicta* of James VC in *Mackenzie v. Coulson*[1] that while 'Courts of Equity do not rectify contracts; they may and do rectify instruments purporting to have been made in pursuance of the terms of contracts'. Similar sentiments have been expressed in a number of recent decisions in this jurisdiction; in *Irish Life Assurance Co. Ltd v. Dublin Land Securities Ltd*[2] Griffin J commented that 'rectification is concerned with defects in the recording, not in the making, of an agreement' a statement echoed by Barron J in *McD. v. McD.*[3]

MUTUAL MISTAKE

Originally, it was necessary to show that there was a valid and enforceable contract antecedent to the instrument sought to be rectified, and that such contract was inaccurately represented in the instrument. However, Clauson

---

1. (1869) LR 8 Eq 368, 375. See also the *dicta* of Buckley LJ in *Lovell and Christmas Ltd v. Wall* (1911) 104 LT 85, 93 that 'the court does not rectify contracts, but what it rectifies is the erroneous expression of contracts in documents.'
2. [1989] IR 253, 260.
3. [1993] ILRM 717, 722.

J suggested *obiter* in *Shipley Urban District Council v. Bradford Corporation*[4] that it was not necessary to find a concluded and binding contract between the parties antecedent to the agreement which it was sought to rectify provided that there was a common continuing intention with regard to a particular provision or aspect of the agreement. Thus if the parties were *ad idem* up to the point in time when they executed the formal instrument which, it transpired, did not correspond with their common agreement, the court might order rectification even though there was no concluded and binding contract between the parties up to the point when the formal instrument was executed. This approach was followed in this jurisdiction in *Monaghan County Council v. Vaughan.*[5] The plaintiff county council invited tenders for demolition work and the removal of valuable materials from a derelict site. Dixon J found that it was the clear intention of both parties that the defendant would pay for the right to carry out the works. Thus when the county council executed a contract which provided that the defendant should be paid for the demolition work, this was an instance of mutual mistake, as the parties had agreed on matters which were not reflected in the written contract. Dixon J rejected the argument that there could be no rectification because there was no antecedent agreement between the parties which was capable of being enforced and granted the plaintiff's claim for rectification.

The reasoning of Clauson J in *Shipley* was followed in England in *Crane v. Hegeman-Harris Co. Inc,*[6] where Simonds J stated that it was not necessary to find a concluded and binding contract between the parties antecedent to the agreement which it is sought to rectify provided there is a common continuing intention in relation to the particular provision of the agreement. Leaving aside questions about enforceability, doubts remained about whether an antecedent complete concluded agreement was necessary, particularly as a result of the views expressed by Denning LJ in *Frederick E. Rose (London) Ltd v. William H. Pim Junior & Co. Ltd,*[7] which were quoted with approval in this jurisdiction in *Lucey v. Laurel Construction Co. Ltd.*[8] The issue appears to have been resolved in England as a result of the judgment of Russell LJ in *Joscelyne v. Nissen*[9] where he stated that in his view the correct position was as enunciated by Simonds J in *Crane* subject to the qualification that there should be some outward expression of accord

---

4. [1936] Ch 375.
5. [1948] IR 306.
6. [1939] 1 All ER 662, 664.
7. [1953] 2 QB 450, 461-462.
8. High Court 1970 No. 3816 (Kenny J) 18 December 1970 at pp.10-11.
9. [1970] 2 QB 86.

between the parties. This question was also considered in Northern Ireland by Lowry LCJ in *Rooney and McParland Ltd v. Carlin*[10] where he laid down the following requirements which must be satisfied where the remedy of rectification is sought:

> 1. There must be a concluded agreement antecedent to the instrument which it is sought to be rectified; but
> 2. The antecedent agreement need not be binding in law (for example, it need not be under seal if made by a public authority or in writing and signed by the party if relating to a sale of land) nor need it be in writing: such incidents merely help to discharge the heavy burden of proof; and
> 3. A complete antecedent concluded contract is not required, as long as there was prior accord on a term of a proposed agreement, outwardly expressed and communicated between the parties, as in *Joscelyne v. Nissen*.

When the matter came before the Supreme Court in *Irish Life Assurance Co. Ltd v. Dublin Land Securities Ltd*[11] Griffin J said unhesitatingly that he would adopt what had been said by Russell LJ in *Joscelyne* and by Lowry LCJ in *Rooney* and pointed out that in *Lucey*, Kenny J did not appear to have been referred to the decision of Russell LJ. Griffin J concluded as follows:

> Applying those principles to the facts of this case, and bearing in mind the heavy burden of proof that lies on those seeking rectification, the question to be addressed is whether there was convincing proof, reflected in some outward expression of accord, that the contract in writing did not represent the common continuing intention of the parties on which the court can act. . . . [12]

As a result it would now seem to be firmly established that an antecedent concluded agreement is not necessary provided there is a common intention to include or exclude a particular term which continues until the contract is executed and which is made manifest by the parties in some way. However it is vital that this common intention can be ascertained with

---

10. [1981] NI 138, 146.
11. [1989] IR 253.
12. *Ibid.* at 263. Quoted with approval by Murphy J in *Lac Minerals Ltd v. Chevron Mineral Corporation of Ireland* [1995] 1 ILRM 161, 172.

precision and a number of claims for rectification have failed on the grounds that the parties' exact intentions cannot be identified with sufficient certainty. This point emerges from the decision of the Supreme Court in *Irish Life Assurance Co. Ltd v. Dublin Land Securities Ltd.*[13] The plaintiff company owned a large portfolio of ground rents and also valuable lands which had been made the subject of compulsory purchase orders. A contract of sale between the plaintiff and the defendant was drawn up and while it was the intention of the plaintiff to exclude the lands subject to the C.P.O.s from the sale, due to a mix up in its legal department, they were included in the contract. The plaintiff's intention to exclude these lands was communicated to an agent of the defendant in a rather imprecise way but was not passed on to the defendant. The plaintiff sought rectification of the contract, while the defendant sought specific performance of the agreement in its original form. Keane J found that the defendant did not know of the plaintiff's intention to exclude the properties in question and dismissed the claim on the grounds that there was no common intention between the parties to this effect. On appeal, the Supreme Court upheld the order of the High Court. Griffin J said that the party seeking rectification must establish by convincing proof that the instrument does not reflect the common intention of the parties and that the plaintiff had failed to discharge this onus as the oral reference to the properties lacked the precision necessary to enable the court to conclude what the common intention of the parties had been.

The lack of precision in relation to the alleged common intention was even more pronounced in the subsequent decision of Murphy J in *Ferguson v. Merchant Banking Ltd.*[14] The plaintiff claimed specific performance of a contract for the sale of land and the official liquidator of the defendant company contested the plaintiff's right to have the contract performed claiming that it was never the intention to include certain development lands in the sale. Murphy J commented that the case before him was far weaker from the defendant's point of view than that presented to the court by the defendant in *Irish Life Assurance Co.* In that case a conscious decision to exclude the lands in question had been made whereas in the case before the court, the liquidator simply did not know of the existence of the valuable vacant land. Murphy J also said that there was a striking similarity in that there was an 'absence of a pre-existing concluded agreement establishing the common intention of the parties with a sufficient degree of particularity'. He concluded that the bargain was too imprecise to con-

---

13. [1986] IR 332 (HC); [1989] IR 253 (SC).
14. [1993] ILRM 136.

stitute a contract and that the question of rectification of the agreement was wholly unstateable.

Lack of precision also proved to be fatal to the plaintiff's case in the recent decision of Barron J in *McD. v. McD.*[15] The plaintiff wife and defendant husband signed an agreement following negotiations to settle proceedings relating to maintenance and the distribution of their property and custody of their children. The plaintiff sought rectification of the agreement to include the fact that the husband had agreed to pay her costs in all outstanding legal proceedings between them. Barron J accepted that: 'In order to rectify the contract the court must be satisfied that there was a common and continuing intention and that the agreement as recorded does not represent [the parties'] common intention'[16] and continued that it 'must also be satisfied as to precisely what that common intention was.' Applying these principles, Barron J said that it was necessary for the evidence to show that there was a common intention that the husband should pay the wife's costs and also the precise nature of such costs. He did not believe that the evidence established either of these matters and said that even if there had been an agreement that the husband was to pay the wife's costs, it was clear from the drafting of the subsequent documents that there was no *consensus ad idem* as to the matters to be dealt with on taxation.

For rectification to be available it is necessary to establish that the instrument in question does not accord with the actual terms agreed by the parties and that if rectified it will do so. In this context it is important to distinguish these actual terms from what the parties might have stipulated if they had not been under some misapprehension about what they were agreeing upon. As Spry[17] has stated 'where there is no lack of conformity between the document and the concurrent intention, the basis for rectification does not exist' so an instrument which truly reflects what the parties agreed cannot be altered even though those involved laboured under a fundamental misapprehension about the consequences of their agreement. This point is well illustrated by the decision of the Court of Appeal in *Frederick E. Rose (London) Ltd v. W.H. Pim Junior & Co. Ltd.*[18] The defendant agreed to supply the plaintiff with 'horsebeans', both parties mistakenly believing that the term was synonymous with 'feveroles'. When the defendant subsequently supplied another type of horsebean which was less valuable in nature the plaintiff sought rectification of the agreement to

---

15. [1993] ILRM 717.
16. *Ibid.* at 722.
17. *The Principles of Equitable Remedies* (5th ed., 1997) at p. 612.
18. [1953] 2 QB 450.

refer specifically to the term 'feverole' but failed on the basis that the contract as recorded accurately reflected the actual terms agreed.

Finally, it emerges from the decision of Murphy J in *Lac Minerals Ltd v. Chevron Mineral Corporation of Ireland*[19] that a claim for rectification cannot succeed where it is not made by either of the parties involved in the original agreement, but by a party who although undoubtedly affected by it was in no sense privy to the manner in which it was negotiated, or the circumstances in which the error occurred. Murphy J concluded that the case law in the area demonstrated that while:

> the action for rectification does not require that the parties to the litigation should be privy to the same contract, they must be privy to or affected by the same mistake in such a way that it would be unconscionable for the defendant in such proceedings to seek to rely on the document which erroneously recorded or mistakenly implemented the true agreement.[20]

UNILATERAL MISTAKE

As Griffin J stated in *Irish Life Assurance Co. Ltd v. Dublin Land Securities Ltd*[21] 'as a general rule, the courts only rectify an agreement in writing where there has been a mutual mistake i.e. where it fails to record the intention of *both* parties'. However, he went on to acknowledge that this statement must now be qualified somewhat and that a party who has entered into an agreement by mistake may be entitled to rectification if he establishes that the other party concluded the agreement with knowledge of this mistake.[22] This position had been accepted by Kenny J in his judgment in *Lucey v. Laurel Construction Co Ltd*[23] in the following manner:

> The Court has jurisdiction to rectify a written agreement made between two parties only when either there is a mutual mistake made by the two parties in the drafting of a written agreement which is to give effect to a prior oral agreement or when one party sees a mistake in the written agreement and when he knows that the other party

---

19. [1995] 1 ILRM 161.
20. *Ibid.* at 178.
21. [1989] IR 253, 260.
22. *Ibid.* at 261. See also *O'Neill v. Ryan (No. 3)* [1992] 1 IR 166, 185 *per* Costello J.
23. High Court 1970 No. 3816P (Kenny J) 18 December 1970, at pp.9-10.

has not seen it and then signs the document knowing that it contains a mistake. . . .

Similar views were expressed by Pennycuick J in *A. Roberts & Co. Ltd v. Leicestershire County Council*[24] where he stated that 'a party is entitled to rectification of a contract on proof that he believed a particular term to be included in the contract and that the other party concluded the contract with the omission or a variation of that term in the knowledge that the first party believed the term to be included'. The plaintiff had undertaken to build a school for the defendant council. The agreement had originally provided that the building should be completed within 18 months, but council officers changed the time for the performance of the contract to 30 months and the plaintiff signed without noticing the alteration. It was held that the council was aware of the mistake and rectification was ordered on this basis. This result can be contrasted with that arrived at in *Riverlate Properties Ltd v. Paul*.[25] The parties executed a lease prepared by the solicitors for the lessor which obliged the lessor to bear all the costs of exterior and structural repairs to the demised premises. Although the lessor had intended that the lessee should be liable to make a contribution towards this expenditure, neither the lessee nor her solicitor were aware of this. The lessor sought rectification of the lease, or if the lessee would not accept this remedy, then rescission. The Court of Appeal held that rectification should not be granted since the lessee neither directly nor through her solicitor knew of the lessor's mistake.

The circumstances in which the so-called doctrine in *Roberts* will apply were considered in some detail by the Court of Appeal in *Thomas Bates & Son Ltd. v. Wyndham's (Lingerie) Ltd.*[26] The defendant tenant was aware of the plaintiff landlord's mistake in not including an arbitration provision in a rent review clause but did not draw its attention to it. The landlord realized the omission only when review was necessary although the tenant had at all times been aware of the mistake. The Court of Appeal ordered that an arbitration clause be inserted into the lease in accordance with the parties' original intention. Buckley LJ stated that for the doctrine to apply the following conditions must be satisfied:

1. One party, A, erroneously believed that the document to be rectified contained a particular term or provision, or mistakenly thought it did

---

24. [1961] Ch 555.
25. [1975] Ch 133.
26. [1981] 1 WLR 505.

not contain a particular term or provision which mistakenly, it did contain.

2. The other party, B, was aware of the mistake and knew that it was due to an error on the part of A.

3. B omitted to draw the mistake to the notice of A.

4. The mistake must be one calculated to benefit B.

Buckley LJ commented that where these requirements are fulfilled, the court may regard it as inequitable to allow B to resist a claim for rectification to give effect to A's intention on the ground that the mistake was not a common one at the time of the execution of the document. One final observation made by Buckley LJ in *Bates* which is worth noting is his comment that while this 'inequitable conduct' may involve some element of sharp practice it depends more 'on the equity of the position'.

Keane J in *Irish Life Assurance Co Ltd v. Dublin Land Securities*[27] said that rectification could be granted in cases of unilateral mistake where it would be inequitable in the circumstances to allow the other party to retain a benefit derived from the mistake. In the case before him there was a mere unilateral mistake and no sharp practice or fraud on the part of the defendant. It would therefore not be equitable to grant rectification because the defendant had not been aware of the plaintiffs' mistake when the contract had been executed.

A further example of circumstances in which a court can decree rectification of a document in a case of unilateral mistake is when the party who is not mistaken is guilty of fraud. Thus in *McCausland v. Young*[28] a son was held to have acquired a right to rectification of an instrument of re-settlement on the grounds that his father, who stood in a fiduciary relationship towards him, had failed to disclose the nature and effect of a forfeiture clause contained in the settlement.

THE ONUS OF PROOF

Clearly the rule that parol evidence is not admissible to add to or vary the terms of a written instrument does not apply to a claim for rectification as it is based on the premise that the written agreement as recorded does not reflect the true intention of the parties. Oral evidence may therefore be

27. [1986] IR 332.
28. [1949] NI 49.

adduced which expressly contradicts the terms of the written agreement and the onus lies firmly on the plaintiff to establish grounds for rectification. Traditionally it was accepted that 'much vigilance and caution' was required in such cases particularly where a claim was based entirely on oral evidence.[29] In *Fowler v. Fowler*[30] Lord Chelmsford LC stated that evidence of the clearest and most satisfactory nature was necessary and that 'something more than the highest degree of probability' was required which would leave 'no fair and reasonable doubt' about the matter. Similar terminology was employed in this jurisdiction by Haugh J in *Nolan v. Graves*[31] where he spoke of an onus of proof 'beyond all reasonable doubt'.

More recently however, the tendency has been to move towards a more lenient approach to this issue. In *Joscelyne v. Nissen*[32] Russell LJ stated that in the view of the Court of Appeal it would be better to use the phrase 'convincing proof' without importing the phrase 'beyond all reasonable doubt' from the criminal law. The matter was also given some consideration by the members of the Court of Appeal in *Thomas Bates & Son Ltd v. Wyndham's (Lingerie) Ltd*[33] where Brightman LJ stated that the standard of proof required in an action for rectification to establish the common intention of the parties is 'the civil standard of balance of probability'. However, he continued by saying that as the alleged common intention will necessarily contradict the written instrument 'convincing proof' is required to counteract the intention of the parties as displayed in the instrument itself. In addition, he was of the opinion that the standard of proof should be no different in cases of unilateral mistake such as that before him, a suggestion which would seem to be in accordance with the view of Griffin J in *Irish Life Assurance Co Ltd v. Dublin Land Securities Ltd*[34] where he spoke of the plaintiff establishing his case by 'convincing evidence'. In this case, Griffin J also gave consideration to the general standard required in cases where a plaintiff seeks to establish the common continuing intention of the parties. He said that bearing in mind 'the heavy burden of proof'[35] that lies on a party seeking rectification, the question which the court must answer is whether there was 'convincing proof' that the written instrument did not reflect the parties' intention.

---

29. *McCormack v. McCormack* (1877) 1 LR Ir 119, 124.
30. (1859) 4 De G & J 250, 265. See also the *dicta* of Thurlow LC in *Countess of Shelburne v. Earl of Inchiquin* (1784) 1 Bro CC 338, 341 that 'strong irrefragable evidence is required'.
31. [1946] IR 376, 389.
32. [1970] 2 QB 86, 98. See also *Westland Savings Bank v. Hancock* [1987] 2 NZLR 21.
33. [1981] 1 WLR 505.
34. [1989] IR 253, 260-261.
35. *Ibid.* at 263. See also p.259.

Therefore, the position would appear to be very similar now both in this jurisdiction and in England, namely that while it has been accepted that the ordinary civil standard of proof should apply, the nature of the case being made inevitably demands that the proof adduced be 'convincing' in view of the fact that it will necessarily contradict the written agreement between the parties.

DISCRETIONARY FACTORS

Rectification as an equitable remedy is discretionary in nature. Haugh J has commented in *Nolan v. Graves*[36] that the jurisdiction of a court to grant rectification and specific performance 'is a delicate jurisdiction ... [which] must be exercised with discretion and care'. However an examination of the case law in this area would suggest that where a convincing case for a right to relief in this form is established, the remedy will only infrequently be withheld on discretionary grounds. The most obvious reason for this finding is that unlike other types of equitable remedy such as injunctions and specific performance, which may be withheld on discretionary grounds leaving the plaintiff to a remedy in damages, if rectification is refused the instrument in question remains effective in its original form and the plaintiff may have no remedy whatsoever.

One clear case in which rectification will not be granted is where a *bona fide* purchaser for value without notice has acquired some interest under the instrument which the plaintiff seeks to rectify.[37] In addition, an order will be withheld where granting it will serve no practical purpose e.g. where the obligations arising under the agreement have already been performed in accordance with the common intention of the parties. Other more general discretionary grounds may relate to the conduct of the parties, such as an absence of clean hands on the part of the plaintiff or laches or acquiescence on his part. Where a plaintiff has delayed unreasonably in seeking relief combined with circumstances which would make it inequitable or unjust to grant relief, such as where the defendant has altered his position on the basis of the plaintiff's statements or actions, relief in the form of rectification may be withheld. Equally even where the plaintiff has in no way been at fault, he may still fail to obtain a remedy on discre-

---

36. [1946] IR 376, 391. See also the comments of Evershed MR in *Whiteside v. Whiteside* [1950] Ch 65, 71 that rectification is a discretionary remedy 'which must be cautiously watched and jealously exercised'.
37. *Smith v. Jones* [1954] 1 WLR 1089.

tionary grounds where the court is satisfied that to make the order sought would cause undue prejudice or hardship to the defendant.

TYPES OF INSTRUMENTS WHICH CAN BE RECTIFIED

Various types of *inter partes* agreements such as leases[38] and share transfers[39] can be rectified. However, where statute requires that an instrument be registered relief may be refused once this has been done, particularly where a statutory mechanism exists for altering the document, and a court will not make an order rectifying the articles of association of a company.[40]

Rectification of a voluntary deed or settlement may be obtained where there is sufficient evidence to satisfy the court that the donor or settlor's intentions were not accurately recorded in the terms of the instrument. As Brightman J stated in *Re Butlin's Settlement Trusts,*[41] there is no doubt that 'the court has power to rectify a settlement notwithstanding that it is a voluntary settlement and not the result of a bargain'. So, in *Fitzgerald v. Fitzgerald*[42] the Irish Court of Appeal granted rectification of a marriage settlement to allow for the insertion of proper words of limitation where the deed itself afforded sufficient evidence of the parties' intention. While such applications will often be made by the settlor himself, a court may entertain a claim by a beneficiary although it will be unlikely to be successful if made during the settlor's lifetime if his consent to the alteration is not forthcoming.[43] However, where the settlor is dead and it is proved either from his instructions or otherwise that the deed was not drawn up in the exact manner which he intended, rectification may be granted.[44] The circumstances in which a court may grant rectification of a voluntary settlement on the application of the settlor, where a trustee does not consent were considered in *Re Butlin's Settlement Trusts,*[45] but it is clearly necessary for such a trustee to have reasonable evidence to support his opposition to the making of an order before he will succeed.

It is generally accepted that a court has no jurisdiction to rectify a will

---

38. *Thomas Bates & Son Ltd v. Wyndham's (Lingerie) Ltd* [1981] 1 WLR 505.
39. *Re International Contract Co.* (1872) 7 Ch App 485.
40. *Scott v. Frank F. Scott (London) Ltd* [1940] Ch 794.
41. [1976] Ch 251, 260.
42. [1902] 1 IR 477.
43. *Thompson v. Whitmore* (1860) 1 J & H 268.
44. *Lister v. Hodgson* (1867) LR 4 Eq 30, 34 *per* Romilly MR.
45. [1976] Ch 251.

apart from where as a matter of construction it finds that a manifest error has occurred.[46] In England, section 20 of the Administration of Justice Act 1982 provides that a will may be rectified where the instrument fails to give effect to the testator's intentions by reason of a clerical error or due to a failure to give effect to his instructions but there is no equivalent provision in this jurisdiction.

---

46. *Re Bacharach's Will Trusts* [1959] Ch 245.

CHAPTER 16

Rescission

INTRODUCTION

The term 'rescission' can be used in a number of different contexts and it is important to appreciate this before examining the circumstances in which rescission in equity may be granted. Where one party has been in breach of a fundamental term of a contract, the innocent party may chose to either affirm it and sue for damages for its breach or, provided the breach goes to the root of the contract, he may treat this conduct as repudiation of the contract by the other party which relieves him from the performance of further contractual obligations and still allows him to sue for damages. This latter option of 'rescission' is a purely common law concept and the decision to pursue this course is essentially one for the innocent party to make. Alternatively the terms of a contract itself may confer on a party the right to terminate or 'rescind' it in certain circumstances e.g. on the occurrence of a specified event or where there is non-compliance with a condition precedent laid down in the contract.

Unlike the forms of rescission just described, rescission in equity involves the setting aside or avoiding of contracts and other instruments by the court, rather than as a result of a decision taken by a party to it where, as Pettit[1] states, 'the contract contains an inherent cause of invalidity' often in the form of mistake, misrepresentation or undue influence. If a court orders the rescission of a contract in the exercise of this equitable jurisdiction the contract is treated as being voidable *ab initio*, so while it is treated as valid until rescission is ordered, it is then retrospectively invalidated from its inception.

The circumstances in which a court will intervene in the exercise of its equitable jurisdiction were summarised by Henchy J in *Northern Bank Finance Corporation Ltd v. Charlton*[2] where he said that relief in the form of rescission 'will be granted when the court considers that it would be just and equitable to do so in order to restore the parties, at least substantially to their respective positions' before the vitiating conduct occurred, a

---

1. *Equity and the Law of Trusts* (8th ed, 1997) p. 654.
2. [1979] IR 149, 197.

point which was echoed by Griffin J in his judgment in the same case.[3] As he went on to say 'the primary purpose of all proceedings for rescission, as contrasted with that of actions for damages is to restore the *status quo* and bring back the original position by undoing all that has intervened between it and the present' and 'the object to be achieved by rescission is the restoration of *both parties* as nearly as may be to the position which each occupied before the transaction'. However, it should be noted that the attitude of equity towards the concept of *restitutio in integrum* in granting rescission is more flexible than that adopted by the common law and as Lord Blackburn commented in *Erlanger v. New Sombrero Phosphate Co.*:[4] 'the practice has always been for a Court of Equity to give this relief whenever, by the exercise of its powers, it can do what is practically just, though it cannot restore the parties precisely to the state they were in before the contract.'

GROUNDS FOR RESCISSION

Mistake

While mistake alone is capable of justifying the refusal of a decree of specific performance, it would be incorrect to assume that it will always automatically justify rescission. However it is equally clear that a party may successfully seek rescission in equity on the grounds of mistake where this result could not be achieved at law. The circumstances in which relief will be granted on this ground were set out as follows by Flanagan J in *Gun v. McCarthy*:[5]

> [W]here there being a clear undoubted mistake by one party in reference to a material term of the contract which he entered into with another, and the other party knowingly seeks to avail himself of that, and seeks to bind the other to the mistake, the law of this Court is, that it will not allow such a contract to be binding on the parties, but will give relief against it.

There are a number of examples of relief being granted in equity on grounds of mistake in England. Thus, in *Cooper v. Phibbs*[6] an individual agreed to

---

3. *Ibid.* at 206. See also the comments of Denning LJ in *Solle v. Butcher* [1950] 1 KB 671, 696.
4. (1878) 3 App Cas 1218, 1278-1279.
5. (1883) 13 LR Ir 304, 310.
6. (1867) LR 2 HL 149.

take a lease of a salmon fishery from the trustee of a settlement in circumstances where, unknown to both parties, it already belonged to him, and the House of Lords agreed to set aside the agreement subject to a lien on the fishery for such monies as had been expended on improvements. As Lord Westbury stated:

> [I]f parties contract under a mutual mistake and misapprehension as to their relative and respective rights, the result is, that that agreement is liable to be set aside as having proceeded upon a common mistake.[7]

This decision also illustrates the ability of equity to set aside a contract on such terms as the court sees fit to impose, in this instance involving the imposition of a lien, and shows the flexible nature of equitable rescission.

Perhaps the most extensive consideration of the circumstances in which rescission will be granted in equity on the grounds of common mistake is contained in the judgment of Denning LJ as he then was in *Solle v. Butcher*.[8] There a lessee leased a flat for a period of years on the basis of an erroneous assumption made by both parties, that it had been so completely reconstructed that it constituted a new flat and as such was no longer controlled by the provisions of the Rent Acts. In fact the maximum permissible rent was substantially less than that paid and the lessee sued to recover the overpaid rent. This action failed and the lease was set aside on the grounds of common mistake. Denning LJ stated as follows:

> It is now clear that a contract will be set aside if the mistake of the one party has been induced by a material misrepresentation of the other, even though it was not fraudulent or fundamental; or if the one party, knowing that the other is mistaken about the terms of an offer, or the identity of the person by whom it is made, lets him remain under his delusion and conclude a contract on the mistaken terms instead of pointing out the mistake.[9]

He continued:

> A contract is also liable in equity to be set aside if the parties were under a common misapprehension either as to facts or as to their relative and respective rights provided that the misapprehension was

---

7.   *Ibid.* at 170.
8.   [1950] 1 KB 671.
9.   *Ibid.* at 692.

fundamental and that the party seeking to set it aside was not himself at fault.[10]

The suggestion of Denning LJ that a contract which although not void as a result of mistake at law, may nevertheless be voidable in equity has met with some criticism,[11] although it appeared to be accepted subsequently by Goff J in *Grist v. Bailey.*[12] The plaintiff agreed to buy the defendant's house at a reduced price because both parties mistakenly believed that it was the subject of a protected tenancy. The plaintiff claimed specific performance and the defendant counter-claimed and sought rescission of the contract. Goff J held that although the mistake did not suffice to nullify the contract at common law, equity could intervene. In relation to the statement made by Denning LJ in *Solle* he commented that this could not be dismissed as a 'mere *dictum*' and was in his judgment the basis of the decision and therefore binding on him. Goff J said that the essential questions to be decided were first, whether there had been a common mistake, secondly, whether it was fundamental and thirdly, whether the defendant was at fault. He was satisfied that in the case before him there had been a common mistake of a fundamental nature. While Goff J said that it was not absolutely clear what Denning LJ had meant by the third requirement, namely that the party seeking to take advantage of the mistake must not be at fault, clearly there must be some degree of blameworthiness beyond the mere fact of having made a mistake. In the circumstances he did not feel that the defendant was at fault to the extent of disentitling herself to relief and he concluded that the plaintiff's action should be dismissed on terms that the defendant would enter into a new contract to sell the house at an appropriate price for vacant possession.

The reasoning in *Solle v. Butcher* was applied again by Denning MR in *Magee v. Pennine Insurance Co. Ltd*[13] although it has been argued[14] that it is difficult to reconcile this approach with that taken by the House of Lords in *Bell v. Lever Brothers Ltd.*[15] While this may be so, there are good grounds for arguing that this equitable basis for intervention should be allowed to continue as it allows for the setting aside of a contract on the grounds that the justice of the case requires it and also permits this to take place on terms which to the court appear just.

---

10. *Ibid.* at 693. See also *Magee v. Pennine Insurance Co. Ltd* [1969] 2 QB 507.
11. Atiyah and Bennion (1961) 24 MLR 421 at 441-442.
12. [1967] Ch 532.
13. [1969] 2 QB 507.
14. Hanbury and Martin, *Modern Equity* (15th ed., 1997) p. 823.
15. [1932] AC 161.

One question which has yet to be satisfactorily resolved is whether a court will grant rescission in a case of unilateral mistake or whether the mistake must be common to both parties before it will intervene. This issue was considered by Russell LJ in *Riverlate Properties Ltd v. Paul*[16] where the parties executed a lease prepared by the lessor's solicitors which obliged the lessor to bear all the costs of exterior and structural repairs to the premises. Although the lessor had intended that the lessee should be liable to make a contribution towards this expenditure, neither the lessee nor her solicitor were aware of this. The Court of Appeal accepted that the mistake was in no way attributable to anything said or done by the lessee and held that it was a case of 'mere unilateral mistake' which could not entitle the plaintiff to rescission of the lease. The opposite approach would seem to have been accepted in Ireland, at least in principle, although it is not clear whether the *dicta* to this effect will be followed. In *Monaghan County Council v. Vaughan*[17] Dixon J commented that 'unilateral mistake arises where one of two or more parties is not *ad idem* with the other party or parties, and there is therefore, no real agreement between them. In such a case rescission may be appropriate. . . .' This statement was referred to by Griffin J in the course of his judgment in *Irish Life Assurance Co. Ltd v. Dublin Land Securities Ltd*,[18] although as the Supreme Court was concerned solely with the issue of rectification in that case, no view was expressed on the circumstances in which the remedy of rescission would be granted.

Regard must also be had to policy considerations and the cases show that rescission in equity on the grounds of mistake is more likely to be available in cases involving mistakes as to private rights than it is in a commercial context where the rights of third parties are likely to be prejudiced by the interference of the court.

Misrepresentation

A contract can be rescinded at common law and in equity where there has been a fraudulent misrepresentation. The most important Irish authority on the right to rescind in equity on grounds of fraudulent misrepresentation is *Northern Bank Finance Corporation Ltd v. Charlton.*[19] The plaintiff bank loaned the defendants a sum of money to facilitate their objective

---

16. [1975] Ch 133.
17. [1948] IR 306, 312.
18. [1989] IR 253.
19. [1979] IR 149.

of acquiring control of a public company. When the defendants defaulted on the loan repayments, the plaintiff claimed the balance and interest and the defendant counter-claimed that it had entered into the original transaction because of the fraudulent misrepresentations of the plaintiff. In the High Court, Finlay P made an order dismissing the plaintiff's claim and allowing the defendants' counter-claim on the basis that the defendant had been induced by a fraudulent misrepresentation to enter into the transactions. The Supreme Court agreed that the plaintiffs' claim should be dismissed but the majority of the court held that the order of rescission granted by the High Court should be set aside because the principle of *restitutio in integrum* could not apply. Extensive consideration was given by a number of members of the Supreme Court to the circumstances in which rescission of a contract may be granted. O'Higgins CJ pointed out that in the case of a fraudulent misrepresentation, the fact that the contract has already been executed or the transaction completed is no bar to rescission unless as a result *restitutio in integrum* has become impossible. In his view it was the duty of the court to do what was 'practically just' in the circumstances, even though the precise restoration of the parties to their previous position was no longer possible. However, the majority view was to the contrary; as Henchy J put it an order of rescission would in the circumstances run counter to the object of the restoration of the *status quo ante*.

However, the principles which apply to rescission in cases of innocent misrepresentation are not as free from doubt.[20] The position where the contract has not yet been completed was examined in *Gahan v. Boland*.[21] Murphy J said that where a false representation was made, even though made in good faith and with no intention to mislead, rescission could be granted where the plaintiff could establish that 'the representation was made by the defendant with the intention of inducing the plaintiff to act thereon and secondly, that the plaintiff did in fact act or rely on the representation.'[22] This view was echoed by Henchy J in the Supreme Court where he stated that an innocent yet false representation could suffice where it was a material one made with the intention of inducing a plaintiff to act on it and where it was one of the factors which induced the plaintiff to enter into the contract. It would appear that it need not be the 'sole cause

---

20. As Keane J commented in *Doolan v. Murray* High Court 1990 No. 7753 P, 21 December 1993: 'An innocent misrepresentation . . . may afford grounds for rescission of a contract'.
21. High Court 1981 No. 4995P (Murphy J) 21 January 1983 and Supreme Court 1983 No. 37, 20 January 1984.
22. *Ibid.* at p.14.

of the transaction' and it is enough that it provides a material inducement to enter into the obligations in question.[23]

It would appear that in circumstances where the contract is complete rescission will only be granted in cases of fraudulent misrepresentation. This point was made by Lord Selborne in *Brownlie v. Campbell*[24] in the following manner: 'it is not ... the principle of equity that relief should afterwards be given against [a] conveyance, unless there be a case of fraud, or a case of misrepresentation amounting to fraud, by which the purchaser may have been deceived'. This would seem to confirm the finding made in the earlier case of *Legge v. Croker*[25] that rescission will not be granted in the case of an innocent as opposed to a fraudulent misrepresentation where the contract has been completed.

A further distinction which must be drawn between cases of fraudulent and innocent misrepresentation in the context of rescission, is that in the former case it is sufficient to show that the misrepresentation has been made 'as to any part of that which induced the party to enter into the contract which he seeks to rescind' whereas in the latter it is necessary to show that as a result there is 'a complete difference in substance' between what was contracted for and what was delivered.[26]

As a general principle, failure to disclose facts material to a contract will not constitute grounds for rescission unless by his silence a person implicitly alters the meaning of a representation previously made by him.[27] However, an exception to this general principle are contracts *uberrimae fidei* of which contracts of insurance and family settlements are the most common examples. In such cases failure to disclose any material fact may justify rescission.

Undue Influence

Gifts or agreements concluded on the basis of wholly inadequate consideration are liable to be set aside in equity where they have been given or made as a result of the exercise of undue influence over the donor or party of whom advantage has been taken. As Lindley LJ made it clear in *Allcard*

---

23. *Lecky v. Walter* [1914] 1 IR 378, 384 *per* O'Connor MR.
24. (1880) 5 App Cas 925, 937. Quoted with approval by O'Connor MR in *Lecky v. Walter* [1914] 1 IR 378, 385-386.
25. (1811) 1 Ba & B 506, 514.
26. *Seddon v. North Eastern Salt Co. Ltd* [1905] 1 Ch 326. Quoted with approval by O'Connor MR in *Lecky v. Walter* [1914] 1 IR 378, 386 and by Fitzgibbon J in *Carbin v. Somerville* [1933] IR 276, 288.
27. *Oakes v. Turquand* (1867) LR 2 HL 325.

v. Skinner[28] equity intervenes not to save individuals 'from the consequences of their own folly' but to prevent them from being victimised by others. He stated as follows in what has been described as a 'famous passage':[29]

> It would obviously be to encourage folly, recklessness, extravagance and vice if persons could get back property which they foolishly made away with, whether by giving it to charitable institutions or by bestowing it on less worthy objects. On the other hand, to protect people from being forced, tricked or misled in any way by others into parting with their property is one of the most legitimate objects of all laws; and the equitable doctrine of undue influence has grown out of and been developed by the necessity of grappling with insidious forms of spiritual tyranny and with the infinite varieties of fraud.[30]

In general the courts have shied away from any attempt to define precisely what constitutes undue influence; but it has been described as where a person has exercised 'unfair, undue and unreasonable mental control'[31] over another. Perhaps the most comprehensive formulation of the type of conduct which will amount to undue influence is that laid down by Lowry LCJ in *R. (Proctor) v. Hutton*[32] where he stated that 'the plaintiff must prove that an unfair advantage has been gained by an unconscientious use of power in the form of some unfair and improper conduct, some coercion from outside, some over reaching, some form of cheating.' Undue influence will therefore arise in circumstances where the defendant has caused the plaintiff's judgment to become clouded through some form of domination and caused him to enter a transaction disadvantageous to him.

Presumed and Actual Undue Influence

Cases of undue influence can be divided into two broad categories, those of presumed and actual undue influence. In cases of actual undue influence as Lord Browne-Wilkinson commented in *Barclays Bank plc v. O'Brien*[33] 'it is necessary for the claimant to prove affirmatively that the wrongdoer exerted undue influence on the complainant to enter into the particular transaction which is impugned'. In addition, undue influence is readily presumed in the case of certain relationships of trust and confi-

---

28. (1887) 36 Ch D 145, 182.
29. By Lord Scarman in *National Westminster Bank plc v. Morgan* [1985] AC 686, 705.
30. *Ibid.* at 182-183.
31. *Harris v. Swordy* High Court 1960 No 71 Sp (Henchy J) 21 December 1967 at p.15.
32. [1978] NI 139, 146.
33. [1994] 1 AC 180, 189.

dence. As Lowry LCJ pointed out in *R. (Proctor) v. Hutton*[34] the undue influence is of the same nature in both cases, the difference being that in the former case it is deemed to have been exercised until this is negatived on a balance of probabilities by evidence.[35] The distinction between these two classes of cases was well summarised by Costello J, as he then was, in *O'Flanagan v. Ray-Ger Ltd*[36] as follows:

> The cases where a plaintiff seeks to set aside a gift or other transaction on the ground that it was procured by undue influence have been divided into two classes; firstly those in which it can be expressly proved that undue influence was exercised, in which circumstances the Court intervenes on the principle that no one should be allowed to retain any benefit arising from his own fraud or wrongful act; secondly those in which the relations between the donor and donee have at or shortly before the execution of a gift been such as to raise a presumption that the donor had influence over the donee.

Within the category of presumed undue influence, Slade LJ in *Aboody* identified two distinct cases. The first, which he termed Class 2(A) was where certain relationships existed which as a matter of law raised the presumption that undue influence had been exercised and the second, Class 2(B) related to cases where 'the complainant proves the *de facto* existence of a relationship under which the complainant generally reposed trust and confidence in the wrongdoer'.

Some of the types of relationship in which the presumption of undue influence arises were referred to by Jones LJ in the decision of the Northern Ireland Court of Appeal in *R. (Proctor) v. Hutton*[37] as follows 'solicitor and client, trustee and *cestui que trust*, doctor and patient or religious adviser and pupil.' To this list could be added the relationships of parent and child and guardian and ward but not the relationships of husband and wife,[38] or today at any rate,[39] the relationship which exists between en-

---

34. [1978] NI 139, 146.
35. It should be noted that in *Healy v. McGillicudy* [1978] ILRM 175, 178 Costello J stated that the authorities established that 'no presumption of undue influence, however, arises in the case of wills and the burden of proving undue influence in relation to wills always rests on the person alleging it'.
36. High Court 1980 No. 2858P (Costello J) 28 April 1983 at p.18. Quoted with approval by Shanley J in *Carroll v. Carroll* [1998] 2 ILRM 218, 229. See also *Allcard v. Skinner* (1887) 36 Ch D 145, 171 *per* Cotton LJ.
37. 30 April 1979, at p. 7.
38. *Bank of Montreal v. Stuart* [1911] AC 120.
39. See the judgments of the Court of Appeal in *Zamet v. Hyman* [1961] 1 WLR 1442.

gaged couples. Some elucidation of the circumstances in which the presumption operates in the context of these various relationships is necessary. First, the case law would suggest that where a person has assumed the role of adviser, whether in a legal sense or otherwise, even where the relationship has ended in the strict sense, the confidence which arises from it may still subsist in relation to matters previously within the scope of this arrangement.[40] Equally, in the context of the relationship of parent/child or guardian/ward the presumption may continue even after the child has reached his majority or married,[41] or provided some element of control remains, where the wardship has ceased,[42] although the view expressed by the English Court of Appeal in *Re Pauling's Settlement's Trusts*[43] was that it should not continue indefinitely. As Budd J made clear in *Gregg v. Kidd*[44] the courts have never attempted to delimit the categories of relationship in which this presumption may arise as 'to do so would fetter that wide jurisdiction to relieve against all manner of constructive fraud which courts administering equitable jurisdiction have always exercised.'[45] In this case the plaintiff executor succeeded in having a voluntary settlement made by the deceased in favour of his nephew set aside on the grounds that the relationship between the testator on the one hand, and the nephew and his mother on the other hand, was such as to raise a presumption of influence which had not been rebutted.

One of the decisions most frequently referred to in this area of presumed undue influence is that of the English Court of Appeal in *Allcard v. Skinner*.[46] The plaintiff joined a sisterhood of nuns and made her will in favour of the superior of the order and also transferred large amounts of money and stock to her. When she left the order, she revoked her will but made no attempt to reclaim her property until five or six years later when she instituted proceedings claiming that it had been transferred as a result of undue influence. The court held that the gifts were made by the plain-

---

40. See *McMaster v. Byrne* [1952] 1 All ER 1362 in the context of a solicitor/client relationship.
41. *Lancashire Loans Ltd v. Black* [1934] 1 KB 380.
42. *Hylton v. Hylton* (1754) 2 Ves Sen 547.
43. [1964] Ch 303, 337.
44. [1956] IR 183, 194. So these categories can be added to as in *O'Sullivan v. Management Agency & Music Ltd* [1985] QB 428 where the presumption of undue influence was found to arise in a relationship between an inexperienced and unknown composer and performer and his manager.
45. See also the comment of Shanley J in *Carroll v. Carroll* [1998] 2 ILRM 218, 229 that 'the categories of relationship which will give rise to the presumption are never "closed"'.
46. (1887) 36 Ch D 145.

tiff, who had received no independent legal advice, as a result of pressure which she could not resist and that they were recoverable in principle. However, the majority of the Court of Appeal held that in the circumstances, the claim was barred by laches and acquiescence.

Once a relationship giving rise to a presumption of undue influence is established, and it is shown that a 'substantial benefit'[47] has been obtained, the onus lies on the donee to establish that the gift or transaction resulted from the 'free exercise of the donor's will.'[48] As Dixon J put it in *Johnson v. Butress,*[49] the evidence must establish that the gift was 'the independent and well-understood act of a man in a position to exercise a free judgment based on information as full as that of the donee.' The manner in which this presumption may be rebutted relates to two main issues; first the question of whether independent legal advice has been received and secondly, whether it can be shown that the decision to make the gift or transfer was 'a spontaneous and independent act'[50] or that the donor 'acted of his own free will.'[51] Where independent legal advice has been given, it will tend to rebut the presumption of undue influence, even where the donor is in a particularly vulnerable position *vis-à-vis* the donee.[52] On the other hand, while it would appear that it is not essential that independent legal advice be given in order to rebut the presumption,[53] equally the complete lack of any such advice may be a deciding factor in whether this will be achieved.[54] Black J made it clear in the course of his judgment in *Provincial Bank of Ireland v. McKeever*[55] that in certain circumstances even where independent advice has been given and rejected, the fact of it having been given may suffice to rebut the presumption of undue influence, although this

---

47. *Johnson v. Buttress* (1936) 56 CLR 113, 134. See also the judgment of Lowry LCJ in *R. (Proctor) v. Hutton* [1978] NI 139, 147 where he referred to the making of a 'substantial gift'.
48. *Gregg v. Kidd* [1956] IR 183, 196.
49. (1936) 56 CLR 113, 134-35.
50. *Re Brocklehurst's Estate* [1978] Ch 14.
51. *Gregg v. Kidd* [1956] IR 183, 196. See also the *dicta* of Lord Hailsham in *Inche Noriah v. Shaik Allie Bin Omar* [1929] AC 127, 135.
52. See e.g. *Leonard v. Leonard* [1988] ILRM 245 where a transfer by an vulnerable elderly lady to her son was upheld despite a claim of undue influence in circumstances where she had obtained proper independent legal advice. It should also be pointed out that MacKenzie J stated that he was satisfied that 'the coercion on [the plaintiff] was because of her situation and was not of [the defendant's] making'. In his view she was alone, afraid and unable to work the land and needed the company and support which transferring the land to her son would bring her.
53. *Provincial Bank of Ireland v. McKeever* [1941] IR 471, 485.
54. *McMakin v. Hibernian Bank* [1905] 1 IR 306.
55. [1941] IR 471, 485. Although note the comments of Farwell J in *Powell v. Powell* [1900] 1 Ch 243, 246.

will not always be the case, as it may only have been rejected as a result of influence exerted. In the view of Black J 'one cannot expect absolute disproof of undue influence' and he suggested that it is sufficient to establish 'a reasonable probability of the exercise of independent will founded upon adequate understanding'.[56] In *McKeever* the sons and widow of the deceased settlor were persuaded by trustees to execute a mortgage to secure an overdraft which these trustees had run up. Black J accepted that on the facts the presumption of undue influence had been rebutted although the only legal advice which they had received was from the trustees' solicitor, who was the sons' uncle. Black J stated that viewing the evidence as a whole, he was satisfied that the consequences of the mortgage transaction had been sufficiently understood and he allowed the claim of the plaintiff bank.

A useful recent summary of the relevant principles in this area is contained in the judgment of Shanley J in *Carroll v. Carroll*.[57] The plaintiffs, who were the daughters and personal representatives of an elderly donor sought to have a transfer of a pub and residential accommodation set aside on the grounds that it had been procured by undue influence and was an improvident transaction. After his wife's death, the donor had transferred the property to his son without disclosing this fact to his daughters. The donor and his son both subsequently died and tensions arose between the plaintiffs and the son's widow, the defendant, which led to the bringing of proceedings to have the original transfer set aside. The donor had discussed making the transfer to his son on two occasions with the solicitor who effected it, although the latter was in reality acting for both parties. While the donor was mentally alert at that time, he was subject to a number of physical infirmities which made him increasingly dependent on others. The plaintiffs submitted that the relationship between the donor and donee was such as to raise a presumption of undue influence, which they argued had not been rebutted. The defendant conceded that the relationship between the parties did give rise to a presumption of undue influence but submitted that it had been rebutted in the circumstances. In setting out the relevant legal principles, Shanley J stated that the law will not concern itself with insignificant transactions and that the presumption of undue influence will only arise where one party has derived a substantial benefit from the transaction. In relation to the circumstances in which the presumption may be rebutted, he stated as follows:

---

56. *Ibid.* at 485.
57. [1998] 2 ILRM 218.

> Where the presumption exists, it may be rebutted by evidence which
> establishes on the balance of probability that the transaction was the
> consequence of the exercise of the donor of his own free will and
> not the result of undue influence. Such evidence may be evidence
> that the donor had independent legal advice — or competent and
> honest lay advice.[58]

Shanley J stated that he was satisfied that the significant benefit obtained
by the donee from the transaction and the relationship between the parties
were such as to raise a presumption of undue influence. He concluded that
he was not satisfied that the defendant had established as a matter of probability that the transaction was the result of the free exercise of the donor's
will such as to rebut presumption of undue influence. Shanley J stated that
while he accepted the evidence that the donor was mentally alert at the
time he made the transfer, he was not satisfied that he had had the necessary independent advice, whether it was from a legal adviser or from a
competent and qualified lay person, such as would persuade him that the
transaction was made of his own free will.

It is important to stress that the presumption of undue influence does
not arise in the context of all relationships which could be described as
'fiduciary' in nature,[59] and that whether a presumption will arise in a particular type of relationship may depend on the facts of the individual case. So,
in *Lloyds Bank Ltd v. Bundy*[60] the presumption was held to apply to the
relationship of banker and client in circumstances where a father had relied entirely on the advice of his bank manager in mortgaging his house as
security for a guarantee relating to his son's debts. However, *Bundy* was
distinguished as turning on special facts by the House of Lords in *National Westminster Bank plc v. Morgan*[61] in which a wife claimed that a
bank manager had exerted undue influence over her to obtain her signature in relation to a mortgage agreement relating to the parties' house,
which was concluded in order to secure a loan to her husband. The House
of Lords was not satisfied that the relationship between Mrs Morgan and
the bank went beyond the normal business relationship of banker and cus-

---

58. *Ibid.* at 229. While it was not relevant in the *Carroll* decision, it is interesting that
    Shanley J adopted the view of Lord Hailsham in *Inche Noriah v. Shaik Allie Bin
    Omar* [1929] AC 127, 135 that independent *legal* advice was not an essential ele-
    ment in rebutting the presumption and that independent advice from a suitably quali-
    fied person could suffice.
59. E.g. *Re Coomber* [1911] 1 Ch 723.
60. [1975] QB 326.
61. [1985] AC 686.

tomer and held that the manager had never assumed a role which would raise the presumption.

Undue Influence and Third Parties

The principles considered above also extend to cases where the party exerting influence does not benefit directly from his conduct and where the person over whom he has exercised this influence enters into obligations to a third party as a result. This issue has recently become very relevant in the context of obligations to financial institutions entered into by wives allegedly as a result of influence exerted over them by their husbands.

Several questions arise in this area; first should the husband/wife relationship give rise to any presumption or should wives be treated as a 'specially protected class'. Secondly, in what circumstances will a debtor be found to be acting as agent of the bank in procuring a surety's consent and thirdly, in the absence of actual knowledge on the part of the bank of the debtor's improper conduct, in what circumstances will the bank be fixed with constructive notice of this conduct?

In relation to the first of these questions, while it appears to be accepted that the relationship of husband and wife does not give rise to any relationship of undue influence,[62] there have been suggestions that wives constitute a special class which deserves protection in these circumstances. This approach was adopted by the majority of the Court of Appeal in *Barclays Bank plc v. O'Brien*[63] where Scott LJ made it clear that the likelihood of a husband exerting influence over his wife, which was the original justification for the 'tenderness of equity' towards married women who gave their property as security for their husband's debts, was still a relevant consideration.[64] He said that if the natural and probable consequences of the relationship between the surety and debtor was that the former would exercise influence over the latter, a bank might be liable where the surety's consent was improperly obtained, if it was aware of this relationship and the consequent likelihood of influence and failed to take reasonable steps to ensure that the surety had given a true and informed consent to the transaction. This 'special equity' theory was referred to by Lord Browne-Wilkinson in the course of his speech in the House of Lords

---

62. *Bank of Montreal v. Stuart* [1911] AC 120, 137; *Bank of Credit and Commerce International SA v. Aboody* [1990] 1 QB 923, 953.
63. [1992] 3 WLR 593. See Dixon [1993] CLJ 24.
64. See also the reference made by Dixon J in the decision of the High Court of Australia in *Yerkey v. Jones* (1930) 63 CLR 649 to the 'invalidating tendency' applied by the courts to transactions between husbands and wives. See further Burton (1997) 4 Comm LP 120.

as meaning that 'equity affords special protection to a protected class of surety viz. those where the relationship between the debtor and the surety is such that influence by the debtor over the surety and reliance by the surety on the debtor are natural features of the relationship'.

The approach of Scott LJ was accepted by Geoghegan J in the High Court in *Bank of Ireland v. Smyth* in holding that the wife's consent to a charge over the family home was not a true consent and that the charge was therefore void. More recently the Supreme Court has suggested in *Bank of Nova Scotia v. Hogan*[65] that it may be possible to identify circumstances which would more readily raise a presumption in favour of a wife than any other third party. Murphy J stated that notwithstanding the fact that the relationship between husband and wife has been held not to raise a presumption of undue influence some special status does appear to have been accorded to wives in a number of decisions. He concluded that whilst the matrimonial relationship as such did not give rise to a presumption of undue influence,[66] in such cases a presumption might more readily be raised in favour of a wife than any outside party.

The second and third questions raised above, relating to agency and notice respectively, have been considered by the House of Lords in two recent decisions. In *Barclays Bank plc v. O'Brien*[67] a wife had joined in a charge over the family home jointly owned by her and her husband as security for overdraft facilities extended by the plaintiff bank to a company in which the husband had an interest. The House of Lords found that as a general principle, where a wife was induced to stand as surety for her husband's debt as a result of his undue influence, misrepresentation or some other legal wrong, she had an equity against him to set aside the transaction and this right would be enforceable against a third party who had actual or constructive notice of the circumstances giving rise to the equity or for whom the husband was acting as agent. In the circumstances, it was held that the bank was fixed with constructive notice of the husband's wrongful misrepresentation and the wife was entitled as against the bank to set aside the legal charge on the matrimonial home securing the husband's liability to the bank. Lord Browne-Wilkinson said that construc-

---

65. [1996] 3 IR 239.
66. Although note that later in his judgment, Murphy J commented (at p.249) that 'assuming, without deciding, that married women in this jurisdiction may in certain circumstances enjoy as against their husbands a presumption that undue influence was exercised. . . .'
67. [1994] 1 AC 180. A number of commentators have written about this decision and its consequences, see Berg [1994] LMCLQ 34; Allen (1995) 58 MLR 87; Lawson [1995] CLJ 280; Sparkes [1995] Conv 250; Felhberg (1996) 59 MLR 675; Richardson (1996) 16 LS 368.

tive notice will exist when a creditor is put on inquiry e.g. by the fact that the transaction is not on its face to the financial advantage of the borrower, and if having been put on inquiry, the lender fails to take reasonable steps to ensure that the borrower understands the nature of the transaction. In terms of what amounts to taking reasonable steps, Lord Browne-Wilkinson stated as follows:

> [A] creditor will have satisfied these requirements if it insists that the wife attend a private meeting (in the absence of the husband) with a representative of the creditor at which she is told of the extent of her liability as surety, warned of the risk she is running and urged to take independent legal advice, If these steps are taken in my judgment the creditor will have taken such reasonable steps as are necessary to preclude a subsequent claim that it had constructive notice of the wife's rights.[68]

The alternative approach, namely the agency theory was also considered by Lord Browne-Wilkinson although he criticised it as having developed in an artificial way. Essentially where it applies, the wrongdoing of the husband will be imputed to the creditor if the former can be regarded as being the agent of the latter in obtaining the wife's consent to the transaction.

It is important to note that in *O'Brien* the bank was held to have constructive notice of the husband's improper conduct because the use of the wife's interest to secure a loan to a company in which she had no interest was *prima facie* not to her advantage, a fact which immediately should have put the bank on inquiry. It was this fact which distinguished the result in *O'Brien* from that in *CIBC Mortgages plc v. Pitt*,[69] where the loan was on its face to both husband and wife for their joint benefit and therefore not apparently to the wife's disadvantage. In *Pitt* the first named defendant persuaded his wife, the second named defendant, to execute a legal charge over their house in favour of the plaintiff in order to obtain a loan to purchase shares which he told her would improve their standard of living. After the stock market crash in 1987, the plaintiff brought proceedings for possession of the matrimonial home when the husband fell into arrears with the payments due under the loan. The Court of Appeal dismissed the wife's appeal against the finding of the trial judge in the plaintiff's favour and held that since the transaction was not manifestly disadvantageous to

---

68. [1994] 1 AC 180 at 196-197.
69. [1994] 1 AC 200.

the wife, she could not establish undue influence and in any event since the plaintiff did not have any actual or constructive notice of any irregularity, the charge was valid as against the plaintiff. In the House of Lords, counsel for the wife argued that the Court of Appeal in *Bank of Credit and Commerce International SA v. Aboody*[70] had erred in extending the need to show manifest disadvantage in cases of actual as opposed to presumed undue influence. Lord Browne-Wilkinson agreed and said that he had no doubt that this requirement laid down in *National Westminster Bank plc v. Morgan,*[71] does not extend to cases of actual undue influence.[72] However the House of Lords held that as the transaction was not *prima facie* disadvantageous to the wife, the bank was not put on inquiry and was not affected by constructive notice of her husband's undue influence and could therefore enforce the security.

An important feature of the decision of the House of Lords was the finding that a person who could prove the exercise of actual undue influence by another in carrying out a transaction was entitled as of right against the other to have the transaction set aside without proof of manifest disadvantage. This had proved to be a major stumbling block to the plaintiff in *Bank of Credit and Commerce International SA v. Aboody*[73] where the Court of Appeal had held that a party who established that a transaction was induced by undue influence was not entitled to have it set aside in reliance on the doctrine without also proving that the transaction was manifestly disadvantageous to him.

Dixon[74] has suggested that once undue influence has been found to exist, whether proved or presumed, the victim should be granted a remedy forthwith. However, the requirement of manifest disadvantage in cases of presumed undue influence would appear to have been retained in England as a number of recent decisions illustrate. As Millett LJ commented in *Dunbar Bank plc v. Nadeem*[75] 'a person who can prove the exercise of actual undue influence by another in respect to a transaction is entitled to have the transaction set aside without proof of manifest disadvantage . . . [b]ut such proof is required when the exercise of undue influence is only

---

70. [1990] 1 QB 923.
71. [1985] AC 686.
72. However, Fehlberg has argued (1994) 57 MLR 467, 473 that by effectively saying that the transaction must not on its face be to the financial advantage of the wife in order for constructive notice to arise, the 'manifest disadvantage' requirement rejected in *Pitt* is being resurrected in another guise.
73. [1990] 1 QB 923.
74. [1994] CLJ 21, 22.
75. [1998] 3 All ER 876, 882. See also *Mahoney v. Purnell* [1996] 3 All ER 61, 82-83.

presumed'. Similarly in *Cheese v. Thomas,*[76] although the requirement of manifest disadvantage was given a fairly flexible interpretation, it was nevertheless insisted upon by the Court of Appeal. The elderly plaintiff agreed to give the defendant, his great nephew, £43,000 towards the purchase of a house in an area in which he wanted to live. The defendant contributed £40,000 by borrowing on the security of the house which was purchased in his sole name, the arrangement being that he would own it outright on the plaintiff's death. When the defendant failed to pay the mortgage instalments and the house had to be sold at a considerable loss, the plaintiff sought to have the transaction set aside. A relationship of presumed influence was conceded by the defendant but he contested the fact that the plaintiff had suffered manifest disadvantage. The Court of Appeal held that the plaintiff had suffered manifest disadvantage, as while he stood to gain to an extent, this was 'manifestly ... outweighed by the drawbacks in the arrangement'. However, the Court of Appeal held that the loss should be shared in the proportions the parties had contributed to the initial purchase price and stressed its concern to achieve practical justice for both parties and not for the plaintiff alone. Chen-Wishart[77] has commented that the court's relaxation of the requirement of manifest disadvantage in *Cheese* made *prima facie* relief for presumed undue influence easier to establish, although in the instant case, this was counterbalanced by the court's approach to the assessment of the appropriate amount of relief.

The circumstances in which a bank will be fixed with constructive notice of undue influence or misrepresentation need to be examined and this question has been considered in a number of recent decisions by the English Court of Appeal.[78] In *Massey v. Midland Bank plc,*[79] a bank was put on inquiry by the circumstances in which a woman had agreed to provide security for an overdraft granted to a business venture in which a man with whom she had a long-standing relationship was involved. However, the Court of Appeal was satisfied that the bank had taken reasonable steps to ensure that her agreement had been properly obtained and held that it was not fixed with constructive notice of the misrepresentation made in this case. Steyn LJ commented that the guidance provided by the House of

---

76. [1994] 1 WLR 129. See Mee [1994] LMCLQ 330
77. (1994) 110 LQR 173.
78. See Mee [1995] CLJ 536. Note that in *Barclays Bank plc v. Boulter* [1997] 1 All ER 1002, 1009 Mummery LJ pointed out that it is for the bank or other creditor to prove that it did not have constructive notice of any equity asserted by the surety. See also *Banco Exterior Internacional v. Mann* [1995] 1 All ER 936, 946 *per* Hobhouse LJ.
79. [1995] 1 All ER 929. See Mee [1995] Conv 148.

Lords in *O'Brien* 'should not be mechanically applied'[80] and said that provided the lender had taken alternative steps to achieve Lord Browne-Wilkinson's aim, failure to follow his guidelines precisely would not be fatal to the creditor's case. In this instance there had been no separate meeting between the surety and and creditor's representative unattended by the debtor but the creditor had required her to be independently advised. Steyn LJ was satisfied that she had received such independent legal advice[81] and that the creditor had therefore complied with the substance of Lord Browne-Wilkinson's guidance.[82] It should be noted that Millett LJ has recently commented in the course of his judgment in *Credit Lyonnais Bank Nederland NV v. Burch*[83] that independent legal advice is 'neither always necessary nor always sufficient' and that the result in such cases 'does not depend mechanically on the presence or absence of legal advice'.

A series of cases appeared to confirm the principle that a financial institution is entitled to rely on the fact that the solicitor in question has undertaken his task in a sufficiently independent manner. In *Banco Exterior Internacional v. Mann*[84] the majority of the Court of Appeal accepted that where a solicitor had certified that he had explained the nature of the charge to the wife, there were no grounds for fixing the bank with constructive notice of her husband's undue influence. Morritt LJ found that the bank was entitled to rely on the fact that the solicitor in question had undertaken this task in a sufficiently independent manner despite the fact that he also acted for the company, owned and controlled by the husband, to whom the loan had been made.[85] As Hoffmann LJ commented in *Bank*

---

80. *Ibid.* at 934. Steyn LJ stated that this guidance 'was intended to strike a fair balance between the need to protect wives (and others in a like position) whose judgmental capacity was impaired and the need to avoid unnecessary impediments to using the matrimonial home as security'.

81. However, it should be noted that earlier in his judgment (at p.931) Steyn LJ mentioned that both debtor and surety had visited this independent legal adviser together and that the solicitor did not see the surety alone but said that he explained the nature of the transaction to her and that she understood it.

82. This can be contrasted with the decision of the Court of Appeal in *TSB Bank plc v. Camfield* [1995] 1 All ER 951 where the bank was fixed with constructive notice of a husband's representation because it had failed in the view of the court to take reasonable steps to ensure that the wife understood the nature of the charge. While the bank had stipulated that the wife should be given independent advice, in fact she was not separately advised from her husband, and the wife executed the charge under the false impression that it was for a limited amount.

83. [1997] 1 All ER 144, 156.

84. [1995] 1 All ER 936. See Dunn [1995] Conv 325.

85. The result in this case can be contrasted with the conclusion reached by the Court of Appeal in *TSB Bank plc v. Camfield* [1995] 1 All ER 951 where the bank was fixed

of Baroda v. Rayarel:[86]

> If a prospective surety deals with a bank through a solicitor, the bank is entitled to assume that the solicitor has given her appropriate advice. If there is a possibility of a conflict of interest between the surety and the other parties whom the solicitor is also advising, the bank is entitled to assume that the solicitor will have told her that she was entitled to take independent advice.

This approach was followed by the Court of Appeal in *Barclays Bank plc v. Thomson;*[87] as Simon Brown LJ has commented: 'I can see no good reason whatever why a bank, perhaps conscientiously instructing solicitors to give independent advice to a signatory who might otherwise go unadvised, should thereby be disabled from relying on the solicitors' certificate that such advice has been properly given'. In this case the court held that the bank was entitled to rely on a solicitor's assurance that he had discharged his professional duty towards the wife and had given her independent advice, although the solicitors' firm in question could have been regarded as having been retained by the bank to carry out their instructions with regard to completing the loan transaction and had also acted for the surety's husband's in relation to his business.

It is interesting to note that a differently constituted Court of Appeal effectively held a few months later in *Royal Bank of Scotland v. Etridge*[88] that a solicitor's certificate that he had explained the nature of the transaction to a surety wife was not conclusive. Hobhouse LJ stated that in his view the bank had appointed the solicitor to act as its agent in performing this function and that it was therefore responsible for ensuring that he discharged his duty. So when the wife disputed the fact that she had received adequate independent advice the Court of Appeal accepted that the matter could not be disposed of summarily and that it gave rise to a triable issue. The essential difference between the reasoning employed in these two decisions is that in the view of Simon Brown LJ in *Thomson* the solicitor is regarded as acting exclusively for the surety when advising her, although he may well have been retained by the bank to do so, whereas in

---

with constructive notice of a husband's misrepresentation because it had failed, in the view of the court, to take reasonable steps to ensure that the wife understood the nature of the charge.

86. [1995] 2 FLR 376.
87. [1997] 4 All ER 816.
88. [1997] 3 All ER 628.

Etridge, Hobhouse LJ was satisfied that the solicitor was acting as the bank's agent in so doing.

It remains to be seen whether this view that the court can look behind a solicitor's certificate where he has been instructed by a financial institution to act on its behalf will win support. In a recent comment on these decisions, Price has expressed the view that the reasoning and result in *Thomson* are to be preferred to those in *Etridge* and that the latter decision should not be followed.[89]

A further point which should be made is that in *Barclays Bank plc v. O'Brien*, Lord Browne-Wilkinson stated that in an exceptional case where a solicitor knows of additional facts rendering the presence of undue influence probable and not just possible, the creditor must insist that the surety be separately advised. The decision of the Court of Appeal in *Credit Lyonnais Bank Nederland NV v. Burch*[90] would appear to be an example of this type of case. The transaction in question was one in which a junior employee mortgaged her flat as security for an increase in the overdraft of a company which employed her at the request of her employer who was the main shareholder in the company. The court found that this transaction was manifestly disadvantageous to the employee and that the presumption of undue influence on the part of her employer was irresistible. In the circumstances it was held that the bank had not taken reasonable steps to avoid being fixed with constructive notice of the employer's undue influence as the extent of the employee's liability had not been explained to her, nor had she received independent legal advice. In the view of the court the circumstances of the case were such that the bank should have insisted that she take independent legal advice before entering into the charge, which it had not done and the court upheld the finding that the transaction should be set aside.

A final question which must be addressed is the type of relationship which the principles laid down in *Barclays Bank plc v. O'Brien* apply to. In the course of his speech in that case, Lord Browne-Wilkinson stressed that the guidelines which he was laying down were not restricted to cases involving spouses and said that they also applied 'if and only if, the creditor is aware that the surety is co-habiting with the principal debtor'.[91] This

---

89. (1998) 114 LQR 186, 187.
90. [1997] 1 All ER 144. See Hooley and O'Sullivan [1997] LMCLQ 17; Tijo (1997) 113 LQR 10 and Chen-Wishart [1997] CLJ 60.
91. [1994] 1 AC 180, 198. Lawson has suggested [1995] CLJ 280, 282 that this should be interpreted as meaning that a creditor should be put on inquiry only if he is actually aware that the surety is co-habiting with the debtor as otherwise it would require creditors to act as 'busybodies'.

requirement of co-habitation was relaxed in *Midland Bank v. Massey*[92] where although the parties had never married or co-habited, they had enjoyed a stable 'sexual and emotional relationship' for many years and had had two children together. Steyn LJ, while recognising that it would constitute an extension of the approach laid down by Lord Browne-Wilkinson said that he had no doubt that 'in terms of impairment of [the surety's] judgmental capacity, this case should be approached as if she was a wife or co-habitee of [the debtor]'.[93]

It should be noted that in *O'Brien*, Lord Browne-Wilkinson stated that the principles he was setting out applied 'where, to the creditor's knowledge, the surety reposes trust and confidence in the principal debtor in relation to his or her financial affairs'.[94] An example of such a relationship is that which existed between an employer and a junior employee in *Credit Lyonnais Bank Nederland NV v. Burch;*[95] as Nourse LJ commented: 'although the relationship between the debtor and the mortgagor was not that of persons living together but employer and employee, it may broadly be said to fall under *Barclays Bank plc v. O'Brien*' and the court proceeded to apply these principles in order to determine whether the bank should be fixed with constructive notice of the employer's wrongdoing.

It remains to consider how the *O'Brien* principles have fared in Ireland where they have been considered in two recent decisions. The first of these, *Bank of Ireland v Smyth*,[96] arose in the context of a wife signing a consent form for the purposes of the Family Home Protection Act 1976 in circumstances where her husband had charged their house and land as security for all present and future liabilities owed to the plaintiffs. Counsel for the wife, the second named defendant, submitted that a consent by a wife under the Family Home Protection Act 1976 to a mortgage or charge in favour of the bank was not valid unless the wife understood the nature and consequences of the transaction and in this regard relied on the decision of the Court of Appeal in *O'Brien*. Geoghegan J stated that he be-

---

92. [1995] 1 All ER 929.
93. *Ibid.* at 933. Mee approves of this approach (see [1995] Conv 148, 150) and suggests, along the same lines as Lawson (*supra*) that if the lender is not actually aware of the nature of the relationship between a surety and a debtor who are not co-habiting, it is not put on inquiry. He asserts that any other conclusion 'would place the lender on a slippery slope' (*ibid.* at 151) and would appear to give constructive notice a far wider scope than that envisaged by Lord Browne-Wilkinson in *O'Brien*.
94. [1994] 1 AC 180, 196.
95. [1997] 1 All ER 144.
96. [1993] ILRM 790 (HC); [1995] 2 IR 459 (SC). See generally Sanfey (1994) 1 Comm LP 99; Doyle (1994) 88 GILSI 187; Sanfey (1996) 3 Comm LP 31 and Mee (1996) 14 ILT (ns) 188; 209.

lieved that decision represented the law in this jurisdiction also and applying the criteria laid down by Scott LJ in *O'Brien* he said that it was obvious that the bank manager was well aware of the husband and wife
relationship with the consequent inherent likelihood of influence and reliance. In his view, the manager should have realized that what he had told
the wife had been inadequate and he had not taken sufficient steps to ensure that she fully understood the transaction; in particular he had not
advised her to take independent legal advice. Geoghegan J concluded that
while there was a document purporting to be a consent there was in fact no
consent within the meaning of the 1976 Act and that the charge over the
property was therefore void. The Supreme Court dismissed the plaintiff's
appeal and held that as the second named defendant's consent was not a
fully informed one — she believed that the charge affected only the land
and not the family home — it was therefore invalid. Blayney J stated that
as the bank ought reasonably to have made inquiries which would have
revealed the wife's lack of consent, the bank was treated as having constructive notice of what the enquires would have revealed. While Blayney
J rejected the argument that the bank had a duty to explain the charge fully
to the wife or to suggest that she should obtain independent legal advice,
he stated that in order to protect its own interests, the bank should have
taken these steps, since if they had it was unlikely that her consent could
have been challenged.

Sanfey has commented that the merit of the Supreme Court decision is
that a bank now knows exactly what it must do to prove a consent valid for
the purposes of the Family Home Protection Act 1976.[97] However, he
stresses that while the decision clarifies the position of banks and the
spouses of debtors who have given consent to the creation of a security
over the family home, its reasoning cannot be extended to the general situation where a spouse has acted as a guarantor of liabilities or created a
charge over assets in respect of the other spouse's liabilities. Mee similarly comments that the Supreme Court decision throws little light on the
impact of third party undue influence or misrepresentation on the validity
of bank guarantees.[98] He puts forward the view that the requirement of
informed consent might suggest a similarly paternalistic approach should
be taken to bank guarantees but points out that Blayney J's invocation of
the concept of constructive notice might indicate a preference for the notice based approach of the House of Lords in *O'Brien*.

Another recent decision which did provide the Supreme Court with

---

97. (1996) 3 Comm LP 31, 34.
98. (1996) 14 ILT (ns) 209, 210.

the opportunity to consider the question of the effect of third party undue influence or misrepresentation on the validity of bank guarantees was *Bank of Nova Scotia v. Hogan*.[99] The first named defendant borrowed money from the plaintiff on the security of equitable mortgages created over properties which he owned. Subsequently in return for releasing the security over two of these properties, the plaintiff took an equitable mortgage over a further property owned by the second named defendant, who was the first named defendant's wife. Prior to depositing the title deeds, a solicitor from a firm which had acted for the second named defendant and her husband in the past, and also for the bank from time to time, explained to her that the plaintiff would be entitled to sell the property in the event of her husband's default. When the plaintiff subsequently brought proceedings to enforce the security, the second named defendant alleged that the security had been improperly obtained. In finding for the plaintiff, Keane J concluded that the legal advice received by the second named defendant had been adequate in all the circumstances.

In considering the appeal brought by the defendants against this order, Murphy J said that while there was a similarity between the facts of the case before him and those in *Bank of Ireland v. Smyth*, the fundamental differences between them rendered the decision of little assistance, although he concluded that the decision of the House of Lords in *O'Brien* was 'both relevant and helpful'. Murphy J concluded that whilst the matrimonial relationship as such did not give rise to a presumption of undue influence, it might be possible to identify circumstances which would more readily raise a presumption in favour of a wife than any outside party. He pointed out the essential issue in this case was the dispute between the rights of the creditor and the wife and in relation to this, he was prepared to adopt and apply the principles of Lord Browne-Wilkinson in *O'Brien* referred to above. These were as follows:

> A wife who has been induced to stand as a surety for her husband's debts by his undue influence, misrepresentation or some other legal wrong has an equity against him to set aside that transaction. Under the ordinary principles of equity, her right to set aside that transaction will be enforceable against third parties (e.g. against a creditor) if either the husband was acting as the third party's agent or the third party had actual or constructive notice of the facts giving rise to her equity.[100]

---

99. High Court 1991 No. 97 Sp (Keane J) 21 December 1992; [1996] 3 IR 239.
100. [1994] 1 AC 180, 195. Quoted with approval [1996] 2 IR 239, 248.

Murphy J stated that even assuming — and he did not decide this issue — that married women in this jurisdiction might in certain circumstances enjoy as against their husbands a presumption that undue influence had been exercised, the fatal flaw in the case before him was that no undue influence was exercised by the husband; the wife had no equity against him to have the transaction set aside and therefore she had no equity on which she could rely to defeat the claim of the bank. Even if such equity had existed, Murphy J was still satisfied that the availability of appropriate legal advice to the wife would have afforded the bank a defence in relation to any claim by her in respect of an equity to set aside the transaction. Furthermore, he was satisfied that there was no evidence to support the claim that the bank itself had exercised undue influence over the wife; the relationship did not give rise to a presumption of undue influence and there was no suggestion of dealings which would raise an inference of wrongdoing.

It was therefore accepted by the Supreme Court in *Bank of Nova Scotia v. Hogan* that where a wife furnishes a guarantee as security for her husband's debts as a result of his undue influence, misrepresentation or some other legal wrong, she has an equity against him to set aside the transaction which may be enforceable against a third party, who had actual or constructive notice of the circumstances giving rise to the equity or for whom the husband was acting as agent. While the facts of this case did not demand any detailed examination by the Supreme Court of the circumstances in which a bank may be deemed to have constructive notice of any wrongdoing, the *dicta* of Murphy J would certainly suggest that the availability of appropriate legal advice to the wife would have been sufficient to enable the bank to reject any claim that they should have been fixed with notice of any impropriety. Clearly to avoid the application of the *O'Brien* principles as adopted by the Supreme Court lending institutions should ensure that where they are put on inquiry by the circumstances of a transaction that they have taken adequate steps to ensure that the wife's agreement has been properly obtained and this requirement should be met by ensuring that an adequate explanation of the potential consequences of her actions have been explained to her by a legal adviser. As stated, it is clear from the judgment of Murphy J that the fact that the wife had received 'appropriate independent legal advice' would have provided the bank with a defence against any equity to set aside the transaction. Whether these words could be used to describe advice received from a firm of solicitors which had previously acted, not only on the wife's behalf but also for her husband and even the bank, is open to some doubt, particularly in view of the differing views expressed by the English Court of Appeal on this point.[101] While the Supreme Court was not required to address this latter issue, the difficulties which such transactions may give rise to would suggest that such a practice it at least undesirable and that attention should be given to ensuring that the advice is not only 'appropriate' but also 'independent' if the spectre of constructive notice is to avoided.[102]

Unconscionable Transactions

A transaction may be set aside in equity where one party is at a serious disadvantage by reason of poverty, ignorance or some other factor such as old age, so that unfair advantage may be taken of that party.[103] Equity will intervene particularly where a transfer of property is made for no consideration at all[104] or at an undervalue and where the transferee acts without the benefit of independent legal advice. The basis of this principle which was set out by Lord Hatherley in *O'Rorke v. Bolingbroke*[105] was summarised as follows by Gavan Duffy J in *Grealish v. Murphy*:[106] 'Equity comes to the rescue whenever the parties to a contract have not met upon equal terms'. A more specific summary of the circumstances which will warrant equitable intervention on this basis was provided by Kitto J in the Australian decision of *Blomley v. Ryan*,[107] namely: 'whenever one party to a transaction is at a special disadvantage in dealing with the other party because

---

101. See *Barclays Bank v. Thomson* [1997] 4 All ER 816; *Royal Bank of Scotland v. Etridge* [1997] 4 All ER 816.
102. Note that Mee has also suggested (1996) ILT (ns) 209, 210 that that common sense dictates a cautious approach so lenders should follow the 'reasonable steps' proposed in *O'Brien*.
103. See generally Clark (1980) 31 NILQ 114; Capper 'Unconscionable bargains' in *One Hundred and Fifty Years of Irish Law* (1996) eds., Dawson, Greer and Ingram p.45 *et seq.* As Nourse LJ commented in *Credit Lyonnais Bank Nederland NV v. Burch* [1997] 1 All ER 144, 151: 'Equity's jurisdiction to relieve against such transactions, although more rarely exercised in modern times, is at least as venerable as its jurisdiction to relieve against those procured by undue influence'.
104. Some doubt was raised about this point by the decision in *Langton v. Langton* [1995] 2 FLR 890, in which A.W.H. Charles QC expressed the view that the doctrine of unconscionable bargains does not apply to gifts. However, as Capper has pointed out [1996] Conv 308, 314 'the weight of principle and authority is against him' and he has recently commented (1998) 114 LQR 479, 492 that 'the better view . . . is that gifts are equally subject to the doctrine of unconscionability and that this concept rather than one of unconscionable bargain should be used in future to avoid confusion'.
105. (1877) 2 App Cas 814, 823.
106. [1946] IR 35, 49. Quoted with approval by McLoughlin J in *Haverty v. Brooks* [1970] IR 214, 219.
107. (1956) 99 CLR 362, 415. See also the *dicta* of Fullgar J at 405 and of Sullivan MR in *Slator v. Nolan* (1876) IR 11 Eq 367, 386 where he spoke of undue advantage being taken 'by reason of distress or recklessness or wildness or want of care' and

illness, ignorance, inexperience, impaired faculties, financial need or other circumstances affect his ability to conserve his own interests, and the other party unconscientiously takes advantage of the opportunity thus placed in his hands.' In *Blomley* a sale of a property at an undervalue was set aside in circumstances where the same solicitor had acted for both parties and where the vendor was elderly and poorly educated and the purchasers had taken advantage of his liking for rum. Similarly, in *McGonigle v. Black*[108] factors which were considered by Barr J as contributing towards what he regarded as an improvident transaction from the point of view of the vendor were 'a combination of bereavement, inability to cope, loneliness, alcoholism and ill-health', which made him vulnerable to manipulation.

According to Hanbury and Martin[109] three elements must be established before equity will intervene, and it is helpful to set these out. First, one party must be at a serious disadvantage to the other by reason of poverty, ignorance or otherwise, so that circumstances existed of which unfair advantage could be taken; secondly, the transaction must be at an undervalue; and thirdly there must be a lack of independent legal advice. One of the most comprehensive statements of the essential preconditions for setting aside a transaction on grounds of unconscionability is set out in the judgment on Peter Millett QC, as he then was in *Alec Lobb (Garages) Ltd v. Total Oil (Great Britain) Ltd*:[110]

> First, one party has been at a serious disadvantage to the other, whether through poverty, or ignorance, or lack of advice, or otherwise, so that circumstances existed of which unfair advantage could be taken. Second, this weakness of the one party has been exploited by the other in some morally culpable manner...And third, the resulting transaction has been not merely hard or improvident, but overreaching and oppressive. . . . In short, there must, in my judgment, be some impropriety, both in the conduct of the stronger party and in the terms of the transaction itself . . . which in the traditional phrase 'shocks the conscience of the court' and makes it against equity and good conscience for the stronger party to retain the benefit of a transaction he has unfairly obtained.

In considering the first of these requirements it is clear that some unfair

---

said that transactions resting on such unconscionable dealing would not be allowed to stand.
108. High Court Circuit Appeal (Barr J) 14 November 1988.
109. *Modern Equity* (15th ed., 1997) p.836-837.
110. [1983] 1 WLR 87, 94-95. (Reversed in part [1985] 1 WLR 173).

advantage must have been gained 'by an unconscientious use of power by a stronger party against a weaker'.[111] On the second point, as Hooley and O'Sullivan have confirmed: 'the courts have repeatedly stressed that it is not sufficient to show that a bargain was a harsh or unreasonable one — it must also be shown that the stronger party acted reprehensibly, exploiting the weaker position of the other party'.[112]

As regards the requirement of undervalue, Gavan Duffy J stated in *Grealish v. Murphy*[113] that a court will be 'very much slower to undo a transaction for value', although he stressed that the principles underlying intervention in either case remain the same. In *Noonan v. O'Connell*[114] a transfer of a half-share in a farm by an elderly man with limited mental capacity to his nephew for what appeared to be a nominal consideration was set aside as was the disposition in *Slator v. Nolan*[115] by a man to his brother-in-law for what was also a grossly inadequate consideration. These decisions can be contrasted with that of Pringle J in *Nyland v. Brennan*[116] where a sale by an elderly lady at a reasonable price was upheld, albeit in circumstances where she had received comprehensive and independent legal advice, and with the decision of McLoughlin J in *Haverty v. Brooks*[117] where he found that 'substantial monetary consideration' had changed hands.

The receipt of full and independent legal advice becomes increasingly important where the consideration paid is low or non-existent or where one party is negotiating from a position of relative weakness, although it will always be a factor which the court will consider in assessing whether a transaction has been improvident. In *Grealish v. Murphy*[118] the plaintiff, an elderly farmer, who according to the medical evidence was mentally deficient, executed a settlement transferring his farm to the defendant subject to a life interest in his favour and charging the land with a right of residence and support for the defendant during the plaintiff's lifetime. While Gavan Duffy J declined to set aside the settlement on the grounds of undue influence, he accepted that the transaction was an improvident one and that the settlement should be rectified on this basis. Gavan Duffy J laid

---

111. *Morrison v. Coast Finance Ltd* (1965) 55 DLR (2d) 710, 713 *per* Davey JA. See also the *dicta* of Lord Brightman in *O'Connor v. Hart* [1985] AC 1000, 1024 where the concept of taking advantage of the weaker party's position was also stressed.
112. [1997] LMCLQ 17, 23.
113. [1946] IR 35, 49-50.
114. High Court 1986 No. 2135P (Lynch J) 10 April 1987.
115. (1876) IR 11 Eq 367.
116. High Court 1970 No. 1548P (Pringle J) 19 December 1970.
117. [1970] IR 214, 219.
118. [1946] IR 35.

emphasis on the plaintiff's weakness of mind and the deficiencies in the legal advice which he had received, pointing to the fact that his solicitor had been unaware of all the material facts and had failed to give the plaintiff a full explanation of the consequences of the settlement or to appreciate the latter's limited mental capacity. Lack of proper legal advice also appeared to be an important factor in the decision of Morris J in *McQuirk v. Branigan*[119] to set aside a deed executed by an elderly lady transferring land to her grandson so that he could build a house on the site. It became necessary to give the grandson an area larger than had been previously envisaged to make the site large enough to accommodate a house and this effectively divested the plaintiff completely of her back garden. Morris J pointed to the total lack of independent legal advice or indeed any advice given to the plaintiff and set aside the transaction as an improvident one from her point of view.

It should be pointed out that as the above consideration of the case law tends to show, there remains a degree of uncertainty about the exact requirements which must be established to support a claim of unconscionability. As Bamforth has recently commented: 'the cases tend to leave the relative importance and requirements of each element unarticulated'[120] and in his view there is still an unacceptable degree of imprecision in the case law. Hooley and O'Sullivan have also recently raised this issue and suggest that the *dicta* of the members of the Court of Appeal in *Credit Lyonnais Bank Nederland NV v. Burch*[121] provides an excellent illustration of Bamforth's point that the juridicial basis and elements of unconscionability as a vitiating factor should be more precisely defined and rooted in principle.[122]

Finally one issue which has provoked considerable academic debate in recent years is whether the doctrines of undue influence and unconscionable transactions or unconscionability should continue to remain separate and distinct or whether they should be merged. It should be noted that the same facts will often cause a court to consider whether to grant relief under both or either heading,[123] and the two have even been combined on occasion.[124] Capper argues that the doctrines of undue influence and

---

119. High Court Circuit Appeal (Morris J) 9 November 1992.
120. [1995] LMCLQ 538, 539.
121. [1997] 1 All ER 144.
122. [1997] LMCLQ 17, 22.
123. *Grealish v. Murphy* [1946] IR 35.
124. *McGonigle v. Black* High Court Circuit Appeal (Barr J) 14 November 1988 in which a transaction was set aside as being a 'grossly improvident' one brought about by undue influence.

unconscionability are 'sufficiently similar in their objectives and effects that they can and may profitably be merged into one'[125] and that unconscionability as the broader of the two doctrines would allow undue influence to be subsumed into it. On the other hand Birks and Chin have argued that the two doctrines are fundamentally distinct and that the existing analytical distinctions should be preserved.[126] In their view undue influence is concerned with the weakness of the plaintiff's consent owing to his excessive dependence on the defendant, while unconscionability is concerned with the defendant's exploitation of the plaintiff's vulnerability. Certainly there are authorities in Canada[127] and Australia[128] which support the approach of Birks and Chin and while the courts in this jurisdiction have not directly addressed this question, it is certainly unlikely in the short term that they would take the step of seeking to merge the doctrines.

LOSS OF THE RIGHT TO RESCIND

Affirmation

If the party is aware of the facts giving rise to the right to rescind and nevertheless affirms the contract by taking some benefit under it he will be taken to have waived his right to rescind.[129] Where a person seeks to rescind a contract he must do so within a reasonable time or he may be taken to have affirmed the contract and in this context the doctrine of laches may operate to defeat a claim. As we have seen, this involves a substantial lapse of time coupled with circumstances which make it inequitable to allow the plaintiff to succeed in his claim. The manner in which laches may defeat an action to have an agreement set aside in the context of an improvident transaction is illustrated by the decision of Keane J in *J.H. v. W.J.H.*[130] As a result of delay by the plaintiff of four years and by reason of the time and money invested in the running of a farm by the defendant on the basis that the plaintiff had abandoned her claim, Keane J refused to

---

125. (1998) 114 LQR 479, 480.
126. 'On the Nature of Undue Influence' in *Good Faith and Fault in Contract Law* eds. Beatson and Friedmann (1995) p.57 *et seq.*
127. *Morrison v. Coast Finance Ltd* (1965) 55 DLR (2d) 710, 713 *per* Bull JA to the effect that while the doctrines are closely related they are 'separate and distinct'
128. *Commercial Bank of Australia Ltd v. Amadio* (1983) 151 CLR 447, 461 *per* Mason J.
129. See *Payman v. Lanjani* [1985] Ch 457.
130. High Court 1977 No. 5831P (Keane J) 20 December 1979.

grant the plaintiff relief although he held that the transaction in question was an improvident one which the courts would normally have set aside.

If Substantial Restitutio in Integrum is Impossible

As Lord Blackburn stated in *Erlanger v. New Sombrero Phosphate Co.*[131] 'as a condition to a rescission there must be a *restitutio in integrum*'. This principle was strictly enforced at common law but equity has taken a more flexible approach and as Lord Blackburn noted there is a considerable difference in the manner in which it has been applied at law and in equity. In the latter case it has not been applied as literally, the aim being to achieve practical justice even where precise restoration of the parties to their previous positions is no longer possible. The attitude of equity towards this concept was well summarised by Griffin J in *Northern Bank Finance Corporation Ltd v. Charlton*[132] as follows: 'Therefore, the rule is that rescission cannot be enforced if events, which have occurred since the contract and in which the representee has participated, make it impossible to restore the parties substantially to their previous position.'

While any property or monies transferred under the contract must in theory be handed back, equity does not insist on precise restoration, and the wrongdoer may be asked to give up his profits in return for compensation for work carried out in performance of his contractual obligations.[133] A further relevant factor may be whether the fact that the parties cannot be restored to their previous positions is attributable to the nature of the subject matter of the agreement or whether it is due to the plaintiff's conduct.[134] Clearly where precise restoration of the parties is impossible the courts will take a more flexible approach if the plaintiff is not in any way responsible for this state of affairs.

Third Party Rights

A contract will not be rescinded where this will prejudice the rights of innocent third parties who have acquired an interest for value in the subject matter of an agreement. So where a *bona fide* purchaser for value without notice has acquired good title to the property in the interim, an action for rescission will not succeed.[135] However, where the third party is a mere volunteer, the right to rescind will not be lost.

---

131. (1878) 3 App Cas 1218, 1278.
132. [1979] IR 149, 206. See also the *dicta* of O'Higgins CJ at p. 183.
133. See *O'Sullivan v. Management Agency & Music Ltd* [1985] QB 428.
134. *Carbin v. Somerville* [1933] IR 276, 289.
135. *Anderson v. Ryan* [1967] IR 34.

CHAPTER 17

Equitable Estoppel

INTRODUCTION

Estoppel is not an exclusively equitable concept and operates today both at common law and in equity. Two main aspects of equitable estoppel are recognised; promissory and proprietary estoppel[1] which both owe their origins to the concept of estoppel by representation.[2] The essential basis of the latter doctrine is the making of a representation by a person whether by words or conduct of an existing fact which causes another party to incur detriment in reliance on this representation. In these circumstances, the person making the representation will not be permitted to act subsequently in a manner inconsistent with that representation. This principle formed the basis of the decision of the House of Lords in *Jorden v. Money*[3] which limited the operation of estoppel to representations of existing fact rather than of a party's intentions. As Lord Cranworth stated:

> [I]f a person makes any false representation to another, and that other acts upon that false representation, the person who has made it shall not afterwards be allowed to set up that what he said was false.[4]

However, he continued by saying that he thought that the doctrine did not apply 'to a case where the representation is not a representation of fact, but a statement of something which the party intends or does not intend to do'. This approach was also followed in Ireland in *Munster & Leinster Bank Ltd v. Croker*[5] in which Black J agreed that this form of estoppel 'only applies to representation of existing facts'. While this reasoning did not appear to leave much scope for development, equity has eroded some of the limitations of this principle in a manner which shall now be examined.

---

1. See Pawlowski, *Proprietary Estoppel* (1996).
2. See generally Spencer-Bower and Turner, *Estoppel by Representation* (3rd ed., 1977).
3. (1854) 5 HLC 185.
4. *Ibid.* at 210.
5. [1940] IR 185, 191.

PROMISSORY ESTOPPEL

One of the guiding principles which arguably has circumscribed the development of the doctrine of promissory estoppel has been that it should not undermine the requirement of consideration. Its operation has been confined to situations where a pre-existing contractual relationship exists or at least a relationship which gives rise to legal rights and obligations.[6] For this reason promissory estoppel is often considered in a contractual context and a fuller treatment of it can be found in the leading texts in this area.[7] It is therefore proposed to briefly outline its early development and examine its main characteristics and later in the chapter to assess whether there is evidence of a move towards a unified doctrine of equitable estoppel.

While the effect of *Jorden v. Money*[8] appeared to be to limit the doctrine of equitable estoppel to representations of existing fact, the decisions of *Hughes v. Metropolitan Railway Co.*[9] and *Birmingham and District Land Co. v. London and North Western Railway Co.*[10] showed that equity would give relief to a person in circumstances where the truth or accuracy of a representation of future intention might be denied in an unconscionable manner. These decisions were in turn employed by Denning J in his landmark judgment in *Central London Property Trust Ltd v. High Trees House Ltd*[11] which can be regarded as the decision in which the foundations of the doctrine known as 'promissory estoppel' were laid. In the view of Denning J, where a promise is made which is 'intended to create legal relations and which, to the knowledge of the person making the promise, was going to be acted on by the person to whom it was made, and which was in fact so acted on'[12] the court should ensure that such a promise is honoured. This reasoning was relied on in this jurisdiction by Kenny J in his decision in *Revenue Commissioners v. Moroney*[13] in which he held that a father who had promised his sons that they would not have to pay the

---

6.   E.g. *Durham Fancy Goods Ltd v. Michael Jackson (Fancy Goods) Ltd* [1968] 2 QB 839, 847 *per* Donaldson J.
7.   See e.g. Clark, *Contract Law in Ireland* (4th ed., 1998); Treitel, *The Law of Contract* (9th ed., 1995).
8.   (1854) 3 HLC 185.
9.   (1877) 2 App Cas 439.
10. (1888) 40 Ch D 268.
11. [1947] 1 KB 130.
12. *Ibid.* at 134. See also *Kenny v. Kelly* [1988] IR 457, 463 where Barron J was satisfied that these elements, necessary to establish a claim based on promissory estoppel, were satisfied in the case before him.
13. [1972] IR 372.

consideration referred to in a deed which they had signed would have been estopped from subsequently seeking this consideration.[14]

While this *'High Trees'* principle appeared to be potentially far-reaching in effect, its scope was circumscribed by the subsequent decision of the English Court of Appeal in *Combe v. Combe*[15] where Denning LJ himself stated that it did not 'create new causes of action where none existed before. It only prevents a party from insisting upon his strict legal rights, when it should be unjust to allow him to enforce them, having regard to the dealings which have taken place between the parties.' It was also in the *Combe* decision that Birkett LJ adopted the now famous expression used by counsel that the *High Trees* doctrine was one which should be 'used as a shield and not a sword'.[16] This reasoning was applied by Barron J in *Chartered Trust Ireland Ltd v. Healy*[17] where he held that estoppel could not confer a cause of action on a plaintiff. The *High Trees* principle also underpinned the decision of Kenny J in *Cullen v Cullen*.[18] The plaintiff purported to transfer his property and business to his wife in return for an undertaking that she would not seek to have him committed to a mental hospital. The plaintiff's wife won a portable house in a competition and gave it to her son. She suggested that he should erect it on the father's lands and the latter expressed the view that as he was making the property over to his wife she could do as she liked. The son erected the house on these lands, rather than on his own as he had originally contemplated, and when the plaintiff instituted proceedings, *inter alia*, claiming injunctions to prevent the son trespassing on the land, the son counter-claimed for a declaration that he was entitled to the house and the site on which it was built. Kenny J held that he was satisfied that the son would have erected the house on his own property had the plaintiff not given his wife permission to erect the house on the disputed lands. However, he rejected the son's claim that he had acquired a right to compel the plaintiff to transfer the site to him although he held that the plaintiff was estopped by his conduct from asserting any title to the site.[19] As Kenny J stated: 'While the estoppel created by the plaintiff's conduct prevents him asserting a title to the site, it does not give [the son] a right to require the plaintiff to

---

14. The Supreme Court dismissed the father's appeal but rested their decision on other grounds and made no comment on the estoppel argument.
15. [1951] 2 KB 215.
16. *Ibid.* at 224.
17. High Court Circuit Appeal (Barron J)10 December 1985.
18. [1962] IR 268. See Brady (1970) 5 Ir Jur (ns) 239.
19. At the end of a 12-year period the son could therefore bring an application under s.52 of the Registration of Title Act 1891 for his registration as owner.

transfer the site to him: if I had jurisdiction to make such an order I would do so, but I do not think I have.'[20]

While the principle had certainly been employed in a defensive context in *Hughes v. Metropolitan Railway Co.*[21] as Jackson[22] has commented 'this does not imply that an action cannot be brought upon a representation' and he argues that any attempt to restrict the effect of such a representation to a defensive mechanism ignores the principle on which it is based, namely that a promise may be enforced. As Mason CJ pointed out in *Waltons Stores (Interstate) Ltd v. Maher,*[23] Denning LJ himself acknowledged in the *Combe* case that estoppel 'may be part of a cause of action' even if not a cause of action in itself. More recently there have been signs in England of a more flexible approach being taken to this traditional limitation on the operation of the doctrine and in *Re Wyvern Developments Ltd*[24] Templeman J rejected the argument that estoppel could not confer a cause of action and said that it applies whenever 'the promissor knows and intends that the promise will irretrievably alter his position on the promise'.[25] Recent High Court decisions in Ireland show that there is a lack of consensus on this question and it would be fair to say that there has been little real analysis of the issues underlying it. In *Re J.R.*[26] Costello J appeared to hold that promissory estoppel could give rise to a cause of action and indeed was capable of creating proprietary rights. However, this approach is at odds with the *dicta* of O'Hanlon J in *Association of General Practitioners Ltd v. Minister for Health,*[27] in which he reasserted the traditional view that promissory estoppel should be regarded as providing a shield and not a sword. The question arose in the context of a claim by the plaintiffs based, *inter alia*, on the doctrine of legitimate expectation which Finlay CJ had described in *Webb v. Ireland*[28] as 'but an aspect of the well-recognised equitable concept of promissory estoppel'. Relying on the position as laid down in *Combe v. Combe,*[29] O'Hanlon J stated that 'the doctrine of equitable or promissory estoppel cannot create any new cause of action where none existed before'[30] and from this proposition he con-

---

20. *Ibid.* at 292.
21. (1877) 2 App Cas 439.
22. (1965) 81 LQR 223, 142.
23. (1988) 164 CLR 387, 400.
24. [1974] 1 WLR 1097.
25. *Ibid.* at 1104.
26. [1993] ILRM 657. See further *infra* pp. 626-626.
27. [1995] 2 ILRM 481.
28. [1988] IR 353.
29. [1951] 2 KB 215.
30. At p. 14 of the unreported judgment.

cluded that where a promise is made which is unsupported by consideration, the promisee cannot bring an action. While no detailed consideration
was given by O'Hanlon J to this issue, his reiteration of the orthodox view
of the limitations of the doctrine of promissory estoppel indicates at the
very least that there is no coherent move towards broadening its perameters
in this jurisdiction.

Another aspect of promissory estoppel which has provoked a degree of
uncertainty is the need for a claimant to establish detriment. There have
been suggestions made by Lord Denning to the effect that it is not an essential requirement,[31] however in *Lowe v. Lombank Ltd*[32] Diplock J disagreed with this viewpoint and said that any representation made to a person
must be acted on by him to his detriment before an estoppel can arise.
Similarly in *Industrial Yarns Ltd v. Greene*[33] Costello J stated that to establish a claim of estoppel, 'the representor must show that what was said
or done by the representor influenced both the belief and conduct of the
representor to his detriment'. The approach adopted by Costello J in his
recent judgment in *Re J.R.*,[34] would tend to confirm the need to establish
detriment if a claim based on promissory estoppel is to succeed in this
jurisdiction.

PROPRIETARY ESTOPPEL

Introduction

The basis of the doctrine of proprietary estoppel is to prevent a person
from insisting on his strict legal rights where to do so would be inequitable
having regard to the dealings which have taken place between the parties.[35] It developed as an exception to the formalities required for the creation of interests in land and the rationale behind the doctrine could be said
to be to prevent unconscionable behaviour. It should be noted at this point
that while proprietary estoppel is almost exclusively invoked in the context of rights in or over land, it can extend to other forms of property.

---

31. *W.J. Alan & Co. Ltd v. El Nasr Export and Import Co* [1972] 2 QB 189, 213. See also
    Brikom Investments Ltd v. Carr [1979] QB 467, 482.
32. [1960] 1 WLR 196. Adopted as a correct statement of the law in this jurisdiction by
    Murphy J in *McCambridge v. Winters* High Court 1983 No. 486Sp (Murphy J) 28
    May 1984.
33. [1984] ILRM 15, 23 *per* Costello J. See also *Dunne v. Molloy* [1976-77] ILRM 266
    in which Gannon J pointed to the fact that there was no evidence of any detrimental
    act done by the plaintiff either with the encouragement or knowledge of the defend-
    ant.
34. [1993] ILRM 657. See further *infra* pp. 625-626.
35. *Crabb v. Arun District Council* [1976] Ch 179, 187-188 *per* Denning MR.

To invoke successfully the doctrine of proprietary estoppel, it is necessary to establish that an assurance has been given, that reliance has been placed by the other party on that assurance and that detriment has been suffered as a result. As Edward Nugee QC (sitting as a High Court judge) stated in *Re Basham*:[36]

> Where one person, A, has acted to his detriment on the faith of a belief which was known to and encouraged by another person, B, that he either has or is going to be given a right in or over B's property, B cannot insist on his strict legal rights if to do so would be inconsistent with A's belief.

The assurance given, while it need not necessarily have been express, must have been made by the party with the intention that it should be relied on and a mere expression of opinion would be insufficient in this context. It will usually consist of encouragement by words or deeds but mere acquiescence or 'conscious silence'[37] may also suffice.

Reliance would seem to be established once it is shown that a representation 'was calculated to influence the judgment of a reasonable man'[38] and there is authority for the proposition that once an assurance on the part of the legal owner has been established, there is a presumption of reliance.[39] The concept of reliance was considered recently by Balcombe LJ in *Wayling v. Jones*[40] in which he stated that '[o]nce it has been established that promises were made, and that there has been conduct by the plaintiff of such a nature that inducement may be inferred then the burden of proof shifts to the defendants to establish that he did not rely on the promises' but he added that 'there must be a sufficient link between the promises relied upon and the conduct which constitutes the detriment'.

Detriment will be suffered where the assurance on which reliance is placed is withdrawn and it is the fact of detriment having been suffered which will render it unconscionable for the legal owner to insist on enforcing his rights. While the detriment suffered by the claimant will usually involve expenditure of money or the building of premises on another's

---

36. [1986] 1 WLR 1498, 1503. Quoted with approval by Balcombe LJ in *Wayling v. Jones* (1993) 69 P & CR 170, 172 and by Carnwath J in *Gillett v. Holt* [1998] 3 All ER 917, 926.

37. *Salvation Army Trustee Co. Ltd v. W. Yorkshire Metropolitan County Council* (1981) 41 P & CR 179.

38. *Brikom Investments Ltd v. Carr* [1979] QB 467, 483 *per* Denning MR.

39. *Greasley v. Cooke* [1980] 1 WLR 1306.

40. (1993) 69 P & CR 170, 173. See Davis [1995] Conv 409 and Cooke (1995) 111 LQR 389.

land, it would appear that this is not the only form of detriment which will suffice. In *Re Basham*[41] Edward Nugee QC stated that 'the expenditure of A.'s money on B.'s property is not the only kind of detriment that gives rise to a proprietary estoppel' and in *McCarron v. McCarron*[42] Murphy J commented *obiter* that 'in a suitable case it may well be argued that a plaintiff suffers as severe a loss or detriment by providing his own labours or services in relation to the lands of another and accordingly should equally qualify for recognition in equity'.

Gray[43] has suggested three categories of situation in which proprietary estoppel may arise: cases where an imperfect gift is made, cases based on common expectation and cases of unilateral mistake. These categories are clearly not mutually exclusive as the effect of the operation of the doctrine may well be to perfect an imperfect gift even in cases where the basis for its operation can be said to be expectation or mistake. An examination of the case law in this area over the last century shows that attempts were made to restrict the cases in which proprietary estoppel could arise to those falling into the mistake category and such an approach undoubtedly restricted the growth of the doctrine. More recently it has come to be recognised that such categorisation is unnecessary and even unhelpful and a broader doctrine based on the general concept of unconscionability has evolved.[44] Nevertheless, it is still useful to build up a picture of how proprietary estoppel has developed by examining the case law by reference to these categories.

Where an Imperfect Gift is Made

While the general principle is that equity will not complete an imperfect gift,[45] in some circumstances the courts will allow the perfection of a gift, usually in the context of a voluntary gift of realty. The main authority for this proposition is the decision of Lord Westbury in *Dillwyn v. Llewelyn.*[46] A son built a house on his father's land with the latter's consent and an informal memorandum was signed which showed that the father's intention was that it should be given to the son for this purpose. After the father

---

41. [1986] 1 WLR 1498, 1509
42. Supreme Court 1995 No. 181, 13 February 1997 at p. 13.
43. *Elements of Land Law* (2nd ed., 1993) p.388.
44. Pawlowski has recently commented in the preface to his book *Proprietary Estoppel* (1996) that these three categories 'remain valid, notwithstanding the modern trend towards applying an underlying concept of unconscionability as the basis for proprietary estoppel claims'.
45. *Milroy v. Lord* (1862) 4 De GF & J 264.
46. (1862) 4 De GF & J 517.

died, it was held by the House of Lords that the father's intention to convey the fee simple estate would be carried into effect by the court, although the land had been left in trust for the benefit of third parties by virtue of the provisions of the father's will. Lord Westbury pointed out that a promise of a gift had been made and on the strength of that promise and with the father's knowledge, the son had incurred substantial expenditure on the land. He stressed that a voluntary agreement would not be completed by a court of equity in the case of a mere gift and that it was instead the subsequent acts of the donor which gave rise to the claim. This decision was stated by Kenny J in *Cullen v. Cullen*[47] to be authority for the proposition that 'a person claiming under a voluntary agreement will not be assisted by a court of equity but that the subsequent acts of the donor may give the donee a ground of claim which he did not acquire from the original gift'.

The principle laid down in *Dillwyn* was applied by the English Court of Appeal in *Pascoe v. Turner.*[48] The parties had lived together for a considerable period of time in a house owned by the plaintiff and when he moved out and went to live with another woman, he assured the defendant that she could remain in the house and that it would henceforth belong to her. On the basis of this assurance, the defendant carried out repairs and improvements to the property. When the plaintiff subsequently brought proceedings for possession, the Court of Appeal held that the fee simple estate in the house should be conveyed to the defendant.

Similarly in *Smyth v. Halpin*[49] the plaintiff had asked his father to provide him with a site on the latter's land so that he could build a house for himself. The father's reply was to the effect that the family house would be his after his mother's death and why would he want two houses and suggested that the plaintiff instead build an extension onto the family home. The father made a number of wills during his lifetime but in the last of these he left the house to his wife for her life and thereafter to the second named defendant, one of his daughters. After the father's death the plaintiff instituted proceedings seeking, *inter alia,* a declaration that he was entitled to the reversionary interest in the property following the life interest in favour of his mother. Geoghegan J stated that the kind of proprietary estoppel invoked in this case has its origins in the decision of *Dillwyn v. Llewelyn* and that the same principles have been applied in a number of other English decisions, including *Pascoe v. Turner*. He stated that the

---

47. [1962] IR 268, 282.
48. [1979] 1 WLR 431.
49. [1997] 2 ILRM 38.

plaintiff's clear expectation in this case was that he would have a fee simple interest in the entire house and concluded that the protection of the equity arising from the expenditure required that an order be made by the court directing a conveyance of that interest to him.

Common Expectation

Proprietary estoppel may also arise where parties have consistently dealt with each other in such a way as reasonably to cause one party to rely on a shared assumption that he would acquire rights in the other party's lands. The accepted classic formulation of this proposition was laid down by Lord Kingsdown in his dissenting speech in *Ramsden v. Dyson*[50] as follows:

> If a man, under a verbal agreement with a landlord for a certain interest in land, or, what amounts to the same thing, under an expectation, created or encouraged by the landlord, that he shall have a certain interest, takes possession of such land, with the consent of the landlord, and upon the faith of such promise or expectation, with the knowledge of the landlord, and without objection by him, lays out money upon the land, a Court of equity will compel the landlord to give effect to such a promise or expectation. ...
>
> If, on the other hand, a tenant being in possession of land, and knowing the nature and extent of his interest, lays out money upon it in the hope and expectation of an extended term or an allowance for expenditure, then, if such expenditure has not been created or encouraged by the landlord, the tenant has no claim which any Court of law or equity can enforce.

Lord Kingsdown's observations were approved of by the Privy Council in *Plimmer v. Mayor of Wellington,*[51] where the landowner rather than merely encouraging the expenditure actually took the initiative in requesting it. A licensee of land had, at the government's request, spent a considerable sum of money on extending a jetty and constructing a warehouse. When the jetty was compulsorily acquired it was held that the appellants had an equity arising from their expenditure on the land and were entitled to 'an indefinite, that is practically a perpetual' right to the jetty for the

---

50. (1866) LR 1 HL 129, 170-171.
51. (1884) 9 App Cas 699. The formulation set out by the Privy Council was quoted by Murphy J in *McCarron v. McCarron* Supreme Court 1995 No. 181, 13 February 1997 at p. 12.

purposes of the original licence. Similarly in *Inwards v. Baker*[52] an estoppel arose on the basis of a common expectation that by reason of one party's expenditure on land, he should be entitled to an interest in it. A father had allowed his son to build a house at his own expense on the former's land, encouraging the son to believe that he would be allowed to remain there during his lifetime. When the father died, the Court of Appeal refused to allow the trustees of the father's will to obtain possession of the lands on the basis that the son had acquired an equity in the land by reason of his expenditure which bound the father and his successors in title. Instead, the court made an order that the son could remain in possession of the property as long as he wished to use the house as his home.

It is important to stress that before Lord Kingsdown's *dicta* will apply it is essential that the expenditure has been requested, or more commonly encouraged, by the landowner. As the second paragraph of Lord Kingsdown's statement makes clear, where the other party merely lays out money in the hope or expectation of acquiring an interest, which has not been encouraged by the landowner, no estoppel will arise. This point is well illustrated by the decision of the Privy Council in *Attorney General of Hong Kong v. Humphrey's Estate.*[53] It was agreed in principle between the Hong Kong government and a group of companies, which included the respondent, that the government would grant the group a lease of specific property in exchange for flats which belonged to the latter. The government took possession of the flats and fitted them out for civil servants but before the contract was concluded, the group withdrew from the transaction. When the government brought an action contesting the group's right to withdraw, the respondent sought a declaration that it was entitled to possession of the flats. The government contended that the group were estopped from withdrawing from what had been agreed in principle but the Privy Council rejected this claim. It was held that to found an estoppel it would have to be established not only that the government had acted to its detriment to the knowledge of the group in the hope that it would not withdraw from the agreement, but also that the group had created or encouraged a belief or expectation on the government's part that they would not withdraw, and that the government had relied on that belief or expectation. While it was accepted that 'the government acted in the confident and not unreasonable hope that the agreement in principle would come into effect,' it was held that the group had not encouraged or allowed a

---

52. [1965] 2 QB 29.
53. [1987] AC 114.

belief or expectation on the government's part that it would not withdraw from the agreement and that in the circumstances no estoppel arose.

This point that a claimant must establish that the legal owner created or encouraged a belief that it would not change its mind was also of importance in the recent decision of *Taylor v. Dickens*.[54] While the plaintiff asserted that he was confident that the defendant would not revoke the provision in her will in which she had left him her house as she had promised, there was no evidence that she had created or encouraged this belief on his behalf.[55] As Milne has recently commented 'proprietary estoppel may prevent unconscionable conduct in respect of property, but it cannot operate unless there has been reliance on an encouraged belief in rights over that property'.[56]

The importance of the fact that any expectation or belief be created or encouraged by a landowner can also be seen from the decision of Blayney J in *Haughan v. Rutledge*.[57] The plaintiffs, who were trustees of an association which promoted harness racing sought to lease the defendant's land for the purpose of holding races. The parties agreed that the defendant would let a field for a trial period and the plaintiffs would construct a racetrack on it. It was further agreed that if at the end of this period the plaintiffs left the property, they would pay no rent and the defendant would retain the benefit of the works carried out. A dispute arose and the defendant re-possessed the lands and the plaintiffs sought specific performance of the alleged agreement to grant a lease of the lands or alternatively an order requiring the defendant to let them into possession. Blayney J held that four conditions would have to be satisfied before an estoppel could arise, namely detriment, expectation or belief, encouragement and finally, that there be no bar to the equity. On the facts of the case before him, he held that the second and third requirements had not been satisfied. The second condition required that the plaintiffs had built the racetrack in the belief that they owned a sufficient interest in the land to justify the expenditure or that they would obtain such an interest and this had not been established. Blayney J added that even if he had been of the view that the plaintiffs had the required belief, he would not have been satisfied that this belief had been encouraged by the defendant. Blayney J referred to the *dicta* of Lord Kingsdown in *Ramsden* and said that the case before him

---

54. [1998] 1 FLR 806. See Thompson [1998] Conv 210.
55. As Gray has commented in *Elements of Land Law* (2nd ed., 1993) p.330 'detrimental reliance upon a self-induced expectation cannot give rise to a valid claim of estoppel'.
56. (1998) 114 LQR 555, 558-559.
57. [1988] IR 295.

came within the second limb of the latter's statement. He concluded as follows:

> I consider that the plaintiffs laid out money on the construction of the track in the hope and expectation that the defendant would continue to make lettings of the track to them, but as that hope and expectation was not created or encouraged by the defendant, the plaintiffs have no claim which can be enforced at law or in equity.[58]

Unilateral Mistake

Proprietary estoppel may also be invoked where one party has made an error as to the nature of his rights, the crucial factor being that detriment is suffered by the party who innocently relies on the mistaken assumption that he has rights in land. The following statement of Lord Cranworth in *Ramsden v. Dyson*[59] provides a summary of the circumstances in which estoppel can arise in such cases:

> If a stranger begins to build on my land supposing it to be his own, and I, perceiving his mistake, abstain from setting him right, and leave him to persevere in his error, a Court of equity will not allow me afterwards to assert my title to the land on which he had expended money on the supposition that the land was his own. It considers that, when I saw the mistake into which he had fallen, it was my duty to be active and to state my adverse title, and that it would be dishonest in me to remain wilfully passive on such an occasion, in order afterwards to profit by the mistake which I might have prevented.

However, he continued: 'If a stranger builds on my land knowing it to be mine, there is no principle of equity which would prevent my claiming the land with the benefit of all the expenditure made on it.' Therefore it is necessary that the person spending the money thought that he was building on his own land and that the real owner knew at the time that the land did in fact belong to him; no estoppel will arise under this heading where the 'stranger' knows that he has no rights over the land. This point is illustrated by the case of *O'Callaghan v. Ballincollig Holdings Ltd.*[60] The plaintiffs claimed that they had acquired title to a house by adverse pos-

---

58. *Ibid.* at 303.
59. (1866) LR 1 HL 129, 140-141.
60. High Court 1987 No. E202 (Blayney J) 31 March 1993.

session and this claim was rejected by the defendants and a notice to quit served. The plaintiffs sought a declaration of their title or alternatively a declaration that they had a lien on the house for monies spent on reinstating it while the defendant counter-claimed for possession. The plaintiffs' claim to a lien was based on the grounds of proprietary estoppel and unjust enrichment. They argued that the defendant had stood idly by while they had spent substantial sums of money reinstating the house and that this precluded it from recovering the property without compensating the plaintiffs for their expenditure. Blayney J was satisfied that this submission was not well founded; as long as the plaintiffs' tenancy continued to subsist, the defendant was not entitled to interfere and it was not a case of the defendant standing idly by. He quoted with approval the second limb of Lord Cranworth's *dicta* in *Ramsden* and concluded that the plaintiffs knew that they held the house as tenants from the defendant and that they were reinstating a house to which the defendant was entitled subject to their tenancy. Therefore they could not prevent the defendant from claiming the house with the benefit of their expenditure on it.

An attempt was made to rely on Lord Cranworth's principle in *Wilmott v. Barber*[61] although on the facts it was clear that both parties were mistaken as to their legal rights and the claim of estoppel was rejected. Neither the plaintiff assignee of a lease nor the lessor had realized that the lease prohibited assignment of the lease without the lessor's consent. Fry J concluded that the lessor could not, by his action in acquiescing in the expenditure incurred by the lessee, be estopped from asserting his right to refuse consent to the assignment since at the date of the purported acquiescence, he was not aware of the right of veto. However, the judgment of Fry J is important in view of the restrictive effects which it had on the development of the doctrine of proprietary estoppel. He laid down the proposition that a person should not be deprived of his strict legal rights unless he has acted in a manner which would make it fraudulent to assert those rights, fraud in this context being dependent on establishing five necessary elements. These were as follows:[62]

1. The claimant must have made a mistake as to his legal rights.

2. The claimant must have expended some money or done some act on the faith of his mistaken belief.

---

61. (1880) 15 Ch D 96.
62. *Ibid.* at 105-106. Quoted with approval by Gannon J in *Dunne v. Molloy* [1976-77] ILRM 266, 268.

3. The owner of the land must know of his own right which is inconsistent with the right claimed by the plaintiff.

4. The owner must know of the claimant's mistaken belief as to his rights.

5. The owner must have encouraged the claimant in relation to the expenditure incurred or other acts done, either directly or by refraining from asserting his legal rights.

These so-called five probanda came to be applied by the courts in cases where a claim of proprietary estoppel was made irrespective of the basis of such a claim and even where it did not involve a case of unilateral mistake. With a few limited exceptions, the most notable being the decision of the Privy Council in *Plimmer v. Mayor of Wellington,*[63] in which a distinction was made between cases of unilateral mistake and common expectation, the courts often sought to construe situations so that they fell within the requirements laid down in *Fry*, even where there was no mistake made, and where this was not possible, a claim might fail. So, in *Cullen v. Cullen*[64] Kenny J appeared to reject a claim based on proprietary estoppel on this basis. In *Hopgood v. Brown,*[65] Evershed MR recognised that these requirements should be limited to cases of unilateral mistake and commented that they were not intended to be a 'comprehensive formulation of the necessary requisites of any case of estoppel by representation.' However, because of the apparently general nature of the probanda, their application resulted in a very restrictive view of the circumstances in which estoppel could arise.[66] Nevertheless, by the 1980s the courts had begun to recognise that the *dicta* of Fry J did not constitute a formula which had to be rigidly adhered to, although the requirements continued to be applied in cases which did not fall within the category of unilateral mistake, albeit less frequently.[67]

A Move Towards a Test of Unconscionability

A view that the five probanda should be used as a guide rather than as a strict requirement began to emerge in England during the 1970s. As Buckley LJ commented in *Shaw v. Applegate*[68] where they were satisfied he had no

---

63. (1884) 9 App Cas 699, 712.
64. [1962] IR 268.
65. [1955] 1 WLR 213, 223.
66. E.g. *E & L Berg Homes Ltd v. Grey* (1979) 253 EG 473.
67. See e.g. *Coombes v. Smith* [1986] 1 WLR 808; *Matharu v. Matharu* (1994) 68 P & CR 93. See Milne (1995) 58 MLR 412.
68. [1977] 1 WLR 970.

doubt that it would be dishonest or unconscionable for the owner of a right to insist upon it, although he doubted whether it was really necessary to comply strictly with all five requirements to establish unconscionability. Similarly in *Crabb v. Arun District Council*[69] Scarman LJ although he did refer to the probanda as a 'valuable guide'[70] expressed the view that it should be necessary to establish that a defendant by asserting a right is taking advantage of a plaintiff in a manner which is 'unconscionable, inequitable or unjust'.[71] However, it was not until the judgment of Oliver J in *Taylor's Fashions Ltd v. Liverpool Victoria Trustees Co. Ltd*[72] that any detailed consideration was given to the idea of a departure from the *Wilmott v. Barber* approach, although on the facts of that case the plaintiff's claim was rejected. Oliver J pointed out that in the example given by Lord Kingsdown in *Ramsden v. Dyson*[73] there was no room for the literal application of the probanda as the circumstances referred to did not presuppose a mistake but rather the fostering of an expectation in the minds of both parties. He said that more recent authorities seemed to support a much wider equitable jurisdiction to interfere in situations where the assertion of legal rights was found by a court to be unconscionable and suggested that the relevance of the probanda even in cases of unilateral mistake was now open to doubt. Oliver J concluded as follows:

> Furthermore, the more recent cases indicate, in my judgment, that the application of the *Ramsden v. Dyson* principle … requires a very much broader approach which is directed rather at ascertaining whether, in particular circumstances, it would be unconscionable for a party to be permitted to deny that which, knowingly or unknowingly, he has allowed or encouraged another to assume to his detriment rather than to inquiring whether the circumstances can be fitted within the confines of some preconceived formula serving as a universal yardstick for every form of unconscionable behaviour.[74]

This more flexible approach was not applied universally in England in the years following the decision in *Taylor's Fashions*,[75] although a Privy Council decision suggested that the strictures of the *Wilmott v. Barber* princi-

---

69. [1976] Ch 179.
70. *Ibid.* at 194.
71. *Ibid.* at 195.
72. [1982] QB 133.
73. (1866) LR 1 HL 129.
74. [1982] QB 133, 151-152.
75. See *Coombes v. Smith* [1986] 1 WLR 808.

ples had been substantially relaxed and that the real question now seemed to be whether or not the assertion of strict legal rights would be unconscionable. In *Lim Teng Huan v. Ang Swee Chuan*[76] the parties entered into an agreement whereby the plaintiff acknowledged his consent to the building of a house by the defendant on land which they had originally purchased jointly[77] and agreed to exchange his share in the property for unspecified land which the defendant expected to acquire. After the defendant had completed the house and gone into occupation of it, the plaintiff sought a declaration that he was the owner of half the land and the defendant counter-claimed for a declaration that he was entitled to the sole beneficial ownership of the plaintiff's share or alternatively sought an injunction to restrain the plaintiff from entering the land. At the trial the plaintiff abandoned his claim and the defendant's counter-claim was dismissed. The Privy Council inferred that the defendant had completed construction of the house in reliance on the agreement made between the parties and found that it would be unconscionable for the plaintiff to renege on the assumption that he would have a sole absolute interest in the land upon paying compensation to the plaintiff. The plaintiff was therefore estopped from denying the defendant's title to the whole of the land. Lord Browne-Wilkinson referred to the decision of Oliver J in *Taylors Fashions* and said that it showed that in order to found a proprietary estoppel, 'it is enough if, in all the circumstances, it is unconscionable for the representor to go back on the assumption which he has permitted the representee to make'.[78]

Despite the attractiveness of such a straightforward formula, there has been a definite lack of consistency in the approach adopted by the English courts since the decision in *Lim*. In *Matharu v. Matharu*[79] despite the fact that adopting a narrow approach did not affect the outcome in the case, Roch LJ seemed to lay down the requirement that the probanda must be satisfied in all cases if proprietary estoppel is to be relied upon and did not refer to the broader approach based on the notion of unconscionability. However, in *Lloyds Bank plc v. Carrick*[80] Morritt LJ made it clear that he agreed with the conclusion of Oliver J in *Taylors Fashions* that 'proof of all those elements or "probanda" is not necessary to found an estoppel.' Thompson, commenting on that decision, stated that 'it is to be welcomed

---

76. [1992] 1 WLR 113.
77. Shortly after the purchase the land was transferred into the name of their respective fathers who both died within a number of years and the plaintiff therefore instituted proceedings as administrator of his father's estate.
78. *Ibid.* at 117.
79. (1994) 69 P & CR 93. See Milne (1995) 58 MLR 412 and Welsted [1995] Conv 61.
80. [1996] 4 All ER 630, 640.

as it continues the trend away from seeking to fit a flexible doctrine into a Procrustean bed, which is frequently not an appropriate thing to do, and should, it is hoped, prevent cases in the future being decided on a somewhat mechanical application of these probanda'.[81] Subsequently in *Taylor v. Dickens*[82] Judge Weeks seemed decidedly hostile to a suggestion that the court might intervene merely where the assertion of strict legal rights was found to be unconscionable, although he stopped short of seeking to adopt the formulation in *Wilmott*. In his view if one were to follow such an approach 'one might as well forget the law of contract and issue every judge with a portable palm tree. The days of justice varying with the size of the Lord Chancellor's foot would have returned'.[83] The most recent decision in this area seems to restore the notion of unconscionability without losing sight of what have traditionally been regarded as the essential elements of a claim of estoppel and for this reason it is to be welcomed. In *Gillett v. Holt*[84] Carnwarth J agreed that the overriding principle was that a defendant should be held to his representation 'only if it would be unconscionable to go back on it' but stressed that estoppel must be founded on an expectation, created or encouraged by the party alleged to be bound, in reliance on which the other party has acted to his detriment.

The concept of unconscionability also emerged in this jurisdiction in the context of a claim based on proprietary estoppel in *McMahon v. Kerry Co. Council*[85] in which Finlay P stressed the importance of assessing the consequences of the actions of the parties both from the point of view of the plaintiff and of the defendant. The plaintiffs bought a plot of land for the purpose of building a school, however shortly afterwards they abandoned their plan and did not visit the site again for a further three years. They then discovered that the defendant council which had originally known of their purchase, was preparing to build on the land and, upon a complaint being made, the work ceased. Four years later the defendant built two houses on the site and the following year the plaintiffs discovered this and instituted proceedings to recover possession of the site. Counsel for the defendant relied on *Ramsden v. Dyson* but Finlay P concluded that the facts of the case did not fall within the principle laid down by Lord Cranworth LC in that case and said that there was no question of the plaintiffs remaining wilfully passive when the defendant commenced to build

---

81. [1996] Conv 295, 298.
82. [1998] 1 FLR 806. This decision has been criticised by Thompson [1998] Conv 210, 217 as representing 'an unduly narrow approach to the doctrine of estoppel'.
83. *Ibid.* at 820.
84. [1998] 3 All ER 917. See Dixon [1999] Conv 46.
85. [1981] ILRM 419.

on their land However, Finlay P held that in the circumstances, it would be unjust and unconscionable that the plaintiffs should recover possession and he held that that they were only entitled to the market value of the site without the houses and to damages. With reference to *Ramsden*, Finlay P stated that the principles of equity stated there depended 'not exclusively on the action or inaction of the plaintiff or on the state of knowledge but have regard also to the action of the defendant.' He continued:

> If a court applying equitable principles is truly to act as a court of conscience then it seems to me unavoidable that it should consider not only conduct on the part of the plaintiff with particular regard to whether it is wrong and wilful but also conduct on the part of the defendant and furthermore the consequences and the justice of the consequences both from the point of view of the plaintiff and of the defendant.[86]

The Extent of the Remedy

As Brennan J commented in the Australian decision of *Waltons Stores (Interstate) Ltd v. Maher*[87] 'the remedy required to satisfy an equity varies according to the circumstances of the case'. This point is particularly apt in the context of proprietary estoppel[88] where the remedy may vary from the conferring of a fee simple interest to the granting of a mere licence. Equally, in some circumstances, it may be inappropriate to grant a remedy which involves any right to occupy property and it may be possible for the court to satisfy the equity raised by an award of damages, e.g. where improvements have been carried out to a premises which are not substantial in nature. As Cooke has recently commented: 'One of the most striking features of estoppel in the context of property claims is the wide range of responses available to the court'.[89]

In the decision of the Privy Council in *Plimmer v. Mayor of Wellington*[90] it was made clear that where an equity has been raised, 'the court must look at the circumstances in each case to decide in what way the equity can be satisfied' and in *Crabb v. Arun DC*[91] Scarman LJ commented

---

86. *Ibid.* at 421.
87. (1987) 164 CLR 387, 419.
88. As Lord Denning MR commented in *Crabb v. Arun District Council* [1976] Ch 179, 189: 'Here equity is displayed at its most flexible'.
89. (1997) 17 LS 258, 266.
90. (1884) 9 App Cas 699, 714. Quoted with approval by Denning MR in *Crabb v. Arun District Council* [1976] Ch 179, 188.
91. [1976] Ch 179, 198.

that the court should formulate the remedy which it will confer in such cases in terms of the 'minimum equity' required to do justice to the claimant. In the latter case the plaintiff acted to his detriment in parting with a portion of his land without having secured a means of access to the rest of it on the basis of a belief encouraged by the defendant that he would be granted a right of way over the latter's land. The Court of Appeal held that an equity arose in the plaintiff's favour and that he was entitled to be granted a right of way free of charge. Examples of the forms of remedy which have been granted in circumstances where an estoppel is made out have already been seen. In some cases such as *Smyth v. Halpin*[92] and *Pascoe v. Turner*[93] an order that a fee simple interest in property be transferred has been made while in the others, such as *Inwards v. Baker*[94] a claimant has been confined to a more limited interest: in this case an irrevocable licence to occupy the property for life. It is possible that as the courts move towards placing greater emphasis on the need to give effect to a claimant's expectations rather than merely seeking to compensate him to the extent of any detrimental reliance that they will inevitably become more generous in the relief which they grant, but it is likely that flexibility will continue to be the touchstone of any remedy based on a claim of proprietary estoppel.

Recent Developments

In order to found a claim based on proprietary estoppel, it has always been accepted that it is necessary that there should have been some form of assurance of entitlement given by the person whom it is sought to estop. However, it has recently been accepted that a claim of proprietary estoppel may succeed on the basis of acts undertaken not in reliance on the fact that the claimant had existing rights but on the faith of an undertaking that such rights would be granted in the future. In *Re Basham*[95] the plaintiff helped to run her mother and stepfather's business for many years on an unpaid basis on the understanding that she would inherit her stepfather's estate. The plaintiff and her husband also expended considerable time and money looking after her stepfather. The stepfather died intestate and the plaintiff sought a declaration against two of his nieces who were administratrixs of his estate that she was entitled to the deceased's house

---

92. [1997] 2 ILRM 38.
93. [1979] 1 WLR 431. See also *Lim Teng Huan v. Ang Swee Chuan* [1992] 1 WLR 113.
94. [1965] 2 QB 29.
95. [1986] 1 WLR 1498.

and to his furniture and other property. Edward Nugee QC held in granting the declaration sought that the principle of proprietary estoppel was not limited to acts done in reliance on a belief relating to an existing right but extended to acts done in reliance on a belief that future rights would be granted. In addition, he accepted that estoppel could extend to non-specific property and held that since the plaintiff had established that she had acted to her detriment in reliance on the belief, which was encouraged by her stepfather that she would ultimately benefit by receiving his property on his death, she was entitled to the residuary estate.

The decision in *Basham* also broke new ground in that Edward Nugee QC appeared to hold that proprietary estoppel will give rise to a constructive trust. It has been accepted that there is a close relationship between the concepts of proprietary estoppel and constructive trusts, in that both involve the application of the equitable principle that it would be unfair to allow a party to enforce his strict legal rights when it would be inequitable to do so on the basis of the dealings which have taken place between the parties. The converse had happened in *Grant v. Edwards*[96] where Browne-Wilkinson VC purported to introduce elements of proprietary estoppel into the doctrine of constructive trusts. As the Vice Chancellor stated, the principles underlying proprietary estoppel are 'closely akin' to those laid down in *Gissing v. Gissing*[97] in relation to constructive trusts and in his view the two principles 'rest on the same foundation'.[98] Undoubtedly the two doctrines possess similarities as both allow for the creation of informal interests in land but as Warburton[99] has pointed out there are also important differences between them, namely in relation to the timing of the interest created and the type of interest which will be acquired by a claimant. While establishing a claim of estoppel may lead to the conferring of a less extensive property right than that conferred by a constructive trust, equally it will often lead to a more far reaching form of relief.[100] It is also clear that both doctrines developed with different aims; proprietary estoppel as a means of compensating detrimental reliance and giving effect to expectations, and constructive trusts as a flexible device for achieving justice in equity. While Cooke P in his judgment in the New Zealand decision of *Gillies v. Keogh*[101] was correct in identifying common factors, principally the concept of unconscionability, it would seem to be incorrect to assert

---

96. [1986] Ch 638.
97. [1971] AC 886.
98. *Ibid.* at 656.
99. (1991) 5 Trust Law Int 9, 10.
100. E.g. *Pascoe v. Turner* [1979] 1 WLR 431.
101. [1989] 2 NZLR 327.

that this alone is evidence of an elision between what are essentially separate and distinct doctrines.[102] Returning to the decision in *Re Basham*, Martin[103] makes the point that if the plaintiff satisfied the requirements for proprietary estoppel, why was it necessary to introduce the concept of the constructive trust into the equation. It would therefore appear that while the relationship between proprietary estoppel and constructive trusts is certainly an interesting one, particularly from an academic perspective, the two doctrines, although linked by the common thread of unconscionability, are likely to continue to develop independently.

Perhaps one of the most controversial recent developments in the area of equitable estoppel has been the judgment of Costello J in *Re J.R.*[104] The committee of an elderly ward of court, who was living in a psychiatric hospital and was unable to manage his own affairs, sought to effect the sale of his house which had fallen into a dilapidated state. He had been living there with the respondent for many years and she maintained that when she went to live with him he had represented to her that he would look after her and that she would be sure of a home for the rest of her life. In his will the ward left everything to the respondent and at the time of its execution said to her that it was no longer his house but their house and that it would eventually be her house. Costello J concluded that the respondent had acted to her detriment on the representation made to her at the time she went to live with the ward that thereafter she could be sure of a home in his house for the rest of her life. He said that accordingly she had made out a case of promissory estoppel as she had acted on the representation made to her. 'It would be plainly inequitable for the ward now to deny that she has a right to live in his house and it seems to me that she has an equity which entitles her to stay in the house rent free for as long as she wishes to which the court must give effect.'[105] Costello J said that the respondent could not claim any enforceable rights by virtue of the ward handing her the will and saying the house was theirs as the gift was an imperfect one which the courts could not enforce — these actions did not confer an immediate beneficial interest under a constructive trust. Instead the ward had intended that she have a right to reside in the house during his life and ownership of it after his death. He concluded that the equity which the respondent had been able to establish was a right to reside in the

---

102. Note that in *Haslemere Estates Ltd v. Baker* [1982] 1 WLR 1109, 1119 Megarry VC rejected the argument that proprietary estoppel arises 'whenever justice and good conscience requires it'.
103. [1987] Conv 211, 213.
104. [1993] ILRM 657.
105. *Ibid.* at 663.

house for her life. However, in the special circumstances of the case as the house was in a serious state of dilapidation, the respondent's equity could be satisfied by selling the house and buying another one suitable for her needs.

While the result achieved was clearly a fair and equitable one in the circumstances, there are a number of difficulties with the reasoning employed by Costello J. First he appears to hold that promissory estoppel is capable of creating proprietary rights. While it has long been accepted that proprietary estoppel may give rise to a cause of action,[106] it would appear to be a novel approach to suggest that promissory estoppel is equally capable of doing so and it is clearly impossible to reconcile with the *dicta* of O'Hanlon J in *Association of General Practitioners Ltd v. Minister for Health*,[107] in which he reasserted the traditional view that promissory estoppel should be regarded as providing a shield and not a sword.[108] Although a more flexible approach appears to have been accepted in Australia by a number of the judges in *Waltons Stores (Interstate) Ltd v. Maher*[109] and in *Commonwealth of Australia v. Verwayen*,[110] Coughlan's[111] comment that in *Re J.R.*[112] Costello J failed to address fully the implications of the step he was taking or to consider the relevant authorities is a fair one. In the context of the facts which were before the court in that case Coughlan's statement that 'it is difficult to envisage situations in which promissory estoppel will be of more utility than proprietary estoppel'[113] is particularly apt.

A further area which may give rise to some confusion is Costello J's treatment of the concept of detriment in that he appeared to treat it as one of the requirements of promissory estoppel. While detriment is undoubtedly a requirement in establishing proprietary estoppel,[114] there is conflicting authority on the question of the need to establish it in cases of

---

106. *Inwards v. Baker* [1965] 2 QB 29, 38; *Crabb v. Arun District Council* [1976] Ch 179, 187 *per* Denning MR. See also the comments of Geoghegan J in *Smyth v. Halpin* [1997] 2 ILRM 38, 42 in which he pointed out that the granting of a remedy to the plaintiff would involve using estoppel 'as a sword and not merely as a shield'.
107. [1995] 2 ILRM 481.
108. See *Combe v. Combe* [1951] 2 KB 215, 224. But see the judgment of Gresson J in *Thomas v. Thomas* [1956] NZLR 785.
109. (1988) 164 CLR 387. See in particular at p.404 *per* Mason CJ; at p.420 *per* Brennan J.
110. (1990) 170 CLR 394.
111. (1993) 15 DULJ (ns) 188.
112. [1993] ILRM 657.
113. (1993) 15 DULJ (ns) 188, 189.
114. See e.g *Haughan v. Rutledge* [1988] IR 295.

promissory estoppel.[115] On the facts of the case before him. Costello J appears to accept that the respondent had acted to her detriment although it could be said that he was prepared to assume its existence as no reference was made to the respondent's circumstances prior to the time she moved in with the ward.

A final issue which has provoked considerable judicial and academic attention is the question of whether the task of the court should be to fulfil the claimant's expectations or merely to compensate him for the detriment which he has suffered, sometimes referred to as the 'expectation-oriented' and 'detriment-oriented' approaches.[116] The latter simply requires the court to provide compensation for the detriment suffered by the claimant because of the assurances made. This approach referred to by Cooke as the 'reliance loss theory'[117] has been consistently applied in Australia.[118] As Brennan J commented in *Waltons Stores (Interstate) Ltd v. Maher*:[119] 'The object of equity is not to compel the party bound to fulfil the assumption or expectation; it is to avoid the detriment which, if the expectation goes unfulfilled, will be suffered by the party who has been induced to act or to abstain from acting thereon.' However, it has generally been the expectation-oriented approach which has found favour with the courts in this jurisdiction and in England as decisions such as *Re J.R.*,[120] *Smyth v. Halpin*[121] and *Pascoe v. Turner*[122] illustrate. While the detriment-oriented approach may be more theoretically acceptable,[123] Cooke has argued that a 'weak version of the reliance loss theory . . . would introduce undesirable uncertainty' into the law and for this reason suggests that the primary function of estoppel should remain the protection of expectations. However, it is submitted that there is one element of the reliance loss theory which might usefully influence the courts in this jurisdiction and in England, even if it is in a more flexible form, namely that 'there must be a

---

115. See *W.J. Alan & Co. Ltd v. EL Nasr Export and Import Co.* [1972] 2 QB 189, 213 but see *Morrow v. Carty* [1957] NI 174, 182. See further *supra* p. 499.
116. Gray *Elements of Land Law* (2nd ed., 1993) pp. 345-347 and Pawlowski *Proprietary Estoppel* (1996) pp.77-82.
117. (1997) 17 LS 258.
118. See e.g. *Grundt v. Great Boulder Proprietary Gold Mines Ltd* (1937) 59 CLR 641.
119. (1988) 164 CLR 387. See also *Commonwealth of Australia v. Verwayen* (1990) 170 CLR 394.
120. [1993] ILRM 657
121. [1997] 2 ILRM 38.
122. [1979] 1 WLR 431.
123. The comment is made in *Modern Equity* (15th ed., 1997) Hanbury and Martin p.886 that reversing detriment is all that is required to prevent unjust enrichment whereas the expectation-oriented approach 'might be said to give a promise unsupported by consideration the effect of a contract'.

proportionality between the remedy and the detriment which is its purpose to avoid.'[124]

LIKELY FUTURE DEVELOPMENTS

As Robert Goff J commented in *Amalgamated Investment & Property Co. v. Texas Commerce International Bank Ltd*:[125] 'Of all doctrines, equitable estoppel is surely one of the most flexible'. While there have been *dicta* suggesting that the distinctions between the concepts of proprietary and promissory estoppel are 'not ... helpful'[126] and recommending that the different species of estoppel should 'merge into one general principle shorn of limitation,'[127] it is questionable whether such an all-embracing doctrine based on the unifying concept of unconscionability would be desirable. Certainly Treitel[128] has suggested that such an approach would provide no basis on which a doctrine capable of yielding predictable results could be developed and Evans[129] has argued that there is no real authority to back up a development of this nature. As against this, recent *dicta* in a number of Australian decisions would suggest that there is 'but one doctrine of estoppel'.[130] In *Waltons Stores (Interstate) Ltd v. Maher*[131] Mason CJ stated as follows:

> One may therefore discern in the cases a common thread which links them together, namely the principle that equity will come to the re-lief of a plaintiff who has acted to his detriment on the basis of a basic assumption in relation to which the other party to the transac-tion has 'played such a part in the adoption of the assumption that it would be unfair or unjust if he were left free to ignore it' *per* Dixon J in *Grundt v. Great Boulder Pty Gold Mines Ltd* (1937) 59 CLR 641 at p.675; see also *Thompson v. Palmer* (1933) 49 CLR 507 at p. 547. Equity comes to the relief of such a plaintiff on the footing that it would be unconscionable conduct on the part of the other party to ignore the assumption.

---

124. *Per* Mason CJ in *Commonwealth of Australia v.Verwayen* (1990) 170 CLR 394.
125. [1982] QB 84, 103. See also *Waltons Stores (Interstate) Ltd v. Maher* (1988) 164 CLR 387, 419.
126. *Crabb v. Arun District Council* [1976] Ch 179, 193 *per* Scarman LJ.
127. *Amalgamated Investment and Property Co. Ltd v. Texas Commerce International Bank Ltd* [1982] QB 84, 122.
128. *The Law of Contract* (9th ed., 1995) p.136.
129. [1988] Conv 346, 347
130. *Commonwealth of Australia v. Verwayen* (1990) 170 CLR 394, 412.
131. (1988) 164 CLR 387, 404.

Similarly, in *Commonwealth of Australia v. Verwayen*[132] Mason CJ spoke of a single doctrine of estoppel which would provide that a court of common law or equity may do what is necessary to prevent a person, who has relied on an assumption as to a present, past or future state of affairs, which he has been induced to hold by the party estopped, from suffering detriment in reliance on this assumption. While Lunney[133] accepts that there is no direct authority in England which supports a unified doctrine of estoppel based on unconscionability raising equities which can be enforced by the other party, he holds the view that the approach advocated in Australia represents a logical advance. Although it could be argued that the reasoning employed by Costello J in *Re J.R.* would support the view that such an approach may be accepted in this jurisdiction, it would probably be unwise to assume such a conclusion based on a judgment which does not fully address the implications of such a step.[134]

Realistically then we are unlikely to see a unified doctrine of estoppel emerging in the near future either in this jurisdiction or in England. Mee[135] suggests that 'there has been nothing resembling a carefully considered (or even conscious) decision to merge the estoppels in Ireland' and states that the present position in this jurisdiction appears to be that the doctrine of proprietary and promissory estoppel retain their separate identities. However, over the past few years there has also been considerable debate about the manner in which the doctrine of proprietary estoppel will develop. Halliwell[136] acknowledges that traditional orthodoxy is being challenged and says that it is now necessary to recognise that 'the organising concept for the doctrine of estoppel is unconscionability'. Yet decisions such as *Taylor v. Dickens*[137] would tend to suggest that such an approach is unlikely to be accepted and as Pawlowski has recently commented 'English law . . . is still a long way from accepting such a universal principle'.[138] As he correctly points out while 'the modern approach is to explain the doctrine in terms of a general concept of unconscionability, the courts

---

132. (1990)170 CLR 394.
133. [1992] Conv 239, 248- 250.
134. Mee has commented (1998) 33 Ir Jur (ns) 187, 219 that 'one must conclude that *Re JR* was simply another example of an Irish judge reaching a conclusion which he regarded as just without paying much attention to strict legal doctrine'.
135. (1998) 33 Ir Jur (ns) 187, 219.
136. (1994) 14 LS 15. However, she suggests that any new doctrine of estoppel freed from traditional labels must still be distinguished from the form of equitable estoppel identified in the *High Trees* case which as she states 'has afforded a defence in circumstances of a gratuitous promise to vary contractual obligations being enforced.'
137. [1998] 1 FLR 806.
138. (1998) 114 LQR 351.

do require the estoppel claimant to prove the three essential elements (i.e. assurance, reliance and detriment) as a prerequisite to a successful claim'[139] and this accurately reflects the approach recently advocated by Carnwath J in *Gillett v. Holt*.[140]

---

139. *Ibid.* at 352.
140. [1998] 3 All ER 917.

CHAPTER 18

Tracing

TRACING AT COMMON LAW

At common law while a person who was wrongfully deprived of his property could follow it into the hands of another party, he could only do so in circumstances where this property was still identifiable and had not been mixed with other funds. Millett J has recently summarised the principles which apply to this form of tracing in his judgment in *Agip (Africa) Ltd v. Jackson*:[1]

> Tracing at common law, unlike its counterpart in equity, is neither a cause of action nor a remedy but serves an evidential purpose. The cause of action is for money had and received. Tracing at common law enables the defendant to be identified as the recipient of the plaintiff's money and the measure of his liability to be determined by the amount of the plaintiff's money he is shown to have received.

So at common law the legal owner of property was entitled to follow it into the hands of another even where it had changed in form provided that there was a means of identifying the asset in its original or converted form. As Lord Ellenborough stated in *Taylor v. Plumer*:[2] 'It makes no difference in reason or law into what other form, different from the original, the change may have been made'. He pointed out that 'the product of or substitute for the original thing still follows the nature of the thing itself, as long as it can be ascertained as such'[3] but this right to follow at common law will cease when the means of identifying the original is lost as, e.g. when the assets are converted into money and 'confounded into a general mass of the same description'. These principles were reiterated by the Court of Appeal in *Re Diplock*[4] where Lord Greene MR commented that the com-

---

1. [1990] Ch 265, 285.
2. (1815) 3 M & S 562, 575. For an alternative interpretation of what this decision establishes, see Smith [1995] LMCLQ 240.
3. *Ibid.* at 575.
4. [1948] 1 Ch 465, 518. See also the comment of Millett J in *Agip (Africa) Ltd v. Jackson* that 'it can only follow a physical asset . . . from one person to another' (at p.285).

mon law 'could only appreciate what might almost be called the "physical" identity of one thing with another'. So the common law could treat money as identifiable provided it was not mixed with other money and could also treat as identifiable other kinds of property acquired with these funds alone.[5]

The inability of the common law to trace into a mixed fund is undoubtedly its greatest limitation and it means that it cannot assist a plaintiff in what is probably the most common situation in practice where a tracing remedy may be required, namely where a defendant has mixed the plaintiff's money with his own and subsequently gone bankrupt.[6] The other major limitation of this form of tracing is that because the common law did not recognise equitable rights and interests, a beneficiary could not follow trust property into the hands of a trustee.[7]

Recently consideration has been given to tracing at common law by the English Court of Appeal in *F.C. Jones & Sons (Trustees) v. Jones,*[8] in which the plaintiff was held entitled to trace not only the property but also any profit made from it. As Nourse LJ commented the decision went further than previous cases 'in that it holds that the action for money had and received entitles the legal owner to trace his property into its product, not only in the sense of property for which it is exchanged, but also in the sense of property representing the original and the profit made by the defendant's use of it'.[9] In considering the rules which apply to tracing at law and in equity Millett LJ stated as follows:

> There is no merit in having distinct and different tracing rules at law and in equity, given that tracing is neither a right nor a remedy but merely the process by which the plaintiff establishes what has happened to his property and makes good his claim that the assets which he claims can properly be regarded as representing his property. The fact that there are different tracing rules at law and in equity is unfortunate though probably inevitable, but unnecessary differences should not be created where they are not required by the different nature of legal and equitable doctrines and remedies. There is in my view, even less merit in the present rule which precludes the invocation of the equitable tracing rules to support a common law claim;

5. *Ibid.* at 518.
6. See Hanbury and Martin, *Modern Equity* (15th ed., 1997) p.660-661.
7. See the judgment of Lord Greene MR in *Re Diplock* [1948] Ch 465, 519-520 where this and other limitations are discussed.
8. [1996] 3 WLR 703.
9. *Ibid.* at 714.

until that rule is swept away unnecessary obstacles to the development of a rational and coherent law of restitution will remain.[10]

TRACING IN EQUITY[11]

Introduction

While a trustee or constructive trustee may be personally liable to beneficiaries, where e.g. he has transferred the trust property to another in breach of trust and has disposed of the proceeds of sale, this remedy will be of little value if the trustee has insufficient assets to meet the claim. Where he no longer has the trust property in his possession and cannot meet any personal claim against him, the alternative of a proprietary remedy must be considered. It is also important to remember that a constructive trust can only be imposed where trust property becomes vested in a person in a manner which amounts to a breach of trust and where property is transferred to an innocent volunteer, no personal liability can be imposed. In both these situations the proprietary remedy of tracing will provide a means whereby a beneficiary may recover property which has been wrongly disposed of. This proprietary remedy has a number of advantages; first, where the trustee is insolvent, the claimant will take in priority to his general creditors[12] and secondly, where trust property comes into the hands of an innocent volunteer, who takes subject to the trust but has neither actual nor constructive knowledge of it, the volunteer will not be liable as constructive trustee but a tracing remedy will lie against him. So the tracing remedy may lie against a person who is not personally liable as a result of a breach of fiduciary duty.

Recently this proprietary remedy has taken on a new significance as a means of tracing the proceeds of international fraud. While, as we have seen, the common law cannot trace into a mixed fund, equity does not require the existence of a physical asset and can follow funds even where they have been the subject of electronic transfer.[13] As Lord Greene MR commented in *Re Diplock*:[14] 'Equity adopted a more metaphysical approach' and 'found no difficulty in regarding a composite fund as an amalgam constituted by the mixture of two or more funds each of which could

---

10. *Ibid.* at 712.
11. For an excellent recent analysis of some of most important issues arising in this area, see Oakley [1995] CLJ 377.
12. *Re Hallett's Estate* (1880) 13 Ch D 696.
13. Millett (1991) 107 LQR 71, 74.
14. [1948] Ch 465, 520. Quoted by Budd J in *Shanahan's Stamp Auctions Ltd v. Farrelly* [1962] IR 386, 436.

be regarded as having, for certain purposes, a continued separate existence.'

General Principles

Tracing in equity is usually sought where property has come into the hands
of trustees and other persons in a fiduciary relationship. It is a remedy *in
rem*, 'a claim to follow and recover property with which, in equity at all
events, [a person] had never really parted'.[15] The right to trace in equity
also exists against third parties into whose hands the funds may have come.
Although it does not extend to purchasers for value of the property without notice of the right to trace, it will apply to an innocent volunteer who
comes into possession of the trust property. It should also be noted that
traditionally it has been accepted that in order to pursue an equitable tracing remedy, a plaintiff should possess an equitable proprietary interest.[16]
	The decision in which the parameters of tracing in equity were first
explored in detail and which illustrated the potential for tracing into a
mixed fund was that of the English Court of Appeal in *Re Hallett's Estate*.[17] As Atkin LJ was later to comment in relation to this decision:[18] 'if
in 1815 the common law halted outside the banker's door, by 1879 equity
had had the courage to lift the latch, walk in and examine the books'. In
Hallett a solicitor had lodged funds from a trust of which he was trustee
and those belonging to a client to his own bank account. He made various
payments from and into the account and after his death it emerged that
there were insufficient funds remaining to pay these monies back and to
meet his personal debts. In an action brought to decide how his estate
should be administered, the question arose whether the trust and the client
could claim priority over the solicitor's general creditors. It was held by
the Court of Appeal that the beneficiaries under the trust and the client
were entitled to trace the misappropriated funds and that they were entitled to a charge on the monies in the bank account in priority to the general
creditors. One important principle to be derived from the judgment to which
we shall return is that the solicitor was presumed to have spent his own
money first and not to have drawn on the trust monies irrespective of the
order in which these funds were paid into his account.[19]

---

15. *Sinclair v. Brougham* [1914] AC 398, 418.
16. Although note the decision of the English Court of Appeal in *Aluminium Industrie
	Vassen BV v. Romalpa Aluminium Ltd* [1976] 1 WLR 676.
17. (1880) 13 Ch D 696.
18. *Banque Belge pour l'Etranger v. Hambrouck* [1921] 1 KB 321, 335.
19. See also *Carroll Group Distributors Ltd v. G. & J.F. Bourke Ltd* [1990] 1 IR 481,
	484.

It has also been established that the equitable tracing remedy is not confined to claims as between a trustee and beneficiary but will extend to any persons in fiduciary relationships and it has become clear that this relationship need not exist between the parties to the action. In *Sinclair v. Brougham*[20] a building society which had operated an *ultra vires* banking business was wound up and a dispute arose in relation to the respective claims of the shareholders and the depositors. The House of Lords found that there was a sufficient fiduciary relationship between the depositors and the directors of the building society 'by reason of the fact that the purposes for which the depositors had handed their money to the directors were by law incapable of fulfilment'.[21] It was held that the depositors had a right to trace the funds into the hands of the society and ranked *pari passu* with the shareholders as regards entitlement to the funds; as Viscount Haldane LC commented: 'I see no reason why either set of claimants should have priority over the other.' As Oakley has commented 'the decision was unquestionably authority for the availability of an equitable proprietary claim to the transferor of property under a transaction which is void *ab initio*'.[22] However, it should be pointed out that the decision in *Sinclair v. Brougham* was effectively overruled by the House of Lords in *Westdeutsche Landesbank Girozentrale v. Islington London Borough Council*,[23] which will be considered in more detail below, where the majority of the House of Lords held that an equitable proprietary claim is not available to a transferor of property under an *ultra vires* transaction which is void *ab initio*.

It was established in *Re Diplock*[24] that an innocent volunteer who receives money or property *bona fide* is in the same position as regards entitlement to this property as an equitable owner who has a right to trace.[25] Mr Diplock left the residue of his estate on trust for 'such charitable institutions or other charitable or benevolent object or objects in England as my executors may in their absolute discretion select'. The executors of the will thinking that it was a valid charitable gift paid out a large part of the

---

20. [1914] AC 398.
21. *Per* Lord Greene MR in *Re Diplock* [1948] Ch 465, 540-541.
22. [1997] Conv 1, 2.
23. Lord Browne-Wilkinson described it as a 'bewildering authority' and commented that all the reasoning in the decision was 'open to serious objection'.
24. [1948] Ch 465.
25. As Lord Greene MR commented at p.539: 'It would be inequitable for the volunteer to claim priority for the reason that he is a volunteer: it would be equally inequitable for the true owner of the money to claim priority over the volunteer for the reason that the volunteer is innocent and cannot be said to act unconscionably if he claims the equal treatment for himself.'

residue amounting to over £200,000 to various charitable institutions. Subsequently, it became clear that the gift was not a valid charitable one,[26] and the next of kin, having exhausted their remedies against the executors, sought to recover these monies from the charities. It was held by the Court of Appeal[27] that they were entitled to trace the funds into the hands of the charities who were innocent volunteers, with whom they had to share rateably. As Lord Greene MR stated:

> [E]quity may operate on the conscience not merely of those who acquire a legal title in breach of some trust, express or constructive, or of some other fiduciary obligation, but of volunteers provided that as a result of what has gone before some equitable proprietary interest has been created and attaches to the property in the hands of the volunteer.[28]

However, he stressed later on in his judgment that although 'equity may operate upon the conscience of a volunteer, it will not operate upon the conscience of a purchaser for value without notice.'[29] It is useful to set out some of Lord Greene MR's conclusions which provide a summary of the principles already considered:

> Where one claimant is a person in a fiduciary relationship to another and has mixed moneys of that other with moneys of his own, that other takes priority. . . . Where the contest is between two claimants to a mixed fund made up entirely of moneys held on behalf of the two of them respectively and mixed together by the fiduciary agent, they share *pari passu*.[30]

---

26. The use of the word 'or' was interpreted to mean that the words of the gift were wide enough to allow the trustees to dispose of the fund or an unascertainable part of it to non-charitable purposes.
27. The appeal to the House of Lords, (*sub nom Ministry of Health v. Simpson* [1951] AC 251) related only to the *in personam* claims of the next of kin.
28. *Ibid.* at 530.
29. *Ibid.* at 544.
30. [1948] Ch 465, 539. The latter principle has recently been reaffirmed and explained further in the context of the purchase of an asset by Scott VC in *Foskett v. McKeown* [1998] Ch 265, 278 in the following terms: '[I]f in purchasing the asset the trustee has used trust money from two different trust sources, neither set of beneficiaries can claim a first charge over the asset to recover its money. The equities as between the two sets of beneficiaries will be equal. Neither will be entitled to priority as against the other. It follows that they must share proportionately in the asset, bearing *pro rata* any shortfall and enjoying *pro rata* any increase in value'.

These principles were applied in Ireland by Budd J in *Shanahan's Stamp Auctions Ltd v. Farrelly.*[31] A company which grouped investors into syndicates and used their funds to buy stamps went into liquidation. Some of these investors had been allocated to syndicates at the time and the liquidator sought directions from the court about priority of payments as between the general creditors and the syndicated and unsyndicated investors. Budd J held that at all material times a fiduciary relationship existed between the company and the investors and that both classes of investors were entitled to trace their money. The stamps allocated to the syndicates were held to be subject to a charge in favour of the syndicated investors for the amount of the investment and the remaining stamps were held by the company subject to a charge in favour of the unsyndicated investors on a rateable basis.

One of the most important cases in this area in recent years is that of *Westdeutsche Landesbank Girozentrale v. Islington London Borough Council.*[32] The parties had entered into a ten-year interest rate swap agreement whereby the plaintiff paid a lump sum to the defendant and the defendant was then obliged to make 'interest' payments to the plaintiff. The House of Lords held in *Hazell v. Hammersmith and Fulham LBC*[33] that such interest rate swap agreements were *ultra vires* the powers of local authorities and following this decision the council made no more payments to the bank. The Court of Appeal held that the bank was entitled to recover the balance owed as money had and received and in equity on the basis of its equitable proprietary interest in the monies advanced and awarded compound interest on this sum. Before the House of Lords the council contested its liability to pay compound interest, the traditional view being that the existence of a claim in equity is a prerequisite for the award of compound as opposed to simple interest. The majority of the House of Lords adhered to this view and held that the type of interest payable depended on whether the bank had a continuing equitable proprietary interest in the sum advanced. They held, overruling *Sinclair v. Brougham,* that an equitable proprietary interest cannot exist in favour of a transferor of property under an *ultra vires* transaction which is void *ab initio* and concluded that as a result only simple interest should be awarded to the bank. The minority disagreed and held that equitable jurisdiction to award compound interest could exist even in relation to personal claims at common law and

---

31. [1962] IR 386.
32. [1996] AC 669. See Cope (1996) 112 LQR 521; Jones [1996] CLJ 432; Oakley [1997] Conv 1; Birks [1997] RLR 3.
33. [1992] AC 1.

dismissed the council's appeal. Lord Browne-Wilkinson summarised the effect of overruling *Sinclair v. Brougham* in the following terms:

> [T]he law can be established in accordance with principle and com-
> mercial common sense: a claimant for restitution of moneys paid
> under an *ultra vires,* and therefore void, contract has a personal ac-
> tion at law to recover the moneys paid as on a total failure of consid-
> eration; he will not have an equitable proprietary claim which gives
> him either rights against third parties or priority in an insolvency;
> nor will he have a personal claim in equity, since the recipient is not
> a trustee.[34]

Tracing into a Bank Account

Where the mixed fund in which trust monies have been lodged is an active bank account, in certain circumstances a principle known as the rule in *Clayton's case*[35] may apply. In theory it applies to competing claims of beneficiaries of different trusts and of beneficiaries and innocent volun-teers and the effect of the rule is 'first in, first out'. So if a trustee pays £1,000 from one trust fund into a bank account and then pays a further sum of £1,000 from another fund into the account and later withdraws £1,000, the loss is borne wholly by the first trust on the basis of the princi-ple of 'first in first out'. It is important to stress that the rule in *Clayton's case* will not apply to the type of situation which arose in *Re Hallett's Estate*[36] as the trustee was presumed to be acting honestly and to have drawn on his own money in the account first. This is sometimes referred to as the rule in *Re Hallett's Estate* and can be summarised as follows:[37] 'the trustee is presumed to be honest rather than dishonest and to make pay-ments out of his own private moneys and not out of the trust fund that was mingled with his private moneys'.

However, this principle will not always be strictly adhered to where this would lead to injustice. In *Re Oatway*[38] a trustee withdrew misappro-priated trust monies from a mixed fund and invested them and subsequently

---

34. *Ibid.* at 714.
35. (1816) 1 Mer 572.
36. (1880) 13 Ch D 696.
37. *Per* Sargant J in *James Roscoe (Bolton) Ltd v. Winder* [1915] 1 Ch 62, 67. See also the *dicta* of Budd J in *Shanahan's Stamp Auctions Ltd v. Farrelly* [1962] IR 386, 428: 'If the person holding the money in a fiduciary capacity mixed it with his own the rule in *Clayton's case* does not apply; such person must be taken to have drawn out his own monies in preference to the trust monies. . . .'
38. [1903] 2 Ch 356.

dissipated the remainder of the fund. Joyce J refused to apply the *Hallett* principle strictly as this would have led to the conclusion that the money withdrawn initially and invested was the trustee's own, and held instead that the beneficiaries were entitled to the assets represented by the investments.

The rule in *Clayton's case* was applied in relation to some of the claims in *Re Diplock*[39] although Lord Greene MR did not seem to be suggesting that it should be automatically applied in such circumstances[40] and said that it was a 'rule of convenience based upon so-called presumed intention'.[41] Similar views were expressed by Woolf LJ in *Barlow Clowes International Ltd v. Vaughan*[42] where he made it clear that 'the rule need only be applied when it is convenient to do so and when its application can be said to do broad justice having regard to the nature of the competing claims.'[43] There companies which had promoted and managed certain investment plans ran into severe financial difficulties and the amount of money owed to investors far exceeded the funds available for distribution. The receivers sought directions as to how the assets in their hands should be distributed. The trial judge held that the rule of first in first out should be applied to the distribution of assets so that the investors who could trace into the funds were to be paid in the reverse order to that in which they had made deposits. The Court of Appeal was of the view that while the first in first out rule would be applied where it provided a convenient method of determining competing claims as between several beneficiaries, where its application would be impractical or would result in injustice between the investors, it would not be applied if a preferable alternative method of distribution was available. It was held that it would be contrary to the presumed intention of the investors to distribute the remaining monies in accordance with the first in first out rule so that those who had invested first could expect least. Instead, it was held that the available assets and moneys should be distributed *pari passu* among all the unpaid investors rateably in proportion to the amounts due to them regardless of the dates on which investors had made their investment.

The rule in *Clayton's case* was also considered by Budd J in the course

---

39. [1948] Ch 465.
40. *Barlow Clowes International Ltd v. Vaughan* [1992] 4 All ER 22, 38 *per* Woolf LJ.
41. [1948] Ch 465, 554.
42. [1992] 4 All ER 22, 39.
43. Oliver has commented (1995) 9 Trust Law Int 78, 79 that 'it is at least clear as a result of the *Barlow Clowes* case that the rule in *Clayton's case* is a rule of convenience and not a rule of law, and accordingly it seems unlikely that the courts will use it where it is impracticable or likely to produce inequitable results'.

of his judgment in *Shanahan's Stamp Auctions Ltd v. Farrelly.*[44] He accepted that the rule is generally applicable to determine the competing claims of beneficiaries, 'that is the first drawings out are to be attributable to the first payments in'.[45] He then went on to state that while it might not be applied apart from where it is sought to trace into a bank account, he was prepared to consider whether it might apply to property acquired by means of a mixed fund. However, Budd J was satisfied that on the facts of the case it could have no application as there had been a 'second mixing of the investor's funds into a second mixed amalgam of property'.

It is certainly unlikely that the suggestion made by Budd J that the rule in *Clayton's case* might apply to property acquired by means of a mixed fund would be followed and Keane's[46] statement that it may be doubtful whether it will continue to be applied to determine the competing claims of beneficiaries to money in a bank account is probably more accurate. The suggestion made by Woolf LJ in *Barlow Clowes* that the rule should only be applied where it can be said to do 'broad justice' has been heralded as 'a welcome relaxation'[47] of what has been labelled a 'capricious and arbitrary'[48] rule. Recently Robert Walker J has pointed out in *El Anjou v. Dollar Land Holdings plc*[49] that the members of the Court of Appeal in *Barlow Clowes* recognised that the rule may be applied as between rival claimants seeking to trace through an active bank account, although he did acknowledge that the court had accepted that it is 'perhaps *prima facie* not appropriate for those who have the common misfortune of being victims of a large scale fraud'.[50] Whether the courts in this jurisdiction follow the approach adopted by the New Zealand Court of Appeal in *Re Registered Securities Ltd*[51] in rejecting the application of the rule outright remains to be seen, but it is in any event unlikely that they would countenance the continued application of the rather inflexible pre-*Barlow* principle.

Traditionally, a beneficiary's right to trace into a mixed fund in a bank account only applied to the extent that the trust monies could be shown to be still there and if the account fell below the sum said to constitute the trust funds, they were then deemed to have been spent. This point is illustrated by the decision of Sargant J in *James Roscoe (Bolton) Ltd v. Winder*[52]

---

44. [1962] IR 386.
45. *Ibid.* at 442.
46. *Equity and the Law of Trusts in the Republic of Ireland* (1988) p. 286.
47. Goff and Jones, *The Law of Restitution* (5th ed., 1998) p.109.
48. *Ibid.* at 108.
49. [1995] 2 All ER 213.
50. *Ibid.* at 222.
51. [1991] 1 NZLR 545, 553 *per* Somers J.
52. [1915] 1 Ch 62.

where an agreement for the sale of the goodwill of a business provided that the purchaser should collect certain book debts and pay this money over to the vendor. The purchaser collected some of these debts and paid part of the money amounting to about £455 into his own account. Subsequently, this balance was reduced to approximately £25 although by the time of the purchaser's death, the balance had risen again to just over £358. Sargant J considered the principles laid down in *Re Hallett's Estate*[53] and said that the general view of that decision was 'that it only applied to such an amount of the balance ultimately standing to the credit of the trustee as did not exceed the lowest balance of the account during the intervening period'.[54] He therefore concluded that the purchaser held the money as trustee but found that the charge was limited to the sum of around £25, which was the lowest intermediate balance after the money had been appropriated.

It is clear from this decision that subsequent payments into an account will not generally be treated as repayments of the trust fund. However, this presumption can be displaced by evidence which establishes that the trustee intended to replace the misappropriated funds. So, in *Re Hughes,*[55] where a solicitor lodged funds to an account after the Law Society had initiated an investigation into his professional activities, Kenny J held that the only possible inference was that he had intended the lodgement to be a replacement for the monies he had withdrawn from the client account.

The question of whether it is possible to trace into an overdrawn bank account has recently been considered in both England and Ireland and the consensus is that it is not possible. In *Bishopsgate Investment Management Ltd v. Homan*[56] the liquidators of a company which was the trustee of the assets of pension schemes from which monies had been improperly paid into the bank account of another company sought to establish an equitable charge in priority to this company's other unsecured creditors. Their claim was rejected by the Court of Appeal on the basis that equitable tracing could not be pursued through an overdrawn and therefore non-existent fund. The same conclusion was reached by Murphy J in *PMPA Ltd v. PMPS Ltd*[57] in which the plaintiff had made an *ultra vires* payment of £450,000 to the defendant which the latter had lodged in an overdrawn account.

---

53. (1880) 13 Ch D 696.
54. [1915] 1 Ch 62, 69.
55. [1970] IR 237.
56. [1994] 3 WLR 1270. See Smith (1994) 8 Trust Law Int 102; Jones [1996] Conv 129. See also *Re Goldcorp Exchange* [1995] 1 AC 74.
57. High Court 1992 No. 702 Sp (Murphy J) 27 June 1994. See also *Carroll Group Distributors Ltd v. G. & J.F. Bourke Ltd* [1990] 1 IR 481, 486-7.

Murphy J was satisfied that the plaintiff could not pursue a tracing remedy as the monies had been dissipated and no longer existed as such, although he concluded that the defendant had had no right to these monies in the first instance and that the plaintiff was entitled to restitution. It would seem therefore that once the balance in an account falls below a certain level or becomes overdrawn, the capacity to trace is limited to the lowest intermediate balance and in the case of an overdrawn account, ceases altogether.

The Extent of the Right to Trace in Equity

Where trust funds have been used to purchase other specific property and have not been mixed with the trustee's own assets, a beneficiary may either elect to take the property purchased, or to have a charge on the property for the amount of the trust money.[58] However, where trust funds have been mixed with others monies, as Jessel MR made clear in *Re Hallett's Estate*,[59] the beneficiary can no longer elect to take the property as it has been purchased with a mixed fund and can only claim an entitlement to a charge on this property to the amount of the trust funds used in the purchase. It would appear that in the latter case, the onus is on the trustee to establish the amount of the mixed fund which actually belongs to him and the beneficiary will be entitled to whatever portion of the fund which the trustee cannot prove is his own.[60]

A further question which arises is where a mixed fund is invested in a manner which yields a profit, should the beneficiary be entitled to a portion of the profit or should he be confined to a charge to the amount of the trust fund initially misappropriated. While a strict reading of *Re Hallett's Estate*[61] and *Sinclair v. Brougham*[62] would suggest the latter conclusion, as Hanbury and Martin[63] point out this would be a 'startling result' given the strict attitude taken by the courts towards any profit-making activities on the part of a trustee. As they suggest, the better solution would be to allow the beneficiary to claim a share of the mixed fund in the proportion which the original fund bore to the mixed fund at the time these monies were mixed. This seems to have been accepted by Ungoed-Thomas J in *Re Tilley's Will Trusts*[64] where he commented as follows: 'If ... it appears that

58. *Re Hallett's Estate* (1880)13 Ch D 696, 709.
59. (1880) 13 Ch D 696, 709. See also *Sinclair v. Brougham* [1914] AC 398, 442.
60. *Lupton v. White* (1808) 15 Ves 432; *Re Tilley's Will Trusts* [1967] Ch 1179, 1182.
61. (1880) 13 Ch D 696, 709.
62. [1914] AC 398, 442.
63. *Modern Equity* (15th ed., 1997) p.676.
64. [1967] Ch 1179. See Jones [1968] CLJ 28.

a trustee has, in fact, whatever his intention, laid out trust moneys in or towards a purchase, then the beneficiaries are entitled to the property purchased and any profits which it produces to the extent to which it has been paid for out of trust moneys.' However, on the facts of the case, Ungoed-Thomas J was satisfied that the misappropriated trust monies had not in fact been invested in this manner. The testator appointed his wife as executrix and gave her a life interest in his estate with remainder to his children. His widow accumulated funds during her lifetime by dealing in properties and mixed these monies with her own. The plaintiff, the executor of her daughter's estate, brought an action seeking to determine what was due to the latter's estate. Ungoed-Thomas held that the trust monies had not been invested in properties at all but had gone in reduction of the widow's overdraft, which was the real source of the purchase money and allowed only the return of the trust money. However, he conceded that if the trust funds had been applied in the purchase of properties, these properties would have been owned partly by Mrs Tilley and partly by the trust, in the proportions in which the monies from those sources had been used to make the purchases.

As Scott VC recently pointed out in *Foskett v. McKeown*,[65] the option of claiming a proportionate interest in the asset set out in the *Tilley* case will obviously be preferable to merely obtaining a charge if the asset has increased in value. However, while Scott VC accepted the former option as a well established principle, Oakley points out that Scott VC made no reference to the more restrictive approach adopted in *Re Hallett's Estate* and suggests that 'the definitive resolution of this matter must clearly await a formal decision on the point'.[66]

The Requirement of a Fiduciary Relationship

While the decision in *Re Hallett's Estate*[67] concerned the relationship of trustee and beneficiary, Jessel MR made it clear in the course of his judgment[68] that he intended that the principles which he laid down should be extended to other types of fiduciary relationships.

The requirement of a fiduciary relationship was also stressed by Kenny J in *Re Shannon Travel Ltd*,[69] where he stated as follows:

---

65. [1998] Ch 265, 278.
66. Parker and Mellows *The Modern Law of Trusts* (7th ed., 1998) p. 733.
67. (1880) 13 Ch D 696.
68. *Ibid.* at 709.
69. High Court 1970 No. 3849 P (Kenny J) 8 May 1972.

> The general principle is that when a person receives money as a trustee or as one occupying a fiduciary relation to another, the person who transferred the property or paid the money may recover the property and has a charge on the account to which the money or cheques have been lodged or on property on which the monies received have been spent provided that the property or money can be traced through the accounts of the debtor into the bank account etc., and provided that there is money to the credit of the account on which the charge can operate.[70]

In *Shannon* Kenny J held that an equitable charge over a bank account containing funds held in trust by an insolvent was liable to abatement so that the liquidator's expenses and remuneration could be paid. This result is in some respects unsatisfactory as Kenny J failed to address adequately the question of why the proprietary remedy should be qualified in such a manner.

In England, as a result of the decision of the House of Lords in *Sinclair v. Brougham*,[71] it became clear that tracing in equity would extend to any persons in fiduciary relationships even where this relationship did not exist between the parties to the action. This requirement of a fiduciary relationship was also accepted unquestioningly by the Court of Appeal in *Re Diplock*[72] and it was regarded in principle as a pre-requisite by Goulding J in *Chase Manhattan Bank NA v. Israel British Bank (London) Ltd*,[73] although it would appear that this 'fiduciary element can be satisfied at the moment the payment is made'.[74] The plaintiff made a duplicate payment of $2,000,000 in error into another bank for the benefit of the defendant. The defendant's bank became insolvent and the question arose whether the plaintiff was entitled to trace this money into the bank's assets or whether it had prove with the other creditors. Goulding J held that the fact that the payment had been mistakenly made gave rise to a constructive trust and that the plaintiff was entitled to trace these funds.[75] He stated that it was

---

70. At pp. 8-9.
71. [1914] Ch 398.
72. [1948] Ch 465.
73. [1981] Ch 105.
74. Collins (1994) 1 Comm L P 211, 213.
75. It should be noted that Lord Browne-Wilkinson in *Westdeutsche Landesbank v. Islington London Borough Council* [1996] AC 669, 715 stated that while he did not accept the reasoning of Goulding J, *Chase Manhatten* may well have been correctly decided. As Jones has pointed out [1996] CLJ 432, 434-5: 'The retention of the money once the [defendant] learnt of the mistake may well have given rise to a constructive trust'. However, Oakley has commented [1997] Conv 1, 3 that although the

common ground that a right to trace money paid by mistake exists in English law and re-iterated that 'an initial fiduciary relationship is a necessary foundation of the equitable right of tracing'.[76] However, it is hard to disagree with the criticism that Goulding J was effectively by-passing the requirement of a fiduciary relationship and he appeared to hold that the payment into the wrong hands itself gave rise to the relationship. His reasoning was approved by Carroll J in *Re Irish Shipping Ltd,*[77] in which a bank made a duplicate payment in error to the bank account in Citibank of Irish Shipping Ltd which subsequently went into liquidation. Citibank, the former bankers of Irish Shipping, claimed to be entitled to set off debts due by the company to them against the mistaken payment. However, it was held by Carroll J that where monies are paid by mistake into the account of a company such monies do not form part of the assets of the company at the date of the liquidation and she concluded that the bank which had made the duplicate payment was entitled to trace the money into the account.

Further comments were made about the requirement of a fiduciary relationship by Millett J at first instance in *Agip (Africa) Ltd v. Jackson*[78] where he stated as follows:

> The only restriction on the ability of equity to follow assets is the requirement that there must be some fiduciary relationship which permits the assistance of equity to be invoked. The requirement has been widely condemned and depends on authority rather than principle, but the law was settled in *In re Diplock* [1948] Ch 465. It may need to be reconsidered but not, I venture to think, at first instance. The requirement may be circumvented since it is not necessary that the fund to be traced should have been the subject of fiduciary obligations before it got into the wrong hands; it is sufficient that the payment to the defendant itself gives rise to a fiduciary relationship: *Chase Manhattan Bank NA v. Israel-British Bank London Ltd* [1981] Ch 105.[79]

---

decision has not been formally overruled, 'it appears unlikely that an equitable proprietary claim will now be available to a transferor of money acting as a result of a mistake of fact'. See also Cope (1996) 112 LQR 521, 523.
76. [1981] Ch 105, 119.
77. [1986] ILRM 518.
78. [1990] Ch 265, 290.
79. Fox LJ also suggested in delivering his decision in the Court of Appeal [1991] Ch 547, 566 that the requirement of a fiduciary relationship remained.

More recently in *Boscawen v. Bajwa*[80] Millett LJ reiterated that '[i]t is still a prerequisite of the right to trace in equity that there must be a fiduciary relationship which calls the equitable jurisdiction into being'. However, the most recent pronouncement which has been interpreted as having relevance to this issue is less clear, namely Lord Browne-Wilkinson's statement in *Westdeutsche Landesbank Girozentrale v. Islington London Borough Council*,[81] that their Lordships 'should not be taken to be casting any doubt on the principles of tracing as established in *Re Diplock*'. As Oakley has commented: 'Since it is generally thought that in this case the Court of Appeal interpreted *Sinclair v. Brougham* as establishing the controversial proposition "that an initial fiduciary relationship is a necessary foundation of the equitable right of tracing" this remark appeared to indicate that Lord Browne-Wilkinson was in favour of the requirement'.[82] As a result of Lord Browne-Wilkinson's statement Cope has commented that 'the extent to which a trust or other fiduciary relationship is still essential to maintain an equitable proprietary claim is not made clear'[83] and Jones has stated that '[t]he condition that there must be a fiduciary relationship to support an equitable proprietary claim is still alive but appears to be increasingly meaningless'.[84]

There are certainly signs of alternative approaches being adopted elsewhere in the common law world, as in New Zealand where it was suggested by Cooke P in *Elders Pastoral Ltd v. Bank of New Zealand*[85] that unconscionability is the key to establishing a right to trace in equity and not the presence of a fiduciary relationship.

The best summary of the likely approach of the courts in this jurisdiction to the question of the need to establish a fiduciary relationship is provided by Collins in the following terms:[86]

> The fiduciary relationship requirement may not be expressly abandoned but the definition of that relationship is proving sufficiently

---

80. [1996] 1 WLR 328, 335. See Birks (1995) 9 Trust Law Intl 124.
81. [1996] AC 669, 714.
82. [1997] Conv 1, 3-4. However, Oakley went on to point out that at a seminar in Oxford in September 1996, Lord Browne-Wilkinson indicated that he had only made that remark to forestall any argument that the whole framework of equitable proprietary claims had been swept away and that he regarded the requirement of establishing a fiduciary relationship as wholly misconceived.
83. (1996) 112 LQR 521, 523.
84. [1996] CLJ 432, 435. Oliver has expressed the hope that the House of Lords will soon eliminate the fiduciary requirement, see (1995) 9 Trust Law Intl 78, 83.
85. [1989] 2 NZLR 180. See Watts (1990) 106 LQR 552.
86. (1994) 1 Comm LP 211, 214.

flexible that it no longer seems to represent a real bar to exercising an equitable tracing remedy if the other conditions for that remedy are satisfied.

Loss of the Right to Trace

In certain circumstances, many of which were referred to by the Court of Appeal in its judgment in *Re Diplock*,[87] the right to trace in equity may be lost. The first example is the obvious one that if the property has been dissipated it cannot be traced. As Lord Greene MR stated in *Re Diplock*:

> The equitable remedies presuppose the continued existence of the money either as a separate fund or as part of a mixed fund or as latent in property acquired by means of such a fund. If, on the facts of any individual case, such continued existence is not established, equity is as helpless as the common law itself. If the fund mixed or unmixed is spent upon a dinner, equity, which dealt only in specific relief and not in damages, could do nothing.[88]

Secondly, where property comes into the hands of a *bona fide* purchaser for value without notice, any equitable tracing claim will be extinguished,[89] and an alternative remedy must be pursued.[90] Thirdly, where it would be inequitable to allow a tracing claim to proceed, such a remedy will not be available. This will happen most frequently where a volunteer uses trust funds to alter or improve property already owned by him. This occurred in *Re Diplock* where some of the charities who received trust funds had used them to carry out improvements to their property. As Lord Greene MR stated: 'In the case of adaptation of property of the volunteer by means of trust money, it by no means necessarily follows that the money can be said to be present in the adapted property.'[91] In such circumstances, he concluded that the trust money could not be traced. The reasoning behind such an approach is that it would be inequitable to allow beneficiaries a charge over the property which would be enforceable by sale. This can be contrasted with the situation where a volunteer has purchased an asset

---

87. [1948] Ch 465.
88. *Ibid.* at 521.
89. *Re Diplock* [1948] Ch 465, 539. It would appear that in Ireland the equitable right to trace is regarded as a mere equity and thus a *bona fide* purchaser for value of an equitable estate will take free of it. See *Re Ffrench's Estate* (1887) 21 LR Ir 283 and *Scott v. Scott* [1924] 1 IR 141 and see *infra* Chapter 2.
90. E.g. a claim against the trustees personally.
91. *Ibid.* at 546-547.

with a mixed fund in which case there would be nothing inequitable in forcing a sale and dividing up the proceeds as he would recover what he invested.

Although there is little evidence of how it would operate in relation to equitable proprietary claims, it would appear that the defence of change of position should also be referred to.[92] In *Lipkin Gorman v. Karpanale Ltd*[93] Lord Goff stated that 'the defence is available to a person whose position has so changed that it would be inequitable in all the circumstances to require him to make restitution, or alternatively to make restitution in full'. He commented that whilst he recognised the different functions of property at law and in equity, in his view 'there may also in due course develop a more consistent approach to tracing claims, in which common defences are recognised as available to such claims, whether advanced at law or in equity'.[94] As Oakley[95] has commented it is clear from this statement that Lord Goff envisaged the application of the defence of change of position to both legal and equitable proprietary claims, although for the present the principles which have been developed relate to the former situation.

It has been accepted that the defence while available to an innocent defendant is not open to a wrongdoer, or to a person who has changed his position in bad faith.[96] In this context it would seem that a defendant who ought to have been aware of the fact that the property in question did not belong to him may not be classified as innocent.[97] It would also appear from the decision of Clark J in *South Tyneside Metropolitan Council v. Svenska International plc*[98] that the change of position would have to occur after the receipt of the property other than in exceptional cases in order for the defence to operate.[99]

---

92. See generally Goff and Jones, *The Law of Restitution* (5th ed., 1998) Chapter 40; Nolan in *Laundering and Tracing* (1995) ed. Birks p.135 *et seq.* and Birks in *Laundering and Tracing* (1995) ed. Birks pp. 323-332.
93. [1991] 2 AC 548, 580.
94. *Ibid.* at 580. However, Lord Goff stated that nothing should be said by him which would inhibit the development of the defence on a case by case basis and Lord Bridge commented that in acknowledging the defence for the first time, 'it would be unwise to attempt to define its scope in abstract terms'.
95. [1995] CLJ 377, 425.
96. *Lipkin Gorman v. Karpanale Ltd* [1991] 2 AC 548, 580 *per* Lord Goff.
97. *South Tyneside Metropolitan Council v. Svenska International plc* [1995] 1 All ER 545, 569.
98. [1995] 1 All ER 545.
99. Jones has submitted [1995] Conv 490, 497 that the approach adopted in *South Tyneside* is an unduly restrictive one and suggests that '[n]one of the reasons given for narrowly limiting the scope of the defence to changes occurring after receipt are convincing'.

CHAPTER 19

Equitable Doctrines

THE DOCTRINE OF CONVERSION

Introduction

The doctrine of conversion is based on the maxim that equity looks on that as done which ought to be done.[1] It operates by regarding one form of property as being another because an obligation to convert it exists. The effect of the doctrine is that in certain circumstances the nature of property is notionally changed so that realty may be treated as personalty with the legal incidents of personalty and vice versa. The reasoning behind the doctrine is that where a person is under a duty to convert realty into personalty or personalty into realty, the property should not be regarded as still being in its original form because the individual concerned has failed to perform his obligations.

Traditionally, the doctrine had an important effect on the passing of property where an individual died intestate, because real estate devolved to the heir-at-law and personalty to the next of kin. However, the practical significance of the doctrine has greatly diminished since the enactment of the Administration of Estates Act 1959 and the Succession Act 1965 which abolished these principles, although it remains relevant where a testator makes separate residuary dispositions of his real and personal property.

The basis of the doctrine was outlined by Sir Thomas Sewell MR in *Fletcher v. Ashburner*:[2]

> [N]othing was better established than this principle, that money directed to be employed in the purchase of land, and land directed to be sold and turned into money, are to be considered as that species of property into which they are directed to be converted; and this in whatever manner the direction is given.

There are a number of situations in which the doctrine of conversion will be applied and these will be examined in turn.

---

1. *McDonnell v. Stenson* [1921] 1 IR 80, 86 *per* Ronan LJ.
2. (1779) 1 Bro CC 497, 499.

Trusts for Sale[3]

Where trustees are directed to sell or purchase realty and there is some person who can insist on their doing so, the property is treated as being converted from the moment when the instrument comes into force. So, in the case of a will, conversion takes place from the date of the testator's death and, in the case of a deed, from the date of its execution. However, as Stirling J stated in *Goodier v. Edmunds*[4] 'nothing short of an absolute and effective trust for sale can in equity create the conversion of realty into personalty'. In order to effect the conversion, the direction to sell or buy must be imperative and a trust for sale, which is mandatory and imposes a duty to sell and which produces an immediate notional conversion, must be distinguished from a power of sale, which merely confers a discretion to sell. As Porter MR stated in *McGwire v. McGwire*:[5] the question which arises is 'whether there is to be found in the settlement an express and imperative direction to convert [the property], or a trust for [its] conversion'. In this case, he concluded that no immediate conversion was effected or intended and that the lands which remained unsold should pass as realty. Similarly, in *Re Tyndall's Estate*[6] where a testator directed that after his wife's death his trustees should invest his residuary personalty in the purchase of realty, it was held by Gavan Duffy J that such a direction did not create an imperative trust for such a conversion. As a matter of construction, it must be shown that the testator intended the conversion to take place and as Sullivan MR made clear in *Norreys v. Franks*[7] this intention must be discerned from the language which he has employed.

It should be noted that in England the Trusts of Land and Appointment of Trustees Act 1996 abolishes the doctrine of conversion in relation to trusts for sale which are now replaced by a 'trust of land', in relation to which trustees have a power of sale, which may be exercised.[8]

---

3. See Boyle [1981] Conv 108.
4. [1893] 3 Ch 455, 462.
5. [1900] 1 IR 200, 203. See also *Owen v. Owen* [1897] 1 IR 580 and the *dicta* of Chatterton VC in *McDonogh v. Nolan* (1881) 9 Lr Ir 262, 270.
6. [1941] Ir Jur Rep 51.
7. (1874) IR 9 Eq 18, 35.
8. Pettit submits (1997) 113 LQR 207 that the Act does not abolish the trust for sale completely and argues that s.3 of the Act clearly assumes that a trust for sale can still exist. S. 3(1) provides: 'Where land is held by trustees subject to a trust for sale, the land is not to be regarded as personal property; and where personal property is subject to a trust for sale in order that the trustees may acquire land, the personal property is not to be regarded as land.'

Contracts or Conditional Contracts for the Sale or Purchase of Land

Where there is a valid contract to sell realty, the realty is treated as part of the vendor's personalty from the time the contract is concluded.[9] Traditionally it was accepted that a contract must be specifically enforceable in order for the doctrine to apply, but this would no longer appear to be the case.[10] Where a vendor dies before completion of the contract, his representatives must convey the realty or will be entitled to enforce specific performance against the purchaser, and the proceeds of the sale will form part of the vendor's estate as personalty. If a purchaser dies before completion, his interest passes to those entitled to his realty, but subject to the obligation to pay the balance of the purchase price.

This principle has been extended to conditional contracts. As Holmes LJ commented in *Re Sherlock's Estate*:[11] 'if the making of an absolute agreement to sell is fixed by judicial authority as the time of conversion, it seems to me that it is both logical and desirable to apply the same rule to a conditional agreement.' The most common example of such a conditional contract is where an option to purchase is created. The operation of this principle is illustrated by the decision of *Lawes v. Bennett*[12] in which a testator leased a farm to an individual for a period of seven years and gave him an option to purchase the reversion on giving written notice before a specified date. This individual assigned the lease to another party who exercised the option and paid the purchase money after the testator's death. It was held that the purchase money formed part of the testator's personalty. The effect of this so-called rule in *Lawes v. Bennett* is therefore that the exercise of an option to purchase after a testator's death will retrospectively convert the property into personalty.

The rationale behind the application of this principle is that a testator is presumed to be aware of the legal result which will flow from granting

---

9. See *Hillingdon Estates Co. v. Stonefield Estates Ltd* [1952] Ch 627, 631 *per* Vaisey J.
10. Keane suggests that all that is necessary is that there is a 'valid contract for sale' (see *Equity and the Law of Trusts in the Republic of Ireland* (1988) p.298) and the most recent edition of Wylie's *Irish Land Law* (3rd ed., 1997 p.139) states that 'arguably all that is needed is a "valid" contract or "binding contract *simpliciter*"'. Pettit also points out (1960) 24 Conv 47, 64-65 that it is doubtful whether the availability of specific performance can be regarded as a satisfactory criterion for determining whether conversion should occur and concludes that 'there do not appear to be any decisions directly and necessarily based on the availability or non-availability of the remedy of specific performance'.
11. [1899] 2 IR 561, 608.
12. (1785) 1 Cox 167.

an option of this nature.[13] However, as the principle is based on the presumed intention of the testator, it will not apply where a contrary intention can be deduced. So as Johnston J stated in *Miley v. Carty*:[14] 'whenever in a will or codicil the testator indicates an intention that, notwithstanding a contract for the sale of the lands, the devisee shall take whatever interest in the lands that the testator may have had at the time of his death, then that intention is to be carried out, and the general rule as established in *Lawes v. Bennett* is not to be followed.' In addition, it has been held that the application of the principle 'should be limited to cases where there was no specific disposition of the property made after the date of the contract giving the option to purchase'.[15] This point was made in the following terms by Page-Wood VC in *Weeding v. Weeding*:[16]

> When you find that, in a will made after a contract giving an option of purchase, the testator, knowing of the existence of the contract, devises the specific property which is the subject of the contract without referring in any way to the contract ... it is considered that there is sufficient indication of an intention to pass that property, to give the devisee all the interest, whatever it may be, that the testator had in it.

Therefore, in the case of a general or residuary devise, the rule operates even where the option cannot be exercised until after the death of the grantor but in the case of a specific devise of the property, it will not operate if the will is made subsequently to the creation of the option or contemporaneously with it. The exception operates not only where a specific devise is made after the granting of the option but also where a will is republished after such grant by the execution of a codicil. These principles are conveniently summarised in *Snell's Equity*[17] in the following terms:

> Where ... there is a specific devise, the operation of the rule depends on the relative dates of the will and the grant of the option. If the will was made before the option was granted, the devise is adeemed by the exercise of the option, just as if the testator had sold

---

13. See *Miley v. Carty* [1927] IR 541, 543. See also *Weeding v. Weeding* (1861) 1 J & H 424.
14. [1927] IR 541, 544.
15. *Duffield v. McMaster* [1896] 1 IR 370, 379.
16. (1861) 1 J & H 424, 431. Quoted with approval by Porter MR in *Duffield v. McMaster* [1896] 1 IR 370, 381 and by Palles CB in *Steele v. Steele* [1913] 1 IR 292, 305.
17. (29th ed., 1990, Baker and Langan), p.493.

the land in his lifetime. But if the will was made or confirmed by codicil after the grant of the option, or substantially contemporaneously with it, the specific devisee is entitled to the proceeds of sale; for the testator will be taken to have been aware of the option and to have intended the devisee to take the property whether it was land or purchase-money.

Where the option can be construed as a gift subject to the payment of the purchase price, it may subsequently be exercised by the personal representatives of the lessee to whom the option was given in the first instance.[18] Finally, the rule in *Lawes v. Bennett* will only be applied as between the competing claims of those entitled to the real and personal property of a grantor on an option and will not apply as between a vendor and purchaser.[19]

Order of the Court

Conversion may occur by reason of a court order directing that property should be bought or sold[20] and such conversion takes effect from the date of the order[21] and not from the date of the sale. This principle is illustrated by the decision of Monroe J in *Re Beamish's Estate*[22] in which he held that an order for sale of an unencumbered estate operated as a conversion into personalty.

An absolute order for the sale of realty made on the petition of an incumbrancer operates as a conversion of only so much of the lands as it is necessary to sell to discharge the incumbrance. This conclusion was reached by Ross J in *Sheane v. Fetherstonhaugh*[23] in which part only of an owner's lands had been sold to discharge incumbrances on the property. After his death the question arose whether the unsold lands had been converted by the order made by the court or whether they remained as real estate. As Ross J concluded: 'because only so much of the land is to be sold as is required for the discharge of incumbrances, no valid order can be deemed to exist for the sale of the remainder. ... It can never become operative in

18. *Belshaw v. Rollins* [1904] 1 IR 284.
19. *Re Sherlock' Estate* [1899] 2 IR 561.
20. Pettit suggests (1997) 113 LQR 207, 210 that the courts have treated such cases as analogous to the situation where there is a trust for sale but states that it is not a trust for sale and would not appear to come within the terms of s.3 of the Trusts of Land and Appointment of Trustees Act 1996.
21. *Re Henry's Estate* (1893) 31 LR Ir 158, 165.
22. (1891) 27 LR Ir 326. See also *Steed v. Preece* (1874) LR 18 Eq 192.
23. [1914] 1 IR 268.

respect of the unsold lands'. In reaching this conclusion, Ross J distinguished his previous decision in *Re Stinson's Estate*[24] where he had held that if more property is actually sold than is necessary to pay off incumbrances, it must pass as personalty to the next of kin.

It should be noted that a court order will not always effect a conversion and section 67 of the Lunacy Regulation (Ireland) Act 1871 provides that any surplus remaining on the sale or mortgage of a lunatic's estate will be treated as if it were of the same character and nature as the property sold.[25] If an order is not made under this section, but is made in the ordinary course of the management of a lunatic's estate, conversion will be effected unless the court makes a direction to the contrary. However, where an order for sale is made outside the ordinary course of managing the estate, the property will retain its original character.

Partnership Property

Section 22 of the Partnership Act 1890[26] provides that unless the contrary intention appears, land which has become partnership property shall be treated as personalty and not as realty as between the partners themselves and those entitled to their estates. The reason for this provision is that on the dissolution of a partnership, the land will have to be sold to be divided amongst the partners.

Settled Land

Section 22(5) of the Settled Land Act 1882 provides that capital money arising from the disposition of property pursuant to the Settled Land Acts 1882-1890 is to be treated as realty.

Failure of Conversion

Where property is subject to a duty to convert but before or at the same time as the direction to convert becomes effective, a total failure of the objects of the conversion occurs, there will be a resulting trust of the property in its actual form. So, if A devises realty on trust for sale for the

---

24. [1910] 1 IR 13.
25. See the *dicta* of Kennedy CJ in *O'Connell v. Harrison* [1927] IR 330, 337-338.
26. It should be noted that s.22 has been repealed in England by the Trusts of Land and Appointment of Trustees Act 1996. Pettit argues (1997) 113 LQR 207, 210-211 that as the section effectively put a pre-existing equitable principle into statutory form, the pre-Partnership Act equitable rule may continue to apply. However, he points out that the effect of this repeal is not entirely clear, see further (1997) 113 LQR 207, 211.

benefit of B and B dies before the sale takes place, a resulting trust of the property, which remains as realty, arises in favour of the settlor. However, where there is a partial failure of the objects for which conversion was directed, the outcome depends on whether the property is left by will or settled by deed. Where the direction to convert is contained in a deed, the property will result subject to the trust for conversion.[27] On the other hand, if the direction is in a will, it will go to the person entitled to the property in its unconverted form, although he will receive it in its converted form because the trustees will be under an obligation to carry out the objects which have not failed.[28]

THE DOCTRINE OF RECONVERSION

In certain circumstances, property which has notionally been converted may be reconverted or theoretically returned to its actual physical form. Reconversion may either occur by act of the party or by operation of law.

By Act of the Party

Where a party is absolutely entitled to property and expresses the desire to take this property in its original unconverted form, it would make no sense for equity to compel the trustees of the property to convert it as the owner could immediately reverse this process. Therefore, on the basis that 'Equity, like nature, will do nothing in vain', the doctrine of reconversion intervenes. So, where beneficiaries who are of full age and capacity and between them absolutely entitled to trust property choose to take property in its actual form, notional reconversion occurs. The decision to reconvert may be expressly stated or it may be inferred from 'evidence of acts and circumstances'.[29] Minors and persons of unsound mind cannot make an election of this nature although where it is necessary to do so, the court may make the decision for such persons or sanction a decision already made.

Normally, 'all persons having interests must concur to effect conversion',[30] although in a limited manner a remainderman may elect to recon-

---

27. *Griffith v. Ricketts* (1849) 7 Hare 299.
28. *Re O'Connor's Estate* [1923] 1 IR 142.
29. *Hart v. McDougall* [1912] 1 IR 62, 75 *per* Barton J. See also the *dicta* of Byrne J in *Re Douglas and Powell's Contract* [1902] 2 Ch 296, 312 to the effect that evidence may be derived from 'declarations or acts and conduct'.
30. *Hart v. McDougall* [1912] 1 IR 62, 72 *per* Barton J.

vert. Clearly, no election made by him can prejudice the interests of those with interests in possession and any decision made may be affected subsequently by any actual conversion which occurs before his interest falls into possession.

In the case of tenants in common, one of them may reconvert without the concurrence of the other(s) in the case of money to be invested in land,[31] but, it would appear not in the case of land to be converted into money on the grounds that land would not be as valuable if divided up in such a manner.[32]

By Operation of Law

Reconversion may also be effected by operation of law where property which has been notionally converted in equity becomes reconverted without any declaration or act of the party entitled. This will occur where, e.g. property which was subject to an obligation to convert comes into the possession of some person who is absolutely entitled, without having been converted, and he dies without making any declaration of intention in relation to it. The important factor here is that there must no longer be anyone who can enforce the obligation to convert and this is illustrated by the decision of Chatterton VC in *McDonogh v. Nolan*.[33] By virtue of a marriage settlement, a sum of money was vested in trustees for the purchase of realty to be held on certain trusts. The realty was never purchased and the parties' only son became absolutely entitled and died unmarried and intestate. It was held that the money should be regarded as personalty and therefore passed to his heir-at-law.

THE DOCTRINE OF ELECTION

Introduction

The doctrine of election can be explained in terms of the principle that 'a man shall not be allowed to approbate and reprobate',[34] in other words one cannot take a benefit and reject an associated burden. The doctrine comes

---

31. *Seeley v. Jago* (1717) P Wms 389.
32. *Holloway v. Radcliffe* (1857) 23 Beav 163.
33. (1881) 9 LR Ir 262.
34. *Re Lord Chesham* (1886) 31 Ch D 466, 473 *per* Chitty J. See also the comments of Lord Redesdale in *Birmingham v. Kirwan* (1805) 2 Sch & Lef 444, 449 that 'a person cannot accept and reject the same instrument' and of Lord Robertson in *Douglas-Menzies v. Umphelby* [1908] AC 224, 232 that 'it is against equity that any one should take against a man's will and also under it'.

into operation where a testator or donor purports to confer a benefit on a donee and in the same instrument purports to transfer some of this donee's property to a third party. A useful recent summary of the effect of the doctrine of election is set out by Histed in the following terms:[35]

> Where a beneficiary receives a gift under a will or deed which also disposes of some of his own property and where the circumstances of the case permit the court to conclude that the donor would not have wanted the beneficiary to receive the gift and keep his own property, then the court will imply a condition that the beneficiary so give up his property before receiving the gift.

As Walsh MR stated in *Williams v. Mayne*:[36] 'In giving effect to an election, the Court professess to enforce a duty; there being two benefits which it is inequitable in the party electing to claim together, it compels him, on the condition of obtaining one, to relinquish the other.' This principle was more fully set out by Lord Hatherley in the course of his judgment in *Cooper v. Cooper*:[37]

> There is an obligation on him who takes a benefit under a will or other instrument to give full effect to that instrument under which he takes a benefit; and if it be found that that instrument purports to deal with something which it was beyond the power of the donor or settlor to dispose of, but to which effect can be given by the concurrence of him who receives a benefit under the same instrument, the law will impose on him who takes the benefit the obligation of carrying the instrument into full and complete force and effect.

This statement was quoted with approval by Ronan LJ in *Re Sullivan*.[38] In that case, a testator gave his wife a legacy of £3,000 to be paid in cash or out of his own or their joint shares as she should select. The Irish Court of Appeal held that the widow was bound to elect between the benefits conferred by the will and any claim to the stocks and shares invested in the joint names of herself and the testator.

---

35. (1998) 114 LQR 621, 634. Histed comments at p.637 that the doctrine is based on the intention of the testator and the willingness of the court to imply a conditional gift where it can be convinced that the intention would be defeated without the condition being placed on the gift.
36. (1867) IR 1 Eq 519, 530.
37. (1874) LR 7 HL 53, 70.
38. [1917] 1 IR 38, 42.

It is important to distinguish such a situation from one in which the gift to the donee is expressly made conditional upon his transferring his property to a third party. Where this condition is not complied with, the gift to the donee cannot take effect and it will fall into residue.

The example provided by Hanbury and Martin[39] best illustrates the operation of the doctrine in practice. This is as follows:

> A is owner of Blackacre. T in his will devises Blackacre to B and bequeaths £10,000 to A. A cannot, of course, be compelled to transfer Blackacre to B. A is put to his election. This means that he can choose to take with the will or against the will. If A takes with the will, he will release Blackacre to B and get his £10,000. If A takes against the will, he will retain Blackacre but the £10,000 will be subject to an equity in B to claim compensation out of it to the extent of the value of Blackacre.

The doctrine has traditionally been described as being based on the implied intention of the testator or donor that effect should be given to every part of the instrument drawn up.[40] However, more recently the view has been expressed that the principle does not depend on 'a conjecture of a presumed intention'[41] and as Meagher, Gummow and Lehane[42] have pointed out 'any such intention will usually be fictional or constructive for it attributes to the donor knowledge of the situation he has created'. In practice where a contrary intention is expressed, the operation of the doctrine may be excluded, although it would not be sufficient merely to show that the testator or donor had not contemplated the circumstances which would give rise to an election. As Buckley LJ pointed out in *Re Mengel's Will Trusts*,[43] 'the case in which the testator frames his will with the conscious intention of bringing the doctrine into play must be very rare' and in the vast majority of cases it will come into effect due to an oversight or mistake on the testator's part.[44]

However, it is necessary to establish an intention on the part of the testator or donor to dispose of the property in question, although it is irrelevant that he did not realise that the property was not in fact his.[45] This

---

39. *Modern Equity* (15th ed., 1997) p. 852.
40. *Re Vardon's Trusts* (1885) 31 Ch D 275, 279 *per* Fry LJ.
41. *Cooper v. Cooper* (1874) LR 7 HL 53, 67 *per* Lord Cairns. See also *Re Sullivan* [1917] 1 IR 38, 43.
42. *Equity Doctrines and Remedies* (3rd ed., 1992) p. 855.
43. [1962] Ch 791, 796-797.
44. *Ibid.* and see Crago (1990) 106 LQR 487, 489.
45. *Re Harris* [1909] 2 Ch 206, 209; *Re Sullivan* [1917] 1 IR 38, 43.

point was considered by Porter MR in *Minchin v. Gabbett*[46] where he stated as follows:

> But the question is, what was the intention of the testator? and that is to be gathered from the whole will, not by speculating, but by an honest endeavour to discover what the testator meant, seeing the language used and what it fairly means. No doubt, in approaching such a question, the Court must *prima facie* construe the words as applying to an estate which the testator had, if the words will fairly apply to it, nay, more than that, in order to raise a question of election, it must be clearly seen that the words used point to an estate which is not the testator's own but another's.

This reasoning was developed by Porter MR in *Galvin v. Devereux*[47] in which it was held that the testatrix intended to dispose only of her own estate and interest in lands and not to dispose of property which was not her own, and that therefore no case of election arose.

Requirements for Election

The doctrine of election applies both to wills and deeds,[48] although it operates more frequently in relation to wills. In circumstances where it applies, the donee is faced with a choice; he may either take under the instrument, in which case he may take the benefit of the gift to himself but must also consent to the transfer of his own property to a third party. Alternatively, he may take against the instrument, in which case he will retain his own property but will lose the benefit of the gift which the donor directed that he should have to the extent to which it is required to compensate the third party for failing to receive the donee's own property. As Sugden LC stated in *Hamilton v. Jackson*,[49] in these circumstances 'the property goes in compensation to the persons disappointed' and in the event of delay, such compensation may carry interest.[50] However, it should be noted that the obligation to compensate is only to the extent of the benefit derived; as Jessel MR pointed out in *Pickersgill v. Rodger*[51] no more compensation can be required than the value of the testator's own

---

46. [1896] 1 IR 1, 12.
47. [1903] 1 IR 185.
48. *Birmingham v. Kirwan* (1805) 2 Sch & Lef 444, 449.
49. (1845) 8 Ir Eq R 195.
50. *Re Saul's Trust* [1951] Ir Jur Rep 34.
51. (1876) 5 Ch D 163, 174. As Jessel MR stated: 'the obligation is only to the extent of the benefit [which the donee] derives: it cannot go beyond that'.

property given to the person called upon to elect, even though this may be inadequate to compensate for the disappointment.

As Crago[52] points out, whatever choice the electing party decides to make, he will not be as well off as the testator in all likelihood intended that he should be. Where the value of the benefit which he is given is no more than the value of his own property, then irrespective of whether he takes under or against the instrument he will derive no net benefit. Even where the value of the benefit is greater than that of his own property, he will only receive a benefit amounting to the difference between these two values. The only circumstances in which the donee will benefit as much as the third party to whom he must give his own property is where the gift made to him by the donor is worth at least twice the value of his own property.

In order to give rise to an election, the testator or donor must not only make a gift to the donee but must also *in the same instrument* make an effective disposition of the donee's property to a third party. It has been accepted in England that a will and any codicils to it will be regarded as the same instrument in this context[53] and a deed and a will have even been treated as one for this purpose. In *Re Woodleys*[54] Palles CB was satisfied that the two documents taken together 'carry out and effectuate one entire and indivisible intention', although he made it clear in the course of his judgment that had they been 'separate and independent', no question of election would have arisen.

The essentials for election were set out as follows by Jenkins LJ in *Re Edwards*:[55] 'there should be an intention on the part of the testator or testatrix to dispose of certain property; secondly, that the property should not in fact be the testator's or testatrix's own property; and, thirdly, that a benefit should be given by the will to the true owner of the property.' So in order for election to be necessary, it is essential that the donor has conferred a benefit on the donee with which he can compensate the third party if he elects to take against the instrument. As Loughborough LC commented in *Bristow v. Warde*:[56] 'in all cases there must be some free disposable property given to the person, which can be made a compensation for what the testator takes away.' In addition, in order for a case for election to arise, it is necessary that the donee's property be directly disposed of to a third party by the terms of the same instrument. This point was laid down

52. (1990) 106 LQR 487, 488.
53. *Cooper v. Cooper* (1874) LR 7 HL 53.
54. (1892) 29 LR Ir 304.
55. [1958] Ch 168, 175.
56. (1794) 2 Ves 336, 350.

as follows by Christian LJ in *Lewis v. Lewis:*[57] 'in order to raise a case of election, a testator must directly by his will assume to dispose of that which is not his; if he merely recites that it *has been* already disposed of in a particular way, and then proceeds to distribute his property on that assumption, and it turns out that he was mistaken, that does not raise a case of election.'

A further requirement is that the donee's property, which the donor purports to give to the third party, must be freely alienable. Election presupposes that the donee will have a choice and if his property cannot be alienated, he will not be required to make an election and will take the donor's gift free from any obligation. This point is illustrated by the decision in *Re Lord Chesham*.[58] A testator bequeathed his residuary estate to his eldest son and purported to dispose of chattels, in relation to which this son enjoyed a life interest but over which he had no power of disposition, in favour of his younger sons. It was held that the eldest son was not put to his election as he had no power to alienate this property and that he was entitled to take the residue of the testator's estate without compensating his younger brothers. However, in this context, it has been held that the application of the doctrine will only be excluded where the donee cannot by any relevant means comply with the testator's intentions and that it will apply even where the donee merely has a contingent interest in the property which he is required to alienate. So, in *Morgan v. Morgan*[59] it was held that the doctrine applied even where the interest in question was a remainder expectant on an estate tail. Equally, the doctrine will apply to property which is subject to a special power of appointment so 'as a general rule when the donee of a power purports to give the property, the subject-matter of the power, to a person not an object, and gives property of his own to the object of the power, the latter is put to his election, and cannot dispute the disposition of the trust property if he takes the benefit out of the donee's own property'.[60] However, the decision of the Irish Court of Appeal in *Re Handcock's Trusts*[61] clearly establishes that no obligation to make an election will arise in such circumstances where this would result in a violation of the rule against perpetuities.

A further important prerequisite for the application of the doctrine is

---

57. (1876) IR 11 Eq 313. Quoted with approval by Palles CB in *Re Woodleys* (1892) 29 LR Ir 304, 313.
58. (1886) 31 Ch D 466. See also *Brown v. Gregson* [1920] AC 860.
59. (1853) 4 Ir Ch R 606.
60. *Re Handcock's Trusts* (1888) 23 LR Ir 34, 46-47. See also *Moriarty v. Martin* (1852) 3 Ir Ch R 26 and *Fearon v. Fearon* (1852) 3 Ir Ch R 19.
61. (1888) 23 LR Ir 34. See also *Re McCormick* [1915]1 IR 315, 319.

that title to the electing party's property must arise independently of the instrument which gives rise to the need for the election to be made. So as James VC stated in *Wollaston v. King*:[62] 'the rule as to election is to be applied as between a gift under the will, and a claim *dehors* the will and adverse to it, and is not to be applied as between one clause in a will and another clause in the same will'. This principle seems to have been accepted in England,[63] although it was not applied by Neville J in the decision of *Re Macartney*[64] which has admittedly been criticised as 'unsatisfactory'[65] and 'aberrant'.[66] The better view would seem to be that no case for election arises where the electing party acquires title to both properties under the same instrument and this approach is supported by the *dicta* of Chatterton VC in *Sweetman v. Sweetman*[67] where he said that the property which the testator purported to devise to a third party must belong 'not by the will, but by an earlier title, to the person who is called upon to elect'.

Making an Election

Romilly MR expressed the view in *Worthington v. Wiginton*[68] that two requirements had to be satisfied in order for a valid election to be made under a will; first, there must be clear proof that the person making the election was aware of the nature and extent of his rights and secondly, it must be shown that having this knowledge, he intended to elect. Chatterton VC expanded these requirements in the following terms in the course of his judgment in *Sweetman v. Sweetman*:[69]

> The requisites for holding a party bound by an election as concluded are, I think, these: first, he must have a knowledge of his rights, that is to say, he must know that the property, which the testator attempted to give to another person, was not the testator's property, and that it would, upon the testator's decease, become independently of the testator's will, the property of the party called upon to elect. It must be known by him, as a matter of fact, that the testator had not the power to give the property which he purported to devise, and that it

---

62. (1869) Lr 8 Eq 165, 174.
63. See e.g. *Bate v. Willats* (1877) 37 LT 221.
64. [1918] 1 Ch 300.
65. Pettit, *Equity and the Law of Trusts* (8th ed., 1997) p.716.
66. Meagher, Gummow and Lehane, *Equity Doctrines and Remedies* (3rd ed., 1992) p. 853.
67. (1868) IR 2 Eq 141, 153.
68. (1855) 20 Beav 67, 74.
69. (1868) IR 2 Eq 141, 152-153.

belongs, not by the will, but by an earlier title, to the person who is called upon to elect. Next he must know the relative values of the properties between which he is called upon to elect; and further, he must know, as a matter of fact, and not as a presumption of law, that the rule of equity exists, that he cannot, under such circumstances, take both estates, but must make an election between the two. And further, the Court must be satisfied that he made a deliberate choice with the intention of making it.

Election may either be express or may be implied from a party's conduct,[70] provided that a clear choice was made with a full knowledge and understanding of the issues involved. When an election is made it relates back to the date of the gift and so any compensation payable in the case of election against the terms of a will depends on the valuation of the property in question at the date of the testator's death. It would appear that where a specified time limit is laid down by the instrument within which election must be made, failure to do so within this time will be considered as election against the instrument, However, where no limitation is expressed, a person is unlikely to lose the right to make an election, even if he has knowledge of his right to do so, merely by reason of lapse of time unless serious prejudice would be caused to third parties as a result.

Disabilities, namely infancy or mental incapacity, will prevent a person exercising a right of election. In such cases an election will generally be made on behalf of the individual once the court has conducted an inquiry as to the most appropriate course of action to take,[71] although in the case of infants, the election may be deferred until majority is attained.

Conclusion

In practice the application of the doctrine of election may lead to rather anomalous results. Although the donee alone has an effective gift under a will, where the doctrine comes into operation, he will generally receive less of a net benefit than a third party to whom he must give either his own property or that which he appeared to be entitled to under the terms of the will, and in some circumstances he may receive no net benefit at all. It has been argued[72] that the doctrine is a 'mischievous' one which tends to de-

---

70. Note that in *Padbury v. Clarke* (1850) 2 McN & G 298 it was found by Lord Cottenham LC that mere receipt of rents and profits of properties could not be construed as election. See also *Morgan v. Morgan* (1853) 4 Ir Ch R 606, 614.
71. *Moore v. Butler* (1805) 2 Sch & Lef 249, 266-267 *per* Lord Redesdale.
72. See Crago (1990) 106 LQR 487, 505.

feat the testator's real intentions and that it is being applied in conditions which no longer correspond to those which may have justified its adoption in the first instance. Any application of the doctrine today will almost inevitably be as a result of a mistake made on the testator's part and the question must be asked whether equity should continue to intervene in a manner which arguably does not give effect to a testator's actual intentions and which so often produces an unfair result from the perspective of the person whom he expressly sought to benefit.

THE DOCTRINE OF SATISFACTION

This equitable doctrine is an illustration of the maxim that 'Equity imputes an intention to fulfil an obligation' and depends on a party's presumed intention to carry out an obligation. Where the doctrine of satisfaction applies, the act performed is of a different nature to that which it had been agreed should be carried out. The question which must be addressed is whether it can be presumed to have been intended to satisfy the original obligation. Cases in which the doctrine may operate are usually grouped into the following classifications.

1. Satisfaction of debts by legacies.

2. Satisfaction of portion debts by legacies.

3. Satisfaction (or ademption) of legacies by portions.

4. Satisfaction of legacies by legacies.

Satisfaction of Debts by Legacies

Where a testator leaves a legacy to a creditor the question arises whether the creditor can claim both the legacy and the debt. The position is straightforward if the legacy is expressed to be in reduction of the debt. However, even if there is no such stipulation, equity presumes that if a debtor leaves a legacy in his will to his creditor of a sum which equals or exceeds the amount of the debt without making any mention of it, the legacy should be treated as being in satisfaction of the debt.[73] The general principle in this area was set out by Trevor MR in *Talbot v. Duke of Shrewsbury*[74] as follows:

---

73. *Garner v. Holmes* (1858) 8 Ir Ch R 469, 476.
74. (1714) Prec Ch 394, 394-395.

> [T]hat if one, being indebted to another in a sum of money, does by his will give him as great, or greater sum of money than the debt amounts to, without taking any notice at all of the debt, that this shall nevertheless be in satisfaction of the debt, so as that he shall not have both the debt and legacy.

Being based on a presumption, the doctrine will not apply where there is an indication of a contrary intention. In practice the presumption may be rebutted where there are any reasonable grounds for doing so and the general trend has been to circumscribe the scope of the circumstances in which it may apply.[75] The doctrine has been held not to apply for a number of different reasons. First, the presumption of satisfaction of a debt by a legacy does not apply where a will contains a direction to pay the testator's debts.[76] Most well-drafted wills now contain such a direction and in practice the application of the doctrine is usually excluded on this basis. Secondly, its application may be excluded for reasons relating to the nature of the debt and the time when it was incurred. Because the doctrine is based on presumed intention, the debt must have existed before the making of the will.[77] In addition, it does not apply to a continuous running account where the debt would have been uncertain at the time of drawing up the will. So in *Buckley v. Buckley*,[78] the testator and another party were involved in ongoing business dealings and their practice was to settle their accounts from time to time. The amounts owed by the testator fluctuated after the date when the will was made and it was held by Porter MR that the testator's indebtedness to the other party at the time of his death was not satisfied by a legacy left in his will. As Porter MR stated:

> The debt here was on a running account, to which the ordinary presumption of satisfaction of debts by legacies does not apply. ... The reason is that the testator could not be presumed to know how the account would stand at his death and therefore he is not deemed to have intended the legacy in satisfaction of it without express words.[79]

---

75. See the comments of Stirling J in *Re Horlock* [1895] 1 Ch 516, 518 that 'no sooner was [the doctrine] established than learned Judges of great eminence expressed their disapproval of it, and invented ways to get out of it'. But note also the comments of Romer J in *Re Stibbe* (1946) 175 LT 198, 201.
76. *Re Manners* [1949] Ch 613, 618 *per* Evershed MR.
77. *Cranmer's Case* (1701) 2 Salk 508.
78. (1888) 19 LR Ir 544.
79. *Ibid.* at 558.

Finally, it is important to stress that the presumption of satisfaction of a debt by a legacy applies only if the legacy is equal to or greater than the debt. In *Ellard v. Phelan*[80] where the testator owed small sums of money in respect of wages to his employees and left them more substantial legacies in his will, Ross J held that these bequests should be held to be a satisfaction of the sums owed by him at the time of his death. This can be contrasted with the situation which arose in *Coates v. Coates*[81] where it was held that where the amount of the legacy was less than the amount of the debt the presumption could not operate. Chatterton VC stressed in the course of his judgment that *pro tanto* satisfaction is not possible either in such cases; as he stated 'a legacy cannot operate in satisfaction of a debt of greater amount, even *pro tanto*'.[82] Therefore, it is even doubtful whether a legacy can be regarded as being in satisfaction of a debt which is for exactly the same amount but subject to the payment of interest.

The presumption will not apply where the legacy is of uncertain amount, and satisfaction is not possible where the gift under the will is the whole or part of the residue of an estate because its value cannot be definitely fixed. So, even where the residue of the testator's estate may clearly exceed the amount of the debt, such a gift will not be regarded as satisfaction of the debt. In *Re Keogh's Estate*,[83] the testator mortgaged his land and in his will directed that the mortgagees, who were relatives and had resided with him prior to his death, should be entitled to remain in his house for a year after his death. The testator also appointed them joint residuary legatees but Monroe J held that these benefits were not regarded as being in satisfaction of the mortgage debt.

In order for the presumption to apply, the legacy must be in every way as beneficial as the debt and where the legacy is different in character to the debt, this will not be the case. So in *Coates v. Coates,*[84] a bequest of the use of a house and furniture for life could not satisfy an obligation to pay a sum of money on a weekly basis. As Chatterton VC stated 'the nature of the gift must correspond with the nature of the obligation'.[85]

Satisfaction of Portion Debts by Legacies

The presumption in favour of the satisfaction of portion debts by legacies

---

80. [1914] 1 IR 76.
81. [1898] 1 IR 258.
82. *Ibid.* at 261. See also *Reade v. Reade* (1880) 9 LR Ir 409.
83. (1889) 23 LR Ir 257.
84. [1898] 1 IR 258.
85. *Ibid.* at 261.

is an aspect of the principle that 'equity leans against double portions'.[86] The effect of the presumption is that where a father, or another person *in loco parentis* to a child makes a gift of a substantial nature or incurs an obligation to do so and subsequently makes provision in his will in the nature of a portion for this child, the portion debt is deemed to be satisfied by the obligation contained in the will. As Lord Cottenham LC stated in *Thynne v. Earl of Glengall*:[87] 'Equity leans in favour of a provision by will being in satisfaction of a portion by contract feeling the great improbability of a parent intending a double portion for one child, to the prejudice generally . . . of other children.'

A number of aspects of this principle require further elaboration. A 'portion' in this context means that the gift must be of a substantial nature, relative to the means of the parent and child, and intended to set a child up in life. As Jessel MR commented in *Taylor v. Taylor*:[88] 'I have always understood that an advancement by way of portion is something given by the parent to establish the child in life, or make what is called a provision for him — not a mere casual payment. . . .' The mere bestowing of a gift by a parent on a child will not suffice to make this gift a portion and equally a number of small gifts or advancements cannot be construed together as amounting to a portion.[89] The most common examples of a 'portion' would be a substantial gift made to a child on the occasion of his marriage or to enable him to set up in business.

The presumption of the satisfaction of portion debts by legacies in this context will only apply where the person making the provision for the child is his father or stands *in loco parentis* to him. Authority would suggest that it does not apply to provision made for a child by his mother[90] or other close relative unless that person can be considered to be *in loco parentis*. The exact interpretation of this phrase has caused difficulties,[91] but it is generally accepted as meaning where a person has assumed 'the office and duty of the parent to make provision for the child'.[92] In *Preston v. Greene*,[93] Meredith MR commented that 'the difference between a father and a mother is this, that in the one case there is a moral obligation to

---

86. See *Keays v. Gilmore* (1873) IR 8 Eq 290, 295 *per* Sullivan MR.
87. (1848) 2 HL Cas 131, 153.
88. (1875) LR 20 Eq 155, 157.
89. *Suisse v. Lord Lowther* (1843) 2 Hare 424, 434 *per* Wigram VC; *Watson v. Watson* (1864) 33 Beav 574.
90. *Re Ashton* [1897] 2 Ch 574.
91. See e.g. *Fowkes v. Pascoe* (1875) 10 Ch App 343, 350 *per* James LJ.
92. *Powys v. Mansfield* (1837) 3 My & Cr 359, 377 *per* Lord Cottenham LC.
93. [1909] 1 IR 172, 177-178.

[advance the child] recognised in equity, while in the case of a mother the moral obligation is there, but the Courts of equity do not recognise it.' While it is unlikely that the courts in this jurisdiction would continue to approve of drawing a distinction between fathers and mothers in this context,[94] until the matter falls to be considered, no definite conclusion can be reached. Where a child's father is still alive it may be more difficult to establish that another individual is acting *in loco parentis*, although it will be easier to do so where this individual is a close relative, and in *Pym v. Lockyer*[95] a grandfather was held to be acting *in loco parentis* to his grandchildren even though their father was still alive. The question of whether a person is acting *in loco parentis* must be answered on the basis of whether there has been 'the assumption of a parent's responsibility'.[96] While Barton J suggested in *Smyth v. Gleeson*[97] that the actions of a brother in making a gift to his older sister were more those of 'an affectionate brother' and said that it was at least doubtful whether the former has ever placed himself *in loco parentis*, he was prepared to assume for the sake of argument that this might have been the case. However, this can be contrasted with the decision of the Supreme Court in *Re Bannon*[98] where it was held that the facts proved did not support the inference that the testator stood *in loco parentis* to his nephew.

It would appear that the question of whether a portion debt may be satisfied by a legacy is one of intention to be determined from the terms of the instrument in the absence of evidence to the contrary. This point was made by Monroe J in *Re Battersby's Estate*[99] in the following terms:

> The question whether a portion given by a settlement is satisfied by a legacy in a subsequent will is entirely one of intention to be gathered in the absence of other evidence from the terms of the two instruments, subject to the consideration, that the presumption of law is against double portions. If the provision made by the later limitations are substantially the same, double portions will not be allowed; the parties entitled will be put to their election. If the limitations are widely different, the presumption is that the provisions were to be cumulative.

---

94. See also *infra* Chapter 7 in relation to the presumption of advancement.
95. (1841) 5 My & Cr 29.
96. *Smyth v. Gleeson* [1911] 1 IR 113, 119. See also *Monck v. Monck* (1810) 1 Ba & B 298.
97. [1911] 1 IR 113.
98. [1934] IR 701.
99. (1887) 19 Lr Ir 359, 363-364.

Unlike in the case of satisfaction of debts by legacies, *pro tanto* satisfaction is possible so if the legacy is of less value than the portion, it is deemed to be a satisfaction *pro tanto*.[100] Although the *dicta* of Monroe J in *Re Battersby*[101] might suggest otherwise, it is likely that this wider construction of *pro tanto* satisfaction would be applied in this jurisdiction.

As a general principle the property left by will must be of the same general nature as the property to which the beneficiary is entitled by virtue of the existing obligation and the interest in the property taken by the beneficiary must be as beneficial to him as this interest. While a greater degree of flexibility may be exercised than in the case of ordinary debts and legacies, generally speaking they 'must be of the same nature and attended with the same degree of certainty'.[102] So, in *Smyth v. Gleeson*[103] the presumption of satisfaction of a portion debt by a legacy was rebutted by the difference in certainty and value between the two benefits.

If the father or person *in loco parentis* has actually advanced a portion to a child and subsequently gives a legacy to the same child, the latter will not be regarded as satisfaction and the child will be entitled to take the benefit of the legacy. The reasoning behind this approach is clear, as if the father has already given the child the gift in the nature of a portion, he would undoubtedly intend that child to benefit in addition from any provision made for him in a subsequent will.

Unlike in the case of ordinary debts, once it is found that the presumption applies, the child is put to his election between the gift under the will and the *inter vivos* portion obligation.[104]

Although designed to promote equality between children, the application of the doctrine of satisfaction has been criticised for penalising an only child in an unfair manner while not applying to more distant relatives of a testator. However, it has been expressly preserved by section 63(9) of the Succession Act 1965. The subsection provides that section 63, which requires that advancements made to a child must be taken into account when determining the child's share on an intestacy, is not to affect the principle of the satisfaction of portion debts by legacies.

---

100. *Warren v. Warren* (1783) 1 Bro CC 305.
101. (1887) 19 LR Ir 359, 363-364.
102. *Bellasis v. Uthwatt* (1737) 1 Atk 426, 427-428.
103. [1911] 1 IR 113.
104. See the *dicta* of Monroe J in *Re Battersby's Estate* (1887) 19 Lr Ir 359, 363-364. This choice must be distinguished from the operation of the doctrine of election discussed above.

Satisfaction of Legacies by Portions and the Doctrine of Ademption

This is essentially a case of ademption, meaning in this context the writing off of a legacy by an advance made during the intended legatee's lifetime. There are two aspects of this principle which must be considered; first the ademption of a legacy by a subsequent portion where the parties are father and child or where the donor is *in loco parentis*, and secondly the ademption of a legacy given for a specific purpose by a subsequent gift made during the donee's lifetime for the same purpose.

The principle of the ademption of a legacy by a portion was set out in the following terms by Lord Selborne LC in *Re Pollock*:[105]

> When a testator gives a legacy to a child, or to any other person towards whom he has taken on himself parental obligations, and afterwards makes a gift or enters into a binding contract in his life-time in favour of the same legatee then (unless there be distinctions between the nature and conditions of the two gifts) there is a presumption that both gifts were made to fulfil the same natural or moral obligation of providing for the legatee and consequently that the gift *inter vivos* is either wholly or in part a substitution for or an ademption of the legacy.

The operation of these principles can be seen in the decision of Sugden LC in *Barry v. Harding*[106] in which he held that an absolute gift in a will to a child would be adeemed by a portion of the same amount subsequently given on her marriage, even thought this sum was settled on her and her husband. The presumption against double portions forms the basis for this principle, as was made clear by Sullivan MR in his judgment in *Curtin v. Evans*:[107]

> There is a presumption raised by the law against double portions; and accordingly, when a parent, or one standing *in loco parentis*, gives by will a sum of money to a child, and afterwards a like or greater sum is secured by a settlement on the marriage of that child, the law presumes the legacy to be adeemed.

However, Sullivan MR went on to stress that this principle is only a presumption and may be rebutted by evidence of intention to the contrary. He

---

105. (1885) 28 Ch D 552, 555.
106. (1844) 7 Ir Eq R 313.
107. (1872) IR 9 Eq 553, 557.

stated that the burden of proving the intention necessary to rebut the presumption rests on the person claiming the double portion and said that parol evidence will be admitted with a view to establishing whether the presumption is well founded. However, he stressed that where the claim rests on oral evidence, 'the Court ought to view and examine it with scrupulous care and great discrimination' and ought not to act on it unless it is free from suspicion and clearly shows the real intention of the person making the advancement.

Where a devise or bequest in the will is followed by a subsequent *inter vivos* gift to the same beneficiary, ademption may operate *pro tanto* if the amount of the gift is less than the value of the legacy.[108] The corollary of this principle is that where a child is left a legacy and is subsequently advanced a smaller sum, he can claim the balance under the terms of the will.[109]

If the portion is paid before the will is drawn up, there can be no question of ademption, as there will be no legacy in existence at the time to be adeemed.[110] Where ademption does take place, equity deems the devise or bequest in the will to have been cancelled. It is therefore no longer treated as being an operable part of the will and the beneficiary cannot claim under it. Thus, unlike in the case of the satisfaction of portions by legacies considered above, there can be no election between the will and the *inter vivos* portion and the beneficiary must take the latter.[111]

The legacy and the portion must be of the same general nature for the presumption of ademption to apply: e.g. there can be no ademption of a pecuniary legacy by a portion consisting of land.[112] However, this requirement will be less strictly applied than in the case of satisfaction and the presumption of ademption will only be displaced by more substantial differences in subject-matter.[113]

As noted above, the doctrine of ademption can operate in a more general context, and a legacy given for a specific purpose may be adeemed by a subsequent gift made during the donee's lifetime for the same purpose. The operation of this principle is well illustrated by the decision of *Griffith v. Bourke.*[114] A legacy was given to a parish priest for the purpose of erecting a new chapel. It was held by Porter MR that this legacy was adeemed

---

108. *Edgeworth v. Johnston* (1877) IR 11 Eq 326.
109. *Pym v. Lockyer* (1841) 5 My & Cr 29. See also *Re Pollock* (1885) 28 Ch D 522.
110. *Re Peacock's Estate* (1872) LR 14 Eq 236.
111. See the *dicta* of Lord Cranworth in *Chichester v. Coventry* (1867) LR 2 HL 71, 87.
112. *Re Wall's Estate* [1922] 1 IR 59.
113. *Chichester v. Coventry* (1867) LR 2 HL 71, 87 *per* Lord Cranworth.
114. (1887) 21 LR Ir 92.

by the gift of a like sum for the same purpose to the archbishop of the diocese by the testator during his lifetime. As Porter MR stated: 'Where there is a gift in a will for an expressed object and afterwards a donation by the testator in his lifetime for the *same* object, the law presumes that he did not intend that both should take effect but that the latter should be in substitution for the former gift.'[115] However, he went on to stress that the object in question must be clearly expressed and it must be plain that the reason for making the *inter vivos* gift was the same as that which motivated the testator to give the legacy; both gifts must be for the 'same identical object'.

It is the requirement of a specific purpose which distinguishes this form of ademption from the variety applying to father and child. A fairly liberal interpretation of the requirement of a specific purpose was given by the English Court of Appeal in *Re Pollock*[116] where Lord Selborne LC stated that the legacy may be adeemed by the subsequent gift where it is expressed to be made 'in fulfilment of some moral obligation recognised by the testator' even though this obligation is not of a kind which the law will recognise. In this case a testatrix bequeathed a sum of £500 to a niece of her deceased husband stating that she was doing so in accordance with the latter's wishes. Subsequently, during her lifetime, she paid the niece the sum of £300 and entered in her diary that this was a legacy from her uncle. It was held by Lord Selborne LC that there was a presumption that the legacy was adeemed to the extent of £300.

Satisfaction of Legacies by Legacies

This process has been described as only 'superficially akin'[117] to the doctrine of satisfaction and is probably better described as an instance of construing a will so as to avoid duplication of legacies which a testator is not likely to have intended. The underlying principle is the desire of the courts to attempt to construe the testamentary documents so as to give effect where possible to the testator's actual intention.

Where two or more legacies are given to the same person either in the same will or more usually in a will and a codicil, the question arises whether these should be regarded as cumulative or substitutional. If the two legacies which are given to the same person are of the same value and are given in the same instrument, equity presumes that they are substitutional

---

115. *Ibid.* at 95.
116. (1885) 28 Ch D 552.
117. Meagher, Gummow and Lehane, *Equity Doctrines and Remedies* (3rd ed., 1992) p.765.

and the legatee can take one only.[118] However, where the two legacies given by the same instrument are for different amounts, the presumption is that they are cumulative. This point was made in the following terms by Smith MR in *Brennan v. Moran*:[119]

> [I]t is a rule of construction that; where two legacies are given by the same testamentary instrument to the same person, of different amount, the legacies are to be considered cumulative, unless a contrary intention appears on the will.

In addition, if the two legacies are given by different instruments, usually by a will and a codicil, it is presumed that they are cumulative irrespective of their value; as Smith MR stated in *Brennan v. Moran*[120] in such a case 'as the testator has given twice, he must *prima facie* be intended to mean two gifts'. This principle was re-iterated by O'Sullivan MR in *Quin v. Armstrong*[121] as follows:

> [W]here a testator by his will gives a benefit to a person, and by a codicil to his will gives a benefit to the same person, the presumption of law is that he means to give twice; and it lies on the party who disputes it to show why that construction of them should not be adopted.

However, this presumption may be rebutted and the legacies may be regarded as substitutional if they are for the same amount and are given for the same motive. So, in *Re Armstrong*[122] it was held that the presumption that legacies given to the same person in a will and in a subsequent testamentary instrument are cumulative was rebutted by the testatrix's intention 'to take away one gift and leave . . . one gift instead of that one which is taken away'.[123]

Despite the guidelines laid down above, the question will ultimately be one of construction of the instruments concerned and as stated above, the primary aim is to give effect as far as possible to the testator's intentions. So, in *Bell v. Park*[124] legacies in a second will were taken as being in

118. *Garth v. Meyrick* (1779)1 Bro CC 30.
119. (1857) 6 Ir Ch R 126, 130.
120. (1857) 6 Ir Ch R 126, 130. See also *Walsh v. Walsh* (1870) IR 4 Eq 396.
121. (1876) IR 11 Eq 161, 168.
122. (1893) 31 LR Ir 154.
123. *Ibid.* at 156.
124. [1914] 1 IR 158.

substitution for those in the first because, on an overall reading of the instruments, it appeared that this was the intention of the testatrix. As Cherry LJ stated: 'Such gifts are undoubtedly *prima facie* cumulative, but it is always permissible to show by the terms of the two instruments that the gifts by the later document were intended to be substitutional and not cumulative'.[125]

If gifts are presumed to be cumulative parol evidence is not admissible to rebut this presumption. However, if gifts are presumed to be substitutional parol evidence is admissible.

THE DOCTRINE OF PERFORMANCE

This equitable doctrine is also based on the maxim that 'Equity imputes an intention to fulfil an obligation' and reflects the principle that 'a person is presumed to do that which he is bound to do'.[126] However, performance can be distinguished from satisfaction because while satisfaction involves fulfilling an obligation by means of an act different in form from the one originally contemplated, performance involves the carrying out of the obligation itself. So, where a person is under an obligation to carry out a particular act and subsequently does an act which can be considered as performance of his obligation, in certain circumstances equity will presume that this subsequent act was done in performance of the earlier obligation. This principle was stated in the following terms by Walker LJ in *Bannatyne v. Ferguson*:[127]

> The principle of performance is that when a person covenants to do an act, and he does that which may either wholly or partially be converted to or towards a completion of the covenant there will be a presumption that he had done the act with the intention to perform his covenant.

There situations in which the doctrine of performance operates can be divided into two categories.

By Act of the Party

The most common example of the operation of the doctrine by act of the

---

125. *Ibid.* at 174.
126. *Tubbs v. Broadwood* (1831) 2 Russ & M 487, 493 *per* Lord Brougham LC.
127. [1896] 1 IR 149, 179.

party is where a person covenants to purchase land and settle it on certain trusts and subsequently purchases land but fails to settle it. In these circumstances, equity may consider that the purchase amounted to performance of the covenant and the land will be considered as being held on the trusts of the settlement. This point is illustrated by the decision of Talbot LC in *Lechmere v. Lechmere.*[128] Prior to his marriage, a husband covenanted to lay out £30,000 in the purchase of freehold land within one year of his marriage. These lands were to be conveyed to trustees and each purchase was to be approved by them. After his marriage but not within the time stipulated and without the consent of the trustees, the husband purchased various interests in land, some of a fee simple nature but others of a reversionary or leasehold character, and also contracted to purchase fee simple estates. The husband died intestate and was survived by his wife. It was held that the freehold land purchased and contracted to be purchased after his marriage, although not amounting to £30,000 in value, should go towards performance of the covenant. However, any lands purchased by the husband before the date of the covenant and the interests which were not of a fee simple nature could not regarded as having been purchased in performance of his obligations.This decision established that where the lands are of lesser value than the lands covenanted to be purchased, they will be considered to have been purchased in part performance of the obligation and also shows that property of a different nature from that covenanted to be purchased will not be available for this purpose.

However, for the doctrine to apply in this context, the act done must be essentially the same as that which the individual has covenanted to do and in *Bannatyne v. Ferguson*[129] the Irish Court of Appeal held that the appointment of a jointure by deed was not performance of an obligation to secure an annuity.

The operation of the doctrine may have important practical consequences in this context because where a covenant to purchase or settle property in the future is deemed to be performed, it may create a specific charge or lien over the property.[130]

By Operation of Law

Where a person covenants to leave a sum of money to another person or covenants that his executors will pay him such a sum and then dies intestate, with the other person taking a share in his intestate estate, that share

---

128. (1735) Cas t Talb 80.
129. [1896] 1 IR 149.
130. *Creed v. Carey* (1857) 7 Ir Ch R 295.

may be regarded as performance, or *pro tanto* performance, of the covenant to leave money. While provision for this individual may be expressly made to be in substitution for any claim which the covenantee may have in relation to an estate,[131] the more common situation is that which arose in *Re Finegan's Estate*.[132] A husband executed a bond which provided that in the event of his death in his wife's lifetime, a sum of money was to be paid to trustees in trust for her. When he predeceased his wife leaving no issue it was held that the sum secured by the bond was to be regarded, in the absence of any contrary intention being expressed, as satisfaction *pro tanto* of the widow's share in her husband's estate. Where there is evidence of a contrary intention, the doctrine will not apply and the covenantee will be entitled to the benefit of the gift and the distributive share.[133]

---

131. See *Re Hogan* [1901] 1 IR 168.
132. [1925] 1 IR 201. See also *Blandy v. Widmore* (1716) 1 P Wms 323.
133. *Re Hood* [1923] 1 IR 109.

Index